Lecture Notes in Computer Science 6084

Commenced Publication in 1973
Founding and Former Series Editors:
Gerhard Goos, Juris Hartmanis, and Jan van Leeuwen

Martin Wirsing Martin Hofmann
Axel Rauschmayer (Eds.)

Trustworthly Global Computing

5th International Symposium, TGC 2010
Munich, Germany, February 24-26, 2010
Revised Selected Papers

Springer

Volume Editors

Martin Wirsing
LMU München
Institut für Informatik
Oettingenstr. 67
80538 Munich, Germany
E-mail: wirsing@pst.ifi.lmu.de

Martin Hofmann
LMU München
Institut für Informatik
Oettingenstr. 67
80538 Munich, Germany
E-mail: mhofmann@informatik.uni-muenchen.de

Axel Rauschmayer
LMU München
Institut für Informatik
Oettingenstr. 67
80538 Munich, Germany
E-mail: axel.rauschmayer@ifi.lmu.de

Library of Congress Control Number: 2010933643

CR Subject Classification (1998): K.6.5, D.4.6, C.2, F.4, E.3, D.2

LNCS Sublibrary: SL 1 – Theoretical Computer Science and General Issues

ISSN 0302-9743
ISBN-10 3-642-15639-8 Springer Berlin Heidelberg New York
ISBN-13 978-3-642-15639-7 Springer Berlin Heidelberg New York

springer.com

Printed in Germany

Typesetting: Camera-ready by author, data conversion by Scientific Publishing Services, Chennai, India
Printed on acid-free paper 06/3180

Preface

Global computing refers to computation over "global computers," i.e., computational infrastructures available globally and able to provide uniform services with variable guarantees for communication, cooperation and mobility, resource usage, security policies and mechanisms, etc., with particular regard to exploiting their universal scale and the programmability of their services. As the scope and computational power of such global infrastructures continue to grow, it becomes more and more important to develop methods, theories and techniques for trustworthy systems running on global computers.

This book constitutes the thoroughly refereed proceedings of the fifth edition of the International Symposium on Trustworthy Global Computing (TGC 2010) that was held in Munich, Germany, February 24-26, 2010. The Symposium on Trustworthy Global Computing is an international annual venue dedicated to safe and reliable computation in global computers. It focuses on providing frameworks, tools, and protocols for constructing well-behaved applications and on reasoning rigorously about their behavior and properties. The related models of computation incorporate code and data mobility over distributed networks with highly dynamic topologies and heterogeneous devices.

At the symposium, there were seven invited talks by Gilles Barthe, Rocco De Nicola, Ugo Montanari, Giuseppe Persiano, Davide Sangiorgi, Don Sannella, and Vladimiro Sassone. They resulted in six papers that are included in this book. It also contains carefully revised versions of the 17 contributed papers; these versions take into account the referees' reports. The Program Committee selected these papers from 31 submissions. Every submission was reviewed by three members of the Program Committee. In addition, the Program Committee sought the opinions of additional referees, selected because of their expertise in particular topics.

Many persons contributed to the success of TGC 2010. We offer sincere thanks to all of them. We are grateful to Andrei Voronkov for his EasyChair system that helped us to manage the submissions, the reviewing process, and the discussions of the Program Committee. We would like to thank the authors who submitted papers to the symposium, the members of the Program Committee, and the additional reviewers for their excellent work. We would also like to thank the invited speakers to TGC 2010. We are particularly grateful to the local organizers Nora Koch, Marianne Busch, Sonja Harrer, Anton Fasching, Christian Kroiß, Philip Mayer, Axel Rauschmayer, and Gefei Zhang for their invaluable work and effort in preparing and running the symposium. We are grateful to Springer for their helpful collaboration and assistance in producing this volume. Finally, we thank all symposium participants for the lively discussions and their deep insights into the subject matter.

May 2010

Martin Hofmann
Martin Wirsing

Organization

Steering Committee

Gilles Barthe	IMDEA Software, Madrid, Spain
Rocco De Nicola	Università di Firenze, Italy
Christos Kaklamanis	University of Patras, Greece
Ugo Montanari	Università di Pisa, Italy
Davide Sangiorgi	Università di Bologna, Italy
Don Sannella	University of Edinburgh, UK
Vladimiro Sassone	University of Southampton, UK
Martin Wirsing	LMU München, Germany

Program Chairs

Martin Hofmann	LMU München, Germany
Martin Wirsing	LMU München, Germany

Programme committee

Gilles Barthe	IMDEA Software, Madrid, Spain
Roberto Bruni	Università di Pisa, Italy
Rocco De Nicola	Università di Firenze, Italy
Howard Foster	Imperial College, UK
Samir Genaim	Universidad Complutense de Madrid, Spain
Stefania Gnesi	Istituto di Scienza e Tecnologie dell'Informazione "A. Faedo", Pisa, Italy
Martin Hofmann	LMU München, Germany (Co-chair)
Thomas Jensen	IRISA, Rennes, France
Christos Kaklamanis	University of Patras, Greece
Alberto Marchetti-Spaccamela	Università di Roma "La Sapienza", Italy
Paddy Nixon	University College Dublin, Ireland
Giuseppe Persiano	Università di Salerno, Italy
Geppino Pucci	Università di Padova, Italy
Paola Quaglia	Università di Trento, Italy
Don Sannella	University of Edinburgh, UK
Vladimiro Sassone	University of Southampton, UK
Maria J. Serna	Universitat Politècnica de Catalunya, Spain
Carolyn Talcott	SRI International, USA
Emilio Tuosto	University of Leicester, UK
Nobuko Yoshida	Imperial College London, UK

Martin Wirsing	LMU München, Germany (Co-chair)
Franco Zambonelli	Università di Modena e Reggio Emilia, Italy

Local Organization

Marianne Busch
Anton Fasching
Sonja Harrer
Nora Koch (Chair)
Christian Kroiß
Philip Mayer
Axel Rauschmayer
Gefei Zhang

External Reviewers

Lucia Acciai
Carme Alvarez
Martin Berger
Nathalie Bertrand
Laura Bocchi
Chiara Bodei
Michele Boreale
Andrea Bracciali
Sara Capecchi
Marco Carbone
Ehab ElSalamouny
Massimo Felici
Rémy Haemmerlé
Daniel Hedin
César Kunz
Diego Latella
Alberto Lluch Lafuente
Michele Loreti
Kenneth MacKenzie
Franco Mazzanti
Carlo Montangero
Alberto Pettarin
Rosario Pugliese
Jaroslav Sevcik
Francesco Tiezzi

Table of Contents

I Invited Talks

II Types and Processes

III Games and Concurrent Systems

IV Certification of Correctness

V Tools and Languages

VI Probabilistic Aspects

Symbolic and Analytic Techniques for Resource Analysis of Java Bytecode

David Aspinall[1], Robert Atkey[2], Kenneth MacKenzie[1], and Donald Sannella[1]

[1] School of Informatics, The University of Edinburgh, Edinburgh
[2] Computer and Information Sciences, University of Strathclyde, Glasgow

Abstract. Recent work in resource analysis has translated the idea of amortised resource analysis to imperative languages using a program logic that allows mixing of assertions about heap shapes, in the tradition of separation logic, and assertions about consumable resources. Separately, polyhedral methods have been used to calculate bounds on numbers of iterations in loop-based programs. We are attempting to combine these ideas to deal with Java programs involving both data structures and loops, focusing on the bytecode level rather than on source code.

1 Introduction

The ability to move code and other active content smoothly between execution sites is a key element of modern computing platforms. However, it presents huge security challenges, aggravating existing security problems and presenting altogether new ones. One challenging security issue in this context is control of resources (space, time, etc.), particularly on small devices, where computational power and memory are very limited.

A promising approach to security is proof-carrying code [31], whereby mobile code is equipped with an independently verifiable certificate consisting of a condensed proof of its security properties. A major advantage of this approach is that it sidesteps the difficult issue of trust: there is no need to trust either the code producer, or a centralized certification authority. Work on the PCC approach to resource security includes [35] and [7].

This approach requires infrastructure on the side of the code producer as well as the code consumer. The code producer needs to produce not just downloadable code, as before, but also a proof of its security properties. The code consumer needs a way of checking such proofs. Arbitrarily complex methods may be used by the code producer to construct proofs, while their verification by the code consumer is a straightforward check of validity. The burden for the code producer is considerably eased by the use of a *certifying compiler* which employs static analysis of the source code alongside standard compilation to supply the information required to produce these proofs automatically. The information provided by the analysis — in the case of resource analysis, concerning upper bounds on usage of space, time, etc. — is potentially of great interest to the code producer as an aid to the development of high-quality code, prior to and independent of its use for producing security certificates.

M. Wirsing, M. Hofmann, and A. Rauschmayer (Eds.): TGC 2010, LNCS 6084, pp. 1–22, 2010.

Recent developments in static analysis methods now makes it feasible to consider an alternative but related approach to security. Instead of requiring the code producer to supply a proof, whether via static analysis of source code or by other means, one can perform an analogous analysis directly on the downloadable bytecode to determine its properties. This could be done by the code consumer on receipt of downloadable code, dispensing with the need for a proof. Alternatively, the code producer could perform the analysis and use the result to produce a proof certificate. An interesting third alternative is that an intermediary, for example a software distributor, could perform such an analysis on uncertified bytecode, transforming it to proof-carrying code. The fact that the original source code is not required is essential to making this feasible in commercial practice.

Here we consider two quite different approaches to the analysis of resource consumption of Java bytecode. The first, in §2, translates the idea of amortised resource analysis to imperative languages to enable automated resource analysis of programs that iterate through data structures. The second, in §3, uses polyhedral methods to calculate resource bounds of iterative procedures controlled by numerical quantities. In §4 we briefly describe some ideas for future work and plans for integrating the two kinds of analysis to deal with Java programs involving both data structures and loops.

2 Amortised Resource Analysis

Amortised resource analysis is a technique for specifying and verifying resource bounds of programs by exploiting the tight link between the structure of the data that programs manipulate and the resources they consume. For instance, a program that iterates through a list doing something for every element can either be thought of as requiring n resources, where n is the length of list, or as requiring 1 resource for every element of the list, where we never know the global length property of the list. Taking the latter view can simplify both the specification and the verification of programs' resource usage.

This work conceptually builds on the work of Tarjan and Sleator on amortised complexity analysis [36], where "credits" and "debits" may be virtually stored within data structures and used to pay for expensive operations. By storing up credit for future operations in a data structure, we *amortise* the cost of operations on the data structure over time. Hofmann and Jost [21] applied this technique to first-order functional programs to yield an automated resource analysis. Atkey [3] has recently adapted this work to integrate with Separation Logic [22,34] to extend the automated technique to pointer-manipulating imperative programs. In this section we give an overview of Atkey's work and describe some examples.

2.1 Integrating the Banker's Method and Separation Logic

Separation Logic is built upon a notion of resources and their separation. The assertion $A * B$ holds for a resource if it can be split into two resources that make A true and B true respectively. Resource separation enables local reasoning about mutation of resources; if the program mutates the resource associated with A, then we know that B is still true on its separate resource.

For the purposes of complexity analysis, we want to consider resource consumption as well as resource mutation, e.g. the consumption of time as a program executes. To see how Separation Logic-style reasoning about resources helps in this case, consider the standard inductively defined list predicate from Separation Logic, augmented with an additional proposition R denoting the presence of a consumable resource for every element of the list:

$$\begin{aligned}\mathsf{list}_{\mathsf{R}}(x) \equiv\ & x = \mathsf{null} \wedge \mathsf{emp} \\ & \vee \exists y, z.\ [x \overset{\mathsf{data}}{\mapsto} y] * [x \overset{\mathsf{next}}{\mapsto} z] * R * \mathsf{list}_{\mathsf{R}}(z)\end{aligned}$$

See Atkey [3] for a complete description of the assertion logic. We can represent a heap H and a consumable resource r that satisfy this predicate graphically:

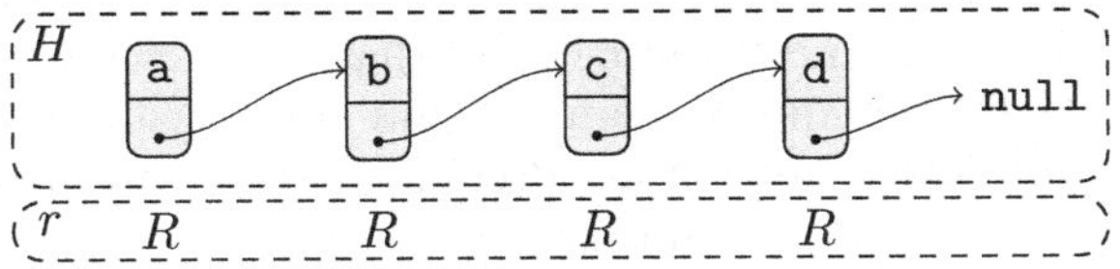

So we have $r, H \models \mathsf{list}_{\mathsf{R}}(x)$, assuming x points to the head of the list. Here $r = R \cdot R \cdot R \cdot R$—we assume that consumable resources form a commutative monoid—and r represents the resource that is available for the program to use in the future. We can split H and r to separate out the head of the list with its associated resource:

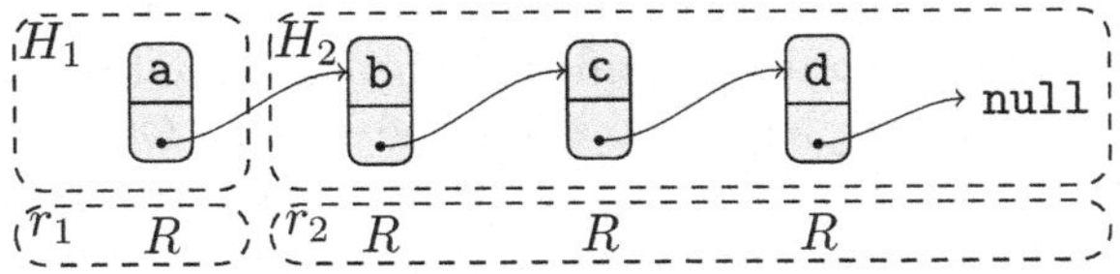

This heap and resource satisfy $r_1 \cdot r_2, H_1 \uplus H_2 \models [x \overset{\mathsf{data}}{\mapsto} \mathsf{a}] * [x \overset{\mathsf{next}}{\mapsto} y] * R * \mathsf{list}_{\mathsf{R}}(y)$, where $H_1 \uplus H_2 = H$, $r_1 \cdot r_2 = r$ and we assume that y points to the b element. Now that we have separated out the head of the list and its associated consumable resource, we are free to mutate the heap H_1 and consume the resource r_1 without affecting the tail of the list, so the program can move to a state:

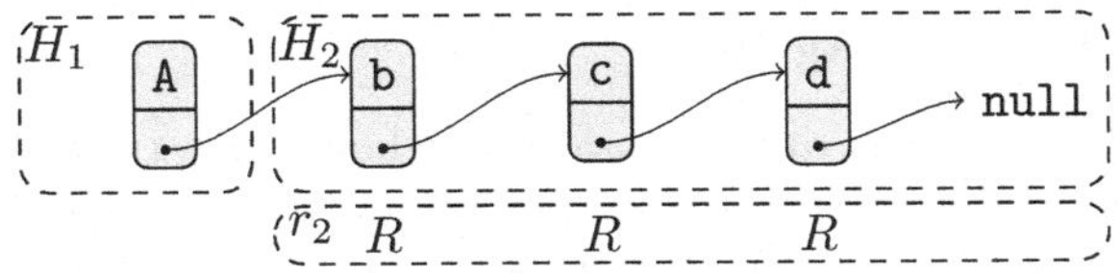

where the head of the list has been mutated to A and the associated resource has been consumed; we do not need to do anything special to reason that the tail of the list and its associated consumable resource are unaffected.

The combined assertion about heap and consumable resource describes the current shape and contents of the heap and also the available resource that the program may consume in the future. By ensuring that, for every state in the program's execution, the resource consumed plus the resource available for consumption in the future is less than or equal to a predefined bound, we can ensure that the entire execution is resource bounded.

Intermixing resource assertions with Separation Logic assertions about the shapes of data structures, as we have done with the resource-carrying list_R predicate above, allow us to specify amounts of resource that depend on the shape of data structures in memory. By the definition of list_R, we know that the amount of resource available to the program is proportional to the length of the list, without having to do any arithmetic reasoning about lengths of lists. The association of resources with parts of a data structure is exactly the banker's approach to amortised complexity analysis proposed by Tarjan [36].

In the exposition above we have used a list predicate $\mathsf{list}_\mathsf{R}(x)$ that describes a list on the heap with a fixed number of resources per element. Using this predicate only allows the specification of resource usage that is linear in the lengths of lists. Recent work by Hoffmann and Hofmann [20] on amortised resource analysis for polynomial bounds lifts this restriction. Preliminary experiments with combining the two techniques have been promising.

2.2 Implementation

The combination of Separation Logic and amortised resource analysis has been implemented in two stages. We have formalised and mechanically checked a proof of soundness for the combined program logic for a simplified subset of Java bytecode in Coq with a shallowly embedded assertion logic. On top of this we have implemented a Coq-verified verification condition generator for a deeply embedded assertion logic and extracted this to OCaml. In OCaml we have implemented a proof search procedure that solves verification conditions using a similar technique to other automated verification tools for Separation Logic [11]. See Atkey [3] for more details. In our proof search implementation, we can leave resource annotations, e.g. the resource associated with each element of a list, as variables to be filled in by a linear program solver. Our tool requires annotation of programs with loop invariants, but can infer the resource portion. This process is demonstrated in the next section.

2.3 A More Complex Example

The example shown in the previous section, where a program iterates through a list consuming resources as it proceeds, only demonstrates an extremely simple, albeit common, pattern. We now describe a more complex list manipulating program that shows the benefits of the amortised approach. This example demonstrates the combination of reasonably complex pointer manipulation with resource reasoning. Most of the technical details arise from dealing with the heap-shape behaviour of the program; the resource bounds simply drop out of shape constraints thanks to the inference of resource annotations.

Consider the Java method declaration shown in Figure 1[1] that describes the inner loop of an in-place merge sort algorithm for linked lists. The method takes two arguments: `list`, a reference to the head node of a linked list; and `k`, an integer. The integer argument dictates the sizes of the sublists that the method will be merging in this pass. In short, the method steps through the list `2*k` elements at a time, merging the two length `k` sublists each time. The outer loop does the `2*k` stepping, and the inner loop does the merging. To accomplish a full merge sort, this method would be called $\log_2(n)$ times with doubling `k`, where n is the length of the list.

Assume that we wish to account for the number of swapping operations performed by this method, i.e. the number of times that the third branch of the `if` statement in the inner loop is executed. We accomplish this in our implementation by inserting a special `consume` instruction at this point.

The pre- and post-conditions of the method are as follows:

$$\begin{aligned} \text{Pre}(\texttt{mergeInner}) &: \texttt{list} \neq \texttt{null} \wedge (\mathit{lseg}(x, \texttt{list}, \texttt{null}) * R^y) \\ \text{Post}(\texttt{mergeInner}) &: \mathit{lseg}(0, \texttt{retval}, \texttt{null}) \end{aligned}$$

The precondition states that the first argument points to a list segment ending with `null`, with x amount of resource associated with every element of the list, and y amount of additional resource that may be used. The values of x and y will be inferred by a linear program solver. The condition $\texttt{list} \neq \texttt{null}$ is a safety condition required for the method to not throw a null pointer exception.

The outer loop in the method needs a disjunctive invariant corresponding to whether this is the first iteration or a later iteration.

$$\begin{aligned} &(\mathit{lseg}(o_1, \texttt{list}, \texttt{tail}) * [\texttt{tail} \overset{\textsf{next}}{\mapsto} ?] * [\texttt{tail} \overset{\textsf{data}}{\mapsto} ?] * \mathit{lseg}(o_2, \texttt{p}, \texttt{null}) * R^{o_3}) \\ \vee\ &((\texttt{list} = \texttt{null} \wedge \texttt{tail} = \texttt{null}) * \mathit{lseg}(o_4, \texttt{p}, \texttt{null}) * R^{o_5}) \end{aligned}$$

The first disjunct is used on normal iterations of loop: the variable `list` points to the list that has been processed so far, ending at `tail`; `p` points to the remainder of the list that is to be processed. We have annotated these lists with the resource variables o_1 and o_2 that will contain the resources associated with each element of these lists. The second disjunct covers the case of the first iteration, when `list` and `tail` are null and `p` points to the complete list to be processed.

Moving on, we consider the first inner loop that advances the pointer `q` by `k` elements forward, thus splitting the list ahead of `p` into a `k`-element segment and the rest of the list. The next loop will merge the first `k`-length segment with the

[1] Adapted from the C code at
`http://www.chiark.greenend.org.uk/~sgtatham/algorithms/listsort.html`.

```
public static Node mergeInner (Node list, int k) {
    Node p      = list;
    Node tail   = null;

    list = null;

    while (p != null) {
        Node q = p;
        for (int i = 0; i < k; i++) {
            q = q.next;
            if (q == null) break;
        }

        Node pstop = q;
        int qsize = k;
        while (p != pstop || (qsize > 0 && q != null)) {
            Node e;
            if (p == pstop) {
                e = q;
                q = q.next;
                qsize--;
            } else if (qsize == 0 || q == null) {
                e = p;
                p = p.next;
            } else if (p.data <= q.data) {
                e = p;
                p = p.next;
            } else {
                e = q;
                q = q.next;
                qsize--;
            }

            if (tail != null)
                tail.next = e;
            else
                list = e;

            tail = e;
        }

        p = q;
    }

    tail.next = null;

    return list;
}
```

Fig. 1. Inner loop of an in-place linked-list merge sort `k`-length prefix of the second segment. It is convenient for our implementation to split out this inner loop into another method[2], with the following signature:

```
public static Node advance (Node l, int k)
```

The argument `l` points to a linked list, and the method will advance `k` elements through the list (or until the end) and return a pointer to the split point. The pre- and post-condition of this method are:

$$\begin{aligned} \text{Pre}(\texttt{advance}) &: \mathit{lseg}(a_0, \texttt{l}, \texttt{null}) \\ \text{Post}(\texttt{advance}) &: \mathit{lseg}(a_0, \texttt{l}, \texttt{retval}) * \mathit{lseg}(a_0, \texttt{retval}, \texttt{null}) \end{aligned}$$

Again, we have left the resource annotation on the elements of the list as a variable a_0, to be filled in by the linear solver. The appearance of the same variable in the pre- and post-condition implies that we expect this resource to be preserved by the method.

Proceeding though our main method, the invariant of the inner loop is as follows, again in two pieces according to whether it is the first or second iteration of the outer loop:

$$\begin{aligned} &(\mathit{lseg}(i_1, \texttt{list}, \texttt{tail}) * [\texttt{tail} \overset{\mathsf{next}}{\mapsto} ?] * [\texttt{tail} \overset{\mathsf{data}}{\mapsto} ?] \\ &\qquad\qquad * \mathit{lseg}(i_2, \texttt{p}, \texttt{pstop}) * \mathit{lseg}(i_3, \texttt{q}, \texttt{null}) * R^{i_4}) \\ \vee\ &((\texttt{list} = \texttt{null} \wedge \texttt{tail} = \texttt{null}) * \mathit{lseg}(i_5, \texttt{p}, \texttt{pstop}) * \mathit{lseg}(i_6, \texttt{q}, \texttt{null}) * R^{i_7}) \end{aligned}$$

The first part of each disjunct is as before, stating that `list` to `tail` contains the part of list that has been processed. Since we have now split the remainder of the list into two pieces we have two separate list segments referenced by `p` and `q` pointing to the parts of the list that are to be merged.

Running this example through our implementation produces the solution $x = 1$, $y = 0$ for the precondition resource annotations. This indicates that each element of the list needs to contain one resource for every element. For the outer loop's invariant, we obtain $o_2 = o_4 = 1$ and all the others are 0. This indicates that the list we have processed has had all its resources consumed, while the list remaining to be processed still has associated resources. This is as expected for a loop iterating through a list. The specification of `advance` is completed by inferring $a_0 = 1$, indicating that `advance` preserves the resources associated with the list. Finally the inner loop's invariant has $i_2 = i_3 = i_5 = i_6 = 1$ and all others 0, indicating that the two list segments that are remaining to be processed have associated resources, while the processed segments do not.

Comparisons to other techniques. While we have had to work to supply the loop invariants for our implementation, we note that these invariants may be inferred by other tools, for example [11], and the resource variables automatically inserted on the list segment parts. The key to the amortised approach is the tight connection between shape invariants, which is a complex but well-studied problem, and resource usage.

[2] This is because our implementation works on unstructured bytecode, and so cannot easily apply Separation Logic's frame rule to modularise the reasoning about the loop. Using a separate method allows application of the frame rule.

Most other techniques for resource usage analysis that handle data structures do so by considering the sizes of structures. The SPEED system of Gulwani et al [19] can infer resource bounds for programs manipulating heap-based data structures, but only via abstract interfaces. The specifications for these abstract interfaces record the effect of the operations on the size of the data structure. Thus, the technique is unable to cope with the kind of program that we have presented above that uses direct pointer manipulation. Nevertheless, Gulwani et al report impressive results on real-world Microsoft product code.

The COSTA system [2] can deal with some uses of direct pointer manipulation, but accounts for the sizes of heap-based data structures by counting the length of the longest path from a given reference. Thus, it cannot deal with programs that demonstrate sharing on the heap; the Java method described above has three pointers all pointing the same list in the inner loop.

One might also consider the use of Separation Logic to deal with sharing on the heap, augmented with information on the sizes of heap-base data structures to account for resource usage. So one would have a predicate $lseg^n(x,y)$ that describes a list segment of length n from x to y, plus a "ghost variable" that accounts for the consumed resources. We argue that the amortised approach described here is simpler due to the differences in reasoning between the *global* property of the length of a whole list, and the *local* property of each list element having an associated amount of resource to be used. For example, consider the specification of the `advance` method using sized structures:

$$\mathrm{Pre}(\texttt{advance}) : lseg^n(\texttt{l},\texttt{null})$$
$$\mathrm{Post}(\texttt{advance}) : \exists n_1, n_2.\ n_1 + n_2 = n \wedge (lseg^{n_1}(\texttt{l},\texttt{retval}) * lseg^{n_2}(\texttt{retval},\texttt{null}))$$

We have had to introduce two existential variables indicating the sizes of the lists returned by the method. These additional values have to then be related back to the length of the original list by the calling method, and thence to the resource consumption, requiring non-straightforward arithmetic reasoning. The amortised approach exploits the shape-reasoning already present in Separation Logic to account for resources. For further elaboration of this point, and a demonstration of the use of amortised specification to improve information hiding in specifications, see the functional queues example in [3].

3 Iteration and Geometry

The previous section has described a technique which can be used to analyse the resource usage of procedures which manipulate heap-based data structures. Here we will describe a mathematical technique which can be used to study iterative procedures controlled by *numerical* quantities. One of our main interests is in producing *certifying* analyses, and our description of the mathematics will highlight aspects which are relevant to this problem.

We will look at some examples of Java methods which use iteration. For simplicity, we will look at the problem of deciding how often the `println` method is called, but we could equally be looking at object allocation or the transmission of SMS messages.

Here is an example with nested loops:

```
public static void m1() {
   for (int i=1; i<=9; i++)
      for (int j=1; j<=i && j<=7; j++)
         System.out.println ("Hello");
}
```

For a more complicated example, consider this Java method where both loops are controlled by method arguments:

```
public static void m2 (int p, int q) {
  for (int i=0; i<=p; j++)
     for (int j=0; j<=9 && i+j<=q; j++)
        System.out.println ("Hello");
}
```

How can one tell how many times `println` is called in these methods? Consider `m1` again. Every time we visit the `println` statement we have the following constraints on the program variables i and j:

$$1 \leq i \leq 9$$
$$1 \leq j \leq i$$
$$1 \leq j \leq 7.$$

Considered as inequalities over the real numbers, these define a trapezoidal region P in the (i, j)-plane, and it is easy to see that the number of times the `println` statement is executed is equal to $|P \cap \mathbb{Z}^2|$, the number of lattice points[3] within the polygon P.

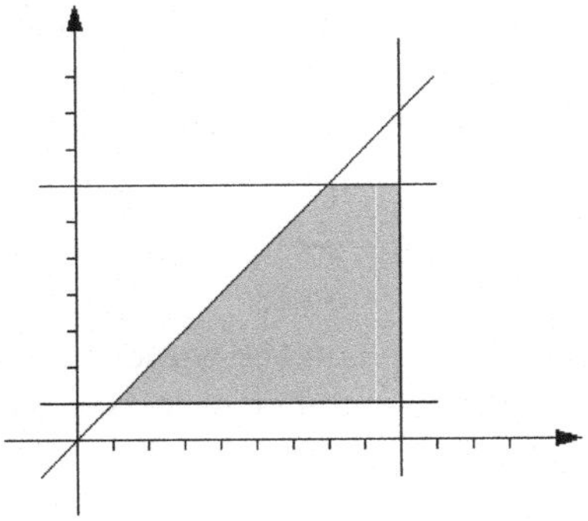

Fig. 2. Polygon P for method `m1`

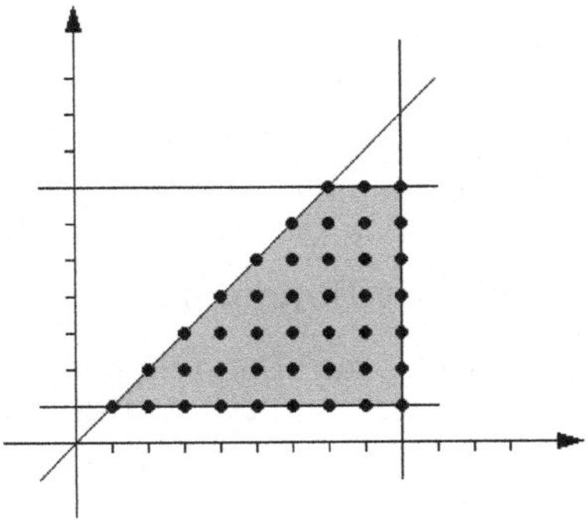

Fig. 3. Lattice points in P

There is a rich mathematical theory of the enumeration of lattice points in polytopes (the generalisation of polygons to higher dimensions) and we will describe some aspects of this theory and its relations to program analysis.

[3] i.e. points with integral coordinates.

3.1 Halfspaces, Polyhedra, and Polytopes

Fix an integer $d \geq 0$ and $a_1, \ldots, a_d \in \mathbb{R}$. We will be interested in solutions $(x_1, \ldots, x_n) \in \mathbb{R}^d$ of inequalities of the form

$$a_1 x_1 + \cdots + a_d x_d \leq b. \tag{1}$$

In our applications, such inequalities will arise in the form of linear constraints on program variables. Putting $\mathbf{a} = (a_1, \ldots, a_d)$ and $\mathbf{x} = (x_1, \ldots, x_d)$ we can rewrite (1) as $\mathbf{a} \cdot \mathbf{x} \leq b$, and if $\mathbf{a} \neq \mathbf{0}$ then the set of $\mathbf{x}$ satisfying the inequality defines a *halfspace* in $\mathbb{R}^d$. For example, in $\mathbb{R}^2$ a halfspace consists of all points lying on one side of some line.

A *convex polyhedron* in $\mathbb{R}^d$ is the intersection of a finite number of halfspaces, and a bounded polyhedron (a polyhedron of finite extent, i.e. one which is contained in some sphere) is called a *polytope.* It can be shown that a polytope can equivalently be defined as the convex hull[4] of a finite set of points in $\mathbb{R}^d$ (the *vertices* of P). Moreover, if the constants in the inequalities defining P are all rational (as will be the case in all of our applications), the vertices of P all have rational co-ordinates. A convex polyhedron is thus the set of simultaneous solutions to a system of n inequalities:

$$\begin{aligned} a_{11}x_1 + \cdots + a_{1d}x_d &\leq b_1 \\ a_{21}x_1 + \cdots + a_{2d}x_d &\leq b_2 \\ &\vdots \\ a_{n1}x_1 + \cdots + a_{nd}x_d &\leq b_n. \end{aligned}$$

The general theory of polyhedra has many applications in mathematics and in computer science. See [6] for a survey of applications in computer science.

Note that if we restrict to natural numbers, then linear inequalities of the type considered above are exactly the type of inequalities that occur in *Presburger arithmetic.* It follows that the lattice point enumeration problem subsumes the problem of counting solutions to systems of Presburger inequalities. This point of view is examined in greater depth by Pugh in [33].

3.2 Ehrhart Polynomials

Many applications of polytope methods have been based on the work of Eugène Ehrhart [17,18], who studied the problem of how the number of lattice points inside a polytope grows as the size of the polytope increases. More precisely, let

$$P = \mathrm{conv}\{\mathbf{y}_1, \ldots, \mathbf{y}_m\}$$

be a polytope and for $n \in \mathbb{N}$, let

$$nP = \mathrm{conv}\{n\mathbf{y}_1, \ldots, n\mathbf{y}_m\}$$

be the *n-fold dilate* of P. Ehrhart showed that $|nP \cap \mathbb{Z}^d|$ is a *quasipolynomial* in n, which may be thought of as a number of polynomials cyclically interleaved.

[4] We denote the convex hull of a set X by $\mathrm{conv}\, X$.

Definition. A *quasipolynomial of degree* d is a function $f : \mathbb{Z} \to \mathbb{Z}$ of the form

$$f(n) = \begin{cases} f_0(n) & \text{if } n \equiv 0 \pmod{k} \\ f_1(n) & \text{if } n \equiv 1 \pmod{k} \\ & \vdots \\ f_{k-1}(n) & \text{if } n \equiv k-1 \pmod{k}. \end{cases}$$

where each f_j is a polynomial of the usual kind and $\max\{\deg f_0, \ldots, \deg f_{k-1}\} = d$. The (minimal) number k of polynomial components is called the *quasiperiod* of f.

Theorem. *Let* $P = \text{conv}\{\mathbf{y}_1, \ldots, \mathbf{y}_n\}$ *be a rational convex polytope in* $\mathbb{Z}^d$ *and let*

$$\mathcal{E}_P(n) = |nP \cap \mathbb{Z}^d|.$$

Then $\mathcal{E}_P(n)$ *is a quasipolynomial of degree* $\dim P$ *and quasiperiod equal to the greatest common denominator of the coordinates of the vertices of* P.

The original proof of this theorem can be found in [17]; see also [9, Chapter 3].

There is a considerable amount of research applying Ehrhart polynomials to program analysis and optimisation, especially in the field of high-performance computing involving array calculations. One of the first papers in this area is due to Clauss [14], with application to problems such as counting the flops executed by a loop, the number of memory locations touched by a loop, the array elements that must be transmitted from one processor to another during parallel array computations, the maximum parallelism induced by a loop from a given time-schedule, and several others. Further work appears in [25,15,38] for example.

The methods of Clauss seem to have remained largely within the high-performance/parallel computing community (see [24,32] for example) until 2006, when Braberman et al [13] (and see also [12]) showed how to adapt these techniques to predict the memory usage of (iterative) Java programs; at present this appears to be the only application of polytope methods within the programming language community.

3.3 Drawbacks of Ehrhart Polynomials

The standard method used to compute Ehrhart polynomials is *interpolation*, where the coefficients of a polynomial f of degree d are derived from the values of the polynomial at $d+1$ distinct points: this data gives a $(d+1) \times (d+1)$ system of linear equations in the coefficients of f which can then be solved by Gaussian elimination or some other technique. In the case of a quasipolynomial of period k and degree d, this requires us to solve k systems of $(d+1) \times (d+1)$ equations. Recalling that the period k of the Ehrhart polynomial associated with a rational polytope P is the greatest common denominator of the coefficients of the vertices of P, it becomes clear that a considerable amount of computation can be required to calculate $\mathcal{E}_P(n)$. In addition to this, the initial $d+1$ values of the k polynomial components of the quasipolynomial have to be computed by explicitly counting the number of lattice points in the dilates $0P, P, 2P, \ldots, (d+1)P$. The number k can be very large, even for relatively simple polytopes. For example, for the triangular polytope

$$P = \text{conv}\{(\tfrac{1}{4}, \tfrac{2}{5}), (\tfrac{5}{7}, \tfrac{2}{11}), (\tfrac{8}{9}, \tfrac{1}{12})\}$$

the quasiperiod of $\mathcal{E}_P(n)$ is 13,680. Calculating the Ehrhart polynomial of P thus requires the solution of 13,680 3×3 systems of linear equations, which would be reasonably time-consuming. In fact, even if the dimension d is fixed, the time taken to compute (via interpolation) the Ehrhart polynomial of a polytope with n vertices can grow exponentially with n (see [38, §2.3]), whereas the methods presented in the next section are polynomial in fixed dimension.

The sheer amount of data required to specify an Ehrhart function is also something of a barrier in the context of certified resource analysis, where such functions would have to be recorded in certificates accompanying mobile programs. This may not in fact be an insurmountable problem. One could possibly find simpler functions which are upper bounds for the exact Ehrhart function (see [30]); this would save space at the expense of a (hopefully small) loss of precision. Another issue is that Ehrhart functions are not arbitrary quasipolynomials: for example it is clear that they are increasing functions, whereas a general quasipolynomial can have polynomial components which are completely unrelated, leading to a function whose value oscillates drastically. It is conceivable that the quasipolynomials arising as Ehrhart functions have special properties which would enable them to be specified by a relatively small amount of data. Unfortunately, it seems that very little is known about exactly which quasipolynomials can occur as Ehrhart polynomials (see [28,10] for some partial results) so at present it is difficult to be precise about the minimum of data required to explicitly specify an Ehrhart function. However, the results discussed in the next section may enable us to bypass this problem.

3.4 Generating Functions

The difficulty of computing Ehrhart polynomials suggests that they would be unsuitable for polytope-based analyses in a certifying framework, but fortunately some more recent results provide a much more efficient means of enumerating lattice points. The basic tool in this theory is the *generating function* of a polytope, which is a multivariate polynomial with a term for every lattice point in the polytope. More concretely, suppose we have a polytope P in R^d. We will consider polynomials in the variables $x_1, \ldots, x_d$. Given $\mathbf{v} = (v_1, ..., v_d) \in \mathbb{Z}^d$ we define

$$\mathbf{x}^{\mathbf{v}} = x_1^{v_1} x_2^{v_2} \cdots x_d^{v_d}$$

and the generating function of P is then defined by

$$\mathcal{G}_P(\mathbf{x}) = \sum\{\mathbf{x}^{\mathbf{v}} : \mathbf{v} \in P \cap \mathbb{Z}^d\}$$

It is easy to see that the number of lattice points in P is given by $\mathcal{G}_P(1,\ldots,1)$. The obvious difficulty here is that the polynomial $\mathcal{G}_P(\mathbf{x})$ will in general be enormous and costly to compute. Recall our earlier example, which gave rise to a trapezoidal region in $\mathbb{R}^2$:

```
for (i=1; i<=9; i++)
    for (j=1; j<=i && j<=7; j++) B
```

For this relatively small example, the full generating function is

$$\begin{aligned}\mathcal{G}_P(x,y) = xy + x^2y + x^3y + x^4y + x^5y + x^6y + x^7y + x^8y + x^9y \\ +x^2y^2 + x^3y^2 + x^4y^2 + x^5y^2 + x^6y^2 + x^7y^2 + x^8y^2 + x^9y^2 \\ +x^3y^3 + x^4y^3 + x^5y^3 + x^6y^3 + x^7y^3 + x^8y^3 + x^9y^3 \\ +x^4y^4 + x^5y^4 + x^6y^4 + x^7y^4 + x^8y^4 + x^9y^4 \\ +x^5y^5 + x^6y^5 + x^7y^5 + x^8y^5 + x^9y^5 \\ +x^6y^6 + x^7y^6 + x^8y^6 + x^9y^6 \\ +x^7y^7 + x^8y^7 + x^9y^7\end{aligned}$$

which is already quite unwieldy.

However, Alexander Barvinok [8] has recently shown how to express the generating function as a sum of short rational functions which are easily determined from local information at the vertices of P. In the case above, we have

$$\begin{aligned}\mathcal{G}_P(x,y) &= \frac{xy}{(1-x)(1-xy)} + \frac{x^9y}{(1-x^{-1})(1-y)} \\ &+ \frac{x^9y^7}{(1-y^{-1})(1-x^{-1})} + \frac{x^7y^7}{(1-x)(1-x^{-1}y^{-1})}\end{aligned}$$

This function is easily computed if one knows the vertices and edges of the polytope. Space constraints prevent us from describing the computation in detail here, but a full explanation can be found in [8] or [9].

There is a problem here, though. To find $|P \cap \mathbb{Z}^2|$ we have to evaluate $\mathcal{G}_P(1,1)$, and the denominators of all of the terms above vanish at $(1,1)$. However, this can be overcome. The singularity at $(1,1)$ is a *removable singularity*[1, §3.1], and various techniques can be used to find $\lim_{(x,y)\to(1,1)} \mathcal{G}_P(x,y)$. For example, we can find a common denominator to obtain

$$\begin{aligned}\mathcal{G}_P(x,y) &= \frac{xy - xy^2 - x^{10}y + x^{11}y^2 + x^{10}y^8 - x^{11}y^9 - x^8y^8 + x^8y^9}{(1-x)(1-y)(1-xy)} \\ &= \frac{xy - xy^2 - x^{10}y + x^{11}y^2 + x^{10}y^8 - x^{11}y^9 - x^8y^8 + x^8y^9}{1 - x - y + x^2y + xy^2 - x^2y^2}\end{aligned}$$

and then repeatedly apply L'Hôpital's rule[5] to obtain

$$\begin{aligned}
\left|P \cap \mathbb{Z}^2\right| &= \mathcal{G}_P(1,1) \\
&= \lim_{(x,y)\to(1,1)} \frac{xy - xy^2 - x^{10}y + x^{11}y^2 + x^{10}y^8 - x^{11}y^9 - x^8y^8 + x^8y^9}{1 - x - y + x^2y + xy^2 - x^2y^2} \\
&= \lim_{(x,y)\to(1,1)} \frac{\frac{\partial}{\partial y}(xy - xy^2 - x^{10}y + x^{11}y^2 + x^{10}y^8 - x^{11}y^9 - x^8y^8 + x^8y^9)}{\frac{\partial}{\partial y}(1 - x - y + x^2y + xy^2 - x^2y^2)} \\
&= \cdots \\
&= \frac{-2 + 22 + 560 - 792 - 448 + 576}{-2} \\
&= 42
\end{aligned}$$

which is indeed equal to the number of lattice points in Figure 3.

This calculation may appear to be quite complex in relation to our relatively small example, but it is easy to automate[6]. Note also that the complexity of the calculation depends only on the shape of the polytope, and not its size. If we took a region of a similar shape but many times larger, all that would change would be the exponents of x and y in the numerator of the generating function; the calculation required to determine the number of lattice points would be essentially identical to that above.

We have only considered Barvinok's construction for integral polytopes here, but the theory can be extended to rational polytopes as well. it is also possible to recover most of the theory of Ehrhart polynomials, which is useful for the study of parametric bounds. This approach is developed in detail by De Loera et al in [26], which describes the implementation of Barvinok's techniques in the `LattE` package. De Loera's work is applied to program analysis problems in [38], where much of Clauss' work is recast in terms of Barvinok's methods. Generating-function methods have recently been applied to the problem of Worst Case Execution Time in [27]. See also [9] for an exposition of the mathematics of the Barvinok theory.

3.5 Implementation

We have implemented (in OCaml) a Java compiler which uses lattice point enumeration techniques to calculate resource bounds for simple imperative programs. This is a preliminary implementation, but the results it produces are quite promising; it can successfully (and automatically) produce precise bounds for realistic matrix manipulation programs, for example (see Appendix A for some examples).

[5] If f and g are continuous at a and $\lim_{x\to a} f(x) = \lim_{x\to a} g(x) = 0$ then $\lim_{x\to a} f(x)/g(x) = \lim_{x\to a} f'(x)/g'(x)$.

[6] The calculation works particularly well for our example because our polygon is specially shaped; in the general case a more complex (but still tractable) computation is required.

Inferring linear constraints. The first phase of the compiler converts the source program to an expression-based form in which all names have been resolved. This form is very similar to the source program, and preserves the explicit control-flow structures of Java.

Our first task is to infer systems of linear constraints on program variables. The expression-based form is converted into a control-flow graph and then between every pair of expressions we infer a polyhedron which bounds the values of the integral variables in the program. This is done using a well-known technique due to Cousot and Halbwachs which involves abstract interpretation over a domain of polyhedra. See [16] for details.

A number of polyhedral operations are required to perform this process. It is necessary to have some representation of polyhedra and the means to convert between vertex and facet representations, and methods for combining polyhedra in various ways (intersection, join (polyhedral hull), widening, ...) are also needed. These can be difficult to program, but fortunately there are a number of high-quality libraries available. We have chosen to use the Parma Polyhedra Library (PPL) [5], which is a large C++ library providing all of the operations we require, including polyhedral widening operators (see [4]) necessary to ensure termination of the abstract interpretation process. The PPL also provides an OCaml interface which was convenient for linking with our OCaml-based compiler.

Using the PPL it was a relatively straightforward task to implement the Cousot-Halbwachs technique and obtain linear bounds on program variables.

Enumerating lattice points. Having determined polytopes controlling loop iteration, it is necessary to enumerate lattice points in order to find bounds on the number of loop executions. We have done this using the `barvinok` library[7] of Sven Verdoolaege, which implements the generating-function methods described in §3.4, and this enables us to automatically find our desired resource bounds.

There are certain difficulties in this approach however; in particular, it can be difficult to decide which variables control iterations, and what the dimension of the relevant polytope should be. Our prototype compiler works with a representation which has a fairly explicit representation of the loop structure of the input program, and we have developed heuristics which enable us to determine the relevant polytopes. This works well in practice, with realistic code examples, but it is possible to devise examples which cause the analysis to give incorrect results. However, we believe that this problem can be solved by methods which will be described below.

3.6 Analysing Compiled Bytecode

We are currently attempting to apply lattice-point methods to the resource analysis of JVM bytecode methods. A basic problem here is that it can be difficult to determine the precise loop structure of a program by examining the bytecode. Consider the following examples.

[7] `http://freshmeat.net/projects/barvinok/`

```
int i=0; int j=9; int k=0;

while (i<5) {
   j=9;
   while (j>0) {
      println ("Hello");
      j--;
   }
   i++;
}
```

Fig. 4.

```
int i=0; int j=100;

while (i<j) {
   println ("Hello");
   if (...) i++;
   else j--;
}
```

Fig. 5.

In Figure 4, the entire inner loop is executed once for each iteration of the outer loop, and the `println` method is called a total of 45 times; however, if the statement `j=9` is altered to `k=9` then the "inner" loop is executed once only, so `println` is executed only 9 times. This example shows that a very small change (only a single instruction in the compiled bytecode will change) can have a major effect on the resource usage of a program. The two versions of the program even have identical control-flow graphs, so it is not easy to see how to perform an accurate analysis of resource usage.

In Figure 5 the loop is controlled by two variables, but the iteration is one-dimensional. How can we recognise such patterns?

Instrumenting the code with counters. Gulwani et al [19] have proposed a technique for instrumenting with *counter variables* which can then be used for resource analysis. The example in Figure 5 would become

```
int i=0; int j=100; int c=0;

while (i<j) {
   println ("Hello");
   if (...) {i++; c++;}
   else {j--; c++}
}
```

The Cousot-Halbwachs technique can successfully analyse this example to deduce that $0 \leq c \leq 99$, allowing us to conclude that the loop is executed at most 100 times.

An algorithm is described in [19] which automatically discovers a collection of counters which can be used to instrument the back-edges in a control-flow graph and then used to analyse the resource usage. The algorithm also gives *dependencies* between counters which enable one to attack nested structures such as the one in Figure 4 above. However, the results of the analysis can be somewhat imprecise due to the fact that bounds associated with "nested" counters are simply multiplied together to obtain an overall bound.

We believe that the Gulwani algorithm can be refined to provide more precise relations between counters which can then be analysed using lattice-point methods to give more precise bounds on loop iterations.

We are currently implementing an analysis for compiled JVM bytecode which will combine the instrumentation technique of Gulwani with lattice-point methods and amortised analysis, and we hope that this will allow us to automatically analyse the resource consumption of many programs.

4 Further Work

The lattice-point techniques described above only apply to single methods. We would like to integrate our work with existing techniques to enable analysis of complete Java applications (including recursion).

Some of the geometrical algorithms are computationally expensive; in particular, the complexity of certain polyhedral operations grows exponentially as the dimension increases. We would like to develop certifying versions of these algorithms so that the output can be verified without excessive effort.

Polyhedral libraries are written in C++ and are very large and complex (PPL is over 100,000 lines long), and also depend on a number of external libraries (for example the `gmp` library for unlimited-precision arithmetic). This provides a lot of opportunities for bugs to creep in, and certifying algorithms would have the added benefit that they would allow us to be sure of the correctness of the output without having to trust the correctness of the libraries. See [29,23] for more on this point of view.

One of our motivations is to measure memory consumption of Java programs. A common assumption in research on this topic is that all objects from a given class are of the same size. However, this will not always be the case: for example, the Java `BigInteger` class represents integers with unlimited precision, and the size of an object will depend on the integer involved. Furthermore, the size of an object returned by a method may depend on the method arguments — consider the `BigInteger multiply` method. We are not aware of any previous research which is able to deal with this type of behaviour. However, there is some recent work by Verdoolaege and Bruynooghe [37] on *weighted generating functions* for polytopes, in which instead of considering the usual generating function $\sum\{\mathbf{x}^{\mathbf{v}} : \mathbf{v} \in P \cap \mathbb{Z}^d\}$, one considers a function of the form $\sum\{f(\mathbf{v})\mathbf{x}^{\mathbf{v}} : \mathbf{v} \in P \cap \mathbb{Z}^d\}$ in which each lattice point is weighted according to some function f. This corresponds to the situation in which a nest of loops indexed by $i_1, \ldots, i_d$ allocates an amount of memory given by the function $f(i_1, \ldots, i_d)$. It seems plausible that this work would be useful for attacking the problem of "dependent allocation" of the type discussed above.

Examination of a large number of examples suggests that most methods which involve loops deal either with iteration over data structures or with iteration controlled by integer variables, but that it is unusual to encounter situations which involve both simultaneously, the most common such situation being the conversion of a list to an array or vice versa. This makes us hopeful that a straightforward combination of our two techniques will enable the automatic analysis of a substantial proportion of Java methods. There are however certain situations where it is difficult to determine the amount of iteration required in advance — for example, worklist algorithms where processing one element of a queue may add an unpredictable number of new elements to the end of the queue, or iterative floating-point numerical algorithms where the number of iterations required is very sensitive to input data — and these remain beyond the scope of our methods at present.

Acknowledgments

This work was funded in part by the Sixth Framework programme of the European Community under the MOBIUS project FP6-015905. This report reflects only the author's views and the European Community is not liable for any use that may be made of the information contained therein.

This work was funded in part by the ReQueST grant (EP/C537068) from the EPSRC e-Science Programme, and by the RESA grant (EP/G006032/1) from the EPSRC Follow-on Fund.

References

1. Ahlfors, L.: Complex Analysis. International Series in Pure and Applied Mathematics. McGraw-Hill, New York (1979)
2. Albert, E., Arenas, P., Genaim, S., Puebla, G., Zanardini, D.: COSTA: Design and implementation of a cost and termination analyzer for Java bytecode. In: de Boer, F.S., Bonsangue, M.M., Graf, S., de Roever, W.-P. (eds.) FMCO 2007. LNCS, vol. 5382, pp. 113–132. Springer, Heidelberg (2008)
3. Atkey, R.: Amortised resource analysis with separation logic. In: Gordon, A.D. (ed.) Programming Languages and Systems. LNCS, vol. 6012, pp. 85–103. Springer, Heidelberg (2010)
4. Bagnara, R., Hill, P.M., Ricci, E., Zaffanella, E.: Precise widening operators for convex polyhedra. Science of Computer Programming 58(1-2), 28–56 (2005)
5. Bagnara, R., Hill, P.M., Zaffanella, E.: The Parma Polyhedra Library: Toward a complete set of numerical abstractions for the analysis and verification of hardware and software systems. Science of Computer Programming 72(1-2), 3–21 (2008)
6. Bagnara, R., Hill, P.M., Zaffanella, E.: Applications of polyhedral computations to the analysis and verification of hardware and software systems. Theor. Comput. Sci. 410(46), 4672–4691 (2009)
7. Barthe, G., Beringer, L., Crégut, P., Grégoire, B., Hofmann, M., Müller, P., Poll, E., Puebla, G., Stark, I., Vétillard, E.: MOBIUS: Mobility, ubiquity, security — objectives and progress report. In: Montanari, U., Sannella, D., Bruni, R. (eds.) TGC 2006. LNCS, vol. 4661, pp. 10–29. Springer, Heidelberg (2007)
8. Barvinok, A., Pommersheim, J.E.: An algorithmic theory of lattice points in polyhedra. In: New Perspectives in Algebraic Combinatorics (Berkeley, CA, 1996-1997). Math. Sci. Res. Inst. Publ, vol. 38, pp. 91–147. Cambridge Univ. Press, Cambridge (1999)

9. Beck, M., Robins, S.: Computing the Continuous Discretely. Undergraduate Texts in Mathematics, p. 226. Springer, Heidelberg (2007)
10. Beck, M., Sam, S., Woods, K.: Maximal periods of (Ehrhart) quasi-polynomials. J. Combin. Theory Ser. A 115, 517–525 (2008)
11. Berdine, J., Calcagno, C., O'Hearn, P.W.: Symbolic execution with separation logic. In: Yi, K. (ed.) APLAS 2005. LNCS, vol. 3780, pp. 52–68. Springer, Heidelberg (2005)
12. Braberman, V., Fernández, F., Garbervetsky, D., Yovine, S.: Symbolic prediction of dynamic memory requirements. In: ISMM (2008)
13. Braberman, V., Garbervetsky, D., Yovine, S.: A static analysis for synthesizing parametric specifications of dynamic memory consumption. Journal of Object Technology 5(5), 31–58 (2006)
14. Clauss, P.: Counting solutions to linear and nonlinear constraints through Ehrhart polynomials: applications to analyze and transform scientific programs. In: ICS 1996: Proceedings of the 10th International Conference on Supercomputing, Philadelphia, Pennsylvania, United States, pp. 278–285 (1996)
15. Clauss, P., Loechner, V.: Parametric analysis of polyhedral iteration spaces. Journal of VLSI Signal Processing 19, 179–194 (1998)
16. Cousot, P., Halbwachs, N.: Automatic discovery of linear restraints among variables of a program. In: POPL 1978: Proceedings of the 5th Annual ACM Symposium on Principles of Programming Languages, pp. 84–97. ACM Press, New York (1978)
17. Ehrhart, E.: Sur un problème de géométrie diophantienne linéaire. I. Polyèdres et réseaux. J. Reine Angew. Math. 226, 1–29 (1967)
18. Ehrhart, E.: Sur un problème de géométrie diophantienne linéaire. II. Systèmes diophantiens linéaires. J. Reine Angew. Math. 227, 25–49 (1967)
19. Gulwani, S., Mehra, K.K., Chilimbi, T.M.: SPEED: precise and efficient static estimation of program computational complexity. In: POPL 2009: Proceedings of the 36th ACM SIGPLAN-SIGACT Symposium on Principles of Programming Languages, pp. 127–139 (2009)
20. Hoffmann, J., Hofmann, M.: Amortized resource analysis with polynomial potential. In: Gordon, A.D. (ed.) Programming Languages and Systems. LNCS, vol. 6012, pp. 287–306. Springer, Heidelberg (2010)
21. Hofmann, M., Jost, S.: Static prediction of heap space usage for first-order functional programs. In: POPL 2003: Proceedings of the 30th ACM SIGPLAN-SIGACT Symposium on Principles of Programming Languages, pp. 185–197 (2003)
22. Ishtiaq, S., O'Hearn, P.W.: BI as an assertion language for mutable data structures. In: POPL 2001: Proceedings of the 28th ACM SIGPLAN-SIGACT Symposium on Principles of Programming Languages, pp. 14–26 (January 2001)
23. Kratsch, D., McConnell, R.M., Mehlhorn, K., Spinrad, J.P.: Certifying algorithms for recognizing interval graphs and permutation graphs. In: SODA 2003: Proceedings of the Fourteenth Annual ACM-SIAM Symposium on Discrete Algorithms, pp. 158–167 (2003)
24. Lengauer, C.: Loop parallelization in the polytope model. In: Best, E. (ed.) CONCUR 1993. LNCS, vol. 715, pp. 398–416. Springer, Heidelberg (1993)
25. Loechner, V., Wilde, D.K.: Parameterized polyhedra and their vertices. Int. J. of Parallel Programming 25, 25–26 (1997)
26. De Loera, J.A., Hemmecke, R., Tauzer, J., Yoshida, R.: Effective lattice point counting in rational convex polytopes. Journal of Symbolic Computation 38, 1273–1302 (2004)

27. Lokuciejewski, P., Cordes, D., Falk, H., Marwedel, P.: A fast and precise static loop analysis based on abstract interpretation, program slicing and polytope models. In: CGO 2009: Proceedings of the 2009 International Symposium on Code Generation and Optimization, pp. 136–146 (2009)
28. McAllister, T.B.: Coefficient functions of the Ehrhart quasi-polynomials of rational polygons. In: ITSL, pp. 114–118. CSREA Press (2008)
29. K. Mehlhorn, A. Eigenwillig, K. Kanegossi, D. Kratsch, R. McConnel, U. Meyer, J. Spinrad. Certifying algorithms (a paper under construction) (2005), `http://www.mpi-inf.mpg.de/~mehlhorn/ftp/CertifyingAlgorithms.pdf`
30. Meister, B.: Approximations of polytope enumerators using linear expansions. Technical report, Universite Louis Pasteur (May 2007)
31. Necula, G.C.: Proof-carrying code. In: POPL 1997: Proceedings of the 24th ACM SIGPLAN-SIGACT Symposium on Principles of Programming Languages, pp. 106–119 (1997)
32. Pouchet, L.-N., Bastoul, C., Cohen, A., Cavazos, J.: Iterative optimization in the polyhedral model: part II, multidimensional time. SIGPLAN Not. 43(6), 90–100 (2008)
33. Pugh, W.: Counting solutions to Presburger formulas: how and why. In: PLDI 1994: Proceedings of the ACM SIGPLAN 1994 Conference on Programming Language Design and Implementation, pp. 121–134. ACM, New York (1994)
34. Reynolds, J.C.: Separation logic: A logic for shared mutable data structures. In: Proceedings of 17th Annual IEEE Symposium on Logic in Computer Science, Copenhagen, Denmark (2002)
35. Sannella, D., Hofmann, M., Aspinall, D., Gilmore, S., Stark, I., Beringer, L., Loidl, H.-W., MacKenzie, K., Momigliano, A., Shkaravska, O.: Mobile resource guarantees. In: Trends in Functional Programming, vol. 6, pp. 211–226. Intellect, Bristol (2007)
36. Tarjan, R.E.: Amortized computational complexity. SIAM Journal on Algebraic and Discrete Methods 6(2), 306–318 (1985)
37. Verdoolaege, S., Bruynooghe, M.: Algorithms for weighted counting over parametric polytopes: A survey and a practical comparison. In: The 2008 International Conference on Information Theory and Statistical Learning, pp. 60–66 (2008)
38. Verdoolaege, S., Seghir, R., Beyls, K., Loechner, V., Bruynooghe, M.: Analytical computation of Ehrhart polynomials: Enabling more compiler analyses and optimizations. In: Proceedings of the 2004 International Conference on Compilers, Architecture, and Synthesis for Embedded Systems (CASES), pp. 248–258 (September 2004)

A Appendix: Examples of Polyhedral Analysis

A.1 Gaussian Elimination

The code below is an implementation of Gaussian elimination for the solution of simultaneous linear equations. This is based on code which was downloaded from the WWW [8], but it has been modified by adding `println` methods to give the analysis something to count, and by replacing references to `A.length` by an integer `N` since our analysis currently only takes account of program variables, and cannot deal with fields.

```
public static double[] lsolve(double[][] A, double[] b, int N) {
  for (int p = 0; p < N; p++) {          System.out.println ("Loop 1");
    int max = p;
    for (int i = p; i < N; i++) {        System.out.println ("Loop 2");
      if (Math.abs(A[i][p]) > Math.abs(A[max][p]))
          max = i;
    }
    double[] temp = A[p]; A[p] = A[max]; A[max] = temp;
    double t      = b[p]; b[p] = b[max]; b[max] = t;

    if (Math.abs(A[p][p]) <= EPSILON)  // EPSILON = 10e-6
      throw new RuntimeException("Matrix is singular or nearly singular");

    for (int i = p+1; i < N; i++) {      System.out.println ("Loop 3");
      double alpha = A[i][p] / A[p][p];
      b[i] -= alpha * b[p];
      for (int j = p; j < N; j++) {      System.out.println ("Loop 4");
        A[i][j] -= alpha * A[p][j];
      }
    }
  }

  double[] x = new double[N];
  for (int i = N - 1; i >= 0; i--) {     System.out.println ("Loop 5");
    double sum = 0.0;
    for (int j = i + 1; j < N; j++) {    System.out.println ("Loop 6");
      sum += A[i][j] * x[j];
    }
    x[i] = (b[i] - sum) / A[i][i];
  }
  return x;
}
```

The output from the analysis appears below, with bounds on the number of calls to each `println` statement in the same order as in the program text. The analysis successfully finds tight bounds for the various nested loops.

[8] `http://www.cs.princeton.edu/introcs/95linear/GaussianElimination.java.html`

```
==== method lsolve ====

 Calls to java.io.PrintStream.println (java.lang.String):
  N                     {1 <= N, 0 <= 1}

 Calls to java.io.PrintStream.println (java.lang.String):
  N^2                   {1 <= N, 0 <= 1}

 Calls to java.io.PrintStream.println (java.lang.String):
  -N/2 + N^2/2          {2 <= N, 0 <= 1}

 Calls to java.io.PrintStream.println (java.lang.String):
  -N/3 + 0 + N^3/3      {2 <= N, 0 <= 1}

 Calls to java.io.PrintStream.println (java.lang.String):
  N                     {1 <= N, 0 <= 1}

 Calls to java.io.PrintStream.println (java.lang.String):
  -N/2 + N^2/2          {2 <= N, 0 <= 1}
```

A.2 Multiple Parameters

We also include a simple example involving multiple parameters which demonstrates the strength of the mathematical techniques underlying our analysis.

```
public static void f (int p, int q) {
  for (int i=0; i <= p; i++)
    for (int j=0; j <= 9 && i+j <= q; j++)
      System.out.println ("Hello");
}
```

The number of iterations depends on the relative values of the arguments p and q, with different Ehrhart polynomials applying for different combinations of arguments. The barvinok library is able to calculate these automatically, and comparatively little programming effort was required on our part to enable the analysis to find results of this type.

```
Calls to java.io.PrintStream.println (java.lang.String):
5 domains in R^2

-35 + 10q                                             {q <= p, 10 <= q, 0 <= 1}

1 + (3/2)q + q^2/2                                    {q <= p, 0 <= q, q <= 9}

(1 + q) + (1/2 + q)p + -p^2/2                         {q <= 9, 0 <= p, p+1 <= q}

10 + 10p                                              {0 <= p, p+10 <= q, 0 <= 1}

(-35 + (19/2)q + -q^2/2) + (1/2 + q)p + -p^2/2 {p+1 <= q, q <= p+9, 10 <= q}
```

Perspectives in Certificate Translation

Gilles Barthe and César Kunz

IMDEA Software, Spain

Abstract. Certificate translation is a general mechanism to transfer evidence across abstraction layers, from source code to executable code. We review the general principles behind certificate translation and the main results achieved so far, and outline directions for future work.

1 Introduction

Certificate translation aims to provide the benefits of (typically interactive) source code verification to code consumers, building upon the notion of certificate used in Proof Carrying Code [14]. More precisely, the primary goal of certificate translation is to transform certificates of source programs into certificates of compiled programs. By design, certificate translation is very general and can be used to enforce arbitrarily complex properties of programs, provided they can be expressed and formally established using source code verification frameworks.

The problem of certificate translation can be expressed informally in a very general form. Consider two programming languages, a source language Prog_s and a target language Prog_t, each equipped with a specification language, respectively Spec_l and Spec_t, and with a verification framework. We assume that the verification frameworks are equipped with a notion of proof object, a.k.a. certificate, and axiomatize the verification frameworks as ternary relations for certificate checkers, written $c : p \models s$, stating that c is a certificate that p adheres to s, where p is a program belonging to Prog_s (resp. Prog_t), s is a specification belonging to Spec_s (resp. Spec_t) and c belongs to the set Prf_s of source certificates (resp. Prf_t of target certificates). Assuming a compiler for programs $\mathcal{C} : \mathsf{Prog}_s \to \mathsf{Prog}_t$, and a compiler for specifications $\mathcal{C}_{\mathrm{spec}} : \mathsf{Spec}_s \to \mathsf{Spec}_t$, the problem is to find a certificate translation, i.e. a function $\mathcal{C}_{\mathrm{cert}} : \mathsf{Prf}_s \to \mathsf{Prf}_t$ such that for all source programs p, policies s, and certificates c,

$$c : p \models s \quad \Longrightarrow \mathcal{C}_{\mathrm{cert}}(c) : \mathcal{C}(p) \models \mathcal{C}_{\mathrm{spec}}(s)$$

The formal study of certificate translation requires that all the parameters are instantiated, and defined formally: source and target programming and specification languages, certificate checkers for source and compiled programs, and finally compilers for programs, specifications, and certificates. Our work focuses on verification infrastructures that rely on verification condition generators (VC Generator), which are used in many interactive verification environments at source level, and in automated verification tools at compile level. A VC Generator can be seen

M. Wirsing, M. Hofmann, and A. Rauschmayer (Eds.): TGC 2010, LNCS 6084, pp. 23–34, 2010.

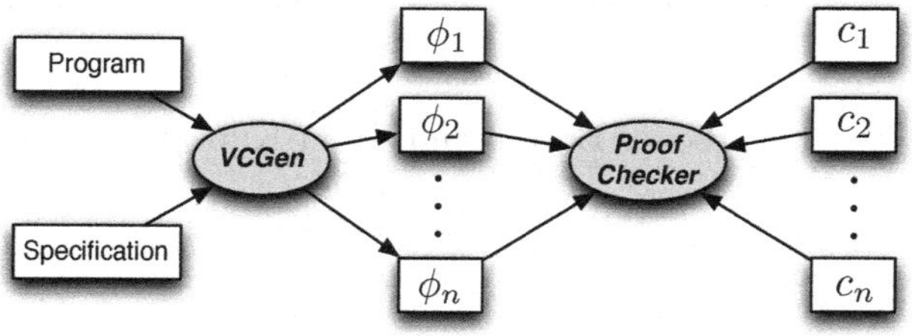

Fig. 1. Verification Infrastructure

as a strategy of applying the rules of an Hoare logic, and extracts automatically a set of proof obligations from an annotated program—annotations include loop invariants, preconditions and postconditions. There are several advantages to verification condition generators, other than their predominance in verification tools: the proof obligations are expressed in the specification language, abstracting away from the programming language; moreover, the certificate does not need to store the application of the rules of the Hoare logic, since the strategy is fixed; hence, standard notions of proof objects can be used as certificates. Figure 1 considers a program verification infrastructure for a specific programming language. The VC Generator takes a program and specification and produces a set of proof obligations attesting the adherence of the program to its specification. A certificate c consists of a set of proof objects $(c_i)_{i \in I}$ such that each proof obligation generated by the VC Generator is validated by a proof object c_i.

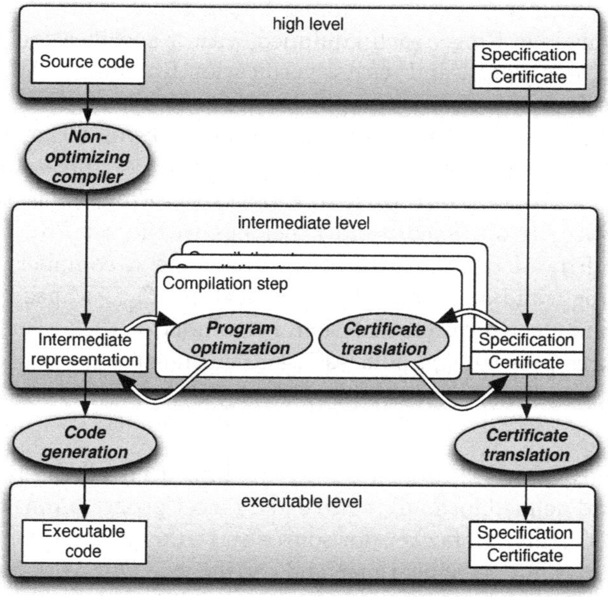

Fig. 2. Overall picture of the Optimizing Infrastructure

Optimizing compilers typically perform several passes over programs and rely on various intermediate program representations. In general, the first pass is handled by a non optimizing that compiler generates, from a source program, a sequence of instructions at the intermediate level language. Then, a series of optimizations are performed successively over the intermediate program, possibly changing the representation language. Finally, executable code is generated from an optimized intermediate representation. In this setting, one must define and prove correct a certificate translator for each validation phase; concretely, it involves: i) defining for each intermediate program representation a verification condition generator; ii) defining for each optimization pass an algorithm to transform specifications and certificates; iii) proving that the certificate transformer is sound. Certificate transformers compose naturally. Figure 2 depicts the overall compilation schema, where the sequence of optimization phases is justified by certificate transformers.

2 Main Results

We have explored certificate translation in different settings: imperative, object-oriented, concurrent and parallel programs, both for non-optimizing and optimizing compilers.

Preservation of proof obligations. The first compilation pass typically transforms programs to an intermediate format, without performing any optimization. Such non-optimizing compilation preserves proof obligations in a very strong sense [7,2]. Let p be a program and $\mathcal{C}(p)$ the result of non-optimizing compilation; typically p is written in a high-level imperative language and $\mathcal{C}(p)$ is written in some intermediate language such as Register Transfer Language (RTL). Assume that a VC Generator vcgen generates a set of proof obligations from a program and its specification s, both at source and intermediate levels. If the set of proof obligations for the original and compiled programs coincide, i.e. the proof obligations are equal up to syntactic equality:

$$\mathsf{vcgen}(p, s) = \mathsf{vcgen}(\mathcal{C}(p), s)$$

then one can reuse the certificates of the source code program for the intermediate program. Formally, one can define $\mathcal{C}_{\mathrm{cert}}$ as the identity function since:

$$c : p \models s \quad \Longleftrightarrow c : \mathcal{C}(p) \models s$$

Preservation of proof obligations requires that proof obligations are syntactically equal, which may be a strong requirement in practice. Often proof obligations are preserved up to minor differences; for example, variable conventions may differ in the source and target languages (named variables vs. indexes), or datatypes may be handled differently (booleans compiled to integers), or syntactic optimizations are performed (e.g. transformations that can be proved sound from the syntax of the programs, such as transforming conditionals with true or false guards). In [1], we report on a prototype compiler from a simple structured language to RTL and show that proof obligations coincide up to minor differences that are easily handled.

Preservation of proof obligations is relevant in the setting of non-optimizing compilation from source code to bytecode that can be executed by a virtual machine. Such compilers are standard for Java or .NET bytecode, where optimizations are delegated to a JIT compiler that operates on the consumer side. Barthe, Grégoire and Pavlova [3] show that proof obligations are preserved for the compilation of Java programs to JVM bytecode, in a simplified setting that avoids the issues of naming, datatype representations, and simple optimizations.

Optimizing compilation. Preservation of proof obligations is invalidated by compiler optimizations. Consider the following piece of code:

$$\begin{array}{l} \mathtt{y} := 2; \\ \mathtt{while}\ b\ \mathsf{do}\ \mathtt{y} := \mathtt{y} + 2; \\ \mathtt{if}\ (\mathsf{even}(\mathtt{y}))\ \mathtt{then}\ c_1\ \mathtt{else}\ c_2; \end{array}$$

with loop invariant Inv and postcondition post. One of the proof obligations returned by the VC Generator is:

$$\mathsf{Inv} \wedge \neg b \Rightarrow (\mathsf{even}(\mathtt{y}) \Rightarrow \mathsf{wp}(c_1, \mathsf{post})) \wedge (\neg\mathsf{even}(\mathtt{y}) \Rightarrow \mathsf{wp}(c_2, \mathsf{post}))$$

One can transform the program by redundant conditional elimination into:

$$\begin{array}{l} \mathtt{y} := 2; \\ \mathtt{while}\ b\ \mathsf{do}\ \mathtt{y} := \mathtt{y} + 2; \\ c_1; \end{array}$$

A VC Generator for the same specification returns the proof obligation

$$\mathsf{Inv} \wedge \neg b \Rightarrow \mathsf{wp}(c_1, \mathsf{post})$$

which does not coincide syntactically with the original one, and thus, the certificate cannot be reused. Furthermore, the transformed proof obligation may become invalid if $\mathsf{Inv} \wedge \neg b$ does not imply $\mathsf{even}(\mathtt{y})$. To recover a valid proof obligation, one must strengthen annotations with the results of the static analyses that are used for justifying the program transformation. In the example above, one must reinforce the invariant with the condition $\mathsf{even}(\mathtt{y})$ that is inferred by the analyzer.

Invariant strengthening introduces an additional set of proof obligations that must be discharged; for the above example, we must in particular prove that $\mathsf{even}(\mathtt{y})$ is an invariant of the loop. These additional proof obligations are valid if the analyzer is correct. Nevertheless, this is not sufficient for our purpose: one must also provide independently verifiable certificates of their validity. For most textbook optimizations, one can implement certifying analyzers that produce, in addition to analysis results, a certificate of their correctness in the underlying verification logic [2]. In the program above, one must assume that the analyzer can produce a certificate of the loop invariant $\mathsf{even}(\mathsf{y})$. This requires discharging the proof obligations $\mathsf{even}(2)$ and $\mathsf{even}(\mathsf{y}) \Rightarrow \mathsf{even}(\mathsf{y}+2)$.

Given a certifying analyzer, one can define a certificate translator that merges the proof of the analysis with the original proof to build a certificate for the optimized program. There are two possible approaches for merging certificates; the first approach is generic and relies on a well-founded induction principle that one can extract from the structure of programs—the verification framework assumes that programs are sufficiently annotated, i.e. all loops must go through an annotated program point. This approach has been applied over a sequence of compilation steps, that includes many program optimizations found on compiler textbooks. The second, so-called direct, approach focuses on optimizations defined as arithmetic simplification, that includes for instance Constant Propagation, Loop Induction Variable Strength Reduction, Common Subexpression Elimination, Copy Propagation. Certificate translation is defined in these cases as an ad-hoc strategy that syntactically compares the transformed proof obligation with the original ones, and computes a set of sufficient conditions under which the proof obligations are equivalent. For this class of optimizations, proof obligations differs on substitutions of expressions. The advantage of this technique is that the certificate translator is not necessarily embedded into the compiler, since proof obligations are analyzed as black-boxes after the optimization. In addition, experimental results show that the size of the final certificate is greatly reduced, and that it is easy to discharge the required proof obligations.

Prototype implementation. A prototype implementation of certificate translation using the direct approach has been implemented [1]. The prototype takes as input a certified imperative program and returns a certified RTL representation. It applies first a non-optimizing transformation from the source language to RTL, and then a sequence of compilation steps that rely on arithmetic simplification. The prototype has been used to show the applicability of certificate translation a common class of textbook optimizations. The additional verification effort required for a certificate translator has been automatically discharged by application of the Coq ring tactic.

Abstract interpretation model. While certificate translators are strongly coupled to a programming language, a verification setting and a compiling infrastructure, it is of interest to develop results asserting a general theory of certificate translation.

Abstract interpretation [9] is a general framework that has been used for automatically analyzing programs, and more globally for reasoning about program analysis and verification methods. Abstract interpretation is a natural setting to model certificate translation, since it provides a common model for the verification environment and the analysis framework used for certifying analysis.

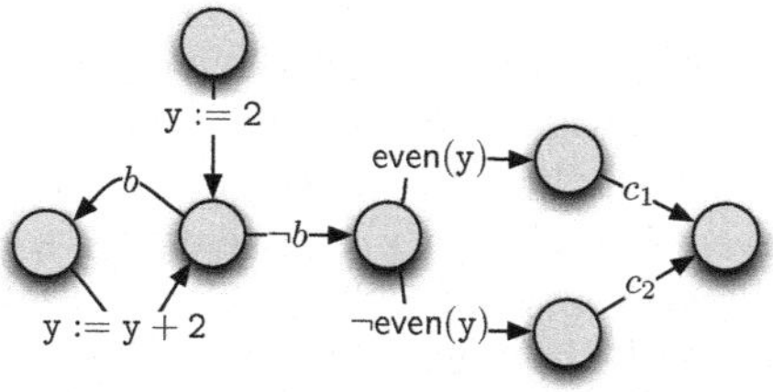

Fig. 3. Program representation as a transition system

A model of certificate translation based on abstract interpretation is developed in [4], allowing to cover a wider range of programming languages, verification settings, and optimizations.

In this work, programs are represented as transition systems, that is, as directed graphs in which nodes represent program points and edges are labeled with a relation that characterizes the program semantics. A transition system representation of the program above is shown in Fig. 3.

Both the verification and analysis frameworks are defined as abstract interpretations, using a very mild extension of the standard framework in which certificates are used to witness the correctness of a solution. In the abstract setting, annotations are represented as partial labellings from program nodes to abstract values and verification consists in checking whether the labeling satisfies a set of inequalities in the abstract domain. We exploit the generality of the abstract interpretation framework to obtain results that apply to backwards verification frameworks such as Verification Condition Generation as well as forward verification frameworks such as Symbolic Execution.

The main results of [4] are a set of sufficient conditions for the existence of certifying analyzers, and of certificate translators. For the latter, we consider basic transformations rather than a particular set of program optimizations; the basic transformations include replacing an edge by another (structure-preserving optimization), duplicating code (loop unrolling, function inlining), and coalescing nodes into a single one (dead code, code motion). These basic transformations can be combined to define many common optimizations, including those considered in [2].

Hybrid verification. Program verification environments typically combine verification condition generation with static analyses. The VC Generator exploits the information of the analysis in two useful ways: on the one hand, verification conditions that originate from spurious edges in the control-flow graph are discarded. This leads to fewer and smaller proof obligations. Furthermore, the VC Generator adds the results of the analysis as additional assumptions to help prove the verification conditions. In the following example, the procedure f is invoked for every element in the range $[0, N)$ of the array a:

```
i := 0
while (i < N) {
  f(a[i]);
  i := i + 1
}
```

Let Inv stand for the loop invariant, $|a|$ denote the length of the array, and assume $N \leq |a|$. A weakest-precondition function that ensures the absence of run-time errors may return a proof obligation of the form

$$\mathsf{Inv} \wedge (\mathtt{i} < N) \Rightarrow 0 \leq \mathtt{i} < |\mathsf{a}| \wedge \mathsf{Inv}'$$

for some formula Inv'. One can simplify such proof obligation by relying on a static analysis that infers that i holds values inside the bounds of the array a.

Thus, hybrid verification methods simplify the task of program verification; however, hybrid verification methods can be embedded into standard methods. In [5], we define a compiler that transforms a hybrid specification (merging logical assertions and analysis results) into a standard one by giving a logical interpretation of the analysis results. This result ensures soundness of the hybrid verification method from the soundness of the standard VC Generator.

Moreover, [5] extends preservation of proof obligations to hybrid verification methods. One well-known difficulty for achieving such a result is the loss of precision of static analysis results by compilation [13]. To solve this difficulty, we achieve preservation of solutions by defining at bytecode level a symbolic execution that decompiles stack instructions, in the style of [8].

Concurrency and parallelism. We have conducted two preliminary studies of certificate translation for concurrent and parallel programming languages. The first extension [6] deals with parallel divide-and-conquer programs over hierarchical memories. It is based on the Sequoia programming language, whose constructions support high-performance computing on modern computer architectures. We use the framework of abstract interpretation to design analysis and verification frameworks to reason about Sequoia programs. A main component of this framework is an analysis that checks whether subtasks operate over disjoint portions of the memory. We use the framework of abstract interpretation to design analysis and verification frameworks to reason about Sequoia programs, and define certificate translation procedures for typical optimizations, including SPMD distribution, Exec Grouping and Copy grouping.

The second extension [10] deals with concurrent programs executing over a shared-memory model. In this setting, sequential components of the concurrent program are defined as simple while programs and optimizations are applied to the sequential program components. In this execution model, the concurrent interference on the shared state space may affect the validity of local specifications. Program verification is thus carried in two steps: first, each program component is certified against its local specification, then the local specifications are proved stable with respect to the global concurrent environment. We extend certifying analyzers to produce, in addition to a local certificate, a formal proof of stability with respect to the concurrent environment. Similarly, certificate translation must deal with the effect that a local component optimization has on the verification conditions for global stability.

3 Issues

Our work on certificate translation has mostly focused on program optimizations in intermediate compiler phases. We briefly review some open issues.

Loop optimizations. Our work has considered a number of loop transformations, e.g., strength reduction, unrolling, and loop-invariant code motion. However, loop optimizations that change the iteration order, or that merge or split loops, are challenging. For instance, it is common to deal with programs of the form:

```
i := 0;
while i < N do {
    c;
    i := i + 1
}
```

For such programs the verification of the invariant depends on the execution order: verifying an invariant $\varphi(\mathtt{i})$ involves discharging the goals $\mathsf{Inv}(0)$ and $\mathsf{Inv}(\mathtt{i}) \wedge \mathtt{i} < N \Rightarrow \varphi'(\mathtt{i}+1)$, for some φ'. Although reversing the iteration order when every pair of iterations are interference-free is semantics-preserving, adapting the original verification result is a hard problem en general.

Assembly code. Our results consider the compilation of source code to an intermediate format. This may be sufficient in a Proof Carrying Code scenario where applications are distributed as interpretable bytecode. However, there is a need to consider certificate translation for the remaining compiler phases, that generates native code from an intermediate representation.

There are a number of issues for extending certificate translation to machine code. First, one must consider a transformation that performs register allocation. In this compilation phase, pseudo-registers used in the intermediate RTL representation are mapped to real machine registers. Since there are a finite number of real registers, the compiler may need to temporarily store some of the pseudo-registers in memory (spilling). A further transformation step is the linearization of the control flow graph. In this step, the control flow graph is flattened as a list of instructions, in which each instruction determines explicitly the set of successor program points. This simple step does not introduce changes in the proof obligations and thus certificates can be reused. Additionally, a compiler step must transform the basic RTL arithmetic operations to the corresponding machine operations. This process is part of the compiler backend and depends on the target executing architecture.

Concurrency. Parallelization techniques exploit the analysis of program interference, allowing the concurrent execution of program fragments that access disjoint regions of the memory space. Parallelizing program transformations have a significant effect on the program structure, making difficult the reuse of verification results. Certificate translation commonly needs to establish a strong connection between the analysis that justifies a program transformation and the verification framework. It seems convenient then to consider a common framework that enables an explicit reasoning on the memory space independence, such as separation logic [18], which has been used recently to discover parallelization opportunities [17].

4 Related Work

The purpose of this section is to compare certificate translation and related techniques from the perspective of an application scenario. A more technical comparison is found e.g. in [2].

4.1 Application Scenario

Certificate translation is useful in scenarios where the reliability and security of software must be independently verifiable: outsourcing safety and security-critical software is an important application, especially for application domains where software must be approved by certification authorities. The purpose of this section is to suggest a possible application scenario.

The scenario involves a software developer, a software integrator, and a software validator. The software developer is a smallish IT company which has developed highly efficient and reliable tools for a specific problem. Their tools are very generic and they can be specialized to many settings according to the needs of their customers. The software developer sells specialized solutions, and does not want to reveal his know-how.

The software integrator is a big company that produces large-scale systems for embedded systems or avionics. The company outsources the production of several critical components of their systems to external software developers, and pass them on the need of producing verifiable evidence of the correctness of their components. Thus, the software developer must provide an independently verifiable correctness proof of the executable code it delivers. Using certificate translation, the software developer can provide verifiable evidence without revealing information about its compiler. Moreover, the software developer is able to reason on the source code, avoiding duplication of efforts for programs that are compiled to multiple platforms.

Finally, the software integrator is able to combine the different certificates to provide verifiable evidence that the system is globally correct, and submit the software system together with the accompanying verifiable evidence to a software validator that can check global correctness.

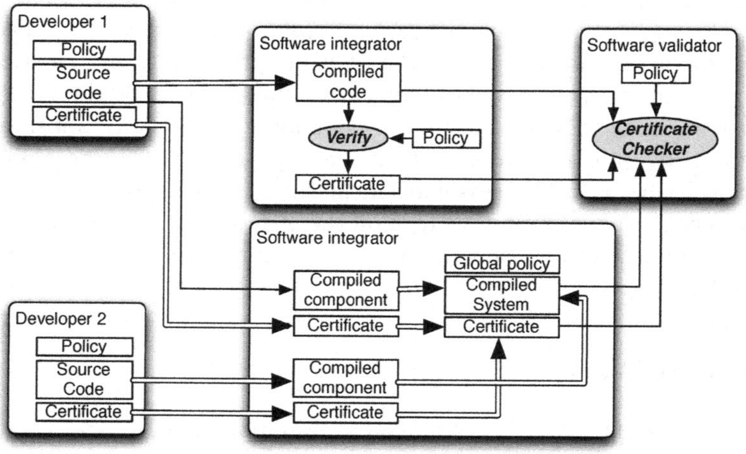

A related scenario involves a software developer, a service provider, and a end-user [7]. The service provider is a mobile phone operator that must decide whether or not to endorse a new application for mobile phones. For liability reasons, the mobile phone operator does not want to see the source code and does not want to engage in costly verification. On the other hand, the mobile phone operator cannot simply release the code without warranty because the permissions of the program will depend on him endorsing the code. Using certificate translation, the software developer can prove that his source code ensures the policy advertised by the mobile phone operator, and rely on certificate translation to obtain verifiable evidence for the code that he eventually ships to the mobile phone operator.

4.2 Related Work from an Application Scenario Perspective

The initial motivation for certificate translation is Proof Carrying Code [14]. Therefore, certificate translators share fundamental characteristics with *certifying compilers* [14], namely targeting the same certificate checking infrastructure on the consumer side, and not forming part of the Trusted Computing Base. However, certificate translators differ from certifying compilers in their scope, and in their level of automation; while certifying compilers focus on generating automatically certificates for a small set of established policies, such as memory safety, type safety or even non-interference, certificate translation aims to provide certificates for arbitrarily rich policies, at the cost of giving up automatic generation of certificates.

Certified compilation [11,12] advocates using proof assistants for verifying compiler correctness. Certified compilation involves: i) defining formally the source, intermediate and target languages; ii) formally specifying the operational semantics of these languages; iii) formally defining the compiler passes, and proving that they preserve the semantics of programs. There are close connections between certificate translation and certified compilation; these connections are captured explicitly in [11,12], where Leroy defines abstract versions of certificate translation and certified compilation and show their equivalence. Nevertheless for our application scenario there are important practical differences between both approaches. Concretely, certificate translation based on certified compilation requires that the software developer provides the source program and the compiler to the software integrator, which is an issue. Moreover, certified compilation is restricted to input/output properties of programs; unfortunately, many interesting properties of programs must be specified using assertions or ghost variables. Finally, generating certificates from certified compilation entails that certificates of executable programs embed the correctness proof of the compiler, which is undesirable.

Translation validation is an alternative to certified compilation that aims at showing, for each individual run of the compiler, that the resulting target program implements correctly the source program, i.e. it has the same semantics. There are two styles of translation validation: in the work of Pnueli, Siegel and Singerman [16], the correctness of the compiler run is established using general purpose verification tools. In contrast, the work of Necula [15] relies on specific and certified verification tools. In comparison with certified compilation, some issues with our application scenarios are overcome with translation validation, e.g. the size of certificates might be significantly smaller. However, issues such as providing source code remain.

Acknowledgments. Thanks to Benjamin Grégoire, Sylvain Heraud, Anne Pacalet, Mariela Pavlova, David Pichardie, Ando Saabas, Jorge Sacchini, Julian Samborski and Tamara Rezk, who contributed to the development of certificate translation. This work benefited from discussion with members of the MOBIUS project. This work is partially funded by the EU projects Mobius and HATS, the Spanish project Desafios 10, and the Community of Madrid project Prometidos.

References

1. Barthe, G., Grégoire, B., Heraud, S., Kunz, C., Pacalet, A.: Implementing a direct method for certificate translation. In: Breitman, K., Cavalcanti, A. (eds.) ICFEM 2009. LNCS, vol. 5885, pp. 541–560. Springer, Heidelberg (2009)
2. Barthe, G., Grégoire, B., Kunz, C., Rezk, T.: Certificate translation for optimizing compilers. ACM Transactions on Programming Languages and Systems 31(5), 18:1–18:45 (2009)
3. Barthe, G., Grégoire, B., Pavlova, M.: Preservation of Proof Obligations from Java to the Java Virtual Machine. In: Armando, A., Baumgartner, P., Dowek, G. (eds.) IJCAR 2008. LNCS (LNAI), vol. 5195, pp. 83–99. Springer, Heidelberg (2008)
4. Barthe, G., Kunz, C.: Certificate translation in abstract interpretation. In: Drossopoulou, S. (ed.) ESOP 2008. LNCS, vol. 4960, pp. 368–382. Springer, Heidelberg (2008)
5. Barthe, G., Kunz, C., Pichardie, D., Samborski-Forlese, J.: Preservation of proof obligations for hybrid verification methods. In: Cerone, A., Gruner, S. (eds.) Software Engineering and Formal Methods, pp. 127–136. IEEE Press, Los Alamitos (2008)

6. Barthe, G., Kunz, C., Sacchini, J.L.: Certified reasoning in memory hierarchies. In: Ramalingam, G. (ed.) APLAS 2008. LNCS, vol. 5356, pp. 75–90. Springer, Heidelberg (2008)
7. Barthe, G., Rezk, T., Saabas, A.: Proof obligations preserving compilation. In: Dimitrakos, T., Martinelli, F., Ryan, P.Y.A., Schneider, S. (eds.) FAST 2005. LNCS, vol. 3866, pp. 112–126. Springer, Heidelberg (2005)
8. Besson, F., Jensen, T., Pichardie, D., Turpin, T.: Result certification for relational program analysis. Research Report 6333, IRISA (September 2007)
9. Cousot, P., Cousot, R.: Abstract interpretation: A unified lattice model for static analysis of programs by construction or approximation of fixpoints. In: Principles of Programming Languages, pp. 238–252 (1977)
10. Kunz, C.: Certificate translation for the verification of concurrent programs. In: Hofmann, M., Wirsing, M. (eds.) TGC 2010. LNCS, vol. 6084, pp. 238–253. Springer, Heidelberg (2010)
11. Leroy, X.: Formal certification of a compiler back-end or: programming a compiler with a proof assistant. In: Morrisett, J.G., Peyton Jones, S.L. (eds.) Principles of Programming Languages, pp. 42–54. ACM Press, New York (2006)
12. Leroy, X.: A formally verified compiler back-end. J. Autom. Reasoning 43(4), 363–446 (2009)
13. Logozzo, F., Fähndrich, M.: On the relative completeness of bytecode analysis versus source code analysis. In: Hendren, L. (ed.) CC 2008. LNCS, vol. 4959, pp. 197–212. Springer, Heidelberg (2008)
14. Necula, G.C.: Compiling with Proofs. PhD thesis, Carnegie Mellon University (October 1998), Available as Technical Report CMU-CS-98-154
15. Necula, G.C.: Translation validation for an optimizing compiler. ACM SIGPLAN Notices 35(5), 83–94 (2000)
16. Pnueli, A., Singerman, E., Siegel, M.: Translation validation. In: Steffen, B. (ed.) TACAS 1998. LNCS, vol. 1384, pp. 151–166. Springer, Heidelberg (1998)
17. Raza, M., Calcagno, C., Gardner, P.: Automatic parallelization with separation logic. In: Castagna, G. (ed.) ESOP 2009. LNCS, vol. 5502, pp. 348–362. Springer, Heidelberg (2009)
18. Reynolds, J.C.: Separation logic: A logic for shared mutable data structures. In: Logic in Computer Science. IEEE Press, Los Alamitos (July 2002)

Uniform Labeled Transition Systems for Nondeterministic, Probabilistic, and Stochastic Processes

Marco Bernardo[1], Rocco De Nicola[2], and Michele Loreti[2]

[1] Dipartimento di Matematica, Fisica e Informatica – Università di Urbino, Italy
[2] Dipartimento di Sistemi e Informatica – Università di Firenze, Italy

Abstract. Rate transition systems (RTS) are a special kind of transition systems introduced for defining the stochastic behavior of processes and for associating continuous-time Markov chains with process terms. The transition relation assigns to each process, for each action, the set of possible futures paired with a measure indicating the rates at which they are reached. RTS have been shown to be a uniform model for providing an operational semantics to many stochastic process algebras. In this paper, we define Uniform Labeled TRAnsition Systems (ULTRAS) as a generalization of RTS that can be exploited to uniformly describe also nondeterministic and probabilistic variants of process algebras. We then present a general notion of behavioral relation for ULTRAS that can be instantiated to capture bisimulation and trace equivalences for fully nondeterministic, fully probabilistic, and fully stochastic processes.

1 Introduction

Process algebras have been successfully used in the last thirty years to model the behavior and prove properties of concurrent systems. The basic ingredients of these formalisms, apart from specific syntactic operators used to define the term algebra, are labeled transition systems (LTS) and behavioral relations in the form of equivalences or preorders. By exploiting the so-called structural operational semantics, a LTS is "compositionally" associated with each term. LTS possibly corresponding to terms describing systems at different levels of abstraction are then compared according to one of the many behavioral relations that have been proposed in the literature.

Initially, the behavioral relations were mainly designed to assess whether two systems have comparable functional (extensional) behavior, i.e., whether they could perform similar actions. However, soon after witnessing the success of the process algebraic approach, it was noticed that other aspects of concurrent systems are at least as important as the functional ones. Thus, many variants of process algebras have been introduced to take into account quantitative aspects of concurrent systems and we have seen proposals of *(deterministically) timed* process algebra, *probabilistic* process algebras, and *stochastic(ally timed)* process

M. Wirsing, M. Hofmann, and A. Rauschmayer (Eds.): TGC 2010, LNCS 6084, pp. 35–56, 2010.

algebras. Their semantics has then been rendered in terms of richer LTS quotiented with new behavioral relations and we have read of (deterministically) timed, probabilistic, and stochastic(ally timed) relations.

The line of research targeted to stochastic variants of process algebras has been particularly productive due to the importance of shared-resource systems. The main aim has been the integration of qualitative descriptions with quantitative (especially performance) ones in a single mathematical framework by building on the combination of LTS and continuous-time Markov chains (CTMC), one of the most successful approaches to modeling and analyzing the performance of computer systems and networks. The common feature of the most prominent stochastic process algebra proposals is that the actions used to label transitions are enriched with rates of exponentially distributed *random variables* characterizing their duration. Although the same class of random variables is assumed in many languages, the underlying models and notions are significantly different, in particular with respect to the issue of the correct representation of the *race condition* principle when modeling the choice operator (see, e.g., [7]).

In [5], two of the authors of the present paper, together with D. Latella and M. Massink, proposed a variant of LTS, namely *rate transition systems* (RTS), as a tool for providing semantics to some of the most representative stochastic process languages. Within LTS, the transition relation describes the evolution of a system from one state to another as determined by the execution of specific actions, thus it is a set of triples (*state*, *action*, *state*). Within RTS, the transition relation $\rightarrowtail$ associates with a given state P and a given transition label (action) a a function, say $\mathscr{P}$, mapping each term into a nonnegative real number. The transition $P \stackrel{a}{\rightarrowtail} \mathscr{P}$ has the following meaning: if $\mathscr{P}(Q) = v$ with $v \neq 0$, then Q is reachable from P by executing a, the duration of such an execution being exponentially distributed with rate v; if $\mathscr{P}(Q) = 0$, then Q is not reachable from P via a.

RTS have been used for providing a uniform semantic framework for modeling many of the different stochastic process languages. This facilitates reasoning about them and throwing light on their similarities as well as on their differences. In [4], we considered a limited number of significant stochastic process calculi. We provided the RTS semantics for TIPP [6], EMPA [3], PEPA [9], and IML [8] as representatives of the class of stochastic languages based on the CSP-like, multipart interaction paradigm. Moreover, we also considered stochastic CCS and stochastic π-calculus [14] as examples of languages based on the two-way interaction paradigm.

In this paper, we aim at performing a step further in the direction of providing a uniform characterization of the semantics of different process calculi. We propose a framework more general than RTS, which can be instantiated to model both classical process algebras usually handled via LTS and process algebras with quantitative information like probability and time. We will introduce ULTRAS – *Uniform Labeled TRAnsition Systems* – as a generalization of RTS and show that they can be used to uniformly describe the nondeterministic, probabilistic, and stochastic variants of process algebras. We will then introduce a general notion of equivalence that can be instantiated to capture the nondeterministic, probabilistic, and stochastic versions of trace and bisimulation equivalence.

Within ULTRAS, the transition relation associates with a state and a given transition label a function mapping each (next) state into an element of a domain D. In order to be uniform with classical nondeterministic calculi, we do encode quantitative information inside the next-state function. More precisely, rather than having transition leading to a next state, we do work with a notion of next-state distribution, meaning that we quantify the possibility of having every process term as the next state after executing a certain action.

By appropriately changing the domain D, we can capture different models of concurrent systems. For example, we will see that if D is the Boolean algebra $\mathbb{B}$ consisting of the two values $\top$ and $\bot$ we can capture classical LTS, while if D is the set $\mathbb{R}_{[0,1]}$ we do capture fully probabilistic models, and when D is the set $\mathbb{R}_{\geq 0}$ we do capture fully stochastic models.

The advantage of the proposed uniform modeling is twofold. On the one hand, we show that the way the semantics for calculi with quantitative information has been defined so far is indeed the natural extension of the definition of the semantics for calculi with only qualitative information. On the other hand, we make calculi with quantitative information more understandable for those people with a process algebraic background who are not familiar with probability/time.

Of course, modeling state transitions and their annotations is one of the key ingredients; however, we need also to worry about how they are combined to obtain computations and how we do deem that from two states we can obtain "equivalent" computation trees. In order to do that, we introduce the notion of *trace* and *measured trace*. Based on them, we define trace equivalence and bisimulation equivalence over ULTRAS and study their relationships with the corresponding equivalences in the literature once we "appropriately" instantiate the domain D to capture well-studied models.

One of the key ingredients of the equivalence definition is a *measure function* that associates a suitable value with every triple composed of a state s, a trace α, and a state subset S'. To capture classical equivalences over nondeterministic systems, the measure of a computation labeled with α from state s to a state in S' yields $\top$ if the computation does exist and $\bot$ otherwise. To capture probabilistic equivalences, the measure yields a value in $\mathbb{R}_{[0,1]}$ that represents the probability of the set of computations labeled with trace α that reach a state in S' from state s. For stochastic equivalences, we consider two cases: the *end-to-end* delay and the *step-by-step* delay of traces. In the first case, the measure function yields the probability that the set of computations labeled with trace α lead to a state in S' from state s within t time units. In the second case, the measure function considers, instead, the probability of the set of computations labeled with α that go from s to S' within a certain number of time units for each single step.

The rest of the paper is organized as follows. In Sect. 2, we introduce ULTRAS and bisimulation and trace equivalences over them. In Sect. 3, we instantiate ULTRAS to obtain, in a row, *fully nondeterministic* processes (i.e., classical LTS), *fully probabilistic* processes (i.e., classical *action-labeled discrete-time*

Markov chains – ADTMC), and *fully stochastic* processes (i.e., classical *action-labeled continuous-time Markov chains* – ACTMC). In Sects. 4, 5, and 6, we prove that bisimulation and trace equivalences for the various instantiations of ULTRAS coincide with the corresponding equivalences defined in the literature for LTS, ADTMC, and ACTMC, respectively. Finally, Sect. 7 concludes the paper and outlines future work.

2 Uniform Labeled Transition Systems

LTS consist of a set of states, a set of transition labels, and a transition relation. States correspond to the configurations processes can reach. Labels describe the actions processes can perform internally or that are used to interact with the environment. The transition relation describes process evolution as determined by the execution of specific actions.

In this section, we introduce a generalization of LTS that aims at providing a uniform framework that can be used for defining the behavior of different kinds of process. In the new model, named ULTRAS from Uniform Labeled TRAnsition Systems, the transition relation associates with any source state and any transition label a function mapping each possible target state into an element of a domain D. The definition of ULTRAS is provided in Sect. 2.1, while in Sect. 2.2 we show how to define behavioral equivalences on ULTRAS.

2.1 Definition of the Uniform Model

In the following, we assume that D is a complete partial order with $\bot$ being its least element. We also denote by $[S \rightarrow D]$ the set of functions from S to D, which is ranged over by $\mathcal{D}$.

Definition 1. *A uniform labeled transition system on D (D-ULTRAS for short) is a triple:*

$$\mathcal{U} = (S, A, \longrightarrow)$$

where:

- *S is a countable set of states.*
- *A is a countable set of transition-labeling actions.*
- *$\longrightarrow \subseteq S \times A \times [S \rightarrow D]$ is a transition relation.*

We say that the D-ULTRAS $\mathcal{U}$ is functional iff $\longrightarrow$ is a function from $S \times A$ to $[S \rightarrow D]$. ■

Every transition $(s, a, \mathcal{D})$ is written $s \xrightarrow{a} \mathcal{D}$, with $\mathcal{D}(s')$ being a D-value quantifying the reachability of s' from s via the execution of a. In order to avoid ambiguity, when considering functional ULTRAS we will often write $\mathcal{D}_{s,a}(s')$ to denote the same value.

2.2 Behavioral Equivalences on the Uniform Model

We now show how two behavioral equivalences lying at the opposite end points of the linear-time/branching-time spectrum [16] like trace equivalence and bisimilarity can be defined on ULTRAS. Later on, we will see that they coincide with their classical definitions in the case of fully nondeterministic, fully probabilistic, and fully stochastic processes when mapping these processes into ULTRAS.

In order to define the two equivalences on ULTRAS, first of all we have to introduce traces and measure functions. The former are sequences of actions and identify possible observable computations in ULTRAS. The latter give measures of reachability of elements in a set of states $S' \subseteq S$ starting from a state $s \in S$ via a fixed trace $\alpha \in A^*$.

Definition 2. *Let $\mathcal{U} = (S, A, \longrightarrow)$ be a D-ULTRAS. A trace α for $\mathcal{U}$ is a finite sequence of transition labels in A^*, where $\alpha = \varepsilon$ denotes the empty sequence while operation "$\_ \circ \_$" denotes sequence concatenation.* ■

Definition 3. *Let $\mathcal{U} = (S, A, \longrightarrow)$ be a D-ULTRAS and M be a lattice. A measure function for $\mathcal{U}$ is a function $\mathcal{M}_M : S \times A^* \times 2^S \to M$.* ■

In the setting of ULTRAS, both trace equivalence and bisimilarity are parameterized with respect to a measure function. Indeed, different measure functions can induce different equivalences on the same D-ULTRAS depending on the support set and the operations of M. Although D and M may share the same support set, this is not necessarily the case as we will see when addressing fully stochastic processes. In fact, while D-values encode one-step reachability, M-values are measures computed (on the basis of D-values) along computations.

Trace equivalence is straightforward: two states are trace equivalent if every trace has the same measure with respect to the entire set of states S when starting from the two considered states.

Definition 4. *Let $\mathcal{U} = (S, A, \longrightarrow)$ be a D-ULTRAS and $\mathcal{M}_M$ be a measure function for $\mathcal{U}$. We say that $s_1, s_2 \in S$ are $\mathcal{M}_M$-trace equivalent, written $s_1 \sim_{\mathrm{Tr},\mathcal{M}_M} s_2$, iff for all traces $\alpha \in A^*$:*

$$\mathcal{M}_M(s_1, \alpha, S) = \mathcal{M}_M(s_2, \alpha, S)$$ ■

While trace equivalence simply compares any two states without taking into account the states reached at the end of the trace, a bisimulation relation also poses constraints on the final states.

Definition 5. *Let $\mathcal{U} = (S, A, \longrightarrow)$ be a D-ULTRAS and $\mathcal{M}_M$ be a measure function for $\mathcal{U}$. An equivalence relation $\mathcal{B}$ over S is an $\mathcal{M}_M$-bisimulation iff, whenever $(s_1, s_2) \in \mathcal{B}$, then for all traces $\alpha \in A^*$ and equivalence classes $C \in S/\mathcal{B}$:*

$$\mathcal{M}_M(s_1, \alpha, C) = \mathcal{M}_M(s_2, \alpha, C)$$

We say that $s_1, s_2 \in S$ are $\mathcal{M}_M$-bisimilar, written $s_1 \sim_{\mathrm{B},\mathcal{M}_M} s_2$, iff there exists an $\mathcal{M}_M$-bisimulation $\mathcal{B}$ over S such that $(s_1, s_2) \in \mathcal{B}$. ■

3 Mapping Classical Models into the Uniform Model

In this section, we show how classical models used for describing fully nondeterministic, fully probabilistic, and fully stochastic processes can be defined in terms of ULTRAS. In particular, we consider labeled transition systems in Sect. 3.1, action-labeled discrete-time Markov chains in Sect. 3.2, and action-labeled continuous-time Markov chains in Sect. 3.3.

3.1 A Fully Nondeterministic Specialization: LTS

Fully nondeterministic processes are traditionally represented through state-transition graphs in which every transition is labeled with the action determining the corresponding state change. In these graphs, there is no information about how to choose among the various transitions departing from a state.

Definition 6. *A labeled transition system (LTS for short) is a triple* $(S, A, \longrightarrow)$ *where:*

- S *is a countable set of states.*
- A *is a countable set of transition-labeling actions.*
- $\longrightarrow \subseteq S \times A \times S$ *is a transition relation.* ■

Every transition (s, a, s') is written $s \xrightarrow{a} s'$ and means that it is possible to reach s' from s by executing a.

It is straightforward to see that a LTS is a functional $\mathbb{B}$-ULTRAS – where $\mathbb{B} = \{\bot, \top\}$ is the Boolean algebra – in which, given a transition $s \xrightarrow{a} \mathcal{D}$, $\mathcal{D}(s') = \bot$ means that it is not possible to reach s' from s by executing a, whereas $\mathcal{D}(s') = \top$ means that it is possible.

3.2 A Fully Probabilistic Specialization: ADTMC

Fully probabilistic processes, also called generative probabilistic processes according to the terminology of [17], can be represented through state-transition graphs in which every transition is labeled with both the action and the probability of the corresponding state change. In other words, each such process can be represented as a discrete-time Markov chain [15] whose transitions are additionally labeled with actions. [1]

In the following, we use $\{\!|$ and $|\!\}$ to delimit multisets. We also assume that the summation over an empty multiset of numbers is zero.

Definition 7. *An action-labeled discrete-time Markov chain (ADTMC for short) is a triple* $(S, A, \longrightarrow)$ *where:*

[1] The name discrete-time Markov chain is used here for historical reasons. Since time does not come into play, a name like time-abstract Markov chain would be better. A discrete-time interpretation is appropriate only when all state changes occur at equidistant time points.

- *S is a countable set of states.*
- *A is a countable set of transition-labeling actions.*
- *$\longrightarrow \subseteq S \times A \times \mathbb{R}_{(0,1]} \times S$ is a transition relation.*
- *For all $s, s' \in S$ and $a \in A$, whenever $(s, a, p_1, s'), (s, a, p_2, s') \in \longrightarrow$, then $p_1 = p_2$.*
- *For all $s \in S$, it holds that $\sum \{\!| p \in \mathbb{R}_{(0,1]} \mid \exists a \in A, s' \in S. (s, a, p, s') \in \longrightarrow |\!\} \in \{0, 1\}$.* ■

Every transition (s, a, p, s') is written $s \xrightarrow{a,p} s'$, with p being the probability with which s' is reached from s by executing a.

It is straightforward to see that an ADTMC is a functional $\mathbb{R}_{[0,1]}$-ULTRAS in which $\sum_{a \in A} \sum_{s' \in S} \mathcal{D}_{s,a}(s') \in \{0, 1\}$ for all $s \in S$. Given a transition $s \xrightarrow{a} \mathcal{D}$, $\mathcal{D}(s') = 0$ means that it is not possible to reach s' from s by executing a, whereas $\mathcal{D}(s') \in \mathbb{R}_{(0,1]}$ means that it is possible with probability $\mathcal{D}(s')$.

3.3 A Fully Stochastic Specialization: ACTMC

Fully stochastic processes in which the notion of time is formalized by means of exponentially distributed durations, also called Markovian processes, can be represented through state-transition graphs in which every transition is labeled with both the action and the rate of the corresponding state change. In other words, each such process can be represented as a continuous-time Markov chain [15] whose transitions are additionally labeled with actions.

This Markov chain can be viewed as an ADTMC in which every state s has associated with it an exponentially distributed sojourn time, which is uniquely identified by a positive real number $\mathrm{E}(s)$ called rate, whose reciprocal coincides with the average sojourn time in s. Assuming that transition firing is governed by a race policy, this is equivalent to replacing the probability labeling each transition departing from s with a rate given by $\mathrm{E}(s)$ multiplied by the transition probability. Consistent with the fact that the minimum of a set of exponentially distributed random variables is exponentially distributed with rate equal to the sum of the original rates, the sum of the transition rates is equal to $\mathrm{E}(s)$.

Definition 8. *An action-labeled continuous-time Markov chain (ACTMC for short) is a triple $(S, A, \longrightarrow)$ where:*

- *S is a countable set of states.*
- *A is a countable set of transition-labeling actions.*
- *$\longrightarrow \subseteq S \times A \times \mathbb{R}_{>0} \times S$ is a transition relation.*
- *For all $s, s' \in S$ and $a \in A$, whenever $(s, a, \lambda_1, s'), (s, a, \lambda_2, s') \in \longrightarrow$, then $\lambda_1 = \lambda_2$.* ■

Every transition (s, a, λ, s') is written $s \xrightarrow{a,\lambda} s'$, with λ being the rate at which s' is reached from s by executing a.

It is straightforward to see that an ACTMC is a functional $\mathbb{R}_{\geq 0}$-ULTRAS. Given a transition $s \xrightarrow{a} \mathcal{D}$, $\mathcal{D}(s') = 0$ means that it is not possible to reach

s' from s by executing a, whereas $\mathcal{D}(s') \in \mathbb{R}_{>0}$ means that it is possible at rate $\mathcal{D}(s')$.

4 Equivalences for Fully Nondeterministic Processes

In this section, we instantiate the two behavioral equivalences of Sect. 2.2 – i.e., bisimilarity and trace equivalence – for fully nondeterministic processes represented as functional $\mathbb{B}$-ULTRAS. This is accomplished by introducing a measure function $\mathcal{M}_{\mathbb{B}}$ that associates a suitable constant $\mathbb{B}$-valued function with every triple composed of a state, a trace, and a state subset.

Definition 9. *Let $\mathcal{U} = (S, A, \longrightarrow)$ be a functional $\mathbb{B}$-ULTRAS. The measure function $\mathcal{M}_{\mathbb{B}} : S \times A^* \times 2^S \to \mathbb{B}$ for $\mathcal{U}$ is inductively defined as follows:*

$$\mathcal{M}_{\mathbb{B}}(s, \alpha, S') = \begin{cases} \bigvee_{s' \in S} \mathcal{D}_{s,a}(s') \wedge \mathcal{M}_{\mathbb{B}}(s', \alpha', S') & \text{if } \alpha = a \circ \alpha' \\ \top & \text{if } \alpha = \varepsilon \text{ and } s \in S' \\ \bot & \text{if } \alpha = \varepsilon \text{ and } s \notin S' \end{cases}$$ ■

The value $\mathcal{M}_{\mathbb{B}}(s, \alpha, S')$ establishes whether there exists a computation labeled with trace α that leads to a state in S' from state s. If such a computation exists, then $\mathcal{M}_{\mathbb{B}}(s, \alpha, S') = \top$, otherwise $\mathcal{M}_{\mathbb{B}}(s, \alpha, S') = \bot$.

We now show that each of the two resulting behavioral equivalences $\sim_{\mathrm{B},\mathcal{M}_{\mathbb{B}}}$ and $\sim_{\mathrm{Tr},\mathcal{M}_{\mathbb{B}}}$ on functional $\mathbb{B}$-ULTRAS coincides with the corresponding behavioral equivalence defined in the literature on LTS.

Given two LTS $(S_i, A_i, \longrightarrow_i)$, $i = 1, 2$, with $S_1 \cap S_2 = \emptyset$, consider the LTS $(S, A, \longrightarrow)$ where $S = S_1 \cup S_2$, $A = A_1 \cup A_2$, and $\longrightarrow \; = \; \longrightarrow_1 \cup \longrightarrow_2$.

Bisimilarity for LTS [13] captures the ability of two states of mimicking each other's behavior step by step.

Definition 10. *A binary relation $\mathcal{B}$ over S is a bisimulation iff, whenever $(s_1, s_2) \in \mathcal{B}$, then for all actions $a \in A$:*

- *Whenever $s_1 \xrightarrow{a} s_1'$, then $s_2 \xrightarrow{a} s_2'$ with $(s_1', s_2') \in \mathcal{B}$.*
- *Whenever $s_2 \xrightarrow{a} s_2'$, then $s_1 \xrightarrow{a} s_1'$ with $(s_1', s_2') \in \mathcal{B}$.*

We say that $s_1, s_2 \in S$ are bisimilar, written $s_1 \sim_{\mathrm{B}} s_2$, iff there exists a bisimulation $\mathcal{B}$ over S such that $(s_1, s_2) \in \mathcal{B}$. ■

Theorem 1. *For all $s_1, s_2 \in S$:*

$$s_1 \sim_{\mathrm{B}} s_2 \iff s_1 \sim_{\mathrm{B},\mathcal{M}_{\mathbb{B}}} s_2$$

Proof. *The proof is divided into two parts:*

- *Let $s_1, s_2 \in S$ be such that $s_1 \sim_{\mathrm{B}} s_2$. From $s_1 \sim_{\mathrm{B}} s_2$, it follows that there exists a bisimulation $\mathcal{B}$ over S such that $(s_1, s_2) \in \mathcal{B}$. Observing that the reflexive and transitive closure $\mathcal{B}'$ of $\mathcal{B}$ is still a bisimulation over S such that $(s_1, s_2) \in \mathcal{B}'$, it turns out that $\mathcal{B}'$ is an $\mathcal{M}_{\mathbb{B}}$-bisimulation and hence*

$s_1 \sim_{\mathrm{B},\mathcal{M}_{\mathbb{B}}} s_2$. *In fact, for all* $s'_1, s'_2 \in S$, *whenever* $(s'_1, s'_2) \in \mathcal{B}'$, *then for all* $\alpha \in A^*$ *and* $C \in S/\mathcal{B}'$:

$$\mathcal{M}_{\mathbb{B}}(s'_1, \alpha, C) \;=\; \mathcal{M}_{\mathbb{B}}(s'_2, \alpha, C)$$

as we now prove by proceeding by induction on $|\alpha|$:

- *If* $|\alpha| = 0$, *then for all* $C \in S/\mathcal{B}'$ *it holds that:*
  $$\mathcal{M}_{\mathbb{B}}(s'_1, \alpha, C) \;=\; \top \;=\; \mathcal{M}_{\mathbb{B}}(s'_2, \alpha, C)$$
  whenever $s'_1, s'_2 \in C$ *and:*
  $$\mathcal{M}_{\mathbb{B}}(s'_1, \alpha, C) \;=\; \bot \;=\; \mathcal{M}_{\mathbb{B}}(s'_2, \alpha, C)$$
  whenever $s'_1, s'_2 \notin C$.
- *Let* $|\alpha| = n \in \mathbb{N}_{>0}$ *and assume that the result holds for all traces of length* $n-1$. *Supposing* $\alpha = a \circ \alpha'$, *we note that for all* $s \in S$ *and* $C \in S/\mathcal{B}'$ *it holds that:*
  $$\begin{aligned}\mathcal{M}_{\mathbb{B}}(s, \alpha, C) &= \bigvee_{s' \in S} \mathcal{D}_{s,a}(s') \wedge \mathcal{M}_{\mathbb{B}}(s', \alpha', C) \\ &= \bigvee_{C' \in S/\mathcal{B}} \bigvee_{s' \in C'} \mathcal{D}_{s,a}(s') \wedge \mathcal{M}_{\mathbb{B}}(s', \alpha', C) \\ &= \bigvee_{C' \in S/\mathcal{B}} \mathcal{M}_{\mathbb{B}}(s_{C'}, \alpha', C) \wedge \bigvee_{s' \in C'} \mathcal{D}_{s,a}(s') \\ &= \bigvee_{C' \in S/\mathcal{B}} \mathcal{M}_{\mathbb{B}}(s_{C'}, \alpha', C) \wedge (\exists s' \in C'.\, s \xrightarrow{a} s')\end{aligned}$$
  where $s_{C'} \in C'$ *and the factorization of* $\mathcal{M}_{\mathbb{B}}(s_{C'}, \alpha', C)$ *stems from the application of the induction hypothesis on* α' *to all states of each equivalence class* C'. *Since* $\exists s' \in C'.\, s'_1 \xrightarrow{a} s'$ *iff* $\exists s' \in C'.\, s'_2 \xrightarrow{a} s'$ *by virtue of* $(s'_1, s'_2) \in \mathcal{B}'$, *we derive that for all* $C \in S/\mathcal{B}'$:
  $$\mathcal{M}_{\mathbb{B}}(s'_1, \alpha, C) \;=\; \mathcal{M}_{\mathbb{B}}(s'_2, \alpha, C)$$

– *Let* $s_1, s_2 \in S$ *be such that* $s_1 \sim_{\mathrm{B},\mathcal{M}_{\mathbb{B}}} s_2$. *From* $s_1 \sim_{\mathrm{B},\mathcal{M}_{\mathbb{B}}} s_2$, *it follows that there exists an* $\mathcal{M}_{\mathbb{B}}$*-bisimulation* $\mathcal{B}$ *over* S *such that* $(s_1, s_2) \in \mathcal{B}$. *It turns out that* $\mathcal{B}$ *is also a bisimulation and hence* $s_1 \sim_{\mathrm{B}} s_2$. *In fact, for all* $s'_1, s'_2 \in S$ *such that* $(s'_1, s'_2) \in \mathcal{B}$, *from the definition of* $\mathcal{M}_{\mathbb{B}}$*-bisimulation it follows in particular that for all* $a \in A$ *and* $C \in S/\mathcal{B}$:
  $$\mathcal{M}_{\mathbb{B}}(s'_1, a, C) \;=\; \mathcal{M}_{\mathbb{B}}(s'_2, a, C)$$
  Since for all $s \in S$, $a \in A$, *and* $C \in S/\mathcal{B}$ *it holds that:*
  $$\mathcal{M}_{\mathbb{B}}(s, a, C) \;=\; \bigvee_{s' \in C} \mathcal{D}_{s,a}(s') \;=\; (\exists s' \in C.\, s \xrightarrow{a} s')$$
  we immediately derive that for all $a \in A$:
  - *Whenever* $s'_1 \xrightarrow{a} s''_1$, *then* $s'_2 \xrightarrow{a} s''_2$ *with* $(s''_1, s''_2) \in \mathcal{B}$.
  - *Whenever* $s'_2 \xrightarrow{a} s''_2$, *then* $s'_1 \xrightarrow{a} s''_1$ *with* $(s''_1, s''_2) \in \mathcal{B}$. ■

Trace equivalence for LTS [10] compares the traces labeling the computations executable from two states. We lift the transition relation $\longrightarrow$ from actions to action sequences by letting $s \xRightarrow{\varepsilon} s$ and $s \xRightarrow{a_1 \ldots a_n} s' \equiv s \xrightarrow{a_1} s_1 \ldots s_{n-1} \xrightarrow{a_n} s'$ for $n \in \mathbb{N}_{>0}$. Given $s \in S$ and $\alpha \in A^*$, we also write $s \xRightarrow{\alpha}$ to denote the existence of $s' \in S$ such that $s \xRightarrow{\alpha} s'$.

Definition 11. *We say that* $s_1, s_2 \in S$ *are trace equivalent, written* $s_1 \sim_{\mathrm{Tr}} s_2$, *iff for all traces* $\alpha \in A^*$:

$$s_1 \xRightarrow{\alpha} \text{ iff } s_2 \xRightarrow{\alpha}$$

■

Theorem 2. *For all* $s_1, s_2 \in S$*:*

$$s_1 \sim_{\mathrm{Tr}} s_2 \iff s_1 \sim_{\mathrm{Tr},\mathcal{M}_{\mathbb{B}}} s_2$$

Proof. Let $s_1, s_2 \in S$ *be such that* $s_1 \sim_{\mathrm{Tr}} s_2$*. The fact that* $s_1 \sim_{\mathrm{Tr}} s_2$ *is equivalent by definition to the fact that for all* $\alpha \in A^*$*:*

$$s_1 \stackrel{\alpha}{\Longrightarrow} \textit{ iff } s_2 \stackrel{\alpha}{\Longrightarrow}$$

Since for all $s \in S$ *it holds that:*

$$(s \stackrel{\alpha}{\Longrightarrow}) = \begin{cases} \bigvee\limits_{s' \in S} \mathcal{D}_{s,a}(s') \wedge (s' \stackrel{\alpha'}{\Longrightarrow}) & \textit{if } \alpha = a \circ \alpha' \\ \top & \textit{if } \alpha = \varepsilon \end{cases}$$

and hence:

$$(s \stackrel{\alpha}{\Longrightarrow}) = \mathcal{M}_{\mathbb{B}}(s, \alpha, S)$$

we immediately derive that the fact that for all $\alpha \in A^*$ $s_1 \stackrel{\alpha}{\Longrightarrow}$ *iff* $s_2 \stackrel{\alpha}{\Longrightarrow}$ *is equivalent to to the fact that for all* $\alpha \in A^*$*:*

$$\mathcal{M}_{\mathbb{B}}(s_1, \alpha, S) = \mathcal{M}_{\mathbb{B}}(s_2, \alpha, S)$$

which in turn is equivalent by definition to $s_1 \sim_{\mathrm{Tr},\mathcal{M}_{\mathbb{B}}} s_2$*.* ■

5 Equivalences for Fully Probabilistic Processes

In this section, we extend the work in the previous section by additionally taking into account the execution probability of transitions. More precisely, we instantiate the two behavioral equivalences of Sect. 2.2 for fully probabilistic processes represented as functional $\mathbb{R}_{[0,1]}$-ULTRAS. This is accomplished by introducing a measure function that associates a suitable constant $\mathbb{R}_{[0,1]}$-valued function with every triple composed of a state, a trace, and a state subset.

Definition 12. *Let* $\mathcal{U} = (S, A, \longrightarrow)$ *be a functional* $\mathbb{R}_{[0,1]}$-ULTRAS*. The measure function* $\mathcal{M}_{\mathbb{R}_{[0,1]}} : S \times A^* \times 2^S \rightarrow \mathbb{R}_{[0,1]}$ *for* $\mathcal{U}$ *is inductively defined as follows:*

$$\mathcal{M}_{\mathbb{R}_{[0,1]}}(s, \alpha, S') = \begin{cases} \sum\limits_{s' \in S} \mathcal{D}_{s,a}(s') \cdot \mathcal{M}_{\mathbb{R}_{[0,1]}}(s', \alpha', S') & \textit{if } \alpha = a \circ \alpha' \\ 1 & \textit{if } \alpha = \varepsilon \textit{ and } s \in S' \\ 0 & \textit{if } \alpha = \varepsilon \textit{ and } s \notin S' \end{cases}$$ ■

The value $\mathcal{M}_{\mathbb{R}_{[0,1]}}(s, \alpha, S')$ is the probability of the set of computations labeled with trace α that lead to a state in S' from state s. If there are no such computations, then $\mathcal{M}_{\mathbb{R}_{[0,1]}}(s, \alpha, S') = 0$, otherwise $\mathcal{M}_{\mathbb{R}_{[0,1]}}(s, \alpha, S') \in \mathbb{R}_{(0,1]}$.

We now show that each of the two resulting behavioral equivalences $\sim_{\mathrm{B},\mathcal{M}_{\mathbb{R}_{[0,1]}}}$ and $\sim_{\mathrm{Tr},\mathcal{M}_{\mathbb{R}_{[0,1]}}}$ on functional $\mathbb{R}_{[0,1]}$-ULTRAS coincides with the corresponding behavioral equivalence defined in the literature on ADTMC.

Given two ADTMC $(S_i, A_i, \longrightarrow_i)$, $i = 1, 2$, with $S_1 \cap S_2 = \emptyset$, consider the ADTMC $(S, A, \longrightarrow)$ where $S = S_1 \cup S_2$, $A = A_1 \cup A_2$, and $\longrightarrow = \longrightarrow_1 \cup \longrightarrow_2$.

Bisimilarity for ADTMC [12] relies on the comparison of state exit probabilities. [2] The exit probability of a state $s \in S$ is the probability with which s can

[2] To be precise, probabilistic bisimilarity was defined in [12] for reactive probabilistic processes, but the same definition applies to fully probabilistic processes too.

execute transitions labeled with a certain action $a \in A$ that lead to a certain destination $S' \subseteq S$: $prob_{\rm e}(s, a, S') = \sum \{\!| p \in \mathbb{R}_{(0,1]} \mid \exists s' \in S'.\, s \xrightarrow{a,p} s' |\!\}$.

Definition 13. *An equivalence relation $\mathcal{B}$ over S is a probabilistic bisimulation iff, whenever $(s_1, s_2) \in \mathcal{B}$, then for all actions $a \in A$ and equivalence classes $C \in S/\mathcal{B}$:*

$$prob_{\rm e}(s_1, a, C) \;=\; prob_{\rm e}(s_2, a, C)$$

We say that $s_1, s_2 \in S$ are probabilistic bisimilar, written $s_1 \sim_{\rm PB} s_2$, iff there exists a probabilistic bisimulation $\mathcal{B}$ over S such that $(s_1, s_2) \in \mathcal{B}$. ■

Theorem 3. *For all $s_1, s_2 \in S$:*

$$s_1 \sim_{\rm PB} s_2 \iff s_1 \sim_{{\rm B},\mathcal{M}_{\mathbb{R}_{[0,1]}}} s_2$$

Proof. *The proof is divided into two parts:*

- *Let $s_1, s_2 \in S$ be such that $s_1 \sim_{\rm PB} s_2$. From $s_1 \sim_{\rm PB} s_2$, it follows that there exists a probabilistic bisimulation $\mathcal{B}$ over S such that $(s_1, s_2) \in \mathcal{B}$. It turns out that $\mathcal{B}$ is also an $\mathcal{M}_{\mathbb{R}_{[0,1]}}$-bisimulation and hence $s_1 \sim_{{\rm B},\mathcal{M}_{\mathbb{R}_{[0,1]}}} s_2$. In fact, for all $s'_1, s'_2 \in S$, whenever $(s'_1, s'_2) \in \mathcal{B}$, then for all $\alpha \in A^*$ and $C \in S/\mathcal{B}$:*

  $$\mathcal{M}_{\mathbb{R}_{[0,1]}}(s'_1, \alpha, C) \;=\; \mathcal{M}_{\mathbb{R}_{[0,1]}}(s'_2, \alpha, C)$$

  as we now prove by proceeding by induction on $|\alpha|$:
  - *If $|\alpha| = 0$, then for all $C \in S/\mathcal{B}$ it holds that:*

    $$\mathcal{M}_{\mathbb{R}_{[0,1]}}(s'_1, \alpha, C) \;=\; 1 \;=\; \mathcal{M}_{\mathbb{R}_{[0,1]}}(s'_2, \alpha, C)$$

    whenever $s'_1, s'_2 \in C$ and:

    $$\mathcal{M}_{\mathbb{R}_{[0,1]}}(s'_1, \alpha, C) \;=\; 0 \;=\; \mathcal{M}_{\mathbb{R}_{[0,1]}}(s'_2, \alpha, C)$$

    whenever $s'_1, s'_2 \notin C$.
  - *Let $|\alpha| = n \in \mathbb{N}_{>0}$ and assume that the result holds for all traces of length $n-1$. Supposing $\alpha = a \circ \alpha'$, we note that for all $s \in S$ and $C \in S/\mathcal{B}$ it holds that:*

    $$\begin{aligned} \mathcal{M}_{\mathbb{R}_{[0,1]}}(s, \alpha, C) &= \sum_{s' \in S} \mathcal{D}_{s,a}(s') \cdot \mathcal{M}_{\mathbb{R}_{[0,1]}}(s', \alpha', C) \\ &= \sum_{C' \in S/\mathcal{B}} \sum_{s' \in C'} \mathcal{D}_{s,a}(s') \cdot \mathcal{M}_{\mathbb{R}_{[0,1]}}(s', \alpha', C) \\ &= \sum_{C' \in S/\mathcal{B}} \mathcal{M}_{\mathbb{R}_{[0,1]}}(s_{C'}, \alpha', C) \cdot \sum_{s' \in C'} \mathcal{D}_{s,a}(s') \\ &= \sum_{C' \in S/\mathcal{B}} \mathcal{M}_{\mathbb{R}_{[0,1]}}(s_{C'}, \alpha', C) \cdot prob_{\rm e}(s, a, C') \end{aligned}$$

    where $s_{C'} \in C'$ and the factorization of $\mathcal{M}_{\mathbb{R}_{[0,1]}}(s_{C'}, \alpha', C)$ stems from the application of the induction hypothesis on α' to all states of each equivalence class C'. Since $prob_{\rm e}(s'_1, a, C') = prob_{\rm e}(s'_2, a, C')$ by virtue of $(s'_1, s'_2) \in \mathcal{B}$, we derive that for all $C \in S/\mathcal{B}$:

    $$\mathcal{M}_{\mathbb{R}_{[0,1]}}(s'_1, \alpha, C) \;=\; \mathcal{M}_{\mathbb{R}_{[0,1]}}(s'_2, \alpha, C)$$
- *Let $s_1, s_2 \in S$ be such that $s_1 \sim_{{\rm B},\mathcal{M}_{\mathbb{R}_{[0,1]}}} s_2$. From $s_1 \sim_{{\rm B},\mathcal{M}_{\mathbb{R}_{[0,1]}}} s_2$, it follows that there exists an $\mathcal{M}_{\mathbb{R}_{[0,1]}}$-bisimulation $\mathcal{B}$ over S such that $(s_1, s_2) \in \mathcal{B}$. It turns out that $\mathcal{B}$ is also a probabilistic bisimulation and hence $s_1 \sim_{\rm PB} s_2$. In fact, for all $s'_1, s'_2 \in S$ such that $(s'_1, s'_2) \in \mathcal{B}$, from the definition of $\mathcal{M}_{\mathbb{R}_{[0,1]}}$-bisimulation it follows in particular that for all $a \in A$ and $C \in S/\mathcal{B}$:*

$$\mathcal{M}_{\mathbb{R}_{[0,1]}}(s_1, a, C) \;=\; \mathcal{M}_{\mathbb{R}_{[0,1]}}(s_2, a, C)$$

Since for all $s \in S$, $a \in A$, and $C \in S/\mathcal{B}$ it holds that:

$$\mathcal{M}_{\mathbb{R}_{[0,1]}}(s, a, C) \;=\; \sum_{s' \in C} \mathcal{D}_{s,a}(s') \;=\; prob_{\mathrm{e}}(s, a, C)$$

we immediately derive that for all $a \in A$ and $C \in S/\mathcal{B}$:

$$prob_{\mathrm{e}}(s'_1, a, C) \;=\; prob_{\mathrm{e}}(s'_2, a, C)$$ ■

Trace equivalence for ADTMC [11] is based on the comparison of the execution probabilities of analogous computations. Given $s \in S$, we denote by $\mathcal{C}_{\mathrm{f}}(s)$ the set of finite-length computations of s and by $|c|$ the length of any $c \in \mathcal{C}_{\mathrm{f}}(s)$. We say that two distinct computations in $\mathcal{C}_{\mathrm{f}}(s)$ are independent of each other iff neither is a proper prefix of the other one. The probability of executing $c \in \mathcal{C}_{\mathrm{f}}(s)$ is the product of the execution probabilities of the transitions of c:

$$prob(c) \;=\; \begin{cases} 1 & \text{if } |c| = 0 \\ p \cdot prob(c') & \text{if } c \equiv s \xrightarrow{a,p} c' \end{cases}$$

which is lifted to $C \subseteq \mathcal{C}_{\mathrm{f}}(s)$ as follows:

$$prob(C) \;=\; \sum_{c \in C} prob(c)$$

whenever C is finite and all of its computations are independent of each other. Indicating with $trace(c)$ the sequence of actions labeling the transitions of $c \in \mathcal{C}_{\mathrm{f}}(s)$, we say that c is compatible with $\alpha \in A^*$ iff $trace(c) = \alpha$ and we denote by $\mathcal{CC}(s, \alpha)$ the set of computations in $\mathcal{C}_{\mathrm{f}}(s)$ that are compatible with α.

Definition 14. *We say that $s_1, s_2 \in S$ are probabilistic trace equivalent, written $s_1 \sim_{\mathrm{PTr}} s_2$, iff for all traces $\alpha \in A^*$:*

$$prob(\mathcal{CC}(s_1, \alpha)) \;=\; prob(\mathcal{CC}(s_2, \alpha))$$ ■

Theorem 4. *For all $s_1, s_2 \in S$:*

$$s_1 \sim_{\mathrm{PTr}} s_2 \iff s_1 \sim_{\mathrm{Tr}, \mathcal{M}_{\mathbb{R}_{[0,1]}}} s_2$$

Proof. *Let $s_1, s_2 \in S$ be such that $s_1 \sim_{\mathrm{PTr}} s_2$. The fact that $s_1 \sim_{\mathrm{PTr}} s_2$ is equivalent by definition to the fact that for all $\alpha \in A^*$:*

$$prob(\mathcal{CC}(s_1, \alpha)) \;=\; prob(\mathcal{CC}(s_2, \alpha))$$

Since for all $s \in S$ it holds that:

$$prob(\mathcal{CC}(s, \alpha)) \;=\; \begin{cases} \sum_{s' \in S} \mathcal{D}_{s,a}(s') \cdot prob(\mathcal{CC}(s', \alpha')) & \text{if } \alpha = a \circ \alpha' \\ 1 & \text{if } \alpha = \varepsilon \end{cases}$$

and hence:

$$prob(\mathcal{CC}(s, \alpha)) \;=\; \mathcal{M}_{\mathbb{R}_{[0,1]}}(s, \alpha, S)$$

we immediately derive that the fact that for all $\alpha \in A^*$ $prob(\mathcal{CC}(s_1, \alpha)) = prob(\mathcal{CC}(s_2, \alpha))$ is equivalent to the fact that for all $\alpha \in A^*$:

$$\mathcal{M}_{\mathbb{R}_{[0,1]}}(s_1, \alpha, S) \;=\; \mathcal{M}_{\mathbb{R}_{[0,1]}}(s_2, \alpha, S)$$

which in turn is equivalent by definition to $s_1 \sim_{\mathrm{Tr}, \mathcal{M}_{\mathbb{R}_{[0,1]}}} s_2$. ■

6 Equivalences for Fully Stochastic Processes

In this section, we further extend the work in the previous two sections by additionally taking into account a notion of time formalized by means of the exponentially distributed durations of transitions. More precisely, we instantiate the two behavioral equivalences of Sect. 2.2 for fully stochastic processes involving only exponential distributions – i.e., fully Markovian processes – represented as functional $\mathbb{R}_{\geq 0}$-ULTRAS. Unlike the previous two sections, when defining the measure function we distinguish between two cases. In Sect. 6.1 we take into account the end-to-end delay of traces, whereas in Sect. 6.2 we consider the step-by-step delay of traces.

6.1 The End-To-End Case

The measure function for the end-to-end case associates a suitable $\mathbb{R}_{[0,1]}$-valued function with every triple composed of a state, a trace, and a state subset, which is parameterized with respect to the end-to-end delay $t \in \mathbb{R}_{\geq 0}$ of the trace.

Definition 15. *Let $\mathcal{U} = (S, A, \longrightarrow)$ be a functional $\mathbb{R}_{\geq 0}$-ULTRAS. The end-to-end measure function $\mathcal{M}_{\mathrm{ete}} : S \times A^* \times 2^S \rightarrow [\mathbb{R}_{\geq 0} \rightarrow \mathbb{R}_{[0,1]}]$ for $\mathcal{U}$ is inductively defined as follows:*

$$\mathcal{M}_{\mathrm{ete}}(s, \alpha, S')(t) = \begin{cases} \int_0^t \mathrm{E}(s) \cdot \mathrm{e}^{-\mathrm{E}(s)\cdot x} \cdot \sum_{s' \in S} \frac{\mathcal{D}_{s,a}(s')}{\mathrm{E}(s)} \cdot \mathcal{M}_{\mathrm{ete}}(s', \alpha', S')(t - x)\, dx & \\ \qquad \text{if } \alpha = a \circ \alpha' \text{ and } \mathrm{E}(s) > 0 & \\ 1 \qquad \text{if } \alpha = \varepsilon \text{ and } s \in S' & \\ 0 \qquad \text{if } \alpha = \varepsilon \text{ and } s \notin S' \text{ or } \alpha \neq \varepsilon \text{ and } \mathrm{E}(s) = 0 & \end{cases}$$

■

Note that subscript "ete" is a symbolic shorthand for $[\mathbb{R}_{\geq 0} \rightarrow \mathbb{R}_{[0,1]}]$. The value $\mathcal{M}_{\mathrm{ete}}(s, \alpha, S')(t)$ is the probability of the set of computations labeled with trace α that lead to a state in S' from state s within t time units. If there are no such computations, then $\mathcal{M}_{\mathrm{ete}}(s, \alpha, S')(t) = 0$, otherwise $\mathcal{M}_{\mathrm{ete}}(s, \alpha, S')(t) \in \mathbb{R}_{(0,1]}$. In the case $\alpha = a \circ \alpha'$ and $\mathrm{E}(s) > 0$, this value is computed as the convolution of probability distributions. Assuming to spend $x \in \mathbb{R}_{[0,t]}$ time units in state s, the first operand of the convolution is the exponentially distributed density function quantifying the sojourn time in s, i.e., the derivative with respect to t of $1 - \mathrm{e}^{-\mathrm{E}(s)\cdot t}$ evaluated in x. For each state s' reachable from s by executing a, the first operand is multiplied by the probability of the set of computations labeled with the remaining trace α' that lead to a state in S' from state s' within the remaining $t - x$ time units.

We now show that each of the two resulting behavioral equivalences $\sim_{\mathrm{B},\mathcal{M}_{\mathrm{ete}}}$ and $\sim_{\mathrm{Tr},\mathcal{M}_{\mathrm{ete}}}$ on functional $\mathbb{R}_{\geq 0}$-ULTRAS coincides with the corresponding behavioral equivalence defined in the literature on ACTMC.

Given two ACTMC $(S_i, A_i, \longrightarrow_i)$, $i = 1, 2$, with $S_1 \cap S_2 = \emptyset$, consider the ACTMC $(S, A, \longrightarrow)$ where $S = S_1 \cup S_2$, $A = A_1 \cup A_2$, and $\longrightarrow = \longrightarrow_1 \cup \longrightarrow_2$.

Bisimilarity for ACTMC [9] relies on the comparison of state exit rates. The exit rate of a state $s \in S$ is the rate at which s can execute transitions labeled with a certain action $a \in A$ that lead to a certain destination $S' \subseteq S$, which is the sum of the rates of those transitions due to the fact that transition firing is governed by the race policy: $rate_{\mathrm{e}}(s, a, S') = \sum\{\!| \lambda \in \mathbb{R}_{>0} \mid \exists s' \in S'.\, s \xrightarrow{a,\lambda} s' |\!\}$.

Definition 16. *An equivalence relation $\mathcal{B}$ over S is a Markovian bisimulation iff, whenever $(s_1, s_2) \in \mathcal{B}$, then for all actions $a \in A$ and equivalence classes $C \in S/\mathcal{B}$:*

$$rate_{\mathrm{e}}(s_1, a, C) \;=\; rate_{\mathrm{e}}(s_2, a, C)$$

We say that $s_1, s_2 \in S$ are Markovian bisimilar, written $s_1 \sim_{\mathrm{MB}} s_2$, iff there exists a Markovian bisimulation $\mathcal{B}$ over S such that $(s_1, s_2) \in \mathcal{B}$. ■

Lemma 1. *For all $s_1, s_2 \in S$:*

$$s_1 \sim_{\mathrm{MB}} s_2 \implies \mathrm{E}(s_1) = \mathrm{E}(s_2)$$

Proof. It stems from the fact that for all $s \in S$:

$$\mathrm{E}(s) \;=\; \sum_{a \in A} rate_{\mathrm{e}}(s, a, S) \;=\; \sum_{a \in A} \sum_{C \in S/\sim_{\mathrm{MB}}} rate_{\mathrm{e}}(s, a, C)$$ ■

Lemma 2. *For all $s_1, s_2 \in S$:*

$$s_1 \sim_{\mathrm{B},\mathcal{M}_{\mathrm{ete}}} s_2 \implies \mathrm{E}(s_1) = \mathrm{E}(s_2)$$

Proof. Let $s_1, s_2 \in S$ be such that $s_1 \sim_{\mathrm{B},\mathcal{M}_{\mathrm{ete}}} s_2$ and assume $\mathrm{E}(s_1) > 0$ and $\mathrm{E}(s_2) > 0$ in order to avoid trivial cases. Since for all $s \in S$ and $a \in A$ it holds that:

$$\mathcal{M}_{\mathrm{ete}}(s, a, S) \;=\; \sum_{C \in S/\sim_{\mathrm{B},\mathcal{M}_{\mathrm{ete}}}} \mathcal{M}_{\mathrm{ete}}(s, a, C)$$

from $s_1 \sim_{\mathrm{B},\mathcal{M}_{\mathrm{ete}}} s_2$ it follows that:

$$\sum_{a \in A} \mathcal{M}_{\mathrm{ete}}(s_1, a, S) \;=\; \sum_{a \in A} \mathcal{M}_{\mathrm{ete}}(s_2, a, S)$$

Since for all $s \in S$ such that $\mathrm{E}(s) > 0$ and $t \in \mathbb{R}_{\geq 0}$ it holds that:

$$\begin{aligned}
\sum_{a \in A} \mathcal{M}_{\mathrm{ete}}(s, a, S)(t) \;&=\; \sum_{a \in A} \int_0^t \mathrm{E}(s) \cdot \mathrm{e}^{-\mathrm{E}(s) \cdot x} \cdot \sum_{s' \in S} \frac{\mathcal{D}_{s,a}(s')}{\mathrm{E}(s)} \, \mathrm{d}x \\
&=\; \sum_{a \in A} \sum_{s' \in S} \frac{\mathcal{D}_{s,a}(s')}{\mathrm{E}(s)} \cdot \int_0^t \mathrm{E}(s) \cdot \mathrm{e}^{-\mathrm{E}(s) \cdot x} \, \mathrm{d}x \\
&=\; \frac{1}{\mathrm{E}(s)} \cdot \sum_{a \in A} \sum_{s' \in S} \mathcal{D}_{s,a}(s') \cdot (1 - \mathrm{e}^{-\mathrm{E}(s) \cdot t}) \\
&=\; 1 - \mathrm{e}^{-\mathrm{E}(s) \cdot t}
\end{aligned}$$

we derive:

$$1 - \mathrm{e}^{-\mathrm{E}(s_1) \cdot t} \;=\; 1 - \mathrm{e}^{-\mathrm{E}(s_2) \cdot t}$$

and hence:

$$\mathrm{E}(s_1) \;=\; \mathrm{E}(s_2)$$ ■

Lemma 3. *Let $s_1, s_2 \in S$. Whenever $s_1 \sim_{\mathrm{B},\mathcal{M}_{\mathrm{ete}}} s_2$, then for all $a \in A$ and $C \in S/\sim_{\mathrm{B},\mathcal{M}_{\mathrm{ete}}}$:*

$$\sum_{s' \in C} \mathcal{D}_{s_1,a}(s') \;=\; \sum_{s' \in C} \mathcal{D}_{s_2,a}(s')$$

Proof. Let $s_1, s_2 \in S$ be such that $s_1 \sim_{\mathrm{B},\mathcal{M}_{\mathrm{ete}}} s_2$ and assume $\mathrm{E}(s_1) > 0$ and $\mathrm{E}(s_2) > 0$ in order to avoid trivial cases. From $s_1 \sim_{\mathrm{B},\mathcal{M}_{\mathrm{ete}}} s_2$, it follows in particular that for all $a \in A$ and $C \in S/\sim_{\mathrm{B},\mathcal{M}_{\mathrm{ete}}}$:

$$\mathcal{M}_{\mathrm{ete}}(s_1, a, C) \;=\; \mathcal{M}_{\mathrm{ete}}(s_2, a, C)$$

Since for all $s \in S$ such that $\mathrm{E}(s) > 0$ and $t \in \mathbb{R}_{\geq 0}$ it holds that:

$$\begin{aligned}\mathcal{M}_{\text{ete}}(s,a,C)(t) &= \int_0^t \mathrm{E}(s)\cdot \mathrm{e}^{-\mathrm{E}(s)\cdot x}\cdot \sum_{s'\in C}\tfrac{\mathcal{D}_{s,a}(s')}{\mathrm{E}(s)}\,\mathrm{d}x\\ &= (\int_0^t \mathrm{E}(s)\cdot \mathrm{e}^{-\mathrm{E}(s)\cdot x}\,\mathrm{d}x)\cdot \tfrac{1}{\mathrm{E}(s)}\cdot \sum_{s'\in C}\mathcal{D}_{s,a}(s')\\ &= \tfrac{1-\mathrm{e}^{-\mathrm{E}(s)\cdot t}}{\mathrm{E}(s)}\cdot \sum_{s'\in C}\mathcal{D}_{s,a}(s')\end{aligned}$$

we derive:

$$\tfrac{1-\mathrm{e}^{-\mathrm{E}(s_1)\cdot t}}{\mathrm{E}(s_1)}\cdot \sum_{s'\in C}\mathcal{D}_{s_1,a}(s') = \tfrac{1-\mathrm{e}^{-\mathrm{E}(s_2)\cdot t}}{\mathrm{E}(s_2)}\cdot \sum_{s'\in C}\mathcal{D}_{s_2,a}(s')$$

and hence:

$$\sum_{s'\in C}\mathcal{D}_{s_1,a}(s') = \sum_{s'\in C}\mathcal{D}_{s_2,a}(s')$$

by virtue of Lemma 2. ■

Theorem 5. *For all $s_1, s_2 \in S$:*

$$s_1 \sim_{\text{MB}} s_2 \iff s_1 \sim_{\text{B},\mathcal{M}_{\text{ete}}} s_2$$

Proof. The proof is divided into two parts:

- *Let $s_1, s_2 \in S$ be such that $s_1 \sim_{\text{MB}} s_2$ and assume $\mathrm{E}(s_1) > 0$ and $\mathrm{E}(s_2) > 0$ in order to avoid trivial cases. From $s_1 \sim_{\text{MB}} s_2$, it follows that there exists a Markovian bisimulation $\mathcal{B}$ over S such that $(s_1, s_2) \in \mathcal{B}$. It turns out that $\mathcal{B}$ is also an $\mathcal{M}_{\text{ete}}$-bisimulation and hence $s_1 \sim_{\text{B},\mathcal{M}_{\text{ete}}} s_2$. In fact, for all $s_1', s_2' \in S$, whenever $(s_1', s_2') \in \mathcal{B}$, then for all $\alpha \in A^*$ and $C \in S/\mathcal{B}$:*
$$\mathcal{M}_{\text{ete}}(s_1',\alpha,C) = \mathcal{M}_{\text{ete}}(s_2',\alpha,C)$$
as we now prove by proceeding by induction on $|\alpha|$:
  - *If $|\alpha| = 0$, then for all $C \in S/\mathcal{B}$ and $t \in \mathbb{R}_{\geq 0}$ it holds that:*
  $$\mathcal{M}_{\text{ete}}(s_1',\alpha,C)(t) = 1 = \mathcal{M}_{\text{ete}}(s_2',\alpha,C)(t)$$
  whenever $s_1', s_2' \in C$ and:
  $$\mathcal{M}_{\text{ete}}(s_1',\alpha,C)(t) = 0 = \mathcal{M}_{\text{ete}}(s_2',\alpha,C)(t)$$
  whenever $s_1', s_2' \notin C$.
  - *Let $|\alpha| = n \in \mathbb{N}_{>0}$ and assume that the result holds for all traces of length $n-1$. Supposing $\alpha = a \circ \alpha'$, we note that for all $s \in S$ such that $\mathrm{E}(s) > 0$, $C \in S/\mathcal{B}$, and $t \in \mathbb{R}_{\geq 0}$ it holds that $\mathcal{M}_{\text{ete}}(s,\alpha,C)(t)$ is equal to:*
  $$\begin{aligned}&\int_0^t \mathrm{E}(s)\cdot \mathrm{e}^{-\mathrm{E}(s)\cdot x}\cdot \sum_{s'\in S}\tfrac{\mathcal{D}_{s,a}(s')}{\mathrm{E}(s)}\cdot \mathcal{M}_{\text{ete}}(s',\alpha',C)(t-x)\,dx\\ &= \int_0^t \mathrm{e}^{-\mathrm{E}(s)\cdot x}\cdot \sum_{C'\in S/\mathcal{B}}\sum_{s'\in C'}\mathcal{D}_{s,a}(s')\cdot \mathcal{M}_{\text{ete}}(s',\alpha',C)(t-x)\,dx\\ &= \int_0^t \mathrm{e}^{-\mathrm{E}(s)\cdot x}\cdot \sum_{C'\in S/\mathcal{B}}\mathcal{M}_{\text{ete}}(s_{C'},\alpha',C)(t-x)\cdot \sum_{s'\in C'}\mathcal{D}_{s,a}(s')\,dx\\ &= \int_0^t \mathrm{e}^{-\mathrm{E}(s)\cdot x}\cdot \sum_{C'\in S/\mathcal{B}}\mathcal{M}_{\text{ete}}(s_{C'},\alpha',C)(t-x)\cdot rate_{\mathrm{e}}(s,a,C')\,dx\end{aligned}$$
  where $s_{C'} \in C'$ and the factorization of $\mathcal{M}_{\text{ete}}(s_{C'},\alpha',C)(t-x)$ stems from the application of the induction hypothesis on α' to all states of each equivalence class C'. Since $\mathrm{E}(s_1') = \mathrm{E}(s_2')$ by virtue of $(s_1', s_2') \in \mathcal{B}$ and

Lemma 1 and $rate_{\mathrm{e}}(s'_1, a, C') = rate_{\mathrm{e}}(s'_2, a, C')$ *by virtue of* $(s'_1, s'_2) \in \mathcal{B}$, *we derive that for all* $C \in S/\mathcal{B}$ *and* $t \in \mathbb{R}_{\geq 0}$:

$$\mathcal{M}_{\mathrm{sbs}}(s'_1, \alpha, C)(t) \ = \ \mathcal{M}_{\mathrm{sbs}}(s'_2, \alpha, C)(t)$$

– *Let* $s_1, s_2 \in S$ *be such that* $s_1 \sim_{\mathrm{B},\mathcal{M}_{\mathrm{ete}}} s_2$. *From* $s_1 \sim_{\mathrm{B},\mathcal{M}_{\mathrm{ete}}} s_2$, *it follows that there exists an* $\mathcal{M}_{\mathrm{ete}}$*-bisimulation* $\mathcal{B}$ *over* S *such that* $(s_1, s_2) \in \mathcal{B}$. *It turns out that* $\mathcal{B}$ *is also a Markovian bisimulation and hence* $s_1 \sim_{\mathrm{MB}} s_2$. *In fact, for all* $s'_1, s'_2 \in S$ *such that* $(s'_1, s'_2) \in \mathcal{B}$, *from Lemma 3 it follows that for all* $a \in A$ *and* $C \in S/\mathcal{B}$:

$$\sum_{s' \in C} \mathcal{D}_{s'_1,a}(s') \ = \ \sum_{s' \in C} \mathcal{D}_{s'_2,a}(s')$$

Since for all $s \in S$, $a \in A$, *and* $C \in S/\mathcal{B}$ *it holds that:*

$$\sum_{s' \in C} \mathcal{D}_{s,a}(s') \ = \ rate_{\mathrm{e}}(s, a, C)$$

we immediately derive that for all $a \in A$ *and* $C \in S/\mathcal{B}$:

$$rate_{\mathrm{e}}(s'_1, a, C) \ = \ rate_{\mathrm{e}}(s'_2, a, C)$$

■

Trace equivalence for ACTMC is based on the comparison of the execution probabilities and the average durations of analogous computations. Here, by average duration of a computation we intend its end-to-end average duration [2]. Given $s \in S$, the probability of executing $c \in \mathcal{C}_{\mathrm{f}}(s)$ is the product of the rate-based execution probabilities of the transitions of c: [3]

$$prob(c) \ = \ \begin{cases} 1 & \text{if } |c| = 0 \\ \frac{\lambda}{\mathrm{E}(s)} \cdot prob(c') & \text{if } c \equiv s \xrightarrow{a,\lambda} c' \end{cases}$$

The end-to-end average duration of c is the sum of the average sojourn times in the states traversed by c:

$$time_{\mathrm{a,ete}}(c) \ = \ \begin{cases} 0 & \text{if } |c| = 0 \\ \frac{1}{\mathrm{E}(s)} + time_{\mathrm{a,ete}}(c') & \text{if } c \equiv s \xrightarrow{a,\lambda} c' \end{cases}$$

and we denote by $C_{\leq t}$ the set of computations in $C \subseteq \mathcal{C}_{\mathrm{f}}(s)$ whose end-to-end average duration is not greater than $t \in \mathbb{R}_{\geq 0}$.

Definition 17. *We say that* $s_1, s_2 \in S$ *are end-to-end Markovian trace equivalent, written* $s_1 \sim_{\mathrm{MTr,ete}} s_2$, *iff for all traces* $\alpha \in A^*$ *and amounts of time* $t \in \mathbb{R}_{\geq 0}$:

$$prob(\mathcal{CC}_{\leq t}(s_1, \alpha)) \ = \ prob(\mathcal{CC}_{\leq t}(s_2, \alpha))$$

■

Theorem 6. *For all* $s_1, s_2 \in S$:

$$s_1 \sim_{\mathrm{MTr,ete}} s_2 \iff s_1 \sim_{\mathrm{Tr},\mathcal{M}_{\mathrm{ete}}} s_2$$

Proof. *Given* $s \in S$, *we define the end-to-end duration of* $c \in \mathcal{C}_{\mathrm{f}}(s)$ *as the sum of the random variables quantifying the average sojourn times in the states traversed by* c:

$$time_{\mathrm{d,ete}}(c) \ = \ \begin{cases} Det_0 & \text{if } |c| = 0 \\ Exp_{\mathrm{E}(s)} + time_{\mathrm{d,ete}}(c') & \text{if } c \equiv s \xrightarrow{a,\lambda} c' \end{cases}$$

[3] With abuse of notation, we use the same name *prob* employed in the ADTMC case.

where Det_0 is the random variable equal to 0 with probability 1, while $Exp_{\mathrm{E}(s)}$ is the exponentially distributed random variable with rate $\mathrm{E}(s)$. Moreover, we define the probability distribution of executing a computation in $C \subseteq \mathcal{C}_{\mathrm{f}}(s)$ within $t \in \mathbb{R}_{\geq 0}$ time units by letting:

$$prob_{\mathrm{d,ete}}(C, t) \;=\; \sum_{c \in C} prob(c) \cdot \Pr\{time_{\mathrm{d,ete}}(c) \leq t\}$$

whenever C is finite and all of its computations are independent of each other.

Let $s_1, s_2 \in S$ be such that $s_1 \sim_{\mathrm{MTr,ete}} s_2$ and assume $\mathrm{E}(s_1) > 0$ and $\mathrm{E}(s_2) > 0$ in order to avoid trivial cases. The fact that $s_1 \sim_{\mathrm{MTr,ete}} s_2$ is equivalent by definition to the fact that for all $\alpha \in A^*$ and $t \in \mathbb{R}_{\geq 0}$:

$$prob(\mathcal{CC}_{\leq t}(s_1, \alpha)) \;=\; prob(\mathcal{CC}_{\leq t}(s_2, \alpha))$$

which in turn is equivalent by virtue of [2] to the fact that for all $\alpha \in A^*$ and $t \in \mathbb{R}_{\geq 0}$:

$$prob_{\mathrm{d,ete}}(\mathcal{CC}(s_1, \alpha), t) \;=\; prob_{\mathrm{d,ete}}(\mathcal{CC}(s_2, \alpha), t)$$

Since for all $s \in S$ such that $\mathrm{E}(s) > 0$, $\alpha \in A^*$, and $t \in \mathbb{R}_{\geq 0}$ it holds that:

$$prob_{\mathrm{d,ete}}(\mathcal{CC}(s, \alpha), t) \;=\; \begin{cases} \sum\limits_{s' \in S} \frac{\mathcal{D}_{s,a}(s')}{\mathrm{E}(s)} \cdot \int\limits_0^t \mathrm{E}(s) \cdot \mathrm{e}^{-\mathrm{E}(s) \cdot x} \cdot & \\ \quad \cdot\, prob_{\mathrm{d,ete}}(\mathcal{CC}(s', \alpha'), t - x)\, \mathrm{d}x & \text{if } \alpha = a \circ \alpha' \\ 1 & \text{if } \alpha = \varepsilon \end{cases}$$

and hence:

$$prob_{\mathrm{d,ete}}(\mathcal{CC}(s, \alpha), t) \;=\; \mathcal{M}_{\mathrm{ete}}(s, \alpha, S)(t)$$

we immediately derive that the fact that for all $\alpha \in A^*$ and $t \in \mathbb{R}_{\geq 0}$ $prob_{\mathrm{d,ete}}(\mathcal{CC}(s_1, \alpha), t) = prob_{\mathrm{d,ete}}(\mathcal{CC}(s_2, \alpha), t)$ is equivalent to the fact that for all $\alpha \in A^*$:

$$\mathcal{M}_{\mathrm{ete}}(s_1, \alpha, S) \;=\; \mathcal{M}_{\mathrm{ete}}(s_2, \alpha, S)$$

which in turn is equivalent by definition to $s_1 \sim_{\mathrm{Tr}, \mathcal{M}_{\mathrm{ete}}} s_2$. ■

6.2 The Step-By-Step Case

The measure function for the step-by-step case associates a suitable $\mathbb{R}_{[0,1]}$-valued function with every triple composed of a state, a trace, and a state subset, which is parameterized with respect to the step-by-step delay $\theta \in (\mathbb{R}_{\geq 0})^*$ of the trace.

Definition 18. *Let $\mathcal{U} = (S, A, \longrightarrow)$ be a functional $\mathbb{R}_{\geq 0}$-ULTRAS. The step-by-step measure function $\mathcal{M}_{\mathrm{sbs}} : S \times A^* \times 2^S \rightarrow [(\mathbb{R}_{\geq 0})^* \rightarrow \mathbb{R}_{[0,1]}]$ for $\mathcal{U}$ is inductively defined as follows:*

$$\mathcal{M}_{\mathrm{sbs}}(s, \alpha, S')(\theta) \;=\; \begin{cases} (1 - e^{-\mathrm{E}(s) \cdot t}) \cdot \sum\limits_{s' \in S} \frac{\mathcal{D}_{s,a}(s')}{\mathrm{E}(s)} \cdot \mathcal{M}_{\mathrm{sbs}}(s', \alpha', S')(\theta') & \\ \qquad \text{if } \alpha = a \circ \alpha' \text{ and } \theta = t \circ \theta' \text{ and } \mathrm{E}(s) > 0 & \\ 1 \qquad \text{if } \alpha = \varepsilon \text{ and } s \in S' & \\ 0 \qquad \text{if } \alpha = \varepsilon \text{ and } s \notin S' \text{ or} & \\ \qquad \alpha \neq \varepsilon \text{ and } \theta = \varepsilon \text{ or} & \\ \qquad \alpha \neq \varepsilon \text{ and } \theta \neq \varepsilon \text{ and } \mathrm{E}(s) = 0 & \end{cases}$$

■

Note that subscript "sbs" is a symbolic shorthand for $[(\mathbb{R}_{\geq 0})^* \rightarrow \mathbb{R}_{[0,1]}]$. The value $\mathcal{M}_{\mathrm{sbs}}(s, \alpha, S')(\theta)$ is the probability of the set of computations labeled with trace α that lead to a state in S' from state s, such that the delay of the i-th transition of any computation is not greater than $\theta[i]$ for each i ranging from 1 to the length of the computation. If there are no such computations, then $\mathcal{M}_{\rm sbs}(s, \alpha, S')(\theta) = 0$, otherwise $\mathcal{M}_{\rm sbs}(s, \alpha, S')(\theta) \in \mathbb{R}_{(0,1]}$. In the case $\alpha = a \circ \alpha'$ and $\theta = t \circ \theta'$ and $\mathrm{E}(s) > 0$, this value is computed on the basis of the probability of leaving state s within t time units, i.e., $1 - \mathrm{e}^{-\mathrm{E}(s) \cdot t}$. For each state s' reachable from s by executing a, this probability is multiplied by the probability of the set of computations labeled with the remaining trace α' that lead to a state in S' from state s' within the remaining time steps θ'.

We now show that each of the two resulting behavioral equivalences $\sim_{\mathrm{B},\mathcal{M}_{\rm sbs}}$ and $\sim_{\mathrm{Tr},\mathcal{M}_{\rm sbs}}$ on functional $\mathbb{R}_{\geq 0}$-ULTRAS coincides with the corresponding behavioral equivalence defined in the literature on ACTMC. In the case of bisimilarity, we consider the same equivalence $\sim_{\rm MB}$ as Sect. 6.1.

Lemma 4. *For all $s_1, s_2 \in S$:*

$$s_1 \sim_{\mathrm{B},\mathcal{M}_{\rm sbs}} s_2 \implies \mathrm{E}(s_1) = \mathrm{E}(s_2)$$

Proof. *Similar to the proof of Lemma 2, with the following different calculation for all $s \in S$ such that $\mathrm{E}(s) > 0$ and $\theta = t \circ \theta' \in (\mathbb{R}_{\geq 0})^*$:*

$$\begin{aligned}
\sum_{a \in A} \mathcal{M}_{\rm sbs}(s, a, S)(\theta) &= \sum_{a \in A} (1 - \mathrm{e}^{-\mathrm{E}(s) \cdot t}) \cdot \sum_{s' \in S} \frac{\mathcal{D}_{s,a}(s')}{\mathrm{E}(s)} \\
&= (1 - \mathrm{e}^{-\mathrm{E}(s) \cdot t}) \cdot \frac{1}{\mathrm{E}(s)} \cdot \sum_{a \in A} \sum_{s' \in S} \mathcal{D}_{s,a}(s') \\
&= 1 - \mathrm{e}^{-\mathrm{E}(s) \cdot t}
\end{aligned}$$

■

Lemma 5. *Let $s_1, s_2 \in S$. Whenever $s_1 \sim_{\mathrm{B},\mathcal{M}_{\rm sbs}} s_2$, then for all $a \in A$ and $C \in S/\sim_{\mathrm{B},\mathcal{M}_{\rm sbs}}$:*

$$\sum_{s' \in C} \mathcal{D}_{s_1,a}(s') = \sum_{s' \in C} \mathcal{D}_{s_2,a}(s')$$

Proof. *Similar to the proof of Lemma 3, with the following different calculation for all $s \in S$ such that $\mathrm{E}(s) > 0$ and $\theta = t \circ \theta' \in (\mathbb{R}_{\geq 0})^*$:*

$$\begin{aligned}
\mathcal{M}_{\rm sbs}(s, a, C)(\theta) &= (1 - \mathrm{e}^{-\mathrm{E}(s) \cdot t}) \cdot \sum_{s' \in C} \frac{\mathcal{D}_{s,a}(s')}{\mathrm{E}(s)} \\
&= \frac{1 - \mathrm{e}^{-\mathrm{E}(s) \cdot t}}{\mathrm{E}(s)} \cdot \sum_{s' \in C} \mathcal{D}_{s,a}(s')
\end{aligned}$$

followed by the exploitation of Lemma 4. ■

Theorem 7. *For all $s_1, s_2 \in S$:*

$$s_1 \sim_{\mathrm{B},\mathcal{M}_{\rm ete}} s_2 \iff s_1 \sim_{\mathrm{B},\mathcal{M}_{\rm sbs}} s_2$$

Proof. *The proof is divided into two parts:*

- *Let $s_1, s_2 \in S$ be such that $s_1 \sim_{\mathrm{B},\mathcal{M}_{\rm ete}} s_2$ and assume $\mathrm{E}(s_1) > 0$ and $\mathrm{E}(s_2) > 0$ in order to avoid trivial cases. From $s_1 \sim_{\mathrm{B},\mathcal{M}_{\rm ete}} s_2$, it follows that there exists an $\mathcal{M}_{\rm ete}$-bisimulation $\mathcal{B}$ over S such that $(s_1, s_2) \in \mathcal{B}$. It turns out that $\mathcal{B}$ is also an $\mathcal{M}_{\rm sbs}$-bisimulation and hence $s_1 \sim_{\mathrm{B},\mathcal{M}_{\rm sbs}} s_2$. In fact, for all $s'_1, s'_2 \in S$, whenever $(s'_1, s'_2) \in \mathcal{B}$, then for all $\alpha \in A^*$ and $C \in S/\mathcal{B}$:*

  $$\mathcal{M}_{\rm sbs}(s'_1, \alpha, C) = \mathcal{M}_{\rm sbs}(s'_2, \alpha, C)$$

  as we now prove by proceeding by induction on $|\alpha|$:

- *If $|\alpha| = 0$, then for all $C \in S/\mathcal{B}$ and $\theta \in (\mathbb{R}_{\geq 0})^*$ it holds that:*
$$\mathcal{M}_{\text{sbs}}(s'_1, \alpha, C)(\theta) \;=\; 1 \;=\; \mathcal{M}_{\text{sbs}}(s'_2, \alpha, C)(\theta)$$
whenever $s'_1, s'_2 \in C$ and:
$$\mathcal{M}_{\text{sbs}}(s'_1, \alpha, C)(\theta) \;=\; 0 \;=\; \mathcal{M}_{\text{sbs}}(s'_2, \alpha, C)(\theta)$$
whenever $s'_1, s'_2 \notin C$.
- *Let $|\alpha| = n \in \mathbb{N}_{>0}$ and assume that the result holds for all traces of length $n-1$. Supposing $\alpha = a \circ \alpha'$, there are two cases for $\theta \in (\mathbb{R}_{\geq 0})^*$:*
  * *If $\theta = \varepsilon$, then for all $C \in S/\mathcal{B}$ it holds that:*
  $$\mathcal{M}_{\text{sbs}}(s'_1, \alpha, C)(\theta) \;=\; 0 \;=\; \mathcal{M}_{\text{sbs}}(s'_2, \alpha, C)(\theta)$$
  * *Let $\theta = t \circ \theta'$. For all $s \in S$ such that $\mathrm{E}(s) > 0$ and $C \in S/\mathcal{B}$ it holds that $\mathcal{M}_{\text{sbs}}(s, \alpha, C)(\theta)$ is equal to:*
  $$\begin{aligned}&(1 - \mathrm{e}^{-\mathrm{E}(s)\cdot t}) \cdot \sum_{s' \in S} \frac{\mathcal{D}_{s,a}(s')}{\mathrm{E}(s)} \cdot \mathcal{M}_{\text{sbs}}(s', \alpha', C)(\theta') \\ &= \frac{1-\mathrm{e}^{-\mathrm{E}(s)\cdot t}}{\mathrm{E}(s)} \cdot \sum_{C' \in S/\mathcal{B}} \sum_{s' \in C'} \mathcal{D}_{s,a}(s') \cdot \mathcal{M}_{\text{sbs}}(s', \alpha', C)(\theta') \\ &= \frac{1-\mathrm{e}^{-\mathrm{E}(s)\cdot t}}{\mathrm{E}(s)} \cdot \sum_{C' \in S/\mathcal{B}} \mathcal{M}_{\text{sbs}}(s_{C'}, \alpha', C)(\theta') \cdot \sum_{s' \in C'} \mathcal{D}_{s,a}(s')\end{aligned}$$
  where $s_{C'} \in C'$ and the factorization of $\mathcal{M}_{\text{sbs}}(s_{C'}, \alpha', C)(\theta')$ stems from the application of the induction hypothesis on α' to all states of each equivalence class C'. Since $\mathrm{E}(s'_1) = \mathrm{E}(s'_2)$ by virtue of $(s'_1, s'_2) \in \mathcal{B}$ and Lemma 2 and $\sum_{s' \in C'} \mathcal{D}_{s'_1,a}(s') = \sum_{s' \in C'} \mathcal{D}_{s'_2,a}(s')$ by virtue of $(s'_1, s'_2) \in \mathcal{B}$ and Lemma 3, we derive that for all $C \in S/\mathcal{B}$:
  $$\mathcal{M}_{\text{sbs}}(s'_1, \alpha, C)(\theta) \;=\; \mathcal{M}_{\text{sbs}}(s'_2, \alpha, C)(\theta)$$

– *The proof of the second part is similar to the proof of the first part, with the following calculation of $\mathcal{M}_{\text{ete}}(s, \alpha, C)(t)$ in the induction case for all $s \in S$ such that $\mathrm{E}(s) > 0$, $C \in S/\mathcal{B}$, and $t \in \mathbb{R}_{\geq 0}$:*
$$\begin{aligned}&\int_0^t \mathrm{E}(s) \cdot \mathrm{e}^{-\mathrm{E}(s)\cdot x} \cdot \sum_{s' \in S} \frac{\mathcal{D}_{s,a}(s')}{\mathrm{E}(s)} \cdot \mathcal{M}_{\text{ete}}(s', \alpha', C)(t - x)\,\mathrm{d}x \\ &= \int_0^t \mathrm{e}^{-\mathrm{E}(s)\cdot x} \cdot \sum_{C' \in S/\mathcal{B}} \sum_{s' \in C'} \mathcal{D}_{s,a}(s') \cdot \mathcal{M}_{\text{ete}}(s', \alpha', C)(t - x)\,\mathrm{d}x \\ &= \int_0^t \mathrm{e}^{-\mathrm{E}(s)\cdot x} \cdot \sum_{C' \in S/\mathcal{B}} \mathcal{M}_{\text{ete}}(s_{C'}, \alpha', C)(t - x) \cdot \sum_{s' \in C'} \mathcal{D}_{s,a}(s')\,\mathrm{d}x\end{aligned}$$
followed by the exploitation of Lemmas 4 and 5. ■

Corollary 1. *For all $s_1, s_2 \in S$:*
$$s_1 \sim_{\text{MB}} s_2 \iff s_1 \sim_{\text{B},\mathcal{M}_{\text{ete}}} s_2 \iff s_1 \sim_{\text{B},\mathcal{M}_{\text{sbs}}} s_2$$ ■

With regard to trace equivalence for ACTMC, unlike Sect. 6.1 here the average duration of a computation is intended as its step-by-step average duration [18]. Given $s \in S$, the step-by-step average duration of $c \in \mathcal{C}_{\text{f}}(s)$ is the sequence of the average sojourn times in the states traversed by c:
$$time_{\text{a,sbs}}(c) \;=\; \begin{cases} \varepsilon & \text{if } |c| = 0 \\ \frac{1}{\mathrm{E}(s)} \circ time_{\text{a,sbs}}(c') & \text{if } c \equiv s \xrightarrow{a,\lambda} c' \end{cases}$$
and we denote by $C_{\leq \theta}$ the set of computations in $C \subseteq \mathcal{C}_{\text{f}}(s)$ whose step-by-step average duration is not greater than $\theta \in (\mathbb{R}_{\geq 0})^*$, i.e., $C_{\leq \theta} = \{c \in C \mid |c| \leq |\theta| \wedge \forall i = 1, \ldots, |c|.\ time_{\text{a,sbs}}(c)[i] \leq \theta[i]\}$.

Definition 19. *We say that $s_1, s_2 \in S$ are step-by-step Markovian trace equivalent, written $s_1 \sim_{\mathrm{MTr,sbs}} s_2$, iff for all traces $\alpha \in A^*$ and sequences of amounts of time $\theta \in (\mathbb{R}_{\geq 0})^*$:*

$$prob(\mathcal{CC}_{\leq\theta}(s_1,\alpha)) \;=\; prob(\mathcal{CC}_{\leq\theta}(s_2,\alpha))$$ ■

Theorem 8. *For all $s_1, s_2 \in S$:*

$$s_1 \sim_{\mathrm{MTr,sbs}} s_2 \iff s_1 \sim_{\mathrm{Tr},\mathcal{M}_{\mathrm{sbs}}} s_2$$

Proof. Given $s \in S$, we define the step-by-step duration of $c \in \mathcal{C}_{\mathrm{f}}(s)$ as the sequence of the random variables quantifying the average sojourn times in the states traversed by c:

$$time_{\mathrm{d,sbs}}(c) \;=\; \begin{cases} Det_0 & \text{if } |c| = 0 \\ Exp_{\mathrm{E}(s)} \circ time_{\mathrm{d,sbs}}(c') & \text{if } c \equiv s \xrightarrow{a,\lambda} c' \end{cases}$$

where Det_0 and $Exp_{\mathrm{E}(s)}$ are the same as those in the proof of Thm. 6. Moreover, we define the probability distribution of executing a computation in $C \subseteq \mathcal{C}_{\mathrm{f}}(s)$ within a sequence $\theta \in (\mathbb{R}_{\geq 0})^*$ of time units by letting:

$$\begin{aligned} prob_{\mathrm{d,sbs}}(C,\theta) \;&=\; \sum_{c\in C}^{|c|\leq|\theta|} prob(c) \cdot \prod_{i=1}^{|c|} \Pr\{time_{\mathrm{d,sbs}}(c)[i] \leq \theta[i]\} \\ &=\; \sum_{c\in C}^{|c|\leq|\theta|} prob(c) \cdot \prod_{i=1}^{|c|} (1 - \mathrm{e}^{-\theta[i]/time_{\mathrm{a,sbs}}(c)[i]}) \end{aligned}$$

whenever C is finite and all of its computations are independent of each other.

Let $s_1, s_2 \in S$ be such that $s_1 \sim_{\mathrm{MTr,sbs}} s_2$ and assume $\mathrm{E}(s_1) > 0$ and $\mathrm{E}(s_2) > 0$ in order to avoid trivial cases. The fact that $s_1 \sim_{\mathrm{MTr,sbs}} s_2$ is equivalent by definition to the fact that for all $\alpha \in A^*$ and $\theta \in (\mathbb{R}_{\geq 0})^*$:

$$prob(\mathcal{CC}_{\leq\theta}(s_1,\alpha)) \;=\; prob(\mathcal{CC}_{\leq\theta}(s_2,\alpha))$$

which in turn is equivalent by virtue of [1] to the fact that for all $\alpha \in A^*$ and $\theta \in (\mathbb{R}_{\geq 0})^*$:

$$prob_{\mathrm{d,sbs}}(\mathcal{CC}(s_1,\alpha),\theta) \;=\; prob_{\mathrm{d,sbs}}(\mathcal{CC}(s_2,\alpha),\theta)$$

Since for all $s \in S$ such that $\mathrm{E}(s) > 0$, $\alpha \in A^*$, and $\theta \in (\mathbb{R}_{\geq 0})^*$ it holds that:

$$prob_{\mathrm{d,sbs}}(\mathcal{CC}(s,\alpha),\theta) \;=\; \begin{cases} \sum\limits_{s'\in S} \frac{\mathcal{D}_{s,a}(s')}{\mathrm{E}(s)} \cdot (1 - \mathrm{e}^{-\mathrm{E}(s)\cdot t}) \cdot prob_{\mathrm{d,sbs}}(\mathcal{CC}(s',\alpha'),\theta') & \\ & \text{if } \alpha = a \circ \alpha' \text{ and } \theta = t \circ \theta' \\ 1 & \text{if } \alpha = \varepsilon \\ 0 & \text{if } \alpha \neq \varepsilon \text{ and } \theta = \varepsilon \end{cases}$$

and hence:

$$prob_{\mathrm{d,sbs}}(\mathcal{CC}(s,\alpha),\theta) \;=\; \mathcal{M}_{\mathrm{sbs}}(s,\alpha,S)(\theta)$$

we immediately derive that the fact that for all $\alpha \in A^*$ and $\theta \in (\mathbb{R}_{\geq 0})^*$ $prob_{\mathrm{d,sbs}}(\mathcal{CC}(s_1,\alpha),\theta) = prob_{\mathrm{d,sbs}}(\mathcal{CC}(s_2,\alpha),\theta)$ is equivalent to the fact that for all $\alpha \in A^*$:

$$\mathcal{M}_{\mathrm{sbs}}(s_1,\alpha,S) \;=\; \mathcal{M}_{\mathrm{sbs}}(s_2,\alpha,S)$$

which in turn is equivalent by definition to $s_1 \sim_{\mathrm{Tr},\mathcal{M}_{\mathrm{sbs}}} s_2$. ■

It is worth observing that $\sim_{\mathrm{MTr,ete}}$ and $\sim_{\mathrm{MTr,sbs}}$ do not coincide. In fact, the latter is finer than the former, because it is somehow able to keep track of the time instants at which the various actions of a trace start/complete their execution. As an example, if we consider the following two ACTMC taken from [1]:

where $\lambda < \mu$ and $b \neq d$, it turns out that $s_1 \sim_{\mathrm{MTr,ete}} s_2$ while $s_1 \not\sim_{\mathrm{MTr,sbs}} s_2$ because $prob(\mathcal{CC}_{\leq\theta}(s_1, \alpha)) = \frac{1}{2} \neq 0 = prob(\mathcal{CC}_{\leq\theta}(s_2, \alpha))$ when $\alpha = g \circ a \circ b$ and $\theta = \frac{1}{2\cdot\gamma} \circ \frac{1}{\lambda} \circ \frac{1}{\mu}$. Therefore, $\sim_{\mathrm{MTr},\mathcal{M}_{\mathrm{ete}}}$ and $\sim_{\mathrm{MTr},\mathcal{M}_{\mathrm{sbs}}}$ do not coincide either.

7 Conclusions and Future Work

In this paper, we have introduced ULTRAS as a general framework to uniformly describe the operational semantics of fully nondeterministic, fully probabilistic, and fully stochastic variants of process algebras. Within ULTRAS, the transition relation associates with a state and a given transition label a function mapping each state into an element of a domain D. Elements in D are used to associate a weight with each transition. By appropriately changing the domain D, different models of concurrent systems can be represented.

We have then defined two of the most classical notions of behavioral equivalences, namely bisimulation and trace equivalences, over ULTRAS and have studied their impact on the characterization as ULTRAS of three classical process models: LTS, ADTMC, and ACTMC. In particular, we have shown that the bisimulation and trace equivalences on the models obtained via the ULTRAS characterization of LTS, ADTMC, and ACTMC are in full agreement with those specifically considered in the literature for the three different models. We consider this general characterization and the proof of correspondence of the equivalences as a vindication for the originally proposed models.

In the near future, we plan to investigate the applicability of the ULTRAS framework to further classes of processes – like deterministically timed processes and processes where nondeterminism and probability or nondeterminism and stochasticity are intertwined – as well as other behavioral equivalences in the linear-time/branching-time spectrum – especially testing equivalences. Moreover, we plan to use ULTRAS for describing the operational semantics of a few of the many process description languages that have been proposed in the literature, in order to assess their relative expressiveness of specific operators and establish general properties for the different languages.

Acknowledgment. We would like to thank Diego Latella and Mieke Massink for their useful comments on a draft of this paper. We would also like to thank Martin Wirsing and Martin Hoffman for having given us the stimulus and the opportunity to write this paper. This work has been funded by MIUR-PRIN project *PaCo – Performability-Aware Computing: Logics, Models, and Languages.*

References

1. Aldini, A., Bernardo, M., Corradini, F.: A Process Algebraic Approach to Software Architecture Design. Springer, Heidelberg (2010)
2. Bernardo, M., Cleaveland, R.: A theory of testing for Markovian processes. In: Palamidessi, C. (ed.) CONCUR 2000. LNCS, vol. 1877, pp. 305–319. Springer, Heidelberg (2000)
3. Bernardo, M., Gorrieri, R.: A tutorial on EMPA: A theory of concurrent processes with nondeterminism, priorities, probabilities and time. Theoretical Computer Science 202(1-2), 1–54 (1998)
4. De Nicola, R., Latella, D., Loreti, M., Massink, M.: On a uniform framework for the definition of stochastic process languages. In: FMICS 2009. LNCS, vol. 5825, pp. 9–25. Springer, Heidelberg (2009)
5. De Nicola, R., Latella, D., Loreti, M., Massink, M.: Rate-based transition systems for stochastic process calculi. In: Albers, S., Marchetti-Spaccamela, A., Matias, Y., Nikoletseas, S., Thomas, W. (eds.) ICALP 2009, Part II. LNCS, vol. 5556, pp. 435–446. Springer, Heidelberg (2009)
6. Götz, N., Herzog, U., Rettelbach, M.: Multiprocessor and distributed systems design: The integration of functional specification and performance analysis using stochastic process algebras. In: Donatiello, L., Nelson, R. (eds.) SIGMETRICS 1993 and Performance 1993. LNCS, vol. 729. Springer, Heidelberg (1993)
7. Haverkort, B.: Performance of Computer Communication Systems. The Weizmann Institute of Science (1999)
8. Hermanns, H. (ed.): Interactive Markov Chains. LNCS, vol. 2428. Springer, Heidelberg (2002)
9. Hillston, J.: A Compositional Approach to Performance Modelling. Cambridge University Press, Cambridge (1996)
10. Hoare, C.A.R.: Communicating Sequential Processes. Prentice-Hall, Englewood Cliffs (1985)
11. Jou, C.-C., Smolka, S.A.: Equivalences, congruences, and complete axiomatizations for probabilistic processes. In: Baeten, J.C.M., Klop, J.W. (eds.) CONCUR 1990. LNCS, vol. 458, pp. 367–383. Springer, Heidelberg (1990)
12. Larsen, K.G., Skou, A.: Bisimulation through probabilistic testing. Information and Computation 94, 1–28 (1991)
13. Milner, R.: Communication and Concurrency. Prentice-Hall, Englewood Cliffs (1989)
14. Priami, C.: Stochastic π-Calculus. The Computer Journal 38(7), 578–589 (1995)
15. Stewart, W.J.: Introduction to the Numerical Solution of Markov Chains. Princeton University Press, Princeton (1994)
16. van Glabbeek, R.J.: The linear time – branching time spectrum I. In: Handbook of Process Algebra, pp. 3–99. Elsevier, Amsterdam (2001)
17. van Glabbeek, R.J., Smolka, S.A., Steffen, B.: Reactive, generative and stratified models of probabilistic processes. Information and Computation 121, 59–80 (1995)
18. Wolf, V., Baier, C., Majster-Cederbaum, M.: Trace machines for observing continuous-time Markov chains. In: Proc. of the 3rd Int. Workshop on Quantitative Aspects of Programming Languages (QAPL 2005). ENTCS, vol. 153(2), pp. 259–277. Elsevier, Amsterdam (2005)

Toward a Game-Theoretic Model of Grid Systems*

Maria Grazia Buscemi[1], Ugo Montanari[2], and Sonia Taneja[1,2,3]

[1] IMT Lucca Institute for Advanced Studies, Italy
{m.buscemi,s.taneja}@imtlucca.it
[2] Dipartimento di Informatica, University of Pisa, Italy
ugo@di.unipi.it
[3] Istituto Nazionale di Fisica Nucleare, Sezione di Pisa, Italy
sonia.taneja@pi.infn.it

Abstract. Computational Grid is a promising platform that provides a vast range of heterogeneous resources for high performance computing. To grasp the full advantage of Grid systems, efficient and effective resource management and Grid job scheduling are key requirements. Particularly, in resource management and job scheduling, conflicts may arise as Grid resources are usually owned by different organizations, which have different goals. In this paper, we study the job scheduling problem in Computational Grid by analyzing it using game theoretic approaches. We consider a hierarchical job scheduling model that is formulated as a repeated non-cooperative game among Grid sites, which may have selfish concerns. We exploit the concept of Nash equilibrium as a stable solution for our game which eventually is convenient for every player.

1 Introduction

Recent years have witnessed dramatic progress of network technology that led to growing interests in distributed computing approaches. As a result, Grid and Global Computing have stood out as preferred research areas. Both of these approaches try to address the problem of utilizing scattered idle resources connected across a network. Grid computing [5] aims at creating an illusion of a simple and yet large virtual computer from a great set of heterogeneous computers sharing various resource types to benefit a (virtual) organization. Grid Technologies enable sharing, exchange, discovery, selection and aggregation of geographically or Internet-wide distributed heterogeneous resources-such as sensors, computers, databases, visualization devices and scientific instruments. Though the research communities of Grid and Global Computing have different concerns, both fields have common focal points such as performance, heterogeneity, scalability, fault tolerance, security, etc.

Game Theory [8] is a mathematical-economic discipline that studies situations in which multiple independent agents take decisions and try to maximize

* Research supported by the EU IST-FP6 16004 Integrated Project SENSORIA.

M. Wirsing, M. Hofmann, and A. Rauschmayer (Eds.): TGC 2010, LNCS 6084, pp. 57–72, 2010.

their returns. Game Theory attempts to formally capture behaviors in *strategic* situations, in which an individual agent's success in making choices depends on the choices of others. A game model consists of three ingredients - a set of players, a set of actions, and a set of player's payoffs. At each round of the game, every player chooses an action and gets a payoff in return. A player's strategy is a sequence of actions such that each action refers to a round of the game. A central notion in Game Theory is that of *Nash Equilibrium* [7], a situation in which no player can improve its own payoff by unilaterally changing its strategy. Game Theory is important as its model can be applied in several situations.

Distributed computing and Game Theory share common problems such as, dealing with systems where there are many agents facing uncertainty, and possibly having different goals. In the context of Grid resource management and job scheduling, game theoretic modeling seems a promising approach. Indeed, in a Grid job scheduling problem, there are Grid *sites* (or *n*odes) that may have conflicting interests as, for instance, some site may prefer first to execute its own local jobs over the Grid jobs, in order to minimize the sum of completion time of its own jobs. Nevertheless, for a Grid to properly work, sites should be incentivated to collaborate for optimizing global objective performance measures such as to minimize the makespan, i.e. the sum of completion times of all Grid jobs. We consider that all sites choose their strategies at the same time. Hence, while taking a decision, a site cannot observe the actions of other players. This context can be thought as a *non-cooperative* Grid scheduling game where a set of players try to optimize their own objective functions, and there is no cooperation in making decision. In such non-cooperative systems, since Grid sites are not under control of a centralized broker, optimization does not amount to maximizing/minimizing a unique common function, but to find a stable situation in which, for instance, sites guarantee to equally treat remote and local jobs.

The main contribution of this work is to propose a rigorous model to reason about job scheduling mechanisms in Grid systems by exploiting key concepts of Game Theory. Specifically, we formulate a repeated non-cooperative Grid scheduling game in which Grid sites are considered as players of the game, while the actions that are available to players range over various job scheduling policies. The state of each player is given by a non-negative number expressing for how many time units the site will be busy (thus not being able to start new job executions). Each time a Grid job is ready to be executed, it is assigned to the site that is able to guarantee the minimum possible completion time for that job among all the other sites that are bidding for executing that job. For l the length of a Grid job, a site p that is elected to execute that job receives a payoff amounting to l and increases its state by $l-1$, given that p will be busy for further l units of time and that one time unit has passed. Similarly, if at a given round of the game, a site p is willing to execute a local job of length l that is in its dispatch queue, p earns a payoff l and its state is increased by $l-1$. Of course, a site cannot accept a local and a Grid job simultaneously at the same time stamp. We consider Earliest estimated Response Time (ERT) as one of the strategies adopted by players, which gives an estimation of the time interval between the job submission and the beginning of the job execution. Note that ERT gives the same result as the Minimum Completion Time strategy since we assume that no preemption is allowed. Moreover, minimizing the completion time of a job will eventually lead to minimal total completion time for all Grid jobs, which eventually contributes to minimizing the makespan.

We first study a general scenario in which sites can execute either local jobs or Grid jobs and we conjecture that in this case the selfish strategy profile, in which every site chooses to execute a local job if there is any in its queue and otherwise bids for executing a Grid job offering its ERT, is a Nash Equilibrium. Next, we restrict to a special case in which there are *no local jobs*. We give a formal proof that, under the above hypothesis, the strategy profile where every site bids its ERT upon arrival of a new Grid job is a Nash Equilibrium. Note that there is a key assumption in both the cases above: during the whole repeated game, *every job has the same fixed length.* Such a requirement is crucial in proving that each site has no benefit (with respect to its payoff) in declining to execute a job (either local or global), while this is not true if jobs may have different length. Indeed, in this last case, a site can benefit from refusing to execute a job in order to be available to accept another job of greater length that might arrive at a subsequent round of the game, hence receiving a higher payoff. Furthermore, in the proof of the special case we require that the Grid are *heavily loaded*, namely the state of each site cannot be zero for two or more consecutive rounds.

Related work. Recently there has been a great interest in game theoretic approaches for analyzing the Grid resource management and job scheduling problems. Regev and Nisan [9] propose a new system, POPCORN, which uses single and double auction schema for job scheduling. Kwok et al. [6] study the impact of local cluster scheduling policies and the selfish behavior at the machine level using Game Theory. In [6] the strategies that are analyzed are those that selfish computers should take inside a Grid site to maximize their utility. It is assumed that each computer is selfish in the way that it only wants to execute jobs from local users, but does not contribute to the execution of Grid jobs. They derive three kinds of strategy namely, Optimal, Nash and random. It is shown that the Optimal strategy consistently outperforms the Random and Nash strategies, and the Nash strategy is very poor. By contrast, our approach focuses on the selfishness at the site level rather than at the machine level and on finding Nash strategies. Local cluster scheduling policies do have impact on Grid scheduling. Wiriyaprasit et al. [12] reported a significant impact of local policies on response time of jobs. A greedy approach has also been proposed to overcome this behavior. Though the techniques reported gives good results, the method adopted is simplistic. The resource management problem in computational Grid is also addressed by Trystram et al. [10] show that when local schedulers change their schedules locally, the game is analogous to Prisoner's Dilemma game. Scheduling the jobs selfishly by executing local jobs first is the only Nash equilibrium for one shot, non-cooperative Grid scheduling game. The scheduling game is analyzed by considering off-line scheduling with dedicated processors. Unlike their approach, we focus on the online scheduling.

Synopsis. The remainder of the paper is organized as follows. In §2, we describe the main features of our reference Grid system. §3 outlines the main assumptions of the Grid model we consider in §5. In §4, we introduce a general framework based on the notion of Labeled Transition Games. In §5 we instantiate the general setting to define a non-cooperative Grid scheduling game and we present the main results. In §6 we draw some conclusions.

2 The Grid System

In this section we introduce the main features of our reference Grid system. We adopt a Grid structure based on the architecture proposed by the Worldwide LHC Computing Grid (WLCG) [3] for our study. The WLCG and the Enabling Grids for E-sciencE (EGEE) [1] projects operate in conjunction and share a large part of their infrastructure. For this reason, we will refer to it as the WLCG/EGEE infrastructure. WLCG/EGEE is a global collaboration linking Grid infrastructures and computer centers worldwide with the purpose of distributing, storing and analyzing the immense amount of data being generated by Large Hadron Collider (LHC) at CERN (European Organization for Nuclear Research). Hence, the WLCG/EGEE project provides computing and analysis infrastructure for thousands of researchers all over the world, from high energy physics community. WLCG/EGEE has deployed a worldwide computational Grid service covering all the computational and storage need of LHC experiments. The WLCG/EGEE is composed of three main layers, or *tiers*, which are made up of computer centres [4] that contribute to different aspects. By using these tiers, the LHC data are processed, stored and analyzed around the globe. The users of a Grid infrastructure are generally divided into *Virtual Organizations* (VOs), abstract entities grouping users, institutions and resources in the same administrative domain. The Grid middleware used is gLite middleware [2]. One of the important components of middleware related to job management is the Workload Management System (WMS). The WMS is responsible for the management of jobs submitted by users; it matches the job requirements to the available resources and schedules the job for execution on an appropriate computing cluster; then, it tracks the job status and allows the user to retrieve the job output when ready. WMS is built on different components, one of them being the Resource Broker (RB), which is being referred to as *global scheduler* in this paper. The Information System (IS) provides information about the WLCG/EGEE resources and their statuses. The informations are published by the individual resources and copied into central databases; it is used by the WMS to match the resources against the job requirements and to rank them. Below, we comment on the main features of our reference Grid.

Overall structure. The Grid consists of several *sites* or resource centers, each of which may provide computational and data-storage resources for user submitted jobs. Each site consists of zero or more *storage elements* (SE), which handle the storage services, and zero or more *computing elements* (CE), which take care of computing resources and distribute jobs among the worker nodes (which are the execution machines). The Grid sites are connected by a communication network. Each site may contain an arbitrary number of identical processors. Furthermore, each site manages its resources in the form of a cluster with its own Local Resource Management System (LRMS), and the machines in a cluster are connected via a high-bandwidth link. Beside the sites, the Grid includes a central global scheduler that is responsible for the scheduling of jobs to computing elements, with the main goal of improving the overall throughput of the Grid. The global scheduler is usually in charge for resource discovery, resource selection, and job assignment to ensure that the user requirements and resource owner objectives are met. A key feature of Grids is *transparency*, i.e. the Grid appears to the users as a single, unified resource. The broker acts as a mediator between users and resources by providing centralized access to distributed resources. In fact, the user requests for executing jobs cannot be submitted directly to the Grid sites but rather to global scheduler.

Hierarchical structure. The physical structure of the reference Grid is *hierarchical.* Accordingly, the scheduling model is two-level and schedulers are implemented at both levels [11], as shown in Fig. 1. At the first level, the global scheduler allocates the jobs to different sites by selecting a site for each job, keeping in mind the effective distribution of workload among the sites. At the second level, if a job is assigned to a given site, the local cluster scheduler of that site schedules the job on one of the worker nodes participating in the cluster, by using some scheduling policy. The model we study in the subsequent sections is only dealt with the first level of scheduling while disregarding the local scheduling mechanism at machine level. The information about the parameters, like number of free CPU's, number of running and waiting jobs, total available storage space, estimated response time etc. are available to the global scheduler for selecting an appropriate site for the job, though the current load of the whole

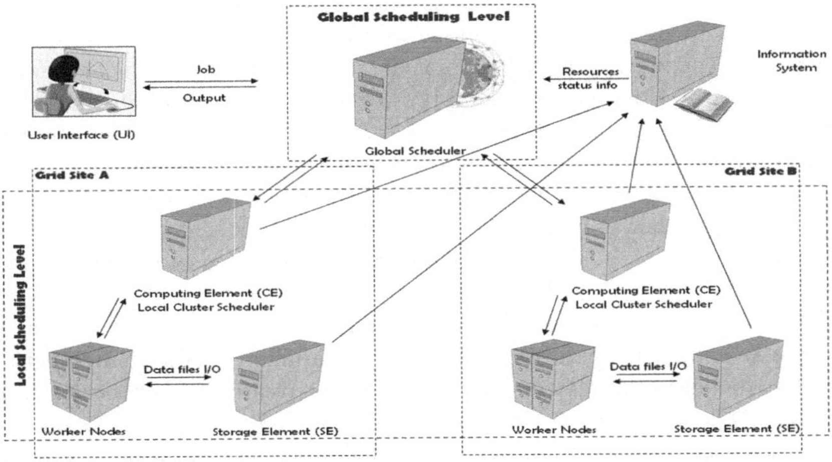

Fig. 1. Operational flow in hierarchical Grid job scheduling

Grid is also taken into account for efficient distribution of workload. One of the most critical issues in the effective utilization of the computational Grid is the *efficiency* of the scheduling of jobs. The global scheduler does not have any hold over the local cluster schedulers as at each site different scheduling policies may be employed on its cluster according to given priorities. While processing a job for scheduling, the global scheduler only knows global capability parameters of each Grid site as a whole represented in the form of computational or storage capability parameters, without regard to details within the sites. Of course, such information are mediated by the local cluster scheduler of each Grid site, which collects the static and dynamic data about the status of participating machines. Jobs are submitted to the global scheduler via the User Interface (UI) specifying the job requirements in the form of Job Description Language (JDL). In JDL, the *Requirements* attribute represents the job requirements on resources in the form of an expression. The global scheduler evaluates this expression during the site selection or matchmaking process. After the matchmaking is done, the job is scheduled to the appropriate site's CE. If two or more sites satisfy the Requirements expression then the global scheduler has to resolve such a tie. While the job runs, any data files required can be accessed either directly from a storage element (SE) or after copying them to the local filesystem on the worker node. After the successful completion of the job, the output is transferred back to the global scheduler's storage and then to the UI. At this point the user can retrieve the output from the UI.

3 System Model

In this section we outline some basic assumptions of the model that we consider in §5 with respect to the reference Grid System described above.

Local and Grid jobs. At any time unit, an arbitrary number of Grid/local jobs can be ready to be executed. We assume that every job can be computed on every cluster (namely, machines are not dedicated). We distinguish among local and remote jobs. Jobs produced by the local users within a site intending to utilize the Grid resources are considered as *local jobs* while all other jobs coming via Grid infrastructure components are referred to as *remote jobs* or *Grid jobs.* In §5 we consider a general model in which there are both kinds of jobs and a restricted model that only includes Grid jobs.

We assume that *jobs have all the same fixed length.* Hence, in turn we assume that jobs can be partitioned into a set of independent sub-tasks of fixed length which can be executed independently on the resources one after the other. After all subtasks end their execution, the result is conjugated as a final output. The above fixed-length requirement plays a crucial role in proving our results. Indeed, suppose that jobs may have different lengths and that the reward assigned to a site for accepting the execution of a job is the length of that job. Then, a site could benefit from refusing the execution of a current job and let its resources free for executing a longer job that might arrive later, thus increasing its gain.

Site states. We consider a discrete-time model in which at each time unit the set of free/busy CPU slots of each site is updated (the time elapses). Every site may have busy slots at any time unit. We assume that if a given job is assigned to a site, than the site's slots will be busy until the end of the execution of that job.

Another key requirement of our model concerns the load of the Grid. We assume the Grid system is *heavily loaded*, in the sense that at any time unit there must be enough incoming jobs so that every site that is free and willing to execute a Grid job cannot be inactive. Roughly, the reason for such a heavy-load requirement is that absence of heavy load could change the order (according to their ERT policies) of the sites that are bidding for executing a given job, thus making the evolution of the system hard to predict.

4 Labeled Transition Games

In this section we introduce the basics of our theory, which combines Game Theory and Labeled Transition Systems. Game Theory [8] can be regarded as a multi-agent decision problem, which means that there are many entities contending for limited rewards/payoffs. These entities have to follow certain rules while making their moves/actions and their payoff depends on those moves. Each player is supposed to behave rationally, i.e. each player tries to maximize its payoff irrespective to what other players are doing. A key issue of Game Theory is that each player has to decide a set of moves which are in accordance with the rules of the game and which maximize its payoff.

Definition 1 (LTS). *A* labeled transition system *is a tuple* $\langle S, L, \rightarrow\rangle$*, where* S *is a set of states,* L *is a set of labels and* $\rightarrow \subseteq S \times L \times S$ *is a ternary relation (of labeled transitions). If* p*,* q *are in* S *and* $a \in L$*, we write* $p \xrightarrow{a} q$ *to mean* $(p, a, q) \in \rightarrow$*.*

Hereafter by $\boldsymbol{k}$ we denote a tuple of elements $\boldsymbol{k} = \langle k_1, \ldots, k_n\rangle$ and by $\boldsymbol{S}$ we denote a Cartesian product $\boldsymbol{S} = S^n$. Furthermore, the usual arithmetic operations over integers, such as summation, extend to tuples by applying the operations elementwise. A *Labeled Transition Game* is meant to model a game in which n players, given a global input g and a tuple of local inputs $\boldsymbol{l}$, make a transition from a state to another such that every player simultaneously takes an action a_i from its respective set of actions. As a result of the execution of a transition, two values are computed: a local payoff u_i that is assigned to each player i, and a global payoff v that represents the benefit for the whole Grid.

Definition 2 (Labeled Transition Game (LTG)). *A Labeled Transition Game is a tuple* $\Gamma = (n, Q, \boldsymbol{q_0}, G, L, A, R, \rightarrow)$ *where*

- n *is the number of* players*.*
- Q *is the set of* states*, ranged over by* p*,*q*, ...*
- $\boldsymbol{q_0} \in Q^n$ *is the vector of* initial *states.*
- G*,* L *are sets of* global/local inputs*, ranged over by* g *and* l*, respectively.*

- *A is a set of player's* actions *(or moves), ranged over by a.*
- *R is a set of payoffs (or rewards), ranged over by u, v, ...*
- *$\rightarrow$ is a relation $\rightarrow \subseteq (\boldsymbol{Q} \times G \times \boldsymbol{L} \times \boldsymbol{A} \times \boldsymbol{Q} \times \boldsymbol{R} \times R)$. Moreover, given $\boldsymbol{p}, g, \boldsymbol{l}$ and $\boldsymbol{a}$, the relation $\rightarrow$ is functional.*

By $\boldsymbol{p} \xrightarrow{g,\boldsymbol{l},\boldsymbol{a}\ \ \boldsymbol{u},v} \boldsymbol{q}$ we mean that $(\boldsymbol{p}, g, \boldsymbol{l}, \boldsymbol{a}, \boldsymbol{u}, v, \boldsymbol{q}) \in \rightarrow$.

In accordance with the definition of labeled transition systems we have defined $\rightarrow$ above as a relation, However, we impose the above requirement on the determinism of the relation as the underlying idea is to have a function that takes $\boldsymbol{p}, g, \boldsymbol{l}$ and $\boldsymbol{a}$ as input and gives in output both a tuple of local payoffs $\boldsymbol{u}$ and a global payoff v.

In a multi-agent scenario, every player has a set of actions available and has to choose an action at each transition step. The decision that a player makes is called the player's *policy*, which is a function that, given a global input, a local input and the state of the player, returns a given action. It would be possible to consider more general policies that also depend on the states and the local inputs of the other players. However, in our framework, it is more reasonable to consider the former kind of policies.

Definition 3 (Policies). *Given an LTG, for every player i, we define a* policy *σ as a function $\sigma : Q \times G \times L \rightarrow A$. Given n players, a* policy profile *is an n-uple of policies $\boldsymbol{\sigma}(\boldsymbol{p}, g, \boldsymbol{l}) = \langle \sigma_1(p_1, g, l_1), \ldots, \sigma_n(p_n, g, l_n)\rangle$.*

By $\boldsymbol{p} \xrightarrow{g,\boldsymbol{l}\ \ \boldsymbol{u},v}_{\boldsymbol{\sigma}} \boldsymbol{q}$ we mean that $\boldsymbol{p} \xrightarrow{g,\boldsymbol{l},\boldsymbol{a}\ \ \boldsymbol{u},v} \boldsymbol{q}$ and $\boldsymbol{\sigma}(\boldsymbol{p}, g, \boldsymbol{l}) = \boldsymbol{a}$.

In this work, we are interested in games that can be repeated for an arbitrary number of times. To this purpose, we generalize the concepts of policies and LTG's to be repeated for a given number of rounds. The *strategy* of a player is a sequence of policies that dictates the player's actions at the different points in the game. The strategies can be pure or mixed. In pure strategies the decision is deterministic while mixed strategies specify the probability distribution used to select the action that the player will perform. In this paper, we only deal with pure strategies. A *Repeated Labeled Transition Game* consists of the repetition of LTGs for an arbitrary number of rounds, in which at each round players accumulate their payoffs.

Definition 4 (strategies). *For N a natural number representing the number of rounds of a game, a* strategy *$\underline{\sigma}_N$ is a sequence of length N of policies $\underline{\sigma}_N = \sigma_1 \cdot \ldots \cdot \sigma_N$. Given n players, a* strategy profile *is an n-uple of strategies $\underline{\boldsymbol{\sigma}}_N = \langle \underline{\sigma}_{N,1}, \ldots, \underline{\sigma}_{N,n}\rangle$.*

Hereafter, if the number of rounds N is clear from the context or irrelevant, we drop the index N and simply denote strategies and strategy profiles as $\underline{\sigma}$ and $\underline{\boldsymbol{\sigma}}$. Furthermore, for $\underline{\tau}$ a strategy, by $\underline{\boldsymbol{\sigma}}[\underline{\tau}/\underline{\sigma}_i]$ we denote the strategy profile obtained from $\underline{\boldsymbol{\sigma}}$ by replacing the strategy $\underline{\sigma}_i$ of the i-th player with $\underline{\tau}$.

Definition 5 (Repeated Labeled Transition Game (RLTG)). *A* Repeated Labeled Transition Game (RLTG) $\boldsymbol{p} \overset{\underline{g},\underline{\boldsymbol{l}}\ \underline{\boldsymbol{u}},\underline{v}}{\Longrightarrow}_{\underline{\sigma}} \boldsymbol{r}$ *is defined by the following inference rules:*

$$\frac{\boldsymbol{p} \xrightarrow{g,\boldsymbol{l}\ \boldsymbol{u},v}_{\sigma} \boldsymbol{r}}{\boldsymbol{p} \overset{g,\boldsymbol{l}\ \boldsymbol{u},v}{\Longrightarrow}_{\sigma} \boldsymbol{r}} \qquad \frac{\boldsymbol{p} \overset{\underline{g},\underline{\boldsymbol{l}}\ \underline{\boldsymbol{u}},\underline{v}}{\Longrightarrow}_{\underline{\sigma}} \boldsymbol{q} \quad and \quad \boldsymbol{q} \xrightarrow{g,\boldsymbol{l}\ \boldsymbol{u},v}_{\sigma} \boldsymbol{r}}{\boldsymbol{p} \xrightarrow{\underline{g}g,\underline{\boldsymbol{l}}\boldsymbol{l}\ \underline{\boldsymbol{u}}\boldsymbol{u},\underline{v}v}_{\underline{\sigma}\sigma} \boldsymbol{r}}$$

In a game, the goal of each player is to maximize the payoff it accumulated during the whole game. Below, we define two types of gains a player can receive: the *local gain* represents the payoff of each player while the *global gain* reflects how effectively the global objective performance measure is achieved. As expected, local and global gains are computed by summing up the local payoffs $\boldsymbol{u}$ and the global payoffs v, respectively.

Definition 6 (global/local gain). *For an* LTG_N $\boldsymbol{p} \overset{\underline{g},\underline{\boldsymbol{l}}\ \underline{\boldsymbol{u}},\underline{v}}{\Longrightarrow}_{\underline{\sigma}} \boldsymbol{r}$, *the* local gain *and the* global gain *are defined respectively as:*

- $\boldsymbol{lgain}(g, \underline{\boldsymbol{l}}, \underline{\sigma}) = \sum_{j \in N} \boldsymbol{u}_j$.
- $ggain(g, \underline{\boldsymbol{l}}, \underline{\sigma}) = \sum_{j \in N} v_j$.

A central notion in Game Theory is that of *Nash equilibrium* [7], a situation in which no player can improve its own payoff function or reward by unilaterally changing its strategy. The *optimal strategy* is the profile of strategies that optimizes the system goal or the global objective performance measure.

Definition 7 (Nash Equilibrium). *Assume an* LTG_N $\boldsymbol{p} \overset{\underline{g},\underline{\boldsymbol{l}}\ \underline{\boldsymbol{u}},\underline{v}}{\Longrightarrow}_{\underline{\sigma}} \boldsymbol{r}$. *The strategy profile* $\underline{\sigma}$ *is a* Nash equilibrium, *written Nash*($\underline{\sigma}$) *iff*

$$\forall \underline{g}, \underline{\boldsymbol{l}}, \underline{\tau}, i \quad lgain(\underline{g}, \underline{\boldsymbol{l}}, \underline{\sigma})_i \geq lgain(\underline{g}, \underline{\boldsymbol{l}}, \underline{\sigma}[\underline{\tau}/\underline{\sigma_i}])_i.$$

Definition 8 (Optimal strategy). *The strategy profile* $\underline{\sigma}$ *of length* N *is* Optimal, *written as Opt*($\underline{\sigma}$) *iff*

$$\forall \underline{g}, \underline{\boldsymbol{l}}, \underline{\tau} \quad ggain(\underline{g}, \underline{\boldsymbol{l}}, \underline{\sigma}) \geq ggain(\underline{g}, \underline{\boldsymbol{l}}, \underline{\tau}).$$

5 A Game-Theoretic Model for Grid

In this section we focus on formulating a Non-cooperative Grid Scheduling (NGS) game, in which each site/organization at each time unit can choose whether to accept executing local or Grid jobs. We exploit the framework developed in §4 to study under which conditions the behavior of sites, in long runs, will be (i) either selfish as, for instance, they prefer to first execute their own local jobs over the Grid jobs, in order to minimize the sum of completion times of their own jobs, or (ii) cooperative, thus contributing toward a proper working of the Grid system. Specifically, assuming M is the fixed length of all jobs, we give a notion of M-LTG, whose players are the Grid sites, actions are dictated by scheduling algorithms, and global and local inputs represent the presence of Grid/local jobs to be executed, respectively.

Definition 9 (An M-LTG for Grid). *Assuming jobs have all a fixed length M, an M-*LTG for Grid *is a tuple $\Gamma = (n, Q, \boldsymbol{q_0}, G, L, A, R, \rightarrow)$ where*

- *n is a set of Grid sites.*
- *Q is a set of natural numbers. Every state $q_i \in Q$ represents the number of future time slots in which site i will be busy according to the present commitments.*
- *$\boldsymbol{q_0} \in \boldsymbol{Q}$ is the tuple of initial states.*
- *$G = L = \{true, false\}$, where $g = true$ (resp. $g = false$) indicates the presence (resp. absence) of a Grid job that is ready to be executed. Similarly, $l_i = true$ (resp. $l_i = false$) expresses that there is (resp., there is not) a job ready to be executed in the queue of site i.*
- *$A = \{loc, glo, no\}$, where $a_i = glo$ (resp., $a_i = loc$) means that the site i, with $1 \leq i \leq n$, bids for executing an incoming Grid job (resp., i is ready to execute a local job); $a_i = no$ means that site i does not accept to execute any job.*
- *R is a set of natural numbers representing the set of payoffs. A local payoff u_i is assigned to player i for executing a local/Grid job, while the global payoff v expresses at which time unit the execution of the Grid job will be completed.*
- *$\rightarrow$ is the relation defined in Def. 10.*

Definition 10 (M-LTG relation $\rightarrow$). *Assuming jobs have all a fixed length M, we define the relation $\rightarrow$ for Grid as $\boldsymbol{p} \xrightarrow{g, \boldsymbol{l}, \boldsymbol{a} \ \ \boldsymbol{u}, v} \boldsymbol{q}$, which is computed as follows:*

1. $\boldsymbol{q} := \boldsymbol{p}$; $\boldsymbol{u} := \boldsymbol{0}$; $v := 0$; $k := 0$; (*initialization*)
2. `if` g `then`
   (a) $k := \min(n, \{h | a_h = glo, \forall i \, a_i = glo \Rightarrow q_h \leq q_i\})$; (*choose the winner*)
   (b) $q_k := q_k + M; u_k := M; v := -(q_k + M)$; (*award the winner*)
3. $\forall i \neq k$. `if` $l_i \wedge (a_i = loc)$ `then` $q_i := q_i + M; u_i := M$;
   (*rewards for local executions*)
4. $\forall i$. `if` $q_i \neq 0$ `then` $q_i := q_i - 1$; `stop`. (*time elapses*)

In the above procedure, step 2 states that if there is a Grid job in the dispatch queue ($g = true$), the global scheduler assigns the job to the site that, among the sites that bid for that job, offers the earliest response time (which eventually leads to lowest completion time, since the model is without preemption and all jobs have the same length). Ties are resolved in favor of the bidder with lowest index. The winner k is granted a payoff amounting to the length M of the job and its state is increased by M (with the intended meaning that k will be busy for further M time units). We assume here that, for every incoming job, there is at least one player, i.e player n, who is always bound to accept the Grid job. Moreover, the global payoff v is assigned the value $-(q_k + M)$: this fact means that the execution of the job will end after $q_k + M$ time units and that from the Grid perspective it is more convenient that the global executions are completed as soon as possible. Step 3 dictates that every site i that is not selected for executing the current Grid job and which accepts executing a job in its local dispatch queue, receives a payoff M and increases its states by M. Step 4 decreases every non-zero state by one, thus simulating that time elapses.

In the present Grid setting, a player's policy is a scheduling algorithm that specifies what jobs that player/site accepts. As mentioned above, once a state q_i, a global input g, and a local input l_i are given, the policy of site i returns a unique action a_i. For instance, if we assume a policy 'Grid Job Otherwise Local Job', i.e. $\sigma_i(p_i, g, l_i) = \texttt{if } g \texttt{ then } \mathit{glo} \texttt{ else } \mathit{loc}$, if there is a Grid job ready to be executed then i bids for that job ($a_i = \mathit{glo}$), otherwise i accepts executing a local job in its dispatch queue ($a_i = \mathit{loc}$).

For M the length of jobs, a repeated LTG for Grid, M-RLTG, is defined by instantiating Def. 5 to the M-LTG for Grid given in Def. 9.

Definition 11. *We define the policy 'Local Job Otherwise Grid Job' (LJOGJ) as a* $\theta : Q \times G \times L \to A$ *such that*

$$\theta(q, g, l) = \texttt{if } l \texttt{ then } \mathit{loc} \texttt{ else } \mathit{glo}$$

We formulate below a conjecture about the policy LJOGJ being Nash. First we give an example that shows the evolution of a repeated game for Grid.

Example 1. Consider a two-round game with jobs of length 5, namely a 5-RLTG with two rounds. In Fig. 2 we summarize the evolution of the game (left-hand table) and report the local and global gains (right-hand table). Specifically, in the left-hand table there are three rows for each time stamp, the first one contains the states of sites q_i's, the second one the boolean values l_i's, the third one the players's actions a_i; the value in the last column represents the boolean value g at each round. The game has three players 1, 2 and 3. Players 1 and 2 can start the execution of a new job after time unit 1, while 3 can start immediately. Suppose that at time stamp 0 there is a Grid job that is ready to be executed. Assume that sites 1 and 2 have no local jobs available while 3 has a job in its dispatch queue (i.e. $l_1 = \mathit{false}$, $l_3 = \mathit{true}$) and that their policies are LJOGJ, namely $\sigma_i = \texttt{if } l_i \texttt{ then } \mathit{loc} \texttt{ else } \mathit{glo}$, for $i = 1, 2, 3$. Hence, 1 and 2 will bid for the Grid job and have the same state but 1 has a smaller index. Hence, according to the rule of the game, the Grid job is assigned to 1, $u_1 = 5$ (amounting to the length of the job) and $u_2 = 0$. On the other hand, 3 opts for executing a local job

Nodes	1	2	3	
	1	1	0	
Time stamp 0	false	false	true	true
	glo	glo	loc	
	5	0	4	
Time stamp 1	false	false	false	true
	glo	glo	glo	
Time stamp 2	4	4	3	

Gains	$\boldsymbol{u}$			v
Nodes	1	2	3	
Time stamp 0	5	0	5	-6
Time stamp 1	0	5	0	-5

Fig. 2. A 5-RLTG for Grid with 3 nodes

and, so, $u_3 = 5$. The global gain v is $-(1+5)$. Then, at time stamp 1, the next free CPU slots of 1 and 3 will be at time stamp $1+5-1$ and $0+5-1$, respectively (with -1 referring to the fact that one time unit has passed). Hence, the states of the sites 1, 2, and 3 will be updated to 5, 0, 4, respectively. Now, assume at time stamp 1 another Grid job of length 5 is ready to be executed and none of the sites has a local job in its queue. Assuming the scheduling policies are LJOGJ as at the previous round, the Grid job will be assigned to 2 because it has the minimum state (i.e. 2 is announcing the minimum response time). Consequently, the local gain of 2 is 5 while the other players receive a null payoff, and the global gain v for round 2 is $-(0+5)$. Furthermore, the states are updated to be 4, 4 and 3, respectively.

Conjecture 1. Consider the M-RLTG for Grid given in Def. 9 and a strategy profile $\underline{\boldsymbol{\theta}} = \langle \underline{\theta}_1, \ldots, \underline{\theta}_n \rangle$, where each strategy $\underline{\theta}_i$ is a sequence of LJOGJ policies θ as defined in Def. 11. Then, *Nash*($\underline{\boldsymbol{\theta}}$).

Example 2. Consider the 5-RLTG depicted in Fig. 3. The left-hand table represents the evolution of the game if all players play the LJOGJ strategy. Suppose that initially there are three players whose states are $q_1 = 1$, $q_2 = 1$, $q_3 = 0$. Moreover, assume that at the first round there is a job that is ready to be executed and all players are bidding for this job. According to the rule of the game, the job is assigned to player 3 and, so, the local payoffs are $u_3 = 5$ and $u_1 = u_2 = 0$ (payoffs are not reported in the picture) and the states are updated to be $q_1 = 0$, $q_2 = 0$, and $q_3 = 4$. At the second round, again there is a job ready to be executed and every players bids for that job. The job is assigned to 1 (remark that ties are resolved in favor of the player with lowest index), the local payoffs are $u_1 = 5$ and $u_2 = u_3 = 0$ and the states are $q_1 = 4$, $q_2 = 0$, and $q_3 = 3$. As mentioned above, the basic idea behind the concept of Nash Equilibrium is to show that any player has no incentive in unilaterally deviating from its own strategy. Suppose now that at the first round, 3 deviates from its policy θ_3 by adopting a policy $\theta_3' =$ `if` l_3 `then` *loc* `else` *no*, while the other players maintain their LJOGJ policies. The evolution of the game is described in the right-hand table of Fig. 3. It is easy to see that at the first round the Grid job will be assigned to 1 rather than to 3. At the next round, 2 exhibits the minimum state. Hence, the local gain of 3 in the deviating case is 0 rather than 5.

This example shows a case in which players have no incentive in deviating from the LJOGJ strategy. Furthermore, this example gives evidence of the importance of the heavy load assumption, which requires that the states of players cannot be zero for two or more consecutive rounds (see Def. 15 below). Indeed, suppose that a player i deviates from its strategy and refuses to execute a job, which is assigned to the second favorite player j. The heavy load assumption guarantees that the order of the states of the players is maintained. Hence, if eventually a new job is ready to be executed, this job will be assigned to i. As a consequence, after an arbitrary number of rounds, the case of the deviating strategy and the case of the original strategies both lead to a situation in which every player has the same state and payoff. By contrast, in this example, if 3 refuses to execute the incoming job at the first round, the job arriving at the second round is assigned

Nodes	1	2	3	
	1	1	0	
Time stamp 0	false	false	false	true
	glo	glo	glo	
	0	0	4	
Time stamp 1	false	false	false	true
	glo	glo	glo	
Time stamp 2	4	0	3	

Nodes	1	2	3	
	1	1	0	
Time stamp 0	false	false	false	true
	glo	glo	no	
	5	0	0	
Time stamp 1	false	false	false	true
	glo	glo	glo	
Time stamp 2	4	4	0	

Fig. 3. Another 5-RLTG

to 2 rather than to 3, since the order of the states has changed and 2 is now the most favorite player. This scenario is formalized in Lemma 1, which in fact does not hold in absence of the heavy load assumption.

5.1 A Special Case

In this section we restrict the theory developed in §5 by introducing the additional requirement that the scheduling problem only takes into account Grid jobs while disregarding local jobs. To this purpose, in the following we adapt some basic concepts defined above to the new 'only-global' setting.

Definition 12 (An only-global M-LTG for Grid). *An* only-global M-LTG for Grid *is a tuple* $\Gamma = (n, Q, \boldsymbol{q_0}, G, A, R, \rightarrow)$ *where*

- n *is a set of Grid sites.*
- Q *is a set of natural numbers. Every state* $q_i \in Q$ *represents the number of future time slots in which site* i *will be busy.*
- $\boldsymbol{q_0} \in \boldsymbol{Q}$ *is the tuple of initial states.*
- $G = \{true, false\}$.
- $A = \{glo, no\}$.
- R *is a set of natural numbers representing the set of payoffs.*
- $\rightarrow$ *is the relation defined in Def. 13.*

Definition 13 (An only-global LTG relation $\rightarrow$). *The relation* $\rightarrow$ *for only-global Grid, represented as* $\boldsymbol{p} \xrightarrow{g,\boldsymbol{a}\ \boldsymbol{u}} \boldsymbol{q}$, *is defined as in Def. 10 apart that local input and global payoff are discarded:*

1. $\boldsymbol{q} := \boldsymbol{p}; \boldsymbol{u} := \boldsymbol{0}$;
2. `if` g `then` $k := \min(n, \{h | a_h$ `= glo,` $\forall i\, a_i = glo \Rightarrow q_h \leq q_i\})$;
   $q_k := q_k + M;\ u_k := M$;
3. $\forall i$. `if` $q_i \neq 0$ `then` $q_i := q_i - 1$; `stop`.

In absence of local jobs, policies and strategies are restricted to be functions that only depend on states and global inputs. For $\boldsymbol{\sigma}$ a policy, by $\boldsymbol{p} \xrightarrow{g\ \boldsymbol{u}}_{\boldsymbol{\sigma}} \boldsymbol{q}$ we mean that $\boldsymbol{p} \xrightarrow{g,\boldsymbol{a}\ \boldsymbol{u}} \boldsymbol{q}$ and $\boldsymbol{\sigma}(\boldsymbol{p}, g) = \boldsymbol{a}$. Below, we consider a variant of the policy Earliest Response Time (ERT) and we give a formal proof that a strategy profile consisting of ERT's policies is a Nash equilibrium. This result exploits the heavy load assumption, which amounts to requiring that the state of each player cannot be zero for two or more consecutive rounds of the game.

Definition 14. *We define a policy Earliest Response Time (ERT) as* $\epsilon : Q \times G \to A$ *such that* $\epsilon(q, g) = glo$.

Hereafter, by $(\boldsymbol{w}, \boldsymbol{p})$ we mean that every player i is in state p_i and has accumulated a payoff w_i and we write $(\boldsymbol{w}, \boldsymbol{p}) \xrightarrow{g}_{\boldsymbol{\sigma}} (\boldsymbol{w} + \boldsymbol{u}, \boldsymbol{q})$ in place of $\boldsymbol{p} \xrightarrow{g\ \boldsymbol{u}}_{\boldsymbol{\sigma}} \boldsymbol{q}$, with w_i and $w_i + u_i$ the payoffs of the i-th player before and after the execution of the transition, respectively. We will use similar notations for sequences of transitions.

Definition 15 (heavy load assumption). *An* M-RLTG *for Grid has* heavy load *if, for every player* i *and for every transition* $\boldsymbol{p} \xrightarrow{g\ \boldsymbol{u}}_{\boldsymbol{\sigma}} \boldsymbol{q}$*, whenever* $p_i = 0$ *then* $q_i \neq 0$.

Lemma 1. *Suppose that the heavy load assumption holds and that, for some* σ*, with* $\sigma \neq \epsilon$ *and* ϵ *as in Def. 14*

$$(\boldsymbol{w}, \boldsymbol{p}) \xrightarrow{g}_{\boldsymbol{\epsilon}} (\boldsymbol{z}, \boldsymbol{q}) \quad \textit{and} \quad (\boldsymbol{w}, \boldsymbol{p}) \xrightarrow{g}_{\boldsymbol{\epsilon}[\sigma/\epsilon_i]} (\boldsymbol{x}, \boldsymbol{r}).$$

1. *If* $q_k = r_k$ *for all* k *then* $z_i = x_i$.
2. *If* $\exists j$ *such that* $q_j \neq r_j$ *then* $z_i > x_i$ *and, if the game continues, there exist two sequences of transitions such that*

$$(\boldsymbol{z}, \boldsymbol{q}) \xrightarrow{g_1}_{\boldsymbol{\epsilon}} (\boldsymbol{z}_1, \boldsymbol{q}_1) \dots \xrightarrow{g_P}_{\boldsymbol{\epsilon}} (\boldsymbol{z}_P, \boldsymbol{q}_P) \textit{ and } (\boldsymbol{x}, \boldsymbol{r}) \xrightarrow{g_1}_{\boldsymbol{\epsilon}} (\boldsymbol{x}_1, \boldsymbol{r}_1) \dots \xrightarrow{g_P}_{\boldsymbol{\epsilon}} (\boldsymbol{x}_P, \boldsymbol{r}_P)$$

and (i) either the game stops at the P*-th round and* $x_{P,i} \leq z_{P,i}$ *or (ii) the game continues and* $q_{P,k} = r_{P,k}$ *for all* $k = 1, \dots, n$*, and* $x_{P,i} = z_{P,i}$.

Proof. If $q_k = r_k$ for all k, it means that the deviating strategy σ has not changed the winner of the game at that round. Hence, the payoff of the i-th player is the same, i.e. $z_i = x_i$. Conversely, suppose that there exists j such that $q_j \neq r_j$. Since every player k with $k \neq i$ is only allowed to play the strategy ϵ_k, necessarily the players are in a precise order given by their states in which i is the most favorite candidate and j is the second favorite, namely $q_i \leq q_j \leq q_{l_1} \leq \dots q_{l_n - 2}$. Hence, by deviating from its strategy ϵ_i, i-th player is not a winner any longer and, so, $z_i > x_i$ and $z_j < x_j$. If the game continues there are two cases. If there is a sequence of rounds in which there is no new job to be executed followed by a last round in which an incoming Grid job arrives, then the heavy load assumption ensures that the order of the players will remain unchanged, namely, in the case of the deviating policy profile $\boldsymbol{\epsilon}[\sigma/\epsilon_i]$ the job will necessarily be assigned to i, while in the case of the original policy profile $\boldsymbol{\epsilon}$ the game will be assigned to j. Hence, i and j arrive in the same state in the two cases and $z_{P,i} = x_{P,j}$. Conversely, if the game ends before such a job arrives, the payoff of i remains greater than in the deviating case, i.e. $x_{P,i} \leq z_{P,i}$.

Theorem 1. *Consider the only-global M-RLTG for Grid given in Def. 12 and the strategy profile* $\underline{\boldsymbol{\epsilon}} = \langle \underline{\epsilon}_1, \ldots, \underline{\epsilon}_n \rangle$*, where each strategy* $\underline{\epsilon}_i$ *is a sequence of ERT policies* ϵ *as defined in Def. 14. If the heavy load assumption holds, then Nash(*$\underline{\boldsymbol{\epsilon}}$*).*

Proof. Starting from the initial state of the game, consider the tree of all the strategy profiles. We propose a proof by induction on the depth N of tree, namely on the number of rounds of the game. Without loss of generality, we can assume that the deviating strategy is applied for the first time at round 1 of the game. Indeed, if this is not the case and the deviating strategy is initially applied at the m-th round, we can discard the first $m-1$ rounds as the payoffs in the two cases will be the same.

Base case. If the game does not start, the thesis trivially holds.

Inductive case. We have to prove the result for $N+1$ rounds. By induction hypothesis, the theorem holds for every tree of depth N. Hence, any strategy profile of length N' that contains at least a σ_i with $\sigma_i \neq \epsilon_i$ is 'dominated' by the strategy profile $\underline{\boldsymbol{\epsilon}}_{N'}$, namely the local gain of the i-th player arising from the deviating strategy is not strictly greater than the local gain of i in the ERT strategy $\underline{\epsilon}_i$. Consequently, we only have to prove that, for any deviating policy $\sigma_i \neq \epsilon_i$, the strategy profile $\boldsymbol{\epsilon}_1[\sigma_i/\epsilon_i] \cdot \boldsymbol{\epsilon}_2 \cdot \ldots \cdot \boldsymbol{\epsilon}_{N+1}$ is dominated by $\underline{\boldsymbol{\epsilon}}_{N+1}$. Suppose that the game starts and that $(\mathbf{0}, \boldsymbol{p}) \xrightarrow{g}_{\boldsymbol{\epsilon}_1} (\boldsymbol{z}, \boldsymbol{q})$, $(\mathbf{0}, \boldsymbol{p}) \xrightarrow{g}_{\boldsymbol{\epsilon}_1[\sigma_i/\epsilon_i]} (\boldsymbol{x}, \boldsymbol{r})$. We apply Lemma 1.

1. If $q_k = r_k$ for all k then $z_i = x_i$. If the game stops the thesis trivially follows by the inductive hypothesis. If the game continues, the theorem holds because all the players have the same positions q_k, for all k, in the two sequences and the continuations are sequences of only strategy ϵ.
2. If $\exists j$ such that $q_j \neq r_j$, then $z_i > x_i$. If the game stops, the theorem trivially holds as $z_i > x_i$. If the game continues, by Lemma 1, there exist two sequences of transitions such that

$$(\boldsymbol{z}, \boldsymbol{q}) \xrightarrow{g_1}_{\boldsymbol{\epsilon}} (\boldsymbol{z}_1, \boldsymbol{q}_1) \ldots \xrightarrow{g_P}_{\boldsymbol{\epsilon}} (\boldsymbol{z}_P, \boldsymbol{q}_P) \text{ and } (\boldsymbol{x}, \boldsymbol{r}) \xrightarrow{g_1}_{\boldsymbol{\epsilon}} (\boldsymbol{x}_1, \boldsymbol{r}_1) \ldots \xrightarrow{g_P}_{\boldsymbol{\epsilon}} (\boldsymbol{x}_P, \boldsymbol{r}_P)$$

   and either the game stops and $x_{P,i} \leq z_{P,i}$ or the game continues and $q_{P,k} = q_{P,k}$ for all $k = 1, \ldots, n$, and $x_{P,i} = z_{P,i}$. If the game stops now, $x_{P,i} \leq z_{P,i}$ and the thesis is proved. If the game continues, as in the above case, all the players have the same positions $q_{P,k}$ in the two sequences and the continuations are both sequences of only strategy ϵ. Hence, again, the theorem holds.

6 Conclusions

In this work, we have addressed the job scheduling problem in heterogeneous computational Grids, by exploiting the concept of Nash Equilibrium in Game Theory. Specifically, we formulated a non-cooperative Grid job scheduling game in which players are Grid sites and actions performed by players are dictated by scheduling algorithms. In the more general scenario including local jobs beside Grid jobs, we have conjectured that the selfish strategy profile is a Nash Equilibrium. By contrast, in the restricted case in which there are no local jobs we have given a formal proof that the strategy profile where every node offers its ERT is a Nash equilibrium. Note that in both the above cases we have required that every job (either Grid or local) must have the same length during the whole repeated game. In the restricted case we have introduced the further requirement that the system must be heavily loaded. Such assumptions are crucial in proving our results. Our future work includes a deeper study of the general scenario in which the above two restrictions have been removed.

References

1. Enabling Grids for E-science in Europe, `http://www.eu-egee.org`
2. gLite Middleware, `http://glite.web.cern.ch/glite/`
3. Worldwide LHC Computing Grid, `http://lcg.web.cern.ch/LCG/public/`
4. Arezzini, S., Boccali, T., Calzolari, F., Ciampa, A., Marini, S., Mazzoni, E., Sarkar, S., Taneja, S., Terreni, G.: Il Grid Data Center Dell'INFN di Pisa. Internal report, `http://www.lnf.infn.it/sis/preprint/pdf/getfile.php?filename=INFN-CCR-09-2.pdf`
5. Foster, I.T., Kesselman, C.: The Grid, Blueprint for a New Computing Infrastructure. Morgan Kaufmann Publishers, San Francisco (1999)
6. Kwok, Y., Song, S., Hwang, K.: Selfish grid computing: Game-theoretic modeling and NAS performance results. In: Proc. CCGrid, pp. 9–12 (2005)
7. Nash, J.: Non-cooperative games. The Annals of Mathematics 54(2), 286–295 (1951)
8. Osborne, M.J.: An introduction to game theory. Oxford Univ. Press, New York (2004)
9. Regev, O., Nisan, N.: The POPCORN market—an online market for computational resources. In: Proc. ICE, pp. 148–157. ACM, New York (1998)
10. Rzadca, K., Trystram, D., Wierzbicki, A.: Fair game-theoretic resource management in dedicated grids. In: Proc. CCGRID, pp. 343–350. IEEE Computer Society, Los Alamitos (2007)
11. Tchernykh, A., Ramírez, J.M., Avetisyan, A., Kuzjurin, N., Grushin, D., Zhuk, S.: Two level job-scheduling strategies for a computational grid. In: Wyrzykowski, R., Dongarra, J., Meyer, N., Waśniewski, J. (eds.) PPAM 2005. LNCS, vol. 3911, pp. 774–781. Springer, Heidelberg (2005)
12. Wiriyaprasit, S., Muangsin, V.: The impact of local priority policies on grid scheduling performance and an adaptive policy-based grid scheduling algorithm. In: Proc. HPCASIA, pp. 343–346. IEEE Computer Society, Los Alamitos (2004)

Functions as Processes: Termination and the $\bar{\lambda}\mu\tilde{\mu}$-Calculus*

Matteo Cimini[1], Claudio Sacerdoti Coen[2], and Davide Sangiorgi[2,3]

[1] School of Computer Science, Reykjavik University, Iceland
[2] Department of Computer Science, University of Bologna, Italy
[3] INRIA, France

Abstract. The $\bar{\lambda}\mu\tilde{\mu}$-calculus is a variant of the λ-calculus with significant differences, including non-confluence and a Curry-Howard isomorphism with the classical sequent calculus.

We present an encoding of the $\bar{\lambda}\mu\tilde{\mu}$-calculus into the π-calculus. We establish the operational correctness of the encoding, and then we extract from it an abstract machine for the $\bar{\lambda}\mu\tilde{\mu}$-calculus. We prove that there is a tight relationship between such a machine and Curien and Herbelin's abstract machine for the $\bar{\lambda}\mu\tilde{\mu}$-calculus. The π-calculus image of the (typed) $\bar{\lambda}\mu\tilde{\mu}$-calculus is a nontrivial set of terminating processes.

1 Introduction

In his seminal paper [10], Milner gave accurate compilations from the call-by-value and call-by-name λ-calculi into the π-calculus. The study of embeddings of λ-calculi into a process calculus has then been continued, by a number of researchers (see [14] for a tutorial), and is interesting for several reasons. From the process calculus point of view, it is a significant test of expressiveness, and helps in getting deeper insight into its theory. From the λ-calculus point of view, it provides the means to study λ-terms in contexts other than purely sequential ones, and with the instruments available in the process calculus. For example, an important behavioural equivalence upon process terms gives rise to an interesting equivalence upon λ-terms. Moreover, the relevance of those λ-calculus evaluation strategies which can be efficiently encoded is strengthened. The study can also be useful to provide a semantic foundation for languages which combine concurrent and functional programming and to develop parallel implementations of functional languages.

Last but not least, the study can give insights into the transfer of results or techniques from the λ-calculus into the process calculus. An example are results about termination of programs. Termination has been studied extensively in the λ-calculus, where it is often called *strong normalisation*. Termination is also important in concurrency. For instance, if we interrogate a server, we may want to know that the interrogation does not cause an infinite computation in the server. Compared to the λ-calculus, results about

* Cimini's work is supported by the project "New Developments in Operational Semantics" (nr. 080039021) of the Icelandic Research Fund.; Sangiorgi's by the EU projects Sensoria and Hats.

M. Wirsing, M. Hofmann, and A. Rauschmayer (Eds.): TGC 2010, LNCS 6084, pp. 73–86, 2010.

termination in the π-calculus are fairly rare [20,15,6,5]. Other interesting results in the λ-calculi concern the Curry-Howard isomorphism, in the sense of [7,17], between the formulae of a logic and the the types of a calculus. An example of a technique widely used in the λ-calculus and that would be interesting to transport onto the π-calculus are logical relations. The technique is used in the λ-calculus to establish various properties including termination, parametricity and representation independence. It remains rather unclear how to transport the technique onto a concurrent language so to capture also processes that are 'non-functional' and non-confluent.

In the present work, we explore the embedding into π-calculus of a variant of the λ-calculus, namely the $\bar{\lambda}\mu\tilde{\mu}$-calculus [4]. The $\bar{\lambda}\mu\tilde{\mu}$-calculus presents some striking differences with respect to the ordinary λ-calculus. A major interest of the $\bar{\lambda}\mu\tilde{\mu}$-calculus is that its typed version is Curry-Howard isomorphic to classical sequent calculus. While in the present work we focus on the untyped version, the Curry-Howard correspondence is still reflected in the untyped calculus in several ways. We discuss all these aspects below.

First of all, the $\bar{\lambda}\mu\tilde{\mu}$-calculus, being Curry-Howard isomorphic to a sequent calculus (as the simpler $\bar{\lambda}$-calculus of Herbelin [8]), can be seen as a calculus whose terms are reduction machine states. In particular, and contrary to the λ-calculus, all head reductions only involve the outermost parts of the term. In the λ-calculus, even in the case of head reduction, the parts of the λ-term that interact need not be at the outermost level, as shown in the term $((\lambda x.\, M)N)P$. Encodings of the λ-calculus into π-calculus have to bring the interacting terms to a topmost position to allow interaction between them. This forces, for instance, the encoding of λ-terms to be parametric on the channels used to interact, which have to be provided dynamically. In the $\bar{\lambda}\mu\tilde{\mu}$-calculus, in contrast, a redex is always at top level. For instance, the previous example becomes $\langle \lambda x.\, M \mid N \cdot (P \cdot \alpha) \rangle$: the λ-abstraction and its argument N are in the outermost parts of the term. The topmost property allows us to avoid the channel parametrization in the encoding into π-calculus: only three channels are needed for reduction, each one corresponding to a different kind of redex.

Secondly, the $\bar{\lambda}\mu\tilde{\mu}$-calculus is strongly normalizing, but non-confluent, as required by Girard's example of non-confluence for cut elimination in classical logic. Thus, one may hope that the subset of the π-calculus obtained as the image of the encoding, restricted to well-typed terms, is a nontrivial example of a non-confluent but strongly normalizing set of processes. In order to achieve non-confluence, the $\bar{\lambda}\mu\tilde{\mu}$-calculus includes the μ control operator that behaves like the μ control operator of Parigot's $\lambda\mu$-calculus [12], introducing a critical pair in the reduction system. The critical pair, however, is only a symptom of a more interesting phenomenon: each topmost subterm (that becomes a process in π-calculus) can always express two different behaviours: either it can be bound and delayed, acting in a passive way, or it can continue its normal behaviour, for instance by capturing another topmost subterm. Moreover, the subterm is actually captured only if it interacts with a capturing term. Since each one is a context for the other and determines the other subterm behaviour, the subterms involved in a reduction interact in an essentially synchronous way. We can see indeed the (encoding of the) $\bar{\lambda}\mu\tilde{\mu}$-calculus as a calculus of peers where each peer can initiate the communication, whereas the λ-calculus (with a fixed strategy) follows the client-server model. These synchrony aspects explain why our encoding of the $\bar{\lambda}\mu\tilde{\mu}$-calculus exploits the synchronous features of the π-calculus, notably mixed choice, i.e. a choice between an input and an output action.

A finally reason of interest for the $\bar{\lambda}\mu\tilde{\mu}$-calculus is that the application of the logical relation technique to it is technically quite different from that for the ordinary λ-calculus. This is partly due to the non-confluence properties of the $\bar{\lambda}\mu\tilde{\mu}$-calculus and partly, but more significantly, to its control operators. These aspects make us believe that the logical relations in the $\bar{\lambda}\mu\tilde{\mu}$-calculus can offer insights for the transport of logical relations onto a concurrent calculus such as the π-calculus, though we do not pursue this line of work in the present paper.

Figure 1 is a summary of the main results. Following the work of Vasconcelos in [19], we identify the reduction machine $M1$ implemented by the encoding and we put it in relation with a previously known reduction machine for the $\bar{\lambda}\mu\tilde{\mu}$-calculus given by Curien and Herbelin in [4], here called $M2$. The operational behaviour of the encoding π-terms is precisely captured by the reduction machine $M1$ (derived in a straightforward way from the $\bar{\lambda}\mu\tilde{\mu}$-to-$\pi$ encoding). This machine $M1$ is essentially equivalent to $M2$. Hence the diagram in the figure commutes and all encodings are correct and complete. Moreover, we also show that some encodings (those marked '1-1,1-1') are *strong operational correspondences*, i.e. the encoding is bijective and every reduction step of the encoded term corresponds exactly to one step of the encoding term and vice versa.

Besides the synchronous encoding, we also present an encoding into the asynchronous π-calculus. As expected, we need to resolve the mixed choice by introducing an arbiter, which yields an heavier encoding. The arbiter is responsible for breaking the critical pair, and it can be biased in order to always give precedence to one side of the pair. Being able to consistently resolve the critical pairs allows to exploit Curien and Herbelin's two encodings of the λ-calculus into the $\bar{\lambda}\mu\tilde{\mu}$-calculus that yields respectively a call-by-value and a call-by-name reduction.

Proofs and examples are here omitted and can be found in [3].

Structure of the paper. In Section 2 we recall the definitions of the $\bar{\lambda}\mu\tilde{\mu}$-calculus and of the Curien and Herbelin's abstract machine. In Section 3 we provide the encoding to π-calculus. Section 4 is devoted to presenting the machine $M1$, whose relationship to the encoding is then addressed in Section 5. In Section 6 we finally prove the correspondence between $M1$ and $M2$, making the diagram of Figure 1 commute. In Section 7 we provide an asynchronous version of the encoding. Conclusions and future work are discussed in Section 8.

2 Preliminaries

2.1 The $\bar{\lambda}\mu\tilde{\mu}$-Calculus

Assuming familiarity with the λ-calculus [1], in this section we recall the definitions of the $\bar{\lambda}\mu\tilde{\mu}$-calculus. A precise description of the $\bar{\lambda}\mu\tilde{\mu}$-calculus is out of the scope of this paper and can be found in [4]. The calculus is characterized by three syntactic categories: terms, contexts (dual to terms) and commands. Syntax and the operational semantics are defined as follows.

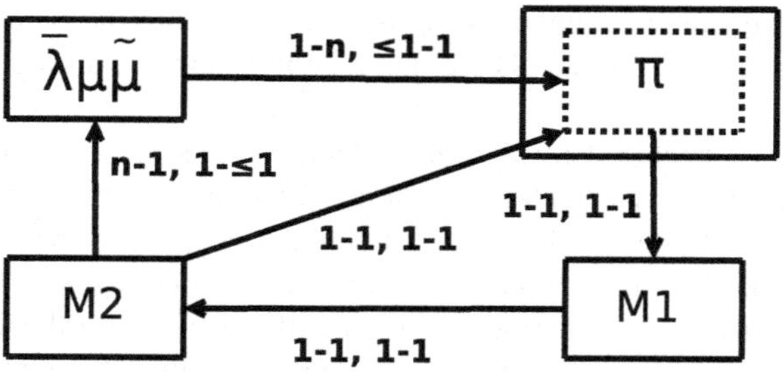

1-n, ≤1-1	Correctness: - if $M \to N$ then $[\![M]\!] \to N'$ where $(N, N') \in \mathcal{R}$ - if $[\![M]\!] \to N$ then $\exists N', M \to^{\leq 1} N' \wedge (N', N) \in \mathcal{R}$ where $\mathcal{R}$ is $1-n$ and modelled after Milner [10]
n-1, 1-≤ 1	Correctness: - if $M \to N$ then $[\![M]\!] \to^{\leq 1} [\![N]\!]$ - if $[\![M]\!] \to N$ then $\exists N', M \to N' \wedge [\![N']\!] = N$ where $[\![\cdot]\!] = \cdot$ is $n-1$ and equal to $\mathcal{R}^{-1}$
1-1, 1-1	Strong Operational Correspondence: - $M \to N$ iff $[\![M]\!] \to [\![N]\!]$

Fig. 1. The main results on the embedding of $\bar{\lambda}\mu\tilde{\mu}$-terms into π-terms

Syntax:	Reduction rules:
$Command\ c = \langle v \mid e \rangle$	$\lambda - reduction :\ \langle \lambda x. v_1 \mid v_2 \cdot e \rangle \to \langle v_2 \mid \tilde{\mu}x. \langle v_1 \mid e \rangle \rangle$
$Term\ v = x \mid \lambda x. v \mid \mu\beta. c$	$\mu - reduction :\ \langle \mu\beta. c \mid e \rangle \to c[e/\beta]$
$Context\ e = \alpha \mid v \cdot e \mid \tilde{\mu}x. c$	$\tilde{\mu} - reduction :\ \langle v \mid \tilde{\mu}x. c \rangle \to c[v/x]$

A command is a closed system containing both the program and the context where it is evaluated. Besides the usual λ-abstraction the calculus has few constructs which deserve some words:

- $\tilde{\mu}x. c$: The (context or continuation) variable β is bound in c. Semantically, the $\tilde{\mu}$ operator is the standard local definition operator of ML: $\langle \cdot \mid \tilde{\mu}x. c \rangle$ is equivalent to `let` $x := \cdot$ `in` c; operationally, it can capture the term in dot position and substitute it in place of x in c, actually delaying its evaluation in a call-by-name fashion.
- $\mu\beta. c$: The (term) variable x is bound in c. Dually to $\tilde{\mu}$, the μ operator binds its evaluation context (like Parigot's μ operator [12] and similarly to the call/cc operator of Scheme) and, operationally, it can capture the context substituting it in place of β in c, actually delaying its evaluation and bringing c in topmost position, in a call-by-value fashion.
- $v \cdot e$: Called the *cons operator*, it is a context for a λ-abstraction that feeds the input v to the λ-abstraction and collects the result of the evaluation by matching it against the context e; operationally, a β-redex is not reduced by performing an immediate substitution (that would correspond to call-by-name): the argument is put in head position and matched by a $\tilde{\mu}$-context that can be fired (like in call-by-name) or that can be delayed (like in call-by-value, if the argument becomes a μ-term).

The reduction takes place at the topmost position, performing the so called *topmost reduction*. This is consistent with the game-theoretic view of the calculus where terms and contexts are players interacting each other in order to perform a computational step. The two players are at the top of the abstract syntax tree and a reduction step is responsible to make them vanish and bring (possibly from the lower levels) the new term and the new context ready to interact again.

As mentioned in the introduction, the calculus is non-confluent. Commands of the form $\langle \mu\beta.\, c_1 \mid \tilde{\mu}x.\, c_2\rangle$ allow indeed for both μ-reduction and $\tilde{\mu}$-reduction to take place and may result into two different reducts:

$$\langle \mu\beta.\, c_1 \mid \tilde{\mu}x.\, c_2\rangle \to c_1[\tilde{\mu}x.\, c_2/\beta]$$
$$\langle \mu\beta.\, c_1 \mid \tilde{\mu}x.\, c_2\rangle \to c_2[\mu\beta.\, c_1/x]$$

with $c_1[\tilde{\mu}x.\, c_2/\beta]$ and $c_2[\mu\beta.\, c_1/x]$ possibly distinct normal forms.

Finally, it is worth noting the dualities between $\mu/\tilde{\mu}$ and term/context variables. In [4] particular attention is devoted to such dualities. Discussing them in detail is out of the scope of this paper and the interested reader is invited to refer to [4].

2.2 The Reduction Machine $M2$

In [4], Curien and Herbelin also provide a reduction machine for the $\bar{\lambda}\mu\tilde{\mu}$-calculus. Before embarking in the definition of such a machine, the formal notion of reduction machine from [19] is repeated here.

Definition 1 (Reduction Machine). *A reduction machine is a triple $\langle S, \to^s, \approx^s\rangle$, where S is a set (the set of states), $\to^s \subset S \times S$ (the reduction relation), and $\approx^s$ is an equivalence relation in $S \times S$, such that $\approx^s\to^s \;\subseteq\; \to^{*s}\approx^s$.*

Definition 1 slightly differs from [19] for the author treats exclusively deterministic machines. We have just dropped the deterministic clause, keeping the name.

The mentioned Curien and Herbelin's machine, here called $M2$ for simplicity, is presented below.

Definition 2 (States and Environments of the machine $M2$**)**

$$\begin{aligned} State\ s\ &= \langle vcl \mid ecl\rangle \\ Term\ Closure\ vcl\ &= v\ in\ \rho \\ Context\ Closure\ ecl\ &= e\ in\ \rho \\ Environment\ \rho\ &= \emptyset \mid [var_v = vcl] + \rho \mid [var_e = ecl] + \rho \end{aligned}$$

with var_v and var_e term and context variables, respectively. We write S_{M2} to refer to the set of the states of the machine $M2$.

The operational behaviour of the machine $M2$ is described by means of the reduction relation $\longrightarrow^{M2} \subset S_{M2} \times S_{M2}$.

Definition 3 (The reduction relation $\longrightarrow^{M2}$)

$$
\begin{aligned}
\langle \mu\beta.\, c\ in\ \rho_1 \mid e\ in\ \rho_2\rangle &\longrightarrow^{M2} c\ in\ \rho_1 + [\beta = e\ in\ \rho_2]\\
\langle v\ in\ \rho_1 \mid \tilde{\mu}x.\, c\ in\ \rho_2\rangle &\longrightarrow^{M2} c\ in\ \rho_2 + [x = v\ in\ \rho_1]\\
\langle x\ in\ \rho_1 + [x = v\ in\ \rho_2] \mid e\ in\ \rho_3\rangle &\longrightarrow^{M2} \langle v\ in\ \rho_2 \mid e\ in\ \rho_3\rangle\\
\langle v\ in\ \rho_1 \mid \beta\ in\ \rho_2 + [\beta = e\ in\ \rho_3]\rangle &\longrightarrow^{M2} \langle v\ in\ \rho_1 \mid e\ in\ \rho_3\rangle\\
\langle \lambda x.\, v_1\ in\ \rho_1 \mid v_2 \cdot e\ in\ \rho_2\rangle &\longrightarrow^{M2} \langle v_1\ in\ \rho_1 + [x = v_2\ in\ \rho_2] \mid e\ in\ \rho_2\rangle
\end{aligned}
$$

The first four rules are simply obtained by replacing immediate substitution with delayed substitution, implemented by means of local explicit substitutions for the topmost term and context. The last rule is more involved: in order to maintain the invariant that the local substitution is applied only to topmost terms and contexts, the λ-reduction rule is twisted a bit. In the rest of the paper we consider a variant of the reduction machine obtained by dropping the twisted rule and by replacing it with the following one, that captures λ-reduction more closely at the price of allowing explicit substitutions on a subterm:

$$\langle \lambda x.\, v_1\ in\ \rho_1 \mid v_2 \cdot e\ in\ \rho_2\rangle \longrightarrow^{M2} \langle v_2\ in\ \rho_2 \mid \tilde{\mu}x.\, \langle v_1\ in\ \rho_1 \mid \delta\ in\ [\delta = e\ in\ \rho_2]\rangle\rangle$$

States in S_{M2} are considered up-to the following equivalence relation $\equiv^{M2}$.

Definition 4 (The equivalence relation $\equiv^{M2}$)

$$
\begin{aligned}
t\ in\ \rho_1 + [var_1 = cl_1] + [var_2 = cl_2] + \rho_2 &\equiv^{M2} t\ in\ \rho_1 + [var_2 = cl_2] + [var_1 = cl_1] + \rho_2\\
t\ in\ \rho_1 + [var = cl] + \rho_2 &\equiv^{M2} t[var'/var]\ in\ \rho_1 + [var' = cl] + \rho_2\\
&\qquad\qquad if\ var' \notin FV(t)\\
t\ in\ \rho_1 + [var = cl] + \rho_2 &\equiv^{M2} t\ in\ +\ \rho_1 + \rho_2 \quad if\ var \notin FV(t)
\end{aligned}
$$

Intuitively, the equivalence relation $\equiv^{M2}$ identifies explicit substitutions up to commutativity, α-equivalence of environment entry names and garbage collection of unused substitutions.

The reduction machine $M2$ is the triple $\langle S_{M2}, \rightarrow^{M2}, \equiv^{M2}\rangle$.

3 From $\bar{\lambda}\mu\tilde{\mu}$ to π

We assuming the reader familiar with the π-calculus [11,16]. We encode the $\bar{\lambda}\mu\tilde{\mu}$-commands into the dialect of the π-calculus with internal mobility, namely the πI-calculus [13], where only the output of fresh new channels is allowed. We employ such a calculus admitting both replication $!P$ and recursion $Rec\ X.\, P$. The encoding is the following one, the reader should bear in mind that, as usual in the πI-calculus, we write $\overline{x}(y).\, P$ for $\nu y\ (\overline{x}\langle y\rangle.\, P)$.

$$
\begin{aligned}
[\![\langle v \mid e\rangle]\!] &= [\![v]\!] \mid [\![e]\!]\\
[\![\mu\beta.\, c]\!] &= Rec\ Y.\ (\overline{\mu}(\beta).\, [\![c]\!] + \tilde{\mu}(x).\, !x.\, Y)\\
[\![\tilde{\mu}x.\, c]\!] &= Rec\ Y.\ (\overline{\tilde{\mu}}(x).\, [\![c]\!] + \mu(\beta).\, !\beta.\, Y)
\end{aligned}
$$

$$
\begin{aligned}
[\![x]\!] &= Rec\ Y.\ (\overline{x} + \tilde{\mu}(z).\,!z.\,Y)\\
[\![\beta]\!] &= Rec\ Y.\ (\overline{\beta} + \mu(\beta).\,!\beta.\,Y)\\
[\![\lambda x.\,v_1]\!] &= Rec\ Y.\ (\lambda(\delta).\,[\![\tilde{\mu}x.\,\langle v_1 \mid \delta\rangle]\!] + \tilde{\mu}(z).\,!z.\,Y)\\
[\![v_2 \cdot e]\!] &= Rec\ Y.\ (\overline{\lambda}(\delta).\,([\![v_2]\!] \mid !\delta.\,[\![e]\!]) + \mu(\beta).\,!\beta.\,Y)
\end{aligned}
$$

The encoding of a command is simply the parallel composition between the encoding of the topmost term and its context, according to the game-theoretic reading of the calculus where every player becomes a process. This property is disrupted in the asynchronous encoding we present in Section 7, which is based on an arbiter.

As for the λ-calculus, substitution is immediate in the $\bar{\lambda}\mu\tilde{\mu}$-calculus, but needs to be delayed both in reduction machines (to achieve efficiency) and in encodings into first order process calculi. We achieve this using the standard technique, already used by Milner, of binding terms by creating fresh channel names and activating them lazily by interacting on the channel. Differently from Milner, however, we let the binding term generate the fresh channel, reusing the variable name coming from the λ-term and thus avoiding to parameterize the encoding or to use syntactical substitution operators.

The encoding uses three selected channels, named μ, $\tilde{\mu}$ and λ to mimic the corresponding redexes. The μ-reduction is implemented by letting every context encoding be of the form $Rec\ Y.\ (\cdot\ + \mu(\beta).\,!\beta.\,Y)$ and letting the encoding of $\mu\beta.\,c$ fire a fresh channel β over μ to its context, activating the right part of the mixed choice and delaying the execution of Y that waits over β for (multiple) activation. A perfectly dual solution is used to mimic $\tilde{\mu}$-reduction, leading to the critical pair obtained by the translation of $[\![\langle \mu\beta.\,c \mid \tilde{\mu}x.\,c'\rangle]\!]$ where two mixed choices can interact both on the μ and the $\tilde{\mu}$ channels to perform either μ-reduction or $\tilde{\mu}$-reduction. In a precise sense, we can see the (encoding of the) $\bar{\lambda}\mu\tilde{\mu}$-calculus as a calculus of peers where each peer can initiate the communication, whereas the λ-calculus (with a fixed strategy) follows the client-server model. It is thus not surprising that the encoding requires a synchronous calculus.

The λ-reduction is more involved since $[\![v_1]\!]$ and $[\![e]\!]$, that belong to different processes, must behave as $[\![\langle v_1 \mid e\rangle]\!]$ where $\langle v_1 \mid e\rangle$ is not a sub-term of the original process, and neither e is accessible in the encoding of $\lambda x.\,v_1$ nor the other way around. We solve the problem by handling $[\![e]\!]$ as an argument, guarding its execution by δ and sending δ to the encoding of $\lambda x.\,v_1$ by means of the channel λ.

The reader may have noticed that having both replication and recursion, albeit unusual and redundant, captures in a natural manner two different behaviours of the processes: bound processes waiting to be activated will be replicated; processes in mixed choice that need to receive a channel and replicate their behaviour on that channel need to be implemented using recursion.

In [3] we provide an example of encoding and we show its reduction steps. The reader can find in [3] also the proof of the correctness of the encoding (the right-headed arrow in Figure 1). In order to establish this result we employ the same technique already used by Milner in [10], that consists in relating (via a relation $\mathcal{R}$) each $\bar{\lambda}\mu\tilde{\mu}$-term M not only to $[\![M]\!]$, but to a larger family of π-terms that are all representations of M up to "delayed substitutions". Indeed, since the π-calculus is first order, the encoding cannot capture precisely immediate substitution, and thus it captures an explicit form of delayed substitution. Thus, during reduction, the same $\bar{\lambda}\mu\tilde{\mu}$-term M receives multiple representations that are all π-processes that are not observationally equivalent, but that can still be "identified" by relating them via $\mathcal{R}$ to M. Formally, $\mathcal{R}$ is the minimal one-to-many relation such that $(M,P) \in \mathcal{R}$ for all M, P, M', N_i, x_i such that $M = M'[N_1/x_1;\dots;N_n/x_n]$ and $P = \nu x_1, x_2, \dots, x_n\ ([\![M']\!] \mid !x_1.[\![N_1]\!] \mid \dots \mid !x_n.[\![N_n]\!])$.

A few points are worth a mention:

- The dualities mentioned in Section 2.1 are preserved. The reader may notice that the encodings concerning μ- and $\tilde{\mu}$-abstractions, as well as the ones concerning term and context variables, are the same modulo the exchange of the channels μ and $\tilde{\mu}$.
- Contrary to the λ-calculus, the encoding is not parametrized.
- The synchronous nature of the $\bar{\lambda}\mu\tilde{\mu}$-calculus discussed in Section 2.1 is reflected by the employment of a synchronous calculus, which uses mixed choice.

4 The Reduction Machine Induced from $[\![\cdot]\!]$

Following the work of Vasconcelos [19] we now question ourself about what reduction machine we are implicitly mimicking through the encoding $[\![\cdot]\!]$. In this section we present the machine $M1$ constructed by inspecting the way the compilation $[\![\cdot]\!]$ simulates the $\bar{\lambda}\mu\tilde{\mu}$-calculus.

By the considerations made in the introduction and at the end of Section 3, it is not surprising that $M1$ turns out to be an environment-based machine. The reader may consider the process

$$P = (\nu x, \beta)([\![\langle x \mid \beta\rangle]\!] \mid !x.[\![v]\!] \mid !\beta.[\![e]\!]).$$

P represents the encoding of the command $\langle x \mid \beta\rangle$ when executed in an environment where x is bound to v and β is bound to e. We can think of P as $[\![\langle x \mid \beta\rangle\ in\ [x = v, \beta = e]]\!]$.

The states of the machine $M1$ are thus pairs consisting of a command and a global environment that maintains the bindings for its free variables. The states of the machine $M1$ are defined as follows.

Definition 5 (States and Environments of the machine $M1$)

$$\begin{aligned} State\ \ s &= c\ in\ \rho \\ Environment\ \ \rho &= \emptyset \mid [var_v = v] + \rho \mid [var_e = e] + \rho \end{aligned}$$

with var_v and var_e term and context variables, respectively. We write S_{M1} to refer to the set of the states of the machine $M1$.

The operational behaviour of the machine $M1$ is described by means of the reduction relation $\longrightarrow^{M1} \subset S_{M1} \times S_{M1}$.

Definition 6 (The reduction relation $\longrightarrow^{M1}$)

$$\begin{aligned} \langle \mu\beta.c \mid e\rangle\ in\ \rho &\longrightarrow^{M1} c[\beta'/\beta]\ in\ \rho\ +\ [\beta' = e] \\ \langle v \mid \tilde{\mu}x.c\rangle\ in\ \rho &\longrightarrow^{M1} c[x'/x]\ in\ \rho\ +\ [x' = v] \\ \langle x \mid e\rangle\ in\ \rho\ +\ [x = v] &\longrightarrow^{M1} \langle v \mid e\rangle\ in\ \rho\ +\ [x = v] \\ \langle v \mid \alpha\rangle\ in\ \rho\ +\ [\alpha = e] &\longrightarrow^{M1} \langle v \mid e\rangle\ in\ \rho\ +\ [\alpha = e] \\ \langle \lambda x.v_1 \mid (v_2 \cdot e)\rangle\ in\ \rho &\longrightarrow^{M1} \langle v_2 \mid \tilde{\mu}x.\langle v_1 \mid \delta\rangle\rangle\ in\ \rho\ +\ [\delta = e] \end{aligned}$$

with β', x' and δ fresh

To understand why a variable change is performed in the first two rules, the reader may consider the way in which the encoding simulates the μ-reductions. In the process $[\![\langle \mu\beta.c \mid e\rangle]\!]$, the encoding of the μ-abstraction sends a fresh new channel to the encoding of e, which we model by means of an α-conversion to a fresh variable.

States in S_{M1} are considered up-to the following equivalence relation $\equiv^{M1}$.

Definition 7 (The equivalence relation $\equiv^{M1}$)

$$c\ in\ \rho_1 + [var_1 = t_1] + [var_2 = t_2] + \rho_2 \equiv^{M1} c\ in\ \rho_1 + [var_2 = t_2] + [var_1 = t_1] + \rho_2$$

$$c\ in\ \rho_1 + [var = t] + \rho_2 \equiv^{M1} c[var'/var]\ in\ \rho_1 + [var' = t] + \rho_2 \quad if\ var' \notin FV(c)$$

$$c\ in\ \rho_1 + [var = t] + \rho_2 \equiv^{M1} c\ in\ +\ \rho_1 + \rho_2 \quad if\ var \notin FV(c)$$

Intuitively, the equivalence relation $\equiv^{M1}$ identifies the states of the machine $M1$ up to commutativity of environment entries, α-equivalence of environment entry names and garbage collection of unused entries.

The reduction machine $M1$ is the triple $\langle S_{M1}, \rightarrow^{M1}, \equiv^{M1}\rangle$.

5 The Relationship between Encoded Terms and $M1$

In the previous section we have extracted the reduction machine $M1$ from the encoding $[\![\cdot]\!]$ following simple intuitions concerning the way it operates. In this section we analyse the relationship between encoded π-calculus terms and terms of the machine $M1$, deferring to Section 6 the question whether $M1$ is a correct abstract machine for the $\bar{\lambda}\mu\tilde{\mu}$-calculus.

Intuitively, an operational correspondence holds whenever a reduction step in the source machine is mimicked by a sequence of steps in the target machine. In our setting we are able to establish a stronger correspondence between the execution of terms in the machine $M1$ and the behaviour of their encoding; we are able in fact to exhibit a 1-1 correspondence between the two.

We set up the notion of *strong operational correspondence*, summarized in Figure 1 and defined here more accurately.

Definition 8 (Strong Operational Correspondence). *Given the two reduction machines $S = \langle St_S, \rightarrow^s, \approx^s\rangle$ and $R = \langle St_R, \rightarrow^r, \approx^r\rangle$, a mapping $(\!|\cdot|\!) : St_S \rightarrow St_R$ is a strong operational correspondence between S and R whenever for all s and s' in St_S*

$$s \rightarrow^s s' \Leftrightarrow (\!|s|\!) \rightarrow^r (\!|s'|\!)$$

where states from S and R are considered equal up-to relations $\approx^s$ and $\approx^r$, respectively.

Proving a mapping $(\!|\cdot|\!)$ to be a strong operational correspondence is strongly demanding since R is required to step-by-step simulates S through the mapping $(\!|\cdot|\!)$.

In order to prove the strong operational correspondence between $M1$ states and π-terms, we need to make explicit the bijective mapping between $M1$ states and images in the π-calculus. The encoding $[\![\cdot]\!]$ is thus completed as follows:

$$\begin{aligned}
[\![c\ in\ \rho]\!] &= \nu var_1, var_2, \ldots, var_n\ ([\![c]\!] \mid [\![\rho]\!]) \\
with\ \rho &= [var_1 = t_1, var_1 = t_2 \ldots\ var_n = t_n] \\
[\![\emptyset]\!] &= \emptyset \\
[\![[var = t]\ +\ \rho]\!] &= !var.\, [\![t]\!] \mid [\![\rho]\!]
\end{aligned}$$

As in the work of Vasconcelos [19], we need to set the π-fragment of Figure 1 as a reduction machine. We denote such a reduction machine by π, which consists of the triple $\langle \mathcal{P}, \rightarrow^{\pi}, \equiv^{\pi} \rangle$, where $\mathcal{P}$ is the codomain of $[\![\cdot]\!]$, $\rightarrow^{\pi}$ is the reduction relation of the π-calculus and $\equiv^{\pi}$ is the structural congruence, see [11,16]. The following theorem ensures that encoded terms and states of the machine $M1$ are (operationally) intimately related to each other.

Theorem 1 (Strong Operational Correspondence between $M1$ and π). *$[\![\cdot]\!]$ is a strong operational correspondence between $M1$ and π, i.e for all s and s'*

$$s \rightarrow^{M1} s' \Leftrightarrow [\![s]\!] \rightarrow^{\pi} [\![s']\!]$$

where states from $M1$ and π are considered equal up-to relations $\equiv^{M1}$ and $\equiv^{\pi}$, respectively.

6 The Relationship between $M1$ and $M2$

Clearly, the machine $M1$ and Theorem 1 are useful only when we prove that the machine $M1$ is correct w.r.t. the operational semantics of the $\bar{\lambda}\mu\tilde{\mu}$-calculus. In this section we prove this by showing a strong operational correspondence between the machine $M2$ and the machine $M1$.

The machine $M1$ and $M2$ are essentially the same, except that the former makes use of a global environment while the latter makes use of local explicit substitutions where terms and contexts carry their own private environment.

The strong operational correspondence is thus proved by mapping the explicit substitutions of $M2$ into the global environment of $M1$, caring that name clashes are avoided. We denote such a mapping by $[\![\cdot]\!]^M$.

Theorem 2 (Strong Operational Correspondence between $M2$ and $M1$). *$[\![\cdot]\!]^M$ is a strong operational correspondence between $M2$ and $M1$, i.e for all s and s'*

$$s \rightarrow^{M2} s' \Leftrightarrow [\![s]\!]^M \rightarrow^{M1} [\![s']\!]^M$$

where states from $M2$ and $M1$ are considered equal up-to relations $\equiv^{M2}$ and $\equiv^{M1}$, respectively.

Theorem 2 makes the diagram of Figure 1 commute. The final result of Figure 1, which is the strong operational correspondence between $M2$ and images in π-calculus, follows by composition of Theorems 1 and 2.

7 An Asynchronous Encoding

In this section we provide an encoding of the $\bar{\lambda}\mu\tilde{\mu}$-calculus into the asynchronous π-calculus $A\pi$ [9,2]. Such an encoding is necessary in order to provide a distributed implementation of the calculus. We employ a variant of the polyadic $A\pi$-calculus able to perform both match and mismatch of channel names. The mapping $[\![\cdot]\!]^a$ is defined below.

$$
\begin{aligned}
[\![\langle v \mid e\rangle]\!]^a &= \nu v, e\,([\![v]\!]^a_v \mid [\![e]\!]^a_e \mid \mathit{arbiter}(v, e))\\
[\![\mu\beta.\, c]\!]^a_v &= \nu x, y\,(\overline{v}\langle \mu, x, y\rangle \mid !x(v).\, \overline{v}\langle \mu, x, y\rangle \mid !y(\beta, \beta Test).\, [\![c]\!]^a)\\
[\![\tilde{\mu}x.\, c]\!]^a_e &= \nu x, y\,(\overline{e}\langle \tilde{\mu}, x, y\rangle \mid !x(e).\, \overline{e}\langle \tilde{\mu}, x, y\rangle \mid !y(x, xTest).\, [\![c]\!]^a)\\
[\![\lambda x.\, v_1]\!]^a_v &= \nu x, y\,(\overline{v}\langle \lambda, x, y\rangle \mid !x(v).\, \overline{v}\langle \lambda, x, y\rangle \mid !y(e, \delta, \delta Test).\, [\![\tilde{\mu}x.\, \langle v_1 \mid \delta\rangle]\!]^a_e)\\
[\![v_2 \cdot e]\!]^a_e &= \nu x, y\,(\overline{e}\langle cons, x, y\rangle \mid !x(e).\, \overline{e}\langle cons, x, y\rangle \mid !y(v, \delta).\, ([\![v_2]\!]^a_v \mid !\delta(e).\, [\![e]\!]^a_e))\\
[\![z]\!]^a_v &= \nu x\,(\overline{v}\langle var, x, z\rangle \mid \overline{v}\langle xTest\rangle \mid !x(v).\, \overline{v}\langle var, x, z\rangle)\\
[\![\beta]\!]^a_e &= \nu x\,(\overline{e}\langle var, x, \beta\rangle \mid \overline{e}\langle \beta Test\rangle \mid !x(v).\, \overline{e}\langle var, x, \beta\rangle)
\end{aligned}
$$

$$
\begin{aligned}
\mathit{arbiter}(v, e) = {} & v(type_v, x_v, y_v).\, e(type_e, x_e, y_e).\\
& [type_v = \mu].\, [type_e \neq var \text{ or } \tilde{\mu}].\, \overline{y_v}\langle x_e, yes\rangle \mid\\
& [type_e = \tilde{\mu}].\, [type_v \neq \mu \text{ or } var].\, \overline{y_e}\langle x_v, yes\rangle \mid\\
& [type_v = \mu].\, [type_e = \tilde{\mu}].\, \nu a\,(\overline{a} \mid a.\, \overline{y_v}\langle x_e\rangle \mid a.\, \overline{y_e}\langle x_v\rangle) \mid\\
& [type_v = var].\, v(bound).\\
& \quad [bound = yes].\, \nu new_v, new_e\,(\overline{y_v}\langle new_v\rangle \mid \overline{new_e}\langle type_e, x_e, y_e\rangle)\\
& \qquad\qquad \mid \mathit{arbiter}(new_v, new_e)\\
& \quad [bound \neq yes].\, \nu new_v, new_e\,(\overline{new_v}\langle varNotBound, x_v, y_v\rangle \mid\\
& \qquad\qquad \overline{new_e}\langle type_e, x_e, y_e\rangle \mid \mathit{arbiter}(new_v, new_e))\\
& [type_e = var].\, [type_v \neq var].\, v(bound).\\
& \quad [bound = yes].\, \nu new_v, new_e\,(\overline{y_e}\langle new_e\rangle \mid \overline{new_v}\langle type_v, x_v, y_v\rangle\\
& \qquad\qquad \mid \mathit{arbiter}(new_v, new_e))\\
& \quad [bound \neq yes].\, \nu new_v, new_e\,(\overline{new_e}\langle varNotBound, x_e, y_e\rangle \mid\\
& \qquad\qquad \overline{new_v}\langle type_v, x_v, y_v\rangle \mid \mathit{arbiter}(new_v, new_e))\\
& [type_v = \lambda].\, [type_e = cons].\\
& \nu new_v, new_e, \delta\,(\overline{y_v}\langle new_e, \delta, yes\rangle \mid \overline{y_e}\langle new_v, \delta\rangle \mid \mathit{arbiter}(new_v, new_e))
\end{aligned}
$$

The encoding of commands is the parallel execution of the term, the context and a third process that acts like an arbiter. Terms and contexts are indeed supposed not to interact each other directly as in the previous encoding, but to interact with an arbiter that mediates the communications. The encoding is parametrized by a channel name that is the channel the term and context use to communicate with the arbiter. Every term and context send to the arbiter three information:

- The type of the construct. This information is discriminated by the name of the channel. For examples μ-abstractions send the channel μ, and cons contexts send the channel *cons*. The full association is straightforward and not listed.

- The private channel x. This channel denotes where the term or context is located.
- The private channel y. The arbiter uses this channel to perform the task associated to the meaning of the term or context.

The arbiter, once taken these information, performs a matching over the names of channels in order to detect the type of the term and context involved. With this information it can discriminate the correct use of the channels xs and ys in order to perform the expected reduction.

The management of the variables is more involved. Every variable needs to carry the information about whether it is bound or it is not. For example the variable x recovers this information by means of the channel named $xTest$; if the variable is bound, the arbiter would set this channel to the distinguished channel yes, exactly dedicated to this purpose. Otherwise, the channel name remains $xTest$ and the arbiter can discriminate the two situations by means of the match and mismatch operator, i.e. whether $xTest$ is, or is not, equal to yes. To understand the reason of such a management, the reader may consider the variables treatment in the arbiter code; when an arbiter does know that a variable is linked to some term or context, it can safely perform an output to liberate a process. If the variable is free, then such an output would just stop the computation even in commands where it is not supposed to, as in $\langle y \mid \tilde{\mu}x.\, c\rangle$, with y free. When the arbiter does know that y is not bound, it iterates again the arbiter tagging the variable as *not bound*, so at least it will be available for capture the second time. Solutions to offer the desired behaviour in a single go using no mixed choices seems to necessarily lead to potential loops in iterating the arbiter.

In order to provide an asynchronous encoding we need to resolve somehow the mixed choice of the previous encoding. This is reflected by introducing an arbiter that mediates the communications between the two players who thus no longer interact directly with each other.

It is worth noting that by straightforward modifications we can bias the arbiter in order to always give the precedence to μ- or $\tilde{\mu}$-reductions when the critical pair occurs. The arbiter can indeed detect such a pair and acts consistently. Being able to resolve the critical pair allows to exploit Curien and Herbelin's two encodings of the λ-calculus into the $\bar{\lambda}\mu\tilde{\mu}$-calculus that yields respectively a call-by-value and a call-by-name reduction.

8 Conclusions and Future Works

We have provided the first encoding of the $\bar{\lambda}\mu\tilde{\mu}$-calculus in π-calculus and, following the ideas by Milner and the technique by Vasconcelos, we have extracted from the encoding and studied a reduction machine $M1$ based on a global environment. The reduction machine turns out to be operationally equivalent to (a variant of) another reduction machine $M2$ previously given for the same calculus.

The $\bar{\lambda}\mu\tilde{\mu}$-calculus, which in its typed version is Curry-Howard isomorphic to classical sequent calculus, has a number of peculiarities that make the study of its embedding into the π-calculus worthwhile: $\bar{\lambda}\mu\tilde{\mu}$-terms are close to machine states (being isomorphic to sequent calculus), and thus the encoding need not be parametric on the channels along which terms interact; terms (and contexts) are fully symmetric and interact in a peer-to-peer way, which makes it useful the use of synchronous features of the π-calculus such as mixed choice in the encoding.

We have provided an asynchronous encoding, which, as expected, needs to resolve the mixed choice and makes use of an arbiter. Such an encoding, albeit less efficient, is easily customisable to tune the reduction strategy and can be a basis for distributed implementations based on asynchronous primitives.

Finally, the reduction in the $\bar{\lambda}\mu\tilde{\mu}$-calculus is strongly normalizing (being isomorphic to cut elimination for classical logic), therefore the encoding into π-calculus may help understanding termination in the π-calculus.

The closest work is due by Cardelli, van Bakel, and Vigliotti in [18], where the authors provide an encoding from the $\mathcal{X}$-calculus into π-calculus. The $\mathcal{X}$-calculus shares with the $\bar{\lambda}\mu\tilde{\mu}$-calculus similar roots; also the former is indeed Curry-Howard isomorphic to classical sequent calculus, but the details of the two calculi are significantly different.

A main objective of future work is the study of the expressiveness of the strongly normalizing π-fragment identified. Related to this, we would like to study whether the techniques for termination in the $\bar{\lambda}\mu\tilde{\mu}$-calculus can be transported onto the π-calculus so to to be able to prove termination properties for larger subsets of processes. In this direction, we first plan to study an extension of the $\bar{\lambda}\mu\tilde{\mu}$-calculus admitting several terms and contexts interacting all together. Whether the new calculus would retain strong normalization for typed terms and contexts appears to be a nontrivial problem.

Another line of future work is the study of typed version of the encodings. In the synchronous case, since three global channels are used to implement the three reduction of the calculus and since redexes of terms with different types are met during reduction, we expect the typing of the global π-channels to pose some difficulties. In the asynchronous case the scenario is even worse: a given channel may be used to accomplish different tasks and also to transmit and receive different numbers of arguments, depending on the particular term or context involved at runtime.

Finally, the symmetry of the calculus suggests that fusion-like calculi might also be interesting target calculi for the encoding.

References

1. Barendregt, H.: The Lambda Calculus: Its Syntax and Semantics. Studies in Logic and the Foundations of Mathematics, vol. 103. North-Holland, Amsterdam (1984) (revised edition)
2. Boudol, G.: Asynchrony and the pi-calculus. Technical Report RR-1702, INRIA (1992)
3. Cimini, M., Coen, C.S., Sangiorgi, D.: Online appendix, `http://nemendur.ru.is/matteo/appendixForFaPTaL.pdf`
4. Curien, P.-L., Herbelin, H.: The duality of computation. In: Proceedings of the Fifth ACM SIGPLAN International Conference on Functional Programming (ICFP 2000), Montreal, Canada, September 18-21. SIGPLAN Notices, vol. 35(9), pp. 233–243. ACM, New York (2000)
5. Demangeon, R., Hirschkoff, D., Sangiorgi, D.: Mobile processes and termination. In: Palsberg, J. (ed.) Semantics and Algebraic Specification. LNCS, vol. 5700, pp. 250–273. Springer, Heidelberg (2009)
6. Deng, Y., Sangiorgi, D.: Ensuring termination by typability. Inf. Comput. 204(7), 1045–1082 (2006)

7. Girard, J.-Y., Lafont, Y., Taylor, P.: Proofs and Types. Cambridge Tracts in Theoretical Computer Science. Cambridge University Press, Cambridge (1989)
8. Herbelin, H.: A lambda-calculus structure isomorphic to Gentzen-style sequent calculus structure. In: Pacholski, L., Tiuryn, J. (eds.) CSL 1994. LNCS, vol. 933, pp. 61–75. Springer, Heidelberg (1994)
9. Honda, K., Tokoro, M.: An object calculus for asynchronous communication. In: America, P. (ed.) ECOOP 1991. LNCS, vol. 512, pp. 133–147. Springer, Heidelberg (1991)
10. Milner, R.: Functions as processes. In: Paterson, M. (ed.) ICALP 1990. LNCS, vol. 443, pp. 167–180. Springer, Heidelberg (1990)
11. Milner, R., Parrow, J., Walker, D.: A calculus of mobile processes, part I. Information and Computation (I&C) 100(1), 1–40 (1992); An earlier version of this paper appeared as Technical Report ECS-LFCS-89-85 of University of Edinburgh (1989)
12. Parigot, M.: Lambda-mu-calculus: An algorithmic interpretation of classical natural deduction. In: Voronkov, A. (ed.) LPAR 1992. LNCS, vol. 624, pp. 190–201. Springer, Heidelberg (1992)
13. Sangiorgi, D.: Internal mobility and agent passing calculi. In: Fülöp, Z., Gecseg, F. (eds.) ICALP 1995. LNCS, vol. 944, pp. 672–684. Springer, Heidelberg (1995)
14. Sangiorgi, D.: From lambda to pi; or, rediscovering continuations. Mathematical Structures in Computer Science 9(4), 367–401 (1999)
15. Sangiorgi, D.: Termination of processes. Mathematical Structures in Computer Science 16(1), 1–39 (2006)
16. Sangiorgi, D., Walker, D.: The π-calculus: A Theory of Mobile Processes. Cambridge University Press, Cambridge (2001)
17. Sørensen, M.H., Urzyczyn, P.: Lectures on the Curry-Howard Isomorphism. Studies in Logic and the Foundations of Mathematics, vol. 149. Elsevier Science Inc., New York (2006)
18. van Bakel, S., Cardelli, L., Vigliotti, M.G.: From X to Pi: Representing Classical Sequent Calculus in Pi-calculus. In: International Workshop on Classical Logic and Computation (CLC 2008) (2009)
19. Vasconcelos, V.T.: Lambda and pi calculi, cam and secd machines. Journal of Functional Programming 15(1), 101–127 (2005)
20. Yoshida, N., Berger, M., Honda, K.: Strong normalisation in the π-Calculus. In: 16th Annual IEEE Symposium on Logic in Computer Science (LICS 2001), pp. 311–322. IEEE Computer Society, Los Alamitos (2001)

Predicate Encryption for Secure Remote Storage

Giuseppe Persiano

Università di Salerno

Abstract. Predicate encryption is a special encryption method that allows one to release keys to compute specific predicates of the plaintext without having to decrypt. This cryptographic primitive is instrumental for executing search on encrypted data and enables remote storage of data. Predicate encryption dispenses with the need of downloading and decrypting the whole data set whenever a search needs to be performed.

In this talk, the author overviewed security models and constructions proposed and suggested a few applications.

M. Wirsing, M. Hofmann, and A. Rauschmayer (Eds.): TGC 2010, LNCS 6084, p. 87, 2010.

Trust in Crowds: Probabilistic Behaviour in Anonymity Protocols

Vladimiro Sassone, Ehab ElSalamouny, and Sardaouna Hamadou

School of Electronics and Computer Science
University of Southampton, United Kingdom

Abstract. The existing analysis of the Crowds anonymity protocol assumes that a participating member is either 'honest' or 'corrupted.' This paper generalises this analysis so that each member is assumed to maliciously disclose the identity of other nodes with a probability determined by her vulnerability to corruption. Within this model, the trust in a principal is defined to be the probability that she behaves honestly. We investigate the effect of such a probabilistic behaviour on the anonymity of the principals participating in the protocol, and formulate the necessary conditions to achieve 'probable innocence.' Using these conditions, we propose a generalised Crowds-Trust protocol which uses trust information to achieves 'probable innocence' for principals exhibiting probabilistic behaviour.

1 Introduction

Anonymity protocols often use random mechanisms. It is therefore natural to think of anonymity in probabilistic terms. Various notions of such probabilistic anonymity have been proposed and a recent line of work in the literature explores formalising these notions through information-theoretic concepts (e.g. [1, 4–6, 12, 15, 18]). Such approaches usually assume that participants in the protocol can be partitioned in two classes: *honest* members, who always behave correctly, and *attackers*, who try to break the protocol. Although a clear separation between trustworthy members and attackers makes the analysis easier, it is not a realistic assumption for open and dynamic systems in the era of ubiquitous computing. Indeed, traditional approaches to security base on *authentication* and *roles* are not sufficient in open systems. A promising approach is to base security and privacy decisions on attributes linked to some level of *trust* a principal can provide evidence for. The principals participating in a protocol will in general have individual trust judgements; accordingly, interactions between any two of them are governed by their mutual levels of trust. As an illustrating example, consider the social network of FACEBOOK, where members can require some of their activities or information to be accessible only to members who they *explicitly* accepted as friends. This could easily (and does) give misplaced confidence to FACEBOOK users, and encourages them to share sensitive information with 'trusted' friends, without considering that those friends' security system may just be vulnerable to attacks: even though they would not maliciously reveal a user's privata data, friends provide different levels of vulnerability according to the robustness of their security systems, such as the strength of their passwords, the quality of their anti-viruses, and so on. In other words, at each

M. Wirsing, M. Hofmann, and A. Rauschmayer (Eds.): TGC 2010, LNCS 6084, pp. 88–102, 2010.

interaction with user i, there is a probability t_i that she is *not corrupted* and hence acts honestly, and a corresponding probability $1 - t_i$ that instead she is *corrupted*. Moreover, between any given two interactions with a given user, her state may change from honest to corrupted (e.g., as a result of being infected) and vice versa (e.g., as a result of running an antiviral software). In this paper we postulate such probabilistic behavioural model for principals, and investigate its effect on the security of anonymity protocols such as Reiter and Rubin's Crowds protocol [16].

Crowds allows Internet users to perform anonymous web transactions by sending their messages through a random chain of users participating in the protocol. Each user in the '*crowd*' establishes a path between her and a set of servers by selecting randomly other users to act as routers. The random selection process is performed in such a way that when a user in the path relays a message, she does not know whether or not the sender is the initiator (or originator) of the message, or just another forwarder. Each user only has access to messages routed through her. It is well known that Crowds cannot ensure strong anonymity [3, 16] in presence of corrupted participants; yet, when the number of corrupted users is sufficiently small, it provides a weaker notion of anonymity known as *probable innocence*: informally, a sender is probably innocent if to an attacker she is no more likely to be the originator than not to be.

This paper is to the best of our knowledge the first to investigate the impact on the security of Crowds of principals alternating in probabilistically between honest and corrupt behaviours.

Related work. The research on quantitative approaches to information-hiding has recently become very active and fruit-bearing. Several formal definitions and frameworks have been proposed for reasoning about *secure information flow analysis* (e.g., [7, 8, 19]), *side-channel analysis* (e.g., [13]) and *anonymity*. Our work follows a recent trend in the analysis of anonymity protocols directed to the application of information-theoretic notions (e.g., [1, 2, 4–6, 9, 12, 15, 17, 18]), whereby the work closer to the present one are those by Reiter and Ruben [16], Halpen and O'Neill [10], Chatzikokolakis and Palamidessi [3], and a recent paper Hamadou et al [12].

In [16] the authors propose a formal definition of probable innocence predicated over the probability of certain observable events induced by the actions of anonymous users participating in the protocol. They require that the probability of an anonymous user producing any observable to be less than one half. In [10] the authors formalise probable innocence in terms of the adversary's confidence that a particular anonymous event happened, after performing an observation. Their definition requires that the probability of an anonymous event should be at most one half, under any observation. In [3] the authors argue that the definition of [16] makes sense only for systems satisfying certain properties, whilst the definition of [10] depends on the probabilities of anonymous events external to the protocol. Thus they propose a definition of probable innocence that combines both by considering both the probability of producing some observable and the adversary's confidence after the observation.

In [12] the authors first generalise the concepts of probable innocence and relate it to Smith's concept of protocol vulnerability [19]. Instead of just comparing the probability of being innocent with the probability of being guilty, they compare such probabilities against a parameter α. Informally, a protocol is α-probable innocent if for any anonymous user the probability of being innocent is less than or equal to α. Then, they extend the definition to deal with the adversary's extra knowledge about the correlation between anonymous events and some observables independent of the protocol. The latter is meant to arise from an independent source such as the environment in which the protocol is executed. The paper shows that the presence of extra knowledge makes probable innocence more difficult to achieve, and quantifies such difficulty.

The main difference between these approaches and the one we present in this paper is that we consider the scenario where each participant in the protocol exhibits honest or malicious behaviours according to a fixed probability. In our opinion, such a scenario is a highly likely in ubiquitous computing. This paper is not intended to propose a new definition of probable innocence; rather, we are interested in studying the impact on the protocol's security of its participants' probabilistic behaviour. To this end, we first extend the scenario of attack by associating to each principal a trust level $t \in [0, 1]$ denoting her robustness against corruption. We then modify the protocol accordingly; rather, than selecting a forwarding node uniformly, the forwarding process is governed by a policy where the probability of selecting a node depends on her trust level. We then establish necessary and sufficient criteria for choosing an appropriate policy of forwarding between members in order to achieve probable innocence. It is important to observe that the trust levels t are parameters representing the real world, and not part of the protocol. However, as will be made clear below, the protocol participants will need to have estimates of them. There are well-studied distributed methods for that, based e.g. on Bayesian analysis (cf. [14]), whilst in the current centralised implementation of Crowds, observation leading to the estimation of t can be made by the mechanism which manages crowd membership, the so-called '*blender*.' We do not cover such issues and the related techniques in the current exposition, as we consider them largely orthogonal and scarcely relevant to the focus of this paper.

Structure of the paper. The paper is organised as follows: in §2 we fix some basic notations and recall the fundamental ideas and properties of the Crowds protocol, including the notion of probable innocence. In §3 we present our first main contribution: Crowds protocol extended with trust information of its participating members; §4 delivers our second main contribution by studying the anonymity provided by the extended protocol and establishing necessary and sufficient conditions for achieving probable innocence.

2 Background

This section describes our conceptual framework and revises the Crowds protocol and its notion of probable innocence. We use capital letters A, B to denote discrete random variables, small letters a, b and calligraphic letters $\mathcal{A}$, $\mathcal{B}$ for their values and set of values, respectively. We denote by $P(a)$ the probability of a and by $P(a, b)$ the *joint probability* of a and b. The *conditional probability* of a given b is defined as

$$P(a \mid b) = \frac{P(a, b)}{P(b)}$$

Bayes' theorem relates the conditional probabilities $P(a \mid b)$ and $P(a \mid b)$ as follows

$$P(a \mid b) = \frac{P(b \mid a)\, P(a)}{P(b)} \tag{1}$$

We consider a framework commonly used in probabilistic approaches to anonymity and information flow (e.g. [5, 11, 15, 19]). This focuses on *total* protocols and programs with one *high level* (or *anonymous*) input A, a random variable over a finite set $\mathcal{A}$, and one *low level* output (observable) O, a random variable over a finite set $\mathcal{O}$. We represent a protocol/program by the matrix of the conditional probabilities $P(o_j \mid a_i)$, where $P(o_j \mid a_i)$ is the probability that the low output is o_j given that the high input is a_i. We assume that the high input is generated according to an *a priori* publicly-known probability distribution. An adversary or eavesdropper can see the output of a protocol, but not the input, and she is interested in deriving the value of the input from the observed output.

2.1 The Crowds protocol

Crowds is a protocol proposed by Reiter and Rubin in [16] to allow Internet users to perform anonymous web transactions, i.e., to protect their identities as originators of request messages. The central mechanism is that the originator forwards the message to a randomly-selected user, which in turn forwards the message to another user, and so on until the message reaches its destination (the end server). This routing process ensures that when a user is detected sending a message, there is a substantial probability that she is not acting for herself but simply forwarding it on behalf of somebody else.

More specifically, a crowd is a *fixed* number of users participating in the protocol. Some members (users) in the crowd may be corrupted (the *attackers*), and they can collaborate in order to discover the originator's identity. The purpose of the protocol is to protect the identity of the message originator from the attackers. When an *originator* – also referred to as *initiator* – wants to communicate with a server, she creates a random *path* between herself and the server through the crowd by the following process.

- *Initial step:* the initiator selects randomly a member of the crowd (possibly herself) and forwards the request to her. We refer to the latter user as the *forwarder*.
- *Forwarding steps:* a forwarder, upon receiving a request, flips a *biased* coin. With probability $1 - p_f$ she delivers the request to the end server or, with probability p_f, she selects randomly a new forwarder (possibly herself) and relays the original request to her, to repeat the forwarding process again.

The response from the server to the originator follows the same path in the opposite direction. Users (including corrupted ones) are assumed to have only access to messages routed through them, so that they only know the identities of their immediate predecessors and successors in the path, and of the destination server.

2.2 Probable Innocence

In [16] Reiter and Rubin have proposed a hierarchy of anonymity notions in the context of Crowds. These range from '*absolute privacy*,' where the attacker cannot perceive the presence of communication, to '*provably exposed*,' where the attacker can prove the sender and receiver relationship to third parties. Clearly enough, CROWDS cannot ensure absolute privacy in presence of attackers or corrupted users; it can only provide weaker notions of anonymity. In particular, in [16] the authors propose an anonymity notion called *probable innocence* and prove that, under suitable conditions on the parameters of the protocol, CROWDS ensures the probable innocence property to the originator. Informally, they define it as follows:

A sender is probably innocent if, from the attacker's point of view, the sender appears no more likely to be the originator than to not be the originator. (2)

In other words, the attacker may have good reasons to consider the sender more likely than any other user to be the originator, yet it still appears at least as likely that she is not.

Let n be the number of users participating in the protocol and let c and m be the number of the corrupted and honest users, respectively, with $n = m+c$. Since anonymity makes only sense for honest users, we define the set of anonymous events as $\mathcal{A} = \{a_1, a_2, \ldots, a_m\}$, where a_i indicates that user i is the initiator of the message.

As it is usually the case in the analysis of CROWDS, we assume that attackers will always deliver a request to forward immediately to the end server, since forwarding it any further cannot help them learn anything more about the identity of the originator. Thus in any given path, there is at most one detected user: the first honest member to forward the message to a corrupted member. We therefore define the set of observable events as $O = \{o_1, o_2, \ldots, o_m\}$, where o_j indicates that user j forwarded a message to a corrupted user. In this case we also say that user j *is detected* by the attacker.

Reiter and Rubin formalise their notion of probable innocence via the conditional probability $P(I \mid H)$ that the initiator is detected given that any user is detected at all. Here H denotes the event that there is an attacker in the path (and thus the user before it will be detected), whilst I is the event that precisely the initiator will forward the message to the attacker.[1] Probable innocence holds if $P(I \mid H) \leq 1/2$.

In our setting the probability that user j is detected given that user i is the initiator, can be written simply as $P(o_j \mid a_i)$. As we are only interested in the case in which a user is detected, for simplicity we do not write such condition explicitly. Therefore, the notion of probable innocence proved in [16] translates in our setting as:

$$P(o_i \mid a_i) \leq \frac{1}{2} \quad \text{for all } i = 1, \ldots, m \tag{3}$$

Reiter and Rubin proved in [16] that the following property holds for CROWDS.

$$P(o_j \mid a_i) = \begin{cases} 1 - \dfrac{m-1}{n} p_f & i = j \\ \dfrac{1}{m} p_f & i \neq j \end{cases} \tag{4}$$

Therefore, probable innocence (3) holds if and only if

$$m \geq \frac{c-1}{p_f - 1/2} p_f \,.$$

[1] Observe that this does not necessarily mean that the attacker is the second user in the path, as the originator could herself be selected as a forwarder in the path she initiated!

As previously noticed in several papers (e.g., [3]), there is a mismatch between the idea of probable innocence expressed informally in (2) and property (3) actually proved by Reiter and Rubin. Indeed, the former seems to correspond to the following interpretation given by Halpern and O'Neill [11]:

$$P(a_i \mid o_i) \leq \frac{1}{2} \quad \text{for all } i = 1, \ldots, m \tag{5}$$

Properties (3) and (5) however coincide under the standard assumption in Crowds that the *a priori* distribution is uniform, i.e., that each honest user has equal probability of being the initiator.

Finally we recall that the concept of probable innocence was recently generalised in [12]. Instead of just comparing the probability of being innocent with the probability of being guilty, *loc. cit.* considers, so to say, 'degrees' of innocence. Formally, given a real number $\alpha \in [0, 1]$, a protocol satisfies α-probable innocence if and only if

$$P(a_i \mid o_i) \leq \alpha \quad \text{for all } i = 1, \ldots, m \tag{6}$$

Clearly, α-probable innocence coincides with the probable innocence for $\alpha = 1/2$.

3 Using Trust Information

In the previous section, we have revised the fundamental ideas of the Crowds protocol and its properties under the assumption that each user participating in the protocol is either always honest or always an attacker, and all members are treated equally. However, as observed in §1, this is not a realistic assumption for open and dynamic systems in ubiquitous computing. Indeed, open and dynamic systems often use attributes related to some level of *trust* to enhance security and privacy. In this section we reformulate Crowds under the novel scenario where interaction between users is governed by their level of trust. We then study the effect of such probabilistic principals' behaviour on the security of the protocol.

3.1 Crowds Protocol Extended

We now extend the Crowds protocol to take into account the trust levels of its participating members. We associate a trust level $t_{ij} \in [0, 1]$ to each pair of users i and j to indicate the trust of user i in user j according to evidence provided by j. Here t_{ij} denotes the probability that when the principal i chooses principal j as a forwarder, j behaves honestly and protects i's identity. Accordingly, each user i defines her *policy of forwarding* to other members (including herself) based on her trust of them. A policy of forwarding for a user i is probability distribution $\{q_{i1}, q_{i2}, \cdots, q_{in}\}$, such that for all i, $\sum_{j=1}^{n} q_{ij} = 1$. Here q_{ij} denotes the probability that j is chosen as a forwarder by i (given that i has decided to forward the message).

Defining trust as an individual judgement as we did above matches the current assumptions in the research on trust (cf. [14]) and is certainly desirable in general. However for some applications – specifically the Crowds protocol – it is more reasonable to consider a simplified notion where trust in a user is common to everybody. In other words $t_{ij} = t_{kj}$ for all i and k. Indeed, in the case of the CROWDS protocol, we want a trust in a user to reflect her robustness to becoming *corrupt* (a.k.a. *infected*). Allowing each member to adopt her own level of trust would make the value of trust subjective and could hardly reflect the user's actual robustness against corruption.

We therefore assume that a trust in a user is shared. Its value could be established cooperatively by the members of the crowd, or by a suitable local authority (e.g., the blender in case of Reiter and Rubin's implementation of CROWDS) based on evidence provided by the user. Accordingly, in the rest of the paper, we will simply write t_i to denote the trust level of user i. Similarly, we require the policy of forwarding to be common to all members of the crowds. This means that all participants treat any given user in the same way, as all of them have the same trust in her. We therefore write $\{q_1, q_2, \cdots, q_n\}$ to represent the common forwarding policy.

Under these assumptions, we extend the protocol. When an initiator wants to communicate with a server, she creates a random *path* between herself and the server through the crowd by the following process.

- *Initial step:* With probability q_j the initiator selects a member j of the crowd (possibly herself) according to the policy of forwarding $\{q_1, q_2, \cdots, q_n\}$ and forwards the request to her. We refer to the latter user as the *forwarder*.
- *Forwarding steps:* a forwarder, upon receiving a request, flips a *biased* coin. With probability $1 - p_f$ she delivers the request to the end server or, with probability $p_f \cdot q_k$, she selects a new forwarder k (possibly herself) and relays the original request to her, to repeat the forwarding process again.

3.2 Probable Innocence Revisited

In order to study the anonymity provided by the extended protocol, we first spell out the hypotheses of our analysis. As is the previous section, we assume that corrupted members will always deliver a request immediately to the end server, since forwarding it any further cannot help the attacker learn anything more about the identity of the originator. Consequently, when an infected user initiates a transaction, her message is delivered directly to the end server.[2]

We also assume that server replies are *short*, so that the status of each user in an anonymous paths from users to servers is maintained for the time it takes for the reply to travel back from server to originator. That is, we do not consider the case where users on a given path may switch to become corrupt (or indeed honest) between request and answer, which might happen if the server's replies are very long or very slow. From servers to users so which would normally follow the same paths in reverse direction. Under these assumptions, there is always at most one corrupted member on a path, it occupies its last position, and detection always occurs while forwarding a request and not while relaying a reply.[3]

[2] Her anonymity is broken at the start, so there is no need to continue the anonymity protocol.

[3] We are currently working on a refined protocol where this assumption is dropped. This means that there can be users on a path which while not infected in the forward direction, become corrupt by the time they receive the response from the server. Hence they report their predecessor as the detected user.

Finally since each user i has probability t_i of being honest when she initiates a request, we extend the set of anonymous events a_i and observable events o_i to the whole set of participating members.

Under these assumption we study the privacy level ensured to each member participating in the protocol, i.e., $P(a_i \mid o_i)$. We remind the reader that by Bayes' theorem (Eq. 1) we have

$$P(a_i \mid o_i) = \frac{P(a_i, o_i)}{P(o_i)} \tag{7}$$

We first evaluate the denominator in the above expression. Let H_k be the event that the first corrupted node in the message path to the server occupies the kth position, where $k \geq 0$. Note that H_0 means that the initiator itself is corrupted.

$$P(o_i, H_k) = \begin{cases} \frac{1}{n}(1 - t_i) & k = 0 \\ \frac{1}{n} t_i \sum_{j=1}^{n} q_j (1 - t_j) & k = 1 \\ \sum_{j=1}^{n} \frac{1}{n} t_j \left(\sum_{j=1}^{n} q_j t_j \right)^{k-2} \cdot \\ \qquad q_i t_i \left(\sum_{j=1}^{n} q_j (1 - t_j) \right) \cdot p_f^{k-1} & k \geq 2 \end{cases} \tag{8}$$

The above equation for the case $k \geq 2$ is implied by the fact that the message is initiated by any honest participant, forwarded to $k - 2$ honest principals before it is passed to the detected principal i, and finally to a corrupted one. For convenience, we will write T for $\sum_{j=1}^{n} q_j t_j$ and S for $\sum_{j=1}^{n} t_j$. Since the joint events $\{o_i, H_k\}$, for $k \geq 0$ are mutually exclusive, we evaluate $P(o_i)$ as follows.

$$\begin{aligned} P(o_i) &= \sum_{k=0}^{\infty} P(o_i, H_k) \\ &= \frac{1}{n}(1 - t_i) + \frac{1}{n} t_i (1 - T) \\ &\quad + \sum_{k=2}^{\infty} \frac{1}{n} S\, T^{k-2} \cdot q_i t_i (1 - T) \cdot p_f^{k-1} \\ &= \frac{1}{n} \left(1 - t_i T + S\, p_f q_i t_i \left(\frac{1 - T}{1 - p_f T} \right) \right) \end{aligned} \tag{9}$$

From Equation (9), it is worth noticing that $P(o_i) = 0$ only if $T = 1$ and $t_i = 1$. Observe that $T = 1$ means that $t_j = 1$ for all participants j where $q_j \neq 0$, i.e., all forwarders are always honest. In this case i is never detected by any forwarder. If moreover $t_i = 1$, the principal i is never detected by herself. Thus in the case where $T = 1$ and $t_i = 1$ the principal i is never detected by any corrupted node.

Now we turn to evaluating the probability $P(a_i, o_i)$ appearing as the numerator in Equation (7). To such purpose, we first formulate the probability $P(a_i, H_k, o_i)$, i.e., the probability that i is the initiator and is also detected by a corrupted node at position k in the message path.

$$P(a_i, H_k, o_i) = \begin{cases} \frac{1}{n}(1 - t_i) & k = 0 \\ \frac{1}{n} t_i \sum_{j=1}^{n} q_j(1 - t_j) & k = 1 \\ \frac{1}{n} t_i \left(\sum_{j=1}^{n} q_j t_j \right)^{k-2} \cdot \\ \qquad q_i t_i \left(\sum_{j=1}^{n} q_j(1 - t_j) \right) \cdot p_f^{k-1} & k \geq 2 \end{cases} \tag{10}$$

Similar to the argument of Equation (8), the formula in the case $k \geq 2$ is implied by the fact that the message is initiated by the principal i, forwarded to $k - 2$ honest principals before it is passed back to i, and finally to a corrupted principal. Since the joint events $\{a_i, H_k, o_i\}$, for $k \geq 0$ are mutually exclusive, we evaluate $P(a_i, o_i)$ as follows.

$$\begin{aligned} P(a_i, o_i) &= \sum_{k=0}^{\infty} P(a_i, H_k, o_i) \\ &= \frac{1}{n}(1 - t_i) + \frac{1}{n} t_i (1 - T) \\ &\quad + \sum_{k=2}^{\infty} \frac{1}{n} t_i T^{k-2} \cdot q_i t_i (1 - T) \cdot p_f^{k-1} \\ &= \frac{1}{n} \left(1 - t_i T + p_f q_i t_i^2 \left(\frac{1 - T}{1 - p_f T} \right) \right) \end{aligned} \tag{11}$$

Assuming $P(o_i) \neq 0$, we substitute Equations (9) and (11) in Equation (7), and we therefore get,

$$P(a_i \mid o_i) = \frac{1 - t_i T + p_f q_i t_i^2 \left(\frac{1-T}{1-p_f T} \right)}{1 - t_i T + S\, p_f q_i t_i \left(\frac{1-T}{1-p_f T} \right)} \tag{12}$$

From Equation (12), we observe that for a detectable principal i (i.e., $P(o_i) \neq 0$), it holds that $P(a_i \mid o_i) > 0$. That is, there is always a non zero probability that i is the initiator if she is detected. This confirms that Crowds never achieves the highest degree of anonymity known as *absolute privacy* in [16].

3.3 Provably Exposed Principals

It would also be interesting to investigate the conditions under which the protocol can only ensure the degree of anonymity known as *provably exposed* to a given principal i. Such a degree, defined in [16], represents the lowest level of anonymity where an attacker can prove the identity of the message initiator. This happens when i is the only possible initiator, given that i is detected, i.e., $P(a_i \mid o_i) = 1$. These conditions are precisely stated by the following proposition.

Proposition 1 (Provably exposed). *For all user i such that $P(o_i) \neq 0$, we have that $P(a_i \mid o_i) = 1$ if and only if one of the following conditions holds:*

- $p_f = 0$;
- $t_i = 0$;
- $q_i = 0$;
- $T = 1$;
- $S = t_i$.

Proof. Solving the following equation $P(a_i \mid o_i) = 1$ using the formula given by Equation (12) yields only the above conditions.

The following paragraphs discuss the meaning of these results. Firstly, we observe that $p_f = 0$ implies that, provided she is not corrupt, the initiator will pick her first forwarder according to the forwarding policy $\{q_1, \cdots, q_n\}$, who then delivers directly the message to the end server, regardless of her being corrupt or not. Thus, in this case a path is always at most of length 2, excluding the end server. Hence, i can only be detected at position 0 (by herself if she is initially corrupted) or at position 1 by her forwarder when the latter is corrupted. Therefore, in both cases, i is the only possible initiator. That is if a principal i is detected, then she must be the initiator.

In the case where $t_i = 0$, i is always corrupted and therefore when she initiates a message, she will detect herself and deliver the message directly to the end server (by assumption). Hence nobody except herself will detect her, and i will be detected if and only if she is the initiator.

Consider the case where $q_i = 0$. This implies that i is never chosen as a forwarder. In this case, i is detected only if she initiates a message and is corrupted at the same time, i.e., she detects herself. Thus, the detection of i implies that i is the initiator.

The case $T = 1$ happens if and only if $t_j = 1$ for all $q_j \neq 0$, which means that only honest members can be chosen as forwarders. In this case too, i is detected only if she originates a message and is corrupted at the same time: she detects herself. Thus, the fact that i is detected, implies that i is the initiator.

Finally, suppose that $S = t_i$. Here $t_j = 0$ for all $j \neq i$, that is all participants other than i are corrupted. In this case if i is detected then it is the only possible initiator because otherwise the initiator would just detect herself at the start of the protocol. Therefore, once again, if i is detected, she must be the initiator.

It is worth noticing that the original Crowds protocol is the protocol obtained by assuming that each principal i is either always honest or always corrupted, i.e., $t_i \in \{0, 1\}$, and by choosing a uniform forwarding policy, that is for all j,

$$q_j = \frac{1}{n} .$$

Thus when the number of corrupted principals is c, we have

$$T = \sum_{j=1}^{n} q_j t_j = \frac{n - c}{n} ,$$

and

$$S = \sum_{j=1}^{n} t_j = n - c .$$

By substituting the values of q_j, T and S in Equation (12) for a honest initiator i, i.e., one for which $t_i = 1$, we get

$$P(a_i \mid o_i) = 1 - p_f \left(\frac{n-c-1}{n} \right) .$$

which is the same expression derived in [16] for standard Crowds and given by (4).

4 Achieving Probable Innocence

For any fixed number of principals n, the extended protocol described in the previous section has three main parameters: the forwarding probability p_f, members' trust values $\{t_1, \cdots, t_n\}$, and the forwarding policy $\{q_1, \cdots, q_n\}$. We study in this section how each of them affect the anonymity of participating members. We begin by the probability of forwarding.

4.1 Probability of Forwarding

The following result states that for fixed trust values $\{t_1, \cdots, t_n\}$ and forwarding policy $\{q_1, \cdots, q_n\}$, the probability $P(a_i \mid o_i)$ for any participant i is a monotonically decreasing function with respect to the forwarding probability p_f.

Theorem 1 (Monotonicity). *For all* $i = 1, \ldots, n$,

$$\frac{\partial P(a_i \mid o_i)}{\partial p_f} \leq 0$$

Proof. By differentiating $P(a_i \mid o_i)$ as given by Equation (12) with respect to p_f, we have

$$\frac{\partial P(a_i \mid o_i)}{\partial p_f} = \frac{t_i q_i (1-T)(1-t_i T)(t_i - S)}{\big((1-p_f T)(1-t_i T) + p_f S q_i t_i (1-T)\big)^2} . \tag{13}$$

Given that $0 \leq t_j \leq 1$ for each principal j, and that $T = \sum_{j=1}^{n} q_j t_j$, we have $0 \leq T \leq 1$ and $0 \leq t_i T \leq 1$. We have also $t_i \leq S$, because $S = \sum_{j=1}^{n} t_j$, and therefore

$$\frac{\partial P(a_i \mid o_i)}{\partial p_f} \leq 0 ,$$

i.e., $P(a_i \mid o_i)$ is either fixed or decreasing with respect to p_f.

From Equation (13) above, $P(a_i \mid o_i)$ is fixed irrespectively of p_f if and only if i is always corrupted ($t_i = 0$), i is never used as a forwarder ($q_i = 0$), all forwarders are honest ($T = 1$), or all participants other than i are corrupted ($S = t_i$). It has been shown by Proposition 1 in the previous section that $P(a_i \mid o_i) = 1$ in these cases.

Theorem 1 justifies using a high value of p_f as it decreases the probability of identifying the initiator and therefore enhance her privacy. However, large p_f implies longer message path to the server, and therefore the performance of the protocol is degraded. Thus a trade-off is required for choosing the forwarding probability p_f.

Corollary 1 (Anonymity range). *For all $i = 1, \ldots, n$,*

$$1 \geq P(a_i \mid o_i) \geq 1 - \frac{q_i t_i \sum_{j \neq i}^{n} t_j}{1 - t_i \sum_{j \neq i}^{n} q_j t_j + q_i t_i \sum_{j \neq i}^{n} t_j}$$

Proof. By Theorem 1, and taking into account that $0 \leq p_f \leq 1$, the above range for $P(a_i \mid o_i)$ is obtained by substituting $p_f = 0$ and $p_f = 1$ in Equation (12).

The corollary above describes the range of probabilities that a principal i is the initiator given that i is detected. Observe that with $p_f = 0$ the message is passed directly to the server, and therefore if i is detected, then she must be the initiator and also detected by herself. Taking $p_f = 1$ minimises $P(a_i \mid o_i)$, but in this case the message never reaches the server.

4.2 Trust Values

We now turn our focus to the trust values. Observe that the anonymity of a member i, indicated by $P(a_i \mid o_i)$, is affected by the trust values t_j of all participating members. Therefore, the above lower bound can be used as a criterion to decide whether a new member i is accepted to join the network or not based on her trust t_i. For instance, such a criterion can be chosen to achieve the *α-probable innocence* according to the following theorem.

Theorem 2 (α-probable innocence). *Let $\alpha \in [0, 1]$ be a positive value. If for all $i = 1, \ldots, n$*

$$\frac{q_i t_i \sum_{j \neq i}^{n} t_j}{1 - t_i \sum_{j \neq i}^{n} q_j t_j + q_i t_i \sum_{j \neq i}^{n} t_j} \geq 1 - \alpha ,$$

then the extended protocol ensures α-probable innocence to all its participating members.

Proof. Results from Corollary 1 and Definition 6.

4.3 Forwarding Policy

We now propose a strategy for choosing a forwarding policy $\{q_1, \cdots, q_n\}$ based on the trust information $\{t_1, \cdots, t_n\}$ in order to achieve α-probable innocence for a given degree of privacy α. The key idea is that the forwarding probabilities q_j are adjusted depending on the given trust information t_j.

Choosing the forwarding policy q_i for a given user i can then be done by maintaining the lower bounds of $P(a_i \mid o_i)$ below a chosen threshold α, i.e., by achieving α-probable innocence. By Theorem 2 the plausible values of q_i are obtained by solving the following system of linear inequalities.

$$1 - \alpha \leq \frac{q_i t_i \sum_{j \neq i}^{n} t_j}{1 - t_i \sum_{j \neq i}^{n} q_j t_j + q_i t_i \sum_{j \neq i}^{n} t_j} \qquad 1 \leq i \leq n$$

$$1 = \sum_{i=1}^{n} q_i$$

Example 1. Consider an instance of Crowds-Trust protocol where three principals are involved. Let the trust values in these principals be:

$$t_1 = 0.70, \qquad t_2 = 0.97, \qquad t_3 = 0.99$$

Solving the above problem for $\alpha = \frac{1}{2}$ yields the two solutions:

$$\begin{aligned} &0.2479 \leq q_2 \leq 0.2620 \\ &1.1411 - 3.4138\, q_2 \leq q_3 \leq 0.5479 - 1.0206\, q_2 \\ &q1 = 1 - q_2 - q_3 \end{aligned}$$

and

$$\begin{aligned} &0.2620 \leq q_2 \leq 0.3074 \\ &0.3197 - 0.2784\, q_2 \leq q_3 \leq 0.5479 - 1.0206\, q_2 \\ &q_1 = 1 - q_2 - q_3 \,. \end{aligned}$$

Thus the following forwarding distribution satisfies the $\frac{1}{2}$-probable innocence:

$$q_1 = 0.4575, \qquad q_2 = 0.2620, \qquad q_3 = 0.2805\,.$$

However, if the uniform distribution is used (as in the original Crowds protocol), i.e., $q_1 = q_2 = q_3 = \frac{1}{3}$, probable innocence is not achievable because according to Corollary 1 the minimum value of $P(a_1 \mid o_1)$ is 0.543, which is greater than $\frac{1}{2}$. Note that such sets of constraints are not always solvable, in which case the required level of anonymity cannot be provided to all members.

Observe that the forwarding distribution above increases the frequency at which the less reliable user 1 will be involved in a message path, so as to make it more difficult for an attacker to detect her with a high degree of confidence. The higher security for 1 is of course achieved at the price of a lower overall security for other two, more reliable users, and can therefore considered a 'social' approach to crowds membership. The flexibility of the protocol means that the forwarding policy can be chosen to provide a lower degree of anonymity to a subset of the members to guarantee probable innocence to a larger crowd ('*social strategy*'), or to reject principals having the low trust values who, therefore, exhibit a greater threat to others ('*rational strategy*').

5 Conclusion

In this paper we focused on the Crowds anonymity protocol and asked the question of how its existing analyses are affected by postulating that each principal behaves honestly or becomes corrupt according to a given probability (as opposed to being either honest or malicious once and for all). This amounts to providing each member i of the crowd with a trust level t_i denoting her robustness against corruption, and a preference level of forwarding q_i denoting the probability of choosing her as the next forwarder in the routing process. Given a probability of forwarding p_f, a level of anonymity α, and the trust levels $t_1, t_2, \cdots, t_n$ of the crowd's members, we have identified the conditions on the probability of choosing a forwarder which are necessary to achieve α-probable innocence. Thus, in presence of untrusted members, the protocol users can exploit these results to derive an interaction policy $q_1, q_2, \cdots, q_n$, if any exists, that guarantees a satisfactory level of anonymity; and in doing so, they can act both 'rationally' or 'socially.'

In conclusion, we remark that although the scenario in which members participating in a protocol can exhibit probabilistic behaviours is highly likely in real-world scenarios, this is the first paper to deal with the question in the context of anonymity protocols. In the near future, we expect to tackle even more interesting scenarios, in particular by extending this work to the case where a possibly slow or long response from the server may follow in the reverse direction to the initiator, as the honesty status of the users on the path has changed since the request was forwarded to the server.

References

1. Bhargava, M., Palamidessi, C.: Probabilistic anonymity. In: Abadi, M., de Alfaro, L. (eds.) CONCUR 2005. LNCS, vol. 3653, pp. 171–185. Springer, Heidelberg (2005)
2. Braun, C., Chatzikokolakis, K., Palamidessi, C.: Compositional methods for information-hiding. In: Amadio, R.M. (ed.) FOSSACS 2008. LNCS, vol. 4962, pp. 443–457. Springer, Heidelberg (2008)
3. Chatzikokolakis, K., Palamidessi, C.: Probable innocence revisited. Theor. Comput. Sci. 367(1-2), 123–138 (2006)
4. Chatzikokolakis, K., Palamidessi, C., Panangaden, P.: Probability of error in information-hiding protocols. In: CSF, pp. 341–354. IEEE Computer Society, Los Alamitos (2007)
5. Chatzikokolakis, K., Palamidessi, C., Panangaden, P.: Anonymity protocols as noisy channels. Inf. Comput. 206(2-4), 378–401 (2008)
6. Chatzikokolakis, K., Palamidessi, C., Panangaden, P.: On the Bayes risk in information-hiding protocols. Journal of Computer Security 16(5), 531–571 (2008)
7. Clark, D., Hunt, S., Malacaria, P.: A static analysis for quantifying information flow in a simple imperative language. Journal of Computer Security 15(3), 321–371 (2007)
8. Clarkson, M.R., Myers, A.C., Schneider, F.B.: Belief in information flow. In: CSFW, pp. 31–45. IEEE Computer Society, Los Alamitos (2005)
9. Deng, Y., Pang, J., Wu, P.: Measuring anonymity with relative entropy. In: Dimitrakos, T., Martinelli, F., Ryan, P.Y.A., Schneider, S. (eds.) FAST 2006. LNCS, vol. 4691, pp. 65–79. Springer, Heidelberg (2007)
10. Halpern, J.Y., O'Neill, K.R.: Anonymity and information hiding in multiagent systems. Journal of Computer Security 13(3), 483–512 (2005)
11. Halpern, J.Y., O'Neill, K.R.: Anonymity and information hiding in multiagent systems. Journal of Computer Security 13(3), 483–512 (2005)
12. Hamadou, S., Palamidessi, C., Sassone, V., ElSalamouny, E.: Probable Innocence in the presence of independent knowledge. In: Degano, P., Guttman, J.D. (eds.) FAST 2009. LNCS, vol. 5983, pp. 141–156. Springer, Heidelberg (2010)
13. Köpf, B., Basin, D.A.: An information-theoretic model for adaptive side-channel attacks. In: Ning, P., di Vimercati, S.D.C., Syverson, P.F. (eds.) ACM Conference on Computer and Communications Security, pp. 286–296. ACM, New York (2007)
14. Krukow, K., Nielsen, M., Sassone, V.: Trust models in ubiquitous computing. Philosophical Transactions of the Royal Society A 366, 3781–3793 (2008)
15. Malacaria, P., Chen, H.: Lagrange multipliers and maximum information leakage in different observational models. In: Erlingsson, Ú., Pistoia, M. (eds.) PLAS, pp. 135–146. ACM, New York (2008)

16. Reiter, M.K., Rubin, A.D.: Crowds: Anonymity for web transactions. ACM Transactions on Information and Systems Security 1(1), 66–92 (1998)
17. Serjantov, A., Danezis, G.: Towards an information theoretic metric for anonymity. In: Dingledine, R., Syverson, P.F. (eds.) PET 2002. LNCS, vol. 2482, pp. 41–53. Springer, Heidelberg (2002)
18. Shmatikov, V., Wang, M.-H.: Measuring relationship anonymity in mix networks. In: Juels, A., Winslett, M. (eds.) WPES, pp. 59–62. ACM, New York (2006)
19. Smith, G.: On the foundations of quantitative information flow. In: de Alfaro, L. (ed.) FOSSACS 2009. LNCS, vol. 5504, pp. 288–302. Springer, Heidelberg (2009)

Expressiveness of Generic Process Shape Types

Jan Jakubův and J.B. Wells

Heriot-Watt University

Abstract. Shape types are a general concept of process types which work for many process calculi. We extend the previously published POLY✶ system of shape types to support name restriction. We evaluate the expressiveness of the extended system by showing that shape types are more expressive than an implicitly typed π-calculus and an explicitly typed Mobile Ambients. We demonstrate that the extended system makes it easier to enjoy advantages of shape types which include polymorphism, principal typings, and a type inference implementation.

1 Introduction

Many type systems for many process calculi have been developed to statically guarantee various important properties of processes. Types differ among these systems and their properties, such as soundness, have to be proved separately for each system. *Shape types* are a general concept of polymorphic process types which can express and verify various properties of processes. POLY✶ [12,11] is a general framework which, for a wide range of process calculi, can be instantiated to make ready-to-use sound type systems which use shape types. Only rewriting rules satisfying common syntactic conditions are needed for instantiating POLY✶.

Many process calculi share semantically equivalent constructions, such as, *parallel composition* ("|"), prefixing a process with an action (sometimes called a *capability*) ("."), and *name restriction* ("ν"). Specific calculi differ mainly in the syntax and semantics of actions (capabilities). META✶ [12,11] is metacalculus which fixes semantics of the shared constructions and provides a way to describe syntax and semantics of actions by a description $\mathcal{R}$ of rewriting rules. Given $\mathcal{R}$, META✶ makes the calculus $C_{\mathcal{R}}$ and POLY✶ makes the type system $S_{\mathcal{R}}$ for $C_{\mathcal{R}}$. $\mathcal{R}$ can describe many calculi including, e.g., the π-calculus, Mobile Ambients, numerous variations of these, and other systems. All instantiations of POLY✶ share *shape predicates* which describe allowed syntactic configurations of META✶ processes. *Shape ($\mathcal{R}$-)types* of $S_{\mathcal{R}}$ are shape predicates whose meaning is guaranteed by a simple test to be closed under rewriting with $\mathcal{R}$. Every $S_{\mathcal{R}}$ has desirable properties such as subject reduction, the existence of principal typings [17], and an already implemented type inference algorithm[1].

[1] `http://www.macs.hw.ac.uk/ultra/polystar` (includes a web demonstration)

M. Wirsing, M. Hofmann, and A. Rauschmayer (Eds.): TGC 2010, LNCS 6084, pp. 103–119, 2010.

1.1 Contributions

This paper extends the POLY✶ system to support name restriction and also proves POLY✶ shape types are more expressive than some previous systems for specific calculi. The contributions are as follows. (1) Sec. 2 presents the extended POLY✶ system. Sections 3, 4 show (2) how to easily use shape types with well-known calculi (the π-calculus [14,13], Mobile Ambients [3]), (3) demonstrate polymorphic abilities of shape types, and (4) prove that shape types are more expressive than predicates of two type systems (*implicitly* typed π-calculus [16], *explicitly* typed Mobile Ambients [4]) custom designed for the above calculi. Finally, (5) we advocate a generic notion of shape types and show that they can be used instead of predicates of many other systems. We consider contributions (4) & (5) to be the main contribution of the paper.

Contribution (2) shows how to use POLY✶ and shape types without needing to fully understand all the details of the underlying formalism. Thus it helps to bridge over the problem of complexity of POLY✶ which is inevitably implied by its high generality and which has been daunting to some readers of earlier papers. Contribution (3) shows an aspect of shape types which is not common for other systems. An accompanying technical report [9] (TR), which extends this paper and contains proofs of main theorems, additionally shows how to use shape types for *flow analysis* of BioAmbients and proves its superior expressiveness to an earlier flow analysis system [15]. This work was left out for space reasons. For all the three systems we have proven not only that shape types are more expressive but also that they can be used to achieve exactly the same results as the original systems which might be important for some of their applications. We believe that the diversity of the mentioned systems and their intended applications provides a reasonable justification for contribution (5).

1.2 Notations and Preliminaries

Let i, j, k range over natural numbers. $\mathcal{P}_{\text{fin}}(U)$ is the set of all finite subsets of a set U, "$\setminus$" denotes set subtraction. Let $u \mapsto v$ be an alternate pair notation used in functions. $f[u \mapsto v]$ stands for the function that maps u to v and other values as f. Moreover, $U \to V$ ($U \to_{\text{fin}} V$) is the set of all (all finite) functions f with $\mathsf{dom}(f) \subseteq U$ and $\mathsf{rng}(f) \subseteq V$.

2 Metacalculus META✶ and Generic Type System POLY✶

2.1 General Syntax of Processes

META✶ process syntax, presented in Fig. 1, allows embeddings of many calculi. A name a^i is a pair of a *basic name* a and a natural number i. The basic part of a name x is denoted $\underline{x}$, that is, $\underline{a^i} = a$. When α-converting, we preserve the basic name and change the number. We write a instead of a^0 when no confusion can arise.

Processes are built from the null process "$\mathsf{0}$" by prefixing with an action ("."), by parallel composition ("$\mid$"), by name restriction ("ν"), and by replication

$a, b \in$	BasicName	$::=$ a $\mid$ b $\mid \cdots \mid$ in $\mid$ out $\mid$ open $\mid \cdots \mid$ [] $\mid \bullet \mid \cdots$
$x, y \in$	Name	$::= a^i$
$F \in$	Form	$::= x_0 \ldots x_k$
$M \in$	Message	$::= F \mid 0 \mid M_0.M_1$
$E \in$	Element	$::= x \mid (x_1, \ldots, x_k) \mid \langle M_1, \ldots, M_k \rangle$
$A \in$	Action	$::= E_0 \ldots E_k$
$P, Q \in$	Process	$::= 0 \mid A.P \mid (P \mid Q) \mid \nu x.P \mid !P$

Fig. 1. Syntax of META✶ processes

$$P \mid Q \equiv Q \mid P \qquad P \mid (Q \mid R) \equiv (P \mid Q) \mid R \qquad P \mid 0 \equiv P$$
$$0 \equiv !0 \qquad \nu x.\nu y.P \equiv \nu y.\nu x.P \qquad !P \equiv P \mid !P$$
$$A.\nu x.P \equiv \nu x.A.P \text{ if } x \notin \mathsf{fn}(A) \cup \mathsf{bn}(A) \qquad P \mid \nu x.Q \equiv \nu x.(P \mid Q) \text{ if } x \notin \mathsf{fn}(P)$$

Fig. 2. META✶ structural equivalence (structural rules omitted)

("!"). Actions can encode prefixes from various calculi such as π-calculus communication actions, Mobile Ambients capabilities, or ambient boundaries. The abbreviation "$x_1 \ldots x_k$ [P]", which further supports ambient syntax, stands for "$x_1 \ldots x_k$ [].P" ([] is a single name).

Process constructors have standard semantics. "0" is an inactive process, "$A.P$" executes the action A and continues as P, "$P \mid Q$" runs P and Q in parallel, "$\nu x.P$" behaves as P with private name x (i.e., x differs from all names outside P), and "$!P$" acts as infinitely many copies of P in parallel ("$P \mid P \mid \cdots$"). Let "." and "ν" bind more tightly than "$\mid$". These constructors have standard properties given by structural equivalence $\equiv$ (Fig. 2), e.g., "$\mid$" is commutative, adjacent "ν" can be interchanged, etc. In contrast, the semantics of actions is defined by instantiating META✶ (see below). Currently, META✶ does not support the choice operator "+" as a built in primitive. However, "$P + Q$" can be encoded as "ch.($P \mid Q$)" provided rewriting rules are extended to use this encoding.

All occurrences x in "$\nu x.P$" are (ν-)bound. When the action A contains an element "$(x_1, \ldots, x_k)$" then all occurrences of the x_i's in "$A.P$" as well as in A on its own are called (input-)bound. An occurrence of x that is not bound is free. The occurrence of a in a^i is bound (resp. free) when this occurrence of a^i is. A bound occurrence of a^i can be α-converted only to a^j with a the same. We identify α-convertible processes. The set of free names of P is denoted $\mathsf{fn}(P)$. The set $\mathsf{fbn}(P)$ (resp. $\mathsf{ibn}(P)$, $\mathsf{nbn}(P)$) contains free (resp. input-bound, ν-bound) basic names of P. The set of bound names of A is written $\mathsf{bn}(A)$.

A process P is *well scoped* when (W1) $\mathsf{fbn}(P)$, $\mathsf{ibn}(P)$, and $\mathsf{nbn}(P)$ do not overlap, (W2) nested input binders do not bind the same basic name, and (W3) no action contains an input-binding of a basic name more than once. These conditions are important for type inference. We allow only well scoped processes.

A META✶ substitution σ is a finite function from Name to Message. Application of σ to P, written $P\sigma$, behaves as usual except the following. (1) It places a special name "•" at positions that would otherwise be syntax errors (e.g., $(\mathsf{in}\ \mathsf{x}.0)\{\mathsf{x} \mapsto \mathsf{out}\ \mathsf{b}\} = \mathsf{in}\ \bullet.0$). (2) When a composed message M is substituted for a single name action x in "x.P", then M's components are pushed from right to left onto $P\sigma$ (e.g., $(\mathsf{x}.0)\{\mathsf{x} \mapsto (\mathsf{a}.\mathsf{b}).\mathsf{c}\} = \mathsf{a}.\mathsf{b}.\mathsf{c}.0$). The full definition of $P\sigma$ is in the TR.

2.2 Instantiations of META✶

META✶ provides syntax to describe rewriting rules that give meaning to actions and also defines how these rules yield a rewriting relation on processes. The syntax is best explained by an example. The following rule description (in which "$\{\mathring{\mathtt{x}} := \mathring{\mathtt{n}}\}\mathring{\mathtt{Q}}$" describes substitution application)

$$\textbf{rewrite}\{\ \mathring{\mathtt{c}}\mathtt{<}\mathring{\mathtt{n}}\mathtt{>}.\mathring{\mathtt{P}} \mid \mathring{\mathtt{c}}(\mathring{\mathtt{x}}).\mathring{\mathtt{Q}} \hookrightarrow \mathring{\mathtt{P}} \mid \{\mathring{\mathtt{x}} := \mathring{\mathtt{n}}\}\mathring{\mathtt{Q}}\ \}$$

directly corresponds to the standard π-calculus communication rule "$c{<}n{>}.P \mid c(x).Q \Rightarrow P \mid Q\{x \mapsto n\}$". The circle-topped letters stand at the place of name, message, and process metavariables. Given a set $\mathcal{R}$ of rule descriptions in the above syntax, META✶ automatically infers the rewriting relation $\overset{\mathcal{R}}{\hookrightarrow}$ which incorporates structural equivalence and congruence rules (e.g., "$P \overset{\mathcal{R}}{\hookrightarrow} Q \Rightarrow \nu x.P \overset{\mathcal{R}}{\hookrightarrow} \nu x.Q$"). A rules description instantiates META✶ to a particular calculus, e.g., the set $\mathcal{R}$ containing only the above rule description instantiates META✶ to the π-calculus.

Further examples of META✶ instantiations are given in Sec. 3.3 and 4.3. A rule description can also contain a concrete META✶ name (e.g. "out") when an exact match is required. We require that these names are never bound in any process. Complete definitions of the syntax of rewriting rules and of the rewriting relation $\overset{\mathcal{R}}{\hookrightarrow}$ is left to the TR [9, Sec. 2.2].

2.3 POLY✶ Shape Predicates and Types for META✶

A *shape predicate* describes possible structures of process syntax trees. When a rewriting rule from $\mathcal{R}$ is applied to a process, its syntax tree changes, and sometimes the new syntax tree no longer satisfies the same shape predicates. All POLY✶ ($\mathcal{R}$-)types are shape predicates that describe process sets closed under rewriting using $\mathcal{R}$. For feasibility, types are defined via a syntactic test that enforces rewriting-closedness. Intuitively, the syntactic test tries to apply the rules from $\mathcal{R}$ to all active positions in a shape graph and checks whether all the edges newly generated by this application are already present in the graph. Further restrictions are used to ensure the existence of principal typings.

Fig. 3 defines shape predicate syntax. Action types are similar to actions except that action types are built from basic names instead of names, and compound messages are described up to commutativity, associativity, and repetitions of their parts. Thus an action type describes a set of actions. A shape predicate

Syntax of POLY✶ *shape predicates:*

$$\begin{array}{lll} \varphi \in \mathsf{FormType} & ::= a_0 \ldots a_k & \alpha \in \mathsf{ActionType} ::= \varepsilon_0\, \varepsilon_1 \ldots \varepsilon_k \\ \Phi \in \mathsf{FormTypeSet} & = \mathcal{P}_{\mathrm{fin}}(\mathsf{FormType}) & \chi \in \mathsf{Node} ::= \mathtt{X} \mid \mathtt{Y} \mid \mathtt{Z} \mid \cdots \\ \mu \in \mathsf{MessageType} & ::= \Phi{*} \mid a & \eta \in \mathsf{Edge} ::= \chi_0 \xrightarrow{\alpha} \chi_1 \\ \varepsilon \in \mathsf{ElementType} & ::= a \mid (a_1, \ldots, a_k) \mid & G \in \mathsf{ShapeGraph} = \mathcal{P}_{\mathrm{fin}}(\mathsf{Edge}) \\ & \quad <\mu_1, \ldots, \mu_k> & \pi \in \mathsf{ShapePredicate} ::= \langle G, \chi \rangle \end{array}$$

Rules for matching META✶ *entities against shape predicates:*

$$\begin{array}{lll} \vdash a^i : a & \vdash (a_1^{i_1}, \ldots, a_k^{i_k}) : (a_1, \ldots, a_k) & (\vdash M_0 : \Phi \mathbin{\&} \vdash M_1 : \Phi) \Rightarrow \vdash M_0.M_1 : \Phi \\ \vdash 0 : \Phi & (\vdash F : \varphi \mathbin{\&} \varphi \in \Phi) \Rightarrow \vdash F : \Phi & (M \notin \mathsf{Name} \mathbin{\&} \vdash M : \Phi) \Rightarrow \vdash M : \Phi{*} \end{array}$$

$$(\forall i \leq k \colon \vdash E_i : \varepsilon_i) \Rightarrow \vdash E_0 \ldots E_k : \varepsilon_0 \ldots \varepsilon_k$$
$$(\forall i \colon 0 < i \leq k \mathbin{\&} \vdash M_i : \mu_i) \Rightarrow \vdash <M_1, \ldots, M_k> : <\mu_1, \ldots, \mu_k>$$

$$\begin{array}{ll} \vdash 0 : \pi & \\ \vdash P : \pi \Rightarrow \vdash \nu x.P : \pi & (\vdash P : \pi \mathbin{\&} \vdash Q : \pi) \Rightarrow \vdash P \mid Q : \pi \\ \vdash P : \pi \Rightarrow \vdash !P : \pi & ((\chi_0 \xrightarrow{\alpha} \chi_1) \in G \mathbin{\&} \vdash A : \alpha \mathbin{\&} \vdash P : \langle G, \chi_1 \rangle) \Rightarrow \vdash A.P : \langle G, \chi_0 \rangle \end{array}$$

Fig. 3. Syntax and semantics of POLY✶ shape predicates

$\langle G, \chi \rangle$ is a directed finite graph with root χ and with edges labeled by action types. A process P matches π when P's syntax tree is a "subgraph" of π. Shape predicate can have loops and thus describe syntax trees of arbitrary height.

Fig. 3 also describes matching META✶ entities against shape predicates. The rule matching actions against action types also matches forms against form types. Matching entities against types does not depend on $\mathcal{R}$, i.e., it works the same in any META✶ instantiation. The *meaning* $[\![\pi]\!]$ of the shape predicate π is the set $\{P \mid \vdash P : \pi\}$ of all processes matching π.

A shape predicate π is *semantically closed* w.r.t. a rule set $\mathcal{R}$ when $[\![\pi]\!]$ is closed under $\mathcal{R}$-rewritings, i.e., when $\vdash P : \pi$ and $P \stackrel{\mathcal{R}}{\hookrightarrow} Q$ imply $\vdash Q : \pi$ for any P and Q. Because deciding semantic closure w.r.t. an arbitrary $\mathcal{R}$ is nontrivial, we use an easier-to-decide property, namely *syntactic closure*, which by design is algorithmically verifiable. $\mathcal{R}$*-types* are shape predicates syntactically closed w.r.t. $\mathcal{R}$. A type π of P is a *principal typing* of P when $[\![\pi]\!] \subseteq [\![\pi_0]\!]$ for any other type π_0 of P. There are *width* and *depth* restrictions to ensure principal typings. Details are left to our TR [9, Sec. 2.4].

2.4 Proving Greater Expressiveness of POLY✶

We now discuss how to consider some process calculus C and its type system S_C and prove the greater expressiveness of the related META✶ and POLY✶ instantiations. Sections 3 and 4 follow this approach. Usually S_C defines predicates (ranged over by φ) which represent properties of processes (ranged over by B) of C. Then S_C defines the relation $\rhd B : \varphi$ which represents statements "B has the property φ" and which is preserved under rewriting of B in C. The META✶ description $\mathcal{R}$ of C's rewriting rules gives us the calculus $C_{\mathcal{R}}$ and its shape type system $S_{\mathcal{R}}$.

Firstly we need to set up a correspondence between C and $C_{\mathcal{R}}$, that is, we need an encoding $(\!|\cdot|\!)$ of processes B into META✶ which preserves C's rewriting relation $\rightarrow$. The following property, which is usually easy to prove, formulates this modulo $\equiv$ because structural equivalences of different calculi might differ.

Property 1. When $B_0 \rightarrow B_1$ then $\exists B_0', B_1'$ such that $B_0 \equiv B_0'$ & $(\!|B_0'|\!) \overset{\mathcal{R}}{\hookrightarrow} (\!|B_1'|\!)$ & $B_1' \equiv B_1$. When $(\!|B_0|\!) \overset{\mathcal{R}}{\hookrightarrow} P_1$ then $\exists B_1$ such that $B_0 \rightarrow B_1$ & $(\!|B_1|\!) \equiv P_1$.

Predicates φ of S_C are commonly preserved under renaming of bound basic names, that is, $\rhd(\nu x)B : \varphi$ usually implies $\rhd(\nu a^0)(B\{x \mapsto a^0\}) : \varphi$ (for a not in B). Predicates of similar systems can not be directly translated to POLY✶ shape types with the corresponding meaning because shape types do not have this property. In other words, the difference in handling of bound names between POLY✶ and other systems makes some straightforward embeddings impossible.

We investigate two reasonable ways to embed S_C in $S_{\mathcal{R}}$, that is, to decide $\rhd B : \varphi$ using $S_{\mathcal{R}}$'s relation "$\Vdash$". (1) In Sec. 4.4 about Mobile Ambients, we translate φ together with information about bound basic names of B into a shape type. (2) In Sec. 3.4 about the π-calculus, we show how to decide $\rhd B : \varphi$ by a simple check on a principal shape type of B. The fact that both embeddings of predicates φ depend on a process B is not a limitation because B is known for desirable applications like type checking.

We stress that these embeddings serve the theoretical purpose of proving greater expressiveness and are not necessary for a practical use of shape types. When S_C is designed to verify a certain fixed property of processes which can be expressed as a property of shape types, then we can use $S_{\mathcal{R}}$ directly for the same purposes as S_C without any embedding. We show how to do this for the two systems in Sec. 3.3 and 4.3. We can also design a property of processes directly on shape types without any reference to another analysis system. Our TR [9, Sec. 3] discusses this further.

2.5 Discussion

POLY✶ presented above extends the previously published POLY✶ [12] with name restriction. The previously published system [12] supports restriction only in META✶ but no processes with ν are typable in POLY✶ instantiations. An earlier attempt in a technical report [11] to handle name restriction was found inconsistent [8, Sec. 3.2-4] and furthermore inadequate [8, Sec. 4] to carry out the proofs of greater expressiveness in sections 3 and 4.

The difficulty with name restriction is because a shape type represents a syntactic structure of a process, and thus presence of bound names in a process has to be somehow reflected by a shape graph. Because bound names can be α-renamed, POLY✶ needs to establish a connection between positions in a process and a shape graph which is preserved by α-conversion. This connection is provided by basic names which are the key concept of name restriction handling in this paper. For example, for the action "a<a>" there is the corresponding action type "a<a>" in its shape type. When the name a were ν-bound and α-renamed to some other name then the correspondence between the action in the process and the action type would be lost. This problem is solved by building shape types from basic names which are preserved under α-conversion.

Syntax of the π-calculus processes:

$$c, n, m \in \mathsf{PiName} \;=\; \mathsf{Name} \setminus \{\bullet\}$$
$$N \in \mathsf{PiAction} ::= c(n_1, \ldots, n_k) \mid c<n_1, \ldots, n_k>$$
$$B \in \mathsf{PiProcess} ::= 0 \mid (B_0 \mathbin{|} B_1) \mid N.B \mid !B \mid (\nu n)B$$

Rewriting relation of the π-calculus (≡ is standard defined in TR [9, Fig. 8]):

$$c(n_1, \ldots, n_k).B_0 \mathbin{|} c<m_1, \ldots, m_k>.B_1 \to B_0\{n_1 \mapsto m_1, \ldots, n_k \mapsto m_k\} \mathbin{|} B_1$$
$$B_0 \to B_1 \Rightarrow (\nu n)B_0 \to (\nu n)B_1 \quad B_0' \equiv B_0 \;\&\; B_0 \to B_1 \;\&\; B_1 \equiv B_1' \Rightarrow B_0' \to B_1'$$
$$B_0 \to B_1 \Rightarrow B_0 \mathbin{|} B_2 \to B_1 \mathbin{|} B_2$$

Fig. 4. The syntax and semantics of the π-calculus

The handling of input-bound names in the previous POLY✶ was reached by disabling their α-conversion which is possible under certain circumstances. But α-conversion of ν-bound names can not be avoided and thus a new approach has been developed.

3 Shape Types for the π-Calculus

3.1 A Polyadic π-Calculus

The π-calculus [14,13] is a process calculus involving process mobility developed by Milner, Parrow, and Walker. Mobility is abstracted as channel-based communication whose objects are atomic names. Channel labels are not distinguished from names and can be passed by communication. This ability, referred as *link passing*, is the π-calculus feature that most distinguishes it from its predecessors. We use a polyadic version of the π-calculus which supports communication of tuples of names.

Fig. 5 presents the syntax and semantics of the π-calculus. Processes are built from META✶ names. The process "$c(n_1, \ldots, n_k).B$", which (input)-binds the names n_i's, waits to receive a k-tuple of names over channel c and then behaves like B with the received values substituted for n_i's. The process "$c<n_1, \ldots, n_k>.B$" sends the k-tuple $n_1, \ldots, n_k$ over channel c and then behaves like B. Other constructors have the meaning as in META✶ (Sec. 2.1). The sets of names $\mathsf{fn}(B)$, $\mathsf{fbn}(B)$, $\mathsf{ibn}(B)$, $\mathsf{nbn}(B)$ are defined as in META✶.

Processes are identified up to α-conversion of bound names which preserves basic names. A substitution in the π-calculus is a finite function from names to names, and its application to B is written postfix, e.g., "$B\{n \mapsto m\}$". A process B is *well scoped* when (S1) $\mathsf{fbn}(B)$, $\mathsf{ibn}(B)$, and $\mathsf{nbn}(B)$ do not overlap, (S2) nested input binders do not bind the same basic name, and (S3) no input action contains the same basic name more then once. Henceforth, we require processes to be well scoped (well-scopedness is preserved by rewriting).

Example 1. Let $B = \mathsf{!s(x,y).x<y>.0 \mid s<a,n>.0 \mid a(v).v(p).0 \mid n<o>.0 \mid s<b,m>.0 \mid b(w).v(q,r).0 \mid m<o,o>.0}$

Using the rewriting relation $\to$ sequentially four times we can obtain (among others) the process "$\mathsf{!s(x,y).x<y>.0 \mid n(p).0 \mid n<o>.0 \mid m(q,r).0 \mid m<o,o>.0}$".

Syntax of TPI *types:*

$$\beta \in \mathsf{PiTypeVariable} ::= \imath \mid \imath' \mid \imath'' \mid \cdots$$
$$\delta \in \mathsf{PiType} ::= \beta \mid \uparrow[\delta_1, \ldots, \delta_k]$$
$$\Delta \in \mathsf{PiContext} = \mathsf{BasicName} \to_{\mathrm{fin}} \mathsf{PiType}$$

Typing rules of TPI:

$$\Delta \vdash \mathsf{0} \qquad \Delta \vdash B_0 \;\&\; \Delta \vdash B_1 \;\Rightarrow\; \Delta \vdash B_0 \mid B_1$$
$$\Delta \vdash B \;\Rightarrow\; \Delta \vdash !B \qquad \Delta[\underline{n} \mapsto \delta] \vdash B \;\Rightarrow\; \Delta \vdash (\nu n)B$$
$$\Delta(\underline{c}) = \uparrow[\delta_1, \ldots, \delta_k] \;\&\; \Delta[\underline{n_1} \mapsto \delta_1, \ldots, \underline{n_k} \mapsto \delta_k] \vdash B \;\Rightarrow\; \Delta \vdash c(n_1, \ldots, n_k).B$$
$$\Delta(\underline{c}) = \uparrow[\Delta(\underline{n_1}), \ldots, \Delta(\underline{n_k})] \;\&\; \Delta \vdash B \;\Rightarrow\; \Delta \vdash c\langle n_1, \ldots, n_k\rangle.B$$

Fig. 5. Syntax of TPI types and typing rules

3.2 Types for the Polyadic π-Calculus (TPI)

We compare POLY✶ with a simple type system [16, Ch. 3] for the polyadic π-calculus presented by Turner which we name TPI. TPI is essentially Milner's sort discipline [13]. In the polyadic settings, an arity mismatch error on channel c can occur when the lengths of the sent and received tuple do not agree, like in "$c(n).\mathsf{0} \mid c\langle m, m\rangle.\mathsf{0}$". Processes which can never evolve to a state with a similar situation are called *communication safe.* TPI verifies communication safety of π-processes.

The syntax and typing rules of TPI are presented in Fig. 5. Recall that $\underline{n}$ denotes the basic name of n. Types δ are assigned to names. Type variables β are types of names which are not used as channel labels. The type "$\uparrow[\delta_1, \ldots, \delta_k]$" describes a channel which can be used to communicate any k-tuple whose i-th name has type δ_i. A context Δ assigns types to free names of a process (via their basic names). The relation $\Delta \vdash B$, which is preserved under rewriting, expresses that the actual usage of channels in B agrees with Δ. When $\Delta \vdash B$ for some Δ then B is communication safe. The opposite does not necessarily hold.

Example 2. Given B from Ex. 1 we can see that there is no Δ such that $\Delta \vdash B$. It is because the parts s<a, n> and s<a, m> imply that types of n and m must be equal while the parts n<o> and m<o, o> force them to be different. On the other hand B is communication safe. We check this using POLY✶ in Sec 3.3.

3.3 Instantiation of META✶ to the π-Calculus

The π-calculus syntax from Sec. 3.1 already matches the META✶ syntax and thus only the following $\mathcal{P}$ is needed to instantiate META✶ to the calculus $C_{\mathcal{P}}$ and POLY✶ to its type system $S_{\mathcal{P}}$. Sec. 3.4 shows that $C_{\mathcal{P}}$ is essentially identical to the above π-calculus.

$$\mathcal{P} = \bigcup_{k=0}^{\infty} \{\textbf{rewrite}\{\, \mathring{c}\langle\mathring{M}_1, \ldots, \mathring{M}_k\rangle.\mathring{P} \mid \mathring{c}(\mathring{a}_1, \ldots, \mathring{a}_k).\mathring{Q} \;\hookrightarrow\; \mathring{P} \mid \{\mathring{a}_1 := \mathring{M}_1, \ldots, \mathring{a}_k := \mathring{M}_k\}\mathring{Q}\,\}\}$$

Each communication prefix length has its own rule; in our implementation, a single rule can uniformly handle all lengths, but the formal META✶ presentation

The set of expected and actual channel types of G:

$$\mathsf{chtypes}(\Delta,G)=\{(\Delta(a),\uparrow[\Delta(b_1),\ldots,\Delta(b_k)]):(\chi\xrightarrow{a\,(b_1,\ldots,b_k)}\chi')\in G\vee(\chi\xrightarrow{a<b_1,\ldots,b_k>}\chi')\in G\}$$

Context Δ and shape type π agreement relation $\cong$:

Write $\Delta \cong \langle G,\chi\rangle$ when there is some Δ' with the domain disjoint from Δ such that $\mathsf{chtypes}(\Delta \cup \Delta', G)$ is defined and is an identity.

Fig. 6. Property of shape types corresponding to $\vdash$ of TPI

is deliberately simpler. The next example shows how to check communication safety in $S_{\mathcal{P}}$ without using TPI.

Example 3. Let P be a META✶ equivalent of B from Ex. 1. We can compute a principal $\mathcal{P}$-type π_P of P which is displayed on the right. Node R is its root. The type π_P contains all computational futures of P in one place. Thus, because there are no two edges from R labeled by "$a\,(b_1,\ldots,b_k)$" and "a<$b'_1,\ldots,b'_j$>" with $k \neq j$, we can conclude that P is communication safe which Ex. 2 shows TPI can not do. Our implementation can be instructed (using an additional rule) to insert the error name • at the place of communication errors. Any type of P without • then implies P's communication safety.

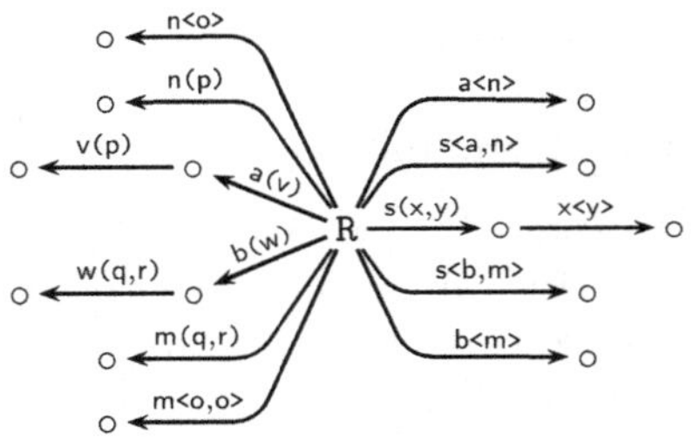

3.4 Embedding of TPI in POLY✶

Using the terminology from Sec. 2.4 we have that C is the π-calculus, S_C is TPI, predicates φ of S_C are contexts Δ, and S_C's relation $\rhd B : \varphi$ is $\Delta \vdash B$. Moreover $\mathcal{R}$ is $\mathcal{P}$ which was introduced with $C_{\mathcal{P}}$ and $S_{\mathcal{P}}$ in Sec. 3.3. This section provides a formal comparison which shows how to, for a given B and Δ, answer the question $\Delta \vdash B$ using $S_{\mathcal{P}}$.

As stated in Sec. 2.4, to relate TPI and $S_{\mathcal{P}}$ we need to provide an encoding $(\!|\cdot|\!)$ of π-processes in META✶. This $(\!|\cdot|\!)$, found in TR [9, Fig. 10] , is almost an identity because the π-calculus syntax (Fig. 4) already agrees with META✶. Thus $(\!|\cdot|\!)$ mainly changes the syntactic category. Prop. 1 holds in the above context.

Given Δ, we define a shape type property which holds for the principal type π_B of $(\!|B|\!)$ iff $\Delta \vdash B$. The property is given by the relation $\Delta \cong \pi$ from Fig. 6. The set $\mathsf{chtypes}(\Delta, G)$ contains pairs of TPI types extracted from G. Each pair corresponds to an edge of G labeled by an action type "$a\,(b_1,\ldots,b_k)$" or "a<$b_1,\ldots,b_k$>". The first member of the pair is a's type expected by Δ, and the second member computes a's actual usage from the types of b_i's. The set $\mathsf{chtypes}(\Delta, G)$ is undefined when some required value of Δ is not defined. The context Δ' from the definition of $\cong$ provides types of names originally bound in

B. These are not mentioned by Δ but are in G. The following theorem shows how to answer $\Delta \vdash B$ by $\cong$.

Theorem 1. *Let no two different binders in B bind the same basic name, π_B be a principal ($\mathcal{P}$-)type of $(\!|B|\!)$, and $\mathsf{dom}(\Delta) = \mathsf{fbn}(B)$. Then $\Delta \vdash B$ iff $\Delta \cong \pi_B$.*

The requirement on different binders (which can be achieved by renaming) is not preserved under rewriting because replication can introduce two same-named binders. However, when all binding basic names differ in B_0, then the theorem holds for any successor B_1 of B_0 even when the requirement is not met for B_1. We want to ensure that the derivation of $\Delta \vdash B$ does not assign different types to different bound names. A slightly stronger assumption of Thm. 1 simplifies its formulation. The theorem uses principal types and does not necessarily hold for a non-principal $\mathcal{P}$-type π of $(\!|B|\!)$ because π's additional edges not needed to match $(\!|B|\!)$ can preclude $\Delta \cong \pi$.

3.5 Conclusions

We showed a process (Ex. 1) that can not be proved communication safe by TPI (Ex. 2) but can be proved so by POLY✶ (Ex. 3). Thm. 1 implies that POLY✶ recognizes safety of all TPI-safe processes. Thus we conclude that POLY✶ is better in recognition of communication safety then TPI. Thm. 1 allows to recognize typability in TPI: B is typable in TPI iff $\emptyset \cong \pi_B$. This is computable because a POLY✶ principal type can always be found (for $S_{\mathcal{P}}$ in polynomial time), and checking $\cong$ is easy.

Turner [16, Ch. 5] presents also a polymorphic system for the π-calculus which recognizes B from Ex. 1 as safe. However, with respect to our best knowledge, it can not recognize safety of the process "B | s<n, a>.0" which POLY✶ can do. We are not aware of any process that can be recognized safe by Turner's polymorphic system but not by POLY✶. It must be noted, there are still processes which POLY✶ can not prove safe, for example, "a(x).a(y, z).0 | a<o>.a<o, o>.0".

Other π-calculus type systems are found in the literature. Kobayashi and Igarashi [7] present types for the π-calculus looking like simplified processes which can verify properties which are hard to express using shape types (race conditions, deadlock detection) but do not support polymorphism. One can expect applications where POLY✶ is more expressive as well as contrariwise. Shape types, however, work for many process calculi, not just the π-calculus.

4 Shape Types for Mobile Ambients

4.1 Mobile Ambients (MA)

Mobile Ambients (MA), introduced by Cardelli and Gordon [3], is a process calculus for representing process mobility. Processes are placed inside named bounded locations called *ambients* which form a tree hierarchy. Processes can change the hierarchy and send messages to nearby processes. Messages contain either ambient names or hierarchy change instructions.

Syntax of MA *processes:*

$$
\begin{array}{rlll}
n \in & \mathsf{AName} & = & \mathsf{Name} \setminus \{\bullet\} \\
N \in & \mathsf{ACapability} & ::= & \varepsilon \mid n \mid \mathsf{in}\ N \mid \mathsf{out}\ N \mid \mathsf{open}\ N \mid N.N' \\
\omega \in & \mathsf{AMessageType} & ::= & \text{definition postponed to Fig. 8} \\
B \in & \mathsf{AProcess} & ::= & \mathsf{0} \mid (B_0 \mid B_1) \mid N[B] \mid N.B \mid !B \mid (\nu n{:}\omega)B \mid \\
 & & & <N_1,\dots,N_k> \mid (n_1{:}\omega_1,\dots,n_k{:}\omega_k).B
\end{array}
$$

Rewriting relation of MA *($\equiv$ is standard defined in TR [9, Fig. 12]):*

$$
\begin{array}{rcl}
n[\mathsf{in}\ m.B_0 \mid B_1] \mid m[B_2] & \rightarrow & m[n[B_0 \mid B_1] \mid B_2] \\
m[n[\mathsf{out}\ m.B_0 \mid B_1] \mid B_2] & \rightarrow & n[B_0 \mid B_1] \mid m[B_2] \\
\mathsf{open}\ n.B_0 \mid n[B_1] & \rightarrow & B_0 \mid B_1 \\
(n_1{:}\omega_1,\dots,n_k{:}\omega_k).B \mid <N_1,\dots,N_k> & \rightarrow & B\{n_1 \mapsto N_1,\dots,n_k \mapsto N_k\}
\end{array}
$$

$$
\begin{array}{ll}
B_0 \rightarrow B_1 \Rightarrow n[B_0] \rightarrow n[B_1] & B_0 \rightarrow B_1 \Rightarrow (\nu n{:}\omega)B_0 \rightarrow (\nu n{:}\omega)B_1 \\
B_0 \rightarrow B_1 \Rightarrow B_0 \mid B_2 \rightarrow B_1 \mid B_2 & B_0' \equiv B_0\ \&\ B_0 \rightarrow B_1\ \&\ B_1 \equiv B_1' \Rightarrow B_0' \rightarrow B_1'
\end{array}
$$

Fig. 7. Syntax and semantics of TMA

Fig. 7 describes MA process syntax. Executing a capability consumes it and instructs the surrounding ambient to change the hierarchy. The capability "in n" causes moving into a sibling ambient named n, the capability "out n" causes moving out of the parent ambient n and becoming its sibling, and "open n" causes dissolving the boundary of a child ambient n. In capability sequences, the left-most capability will be executed first.

The constructors "0", "|", ".", "!", and "ν" have standard meanings. Binders contain explicit type annotations (Sec. 4.2 below). The expression $n[B]$ describes the process B running inside ambient n. Capabilities can be communicated in messages. $<N_1,\dots,N_k>$ is a process that sends a k-tuple of messages. $(n_1:\omega_1,\dots,n_k:\omega_k).B$ is a process that receives a k-tuple of messages, substitutes them for appropriate n_i's in B, and continues as this new process. Free and bound (basic) names are defined like in META✶. Processes that are α-convertible are identified. A substitution σ is a finite function from names to messages and its application to B is written $B\sigma$. Fig. 7 also describes structural equivalence and semantics of MA processes. The only thing the semantics does with type annotations is copy them around. We require all processes to be well-scoped w.r.t. conditions S1-3 from Sec. 3.1, and the additional condition (S4) that the same message type is assigned to bound names with the same basic name. Ambients and capabilities where N is not a single name, which the presentation allows for simplicity, are inert and meaningless.

Example 4. In this example, packet ambient p delivers a synchronization message to destination ambient d by following instructions x. As we have not yet properly defined message types, we only suppose $\omega_{\mathsf{p}} = \mathsf{Amb}[\kappa]$ for some κ.

$$
\begin{array}{l}
B = <\mathsf{in\ d}> \mid (\nu\mathsf{p}{:}\omega_{\mathsf{p}})(\mathsf{d}[\mathsf{open\ p.0}] \mid (\mathsf{x}:\omega_{\mathsf{x}}).\mathsf{p}[\mathsf{x}.<>]) \rightarrow \\
\quad (\nu\mathsf{p}{:}\omega_{\mathsf{p}})(\mathsf{d}[\mathsf{open\ p.0}] \mid \mathsf{p}[\mathsf{in\ d}.<>]) \rightarrow (\nu\mathsf{p}{:}\omega_{\mathsf{p}})(\mathsf{d}[\mathsf{open\ p.0} \mid \mathsf{p}[<>]]) \rightarrow \mathsf{d}[<>]
\end{array}
$$

Syntax of TMA *types:*

$$\omega \in \mathsf{AMessageType} ::= \mathsf{Amb}[\kappa] \mid \mathsf{Cap}[\kappa]$$
$$\kappa \in \mathsf{AExchangeType} ::= \mathsf{Shh} \mid \omega_1 \otimes \cdots \otimes \omega_k$$
$$\Delta \in \mathsf{AEnvironment} = \mathsf{AName} \to_{\text{fin}} \mathsf{AMessageType}$$

Typing rules of TMA*:*

$$\Delta(n) = \omega \Rightarrow \Delta \vdash n : \omega$$
$$\Delta \vdash N : \mathsf{Amb}[\kappa'] \Rightarrow \Delta \vdash \mathsf{in}\ N : \mathsf{Cap}[\kappa]$$
$$\Delta \vdash N : \mathsf{Amb}[\kappa'] \Rightarrow \Delta \vdash \mathsf{out}\ N : \mathsf{Cap}[\kappa]$$
$$\Delta \vdash N : \mathsf{Amb}[\kappa] \Rightarrow \Delta \vdash \mathsf{open}\ N : \mathsf{Cap}[\kappa]$$
$$\Delta \vdash \varepsilon : \mathsf{Cap}[\kappa]$$
$$\Delta \vdash N : \mathsf{Cap}[\kappa]\ \&\ \Delta \vdash N' : \mathsf{Cap}[\kappa] \Rightarrow \Delta \vdash N.N' : \mathsf{Cap}[\kappa]$$

$$\Delta \vdash B : \kappa \Rightarrow \Delta \vdash\ !B : \kappa$$
$$\Delta \vdash \mathsf{0} : \kappa$$
$$\Delta \vdash N : \mathsf{Cap}[\kappa]\ \&\ \Delta \vdash B : \kappa \Rightarrow \Delta \vdash N.B : \kappa$$
$$\Delta \vdash N : \mathsf{Amb}[\kappa]\ \&\ \Delta \vdash B : \kappa \Rightarrow \Delta \vdash N[B] : \kappa'$$
$$\Delta \vdash B_0 : \kappa\ \&\ \Delta \vdash B_1 : \kappa \Rightarrow \Delta \vdash B_0 \mid B_1 : \kappa$$

$$\Delta[n \mapsto \mathsf{Amb}[\kappa']] \vdash B : \kappa \Rightarrow \Delta \vdash (\nu n{:}\mathsf{Amb}[\kappa'])B : \kappa$$
$$\forall i\colon 0 < i \le k\ \&\ \Delta \vdash N_i : \omega_i \Rightarrow \Delta \vdash \langle N_1, \ldots, N_k \rangle : \omega_1 \otimes \cdots \otimes \omega_k$$
$$\Delta[n_1 \mapsto \omega_1, \ldots, n_k \mapsto \omega_k] \vdash B : \omega_1 \otimes \cdots \otimes \omega_k \Rightarrow \Delta \vdash (n_1{:}\omega_1, \ldots, n_k{:}\omega_k).B : \omega_1 \otimes \cdots \otimes \omega_k$$

Fig. 8. Syntax of TMA types and typing rules

4.2 Types for Mobile Ambients (TMA)

An arity mismatch error, like in "<a, b>.0 | (x).in x.0", can occur in polyadic MA. Another communication error can be encountered when a sender sends a capability while a receiver expects a single name. For example "<in a>.0 | (x).out x.0" can rewrite to a meaningless "out (in a).0". Yet another error happens when a process is to execute a single name capability, like in "a.0". Processes which can never evolve to a state with any of the above errors are called *communication safe*. A typed MA introduced by Cardelli and Gordon [4], which we name TMA, verifies communication safety.

TMA assigns an allowed communication topic to each ambient location and ensures that processes respect the topics. Fig. 8 describes TMA type syntax. Exchange types, which describe communication topics, are assigned to processes and ambient locations. The type Shh indicates silence (no communication). $\omega_1 \otimes \cdots \otimes \omega_k$ indicates communication of k-tuples of messages whose i-th member has the message type ω_i. For $k = 0$ we write **1** which allows only synchronization actions <> and (). $\mathsf{Amb}[\kappa]$ is the type of an ambient where communication described by κ is allowed. $\mathsf{Cap}[\kappa]$ describes capabilities whose execution can unleash exchange κ (by opening some ambient). Environments assign message types to free names (via basic names). Fig. 8 also describes the TMA typing rules. Types from conclusions not mentioned in the assumption can be arbitrary. For example, the type of $N[B]$ can be arbitrary provided B is well-typed. It reflects the fact that the communication inside N does not directly interact with N's outside. Existence of some Δ and κ such that Δ does not assign a Cap-type to any free name and $\Delta \vdash B : \kappa$ holds implies that B is communication safe.

Example 5. Take B from Ex. 4, $\Delta = \{\mathsf{d} \mapsto \mathsf{Amb[1]}\}$, and $\omega_{\mathsf{p}} = \mathsf{Amb[1]}$, and $\omega_{\mathsf{x}} = \mathsf{Cap[1]}$. We can see that $\Delta \vdash B : \mathsf{Cap[1]}$ but, for example, $\Delta \nvdash B : \mathbf{1}$.

4.3 Instantiation of META✶ to MA

When we omit type annotations, add "0" after output actions, and write capability prefixes always in a right associative manner (like "in a.(out b.(in c.0))"), we see that the MA syntax is included in the META✶ syntax. The following set $\mathcal{A}$ instantiates META✶ to MA.

$$\begin{aligned}\mathcal{A} = \{\ & \textbf{active}\{\,\mathring{\mathsf{P}}\ \textbf{in}\ \mathring{\mathsf{a}}[\mathring{\mathsf{P}}]\,\},\\ & \textbf{rewrite}\{\,\mathring{\mathsf{a}}[\mathsf{in}\ \mathring{\mathsf{b}}.\mathring{\mathsf{P}} \mid \mathring{\mathsf{Q}}] \mid \mathring{\mathsf{b}}[\mathring{\mathsf{R}}] \hookrightarrow \mathring{\mathsf{b}}[\mathring{\mathsf{a}}[\mathring{\mathsf{P}} \mid \mathring{\mathsf{Q}}] \mid \mathring{\mathsf{R}}]\,\},\\ & \textbf{rewrite}\{\,\mathring{\mathsf{a}}[\mathring{\mathsf{b}}[\mathsf{out}\ \mathring{\mathsf{a}}.\mathring{\mathsf{P}} \mid \mathring{\mathsf{Q}}] \mid \mathring{\mathsf{R}}] \hookrightarrow \mathring{\mathsf{a}}[\mathring{\mathsf{R}}] \mid \mathring{\mathsf{b}}[\mathring{\mathsf{P}} \mid \mathring{\mathsf{Q}}]\,\},\\ & \textbf{rewrite}\{\,\mathsf{open}\ \mathring{\mathsf{a}}.\mathring{\mathsf{P}} \mid \mathring{\mathsf{a}}[\mathring{\mathsf{R}}] \hookrightarrow \mathring{\mathsf{P}} \mid \mathring{\mathsf{R}}\,\}\ \} \cup\\ \textstyle\bigcup_{k=0}^{\infty} \{\ & \textbf{rewrite}\{\,\langle\mathring{\mathsf{M}}_1,\ldots,\mathring{\mathsf{M}}_k\rangle.\mathring{\mathsf{P}} \mid (\mathring{\mathsf{a}}_1,\ldots,\mathring{\mathsf{a}}_k).\mathring{\mathsf{Q}} \hookrightarrow \mathring{\mathsf{P}} \mid \{\mathring{\mathsf{a}}_1 := \mathring{\mathsf{M}}_1,\ldots,\mathring{\mathsf{a}}_k := \mathring{\mathsf{M}}_k\}\,\mathring{\mathsf{Q}}\,\}\ \}\end{aligned}$$

The **active** rule lets rewriting be done inside ambients. It corresponds to the rule "$B_0 \to B_1 \Rightarrow n[B_0] \to n[B_1]$". Each communication prefix length has its own rule as in the case of the π-calculus. $\mathcal{A}$ defines the calculus $C_{\mathcal{A}}$ and the type system $S_{\mathcal{A}}$.

Communication safety of P can be checked on an $\mathcal{A}$-type as follows. Two edges with the same source labeled by $(a_1,\ldots,a_k)$ and $\langle b_1,\ldots,b_j\rangle$ with $k \neq j$ indicates an arity mismatch error (but only at active positions). Every label containing $\bullet$ (introduced by a substitution) indicates that a capability was sent instead of a name. Moreover, an edge labeled with a name $a \notin \mathsf{ibn}(P)$ at active position indicates an execution of a single name capability. A type of P not indicating any error proves P's safety. Checking safety this way is easy.

Example 6. $C_{\mathcal{A}}$'s equivalent of B from Ex. 4 is $P = \langle\mathsf{in\ d}\rangle.0 \mid \nu\mathsf{p}.(\mathsf{d}[\mathsf{open\ p}.0] \mid (\mathsf{x}).\mathsf{p}[\mathsf{x}.\langle\rangle.0])$. Its principal $\mathcal{A}$-type is displayed on the right. Its root is R and other node names are omitted. Checking the edge labels as described above easily proves P's safety. The edge labeled by x is not a communication error because x is input-bound in P.

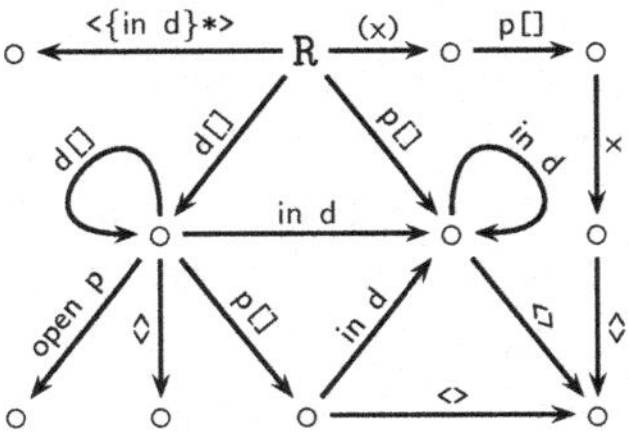

4.4 Embedding of TMA in POLY✶

Using the notation from Sec.2.4 we have that C is MA, S_C is TMA, predicates φ are pairs (Δ,κ), and S_C's relation $\rhd B : \varphi$ is $\Delta \vdash B : \kappa$. Moreover $\mathcal{R}$ is $\mathcal{A}$ which was introduced with $C_{\mathcal{A}}$ and $S_{\mathcal{A}}$ in Sec. 4.3. This section provides an embedding which shows how to, for a given B, Δ, and κ, answer the question $\Delta \vdash B : \kappa$ using $S_{\mathcal{A}}$. We stress that it is primarily a theoretical embedding for proving greater expressiveness which is not intended for use in practice.

An encoding $(\!|\cdot|\!)$ of MA processes in META✶, found in TR [9, Fig. 14], is again almost an identity except for the following. (1) Meaningless expressions allowed by MA's syntax are translated using the special name $\bullet$, e.g., "$(\!|\mathsf{in\ (out\ a)}|\!) = \mathsf{in}\ \bullet$". (2) The encoding erases type annotations which is okay because MA's rewriting rules only copy them around. The type embedding below recovers type information by different means. Prop. 1 holds in the given context.

As discussed in Sec. 2.4, we can not translate (Δ, κ) to a shape type with an equivalent meaning because $\vdash$ is preserved under renaming of bound basic names. Nevertheless this becomes possible when we specify the sets of allowed input- and ν-bound basic names and their types. These can be easily extracted from a given process B. An environment Δ^{ν}_{B} (resp. Δ^{in}_{B}) from the top part of Fig. 9 describes ν-bound (resp. input-bound) basic names of B. The definition reflects that ν-bound names in typable processes can only have Amb-types. For a given Δ, B, and κ we construct the shape type $\langle\!| \Delta \cup \Delta^{\nu}_{B}, \Delta^{\mathsf{in}}_{B}, \kappa |\!\rangle$ such that $\Delta \vdash B : \kappa$ iff $\vdash (\!|B|\!) : \langle\!| \Delta \cup \Delta^{\nu}_{B}, \Delta^{\mathsf{in}}_{B}, \kappa |\!\rangle$. The construction needs to know which names are input-bound and thus they are separated from the other names. The well-scopedness rules S1-4 ensure that there is no ambiguity in using only basic names to refer to typed names in a process. The type information I (Fig. 9, 2nd part) collects what is needed to construct a shape type. For $I = (\Delta \cup \Delta^{\nu}_{B}, \Delta^{\mathsf{in}}_{B}, \kappa)$ we define Δ_I, Δ^{in}_{I}, and κ_I such that Δ_I describes types of all names in Δ and B, and Δ^{in}_{I} describes types of B's input-bound names, and κ_I is simply κ.

Example 7. Δ, B, and κ from the previous examples (Ex. 4 and Ex. 5) give us $I = (\Delta \cup \Delta^{\nu}_{B}, \Delta^{\mathsf{in}}_{B}, \mathsf{Cap[1]})$ and we have:

$$\Delta \cup \Delta^{\nu}_{B} = \{\mathsf{d} \mapsto \mathsf{Amb[1]}, \mathsf{p} \mapsto \mathsf{Amb[1]}\} \quad \Delta^{\mathsf{in}}_{I} = \{\mathsf{x} \mapsto \mathsf{Cap[1]}\} \quad \Delta_I = \Delta \cup \Delta^{\nu}_{B} \cup \Delta^{\mathsf{in}}_{I}$$

The main idea of the construction of the shape type $\langle\!| I |\!\rangle$ from I is that $\langle\!| I |\!\rangle$ contains exactly one node for every exchange type of some ambient location, that is, one node for the top-level type κ_I, and one node for κ' whenever $\mathsf{Amb[}\kappa'\mathsf{]}$ is in I. The top-level type corresponds to the shape type root. Each node corresponding to some κ has self-loops which describe all capabilities and communication actions which a process of the type κ can execute. When $\Delta_I(\mathsf{d}) = \mathsf{Amb[1]}$ then every node would have a self-loop labeled by "in d" because in-capabilities can be executed by any process. On the other hand only the node corresponding to **1** would allow "open d" because only processes of type **1** can legally execute it. Finally, following an edge labeled with "d[]" means entering d. Thus the edge has led to the node χ_{d} that corresponds to **1**. In the above example, the shape graph would contain edges labeled with "d[]" from any node to χ_{d}.

The construction starts by building the node set of a shape predicate (Fig. 9, 3rd part). All the exchange types of ambient locations are gathered in the set types_I. These types are put in bijective correspondence with the set nodes_I.

Example 8. Our example gives $\mathsf{types}_I = \{\mathsf{Cap[1]}, \mathbf{1}\}$. Let us take $\mathsf{nodes}_I = \{\mathsf{R}, \mathsf{1}\}$ and define the bijections such that $\mathsf{nodeof}_I(\mathsf{Cap[1]}) = \mathsf{R}$ and $\mathsf{nodeof}_I(\mathbf{1}) = \mathsf{1}$.

The 4th part of Fig. 9 defines some auxiliary functions. The set $\mathsf{namesof}_I(\omega)$ contains all basic names declared with the type ω by I. The set $\mathsf{allowedin}_I(\kappa)$ contains all POLY★ action types which describe (translations of) all capabilities and action prefixes which are allowed to be legally executed by a process of the type κ. The set $\mathsf{allowedin}_I(\kappa)$ consists of three parts: moves_I, $\mathsf{opens}_I(\kappa)$, and $\mathsf{comms}_I(\kappa)$. The action types in moves_I describe all in/out capabilities constructible from ambient

Extraction of types of bound names: $\Delta^{\mathsf{in}}_B(a) = \omega$ iff B has a subprocess $(\ldots, a^i : \omega, \ldots).B_0$ $\Delta^{\nu}_B(a) = \omega$ iff $\omega = \mathsf{Amb}[\kappa]$ & B has a subprocess $(\nu a^i : \omega)B_0$
Type information: $I \in \mathsf{TypeInfo} = \mathsf{AEnvironment} \times \mathsf{AEnvironment} \times \mathsf{AExchangeType}$ For a given $I = (\Delta_0, \Delta_1, \kappa)$ we write Δ_I for $\Delta_0 \cup \Delta_1$, and Δ^{in}_I for Δ_1, and κ_I for κ.
Set of nodes of a shape graph (and correspondence functions): $\mathsf{types}_I = \{\kappa_I\} \cup \{\kappa \colon \mathsf{Amb}[\kappa] \in \mathsf{rng}(\Delta_I)\} \qquad \mathsf{nodeof}_I = \mathsf{typeof}_I^{-1}$ Let nodes_I be an arbitrary but fixed set of nodes such that there exist the bijection typeof_I from nodes_I into types_I.
Action types describing legal capabilities: $\mathsf{namesof}_I(\omega) = \{a \colon \Delta_I(a) = \omega\} \qquad \mathsf{allowedin}_I(\kappa) = \mathsf{moves}_I \cup \mathsf{opens}_I(\kappa) \cup \mathsf{comms}_I(\kappa)$ $\mathsf{moves}_I = \{\mathsf{in}\ a, \mathsf{out}\ a \colon \exists \kappa.\, a \in \mathsf{namesof}_I(\mathsf{Amb}[\kappa])\}$ $\mathsf{opens}_I(\kappa) = \{\mathsf{open}\ a \colon a \in \mathsf{namesof}_I(\mathsf{Amb}[\kappa])\} \cup \mathsf{namesof}_I(\mathsf{Cap}[\kappa])$ $\mathsf{msgs}_I(\mathsf{Amb}[\kappa]) = \mathsf{namesof}_I(\mathsf{Amb}[\kappa])$ $\mathsf{msgs}_I(\mathsf{Cap}[\kappa]) = \mathsf{namesof}_I(\mathsf{Cap}[\kappa]) \cup \{(\mathsf{moves}_I \cup \mathsf{opens}_I(\kappa))*\}$ $\mathsf{comms}_I(\mathsf{Shh}) = \emptyset \qquad \mathsf{comms}_I(\omega_1 \otimes \cdots \otimes \omega_k) = \{\langle \mu_1, \ldots, \mu_k \rangle \colon \mu_i \in \mathsf{msgs}_I(\omega_i)\} \cup$ $\{(a_1, \ldots, a_k) \colon \Delta^{\mathsf{in}}_I(a_i) = \omega_i\ \&\ (i \neq j \Rightarrow a_i \neq a_j)\}$
Construction of shape predicates: $\{\!\|I\|\!\} = \langle \{\!\|I\|\!\}, \mathsf{nodeof}_I(\kappa_I)\rangle \quad \{\!\|I\|\!\} = \{\chi \xrightarrow{\alpha} \chi \colon \alpha \in \mathsf{allowedin}_I(\mathsf{typeof}_I(\chi))\ \&\ \chi \in \mathsf{nodes}_I\} \cup$ $\{\chi \xrightarrow{a[]} \chi' \colon a \in \mathsf{namesof}_I(\mathsf{Amb}[\mathsf{typeof}_I(\chi')])\ \&\ \chi, \chi' \in \mathsf{nodes}_I\}$

Fig. 9. Construction of POLY✶ type embedding

basic names in I. The set does not depend on κ because in/out capabilities can be executed by any process. The set $\mathsf{opens}_I(\kappa)$ describe open-capabilities which can be executed by a process of the type κ. The second part of $\mathsf{opens}_I(\kappa)$ describes names of the type $\mathsf{Cap}[\kappa]$ which might be instantiated to some executable capabilities. The set $\mathsf{comms}_I(\kappa)$ describes communication actions which can be executed by a process of the type κ. Its first part describes output- and the second input-actions. The auxiliary set $\mathsf{msgs}_I(\omega)$ describes all messages of the type ω constructible from names in I.

Example 9. Relevant sets for our example are:

$$\begin{array}{ll}
\mathsf{namesof}_I(\mathsf{Amb}[\mathbf{1}]) = \{\mathsf{d}, \mathsf{p}\} & \mathsf{opens}_I(\mathbf{1}) = \{\mathsf{open\ d}, \mathsf{open\ p}, \mathsf{x}\} \\
\mathsf{namesof}_I(\mathsf{Cap}[\mathbf{1}]) = \{\mathsf{x}\} & \mathsf{opens}_I(\mathsf{Cap}[\mathbf{1}]) = \emptyset \\
\mathsf{comms}_I(\mathbf{1}) = \{\langle\rangle, ()\} & \mathsf{moves}_I = \{\mathsf{in\ d}, \mathsf{in\ p}, \mathsf{out\ d}, \mathsf{out\ p}\} \\
\multicolumn{2}{l}{\mathsf{comms}_I(\mathsf{Cap}[\mathbf{1}]) = \{\langle \mathsf{x}\rangle, \langle\{\mathsf{in\ d}, \mathsf{in\ p}, \mathsf{out\ d}, \mathsf{out\ p}, \mathsf{open\ d}, \mathsf{open\ p}, \mathsf{x}\}*\rangle, (\mathsf{x})\}}
\end{array}$$

The bottom part of Fig. 9 constructs the shape graph $\{\!\|I\|\!\}$ and the shape predicate $\{\!\|I\|\!\}$ from I. The first part of $\{\!\|I\|\!\}$ describes self-loops of χ which describe actions allowed to be executed by a process of $\mathsf{typeof}_I(\chi)$. The second part of $\{\!\|I\|\!\}$ describe transitions among nodes. Any edge labeled by "a[]" always leads to the node which corresponds to the exchange type allowed inside a.

Example 10. The resulting shape predicate $\langle\!| I |\!\rangle = \langle G, \mathtt{R}\rangle$ in our example is as follows. We merge edges with the same source and destination using "|".

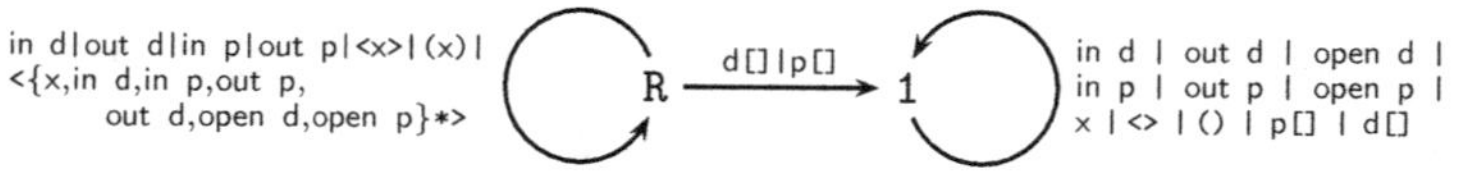

Correctness of the translation is expressed by Thm. 2. The assumptions ensure that no ν-bound name is mentioned by Δ or has a Cap-type assigned by an annotation. Here we just claim that $\langle\!| I |\!\rangle$ is always an $\mathcal{A}$-type.

Theorem 2. *Let* $\mathsf{dom}(\Delta) \cap \mathsf{nbn}(B) = \emptyset$ *and* $\mathsf{dom}(\Delta^{\nu}_{B}) = \mathsf{nbn}(B)$. *Then it holds that* $\Delta \vdash B : \kappa$ *if and only if* $\vdash (\!| B |\!) : \langle\!| (\Delta \cup \Delta^{\nu}_{B}, \Delta^{\mathsf{in}}_{B}, \kappa) |\!\rangle$.

5 Conclusions

We embedded TMA's typing relation in $S_{\mathcal{A}}$ (Sec. 4.4) and showed how to recognize communication safety in $S_{\mathcal{A}}$ directly (Sec. 4.3). The type $\langle\!| I |\!\rangle$ constructed in Sec. 4.4 can also be used to prove the safety of B. But then, it follows from the properties of principal types, that the safety of B can be recognized directly from its principal $\mathcal{A}$-type. Thus any process proved safe by TMA can be proved safe by $S_{\mathcal{A}}$ on its own.

Some processes are recognized safe by $S_{\mathcal{A}}$ but not by TMA. For example, "(x : ω).x.0 | <in a>" is not typable in TMA but it is trivially safe. Another examples show polymorphic abilities of shape types, for example, the $C_{\mathcal{A}}$ process

```
!(x, y, m).x[in y.<m>.0] | <p, a, c>.0 | a[open p.0] | <q, b, in a>.0 | b[open q.0]
```

can be proved safe by POLY★ but it constitutes a challenge for TMA-like non-polymorphic type systems. We are not aware of other type systems for MA and its successors that can handle this kind of polymorphism.

The expressiveness of shape types $\langle\!| I |\!\rangle$ from Sec. 4.4 can be improved. In subsequent work [1], Cardelli, Ghelli, and Gordon define a type system which can ensure that some ambients stay immobile or that their boundaries are never dissolved. This can be achieved easily by removing appropriate self loops of nodes. We can also assign nodes to (groups of) ambients instead of exchange types. This gives us similar possibilities as another TMA successor [2]. Moreover, we can use shape type polymorphism to express location-dependent properties of ambients, like that ambient a can be opened only inside ambient b.

6 Conclusions and Future Work

We discussed already the contributions (Sec. 1.1, 2.5). Conclusions for the embeddings were given separately (Sec. 3.5, 5). Future work is as follows. For extensions, priorities are better handling of choice (e.g., because of its use in biological system modeling), and handling of **rec** which is in many calculi more expressive than replication and better describes recursive behavior. Moreover we would like to generalize actions so that calculi with structured messages, like the Spi calculus [5], can be handled. For applications, we would like to (1) relate shape types with other systems which also use graphs to represent types [18,10], and (2) to study the relationship between shape types and session types [6].

References

1. Cardelli, L., Ghelli, G., Gordon, A.D.: Mobility types for mobile ambients. In: Wiedermann, J., Van Emde Boas, P., Nielsen, M. (eds.) ICALP 1999. LNCS, vol. 1644, pp. 230–239. Springer, Heidelberg (1999)
2. Cardelli, L., Ghelli, G., Gordon, A.D.: Ambient groups and mobility types. In: Watanabe, O., Hagiya, M., Ito, T., van Leeuwen, J., Mosses, P.D. (eds.) TCS 2000. LNCS, vol. 1872, pp. 333–347. Springer, Heidelberg (2000)
3. Cardelli, L., Gordon, A.D.: Mobile ambients. In: Nivat, M. (ed.) FOSSACS 1998. LNCS, vol. 1378, pp. 140–155. Springer, Heidelberg (1998)
4. Cardelli, L., Gordon, A.D.: Types for mobile ambients. In: POPL, pp. 79–92 (1999)
5. Gordon, M.A.D.: A calculus for cryptographic protocols: The spi calculus. Inf. & Comp. 148(1), 1–70 (1999)
6. Honda, K.: Types for dyadic interaction. In: Best, E. (ed.) CONCUR 1993. LNCS, vol. 715, pp. 509–523. Springer, Heidelberg (1993)
7. Igarashi, A., Kobayashi, N.: A generic type system for the pi-calculus. In: POPL, pp. 128–141 (2001)
8. Jakubův, J.: A Second Year Report. Heriot-Watt Univ., MACS (2009), `http://www.macs.hw.ac.uk/~jj36`
9. Jakubův, J., Wells, J.B.: The expressiveness of generic process shape types. Technical Report HW-MACS-TR-0069. Heriot-Watt Univ. (July 2009)
10. König, B.: Generating type systems for process graphs. In: Baeten, J.C.M., Mauw, S. (eds.) CONCUR 1999. LNCS, vol. 1664, pp. 352–367. Springer, Heidelberg (1999)
11. Makholm, H., Wells, J.B.: Instant polymorphic type systems for mobile process calculi: Just add reduction rules and close. Technical Report HW-MACS-TR-0022. Heriot-Watt Univ. (November 2004)
12. Makholm, H., Wells, J.B.: Instant polymorphic type systems for mobile process calculi: Just add reduction rules and close. In: Sagiv, M. (ed.) ESOP 2005. LNCS, vol. 3444, pp. 389–407. Springer, Heidelberg (2005)
13. Milner, R.: Communicating and Mobile Systems: The π-Calculus. Cambridge Press, Cambridge (1999)
14. Milner, R., Parrow, J., Walker, D.: A calculus of mobile processes. Inf. & Comp. 100(1), 1–77 (1992)
15. Nielson, F., Nielson, H.R., Priami, C., Rosa, D.: Control flow analysis for bioambients. ENTCS 180(3), 65–79 (2007)
16. Turner, D.N.: The Polymorphic Pi-Calculus: Theory and Implementation. PhD thesis, Uni. of Edinburgh (1995) Rep. ECS-LFCS-96-345
17. Wells, J.B.: The essence of principal typings. In: Widmayer, P., Triguero, F., Morales, R., Hennessy, M., Eidenbenz, S., Conejo, R. (eds.) ICALP 2002. LNCS, vol. 2380, pp. 913–925. Springer, Heidelberg (2002)
18. Yoshida, N.: Graph types for monadic mobile processes. In: Chandru, V., Vinay, V. (eds.) FSTTCS 1996. LNCS, vol. 1180, pp. 371–386. Springer, Heidelberg (1996)

A Java Inspired Semantics for Transactions in SOC*

Laura Bocchi and Emilio Tuosto

Department of Computer Science, University of Leicester, UK

Abstract. We propose a formal semantics for distributed transactions inspired by the attribute mechanisms of the Java Transaction API. Technically, we model services in a process calculus featuring transactional scope mechanisms borrowed from the so called *container-managed* transactions of Java. We equip our calculus with a type system for our calculus and show that, in well-typed systems, it guarantees absence of run-time errors due to misuse of transactional mechanisms.

1 Introduction

The *Service-Oriented Computing* (SOC) paradigm envisages distributed systems as loosely-coupled computational entities which dynamically discover each other and bind together. Although appealing, SOC has imposed to re-think, among other classic concepts, the notion of transaction. The long lasting and cross-domain nature of SOC makes typically unfeasible to adopt ACID transactions, which are implemented by locking the involved resources. The investigation of formal semantics of SOC transactions (often referred to as long-running transactions) has been a topic of focus in the last few years (see § 6 for a non-exhaustive overview). Central to this investigation is the notion of *compensation* (a weaker and "ad hoc" version of the classic rollback of database systems) which has mainly been studied in relation to mechanisms of failure propagation.

In this paper we address an orthogonal topic, namely the semantics of dynamic reconfiguration of transactions in SOC which, to the best of our knowledge, has not been explicitly considered. In SOC, the configuration of a system can change at each service invocation to include a new instance of the service in the ongoing computation. There is still a lack of agreement on how the run-time reconfiguration should affect the relationships between existing and newly created transactional scopes. To illustrate the main problems, we consider the following example:

$$\langle \texttt{invoke}\ s.P \mid (\!|C|\!) \rangle \qquad \text{with } s \text{ implemented as } Q \tag{1}$$

where a process in a transactional scope (represented by the angled brackets) with compensation C invokes a service s and then behaves like P; the invocation triggers a (possibly remote) instance Q of the service s. Should the system in (1) evolve to a transactional scope that includes Q (i.e., $\langle P \mid Q \mid (\!|C|\!) \rangle$)? Should instead Q be running in a

* This work has been partially sponsored by the project Leverhulme Trust Award "Tracing Networks". The authors also thank Hernan Melgratti for his valuable comments on a preliminary draft of this paper.

M. Wirsing, M. Hofmann, and A. Rauschmayer (Eds.): TGC 2010, LNCS 6084, pp. 120–134, 2010.

different scope (i.e., $\langle P \mid (\!|C|\!) \rangle \mid \langle Q \rangle$)? Or should Q be executed outside any transactional scope (i.e., $\langle P \mid (\!|C|\!) \rangle \mid Q$) or else raise an exception triggering the compensation C? Notice that each alternative is valid and has an impact on failure propagation.

Enterprise Java Beans (EJB) promote *Container Managed Transactions* (CMT) as a mechanism to control dynamic reconfigurations. We take inspiration from the EJB mechanism and adapt it to SOC transactions. A *container* can be used to publish objects and can specify:

- the transactional modality of method calls (e.g., "*calling the method* `fooBar` *from outside a transactional scope throws an exception*"),
- how the scope of transactions dynamically reconfigure (e.g., "`fooBar` *is always executed in a newly created transactional scope*").

A limitation of CMT is that it only permits to declare transactional modalities for the methods to be invoked and does not allow invokers to specify their own requirements on the needed transactional support. On the contrary service invocations are resolved at run-time and different providers may publish different implementations of a service. Hence, it is natural to give the invoker the opportunity to express some requirements on the transactional behaviour of the invoked services. For instance, in (1) the invocation to s may require that Q must be executed in the same transactional scope of P.

We do not aim to provide a semantics for CMT but rather investigate how CMT could be borrowed to address the issues described above for SOC transactions. We promote some CMT inspired primitives for SOC which allow invokers (and not just callees) to specify their own transactional requirements. Furthermore, we give a typing discipline to ensure that invocations do not yield run-time errors due to the incompatibility of the transactional modalities required by callers and those guaranteed by callees.

Our main contributions are

1. a semantics to specify dynamic reconfiguration of SOC transactions inspired by the CMT mechanisms of EJB; namely, we introduce a CCS-like process calculus called ATc (after *Attribute-based Transactional calculus*)
2. a type system that guarantees that no error will occur for a method invocation due to the incompatibility of the transactional scopes of caller and callee
3. a methodology for designing SOC transactions based on our typing discipline.

Synopsis. The transactional mechanisms of EJB are summarised in § 2. The syntax and semantics of ATc are introduced in § 3. The typing discipline of ATc is in § 4. In § 5 we give a gist of how our type system can be used to design systems correct wrt dynamic reconfigurations of transactions. Conclusions and related work are discussed in § 6.

2 EJB Transactional Attributes

Roughly, a *Java bean* can be thought of as on object amenable to be executed in a specialised run-time environment called *container* (see e.g., [19,18]). An EJB container supports typical functionalities to manage e.g. the life-cycle of a bean and to make components accessible to other components by binding it to a naming service[1].

[1] `http://docs.sun.com/app/docs/doc/819-3658/ablmw?a=view`

For the sake of this paper, we focus on the transactional mechanisms offered by EJB-containers. Specifically, we consider *Container Managed Transactions* (CMT) whereby a container associates each method of a bean with a *transactional attribute* specifying the modality of reconfiguring transactional scopes. We denote the set of EJB transactional attributes as

$$\text{(EJB Transactional Attributes)} \qquad \mathcal{A} \stackrel{def}{=} \{\mathtt{m}, \mathtt{s}, \mathtt{n}, \mathtt{ns}, \mathtt{r}, \mathtt{rn}\}$$

where, following the EJB terminology, m stands for *mandatory*, s for *supported*, n for *never*, ns for *not supported*, r for *requires*, and rn for *requires new*.

The intuitive semantics of EJB attributes $\mathcal{A}$ (ranged over by $a, a_1, a_2, \ldots$) is illustrated in Figure 1 where each row represents the behaviour of one transactional attribute and shows how the transactional scope (represented by a rectangular box) of the caller (represented by a filled circle) and callee (represented by an empty circle) behave upon invocation. The first two columns of Figure 1 represent, respectively, invocations from outside and from within a transactional scope. More precisely, (1) a callee supporting r is always executed in a transactional scope which happens to be the same as the caller's if the latter is already running in a transactional scope; (2) a callee supporting rn is always executed in a new transactional scope; (3) a callee supporting ns is always executed outside a transactional scope; (4) the invocation to a method supporting m fails if the caller is not in a transactional scope (first column of the fourth row in Figure 1), otherwise the method is executed in the transactional scope of the caller; (5) the invocation to a method supporting n is successful only if the caller is outside a transactional scope, and it fails if the caller is running in a transactional scope (in this case an exception is triggered in the caller); (6) a method supporting s is executed inside (resp. outside) the caller's scope if the caller is executing in (resp. outside) a scope.

In this paper, we adapt the transactional model of EJB to the context of SOC, where each provider can be thought of as a container specifying a number of services together with their transactional attribute. A transactional attribute declares whether a published service must or must not be executed within a transactional scope and the modality of

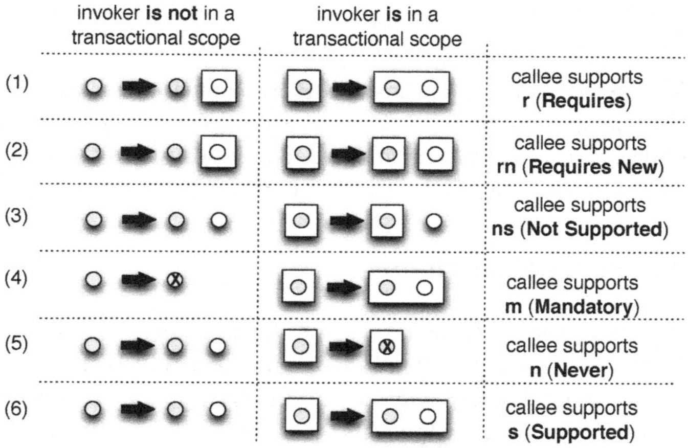

Fig. 1. EJB transactional attributes synopsis

dynamic reconfiguration of the transactional scope (e.g., whether a new scope has to be created, how the scope of the invoking party has to be extended, etc.). We formally model the behaviour illustrated in Figure 1 by embedding EJB attributes in a simple process calculus to give a general model for SOC[2]. Hereafter, according to this interpretation, the terms *service provider* and *container* will be used interchangeably.

3 Attribute-Based Transaction Calculus (ATc)

The ATc calculus is built on top of two layers; *processes* (§ 3.1) and *systems* (§ 3.2). The former specify how communication takes place in presence of (nested) transactional scopes while the latter provide a formal framework for defining and invoking transactional services and the run-time reconfiguration of the transactional scopes.

3.1 ATc Processes

An ATc process is a CCS-like process with three additional capabilities: *service invocation, transactional scope*, and *compensation installation*. Let $\mathcal{S}$ and $\mathcal{N}$ be two countably infinite and disjoint sets of names for *service* and *channel*, respectively.

Definition 1. *The set* ATc processes $\mathcal{P}$ *is defined by following grammar:*

$$
\begin{array}{rlll}
P, Q ::= & 0 & \textit{empty process} & \pi ::= x \quad \textit{input} \\
\mid & \nu x\, P & \textit{channel restriction} & \quad\mid \overline{x} \quad \textit{output} \\
\mid & P \mid Q & \textit{parallel} & \\
\mid & !P & \textit{replication} & A \subseteq \mathcal{A} \\
\mid & s \leftharpoondown A.P & \textit{service invocation} & s, s', \ldots \textit{ range over } \mathcal{S} \\
\mid & \langle P \mid (\!|Q|\!) \rangle & \textit{transactional scope} & x, y, z, \ldots \textit{ range over } \mathcal{N} \\
\mid & \pi[\![Q]\!].P & \textit{compensation installation} & u \textit{ ranges over } \mathcal{S} \cup \mathcal{N}
\end{array}
$$

Restriction $\nu x\, P$ *binds* x *in* P *and the sets of* free *and* bound *channels of* $P \in \mathcal{P}$ *are defined as usual and respectively denoted by* $\mathsf{fc}(P)$ *and* $\mathsf{bc}(P)$*. Finally, we assume* $\pi = \overline{\overline{\pi}}$.

The standard process algebraic syntax is adopted for idle process, restriction, parallel composition, and replication. Process $s \leftharpoondown A.P$ invokes a service s required to support a transactional attributes in $A \subseteq \mathcal{A}$; a transactional scope $\langle P \mid (\!|Q|\!) \rangle$ consists of a running process P and a compensation Q (confined in the scope) executed only upon failure; $\pi[\![Q]\!].P$ executes π and installs the compensation Q in the enclosing transactional scope then behaves as P. Service definition and invocation are dealt with in § 3.2.

Definition 2. *The* structural congruence $\equiv \subseteq \mathcal{P} \times \mathcal{P}$*, is the smallest equivalence relation containing α-renaming, the monoidal axioms for* $\mid$ *and* 0*, and satisfying:*

$$
!P \mid P \equiv !P \quad \langle 0 \mid (\!|Q|\!) \rangle \equiv 0 \equiv (\!|0|\!) \quad (\!|P|\!) \mid (\!|Q|\!) \equiv (\!|P \mid Q|\!)
$$

$$
\textit{if } P \equiv Q \textit{ then } \langle P \rangle \equiv \langle Q \rangle \textit{ and } (\!|P|\!) \equiv (\!|Q|\!)
$$

$$
\nu x\, \langle P \rangle \equiv \langle \nu x\, P \rangle \quad \nu x\, \nu y\, P \equiv \nu y\, \nu x\, P \quad \nu x\, 0 \equiv 0 \quad \nu x\, (P \mid Q) \equiv (\nu x\, P) \mid Q, \textit{ if } x \notin \mathsf{fc}(Q)
$$

Hereafter, $\pi.P$ *stands for* $\pi[\![Q]\!].P$ *when* $Q \equiv 0$ *and trailing occurrences of* 0 *are omitted.*

[2] We refer to the service-oriented paradigm in a technology-agnostic way, abstracting from its actual realisations (e.g., the Web Service Architecture).

In ATc, transactional scopes can be nested up to an arbitrary level. The fact that a process is inside a transactional scope does not alter its communication capabilities, since we assume that transactional scopes influence the behaviour of processes only in case of failure. To model the semantics of communications we use *contexts*[3].

Definition 3. *A* context *is a term generated by the following productions:*

$$C[\_] ::= \_ \;\big|\; 0 \;\big|\; \langle \_ \mid P \mid \llparenthesis Q \rrparenthesis \rangle \;\big|\; P \mid C[\_] \;\big|\; C[\_] \mid P$$

A context $C[\_]$ *is* scope-avoiding *if there are no* $P, Q \in \mathcal{P}$ *and context* $C'[\_]$ *such that* $C[\_] = C'[\langle \_ \mid P \mid \llparenthesis Q \rrparenthesis \rangle]$.

Definition 3 does not consider $\nu x\ C[\_]$ to avoid name capture while prefix contexts $\alpha.C[\_]$ (where α is either of the prefixes of ATc) are ruled out as they prevent inner reductions. The semantics of ATc is defined by means of two reduction relations, one (Definition 4) for process communication and the other (Definition 6) for service invocations (and, correspondingly, reconfigurations of transactional scopes).

Definition 4. *The* reduction relation of ATc processes *is the smallest relation* $\rightarrow \subseteq \mathcal{P} \times \mathcal{P}$ *closed under the following axioms and rules:*

$$C[\langle \pi\llbracket Q \rrbracket.P \mid \llparenthesis R \rrparenthesis \rangle] \mid C'[\langle \bar{\pi}\llbracket Q' \rrbracket.P' \mid \llparenthesis R' \rrparenthesis \rangle] \rightarrow C[\langle P \mid \llparenthesis R \mid Q \rrparenthesis \rangle] \mid C'[\langle P' \mid \llparenthesis R' \mid Q' \rrparenthesis \rangle]$$

$$C[\langle \pi\llbracket Q \rrbracket.P \mid \llparenthesis R \rrparenthesis \rangle] \mid C'[\bar{\pi}\llbracket Q' \rrbracket.P'] \rightarrow C[\langle P \mid \llparenthesis R \mid Q \rrparenthesis \rangle] \mid C'[P'], \quad \text{if } C'[\_] \text{ is scope-avoiding}$$

$$C[\pi\llbracket Q \rrbracket.P] \mid C'[\bar{\pi}\llbracket Q' \rrbracket.P'] \rightarrow C[P] \mid C'[P'], \quad \text{if } C[\_] \text{ and } C'[\_] \text{ are scope-avoiding}$$

$$\frac{P \rightarrow P'}{P \mid R \rightarrow P' \mid R} \qquad \frac{P \rightarrow P'}{\nu x\, P \rightarrow \nu x\, P'} \qquad \frac{P \equiv P' \rightarrow Q' \equiv Q}{P \rightarrow Q}$$

Notice that sender and receiver synchronise regardless the relative nesting of transactional scopes. As in [12], when communication actions are executed compensations are installed in parallel to the other compensations of the enclosing transactional scope if any, otherwise they are discarded. In case of failure, only the actions executed before the failure are compensated, as illustrated by Example 1.

Example 1. Consider the transactional scope $P_{\text{bookNight}} = \langle P_{\text{theatre}} \mid P_{\text{dinner}} \rangle$ where:

$$P_{\text{theatre}} = \overline{\text{askSeat}}.\text{getSeat}.\overline{\text{pay}}\llbracket \overline{\text{getRefund}} \rrbracket \qquad P_{\text{dinner}} = \overline{\text{askTable}}.\text{getTable}.\overline{\text{confirm}}\llbracket \overline{\text{freeTable}} \rrbracket$$

Action $\overline{\text{getRefund}}$ compensates $\overline{\text{pay}}$ and action $\overline{\text{freeTable}}$ compensates $\overline{\text{confirm}}$. The process dynamically installs the compensations of its actions. The two executions show that different compensations may be executed in case of failure.

$$\langle P_{\text{theatre}} \mid P_{\text{dinner}} \rangle \rightarrow^{*} \langle \text{getTable}.\overline{\text{confirm}}\llbracket \overline{\text{freeTable}} \rrbracket \mid \llparenthesis \overline{\text{getRefund}} \rrparenthesis \rangle \rightarrow^{*} \langle 0 \mid \llparenthesis \overline{\text{freeTable}} \mid \overline{\text{getRefund}} \rrparenthesis \rangle$$

$$\langle P_{\text{theatre}} \mid P_{\text{dinner}} \rangle \rightarrow^{*} \langle \text{getSeat}.\overline{\text{pay}}\llbracket \overline{\text{getRefund}} \rrbracket \mid \llparenthesis \overline{\text{freeTable}} \rrparenthesis \rangle \rightarrow^{*} \langle 0 \mid \llparenthesis \overline{\text{freeTable}} \mid \overline{\text{getRefund}} \rrparenthesis \rangle$$

◇

[3] Other and more standard techniques could have been used (e.g., LTS); however, contexts enable us to easily define the semantics of communication and service invocation of ATc.

3.2 ATc Systems

The semantics of transactional scoping of service invocations is given at the level of *systems* (Definition 5). Systems can be thought of as an abstraction for EJB and consist of processes wrapped by *containers* defined as a partial finite maps $\gamma : \mathcal{S} \to \mathcal{A} \times \mathcal{P}$; containers assign a transactional attribute and a process (the "body") to service names. When defined, $\gamma(s) = (a, P)$ ensures that, if invoked in γ, the service s supports the attribute a and activates an end-point that executes as P.

Definition 5. *A* system *in ATc is a pair $\Gamma \vdash P$ where the* environment *Γ is a set of containers and is derived by the productions in Definition 1 augmented with $P ::= \mathtt{err}$ to represent* erroneous processes. *Also, the following axioms*

$$!\mathtt{err} \equiv \mathtt{err} \qquad \nu x\ \mathtt{err} \equiv \mathtt{err} \qquad \langle \mathtt{err} \mid (\!| Q |\!) \rangle \equiv \mathtt{err}$$

extend the congruence relation to erroneous processes.

Given $A \subseteq \mathcal{A}$, $P \in \Gamma(s, A)$ shortens $\exists \gamma \in \Gamma\ \exists a \in A\ :\ \gamma(s) = (a, P)$ and $P \in \Gamma(s, \{a\})$ is abbreviated as $P \in \Gamma(s, a)$. Hereafter, we use P, Q to range over both $\mathcal{P}$ and erroneous processes. We rule out terms where compensations contain err; basically, err represent a run-time error and cannot be used by the programmer. A service invocation is *transactional* (resp. *non-transactional*) if it is (resp. not) executed a transaction scope.

Definition 6 formalises the informal presentation in Figure 1 of the CMT mechanisms which are rendered in SOC by allowing environments Γ to offer different implementations of the same service possibly with different attributes. This results in a non-deterministic semantics where one of several possible reductions is chosen.

Definition 6. *The* reduction relation of ATc systems *is the smallest relation $\rightsquigarrow$ closed under the following rule and axioms of Figure 2 where $C[\_] \neq 0$ and $C[\_]$ is scope avoiding in* (ntx1 ÷ 3).

Axioms (ntx1÷3) rule non-transactional invocations; (ntx1) states that an invocation results in an error when a service supporting attribute m is required[4]; when a non-transactional invocation is made to a service supporting either s, or n, or ns, by (ntx2), the end-point of the service is executed in parallel with the continuation of the caller; finally by (ntx3), the end-point of a service supporting r or rn will be executed in a new scope (initially with idle compensation).

Axioms (tx1÷4) determine how transactional invocations modify the scope; by (tx1), the end-point of the service is executed in the same scope of the caller when the requested attribute is m, s, or r; instead by (tx2), transactional invocations to a service supporting n yields a failure which triggers the compensation of the caller; by (tx3) a transactional invocation requesting ns will let the service end-point to run outside the

[4] Axiom (ntx1) may seem odd as it introduces an error even if Γ may offer a service supporting other attributes in A. An actual implementation may in fact select more suitable services with an appropriate negotiation in the search phase. Here, more simply, we define the conditions to correctly use attributes avoiding errors in *any* possible environment; therefore (ntx1) models the worst case scenario. As shows in § 4, in well-typed processes, invocations requiring m never occur in scope-avoiding contexts.

(ntx1) $\Gamma \vdash C[s \Leftarrow A.P] \rightsquigarrow \Gamma \vdash C[\mathtt{err}]$ $\mathtt{m} \in A$

(ntx2) $\Gamma \vdash C[s \Leftarrow A.P] \rightsquigarrow \Gamma \vdash C[P] \mid R$ $R \in \Gamma(s, \{\mathtt{s}, \mathtt{n}, \mathtt{ns}\} \cap A)$

(ntx3) $\Gamma \vdash C[s \Leftarrow A.P] \rightsquigarrow \Gamma \vdash C[P] \mid \langle R \rangle$ $R \in \Gamma(s, \{\mathtt{r}, \mathtt{rn}\} \cap A)$

(tx1) $\dfrac{P = C[\langle s \Leftarrow A.P_1 \mid P_2 \mid (\!|Q|\!) \rangle] \qquad \mathsf{bc}(P) \cap \mathsf{fc}(R) = \emptyset}{\Gamma \vdash P \rightsquigarrow \Gamma \vdash C[\langle P_1 \mid P_2 \mid R \mid (\!|Q|\!) \rangle]}$ $R \in \Gamma(s, \{\mathtt{m}, \mathtt{s}, \mathtt{r}\} \cap A)$

(tx2) $\Gamma \vdash C[\langle s \Leftarrow A.P_1 \mid P_2 \mid (\!|Q|\!) \rangle] \rightsquigarrow \Gamma \vdash C[Q]$ $\mathtt{n} \in A$

(tx3) $\Gamma \vdash C[\langle s \Leftarrow A.P_1 \mid P_2 \mid (\!|Q|\!) \rangle] \rightsquigarrow \Gamma \vdash C[\langle P_1 \mid P_2 \mid (\!|Q|\!) \rangle] \mid R$ $\mathtt{ns} \in A \land R \in \Gamma(s, \mathtt{ns})$

(tx4) $\Gamma \vdash C[\langle s \Leftarrow A.P_1 \mid P_2 \mid (\!|Q|\!) \rangle] \rightsquigarrow \Gamma \vdash C[\langle P_1 \mid P_2 \mid (\!|Q|\!) \rangle] \mid \langle R \rangle$ $\mathtt{rn} \in A \land R \in \Gamma(s, \mathtt{rn})$

(s-p) $\dfrac{P \to P'}{\Gamma \vdash P \rightsquigarrow \Gamma \vdash P'}$

Fig. 2. Semantics of ATc

caller's scope; finally, (tx4) states that a transactional invocation requesting rn will let the service end-point to run in a new scope with idle compensation.

Rule (s-p) lifts process reduction relation to systems.

Communication failures occurring within transactional scopes trigger compensations while those occurring outside result in an error. Formally, this can be achieved by adding to Definition 6 the axioms

$$C[\langle \pi[\![Q]\!].P \mid (\!|R|\!) \rangle] \to C[Q] \quad \text{and} \quad C[\pi[\![Q]\!].P] \to C[\mathtt{err}], \text{ if } C[\_] \text{ is scope avoiding} \quad (2)$$

For simplicity, we gloss over this point in order to focus on failures due to misuse of transactional attributes and scope reconfigurations. We are currently working on a semantics of communication failures for ATc systems briefly outlined in § 6. The semantics of failures is based on the notion of testing equivalence [10] (see [5] for an extended report of this paper including further details).

3.3 Some Examples of Failing Invocations

The following examples motivate the need of a disciplined use of transactional attributes. The typing system presented in § 4 ensures that a well-typed process will incur in errors due to the fact that the attributes required by an invoker do not match those guaranteed by the service.

Example 2. Let $P_{\text{bookTheatre}} = \langle s_{\text{tickets}} \Leftarrow \{\mathtt{m}\}.P_{\text{theatre}} \mid (\!| s_{\text{compensate}} \Leftarrow \{\mathtt{m}\} |\!) \rangle$ be a process that invokes s_{tickets} and behaves as $P_{\text{theatre}} = \text{askSeat}.\text{getSeat}.\overline{\text{pay}}[\![\overline{\text{getRefund}}]\!]$. If a communication of P_{theatre} fails (i.e., the left-most axiom in (2) is applied), then the compensation is executed outside a transactional scope. Therefore, the non-transactional invocation to $s_{\text{compensate}}$ will result in an error. ◇

Example 3. Let P_{theatre} as in Example 2 and consider

$$P_{\text{bookTheatre}} = s_{\text{tickets}} \,\&\!\!- \{\mathtt{m}, \mathtt{s}, \mathtt{n}, \mathtt{ns}, \mathtt{r}, \mathtt{rn}\}.P_{\text{theatre}} \qquad P_{\text{tickets}} = \text{askSeats}.\overline{\text{getSeats}}.s_{\text{bank}} \,\&\!\!- \{\mathtt{m}\}$$

The non-transactional invocation s_{tickets} in a Γ for which $P_{\text{tickets}} \in \Gamma(s_{\text{tickets}}, \mathtt{s})$ causes P_{tickets} to run outside a transactional scope; hence, invoking s_{bank} leads to an error. ◇

A provider must guarantee that none of its services yield errors; namely, the execution of (the body of) a service in any context resulting from its supported attributes should be safe. For instance, since s_{tickets} in Example 3 supports $\mathtt{s}$, the execution P_{tickets} should be safe regardless it will run inside or outside a transactional scope. In fact, whether or not P_{tickets} will be running in a scope depends on the caller.

4 A Type System for Transactional Services

This section yields a type system for ATc that can determine if a system may fail for a service invocation due to misuse of the transactional attributes. We give an algebra of types (§ 4.1), then define a type system for ATc (§ 4.2), and finally we give a suitable notion of well-typedness for ATc systems (§ 4.3) which is preserved by the reduction relation (Theorem 1) and ensures error-freedom (Corollary 1). All the proofs are reported in [5].

4.1 Types for ATc

Our types record which transactional attributes may be required/supported in service invocations of processes. Basically, for each possible invocation, a type specifies if it is transactional or not and which transactional attributes are declared for the invocation.

Definition 7. *Let $I \subseteq \{\mathtt{i}, \mathtt{o}\} \times \mathcal{A}$ where labels* $\mathtt{i}$ *and* $\mathtt{o}$ *are the* transactional modalities *used to keep track of transactional and non-transactional invocations, respectively. Types are defined as*

$$(Types) \quad t ::= \mathsf{0} \;\big|\; (I, t, t)$$

Let $P \triangleright t$ state that $P \in \mathcal{P}$ has type t. If $P \triangleright \mathsf{0}$ then P does not make any invocations; if $P \triangleright (I, t_c, t_u)$,

- I records the transactional modality/attribute pairs of the service invocations of P;
- t_c collects the transactional modality/attribute pairs relative to the service invocations in the compensations of the transactional scopes of P;
- t_u yields modality/attribute pairs for the invocations in the compensation installation prefixes[5] of P;

Example 4. Consider $P_2 = s \,\&\!\!- A.y[\![P_1]\!]$ with $P_1 \triangleright t_1$. As more clear in § 4.2, $P_2 \triangleright t_2 = (\{\mathtt{o}\} \times A, \mathsf{0}, t_1)$. In fact, the invocation in P_2 is non-transactional and the third component of t_2 is t_1 as P_1 is used to compensate prefix y. ◇

Types of processes become more complex in presence of nested scopes.

[5] By Definition 6 compensations vanish for synchronisations outside transactional scopes.

Example 5. Take the process $P_3 = \langle P_2 \mid (\!| s' \,\&\!\!-\, A' |\!) \rangle \mid \langle\langle P_2 \mid (\!| s' \,\&\!\!-\, A'' |\!)\rangle\rangle$, where P_2 is defined in Example 4. The type of P_3 is

$$t_3 = (\{\mathtt{i}\} \times (A \cup A''), (\{\mathtt{o}\} \times A', 0, 0), 0)$$

In fact, the invocations in P_2 and in the nested compensation in the rightmost scope of P_3 will be transactional; therefore the first component of t_3 is $\{\mathtt{i}\} \times (A \cup A'')$. Moreover, the leftmost scope of P_3 may possibly have a non-transactional invocation (thereby the second component of t_3). ◇

The next example illustrates the installation of a non-trivial compensation.

Example 6. The type of $P_4 = \bar{z}[\![s_1 \,\&\!\!-\, A_1]\!].\langle \bar{z}[\![s_1 \,\&\!\!-\, A_1]\!] \mid (\!| s_2 \,\&\!\!-\, A_2.z[\![s_3 \,\&\!\!-\, A_3]\!] |\!)\rangle$ is

$$t_4 = (0, (\{\mathtt{o}\} \times (A_1 \cup A_2), 0, \{\mathtt{o}\} \times A_3), \{\mathtt{o}\} \times A_1)$$

In fact, P_4 does not invoke services but installs compensations that do so. Observe that the third component of t_4 corresponds to the first installation of P_4, while the second component of t_4 is the type of the scope occurring in P_4. ◇

It is convenient to treat types as binary trees whose nodes are labelled with subsets of $\{\mathtt{i}, \mathtt{o}\} \times \mathcal{A}$. More precisely, the type (I, t_c, t_u) can be represented as a tree where the root is labelled I, t_c is the left child, and t_u is the right child (0 is the empty tree which is conventionally labelled with the empty set). The operators $\_^{\&\!-}$, $\_^{\downarrow}$, and $\_^{?}$ are used to "traverse" types and $\_ \oplus \_$ to "sum" them as per the following definitions:

$$0^{\&\!-} = \emptyset, \qquad 0^{\downarrow} = 0^{?} = 0 \qquad (I, t_c, t_u)^{\&\!-} = I, \qquad (I, t_c, t_u)^{\downarrow} = t_c, \qquad (I, t_c, t_u)^{?} = t_u$$

$$0 \oplus t = t, \qquad (I, t_c, t_u) \oplus (I', t'_c, t'_u) = (I \cup I', t_c \oplus t'_c, t_u \oplus t'_u)$$

We assume that $\_ \oplus \_$ has lower precedence than unary operators.

Propositions 1 and 2 will be tacitly used in the proofs of the lemmas and Theorem 1.

Proposition 1. *The operator $\_ \oplus \_$ is idempotent, associative and commutative.*

Proposition 2. *Operators $\_^{\&\!-}$, $\_^{\downarrow}$, and $\_^{?}$ distribute over $\_ \oplus \_$ and $(t_1 \oplus t_2)^{\&\!-} = t_1{}^{\&\!-} \cup t_2{}^{\&\!-}$.*

4.2 Typing ATc

This section introduces a typing system for ATc. We recall that the ATc programmer has to write non-erroneous processes for which we give the following typing rules.

Definition 8. *The typing rules for non-erroneous processes (cf. Definition 5) are*

$$\texttt{(idle)}\frac{}{0 \triangleright 0} \qquad \texttt{(res)}\frac{P \triangleright t}{\nu x\, P \triangleright t} \qquad \frac{P \triangleright t \qquad P' \triangleright t'}{P \mid P' \triangleright t \oplus t'}\texttt{(par)} \qquad \frac{P \triangleright t}{!P \triangleright t}\texttt{(repl)}$$

$$\texttt{(inv)}\frac{P \triangleright t_p \qquad I = \{\mathtt{o}\} \times A}{s \,\&\!\!-\, A.P \triangleright (I \cup t_p{}^{\&\!-}, t_p{}^{\downarrow}, t_p{}^{?})} \qquad \frac{P \triangleright t_p \qquad Q \triangleright t_q}{\pi[\![Q]\!].P \triangleright (t_p{}^{\&\!-}, t_p{}^{\downarrow}, t_q \oplus t_p{}^{?})}\texttt{(comp)}$$

$$\texttt{(scope}_1\texttt{)}\frac{P \triangleright (I, t_c, t_u) \qquad Q \triangleright t_q}{\langle P \mid (\!|Q|\!)\rangle \triangleright ((I \cup t_c{}^{\&\!-})[\![\mathtt{o} \mapsto \mathtt{i}]\!], t_u \oplus t_c{}^{\downarrow} \oplus t_c{}^{?} \oplus t_q, 0)} \qquad \frac{P \triangleright 0}{\langle P \mid (\!|Q|\!)\rangle \triangleright 0}\texttt{(scope}_2\texttt{)}$$

where, for $I \subset \{\mathtt{i}, \mathtt{o}\} \times \mathcal{A}$, $I[\![\mathtt{o} \mapsto \mathtt{i}]\!] \stackrel{def}{=} \{(\mathtt{i}, a) : (\mathtt{o}, a) \in I\} \cup (I \cap \{\mathtt{i}\} \times \mathcal{A})$.

The first five rules are straightforward. Rule (comp) states that the type of the installation of a compensation Q records the invocations in Q as possible invocations of P by adding them to the third component of the type of $\pi[\![Q]\!].P$. The last two rules regulate the typing of transactional scopes. By rule (scope$_1$), when P is in a transactional scope the invocations done by the compensations installed by P (recorded in t_u) become possible; therefore they are removed from the third component and added to the second component with the compensations nested in P (recorded in $t_c{}^{\downarrow}$ and $t_c{}^{?}$) and to those of Q (recorded in t_q). Also, $t_c{}^{\&}$ records the invocation of the compensation of P when P is itself defined s a transactional scope (e.g., $P = \langle Q \mid (\!|C|\!) \rangle$); in this case the compensations of P will be surely executed inside a transactional scope thus they are included in the first component with the substitution $[\![\mathtt{o} \mapsto \mathtt{i}]\!]$. A transactional scope whose process does not invoke/install anything is simply typed as 0 by rule (scope$_2$).

Example 7. Consider the process $P = \pi_1[\![Q]\!]$ where

$$Q = \pi_2[\![R]\!] \qquad \text{and} \qquad R = s_1 \,\&\!- A_1.\pi_3[\![s_2 \,\&\!- A_2]\!]$$

The typing of P is $t = (0, 0, (0, 0, (I_1, 0, I_2)))$ as proved by the type inference below.

$$
\dfrac{
 \dfrac{
  \dfrac{
   \dfrac{
    \dfrac{I_2 = \{\mathtt{o}\} \times A_2 \qquad 0 \triangleright 0}{s_2 \,\&\!- A_2 \triangleright (I_2, 0, 0)}\,(\mathtt{inv}) \qquad 0 \triangleright 0
   }{\pi_3[\![s_2 \,\&\!- A_2]\!] \triangleright (0, 0, I_2)}\,(\mathtt{Comp}) \qquad I_1 = \{\mathtt{o}\} \times A_1
  }{s_1 \,\&\!- A_1.\pi_3[\![s_2 \,\&\!- A_2]\!] \triangleright (I_1, 0, I_2)}\,(\mathtt{inv}) \qquad 0 \triangleright 0
 }{\pi_2[\![R]\!] \triangleright (0, 0, (I_1, 0, I_2))}\,(\mathtt{Comp}) \qquad 0 \triangleright 0
}{\pi_1[\![Q]\!] \triangleright (0, 0, (0, 0, (I_1, 0, I_2)))}\,(\mathtt{Comp})
$$

◇

Proposition 3. *For each non-erroneous $P \in \mathcal{P}$ there is a unique type t such that $P \triangleright t$.*

Proposition 4. *For any non-erroneous $P, Q \in \mathcal{P}$, if $P \equiv Q$ and $P \triangleright t$ then $Q \triangleright t$.*

Definition 9. *Let t be a type. The* flat type $\widehat{t}$ *of t is defined as follows:*

$$\widehat{0} = \emptyset \qquad \widehat{t} = t^{\&} \cup \textsc{Flatten}(t^{\downarrow}), \ \textit{if } t \neq 0$$

$$\textsc{Flatten}(0) = \emptyset \qquad \textsc{Flatten}(t) = t^{\&} \cup \textsc{Flatten}(t^{\downarrow}) \cup \textsc{Flatten}(t^{?}), \ \textit{if } t \neq 0$$

Notice that $\widehat{t_1 \oplus t_2} = \widehat{t_1} \cup \widehat{t_2}$. In the interpretation of t as a tree, the flat type of t is the union of the set labelling all the nodes of t, excluding those of the subtree $t^{?}$ which corresponds to dead code (cf. Example 8); in other words, either the typed process is outside a scope (in which case its pending compensations can be ignored) or the typed process is inside a scope (hence $t^{?}$ is empty because of rule (Scope1)).

4.3 Well-Typedness in ATc

The definition of well-typedness requires some care. In ATc, invocations to services can be statically typed as transactional or not. However, there is a different notion of well-typedness to adopt for services.

If P is not published as a service then it is possible to determine the nature of the service invocations of P by inspecting its code. Therefore, it suffices to specify, for each service invocation, the attributes for which no run-time errors are possible. This enables us to adopt the following definition.

Definition 10. *Let $P \in \mathcal{P}$ such that $P \triangleright t$. The process P is* well-typed *iff* $(\mathtt{o}, \mathtt{m}) \notin \widehat{t}$.

Example 8. Process P in Example 7 is (trivially) well-typed since $\widehat{t} = \emptyset$. In fact, the only service invocations of P are in the compensations to install (that are dead code since P is not included in any transactional scope). ◇

Correctness depends on the (correctness of the) services invoked by a process. Remarkably, the fact that the invoked service is well-typed could be guaranteed by the service provider (as part of the service interface) and required as an obligation by the service requester in the service discovery phase. Namely, negotiation of transactional attributes should be part of the "contract" between requester and provider. The study of the mechanisms used to require/negotiate/certify transactional aspects of published services is out of the our scopes. However, our type system provides an effective framework to certify compatibility of transactional aspects between services and invokers.

Ensuring correctness for services is a bit more complex. Whether or not the invocations in the body of (the end-point of) a service, say s, are transactional depends on which attribute s supports and if the invocation to s happened from within or outside a transactional scope. Therefore, well-typedness of services takes into account both cases.

Definition 11. *Let γ be a container and s be a service such that $\gamma(s) = (a, P)$ for some $a \in \mathcal{A}$ and $P \in \mathcal{P}$. Service s is* well-typed *in γ, if both (3) and (4) below hold.*

$$\langle P \rangle \triangleright t \wedge a \in \{\mathtt{r}, \mathtt{rn}, \mathtt{m}, \mathtt{s}\} \implies (\mathtt{o}, \mathtt{m}) \notin \widehat{t} \tag{3}$$

$$P \triangleright t \wedge a \in \{\mathtt{s}, \mathtt{n}, \mathtt{ns}\} \implies (\mathtt{o}, \mathtt{m}) \notin \widehat{t} \tag{4}$$

An environment Γ is well-typed *iff all the services in the domain of any $\gamma \in \Gamma$ are well-typed.*

We only consider the errors generated by the invocation of a service when attributes and transactional scopes mismatch. Errors due to other causes (e.g., failure of a communication channel) have been modelled in [5] by introducing *observers*, namely processes which can interfere in communications.

Example 9. Let the process P in Example 7 be the body of a service s supporting $\mathtt{s} \in \mathcal{A}$. Both the well-typedness of P and of $\langle P \rangle$ must be checked. As argued in Example 8, P is well-typed while for $\langle P \rangle$ we just need to apply rule (Scope1) as follows:

$$\frac{\pi_1 [\![Q]\!] \triangleright (0, 0, (0, 0, (I_1, 0, I_2))) \qquad 0 \triangleright 0}{\langle \pi_1 [\![Q]\!] \mid (\!|0|\!) \rangle \triangleright (0, (0, 0, (I_1, 0, I_2)), 0)} \ \mathtt{(Scope1)}$$

Clearly, well-typedness of $\langle P \rangle$ depends on whether $(\mathtt{o}, \mathtt{m}) \in I_1 \cup I_2$ or not. ◇

Theorem 1. *Let $P \in \mathcal{P}$ be well-typed. For every well-typed environment Γ, if $\Gamma \vdash P \leadsto \Gamma \vdash Q$ then Q is well-typed.*

A straightforward corollary of Theorem 1 is

Corollary 1. *If Γ and $P \in \mathcal{P}$ are well-typed and $\Gamma \vdash P \leadsto \Gamma \vdash Q$ then Q is a non-erroneous process.*

Our notion of well-typedness is stricter than necessary. In fact, a weaker notion can be adopted by taking a definition of flat type where the labels of some of the 'right children' of types are not considered. Though yielding less restrictive types, this would make the theory more complex, therefore we opted for simplicity rather than generality.

5 ATc Type System at Work

The type system in § 4 checks that any possible invocation to a service requires a safe set of attributes so to avoid errors due to misuse of transactional scopes and attributes.

The design of SOC transactions could be easier if we knew, for each service invocation in a process, the maximal set of attributes that satisfies the typing. As a matter of fact, specifying a larger set of attributes in a service invocation increases the chances of finding a suitable service supporting one of the attributes. The trade-off is however that a too large set of attributes may cause a run-time error due to a service instance running in a wrongly nested transactional scopes.

Arguably, non well-typed processes can be turned into well-typed ones by changing the attributes of some invocations. We show through an example a method for designing a well-typed process based on an alternative usage of the typing system in § 4. First, consider the types obtained as in Definition 7 but for set $\mathcal{A}$ which is replaced by an infinite countable set Ξ of symbolic identifiers. A *symbolic* process corresponding to $P \in \mathcal{P}$ is a term *sym*(P) obtained by replacing each set of attributes with a distinct formal identifier in Ξ meant to be substituted by a subset of $\mathcal{A}$.

Example 10. A symbolic process corresponding to $P_{\text{bookTheatre}}$ in Example 2 is

$$sym(P_{\text{bookTheatre}}) = \langle s_{\text{tickets}} \between X_1.\overline{\text{askSeat}}.\text{getSeat}.\overline{\text{pay}}[\![\overline{\text{getRefund}}]\!] \mid (\!| s_{\text{compensate}} \between X_2 |\!) \rangle$$

(the sets of attributes in $P_{\text{bookTheatre}}$ are replaced by X_1 and X_2). ◇

A *maximal process* is a well-typed process for which augmenting any of the sets of attributes of its invocations yields the same process or a non-well typed process. Given a well-typed $P \in \mathcal{P}$, max(P) is the maximal process corresponding to P. (Notice that if P does not make any invocation then $P = \max(P)$.)

The typing system of Definition 8 is adapted to symbolic processes by replacing rule (inv) with

$$(\texttt{invSym})\ \frac{P \rhd t_p \qquad I = \{\mathfrak{o}\} \times X}{s \between X.P \rhd (I \cup t_p^{\between}, t_p^{\downarrow}, t_p^{?})}, \quad \text{where } X \text{ not occurs in } P$$

Example 11. By straightforward application of the typing system for symbolic processes $sym(P_{\text{bookTheatre}}) \triangleright t_{sym}$, where $t_{sym} = (\{\mathtt{i}\} \times X_1, (\{\mathtt{o}\} \times X_2, 0, 0), 0, 0)$. Hence, the flattened type of $sym(P_{\text{bookTheatre}})$ is $\widehat{t_{sym}} = \{(\mathtt{i}, X_1),\ (\mathtt{o}, X_2)\}$. ◇

Finally, the maximal process is obtained by replacing each formal identifies with a suitable set of attributes. For example,

$$\max(P_{\text{bookTheatre}}) = \langle s_{\text{tickets}} \mathrel{\text{ε}\!-} \mathcal{A}.\overline{\text{askSeat}}.\text{getSeat}.\overline{\text{pay}}[\![\overline{\text{getRefund}}]\!] \mid (\!| s_{\text{compensate}} \mathrel{\text{ε}\!-} \mathcal{A} \setminus \{\mathtt{m}\} |\!) \rangle$$

is obtained by replacing X_1 with $\mathcal{A}$ and X_2 with $\mathcal{A} \setminus \{\mathtt{m}\}$ in $sym(P_{\text{bookTheatre}})$. In fact, the invocation to s_{tickets} (i.e., the one associated with X_1) can possibly contain all attributes since they are transactional while the other invocation (i.e., the one to $s_{\text{compensate}}$ associated with X_2) can contain all attributes except $\mathtt{m}$.

In general, one is interested only in some policies for transactional scopes and will typically choose, for each invocation in a process P, a subset of the attributes of the corresponding invocation in $\max(P)$.

6 Concluding Remarks and Related Work

An original contribution of this paper is the definition of mechanisms to *determine* and *control* the dynamic reconfiguration of distributed transactions. Namely, we embed a few primitives for managing the dynamic reconfiguration of transactional scopes in ATc to generalise the transactional mechanisms of EJB to SOC so to have consistent and predictable failure propagation. We give a type system that guarantees absence of failures due to misuse of transactional attributes. Since both dynamic reconfiguration and LRT are a key aspects in SOC, it is crucial to provide a formal account of their interrelationships and to understand and control the mechanisms of failure. The aim of this paper is to address the lack of agreement on the semantics of dynamic reconfigurations of transactional scopes in SOC. In fact, service invocations cause systems reconfiguration as they may dynamically introduce new transactional scopes or rearrange the old ones. Such problem is amplified when services support and rely on different kinds of transactional behaviour.

Languages for service orchestration (e.g., WS-BPEL [16]) providing support for distributed transactions have been modelled extending some process calculi like those in [3,11,13,14] with primitives that allow a party to define the scopes, failure handlers, and compensation mechanisms (see [20] for an overview and a comparison of such approaches). StAC [8] and CJoin [6] are process calculi which model arbitrarily nested transactions and focus on the separation of process management with error/compensation. The latter offers a mechanism to merge different scopes but it is not offering the flexibility of the transactional attributes of ATc. At the best of our knowledge, none of the proposed framework has been given a type system as the one proposed here (a formal comparison of different approaches for compensations in flow composition languages can be found in [7]). The existing literature addresses only part of the dynamic aspects involved in error management. For example, [12] proposes a model for dynamic installations of compensation processes, however, dynamic reconfigurations of transactional scopes have not been considered.

We are currently extending ATc with a theory of testing [10] where observers can cause communication failures. The aim is to test the correctness of the system behaviour, including failure handling and compensations. On this basis it is possible to define a notion of equivalence for ATc systems. The intuition is that two systems are equivalent if they satisfy the same set of tests; some preliminary results are summarised below (the interested reader is referred to [5] for a detailed presentation). The theory of testing of ATc shows that under some conditions some transactional attributes are equivalent. Namely, it is possible to replace a transactional attribute with an equivalent one without altering the behaviour of the system. Notice that this also allows one to specify a larger set of transactional attributes for service invocations. For example, $\langle s \Leftarrow A.P \mid (\!|Q|\!) \rangle$ maintain the same behaviour if A is any of the subsets of $\{\mathtt{r}, \mathtt{m}, \mathtt{s}\}$ since the invocation of s happens inside a transaction.

A limitation of our approach is the lack of link mobility à la π-calculus; extending ATc with name passing is left as future work. We argue that the type discipline proposed here can be simply adapted to a name passing version of ATc. In fact, our type system is orthogonal to the communication mechanisms. On the contrary, the testing theory of ATc will be greatly affected by the introduction of name passing features. Allowing attributes to be communicated is anther interesting extension of ATc also, a primitive enabling a service s to make a parametrised invocation to a service s' using the same attribute supported by s (attributes are set when services are published in containers). Such extensions increase expressiveness but require more sophisticated type disciplines.

An orthogonal topic is the modelling of protocols for deciding the outcome of distributed transactions (e.g., the work in [1]). Some standards like Business Transaction Protocol (BTP) [15] and Web Service Transaction (WS-Tx [17]) have been proposed for LRTs. Such protocols involve a more general scenario than the classic *atomic commit*: the global consensus is no longer necessary and is substituted by weaker constraints. In [2,4] BTP cohesion along with the properties ensured by the "weakened" constraints have been studied via a formalisation in the asynchronous π-calculus (see [9] for an overview on the *cohesion*-base approach of BTP). The present paper provides a high level semantics of failure propagation, compensation and scope reconfiguration, while abstracting from protocols necessary to implement them. Consider, for example, the process $\langle s \Leftarrow \{\mathtt{r}\}.P \mid (\!|Q|\!) \rangle$ invoking a service s whose body is $x[\![P']\!].Q'$. Since service s supports the attribute $\mathtt{r}$, its body is executed inside the same scope (if any) of the caller, according to Definition 6.

$$\Gamma \vdash \langle s \Leftarrow \{\mathtt{r}\}.P \mid (\!|Q|\!) \rangle \rightsquigarrow^{*} \Gamma \vdash \langle P \mid P' \mid (\!|Q \mid Q'|\!) \rangle$$

The same above includes compensations of different possibly cross-domain and distributed processes. Noteworthy, the mechanism that trigger Q and Q' are not trivial The higher level perspective we adopted has the advantage of providing a concise but rigorous understanding of dynamic scope reconfigurations. We leave the investigation of the underneath coordination protocols, which would provide a skeleton for the implementation of the higher level mechanisms, as a future work. (We remark that this issue is common to any theory of distributed transactions.)

References

1. Berger, M., Honda, K.: The two-phase commitment protocol in an extended pi-calculus. Electr. Notes Theor. Comput. Sci. 39(1) (2000)
2. Bocchi, L.: Compositional nested long running transactions. In: Wermelinger, M., Margaria-Steffen, T. (eds.) FASE 2004. LNCS, vol. 2984, pp. 194–208. Springer, Heidelberg (2004)
3. Bocchi, L., Laneve, C., Zavattaro, G.: A calculus for long-running transactions. In: Najm, E., Nestmann, U., Stevens, P. (eds.) FMOODS 2003. LNCS, vol. 2884, pp. 124–138. Springer, Heidelberg (2003)
4. Bocchi, L., Lucchi, R.: Atomic commit and negotiation in service oriented computing. In: Ciancarini, P., Wiklicky, H. (eds.) COORDINATION 2006. LNCS, vol. 4038, pp. 16–27. Springer, Heidelberg (2006)
5. Bocchi, L., Tuosto, E.: A Java Inspired Semantics for Transactions in SOC, extended report (2009), http://www.cs.le.ac.uk/people/lb148/javatransactions.html
6. Bruni, R., Melgratti, H.C., Montanari, U.: Nested commits for mobile calculi: extending Join. In: Lévy, J.-J., Mayr, E., Mitchell, J. (eds.) IFIP TCS 2004, pp. 563–576. Kluwer, Dordrecht (2004)
7. Bruni, R., Melgratti, H.C., Montanari, U.: Theoretical foundations for compensations in flow composition languages. In: POPL, pp. 209–220. ACM, New York (2005)
8. Butler, M., Ferreira, C.: An operational semantics for StAC, a language for modelling long-running business transactions. In: De Nicola, R., Ferrari, G.-L., Meredith, G. (eds.) COORDINATION 2004. LNCS, vol. 2949, pp. 87–104. Springer, Heidelberg (2004)
9. Dalal, S., Temel, S., Little, M., Potts, M., Webber, J.: Coordinating business transactions on the web. IEEE Internet Computing 7(1), 30–39 (2003)
10. De Nicola, R., Hennessy, M.C.B.: Testing equivalences for processes. Theoretical Comput. Sci. 34(1-2), 83–133 (1984)
11. Guidi, C., Lanese, I., Montesi, F., Zavattaro, G.: On the interplay between fault handling and request-response service invocations. In: ACSD, pp. 190–198. IEEE, Los Alamitos (2008)
12. Guidi, C., Lanese, I., Montesi, F., Zavattaro, G.: Dynamic error handling in service oriented applications. Fundam. Inf. 95(1), 73–102 (2009)
13. Laneve, C., Zavattaro, G.: Foundations of web transactions. In: Sassone, V. (ed.) FOSSACS 2005. LNCS, vol. 3441, pp. 282–298. Springer, Heidelberg (2005)
14. Mazzara, M., Lanese, I.: Towards a unifying theory for web services composition. In: Bravetti, M., Núñez, M., Zavattaro, G. (eds.) WS-FM 2006. LNCS, vol. 4184, pp. 257–272. Springer, Heidelberg (2006)
15. Business Transaction Protocol (BTP) (2002)
16. Web Services Business Process Execution Language (WS-BPEL). Technical report (2007)
17. Web Services Transaction (WS-TX) (2009)
18. Panda, D., Rahman, R., Lane, D.: EJB 3 in action. Manning (2007)
19. Sun Microsystems. Enterprise JavaBeans (EJB) technology (2009), http://java.sun.com/products/ejb/.
20. Vaz, C., Ferreira, C., Ravara, A.: Dynamic recovering of long running transactions. In: Kaklamanis, C., Nielson, F. (eds.) TGC 2008. LNCS, vol. 5474, pp. 201–215. Springer, Heidelberg (2008)

Responsive Choice in Mobile Processes

Maxime Gamboni and António Ravara*

SQIG, Instituto de Telecomunicações and Mathematics Dept.
IST, Technical University of Lisbon

Abstract. We propose a general type notation, formal semantics and a sound, compositional, and decidable type system to characterise some liveness properties of distributed systems. In the context of mobile processes, we define two concepts, *activeness* (ability to send/receive on a channel) and *responsiveness* (ability to reliably conduct a conversation on a channel), that make the above properties precise. The type system respects the semantic definitions of the concepts, in the sense that the logical statements it outputs are, according to the semantics, correct descriptions of the analysed process. Our work is novel in two aspects. First, since mobile processes can make and communicate choices, a fundamental component of data representation (where a piece of data matches one of a set of patterns) or conversations (where the protocol may permit more than one message at each point), our types and type system use *branching* and *selection* to capture activeness and responsiveness in process constructs necessary for such usage patterns. Secondly, *conditional properties* offer *compositionality* features that permit analysing components of a system individually, and indicate, when applicable, what should be provided to the given process before the properties hold.

Keywords: π-calculus, liveness properties, choice, static analysis.

1 Introduction

When describing a distributed or service-oriented system using mobile processes [12,15], it is important to provide a number of liveness guarantees, such as, from a client's point of view, "If I send a request, will it eventually be received? Will it eventually be processed, and will I eventually obtain an answer?", or, from a server's point of view, "Will I eventually receive a request? Will my clients respect my communication protocol?". The work we present herein ensures these properties statically, allowing, e.g., to guarantee reliability of actual software or distributed protocols, or to prove validity of calculus encodings. The main contribution of this work is an integration of *choice* with activeness and responsiveness, through a general type notation, formal semantics and a sound, compositional, and decidable type system. This work has three main ingredients:

First, *activeness* (ability to establish a connection) and *responsiveness* (ability to conduct a conversation for each connection) are liveness properties that have

* CITI and Dep of Informatics, FCT, New University of Lisbon.

M. Wirsing, M. Hofmann, and A. Rauschmayer (Eds.): TGC 2010, LNCS 6084, pp. 135–152, 2010.

been studied, in more restricted forms, under the names of receptiveness [14], lock-freedom [8] or responsiveness [1]. Activeness is a generalisation of receptiveness both because communication is not required to succeed immediately but also because we may talk of output activeness, whereas receptiveness is only for inputs. Activeness of a channel end point (henceforth called *port*) is equivalent to lock-freedom of every instance of the complement port (including those in the environment). Acciai and Boreale's responsiveness is actually closer to what we call activeness than our concept of responsiveness.

Secondly, *conditional properties* are statements of the form $\Delta \lhd \Theta$, where Δ and Θ are logical statements on channel activeness meaning that "Δ holds *provided* Θ is made available (e.g. through parallel composition)".

Thirdly, the language of processes, as well as the language of types, support the concepts of *selection* (or "internal choice") and *branching* (or "external choice"), abstract descriptions of *choices* made and communicated by processes.

Conversations are an example where responsiveness and choice appear together. A conversation is a sequence of exchanges between a *server* and a *client*, guided by a *protocol* that describes what data type may be transmitted and in which direction, as well as choices that may be performed and by which party. The following example (in a π-calculus extended with numbers and a multiplication operator) is a *multiplication service* that receives numbers and returns their product. At every step the client *selects* to send more numbers ("*more*") or request the result ("*done*"). Input (respectively, output) responsiveness of channel *prod* in this scenario means that the server (respectively, the client) will keep *progressing* until reaching a terminal state, i.e. until t is sent over r.

$$\text{Server} = {!\,} \mathit{prod}(s).\overline{p_0}\langle s, 1\rangle \quad | \quad {!\,} p_0(s,t).\overline{s}(\boldsymbol{\nu} \mathit{more}, \mathit{done}).\\ \big(\mathit{more}(s,n).\overline{p_0}\langle s, t \times n\rangle + \mathit{done}(r).\overline{r}\langle t\rangle\big)$$

$$\text{Client} = \overline{\mathit{prod}}(\boldsymbol{\nu} s).s(\mathit{more}, \mathit{done}).\overline{\mathit{more}}(\boldsymbol{\nu} s, 2).s(\mathit{more}, \mathit{done}).\overline{\mathit{more}}(\boldsymbol{\nu} s, 5).\\ s(\mathit{more}, \mathit{done}).\overline{\mathit{done}}(\boldsymbol{\nu} r).r(t).\overline{\mathit{print}}\langle t\rangle$$

A second application is Milner's encoding of Boolean values in the π-calculus [11], which represents them as receivers on two parameter channels: True replies to queries with a signal on the first parameter (${!\,}b(tf).\bar{t}$) and False on the second one (${!\,}b(tf).\bar{f}$). A Boolean is (input) active if it is able to receive a request, and (input) responsive if it is able to reply to all requests. Those two processes are instances of *selection* because they pick one behaviour out of a set of mutually exclusive permissions, by sending a signal to one parameter rather than to the other. A Random Boolean can be written ${!\,}b(tf).(\boldsymbol{\nu} x)\,(\bar{x} \mid (x.\bar{t} + x.\bar{f}))$, in which the selection is performed "at run-time" by the sum ("+"). A selection made by one process may cause *branching* in another process. Branching is typically implemented with the π-calculus sum operator, as in $\bar{b}(\boldsymbol{\nu} tf).(t.P + f.Q)$, which runs P if b is True, and Q if b is False. The "$r = a$ and b" logical circuit is implemented as follows.

$$A = {!\,} r(tf).\bar{a}(\boldsymbol{\nu} t'f').(t'.\bar{b}\langle tf\rangle + f'.\bar{f}) \tag{1}$$

Upon receiving a request on r, process A first queries a. If it returns True (t') then the process returns on b the same channels received on r. If a returns False instead (f'), the process returns False ($\bar{f}$). So, depending on a and b's behaviour, either a signal will be sent on t, or one will be sent on f (but never both). We shall use this process as a running example in the course of this paper. First by formally stating the property "r is responsive provided that both a and b are active and responsive" into a type, then we will prove that this statement is correct using semantic definitions, and finally, to illustrate our type system, we will show how to automatically infer that property from the process alone (and given that a, b and r are all Booleans).

To the best of our knowledge, no existing work is able to perform a static analysis of processes such as (1). The usual approach for deciding whether names are active is to assign a single numerical level to name occurrences. But this does not allow for conditional properties, and moreover does not deal nicely with choice (specifically, with selection). In this case, when analysing r's continuation, as $\bar{t}$ may never get triggered (in case r returns False), it would require an infinite level, and similarly for $\bar{f}$. In other words, all a level-based system is able to say is "neither $\bar{t}$ nor $\bar{f}$ is guaranteed to ever be fired". We need a typing system able to capture the fact that *exactly one* of $\bar{t}$ and $\bar{f}$ will eventually get triggered when r is queried. In contrast to level-based analysis, dependency-based systems as we have been developing naturally incorporate choice and branching operators, to express that sort of properties (a short abstract presents the approach [5]).

These three ingredients, responsiveness, choice and conditional properties, are put together into *behavioural statements*. Given a process and for every channel a *channel type* specifying its communication protocol, the type system constructs a *process type* containing a behavioural statement describing every property it was able to infer from the process (unless the process risks violating constraints such as linearity or arity of a channel, in which case it is rejected).

This extended abstract is intended as only an overview of our work, and some technical details have been deliberately left out or put in appendices. A complete technical report including proofs can be found on-line [6].

Section 2 describes our type syntax and algebra, Section 3 gives precise semantics for our types and finally Section 4 presents our type system.

2 Processes, Types and Dependencies

After a word on the process calculus used, we describe in this section our type syntax and algebra in detail.

2.1 Processes

Our target process calculus is the synchronous polyadic π-calculus with mixed guarded sums and replication, according to the grammar given in Table 1. The symbol σ (hereafter usually omitted) stands for x's *channel type*, whose definition is given later. The letters a, b, c, d, r, x, y, z denote channel names (sometimes

Table 1. Process Syntax

Processes: $P ::= (P|P) \mid (\boldsymbol{\nu}x:\sigma)\,P \mid S \mid \mathbf{0}$
Components of a parallel composition: $S ::= (S{+}S) \mid G.P$
Guards: $G ::= T \mid\, !\,T$
Non-replicated guards: $T ::= (\boldsymbol{\nu}z:\sigma)\,T \mid a(\tilde{y}) \mid \overline{a}\langle\tilde{x}\rangle$

simply called *names*), taken from a countable set. Every channel x has two *ports*, its input (x) and output ($\bar{x}$) end points. Letter p ranges over ports.

Free names $\text{fn}(P)$ of a process P are defined as usual, binders being $(\boldsymbol{\nu}x)\,P$ (binding x in P) and $a(\tilde{y}).P$ (binding $\tilde{y}$ in P). A guard G has a *subject port* $\mathsf{sub}(G)$, defined by the axioms $\mathsf{sub}(!\,T) \stackrel{\text{def}}{=} \mathsf{sub}((\boldsymbol{\nu}x:\sigma)\,T) \stackrel{\text{def}}{=} \mathsf{sub}(T)$, $\mathsf{sub}(a(\tilde{y})) \stackrel{\text{def}}{=} a$ and $\mathsf{sub}(\overline{a}\langle\tilde{x}\rangle) \stackrel{\text{def}}{=} \bar{a}$, and a set of *object names* $\mathsf{obj}(G)$, defined by $\mathsf{obj}(!\,T) \stackrel{\text{def}}{=} \mathsf{obj}((\boldsymbol{\nu}x:\sigma)\,T) \stackrel{\text{def}}{=} \mathsf{obj}(T)$, $\mathsf{obj}(a(\tilde{y})) \stackrel{\text{def}}{=} \{\tilde{y}\}$ and $\mathsf{obj}(\overline{a}\langle\tilde{x}\rangle) \stackrel{\text{def}}{=} \{\tilde{x}\}$, of which the *bound names* $\text{bn}(G)$ are a subset: $\text{bn}(a(\tilde{y})) \stackrel{\text{def}}{=} \{\tilde{y}\}$ and $\text{bn}((\boldsymbol{\nu}\tilde{z})\,\overline{a}\langle\tilde{x}\rangle) \stackrel{\text{def}}{=} \{\tilde{z}\}$. Finally, the *multiplicity* $\#(G)$ of a guard G is ω if it is replicated, or 1 otherwise. The operational semantics of the calculus is given, as usual, by a labelled transition system (Appendix A).

2.2 Syntax of Types

Types contain annotations on channels to record the liveness properties they enjoy (activeness and/or responsiveness), as well as the number of times they may be used: *Activeness* and *multiplicities* specify, respectively, lower and upper bounds on the number of times a port is going to be used. We write p^m, where p is a port and m is a multiplicity that can be 0, 1, ω (one replicated occurrence) or $\star$ (unbounded), to specify an upper bound on the use of p. We write $p_{\mathbf{A}}$ to specify a non-zero lower bound on the use of p. Note that multiplicity is a *safety* property (broken by using a channel too often), while activeness is a *liveness* property, satisfied once a message is ready to be sent or received. We focus on liveness properties, and use multiplicities merely as a tool for establishing them.

Behavioural statements. Just like $p_{\mathbf{A}}$, activeness of a port p, tells that a p-guarded process eventually comes to top-level[1], activeness of a branching $s_{\mathbf{A}}$ where $s = \sum_i p_i$ requires a sum to eventually come to top-level, with one p_i-guarded branch for each i.

A port a or $\bar{a}$ is *responsive* in a process (written $a_{\mathbf{R}}$ or $\bar{a}_{\mathbf{R}}$) if a-receivers (or $\bar{a}$-senders) respect the channel *protocol*. Protocols, expressed using *channel types*, will be described later on.

These three expressions — p^m, $s_{\mathbf{A}}$ and $p_{\mathbf{R}}$ — are the fundamental building blocks of *behavioural statements*, logical expressions describing the behaviour of a process. The *dependency statement* $\Delta \triangleleft \Theta$ (read "Δ if Θ" and also called *rely-guarantee* construct in the literature), says that whenever Θ holds in a process's

[1] Q is *at top-level* in P if $P \equiv (\boldsymbol{\nu}\tilde{z})\,(P \mid Q)$.

Table 2. Behavioural Statement Syntax

Behavioural statements Δ	$::=$	$\Delta \vee \Delta \mid \Delta \wedge \Delta \mid \Delta \lhd \Delta \mid \gamma \mid p^m \mid \bot \mid \top$
Resources γ	$::=$	$s_{\mathbf{A}} \mid p_{\mathbf{R}}$
Sums s	$::=$	$s + s \mid p$

environment, Δ will hold in that process. For instance $a_{\mathbf{A}} \lhd \bar{b}_{\mathbf{A}}$ holds for the process $b.a$ because, should a third-party process provide an output at b ("$\bar{b}_{\mathbf{A}}$"), this process will provide an input at a ("$a_{\mathbf{A}}$"). Dependency "$\Delta \lhd \Theta$" can be understood as an implication "$\Delta \Leftarrow \Theta$", and indeed shares many properties with logical implication.

The usual logical connectives $\vee$ (disjunction), $\wedge$ (conjunction), $\top$ (truth) and $\bot$ (falsity) are used to build complex behavioural statements (ranged over by ε, Δ, Θ or Ξ and given by the grammar in Table 2) about a process. In this work, multiplicities p^m may appear neither on the left nor on the right of a $\lhd$ connective, and in $\Delta \lhd \Theta$, Δ and Θ may not themselves use the $\lhd$ connective. By convention ε denotes the dependencies of a particular resource. We often group statements about a particular port into a single abbreviated expression: $p^m_{\mathbf{A}} \stackrel{\text{def}}{=} p^m \wedge p_{\mathbf{A}}$ ("p is used at least once and at most m times") and $p_{\mathbf{AR}} \stackrel{\text{def}}{=} p_{\mathbf{A}} \wedge p_{\mathbf{R}}$ ("p is active and responsive"). For instance $p^1_{\mathbf{A}}$ is a linear port (used precisely once), $p^\star_{\mathbf{A}}$ is a port used *at least* once, and p^1 is a port used *at most* once.

Channel Types give, separately for the input and output ports of a channel, behavioural statements that *must* hold for every receiver, respectively sender, at the corresponding channel, using natural numbers (starting from 1) to refer to the parameter channels. Specifically, multiplicities indicate which capabilities (input or output) of the parameters may be used, activeness resources tell which parameter must be active, selection "$\vee$" tells what choices may be performed, and branching "+" tells what branching they must offer. Note how the type of some channel a only talks about the parameters carried on a — it does not include a's multiplicities or activeness which are given by the *process type.*

The input port of a Boolean channel (such as r, a and b in (1)) has type

$$\bar{1}^1_{\mathbf{A}} \vee \bar{2}^1_{\mathbf{A}} \tag{2}$$

that says that either the first parameter ("1") must be output ("$\bar{1}$") active ("$_{\mathbf{A}}$"), and the second parameter unused, or ("$\vee$") the opposite ("$\bar{2}^1_{\mathbf{A}}$") — by convention we don't mention ports with multiplicity zero. The output port has type

$$(1^1 \vee 2^1) \wedge (1+2)_{\mathbf{A}}, \tag{3}$$

which has a similar meaning, but where one of its parameters (t and f in the example) should be *input* rather than output. Additionally ("$\wedge$"), inputs at the parameters ("1" and "2") must be the guards of a sum ("+"). A Boolean channel is now said input (resp., output) *responsive* if its input port (resp., output port) respects this protocol. A *channel type* σ is a triple $(\tilde{\sigma}; \xi_{\mathrm{I}}; \xi_{\mathrm{O}})$ where

$\tilde{\sigma}$ are the types of the parameters, ξ_{I} and ξ_{O} are behavioural statements (only using *numbers* for channels) standing for the behaviour required respectively of inputs and outputs at that channel. For instance, abbreviating the parameterless channel type $(\varnothing; \top; \top)$ as $()$, the Boolean type gathers (2) and (3) as

$$\mathsf{Bool} \stackrel{\text{def}}{=} \big(()() \; ; \; \bar{1}^1_{\mathbf{A}} \vee \bar{2}^1_{\mathbf{A}} \; ; \; (1^1 \vee 2^1) \wedge (1+2)_{\mathbf{A}}\big)$$

The type σ_p of channel *prod* in the conversation example from the introduction nicely illustrates how a channel type describes the protocol used at a channel:

1. Connection: $\sigma_p = (\sigma_s; \bar{1}_{\mathbf{AR}}; 1_{\mathbf{AR}})$,
2. Client selects m or d: $\sigma_s = (\sigma_m, \sigma_d; \bar{1}_{\mathbf{AR}} \vee \bar{2}_{\mathbf{AR}}; (1+2)_{\mathbf{A}} \wedge (1_{\mathbf{R}} \vee 2_{\mathbf{R}}))$,
3. If m, client sends a number: $\sigma_m = (\sigma_s, \mathsf{Int}; \bar{1}_{\mathbf{AR}}; 1_{\mathbf{AR}})$,
4. If d, client requests result: $\sigma_d = (\sigma_r; \bar{1}_{\mathbf{AR}}; 1_{\mathbf{AR}})$,
5. Server returns result: $\sigma_r = (\mathsf{Int}; \top; \top)$.

Process Types are similar to channel types, but refer to channels by names rather than parameter numbers. A process type Γ is a structure $(\Sigma \; ; \; \Xi_{\mathrm{L}} \blacktriangleleft \Xi_{\mathrm{E}})$ where $\Sigma = \tilde{a} : \tilde{\sigma}$ is the *channel type mapping* giving the channel types of free names used by the process, while Ξ_{L} and Ξ_{E} are behavioural statements using names in $\tilde{a}$, respectively the *local component* (constraints what the process does) and the *environment component* (constraints what any third-party process may do). Unless specified otherwise, Ξ_{E} contains no activeness or responsiveness statements.

Typing the running example. The process (1) can be given the following type, where the local component says that r is active with multiplicity ω (i.e. has precisely one occurrence and it is replicated), and its responsiveness depends on both a and b being active and responsive. The environment component specifies that a and b must both have at most one replicated instance, and there are no additional input on r.

$$\Gamma_A = \big(a : \mathsf{Bool}, b : \mathsf{Bool}, r : \mathsf{Bool}; r^{\omega}_{\mathbf{A}} \wedge \big(r_{\mathbf{R}} \triangleleft (a_{\mathbf{AR}} \wedge b_{\mathbf{AR}})\big) \blacktriangleleft a^{\omega} \wedge b^{\omega} \wedge r^0\big) \quad (4)$$

Apart from some informal descriptions, behavioural statements have so far been purely syntactical constructs. Some operators and relations we present ahead clarify their semantics: (1) equivalence and weakening relations highlight their *logical* aspect (a statement may *imply* another); (2) composition, restriction and prefixing operators highlight their *spatial* aspect by mirroring process constructs; and (3) the transition operator and the typed transition relation highlight their *dynamical* aspect (types, like processes, may evolve over time).

2.3 Logical Aspects

We define weakening and reduction relations on behavioural statements.

A weakening relation on behavioural statements (and, by extension, on process types) builds on the idea that a statement A can be said *weaker* than a statement

B (written $A \succeq B$) if all worlds (processes) satisfying B also satisfy A. Similarly, statements are *equivalent* (written $A \cong B$) if they hold in the same set of worlds (i.e., if $A \succeq B$ and $B \succeq A$).

The weakening relation is inductively defined by the rules in Appendix B. We present now the most significant rules, useful to analyse the running example.

- $\Delta_1 \wedge \Delta_2 \preceq \Delta_1 \preceq \Delta_1 \vee \Delta_2$, and $\bot \preceq \Delta \preceq \top$. $\Delta \wedge (\Delta_1 \vee \Delta_2) \cong (\Delta \wedge \Delta_1) \vee (\Delta \wedge \Delta_2)$.
- $\wedge$ and $\vee$ are commutative, associative and idempotent, up to $\cong$.
- On multiplicities, $p^{m_1} \preceq p^{m_2}$ if $m_1 = 0$ or $m_2 \in \{m_1, \star\}$. Also, $p^\star \cong \top$.
- $(\gamma \triangleleft \varepsilon_1) \wedge (\gamma \triangleleft \varepsilon_2) \cong \gamma \triangleleft (\varepsilon_1 \vee \varepsilon_2)$ and $(\gamma \triangleleft \varepsilon_1) \vee (\gamma \triangleleft \varepsilon_2) \cong \gamma \triangleleft (\varepsilon_1 \wedge \varepsilon_2)$.

The Technical report ("Weakening Decidability" in [6], Section 2) describes a way to decide if two behavioural statements are related by weakening. From now on we consider process types and dependencies up to $\cong$ as equal, since every operator and relation considered commutes with $\cong$ (Lemma "Types may be seen up to $\cong$" in [6], Section 2).

Dependency reduction. Another relation highlighting the logical aspect of behavioural statements is the *reduction* relation, analogous to the *modus ponens* rule in logic. It occurs with process composition which may create dependency chains that must then be reduced. For example $a.\bar{b}$ and $b.\bar{c}$ satisfy respectively $\bar{b}_{\mathbf{A}} \triangleleft \bar{a}_{\mathbf{A}}$ and $\bar{c}_{\mathbf{A}} \triangleleft \bar{b}_{\mathbf{A}}$, while their composition $a.\bar{b} \mid b.\bar{c}$ satisfies $(\bar{b}_{\mathbf{A}} \triangleleft \bar{a}_{\mathbf{A}}) \wedge (\bar{c}_{\mathbf{A}} \triangleleft \bar{b}_{\mathbf{A}}) \wedge \underline{(\bar{c}_{\mathbf{A}} \triangleleft \bar{a}_{\mathbf{A}})}$ (where the underlined statement was derived from the other two) or, applying type equivalence, $(\bar{b}_{\mathbf{A}} \triangleleft \bar{a}_{\mathbf{A}}) \wedge \big(\bar{c}_{\mathbf{A}} \triangleleft (\bar{a}_{\mathbf{A}} \vee \bar{b}_{\mathbf{A}})\big)$. More generally:

Definition 1 (Dependency Reduction). *The* reduction relation $\hookrightarrow$ *on behavioural statements is a partial order relation satisfying*
1. $(s_{\mathbf{A}} \triangleleft \varepsilon) \wedge (\gamma \triangleleft \varepsilon') \;\hookrightarrow\; (s_{\mathbf{A}} \triangleleft \varepsilon) \wedge (\gamma \triangleleft \varepsilon'\{^{\varepsilon\{^{\bot}/_{\gamma}\} \vee s_{\mathbf{A}}}/_{s_{\mathbf{A}}}\})$,
2. $(p_{\mathbf{R}} \triangleleft \varepsilon) \wedge (\gamma \triangleleft \varepsilon') \;\hookrightarrow\; (p_{\mathbf{R}} \triangleleft \varepsilon) \wedge (\gamma \triangleleft \varepsilon'\{^{\varepsilon\{^{\bot}/_{\gamma}\} \wedge p_{\mathbf{R}}}/_{p_{\mathbf{R}}}\})$.
A closure *of a behavioural statement* Ξ, *written* close (Ξ), *is* Ξ' *such that* $\Xi \hookrightarrow \Xi'$ *and if* $\Xi' \hookrightarrow \Xi''$ *then* $\Xi' \cong \Xi''$.

The different treatment of activeness and responsiveness (in γ's dependencies, the former gets a $\vee$ and the latter a $\wedge$), can be understood as follows: If two processes P_1 and P_2 both provide an a-input, it is enough that one of them is able to receive a request to have a active in $P_1|P_2$. On the other hand, they must both be responsive in order to guarantee that all a-requests will get a response. Also note how *self-dependencies* $\gamma \triangleleft \gamma$ are replaced by $\gamma \triangleleft \bot$. Activeness self-dependencies are found in deadlocks such as $\bar{a}.!\,b \mid \bar{b}.!\,a$ where $a_{\mathbf{A}}$ and $b_{\mathbf{A}}$ depend on each other, and responsiveness self-dependencies are found in livelocks such as $!\,a(x).\bar{b}\langle x\rangle \mid !\,b(x).\bar{a}\langle x\rangle$ where $a_{\mathbf{R}}$ and $b_{\mathbf{R}}$ depend on each other.

Most operators commute with the logical connectives: A *logical homomorphism* is a function f on behavioural statements or process types such that $f(X \vee Y) = f(X) \vee f(Y)$ and $f(X \wedge Y) = f(X) \wedge f(Y)$. It is now sufficient to describe how operators behave on behavioural statements not using $\wedge$ or $\vee$, as the general behaviour can be derived from the above.

2.4 Spatial Aspects

Every process constructor has a corresponding operator on types, which is the essence of any syntax directed type system such as ours. We focus on the (parallel) composition operation "$\Gamma_1 \odot \Gamma_2$" that, given the types Γ_1 and Γ_2 of two processes P_1 and P_2, constructs the type of $P_1|P_2$. On behavioural statements, $\odot$ is the logical homomorphism such that:

1. $(p^m) \odot (p^{m'}) \stackrel{\text{def}}{=} p^{m+m'}$
2. $(s_{\mathbf{A}} \lhd \varepsilon) \odot (s_{\mathbf{A}} \lhd \varepsilon') \stackrel{\text{def}}{=} (s_{\mathbf{A}} \lhd \varepsilon) \vee (s_{\mathbf{A}} \lhd \varepsilon')$
3. $(p_{\mathbf{R}} \lhd \varepsilon) \odot (p_{\mathbf{R}} \lhd \varepsilon') \stackrel{\text{def}}{=} (p_{\mathbf{R}} \lhd \varepsilon) \wedge (p_{\mathbf{R}} \lhd \varepsilon')$
4. When they don't have resources in common, $\Xi \odot \Xi' \stackrel{\text{def}}{=} \Xi \wedge \Xi'$.

When composing full process types, the *local* component of the whole is the composition of the local components of the parts, and the *environment* of the whole is the environment of one part, without the local component of the other part (we omit the formal definition of "\" that does just that). Formally:

$$(\Sigma;\Xi_{\mathrm{L}1} \blacktriangleleft \Xi_{\mathrm{E}1}) \odot (\Sigma; \Xi_{\mathrm{L}2} \blacktriangleleft \Xi_{\mathrm{E}2}) \stackrel{\text{def}}{=} (\Sigma; \Xi_{\mathrm{L}1} \odot \Xi_{\mathrm{L}2} \blacktriangleleft (\Xi_{\mathrm{E}1} \setminus \Xi_{\mathrm{L}2}) \wedge (\Xi_{\mathrm{E}2} \setminus \Xi_{\mathrm{L}1}))$$

The $\odot$ operator is *associative, commutative* and has $(\varnothing; \top \blacktriangleleft \top)$ as a *neutral element* (Lemma "Composition Properties" in [6], Section 2). See Sections 2.5 and 4 for examples.

2.5 Dynamical Aspects

We describe in this section a *transition operator* "$\Gamma \wr \mu$" on types, to answer to the following question: If a process P has type Γ, and $P \xrightarrow{\mu} P'$, what is the type of P'? The motivation for such an operator is three-fold:

Ruling out transitions that a well-behaved third party process can't cause and that force a process to misbehave. E.g. interference on a linear channel (a transition $l|\bar{l} \xrightarrow{l} \bar{l}$ is ruled out, as it contradicts $\bar{l}^0$ in the environment) and channel mismatches ($a(x).\overline{x}\langle 3\rangle \mid b(yz) \xrightarrow{a(b)} \overline{b}\langle 3\rangle \mid b(yz)$ introduces an arity mismatch and is ruled out, as a's parameter type is incompatible with b's type).

Secondly, to avoid semantics with universal quantification on third-party processes, we characterise the $\lhd$ connective with labelled transitions. However, those change the properties of processes: assume P and E represent a process and its environment. A request $P \xrightarrow{\overline{a}\langle b\rangle}$ is then received as $E \xrightarrow{a(b)} E'$, and if a was responsive in E then $\bar{b}$ is active and responsive and a is no longer active in E' (for linear a with a typical input-output-alternating channel type). The transition operator predicts the evolution of both the process and its environment.

Thirdly, to prove that the previous point is sound, subject reduction works with arbitrary labelled-transitions (see Proposition 1 on page 147).

For transitions not carrying parameters, we have the following equality:

$$(\Sigma; \Xi_\mathrm{L} \blacktriangleleft \Xi_\mathrm{E}) \wr p \stackrel{\mathrm{def}}{=} (\Sigma; \Xi_\mathrm{L} \setminus p \blacktriangleleft \Xi_\mathrm{E} \setminus \bar{p})$$

Based on $\odot$ and *channel type instantiation* $\sigma[\tilde{x}]$ (which transforms a channel type σ into a process type, essentially by substituting parameter references $1 \dots n$ by $x_1 \dots x_n$, but with extra care in case two x_i are equal), input transitions are simulated as follows. Let $\Gamma = (\Sigma; \Xi_\mathrm{L} \blacktriangleleft \Xi_\mathrm{E})$ with $\Sigma(a) = \sigma$.

$$\Gamma \wr a(\tilde{x}) \stackrel{\mathrm{def}}{=} \Gamma \wr a \odot \sigma[\tilde{x}] \lhd (a_\mathbf{R} \blacktriangleleft \bar{a}_\mathbf{R})$$

The $\Gamma \lhd (a_\mathbf{R} \blacktriangleleft \bar{a}_\mathbf{R})$ operation makes Γ's local component depend on $a_\mathbf{R}$ and its environment component depend on $\bar{a}_\mathbf{R}$. An output transition can be done by swapping the local and environment components, doing an input transition, and swapping the two resulting components back. We illustrate the above operator on the transition $A \xrightarrow{r(uv)} A' = A \,|\, \bar{a}(\boldsymbol{\nu} t' f').(t'.\bar{b}\langle uv\rangle + f'.\bar{v})$ where A is (1) and its type (4) is $\Gamma_A = \big(\Sigma \,;\, r^\omega_\mathbf{A} \wedge r_\mathbf{R} \lhd (a_\mathbf{AR} \wedge b_\mathbf{AR}) \;\blacktriangleleft\; a^\omega \wedge b^\omega \wedge r^0\big)$:

$$\Gamma_A \wr r(uv) = \Gamma_A \wr r \odot \big(u : (), v : (); (\bar{u}_\mathbf{A} \vee \bar{v}_\mathbf{A}) \lhd r_\mathbf{R} \blacktriangleleft (u^1 \vee v^1) \wedge (u+v)_\mathbf{A} \lhd \bar{r}_\mathbf{R}\big)$$

1. The "$\wr r$" part has no effect as $r^\omega \setminus r = r^\omega$ and $\bar{r}^\star \setminus \bar{r} = \bar{r}^\star$.
2. The channel type mapping is $\Sigma' = a : \mathsf{Bool}, b : \mathsf{Bool}, r : \mathsf{Bool}, u : (), v : ()$.
3. the remote component "Ξ_E" is just the conjunction of $(a^\omega \wedge b^\omega \wedge r^0)$ from Γ_A and $\big((u^1 \vee v^1) \wedge (u+v)_\mathbf{A} \lhd \bar{r}_\mathbf{R}\big)$.
4. The local component is $\Xi_\mathrm{L} = \Big(r^\omega_\mathbf{A} \wedge r_\mathbf{R} \lhd (a_\mathbf{AR} \wedge b_\mathbf{AR})\Big) \odot \Big((\bar{u}_\mathbf{A} \vee \bar{v}_\mathbf{A}) \lhd r_\mathbf{R}\Big) = \Big(r^\omega_\mathbf{A} \wedge r_\mathbf{R} \lhd (a_\mathbf{AR} \wedge b_\mathbf{AR})\Big) \wedge \Big((\bar{u}_\mathbf{A} \vee \bar{v}_\mathbf{A}) \lhd r_\mathbf{R}\Big)$.
5. Closure of Ξ_L reduces the $(\bar{u}_\mathbf{A} \vee \bar{v}_\mathbf{A}) \lhd r_\mathbf{R} \;\wedge\; r_\mathbf{R} \lhd (a_\mathbf{AR} \wedge b_\mathbf{AR})$ dependency chain into $(\bar{u}_\mathbf{A} \vee \bar{v}_\mathbf{A}) \lhd (r_\mathbf{R} \wedge a_\mathbf{AR} \wedge b_\mathbf{AR})$.
6. Finally, because of r^0 in the remote side Ξ_E, the dependency on $r_\mathbf{R}$ can be replaced[2] by $\top$ in the above statement, resulting in $(\bar{u}_\mathbf{A} \vee \bar{v}_\mathbf{A}) \lhd (a_\mathbf{AR} \wedge b_\mathbf{AR})$.
7. Omitting irrelevant parts, we end up with

$$(\Sigma'; (\bar{u}_\mathbf{A} \vee \bar{v}_\mathbf{A}) \lhd (a_\mathbf{AR} \wedge b_\mathbf{AR}) \blacktriangleleft a^\omega \wedge b^\omega \wedge r^0 \wedge (u^1 \vee v^1)) \tag{5}$$

as a type for $A \,|\, \bar{a}(\boldsymbol{\nu} t' f').(t'.\bar{b}\langle uv\rangle + f'.\bar{v})$, where the local component is read as "if active and responsive a and b inputs are provided, then an output will be sent on (exactly) one of u and v," which is indeed a correct statement for that process A'. Remember that this type was not obtained by analysing A', but is a prediction of the effect of a transition $\xrightarrow{r(uv)}$ on a process of type Γ_A.

Transitions on types and on processes are combined to form transitions on *typed processes*: $(\Gamma; P) \xrightarrow{\mu} (\Gamma \wr \mu; P')$ if $P \xrightarrow{\mu} P'$ and $\Gamma \wr \mu$ is well-defined.

[2] An unused port is vacuously responsive. Inversely, $r_\mathbf{A}$ could be replaced by $\bot$.

3 Activeness and Responsiveness

In this section we define *correctness* of a type Γ for a process P, denoted $\Gamma \models P$.

The *projection relation* "$\searrow$" permits extracting an "elementary" part of a process type for testing its validity. It simulates selections done by the environment by reducing any $\Delta_1 \wedge \Delta_2 \ldots$ to Δ_i and any $\gamma \triangleleft (\varepsilon_1 \vee \varepsilon_2 \ldots)$ to $\gamma \triangleleft \varepsilon_j$ for some i and j. Then, proving that a projection $\bigvee_i \gamma_i \triangleleft \varepsilon_i$ is correct for P is done with a *strategy* — a function f mapping typed processes to pairs of transition labels and typed processes such that $f(\Gamma; P) = (\mu; \Gamma'; P')$, also written $(\Gamma; P) \xrightarrow{f} (\Gamma'; P')$, implies $(\Gamma; P) \xrightarrow{\mu} (\Gamma'; P')$. For $(\Gamma; P) \notin \mathrm{dom}(f)$ we write $(\Gamma; P) \xrightarrow{f} (\Gamma; P)$. A valid strategy "leads to" a process where one of the γ_i is immediately available, using no more external resources than declared in ε_i. While projections deal with disjunctions on the right of the $\triangleleft$ connective, disjunctions on its left need to be handled specially: $(\Xi_1 \vee \Xi_2) \models P$ is weaker than $(\Xi_1 \models P) \vee (\Xi_2 \models P)$ as it could be that the selection is not yet decided in P, but will only be after a few transitions. This is addressed by first picking a full transition sequence and *then only* requiring the outcome of the selection to be decided, which can be seen in the definition in "$\exists \alpha$ s.t.". Correctness is stated similarly to the usual notion of *fairness* ("if a particular transition is constantly available, it will eventually occur") but with a strategy instead of a particular transition. Note how the transition sequence interleaves single invocations of the strategy between arbitrarily long transition sequences: this permits stating results in presence of divergence but still correct with a stochastic scheduler. The "eventually" aspect of activeness is given by "$\exists n$ s.t.". "Immediately correct" essentially means the corresponding port or sum is at top-level.

If a type Γ is correct for a process then so is any Γ' with $\Gamma' \succeq \Gamma$ (Lemma "Bisimulations and Type Equivalence" in [6], Section 4).

Definition 2 (Correctness). *Let Γ be a type and P a process. We say that or Γ is* correct *for P if, for some strategy f, for any infinite sequence of the form $(\Gamma; P) = (\Gamma_0; P_0) \xrightarrow{\tilde{\mu}_0}\searrow (\Gamma'_0; P'_0) \xrightarrow{f} (\Gamma'_1; P'_1) \cdots \xrightarrow{\tilde{\mu}_i}\searrow (\Gamma'_i; P'_i) \xrightarrow{f} (\Gamma_{i+1}; P_{i+1}) \cdots$: Let (for all i) p_i be the subject of the $(\Gamma'_i; P'_i) \xrightarrow{f} (\Gamma_{i+1}; P_{i+1})$ transition (or "τ" if it is the identity or a τ-transition). Then there is a number n and a resource α such that:*

1. *for all i with $p_i \neq \tau$, $(\alpha \triangleleft \overline{p_i}_{\mathbf{A}}) \preceq \Gamma'_i$*
2. *For some ε with $(\alpha \triangleleft \varepsilon) \preceq \Gamma_n$, $\alpha \triangleleft \varepsilon$ is immediately correct for $(\Gamma_n; P_n)$.*

We now sketch a proof that Γ_A given in (4) is a correct type for A given in (1). We only pick a representative transition sequence, but of course a complete proof would have to take all possible transitions into account. Following the pattern given in Definition 2 we alternate arbitrary transition sequences $\tilde{\mu}_i$ (odd-numbered steps) and those provided by the strategy (even-numbered steps).

1. We first send a request $\tilde{\mu}_0 = r(uv)$. The resulting type is (5) on page 143.
2. The strategy executes $\overline{a}(\boldsymbol{\nu} t' f')$ to bring the process closer to an output on u or v. This is allowed, as the subject's complement a is active in the dependencies. The local dependency network is now $(\bar{u}_{\mathbf{A}} \vee \bar{v}_{\mathbf{A}}) \bowtie (a_{\mathbf{AR}} \wedge (\bar{t}'_{\mathbf{A}} \vee \bar{f}'_{\mathbf{A}}) \wedge b_{\mathbf{AR}})$.
3. As we do not want to help the strategy find the way out we set $\tilde{\mu}_1 = \varnothing$. However we must still do a projection "$\searrow$", i.e. simulate the choice made by the a-input. Let's pick $\bar{f}'$: $(\bar{u}_{\mathbf{A}} \vee \bar{v}_{\mathbf{A}}) \triangleleft (a_{\mathbf{AR}} \wedge \bar{f}'_{\mathbf{A}} \wedge b_{\mathbf{AR}})$.
4. The process is now $A \mid (t'.\bar{b}\langle uv\rangle + f'.\bar{v})$, so the strategy is just to consume the f' prefix, which is permitted because its complement is active $(\bar{f}'_{\mathbf{A}})$.
5. We are now at $A|\bar{v}$. If we set $\tilde{\mu}_2 = \varnothing$ at this point, $n = 2$ satisfies the requirement as $\bar{v}$ is at top-level. If instead we consume $\bar{v}$ with $\tilde{\mu}_2 = \bar{v}$, the transition operator removes activeness of both $\bar{u}$ and $\bar{v}$, and the process type becomes $(\bar{u}_{\mathbf{A}} \vee \bar{v}_{\mathbf{A}}) \triangleleft \bot \cong \top$ which is vacuously correct.

4 Type System

Given a process P, a mapping Σ of channel types for all free names, and optionally multiplicities for some names, our type system constructs a process type Γ for P. Processes that may violate multiplicity constraints or mismatch channel types are rejected. Typing is decidable and sound, but necessarily not complete (may reject safe processes, or construct a behavioural statement weaker than what is actually correct for the process). Most rules of the type system are straightforward (every process constructor has a corresponding process type operator). Appendix C presents the full system.

We focus on the *prefix* rule. It $\odot$-composes five statements, in order: subject type and total multiplicities, subject activeness, continuation, expected remote behaviour and subject responsiveness.

$$\frac{\Gamma \vdash P \quad \mathsf{sub}(G) = p \quad \mathsf{obj}(G) = \tilde{x} \qquad (\#(G) = 1 \text{ and } m' = \star) \Rightarrow \varepsilon = \bot}{\begin{array}{r}\left(p : \sigma;\ \blacktriangleleft p^m \wedge \bar{p}^{m'}\right) \odot \\ \left(;p_{\mathbf{A}}^{\#(G)} \triangleleft \varepsilon \blacktriangleleft\right) \odot \\ !_{\text{if } \#(G) = \omega}\, (\boldsymbol{\nu}\mathrm{bn}(G)) \Big(\Gamma \triangleleft \bar{p}_{\mathbf{A}} \odot \\ \overline{\sigma}[\tilde{x}] \triangleleft \bar{p}_{\mathbf{AR}} \odot \\ (;p_{\mathbf{R}} \triangleleft \sigma[\tilde{x}] \blacktriangleleft)\Big) \vdash G.P\end{array}} \quad (\text{R-Pre})$$

We illustrate the five factors in order with the derivation of $r_{\mathbf{R}} \triangleleft (a_{\mathbf{AR}} \wedge b_{\mathbf{AR}})$ as a type for (1) on page 136. We omit parts not needed to get $r_{\mathbf{R}}$'s dependencies.

Subject type, multiplicities and activeness. The parameter-less output $\bar{f}$ is typed using (R-Pre). The name is linear $(m = m' = 1)$ and, since there are no parameters or continuation, all but the first two factors of the typing are empty, leaving us with: $(f : ();\ \blacktriangleleft \bar{f}^1 \wedge f^1) \odot (;\bar{f}^1_{\mathbf{A}} \triangleleft \top \blacktriangleleft)$, or:

$$\Gamma_6 = (f : ();\bar{f}^1_{\mathbf{A}} \blacktriangleleft \bar{f}^0 \wedge f^1) \vdash \bar{f} \tag{6}$$

Continuation. A sequence $G.P$ is typed like composition $G|P$, except that activeness resources in P additionally depend on $\bar{p}_{\mathbf{A}}$, p being G's subject port. Here, $f'.\bar{f}$ is again typed with (R-PRE), where the first three terms are now non-null:

$$\left(f' : (); \blacktriangleleft f'^1 \wedge \bar{f}'^1\right) \odot \left(; f'^1_{\mathbf{A}} \lhd \top \blacktriangleleft\right) \odot \Gamma_6 \lhd \bar{f}'_{\mathbf{A}} \vdash f'.\bar{f}$$

Dropping the unneeded $f'^1_{\mathbf{A}}$ statement we get

$$\Gamma_T = \left(f : (), f' : (); \bar{f}_{\mathbf{A}} \lhd \bar{f}'_{\mathbf{A}} \blacktriangleleft \bar{f}^0 \wedge f^1 \wedge f'^0 \wedge \bar{f}'^1\right) \vdash f'.\bar{f} \tag{7}$$

Remote behaviour plays two roles, respectively through the local and environment parts of the instantiated channel $\overline{\sigma}[tf]$. First, if the input on a channel is active and responsive, it will behave according to the protocol specified in the channel type whenever queries are sent to it. For $\bar{b}\langle tf\rangle$, this is $(\bar{t}_{\mathbf{A}} \vee \bar{f}_{\mathbf{A}}) \lhd b_{\mathbf{AR}}$, where the left side is (3) from page 139 with t and f replacing 1 and 2. Second, it sets upper bounds on the local side's use of parameters ports. In this case we get $t^1 \vee f^1$ in the environment side, which effectively prevents any part of the process to do at t and f anything more than an input-guarded sum at t and f. Together with the subject b handled as in (6), we get the following:

$$\left(b : \mathsf{Bool}, t : (), f : (); (\bar{t}_{\mathbf{A}} \vee \bar{f}_{\mathbf{A}}) \lhd b_{\mathbf{AR}} \blacktriangleleft (t^1 \vee f^1) \wedge (\bar{b}^\star \wedge b^\omega)\right) \vdash \bar{b}\langle tf\rangle \tag{8}$$

As in (7), the t'-prefix adds a dependency on $\bar{t}'_{\mathbf{A}}$ to all activeness resources:

$$\Gamma_F = \left(\Sigma; (\bar{t}_{\mathbf{A}} \vee \bar{f}_{\mathbf{A}}) \lhd (b_{\mathbf{AR}} \wedge \bar{t}'_{\mathbf{A}}) \blacktriangleleft (t^1 \vee f^1) \wedge (\bar{b}^\star \wedge b^\omega)\right) \vdash t'.\bar{b}\langle tf\rangle \tag{9}$$

A sum $T + F$ is given the type $(t' + f')_{\mathbf{A}} \wedge (\Gamma_T \vee \Gamma_F)$, where Γ_T (here (7)) and Γ_F (here (9)) are respectively the types of T and F, and t', f' their guards: the process offers a branching $t'+f'$, and ("$\wedge$") selects ("$\vee$") one of Γ_T and Γ_F (we use $(\Sigma; \Xi_{\mathrm{L1}} \blacktriangleleft \Xi_{\mathrm{E1}}) \vee (\Sigma; \Xi_{\mathrm{L2}} \blacktriangleleft \Xi_{\mathrm{E2}}) \stackrel{\mathrm{def}}{=} (\Sigma; \Xi_{\mathrm{L1}} \vee \Xi_{\mathrm{L2}} \blacktriangleleft \Xi_{\mathrm{E1}} \wedge \Xi_{\mathrm{E2}})$ for $\Gamma_T \vee \Gamma_F$). The decoupling between the guards and the continuations is done to make explicit which channels must be used to make the process branch.

$$\begin{aligned}\Big(\Sigma; (t' + f')_{\mathbf{A}} \wedge \Big(((\bar{t}_{\mathbf{A}} \vee \bar{f}_{\mathbf{A}}) \lhd (b_{\mathbf{AR}} \wedge \bar{t}'_{\mathbf{A}}))\ \vee\ (\bar{f}_{\mathbf{A}} \lhd \bar{f}'_{\mathbf{A}})\Big) \blacktriangleleft \\ \left(\bar{f}^0 \wedge f'^0 \wedge \bar{f}'^1\right) \wedge \left((t^1 \vee f^1) \wedge \bar{b}^\star \wedge b^\omega\right)\Big) \vdash t'.\bar{b}\langle tf\rangle + f'.\bar{f}\end{aligned} \tag{10}$$

We run (R-PRE) once more for the full a-output. Now two names are bound ($\mathrm{bn}(\overline{a}(\boldsymbol{\nu} t'f')) = \{t', f'\}$), and we only need the third and fourth factors:

Remote behaviour $\left(t' : (), f' : (); (\bar{t}'_{\mathbf{A}} \vee \bar{f}'_{\mathbf{A}}) \lhd a_{\mathbf{AR}} \blacktriangleleft t'^1 \vee f'^1\right)$ and
Continuation $\big(\Sigma; (\bar{t}_{\mathbf{A}} \vee \bar{f}_{\mathbf{A}}) \lhd (b_{\mathbf{AR}} \wedge \bar{t}'_{\mathbf{A}} \wedge a_{\mathbf{A}}) \vee (\bar{f}_{\mathbf{A}} \lhd (\bar{f}'_{\mathbf{A}} \wedge a_{\mathbf{A}})) \blacktriangleleft$
$(t^1 \vee f^1) \wedge \bar{b}^\star \wedge b^\omega \wedge \bar{f}^0 \wedge f'^0 \wedge \bar{f}'^1\big)$.

The $\odot$ operator now does some dependency reduction (Definition 1 on page 141): The remote behaviour provides $(\bar{t}'_{\mathbf{A}} \lhd a_{\mathbf{AR}}) \vee (\bar{f}'_{\mathbf{A}} \lhd a_{\mathbf{AR}})$, and the continuation $(\bar{t}_{\mathbf{A}} \vee \bar{f}_{\mathbf{A}}) \lhd t'_{\mathbf{A}} \ \vee \ (\bar{f}_{\mathbf{A}} \lhd f'_{\mathbf{A}})$. Remember that $(p_{\mathbf{A}} \lhd \gamma) \wedge (\alpha \lhd p_{\mathbf{A}}) \hookrightarrow (p_{\mathbf{A}} \lhd \gamma) \wedge \alpha \lhd (p_{\mathbf{A}} \vee \gamma)$, so the two dependency statements in the continuation become respectively $(\bar{t}_{\mathbf{A}} \vee \bar{f}_{\mathbf{A}}) \lhd (t'_{\mathbf{A}} \vee a_{\mathbf{AR}})$ and $\bar{f}_{\mathbf{A}} \lhd (f'_{\mathbf{A}} \vee a_{\mathbf{AR}})$. Therefore composing remote behaviour and continuation and binding (dropping) t' and f' yields:

$$(a : \mathsf{Bool}, t : (), f : (); (\bar{t}_{\mathbf{A}} \vee \bar{f}_{\mathbf{A}}) \lhd (b_{\mathbf{AR}} \wedge a_{\mathbf{AR}}) \vee \bar{f}_{\mathbf{A}} \lhd a_{\mathbf{AR}} \blacktriangleleft a^{\omega} \wedge (t^1 \vee f^1)) \vdash \bar{a}(\boldsymbol{\nu} t' f').(t'.\bar{b}\langle tf \rangle + f'.\bar{f}) \quad (11)$$

Subject responsiveness. A port is responsive if it provides all resources given in the channel type, which is what the last statement in the (R-PRE) rule states. For $r(tf)$, this is written $r_{\mathbf{R}} \lhd (\bar{t}_{\mathbf{A}} \vee \bar{f}_{\mathbf{A}})$, where the right hand side is just (2) from page 139 with t and f replacing 1 and 2. Composing with (11) reduces the dependency chain and we obtain $r_{\mathbf{R}} \lhd (b_{\mathbf{AR}} \wedge a_{\mathbf{AR}})$, as required.

The type system sketched above has two important properties. It agrees with the transition operator on the type of a process after a transition...

Proposition 1 (Subject Reduction). *$(\Gamma; P) \xrightarrow{\mu} (\Gamma \wr \mu; P')$ implies $\exists \Gamma'$ s.t. $\Gamma' \preceq \Gamma \wr \mu$ and $\Gamma' \vdash P'$.*

...and decidable typability implies undecidable correctness.

Proposition 2 (Type Soundness). *If $\Gamma \vdash P$ then $\Gamma \models P$.*

5 Related Works

Acciai and Boreale's work on *Responsiveness* [1] (essentially our activeness, except that they work in a reduction-based setting, while we have to take the environment into account) addresses concerns very close to ours. It does not support choice or conditional properties, as it uses numerical levels to track dependencies, but presents an extension for recursive processes, in that it permits handling unbounded recursion such as a "factorial" function. Our dependency analysis would reject such a process, as the recursive call would create a dependency $f_{\mathbf{R}} \lhd f_{\mathbf{R}}$, that reduces to $f_{\mathbf{R}} \lhd \bot$. We conjecture that "delayed dependencies" [6] would permit integrating their recursion analysis with our work.

Kobayashi's *Livelock-Freedom Type System* (implemented as TyPiCal [8,9]), does a very fine analysis of channel *usages*. Instead of counting how many times a port may be used, they permit arbitrary *channel usages* that describe using a CCS-like language in what way and order the two ports of a channel may be used. This permits describing usages such as "every input must be followed by an output". Using numerical levels, basic dependency relations can be forced between elements of the usages of different channels. This prevents encoding of selection and branching as it amounts to having no "$\vee$" in behavioural statements, but permits analysing other usage patterns such as semaphores, which the present work would dismiss as unreliable $\star$-multiplicities.

Kobayashi and Sangiorgi's *Hybrid Type System* for lock-freedom [10] combines (arbitrary) deadlock, termination and confluence type systems on *sub-processes* of the one being analysed (thereby permitting analysis of globally divergent processes). This work uses typed transitions reminiscent of ours, and their "robust" properties are analogous to our semantics permitting arbitrary transition sequences $\tilde{\mu}_i$. Channel usages are like those used by Kobayashi in previous works [8,9], with the same expressive power and limitations. The typing rules discard those processes that rely on the environment in order to fulfil their obligation. Hence well-typed processes are lock-free without making any assumption on the environment. Advanced termination type systems such as those proposed by Deng and Sangiorgi [4] permit this hybrid system to deal with complex recursive functions like tree traversal.

The three following papers have a *generic* approach, as opposed to the previous ones (and the present paper) that are aimed at specific properties. They have to be *instantiated* with the desired property, expressed in various ways.

Kobayashi's *Generic Type System* [7] is a general purpose type system that can be *instantiated* with a subtyping relation and a consistency condition on types, resulting in type systems for various safety properties (unlike activeness which is a liveness property). Types are CCS-like abstractions of the process, and the consistency condition verifies that the type enjoys the desired property. Its types use "+" in essentially the same sense as we do, and "&" corresponds precisely to our $\vee$. The paper includes as examples of instantiations, arity-mismatch checking, race-freedom and deadlock-freedom type systems. However, simply by providing a subtyping relation and a consistency predicate one does not get the desired results "for free". It is still necessary to prove several technical lemmas.

Caires and Vieira's *Spatial Logic Model Checker* [3] checks processes for a wide range of properties, expressed by expressions in a *spatial logic*. Activeness of a port p can be written $\mu X.(\langle p\rangle \vee \Box\Diamond X)$. Responsiveness of a port depends on the channel type, but it should be possible to give an inductive translation of channel types to modal formulæ corresponding to responsiveness on it. The selection connective $\vee$ is also present, with the same meaning. There is no direct equivalent of $\triangleleft$, so conditional properties need to be encoded by modifying the activeness formulæ, which may become too complex with dependencies on responsiveness as in $r_{\mathbf{R}}\triangleleft(a_{\mathbf{AR}}\wedge b_{\mathbf{AR}})$ (Section 4). Both its strengths and limitations come from it being a *model checker*. On the one hand, it takes logical formulæ in *input* rather than constructing them, it has a large complexity due to exhaustively exploring the state space, and doesn't terminate when given unbounded processes (our type system is polynomial in the process size and always terminates). On the other hand it is *complete* for bounded processes, and recognises activeness in cases deemed unsafe by our system due to over-approximation.

Acciai and Boreale's *Spatial Type System* [2] combines ideas from Kobayashi's Generic Type System (types abstract the behaviour of processes) and Spatial Logic, by performing model checking with spatial formulæ on the types rather than on the processes. This results in a generic type system able to characterise liveness properties such as activeness and supporting choice, both through the process constructor + and logical connective $\vee$. It is parametrised by "shallow" (without direct access to the object parts of transitions) logical formulæ, that it verifies using model-checking. Being based on model checking, it suffers from the same limitations as the previous work, in terms of computation complexity, and difficulty of expressing conditional properties or responsiveness (again, "responsiveness" in that paper corresponds to our "activeness"). On the other hand, restricting it to shallow logic formulæ allows working on the abstracted process, making it more efficient than a fully general model checker. Like the previous work and unlike the Generic Type System, it doesn't require proving soundness of a consistency predicate, as it is based on a fixed formula language.

6 Conclusion

We described a type notation and semantics that combine statements about liveness properties ($s_{\mathbf{A}}$ and $p_{\mathbf{R}}$), choice (through branching $(p+q)_{\mathbf{A}}$ and selection $\Delta \vee \Delta$) and conditional properties ($\Delta \triangleleft \Theta$). Then the type system outlined in Section 4 is able, given a process P, channel types and optionally port multiplicities, to construct a process type whose local component Ξ_{L} contains all information the type system was able to gather about P's behaviour. As the type system is sound and decidable, it is necessarily incomplete, but still powerful enough to recognise activeness and responsiveness in many important applications such as data representation or conversation-based programming. We chose to focus on choice itself, leaving out features like recursivity [1] subtyping [13], and complex channel usages such as locks [8], well explored before in a choice-less context.

References

1. Acciai, L., Boreale, M.: Responsiveness in process calculi. Theoretical Computer Science 409(1), 59–93 (2008)
2. Acciai, L., Boreale, M.: Spatial and behavioral types in the pi-calculus. In: van Breugel, F., Chechik, M. (eds.) CONCUR 2008. LNCS, vol. 5201, pp. 372–386. Springer, Heidelberg (2008)
3. Caires, L.: Behavioral and spatial observations in a logic for the π-calculus. In: Walukiewicz, I. (ed.) FOSSACS 2004. LNCS, vol. 2987, pp. 72–89. Springer, Heidelberg (2004)
4. Deng, Y., Sangiorgi, D.: Ensuring termination by typability. Information and Computation 204(7), 1045–1082 (2006)
5. Gamboni, M., Ravara, A.: Activeness and responsiveness in mobile processes. In: 7th Conference on Telecommunications, pp. 429–432. Instituto de TelecomunicaÇões (2009)
6. Gamboni, M., Ravara, A.: Responsive choice in process calculi. Technical report, SQIG — IT and IST, UTL Portugal (2009), `http://gamboni.org/i.pdf`
7. Igarashi, A., Kobayashi, N.: A generic type system for the Pi-calculus. ACM SIGPLAN Notices 36(3), 128–141 (2001)
8. Kobayashi, N.: A type system for lock-free processes. Information and Computation 177(2), 122–159 (2002)

9. Kobayashi, N.: Typical 1.6.2 (2008)
10. Kobayashi, N., Sangiorgi, D.: A hybrid type system for lock-freedom of mobile processes. In: Gupta, A., Malik, S. (eds.) CAV 2008. LNCS, vol. 5123, pp. 80–93. Springer, Heidelberg (2008)
11. Milner, R.: The polyadic π-calculus: A tutorial. In: Logic and Algebra of Specification, Proceedings of the International NATO Summer School (Marktoberdorf, Germany, 1991). NATO ASI Series F, vol. 94, Springer, Heidelberg (1993)
12. Milner, R., Parrow, J., Walker, D.: A calculus of mobile processes, i and ii. Information and Computation 100(1), 1–77 (1992)
13. Pierce, B.C., Sangiorgi, D.: Typing and subtyping for mobile processes. In: Proceedings of LICS 1993, pp. 376–385. IEEE Computer Society, Los Alamitos (1993)
14. Sangiorgi, D.: The name discipline of uniform receptiveness. Theoretical Computer Science 221(1-2), 457–493 (1999)
15. Sangiorgi, D., Walker, D.: PI-Calculus: A Theory of Mobile Processes. Cambridge University Press, Cambridge (2001)

A Labelled Transition System

The labelled transition system is inductively defined by the following rules. Labels, ranged over by μ, are τ, input $a(\tilde{x})$ and output $(\boldsymbol{\nu}\tilde{z}:\tilde{\sigma})\,\overline{a}\langle\tilde{x}\rangle$ where $a \notin \tilde{z} \subseteq \tilde{x}$.

$$\frac{-}{\overline{a}\langle\tilde{x}\rangle.P \xrightarrow{\overline{a}\langle\tilde{x}\rangle} P}\ (\text{OUT}) \qquad \frac{-}{a(\tilde{y}).P \xrightarrow{a(\tilde{x})} P\{^{\tilde{x}}/_{\tilde{y}}\}}\ (\text{INP})$$

$$\frac{P \xrightarrow{(\boldsymbol{\nu}\tilde{y}:\tilde{\theta})\,\overline{a}\langle\tilde{x}\rangle} Q \quad z \in \tilde{x} \setminus (\{a\} \cup \tilde{y})}{(\boldsymbol{\nu}z:\sigma)\,P \xrightarrow{(\boldsymbol{\nu}z:\sigma,\tilde{y}:\tilde{\theta})\,\overline{a}\langle\tilde{x}\rangle} Q}\ (\text{OPEN})$$

$$\frac{P \xrightarrow{\mu} P'}{!P \xrightarrow{\mu} P' \,|\, !P}\ (\text{REP}) \qquad \frac{P \xrightarrow{\mu} Q \quad z \notin \mathrm{n}(\mu)}{(\boldsymbol{\nu}z:\sigma)\,P \xrightarrow{\mu} (\boldsymbol{\nu}z:\sigma)\,Q}\ (\text{NEW})$$

$$\frac{P \xrightarrow{\mu} P' \quad \mathrm{bn}(\mu) \cap \mathrm{fn}(Q) = \varnothing}{P \,|\, Q \xrightarrow{\mu} P' \,|\, Q \qquad Q \,|\, P \xrightarrow{\mu} Q \,|\, P'}\ (\text{PAR})$$

$$\frac{P \xrightarrow{(\boldsymbol{\nu}\tilde{z}:\tilde{\sigma})\,\overline{a}\langle\tilde{x}\rangle} P' \quad Q \xrightarrow{a(\tilde{x})} Q' \quad \tilde{z} \cap \mathrm{fn}(Q) = \varnothing}{\begin{array}{c} P \,|\, Q \xrightarrow{\tau} (\boldsymbol{\nu}\tilde{z}:\tilde{\sigma})\,(P' \,|\, Q') \\ Q \,|\, P \xrightarrow{\tau} (\boldsymbol{\nu}\tilde{z}:\tilde{\sigma})\,(Q' \,|\, P') \end{array}}\ (\text{COM})$$

$$\frac{P \xrightarrow{\mu} P'}{P{+}Q \xrightarrow{\mu} P' \quad Q{+}P \xrightarrow{\mu} P'}\ (\text{SUM})$$

$$\frac{P \equiv_\alpha P' \quad P' \xrightarrow{\mu} Q' \quad Q' \equiv_\alpha Q}{P \xrightarrow{\mu} Q}\ (\text{CONG})$$

B Weakening on behavioural statements

Definition 3 (Weakening Relation).
Relation $\preceq$ is the smallest preorder defined by the following rules, where $\cong$ is its symmetric closure.

1. *On behavioural statements or process types (ranged over by η):*
   - $\eta_1 \wedge \eta_2 \preceq \eta_1 \preceq \eta_1 \vee \eta_2$, *and* $\bot \preceq \eta \preceq \top$. $\eta \wedge (\eta_1 \vee \eta_2) \cong (\eta \wedge \eta_1) \vee (\eta \wedge \eta_2)$.
   - $\wedge$ *and* $\vee$ *are commutative, associative and idempotent, up to* $\cong$.
   - *If* $\eta_1 \preceq \eta_2$ *then* $\eta \wedge \eta_1 \preceq \eta \wedge \eta_2$ *and* $\eta \vee \eta_1 \preceq \eta \vee \eta_2$.
   - *If* $\eta_1 \cong \eta_2$ *then* $\gamma \lhd \eta_1 \cong \gamma \lhd \eta_2$, $(\eta \blacktriangleleft \eta_1) \cong (\eta \blacktriangleleft \eta_2)$ *and* $(\eta_1 \blacktriangleleft \eta) \cong (\eta_2 \blacktriangleleft \eta)$.

2. *On multiplicities,* $m_1 \preceq m_2$ *and* $p^{m_1} \preceq p^{m_2}$ *if* $m_1 = 0$ *or* $m_2 \in \{m_1, \star\}$. *Also,* $p^\star \cong \top$.
3. *On dependency statements:* $(\gamma \triangleleft \varepsilon_1) \wedge (\gamma \triangleleft \varepsilon_2) \cong \gamma \triangleleft (\varepsilon_1 \vee \varepsilon_2)$, $(\gamma \triangleleft \varepsilon_1) \vee (\gamma \triangleleft \varepsilon_2) \cong \gamma \triangleleft (\varepsilon_1 \wedge \varepsilon_2)$ *and* $\gamma \triangleleft \bot \cong \top$

C Type System

The type system is constituted by the following rules. (R-Pre) is detailed in Section 4, and the reader is invited to have a look at the technical report for a detailed discussion of the notation and operators used in the other rules.

$$\frac{-}{(\varnothing; \top \blacktriangleleft \top) \vdash \mathbf{0}} \text{ (R-Nil)}$$

$$\frac{\forall i : \Gamma_i \vdash P_i}{\Gamma_1 \odot \Gamma_2 \vdash P_1 \mid P_2} \text{ (R-Par)} \qquad \frac{\Gamma \vdash P \qquad \Gamma(x) = \sigma}{(\boldsymbol{\nu} x)\,\Gamma \vdash (\boldsymbol{\nu} x : \sigma)\,P} \text{ (R-Res)}$$

$$\frac{\begin{array}{c}\forall i : \big(\mathsf{sub}(G_i) = \{p_i\},\quad (\Sigma_i; \Xi_{\mathrm{L}i} \blacktriangleleft \Xi_{\mathrm{E}i}) \vdash G_i.P_i\big)\\ \Xi_{\mathrm{E}} \preceq \bigwedge_i \Xi_{\mathrm{E}i}\\ \big(\Xi_{\mathrm{E}} \text{ has concurrent environment } p_{i'}\big) \Rightarrow \varepsilon = \bot\end{array}}{\big(\bigwedge_i \Sigma_i; (\sum_i p_i)_{\mathbf{A}} \triangleleft \varepsilon \wedge \bigvee_i \Xi_{\mathrm{L}i} \blacktriangleleft \Xi_{\mathrm{E}}\big) \vdash \sum_i G_i.P_i} \text{ (R-Sum)}$$

$$\frac{\begin{array}{c}\Gamma \vdash P \quad \mathsf{sub}(G) = p \quad \mathsf{obj}(G) = \tilde{x}\\ (\#(G) = 1 \text{ and } m' = \star) \Rightarrow \varepsilon = \bot\end{array}}{\begin{array}{l}\left(p : \sigma; \blacktriangleleft p^m \wedge \bar{p}^{m'}\right) \odot\\ \left(; p_{\mathbf{A}}^{\#(G)} \triangleleft \varepsilon \blacktriangleleft\right) \odot\\ !_{\text{if } \#(G) = \omega}\, (\boldsymbol{\nu}\mathrm{bn}(G)) \Big(\Gamma \triangleleft \bar{p}_{\mathbf{A}} \odot\\ \quad \overline{\sigma}[\tilde{x}] \triangleleft \bar{p}_{\mathbf{AR}} \odot\\ \quad (; p_{\mathbf{R}} \triangleleft \sigma[\tilde{x}] \blacktriangleleft) \Big) \vdash G.P\end{array}} \text{ (R-Pre)}$$

In the rule (R-Sum), a process type having no "concurrent environment $p_{i'}$" prevents a third-party process to attempt selecting more than one branch of the sum, and, by contraposition, guarantees that any attempt to select a branch of the sum (by communicating with its guard) will succeed, which is what activeness of the branching means.

A Model of Evolvable Components*

Fabrizio Montesi and Davide Sangiorgi

Focus Research Team, Inria/University of Bologna

Abstract. We present a model of components following the process calculus approach. The main problem was isolating primitives that capture the relevant concepts of component-based systems. The key features of the calculus are: a hierarchical structure of components; a prominent role to input/output interfaces; the possibility of stopping and capturing components; a mechanism of channel interactions, orthogonal to the activity of components, which may produce tunneling effects that bypass the component hierarchy.

We present the calculus, explain the syntax, formulate its operational semantics and a basic type system. We show a number of examples of use of the calculus, with particular emphasis to common evolvability patterns for components.

1 Introduction

Complex software systems, in particular distributed systems, are often being thought and designed as structured composition of computational units referred to as *components*. These components are supposed to interact with each other following some predefined patterns or protocols. The notion of component is widely used in industry but there is no single answer to the question of what is, exactly, a software component. In industry, the following informal definition, from Szyperski et al. [SGM02], is often used: "A software component is a unit of composition with contractually specified interfaces and explicit context dependencies. An interface is a set of named operations that can be invoked by clients. Context dependencies are specifications of what the deployment environment needs to provide, such that the components can function." Key ingredients of a component are therefore their input and output interfaces. Moreover, to promote composition, the structure of a component system is often hierarchical.

In this paper we study models of components following the process calculus approach. Process calculi have been successfully employed in the modeling, analysis, and verification of concurrent and distributed systems. In recent years, proposals of calculi for distributed systems have been put forward with explicit notions of *location*, or *site*. While locations may be suggestive components, the differences between the two concepts remain noticeable. In particular locations do not have explicit input and output interfaces.

An important issue in complex software system is *evolvability*. The needs and the requirements on a system change over time. This may happen because the

* Work supported by the EU project "Hats".

M. Wirsing, M. Hofmann, and A. Rauschmayer (Eds.): TGC 2010, LNCS 6084, pp. 153–171, 2010.

original specification was incomplete or ambiguous, or because new needs arise that had not been predicted at design time. As designing and deploying a system is costly, it is important that the system be capable of adapting itself to changes in the surrounding environment. Evolvability was another major target in this work.

The challenge in the formalisation of a calculus of components was to isolate key aspects of component-based systems and reflect these into specific constructs. The main features that we have decided to retain are: a hierarchical structure of components; a prominent role to input/output interfaces; the possibility of stopping and capturing components to produce dynamicity; a mechanism of channel interactions, orthogonal to the activity of components, with tunneling effects that bypass the component hierarchy. Interactions along channels may be triggered when a method in the input interface of a component is invoked. Channels can be used to implement sessions of interactions between components.

Components are stopped by means of a construct, `extract`, reminiscent of the passivation operator of calculi such as Kell [SS05] and Homer [HGB04, BHG06]. The `extract` operator is the only one that permits modifications of the structure of components, which is otherwise static.

In the paper we first present the calculus and explain the syntax. Then we formulate its operational semantics. We found it convenient to formulate the component activity by means of a reduction semantics, and channel interaction by means of a labelled semantics. We equip the calculus with a basic type system to avoid run-time errors. A number of examples of use of the calculus are presented. In particular, we show how various patterns of evolvability of components are captured.

2 Syntax

Table 1 presents the syntax of the calculus, MECo (Model of Evolvable Components). Components are the unit of composition. Each component has: an identity; a set of *input ports* that represent the functionalities that the component offers to the environment; a set of *output ports* that specify the dependencies of the components, that is, what the deployment environment has to provide for the components to function; an internal structure, itself containing components (which gives the hierarchical structure). Thus the general form of a component is

$$a \ \{_{i \in 1..h} \, m_i = (x).\, P_i\} \, [\, P \,] \{\, _{j \in 1..k} \, n_j \mapsto f_j \,\} \,, \tag{1}$$

where: a is the component identity; m_i is an input port and $m_i = (x).\, P_i$ the *method* implementing the port; n_j is an output port and $n_j \mapsto f_j$ a *link* specifying the binding for the port; P is the internal structure of the component. Both the m_i's and the n_j's should all be distinct. The method bodies P_i may refer to inner components (i.e., components inside P) as well as to the output ports n_j's. An output port of the component may be bound to the input port of a sibling component or to an output port of the enclosing component. The set of input ports form the *input interface*; the set of output ports form the *output interface*.

Table 1. The syntax of the calculus

Input/output ports m, n			
Unit value	$\star$		
Names $a, b, \ldots, p, q \ldots, r, s \ldots, x, y$			
Method set	$I ::=$	$m = (x).\, P,\ I$	method
	$\mid$	$\emptyset$	empty list
Link set	$O ::=$	$m \mapsto f,\ O$	link
	$\mid$	$\emptyset$	empty list
Skeleton	$K ::=$	$\{\, I \,\}[\, P \,]$	
Values	$v ::=$	$p \mid K \mid \star$	
Process	$P ::=$	$P \mid P$	parallel comp.
	$\mid$	$\nu p\, P$	restriction
	$\mid$	$v\, w\{\, O \,\}$	component
	$\mid$	`extract` v `as` x `in` P	passivation
	$\mid$	$f\, v$	call
	$\mid$	$\overline{v}\, w.\, P$	channel output
	$\mid$	$v(x).\, P$	channel input
	$\mid$	$\mathbf{0}$	nil
Call subject	$f ::=$	v_m	method selection
	$\mid$	m	port

The activity of components is local: when the body of the method of a component is executed, calls may only be issued to inner components or to components that are reachable via output port bindings. In particular, the environment surrounding a component a may call a but not components internal to a. Such components may only be reached if some input port of a forwards messages to them.

Other than through component methods, interactions can take place through channels. When a component calls another one, the first may pass a private channel to the second; this channel may be used for further interactions, thus creating sessions of interaction between the two components (other components may actually get involved, if the channel is sent around). Creation and communication of channels may have tunneling effects: for instance a component a may call a component b and this may forward the message to some inner component c. If the message contains a channel, then a and c may use the channel for direct interactions.

In a link $m \mapsto f$, the binding f for the output port m can either be of the form a_n, meaning that m is bound to the input port n of the sibling component a, or n, meaning that m is bound to the output port n of the enclosing component.

On the terminology, we should stress that an input interface refers to the signature of the methods of a components, excluding their actual implementation as a method set. Similarly for output interface with respect to link sets.

In (1), the body $[P]$ of the component together with its set of methods form its *skeleton*. The `extract` construct permits to stop a component and extract its skeleton. This skeleton may then be manipulated, as a first-class value. Skeleton extraction is a form of passivation as found in calculi such as Kell and Homer, and is the basis for expressing modifications of components and thus modelling evolvability.

The set of values includes, besides skeletons, also component identities, channels, and the unit value $\star$ (other basic values such as integers and booleans could be added). In contrast, input and output ports are not values; this because the ports associated to a component are specified by the type of the component. Similarly, method and link sets are not values; this is both for simplicity in the calculus, and because it is unclear how useful this extensions would be (given that the calculus is typed). We discuss types in the next section.

The syntax does not distinguish between channels and component identities: they are all names. The distinction will be made by the typing. However, in examples and explanations, a, b will be component identities and r, s channels. Similarly, as in the π-calculus, we do not have a separate syntactic class for variables. In Table 1, in the definitions of method, channel input, and `extract`, variable x is bound in P. Similarly, a restriction $\boldsymbol{\nu} p\, P$ binds the free occurrences of p in P. The definitions of free (`fn`) and bound name (`bn`) of a term are as expected. We use i, j, h, k for integers.

We require that a method $p = (x).\, P$ has no free channels: the only channels that the method can use are those provided by the callee, and those that are created in P itself. This constraint will be enforced by the type system.

The forwarding action of output ports makes calls to components naturally asynchronous; hence the call construct, $f\ v$, has no continuation. In contrast, channel interaction could be asynchronous or synchronous; we have preferred it synchronous because it fits well with the use of channels for session interactions.

3 Operational Semantics

The operational meaning of a process calculus is usually explained either by means of a reduction semantics, or by means of a labelled transition semantics. A reduction semantics uses the auxiliary relation of structural congruence, with which the participants of an interaction are brought into contiguous positions. This makes it possible to express interaction by means of simple term-rewriting rules. In a labelled transition semantics, by contrast, the rules are given in a purely SOS style, without a prior rewriting of the structure of terms. The participants of an interaction therefore need not be contiguous. This makes it necessary to define also transitions that describe the potential interaction of a term with its environment (the input and output actions of CCS and π-calculus).

For our calculus, we explain component activities (use of input and output ports, passivation) by means of a reduction semantics, whereas we explain channel interaction by means of a labelled semantics. The reason for the separation is that component activity is local, whereas channel interaction is global (the component structure is transparent to them). A reduction semantics makes it possible to express component activity in a simple and neat way. A reduction semantics for channel interaction, in contrast, would be more complex; due to tunneling, interacting particles could be located far away in the structure of a term. To bring such particles into contiguous positions we would have to allow, in the structural congruence, the possibility of moving them in and out of a component. This is however unsound in presence of passivation (unsound in the sense that one could derive undesired reductions). For the same reasons, in structural congruence restrictions cannot escape the boundaries of components.

We write $P \longrightarrow_{\mathtt{R}} P'$ for an internal step of the process P that is derived using the reduction semantics, and that therefore represents a component activity; and $P \xrightarrow{\tau} P'$ for an internal step derived using the labeled semantics, and that therefore represents a channel interaction. Finally, $\longrightarrow$ is the unions of the two relations $\longrightarrow_{\mathtt{R}}$ and $\xrightarrow{\tau}$, and $\Longrightarrow$ is the reflexive and transitive closure of $\longrightarrow$. Relation $\longrightarrow_{\mathtt{R}}$ and $\xrightarrow{\tau}$ are explained in the following two sections. We assume that at any point bound names can be renamed (alpha-conversion).

3.1 Component Activity

Structural congruence As explained above, the presence of passivation makes the component boundaries rigid for structural congruence. The structural congruence relation is written $\equiv$, and defined as the smallest congruence satisfying the following rules:

$$P_1 \mid P_2 \equiv P_2 \mid P_1 \qquad P_1 \mid (P_2 \mid P_3) \equiv (P_1 \mid P_2) \mid P_3$$
$$P \mid \boldsymbol{\nu} p\, Q \equiv \boldsymbol{\nu} p\,(P \mid Q) \text{ if } p \notin \mathsf{fn}(P) \quad \boldsymbol{\nu} p\, \boldsymbol{\nu} q\, P \equiv \boldsymbol{\nu} q\, \boldsymbol{\nu} p\, P$$

Reduction rules. There are three reduction axioms. The first axiom shows a call to an input port. The second axiom explains the forwarding action of an output port. The third axiom is a skeleton extraction. In calculi with passivation, some care is needed when extruding restricted names out of "boxes" that may be passivated: the extrusion takes place only when messages containing that name are sent. This corresponds to the extrusion of names $\widetilde{p}$ in rule `R-Oport` below.

$$[\mathtt{R-Iport}]\quad \frac{m = (x).\,Q \in I}{a\_m\, v \mid a\,\{\, I\,\}[\, P\,]\{\, O\,\} \longrightarrow_{\mathtt{R}} a\,\{\, I\,\}[\, P \mid Q\{^{v}/_{x}\}\,]\{\, O\,\}}$$

$$[\mathtt{R-Oport}]\quad \frac{m \mapsto f \in O \qquad \widetilde{p} \subseteq \mathsf{fn}(v)}{a\,\{\, I\,\}[\, \boldsymbol{\nu}\widetilde{p}\,(P \mid m\, v)\,]\{\, O\,\} \longrightarrow_{\mathtt{R}} \boldsymbol{\nu}\widetilde{p}\,(\, a\,\{\, I\,\}[\, P\,]\{\, O\,\} \mid f\, v)}$$

$$[\mathtt{R-extract}]\quad \frac{}{a\, K\{\, O\,\} \mid \mathtt{extract}\; a\; \mathtt{as}\; x\; \mathtt{in}\; P \longrightarrow_{\mathtt{R}} P\{^{K}/_{x}\}}$$

Now the inference rules for reduction. Reduction can occur within a parallel composition, a restriction, or a component boundary. The final rule introduces structural congruence.

$$[\mathtt{R-par}]\quad \frac{P \longrightarrow_{\mathtt{R}} P'}{P \mid Q \longrightarrow_{\mathtt{R}} P' \mid Q}$$

$$[\mathtt{R-res}]\quad \frac{P \longrightarrow_{\mathtt{R}} P'}{\boldsymbol{\nu} p\, P \longrightarrow_{\mathtt{R}} \boldsymbol{\nu} p\, P'}$$

$$[\mathtt{R-comp}]\quad \frac{P \longrightarrow_{\mathtt{R}} P'}{a\{\, I\,\}[\, P\,]\{\, O\,\} \longrightarrow_{\mathtt{R}} a\{\, I\,\}[\, P'\,]\{\, O\,\}}$$

$$[\mathtt{R-equiv}]\quad \frac{P \equiv P' \longrightarrow_{\mathtt{R}} P'' \equiv P'''}{P \longrightarrow_{\mathtt{R}} P'''}$$

3.2 Channel Interaction

Communications along channels is explained with an LTS. The rules are entirely standard, following the SOS of message-passing calculi such as π-calculus and Higher-Order π-calculus, as channel communications are independent of the component hierarchy. The label (or action) of a transition can be τ, rv (input), and $(\boldsymbol{\nu}\widetilde{p}\,)\overline{r}\,v$ (output). In the output label, $\widetilde{p}$ are private names, appearing free in v, that are being extruded. We use μ to range over actions. The bound names of an action μ, written $\mathsf{bn}(\mu)$, is the empty set for an input or silent action, they are $\widetilde{p}$ for an output action $(\boldsymbol{\nu}\widetilde{p}\,)\overline{r}\,v$. We omit the definitions of free names and names of μ, respectively written $\mathsf{fn}(\mu)$ and $\mathsf{n}(\mu)$, which are the expected ones. We have omitted the symmetric of L-parR and L-comR.

$$[\mathtt{L-out}]\quad \frac{}{\overline{r}\,v.\,P \xrightarrow{\overline{r}\,v} P}$$

$$[\mathtt{L-inp}]\quad \frac{}{r(x).\,P \xrightarrow{rv} P\{^{v}\!/_{x}\}}$$

$$[\mathtt{L-parR}]\quad \frac{P \xrightarrow{\mu} P' \qquad \mathsf{bn}(\mu) \cap \mathsf{fn}(Q) = \emptyset}{P \mid Q \xrightarrow{\mu} P' \mid Q}$$

$$[\mathtt{L-comR}]\quad \frac{P \xrightarrow{rv} P' \qquad Q \xrightarrow{(\boldsymbol{\nu}\widetilde{p}\,)\overline{r}\,v} Q' \qquad \widetilde{p} \cap \mathsf{fn}(P) = \emptyset}{P \mid Q \xrightarrow{\tau} \boldsymbol{\nu}\widetilde{p}\,(P' \mid Q')}$$

$$[\mathtt{L-res}]\quad \frac{P \xrightarrow{\mu} P' \qquad p \notin \mathsf{n}(\mu)}{\boldsymbol{\nu} p\, P \xrightarrow{\mu} \boldsymbol{\nu} p\, P'}$$

$$[\mathtt{L-open}]\quad \frac{P \xrightarrow{(\boldsymbol{\nu}\widetilde{p}\,)\overline{r}\,v} P' \qquad p \neq r \qquad p \in \mathsf{fn}(v) - \widetilde{p}}{\boldsymbol{\nu} p\, P \xrightarrow{(\boldsymbol{\nu} p, \widetilde{p}\,)\overline{r}\,v} \boldsymbol{\nu} p\, P'}$$

$$[\mathtt{L-comp}]\quad \frac{P \xrightarrow{\mu} P' \qquad \mathsf{bn}(\mu) \cap (a \cup \mathsf{fn}(I, O)) = \emptyset}{a\{\, I\,\}[\, P\,]\{\, O\,\} \xrightarrow{\mu} a\{\, I\,\}[\, P'\,]\{\, O\,\}}$$

4 Types

We comment the form of types with which the terms of the calculus are typed. The syntax is in Table 2. An input (or output) interface is a set of ports, say $m_1..m_h$. The type $[_{j\in 1..h}\, m_j : T_j]$ of such an interface shows what are the ports and, for each of them, say m_j, the type T_j of the values that may be sent along m_j. We use A, B to range over interface types.

A skeleton has type $A \triangleright B$, in which A is the type of the input interface of the skeleton, and B the type of its output interface. This means that a component using such skeleton offers the functionalities specified in A, and requires binders for the output ports as specified in B. Using H for a skeleton type, $\diamond H$ is then the type of the name of a component whose skeleton has type H.

We also assign a skeleton type to sets of methods or links; in this case a type $A \triangleright B$ means that the methods or links implement an (input or output) interface of type A and their body use output ports in the interface B. The type of a process is an interface type; it tells us the use of output ports made from the process.

The assignment of an output interface type A to a term means that the term uses output ports in A; it need not use all of them, though. This implicitly introduces a form of subtyping. We deliberately avoid however subtyping judgements. As in object-oriented languages, so here subtyping brings in subtle issues, outside the scope of the present paper.

The type $\sharp T$ for channels is as in π-calculus: T is the type of the values that may be carried along that channel.

Table 2. The syntax of types

Value types	$T ::=$	$\sharp T$	channel type
	$\mid$	H	skeleton type
	$\mid$	$\diamond H$	component id. type
	$\mid$	`unit`	unit type
Interface type	$A, B ::=$	$[_{j\in 1..h}\, m_j : T_j]$	
Skeleton type	$H ::=$	$A \triangleright B$	

4.1 Typing

Typing environments, ranged over by Γ, are partial functions from names to value types; $\mathsf{dom}(\Gamma)$ is the domain of Γ, i.e., the set of names on which Γ is defined. A typing judgement $\Gamma \vdash P : A$ says that under the assumptions in Γ, process P has an output interface type A. Similarly for other syntactic objects of the calculus. In the typing rules:

- we write $m : T \in A$ if the type A has a component $m : T$ (that is, A is $\lfloor_{j\in 1..h}\, m_j : T_j\rfloor$ and, for some j, $m = m_j$ and $T = T_j$);
- we write $\Gamma(a\_m) = T$ if a is typed in Γ as a component identity with an input interface in which there is a method m of type T; that is, $\Gamma(a) = \diamond(A \triangleright B)$ and $m : T \in A$.

Typing rules for methods, links, and values. In rule `T-method-set`, a skeleton type $A \triangleright B$ is assigned to a set of methods. The rule checks that the set implements the input interface A and that the body of each method only needs output ports in B. In the premise of the rule, $\Gamma/\mathtt{ch}$ indicates the removal from Γ of all names with a channel type. This constraint ensures us that the methods of a component have no free channels.

Rule `T-link-set`, for typing a set of links, is similar. A case distinction is made in the premise of the rule for the two possible forms of a link (binding to an output port or to the input port of another component). In `T-skeleton`, for typing a skeleton, we check that the skeleton offers the correct input interface A, and that both the methods and the body of the skeleton use output ports in B.

$$\mathtt{T-method-set}\ \frac{\forall j \quad \Gamma/\mathtt{ch}, x_j : T_j \vdash P_j : B}{\Gamma \vdash \{_{j\in 1..h}\, m_j = (x_j).\, P_j\} : \lfloor_{j\in 1..h}\, m_j : T_j\rfloor \triangleright B}$$

$$\mathtt{T-link-set}\ \frac{\forall j \quad \text{either } f_j = n \text{ and } n : T_j \in B, \text{ or } f_j = p\_n \text{ and } \Gamma(p\_n) = T_j}{\Gamma \vdash \{_{j\in 1..h}\, m_j \mapsto f_j\} : \lfloor_{j\in i..h}\, m_j : T_j\rfloor \triangleright B}$$

$$\mathtt{T-unit}\ \frac{}{\Gamma \vdash \star : \mathtt{unit}}$$

$$\mathtt{T-skeleton}\ \frac{\Gamma \vdash I : A \triangleright B \qquad \Gamma \vdash P : B}{\Gamma \vdash \{\, I\,\}[\, P\,] : A \triangleright B}$$

$$\mathtt{T-names}\ \frac{\Gamma(p) = T}{\Gamma \vdash p : T}$$

Typing rules for processes. The interesting rules for processes are those for components and for the `extract` construct. In `T-comp`, we check that the types of the component identity and of the skeleton agree, and that the skeleton can be composed with the links. In `T-extract`, we type the body P under the typing extended with the skeleton type for the variable x derived from the type of the component identity p. The remaining rules are the usual one of process calculi.

$$\mathtt{T-comp}\ \frac{\Gamma(p) = \diamond(A \triangleright B') \qquad \Gamma \vdash v : A \triangleright B' \qquad \Gamma \vdash O : B' \triangleright B}{\Gamma \vdash p\, v\{\, O\,\} : B}$$

$$\mathtt{T-extract}\ \frac{\Gamma(p) = \diamond H \qquad \Gamma, x : H \vdash P : B}{\Gamma \vdash \mathtt{extract}\, p\, \mathtt{as}\, x\, \mathtt{in}\, P : B}$$

$$\mathtt{T-par}\ \frac{\Gamma \vdash P_i : B \quad i = 1, 2}{\Gamma \vdash P_1 \mid P_2 : B}$$

$$\mathtt{T-res1}\ \frac{\Gamma, p : \diamond H \vdash P : B}{\Gamma \vdash \boldsymbol{\nu} p\, P : B}$$

$$\mathtt{T-res2}\ \frac{\Gamma, p : \sharp T \vdash P : B}{\Gamma \vdash \boldsymbol{\nu} p\, P : B}$$

$$\mathtt{T-call-Iport}\ \frac{\Gamma(p\_m) = T \qquad \Gamma \vdash v : T}{\Gamma \vdash p\_m\, v : B}$$

$$\mathtt{T-call-Oport}\ \frac{m : T \in B \qquad \Gamma \vdash v : T}{\Gamma \vdash m\, v : B}$$

$$\mathtt{T-out}\ \frac{\Gamma(p) = \sharp T \qquad \Gamma \vdash v : T \qquad \Gamma \vdash P : B}{\Gamma \vdash \overline{p} v. P : B}$$

$$\mathtt{T-inp}\ \frac{\Gamma(p) = \sharp T \qquad \Gamma, x : T \vdash P : B}{\Gamma \vdash p(x). P : B}$$

$$\mathtt{T-nil}\ \frac{}{\Gamma \vdash \mathbf{0} : B}$$

Suppose $\Gamma \vdash P : B$. Then P is *closed* if the type of each name in Γ is either a channel type or a component identity type.

4.2 Soundness

Lemma 1 (Weakening). *If $\Gamma \vdash P : A$ and $p \notin \mathsf{dom}(\Gamma)$ then also $\Gamma, p : T \vdash P : A$, for any T.*

The fundamental theorem for typing is Subject Reduction. It is stated for arbitrary processes, though it would be reasonable to admit reductions only on closed processes.

Theorem 1 (Subject Reduction). *If $\Gamma \vdash P : A$ and $P \longrightarrow P'$, then $\Gamma \vdash P' : A$.*

The proof of the theorem is along the lines of Subject Reduction theorems in process calculi. Thus one first establishes invariance for typing under structural congruence.

In the calculus, there are four kinds of values: component identities, channels, skeletons, unit. Each of them has a specific role, and a use in wrong places may produce run-time errors. Typing guarantees absence of run-time errors. This is proved by defining a tagged semantics of the calculus as follows. Given a well-typed process P and a typing derivation for it, we tag each occurrence of a value in P with one of the symbols $\sharp, \diamond, \triangleright,$ **unit**, depending on whether in the typing derivation the value is assigned a channel type, a component identity type, a skeleton type, or the unit type. The operational semantics of tagged processes is defined as that of ordinary processes except that the following rules are added. They indicate the appearance of a run-time error by the introduction of the special process `wrong`. The rules are added to the reduction semantics (they could have been equally placed in the labeled semantics). There is one rule for each process construct making use of values. We use γ, δ to range over $\sharp, \diamond, \triangleright,$ **unit**.

- $v_\gamma\, w_\delta\{\, O \,\} \longrightarrow_{\mathtt{R}} \mathtt{wrong}$, if $\gamma \neq \diamond$ and $\delta \neq \triangleright$;
- $\mathtt{extract}\ v_\gamma\ \mathtt{as}\ x_\delta\ \mathtt{in}\ P \longrightarrow_{\mathtt{R}} \mathtt{wrong}$, if $\gamma \neq \diamond$ and $\delta \neq \triangleright$;
- $v_\gamma\_m\, w_\delta \longrightarrow_{\mathtt{R}} \mathtt{wrong}$, if $\gamma \neq \diamond$;
- $\overline{v_\gamma}\, w_\delta.\, P \longrightarrow_{\mathtt{R}} \mathtt{wrong}$, if $\gamma \neq \sharp$;
- $v_\gamma(x_\delta).\, P \longrightarrow_{\mathtt{R}} \mathtt{wrong}$, if $\gamma \neq \sharp$.

We then say that a well-typed process P *has a run-time error* if there is a typing derivation for P and a tagging R of P under the typing derivation such that $R \Longrightarrow R'$ for some tagged R' containing `wrong`. Exploiting type information and a correspondence between the two semantics (that in turn, uses Subject Reduction and tag preservation under substitutions), we prove that no run-time error can occur.

Theorem 2. *If P is well-typed then P has no run-time error.*

Other forms of error that typing avoids are: emission on an output port that is not bound, that is, the appearance of a process

$$a\,\{\, I \,\}[\, \boldsymbol{\nu}\widetilde{p}\,(P \mid m\, v)\,]\{\, O \,\}$$

where O contains no link at m; calls to a component that exists but does not have the expected method, that is, the appearance of a process

$$a\_m\, v \mid a\,\{\, I \,\}[\, P \,]\{\, O \,\}$$

where I contains no m method.

The absence of such run-time errors can be formalised similarly to above, using the special process `wrong`; in this case, however, we do not need tagged processes, as the rules producing `wrong` can be inserted directly into the ordinary operational semantics.

The type system can be refined in various ways, following existing type systems for process calculi. In particular, using linearity, one can enforce unicity of component identities, which may often be a desirable feature.

5 Examples

In this section we discuss some simple examples. The first is about mutable storage, the others are evolvability-related patterns. The examples show the various constructs of the language, including tunneling on channels. They also show how to implement atomicity constrains on methods via a lock mechanism. We present a larger example in Section A. We omit the typing judgements, as they are very simple. We write $r.\,P$ and $\overline{r}.\,P$ for inputs and outputs of unit type; we omit trailing $\mathbf{0}$, e.g., writing $\overline{r}\,v$ for $\overline{r}\,v.\,\mathbf{0}$.

5.1 Store

$\mathtt{Cell}\langle v, P\rangle$ is a memory cell that stores the value v. It is realised as a component, called *cell*, with a single method *read*, whose parameter is a channel on which the stored value is sent. As we shall see, it is also useful to have a second parameter for the cell, as a process P that runs inside the cell:

$$\mathtt{Cell}\langle v, P\rangle \stackrel{\text{def}}{=} \mathit{cell}\{\, \mathit{read} = (r).\overline{r}\,v \,\}[\, P\,]\{\, \emptyset\,\}$$

We can use this component to implement a mutable variable $\mathtt{Var}\langle v\rangle$. This becomes a component *var*, with methods *get* and *set* for reading and changing the value stored, and with intial value v. Return channels in the methods implement a rendez-vous synchronisation with the callees.

$$\begin{aligned}\mathtt{Var}\langle v\rangle \stackrel{\text{def}}{=} \mathit{var}\{\; & \mathit{get} = (r).\, \mathit{cell\_read}\, r,\\ & \mathit{set} = (y,s).\, \mathtt{extract}\ \mathit{cell}\ \mathtt{as}\ x\ \mathtt{in}\,(\overline{s} \mid \mathtt{Cell}\langle y, \boldsymbol{\nu} a\ a\, x\{\, \emptyset\,\}\rangle)\,\}\\ & [\mathtt{Cell}\langle v, \mathbf{0}\rangle]\ \{\emptyset\}\end{aligned}$$

The skeleton x resulting from the extract of *cell* is run inside the new cell because x may contain uncompleted calls to the *read* method. Note the tunneling on the *get* method: the callee of the *var* component receives the answer directly from the inner *cell* component. As an example, we show an evolution of a system composed by $\mathtt{Var}\langle 5\rangle$, a reader, and a writer; we abbreviate the methods of *var* as I, and those of *cell* as I'; we omit empty output interfaces.

$$\begin{aligned}
& (\boldsymbol{\nu} r, s\,)(\;\; \mathit{var_get}\, r.\, r(x).\, P\\
&\qquad\qquad \mid \mathit{var_set}\,\langle 3, s\rangle.\, s.\, Q\;\;)\\
&\qquad\qquad \mid \; \mathit{var}\{\, I\,\}[\,\mathtt{Cell}\langle 5, \mathbf{0}\rangle\,]\\
\longrightarrow\!\!\longrightarrow\; & (\boldsymbol{\nu} r, s\,)(\;\; r(x).\, P\\
&\qquad\qquad \mid \mathit{var_set}\,\langle 3, s\rangle.\, s.\, Q\\
&\qquad\qquad \mid \; \mathit{var}\{\, I\,\}[\,\mathtt{Cell}\langle 5, \overline{r}\,5\rangle\,]\;\;)\\
\longrightarrow\!\!\longrightarrow\; & (\boldsymbol{\nu} r, s\,)(\;\; r(x).\, P \mid s.\, Q\\
&\qquad\qquad \mid \; \mathit{var}\{\, I\,\}[\,\overline{s} \mid \mathtt{Cell}\langle 3, \boldsymbol{\nu} a\;\; a\,\{\, I'\,\}[\,\overline{r}\,5\,]\rangle\,]\;\;)\\
\longrightarrow\!\!\longrightarrow\; & (\boldsymbol{\nu} r, s\,)(\;\; P\{5/x\} \mid Q\\
&\qquad\qquad \mid \; \mathit{var}\{\, I\,\}[\,\mathtt{Cell}\langle 3, \boldsymbol{\nu} a\;\; a\,\{\, I'\,\}[\,\mathbf{0}\,]\rangle\,]\;\;)\\
\simeq\; & \qquad P\{5/x\} \mid Q\\
&\quad \mid \; \mathit{var}\{\, I\,\}[\,\mathtt{Cell}\langle 3, \mathbf{0}\rangle\,]\{\, \emptyset\,\}
\end{aligned}$$

where $\simeq$ is *barbed congruence* [SW01], defined in the expected way, and obtained by application of the garbage-collection law $\boldsymbol{\nu} a\, a\{\, I\,\}[\mathbf{0}]\{\, O\,\} \simeq \mathbf{0}$, and assuming r, s not free in P and Q.

Next we implement a counter, initially set to v; it offers methods for reading and incrementing its internal value. There is an atomicity issue now: multiple executions of the increment method should not be allowed as they might interfere with each other. This synchronisation is achieved by means of a lock. We use, as abbreviations, $\texttt{remove}\ a\,.\,P$ for $\texttt{extract}\ a\ \texttt{as}\ x\ \texttt{in}\ P$ if x not free in P, and $\boldsymbol{\nu} r\ a\_m\, r.\, r.\, P$ for $\boldsymbol{\nu} r\ (a\_m\, r \mid r.\, P)$.

$$\begin{array}{l}\texttt{Counter}\langle v\rangle \stackrel{\text{def}}{=} \\ counter\{\ read = (r).\ var\_get\, r, \\ \qquad\qquad incr = (s).\,\texttt{remove}\ lock\,.\,\boldsymbol{\nu} r\ var\_get\, r.\, r(x).\,\boldsymbol{\nu} r'\ var\_set\,\langle x+1, r'\rangle.\, r'.\,(\overline{s} \mid \texttt{Lock})\ \} \\ \qquad [\,\texttt{Var}\langle v\rangle \mid \texttt{Lock}\,] \\ \qquad \{\,\emptyset\,\}\end{array}$$

and with $\texttt{Lock} \stackrel{\text{def}}{=} lock\{\,\emptyset\,\}[\,\mathbf{0}\,]\{\,\emptyset\,\}$. The use of locks could also be forced on the *read* method.

A different design for the counter exploits *var* as an external (rather than internal) component reachable via output ports *oget* and *oset*:

$$\begin{array}{l}\texttt{CAux} \stackrel{\text{def}}{=} counter\{\ read = (r).\ oget\, r, \\ \qquad\qquad incr = (s).\,\texttt{remove}\ lock\,.\,\boldsymbol{\nu} r\ oget\, r.\, r(x).\,\boldsymbol{\nu} r'\ oset\,\langle x+1, r'\rangle.\, r'.\,(\overline{s} \mid \texttt{Lock})\ \} \\ \qquad [\,\texttt{Lock}\,] \\ \qquad \{\ oget \mapsto var\_get,\ oset \mapsto var\_set\,\}\end{array}$$

and then the system is

$$\texttt{Counter}'\langle v\rangle \stackrel{\text{def}}{=} \boldsymbol{\nu}\ var\,(\texttt{CAux} \mid \texttt{Var}\langle v\rangle)$$

The difference between $\texttt{Counter}\langle v\rangle$ and $\texttt{Counter}'\langle v\rangle$ is similar to that between interceptors and wrappers discussed in Section 5.3.

5.2 Rebinding

Rebinding is a tecnique for modifying the output port bindings of a component at runtime. This is done by extracting the component and putting it into execution with the new output port definitions. Below, the component is c, its current output binders are O, and the new ones are O'.

$$c\{\,I\,\}[\,P\,]\{\,O\,\} \mid \texttt{extract}\ c\ \texttt{as}\ x\ \texttt{in}\ c\, x\{\,O'\,\} \longrightarrow c\{\,I\,\}[\,P\,]\{\,O'\,\}$$

5.3 Interceptors and Wrappers

Both the *interceptor* and the *wrapper* patterns are about modifications of the functionality of a given legacy component. The two techniques are similar in their basic concepts but the structures resulting from their applications are different, and this may affect the interactions with other components, as commented at the end of the section.

Interceptors. There are two kinds of interceptors: input interceptors and output interceptors. Input interceptors are used to adapt the input interface of the legacy component by intercepting calls for it from other components, whereas output interceptors intercept calls coming out of the output ports of the legacy component. Below the legacy component is $c\{_{i\in 1..h} m_i(x).\, P_i\}[P]\{_{j\in 1..k} n_j \mapsto f_j\}$.

Input interceptors. The simplest input interceptor is the *direct forwarder.* It exposes the same input interface as the legacy component and simply forwards method calls to it. For this, the output port of the forwarder are mapped onto the input ports of the legacy component:

$$a\,\{_{i\in 1..h}\, m_i = (x).\, n_i\, x\}[\mathbf{0}]\{\,_{j\in 1..h}\, n_j \mapsto c\_m_j\,\}$$

Direct forwarders can be used for making the same component available under multiple identities. Input interceptors can also be used for exposing a different interface; there are three possible cases: offering a new method (the system may have more requirements than what the legacy component supports); hiding a method (for encapsulation or security purposes); changing the behaviour of a method. In the first two cases, and sometimes also in the third, the types of the direct forwarder and of the legacy component are different.

Exposing a new method $m_{h+1}(x).\, P_{h+1}$, where m_{h+1} was not in the input interface of the legacy component, can be done by augmenting the interface of the direct forwarder:

$$a\,\{_{i\in 1..h}\, m_i = (x).\, n_i\, x, m_{h+1} = (x).\, P_{h+1}\}[\mathbf{0}]\{\,_{j\in 1..h}\, n_j \mapsto c\_m_j, O_{new}\,\}$$

where O_{new} collects all the links necessary for the execution of P_{h+1}.

Hiding a method can be done by removing this, and its related link, from the definition of the forwarder. The following is an example that hides method m_h:

$$a\,\{_{i\in 1..h-1}\, m_i = (x).\, n_i\, x\}[\mathbf{0}]\{\,_{j\in 1..h-1}\, n_j \mapsto c\_m_j\,\}$$

The case in which the body of a method is modified is similar — we change the body of such method in the definition of the forwarder.

Output interceptors. Output interceptors are supposed to capture outgoing calls issued by the legacy component and then trigger some actions.

We consider a component a that relies on a mail server b for its functioning. In particular, a makes use of the *sendMail* method of b in some of its method bodies. This system is:

$$\begin{array}{l} a\,\{_{i\in 1..h}\, m_i(x).\, P_i\}[\mathbf{0}]\{\, sendMail \mapsto b\_sendMail\,\} \\ \mid\ b\,\{\, sendMail = (x).\, P_{sendMail}\,\}[\,Q\,]\{\,O\,\} \end{array}$$

Now we want to log how many times a makes use of the *sendMail* functionality. Doing this with an input interceptor could be hard, because we do not know, a priori, how many times the execution of a method m_i will cause *sendMail* to be invoked. Instead, we contruct an output interceptor c that is responsible for executing process P_{log} whenever it receives a call for method *sendMail* and we rebind component a so that its link for *sendMail* points to c. Process P_{log} is executed together with a forwarding of the original *sendMail* request to the mail server b. These modifications are realised by the `extract` construct below:

$$
\begin{array}{l}
Sys \stackrel{\text{def}}{=} \\
\quad a\,\{_{i\in 1..h}\, m_i = (x).\, P_i\}[\mathbf{0}]\{\, sendMail \mapsto b\_sendMail\,\} \\
\mid b\,\{\, sendMail = (x).\, P_{sendMail}\,\}[\,Q\,]\{\,O\,\} \\
\mid \texttt{extract}\ a\ \texttt{as}\ x\ \texttt{in}\,(\quad a\,x\{\, sendMail \mapsto c\_sendMail\,\} \\
\qquad\qquad\qquad\qquad\quad \mid c\,\{\, sendMail = (x).\,(P_{log} \mid sendMail\ x)\,\}[\,\mathbf{0}\,]\{\, sendMail \mapsto \\
\qquad\qquad\qquad\qquad\quad b\_sendMail\,\}\ )
\end{array}
$$

We have:

$$
\begin{array}{rl}
Sys \longrightarrow & b\,\{\, sendMail = (x).\, P_{sendMail}\,\}[\,Q\,]\{\,O\,\} \\
\mid & a\,\{_{i\in 1..h}\, m_i = (x).\, P_i\}[\mathbf{0}]\{\, sendMail \mapsto c\_sendMail\,\} \\
\mid & c\,\{\, sendMail = (x).\,(P_{log} \mid sendMail\ x)\,\}[\,\mathbf{0}\,]\{\, sendMail \mapsto b\_sendMail\,\}
\end{array}
$$

Wrappers. While interceptors execute as siblings of the legacy component, a wrapper captures the legacy component (the *wrapped component*) and executes it as an inner component of another one (the *wrapper*), that is responsible for offering a modified view of the wrapped component. Wrapping can be applied in all the scenarios considered above with interceptors. For brevity, we only analyze the case of addition a method to a component interface.

As usual, the given legacy component is $\texttt{LC} \stackrel{\text{def}}{=} c\{_{i\in 1..h} m_i = (x).\, P_i\}[P]\{_{j\in 1..k}\, n_j \mapsto f_j\,\}$. We want to use this component so to create a new one, called a, that exposes an additional method $m_{h+1}(x).\, P_{h+1}$. We do so by wrapping the legacy component inside a new component a that implements the new method and forwards calls for the other methods to the legacy component:

$$
\begin{array}{l}
\texttt{WR} \stackrel{\text{def}}{=} \texttt{extract}\ c\ \texttt{as}\ x\ \texttt{in} \\
\qquad a\{_{i\in 1..h}\, m_i(x).\, c\_m_i\ x, m_{h+1} = (x).\, P_{h+1}\} \\
\qquad\ [\,c\,x\{\,_{j\in 1..k}\, n_j \mapsto n'_j\,\}] \\
\qquad \{_{j\in 1..h}\, n'_j \mapsto f_j, O_{new}\}
\end{array}
$$

where O_{new} collects the output port binders necessary for the execution of P_{h+1}. The wrapper defines, in its output ports, all the links needed by the wrapped component, whereas the output ports of the wrapped component refer to the wrapper for communicating with the outside world. We have:

$$
\begin{array}{rl}
\texttt{LC} \mid \texttt{WR} \longrightarrow & a\{_{i\in 1..h}\, m_i = (x).\, c\_m_i\ x, m_{h+1} = (x).\, P_{h+1}\} \\
& [\,c\,\{_{i\in 1..h}\, m_i = (x).\, P_i\}[P]\{\,_{j\in 1..k}\, n_j \mapsto n'_j\,\}] \\
& \{_{j\in 1..h}\, n'_j \mapsto f_j, O_{new}\}
\end{array}
$$

A client that invokes a at one of the "old" methods will have its message forwarded to c; then the client will be able to start a dialogue directly with c, exploiting the tunneling effect of channels.

Discussion. There are important differences between interceptors and wrappers when adapting a legacy component. A wrapper has a tighter control on the legacy component since only with the wrapper the legacy component becomes an inner component. It can thus be captured by the wrapper with the `extract` operator. Moreover, wrapping and wrapper components can be treated as a single unit. For instance, in the wrapping example above, we can throw this unit away thus:

$$\texttt{extract}\ a\ \texttt{as}\ x\ \texttt{in}\ \mathbf{0} \mid a\{\,..\,\}[\,..\,]\{\,..\,\} \longrightarrow \mathbf{0}$$

This is not possible with interceptors, as these are run in parallel with the legacy components and therefore both components are reachable from the environment.

On the other hand, a wrapped legacy component is not anymore reachable from the rest of the system other than through the wrapper itself, whereas with interceptors the legacy component remains reachable by those components that know its identity.

6 Conclusions and Extensions

We have presented a basic calculus of components, MECo, that tries to formalise the notion of component and evolvability patterns for components. We have experimented with a number of operators, especially related to adaptability and evolvability: those retained for MECo seemed to us a reasonable compromise between practical component needs (as in, e.g., Fractal component systems) and conciseness. Key component concepts that we wished to have were input and output interfaces, hierarchical structures, local interaction with possibile tunneling sessions that bypass the hierarchy. On top of this, for evolvability, MECo has a construct that allows one to stop a component and extract its skeleton.

The study of MECo is, admittedly, in a preliminary stage; for instance, as discussed below, typing is very rigid, and behavioural equivalences remain unexplored. We hope however that the work reported conveys the idea of component that MECo tries to formalise, and that this may trigger further study.

The closest process calculi to ours are Kell [SS05] and Homer [HGB04, BHG06]. These are calculi of mobile distributed processes in which computational entities may move in a dynamic hierarchy of locations. They have passivation operators that behave similarly to the `extract` of MECo. We may also see these calculi as calculi of components, thinking of locations as component boundaries (indeed, one of the main motivations behind Kell is to provide a model for Fractal components [Fra]). The main differences between Kell/Homer and MECo is the explicit use of input/output interfaces in MECo (input interfaces make MECo components look like objects, in fact, more than Kell/Homer locations;

but even in objects the notion of output interface is usually absent). Another difference is the presence of channels in MECo; the resulting tunneling effects are not possible in Kell or Homer where communication is local. The relations of MECo with other process calculi with locations, e.g., Ambients [CG98] and Seal [VC99], is weaker. The following are component models more loosely related (in particular they are not process calculi): Barros et al. [BHM05], also inspired by Fractal, model component behaviours as hierarchical synchronised transition systems and a composite system as a product of these, with the goal of applying model-checking techniques; Pucella [Puc02] proposes a form of typed λ-calculus targeted to modeling execution aspects of Microsoft Component Object Model; van Ommering et al. [vOvdLKM00] give an account of the architecture of Philips Koala component systems; Larsen et al. [LNW06], building on earlier work by de Alfaro and Henzinger [dAH01], study an interface language based on automata that separates the behavioural assumptions and guarantees for a component towards its environment.

Among the directions for future work, we are interested in exploring refinement of the basic type system, especially subtyping. Ideas from object-oriented languages should be useful here too, though output interfaces will require extra care. This may also lead to refining the present channel interactions of MECo into notions of session from Service-Oriented calculi, e.g., [CHY07, LMVR07, Vas09].

On another direction, we would like to examine stronger forms of run time error, whereby if a_m appears in a process, then one is ensured that a component a capable of consuming the message exists. For this one would probably have to record the set of components that a process needs for its execution. This is non-trivial, as component identities may be communicated and components may be passivated.

Another issue to study in MECo may be behavioural equivalence; for instance, one may be able to establish behavioural properties on the evolvability patterns of Section 5. For this, recent advances in bisimulation for higher-order process calculi (e.g., [LSS09, SKS07, JR05]) should be useful.

MECo has been partly inspired by the Fractal component system [Fra]. Modelling in MECo some of the applications built in Fractal should be useful both to understand the expressiveness of MECo and to provide a formal description of such applications.

Acknowledgements. We have benefited from discussions and many useful suggestions from A. Poetzsch-Heffter, I. Lanese, A. Schmitt, and J.-B. Stefani.

References

[BHG06] Bundgaard, M., Hildebrandt, T.T., Godskesen, J.C.: A cps encoding of name-passing in higher-order mobile embedded resources. Theor. Comput. Sci. 356(3), 422–439 (2006)

[BHM05] Barros, T., Henrio, L., Madelaine, E.: Behavioural models for hierarchical components. In: Godefroid, P. (ed.) SPIN 2005. LNCS, vol. 3639, pp. 154–168. Springer, Heidelberg (2005)

[CG98] Cardelli, L., Gordon, A.D.: Mobile ambients. In: Nivat, M. (ed.) FOSSACS 1998. LNCS, vol. 1378, pp. 140–155. Springer, Heidelberg (1998)

[CHY07] Carbone, M., Honda, K., Yoshida, N.: Structured communication-centred programming for web services. In: De Nicola, R. (ed.) ESOP 2007. LNCS, vol. 4421, pp. 2–17. Springer, Heidelberg (2007)

[dAH01] de Alfaro, L., Henzinger, T.A.: Interface automata. In: ESEC/SIGSOFT FSE, pp. 109–120 (2001)

[Fra] The fractal project, `http://fractal.ow2.org`

[HGB04] Hildebrandt, T., Godskesen, J.C., Bundgaard, M.: Bisimulation congruences for homer, a calculus of higher order mobile embedded resources. Technical Report ITU-TR-2004-52, IT University of Copenhagen (2004)

[JR05] Jeffrey, A., Rathke, J.: Contextual equivalence for higher-order pi-calculus revisited. Logical Methods in Computer Science 1(1) (2005)

[LMVR07] Lanese, I., Martins, F., Vasconcelos, V.T., Ravara, A.: Disciplining orchestration and conversation in service-oriented computing. In: SEFM 2007, pp. 305–314. IEEE, Los Alamitos (2007)

[LNW06] Larsen, K.G., Nyman, U., Wasowski, A.: Interface input/output automata. In: Misra, J., Nipkow, T., Sekerinski, E. (eds.) FM 2006. LNCS, vol. 4085, pp. 82–97. Springer, Heidelberg (2006)

[LSS09] Lenglet, S., Schmitt, A., Stefani, J.-B.: Howe's method for calculi with passivation. In: Bravetti, M., Zavattaro, G. (eds.) CONCUR 2009. LNCS, vol. 5710, pp. 448–462. Springer, Heidelberg (2009)

[Puc02] Pucella, R.: Towards a formalization for com part i: the primitive calculus. In: OOPSLA, pp. 331–342 (2002)

[SGM02] Szyperski, C., Gruntz, D., Murer, S.: Component Software: Beyond Object-Oriented Programming. Addison-Wesley, Reading (2002)

[SKS07] Sangiorgi, D., Kobayashi, N., Sumii, E.: Environmental bisimulations for higher-order languages. In: LICS 2007, pp. 293–302. IEEE Comp. Soc., Los Alamitos (2007)

[SS05] Schmitt, A., Stefani, J.-B.: The kell calculus: A family of higher-order distributed process calculi. In: Priami, C., Quaglia, P. (eds.) GC 2004. LNCS, vol. 3267, pp. 146–178. Springer, Heidelberg (2005)

[SW01] Sangiorgi, D., Walker, D.: The π-calculus: a Theory of Mobile Processes. Cambridge University Press, Cambridge (2001)

[Vas09] Vasconcelos, V.T.: Fundamentals of session types. In: Bernardo, M., Padovani, L., Zavattaro, G. (eds.) SFM 2009. LNCS, vol. 5569, pp. 158–186. Springer, Heidelberg (2009)

[VC99] Vitek, J., Castagna, G.: Seal: A framework for secure mobile computations. In: Bal, H.E., Cardelli, L., Belkhouche, B. (eds.) ICCL-WS 1998. LNCS, vol. 1686, p. 47. Springer, Heidelberg (1999)

[vOvdLKM00] van Ommering, R.C., van der Linden, F., Kramer, J., Magee, J.: The koala component model for consumer electronics software. IEEE Computer 33(3), 78–85 (2000)

A An Electronic Store Example

In the example in this section, a music store wants to build an E-Commerce business by means of an online service. The store already possesses a simple application for handling their products and selling them to customers. We represent such application as a component:

$$\begin{aligned}\texttt{STORE} \stackrel{\text{def}}{=} store\{\ & buy = (data, r).\, P_{buy},\\ & listProducts = (r).\, P_{listProducts},\\ & I_{store}\ \}\\ [\ & P_{store}\ ]\\ \{\ & _{j\in 1..h}\ n_j \mapsto f_j\ \}\end{aligned}$$

Component STORE offers a method $buy(data, r)$, for buying a product (where $data$ contains both the name of the product and the money that the client is willing to spend for it) and performing the appropriate bank transaction; then STORE confirms the execution of the transaction along channel r. STORE also offers method $listProducts(r)$ which sends a list of the available products at r. Other methods may be available at STORE, indicated by I_{store}. The set of links in STORE, namely $_{j\in 1..h}\ n_j \mapsto f_j$, represent its deployment requirements.

Component STORE was designed to run in a local environment that guarantees at most one buy transaction (one execution of the buy method) at a time.

Now we reuse STORE to implement a new component, E-STORE, that is meant to be exposed on a public network (e.g. the Internet). Other than adapting the behaviour of the legacy component, we want E-STORE to offer a new method $getVisits$ for reading the number of visits received by the online store. The implementation of E-STORE with its explanation follows. The parameter z is the skeleton of the inner $store$ component.

$$\begin{aligned}&\texttt{E} - \texttt{STORE}(z) \stackrel{\text{def}}{=}\\ &estore\{\ buy = (data, r).\,\texttt{extract}\ lock\ \texttt{as}\ x\ \texttt{in}\ \boldsymbol{\nu} s\ (store\_buy\ \langle data, s\rangle \mid s.\overline{r}.\,\texttt{Lock}),\\ &\qquad listProducts = (r).\,\boldsymbol{\nu} s\ (counter\_incr\ s \mid s.\, store\_listProducts\ r),\\ &\qquad getVisits = (r).\, counter\_read\ r\\ &\quad [\ store\ z\ \{\ _{j\in 1..h}\ n_j \mapsto n'_j\ \} \mid \texttt{Lock} \mid \texttt{Counter}(0)\ ]\\ &\quad \{\ _{j\in 1..h}\, n'_j \mapsto f_j\}\end{aligned}$$

Components Lock and $\texttt{Counter}\langle v\rangle$ are defined in Section 5. concurrent invocations of buy are prevented using a lock mechanism. Whenever buy is called, we first extract the Lock component. Thus other concurrent invocations of method buy will not proceed because $lock$ is not anymore available and their extract instructions is blocking. After extracting $lock$, the necessary data exchanges between the client and the legacy component are performed; the final message from the legacy component is however intercepted; this is necessary because we need to know when we can put Lockback into execution and allow for another instance of buy in E-STORE to continue.

We take the number of received visits that should be monitor as the number of invocations for method $listProducts$. This number, v, is stored in the counter $\texttt{Counter}\langle v\rangle$.

We can finally obtain the desired system using the extract instruction:

$$\begin{array}{l} \quad \texttt{extract}\ store\ \texttt{as}\ z\ \texttt{in}\,\texttt{E}-\texttt{STORE}(z) \mid \texttt{STORE} \\ \longrightarrow \{\ buy = (data, r).\,\texttt{extract}\ lock\ \texttt{as}\ x\ \texttt{in}\,\boldsymbol{\nu} s\,(store\_buy\ \langle data, s\rangle \mid s.\,\overline{r}.\,\texttt{Lock}), \\ \quad\quad listProducts = (r).\,\boldsymbol{\nu} s\,(counter\_incr\ s \mid s.\,store\_listProducts\ r), \\ \quad\quad getVisits = (r).\,counter\_read\ r \\ \quad [\ store\,\{\dots\}[\dots]\,\{\,_{j\in 1..h}\ n_j \mapsto n'_j\,\} \mid \texttt{Lock} \mid \texttt{Counter}(0)\ ] \\ \quad \{\,_{j\in 1..h}\, n'_j \mapsto f_j\} \end{array}$$

Note that the use of channels enables direct communications between a client and inner components. For instance, when a client calls method *getVisits* the answer is sent back directly from component *cell* situated inside component *counter*; this can be seen graphically in Figure 1 (which, for the sake of clarity, does not report communications with the internal lock).

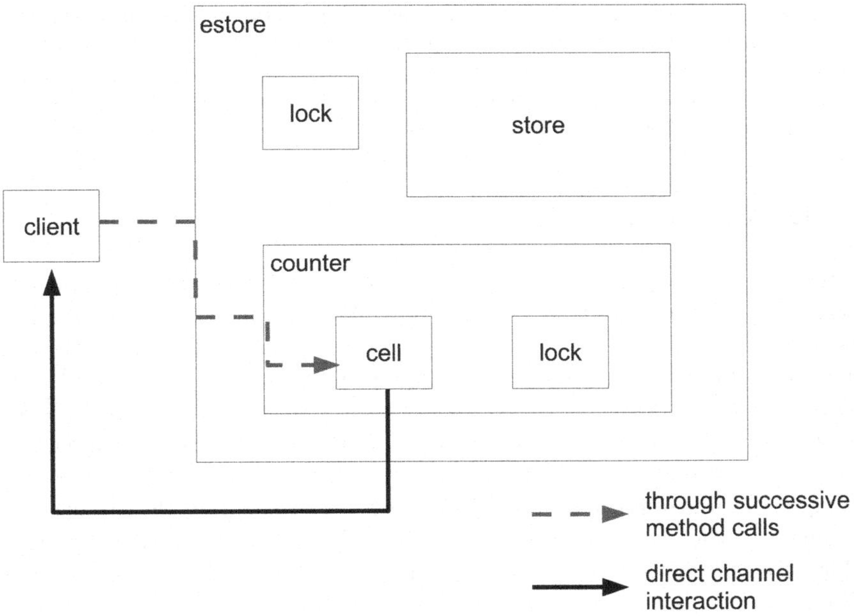

Fig. 1. An abstract graphical representation of the communication flow of method *getVisits*

The Impact of Altruism on the Efficiency of Atomic Congestion Games*

Ioannis Caragiannis, Christos Kaklamanis, Panagiotis Kanellopoulos, Maria Kyropoulou, and Evi Papaioannou

Research Academic Computer Technology Institute and
Department of Computer Engineering and Informatics
University of Patras, 26504 Rio, Greece

Abstract. We study the effect of combining selfishness and altruism in atomic congestion games. We allow players to be partially altruistic and partially selfish and determine the impact of this behavior on the overall system performance. Surprisingly, our results indicate that, in general, by allowing players to be (even partially) altruistic, the overall system performance deteriorates. Instead, for the class of symmetric load balancing games, a balance between selfish and altruistic behavior improves system performance to optimality.

1 Introduction

Congestion games provide a natural model for antagonistic resource allocation in large-scale systems and have recently played a central role in algorithmic game theory. In a congestion game, a set of non-cooperative players, each controlling an unsplittable unit demand, compete over a set of resources. All players using a resource experience a latency (or cost) given by a non-negative and non-decreasing function of the total demand (or congestion) of the resource. Among a given set of resource subsets (or strategies), each player selects one selfishly trying to minimize her individual total cost, i.e., the sum of the latencies on the resources in the chosen strategy. Load balancing games are congestion games in which the strategies of the players are singletons. Load balancing games in which all players have all resources as singleton strategies are called symmetric.

A typical example of a congestion game stems from antagonistic routing on a communication network. In this setting, we have several network users, where each user wishes to send traffic between a source-destination pair of network nodes. Each user may select among all possible paths connecting her source-destination pair of nodes. A natural objective for a user is to route her traffic using as less congested links as possible. This situation can be modelled by a congestion game where the users of the network are the players and the communication links correspond to the resources. In a load balancing game, we may

* This work is partially supported by the European Union under IST FET Integrated Project FP6-015964 AEOLUS and Cost Action IC0602 "Algorithmic Decision Theory", and by a "Caratheodory" basic research grant from the University of Patras.

M. Wirsing, M. Hofmann, and A. Rauschmayer (Eds.): TGC 2010, LNCS 6084, pp. 172–188, 2010.

think of the resources as servers and the players as clients wishing to get served by one of the servers. Then, the load balancing game is used to model the inherent selfishness of the clients in the sense that each of them desires to be served by the least loaded server.

A natural solution concept that captures stable outcomes in a (congestion) game is that of a pure Nash equilibrium (PNE), a configuration where no player can decrease her individual cost by unilaterally changing her strategy. Rosenthal [13] proved that the PNE of congestion games correspond to the local optima of a natural potential function, and thus every congestion game admits a PNE. Much of the recent literature on congestion games has focused on quantifying the inefficiency due to the players' selfish behavior. It is well known that a PNE may not optimize the system performance, usually measured by the total cost incurred by all players. The main tool for quantifying and understanding the performance degradation due to selfishness has been the *price of anarchy*, introduced by Koutsoupias and Papadimitriou [10] (see also [12]). The price of anarchy is the worst-case ratio of the total cost of a PNE to the optimal total cost.

Many recent papers have provided tight upper and lower bounds on the price of anarchy for several interesting classes of congestion games, mostly congestion games with linear and polynomial latencies. Awerbuch et al. [2] and Christodoulou and Koutsoupias [7] proved that the price of anarchy of congestion games is $5/2$ for linear latencies and $d^{\Theta(d)}$ for polynomial latencies of degree d. Subsequently, Aland et al. [1] obtained exact bounds on the price of anarchy for congestion games with polynomial latencies. Caragiannis et al. [4] proved that the same bounds hold for load balancing games as well. For symmetric load balancing games, Lücking et al. [11] proved that the price of anarchy is $4/3$.

In this paper, we are interested in the impact of altruistic behavior on the efficiency of atomic congestion games with linear latency functions. We assume that a player with completely altruistic behavior aims to minimize the total latency incurred by the other players. We also consider types of behavior that lie between completely altruistic behavior and selfishness. In this respect, we use a parameter $\xi \in [0, 1]$ and consider a player to be ξ-altruistic is she aims to minimize the linear combination of the total latency incurred by the other players and her latency with coefficients ξ and $1 - \xi$ respectively. Hence, an 1-altruistic player acts completely altruistically while a 0-altruistic one is selfish.

Intuitively, altruism should be considered as a synonym for trustworthy behavior. In contrast to this intuition, we demonstrate rather surprising results. We show that having players that behave completely altruistically may lead to a significant deterioration of performance. More importantly, even a small degree of altruism may have a negative effect on performance compared to the case of selfish players. These results hold for general atomic congestion games in which players may have different strategy sets. This asymmetry seems to be incompatible with altruism. On the contrary, in simpler games such as symmetric load balancing games, we prove that a balance between altruism and selfishness in the players' behavior leads to optimal performance.

In technical terms, we show the following results which extend the known bounds on the price of anarchy of games with selfish players to games with ξ-altruistic ones:

- The price of anarchy of atomic congestion games with ξ-altruistic players is at most $\frac{5-\xi}{2-\xi}$ when $\xi \in [0, 1/2]$ and at most $\frac{2-\xi}{1-\xi}$ when $\xi \in [1/2, 1]$. These bounds are proved to be tight for all values of ξ. The corresponding lower bound proofs are based on the construction of load balancing games with the desired price of anarchy.
- For symmetric load balancing games, we show that the price of anarchy with ξ-altruistic players is at most $\frac{4(1-\xi)}{3-2\xi}$ when $\xi \in [0, 1/2]$ and at most $\frac{3-2\xi}{4(1-\xi)}$ when $\xi \in [1/2, 1]$. These bounds are proved to be tight as well; the lower bound constructions are very simple and use symmetric load balancing games with two machines and two players.

Surprisingly, our first set of results indicates that altruism may be harmful in general since the price of anarchy increases from $5/2$ to unbounded as the degree of altruism increases from 0 to 1. Hence, selfishness is more beneficial than altruism in general. Our second set of results establishes a different setting for symmetric load balancing games. Interestingly, a balance between altruistic and selfish behavior leads to optimal performance (i.e., the price of anarchy is 1 and the equilibria reached are optimal). This has to be compared to the tight bound of $4/3$ on the price of anarchy with selfish players. Again, completely altruistic behavior leads to an unbounded price of anarchy.

In our upper bound proofs, we follow the standard high-level analysis ideas that have been used in the literature (see [3]) in order to compare the cost of equilibria to the cost of optimal assignments but adapt it to the case of altruistic players. For each player, we express with an inequality its preference to the strategy she uses in the equilibrium instead of the one she uses in the optimal assignment. For general atomic congestion games, by summing these inequalities over all players, we obtain an upper bound on the cost of the equilibrium in terms of quantities characterizing both the equilibrium and the optimal assignment. Then, we need to use new inequalities on the non-negative integers in order to obtain a direct relation between the cost of the equilibrium and the optimal assignment. In symmetric load balancing, we exploit the symmetry in order to obtain a better relation between the cost of the equilibrium and the optimal cost. In our analysis, we use the inequalities expressing the preference of a carefully selected set of players and develop new inequalities over non-negative integers in order to obtain our upper bound.

Chen and Kempe [6] have considered similar questions in non-atomic congestion games, i.e., games with an infinite number of players each controlling a negligibly small amount of traffic. Our findings are inherently different than theirs as in non-atomic congestion games the system performance improves as the degree of altruism of the players increases. Hoefer and Skopalik [9] consider atomic congestion games using a slightly different definition of altruism, which corresponds to ξ-altruistic behavior with $\xi \in [0, 1/2]$ in our model. They mainly present complexity results for the computation of equilibria in the corresponding congestion games and do not address questions related to the price of anarchy.

The rest of the paper is structured as follows. We begin with preliminary definitions and properties of altruistic players in Section 2. Our upper bounds for atomic congestion games and the corresponding lower bounds are presented in Sections 3 and 4, respectively. Section 5 is devoted to our results regarding symmetric load balancing. We conclude in Section 6 with a discussion on possible extensions of our work.

2 Preliminaries

In this section we formally define the model and establish characteristic inequalities that capture the players' behavior.

In *atomic congestion games* there is a set E of resources, each resource e having a non-negative and non-decreasing latency function f_e defined over non-negative numbers, and a set of n players. Each player i has a set of strategies $S_i \subseteq 2^E$ (each strategy of player i is a set of resources) and controls an unsplittable unit demand. An assignment $A = (A_1, ..., A_n)$ is a vector of strategies, one strategy for each player. The cost of player i for an assignment A is defined as $cost_i(A) = \sum_{e \in A_i} f_e(n_e(A))$, where $n_e(A)$ is the number of players using resource e in A, while the *social cost* of an assignment is the total cost of all players. An assignment is a *pure Nash equilibrium* if no player has an incentive to unilaterally deviate to another strategy, i.e., $cost_i(A) \leq cost_i(A_{-i}, s)$ for any player i and for any $s \in S_i$, where (A_{-i}, s) is the assignment produced from A if player i deviates from A_i to s. This inequality is also known as the *Nash condition*. A congestion game is called *symmetric* when all players share the same set of strategies. Load balancing games are congestion games where the strategies of the players are singleton sets. The *price of anarchy* of a congestion game is defined as the ratio of the maximum social cost over all Nash equilibria over the optimal cost. The price of anarchy for a class of congestion games is simply the highest price of anarchy among all games belonging to that class.

In this paper, we consider latency functions of the form $f_e(x) = \alpha_e x + \beta_e$ for each resource e, where α_e, β_e are non-negative constants. Then, the cost of a player i for an assignment A becomes $cost_i(A) = \sum_{e \in A_i} (\alpha_e n_e(A) + \beta_e)$, while the social cost becomes

$$\sum_i cost_i(A) = \sum_i \sum_{e \in A_i} (\alpha_e n_e(A) + \beta_e) = \sum_e \left(\alpha_e n_e^2(A) + \beta_e n_e(A)\right).$$

We now proceed to modify the model so that altruism is taken into account. We assume that each player i is partially altruistic, in the sense that she tries to minimize a function depending on the total cost of all other players and the total latency she experiences. We say that player i following a strategy A_i is *ξ-altruistic*, where $\xi \in [0, 1]$, when her cost function is

$$cost_i(A) = \xi \left(\sum_e (\alpha_e n_e^2(A) + \beta_e n_e(A)) - \sum_{e \in A_i} (\alpha_e n_e(A) + \beta_e) \right)$$

$$+ (1-\xi) \sum_{e \in A_i} (\alpha_e n_e(A) + \beta_e).$$

Clearly, when $\xi = 0$ then player i wishes to minimize her total latency, while when $\xi = 1$ player i wishes to minimize the total latency of all other players.

Now, consider two assignments A and A' that differ in the strategy of player i and let p_1 and p_2 be the strategies of i in the two assignments. Furthermore, by slightly abusing notation, we let $n_e = n_e(A)$ and $n'_e = n_e(A')$.

Assume that assignment A is an equilibrium; the cost of player i under A is

$$\begin{aligned} cost_i(A) &= \xi \left(\sum_e (\alpha_e n_e^2 + \beta_e n_e) - \sum_{e \in p_1} (\alpha_e n_e + \beta_e) \right) + (1-\xi) \sum_{e \in p_1} (\alpha_e n_e + \beta_e) \\ &= \xi \left(\sum_{e \notin p_1 \ominus p_2} (\alpha_e n_e^2 + \beta_e n_e) + \sum_{e \in p_1 \ominus p_2} (\alpha_e n_e^2 + \beta_e n_e) \right) \\ &\quad + (1-2\xi) \left(\sum_{e \in p_1 \cap p_2} (\alpha_e n_e + \beta_e) + \sum_{e \in p_1 \setminus p_2} (\alpha_e n_e + \beta_e) \right), \end{aligned}$$

where $\ominus$ is the symmetric difference operator in set theory, i.e., for two sets a, b it holds that $a \ominus b = (a \setminus b) \cup (b \setminus a)$.

Consider now the second assignment $A' = (A_{-i}, p_2)$ in which player i has changed her strategy from p_1 to p_2. Observe that $n'_e = n_e + 1$ for $e \in p_2 \setminus p_1$, $n'_e = n_e - 1$ for $e \in p_1 \setminus p_2$ and $n'_e = n_e$ otherwise. Her cost under the second assignment is

$$\begin{aligned} cost_i(A') &= \xi \left(\sum_e (\alpha_e n_e'^2 + \beta_e n'_e) - \sum_{e \in p_2} (\alpha_e n'_e + \beta_e) \right) + (1-\xi) \sum_{e \in p_2} (\alpha_e n'_e + \beta_e) \\ &= \xi \left(\sum_{e \notin p_1 \ominus p_2} (\alpha_e n_e'^2 + \beta_e n'_e) + \sum_{e \in p_1 \ominus p_2} (\alpha_e n_e'^2 + \beta_e n'_e) \right) \\ &\quad + (1-2\xi) \left(\sum_{e \in p_1 \cap p_2} (\alpha_e n'_e + \beta_e) + \sum_{e \in p_2 \setminus p_1} (\alpha_e n'_e + \beta_e) \right) \\ &= \xi \left(\sum_{e \notin p_1 \ominus p_2} (\alpha_e n_e^2 + \beta_e n_e) + \sum_{e \in p_1 \setminus p_2} \left(\alpha_e (n_e - 1)^2 + \beta_e (n_e - 1) \right) \right. \\ &\quad \left. + \sum_{e \in p_2 \setminus p_1} \left(\alpha_e (n_e + 1)^2 + \beta_e (n_e + 1) \right) \right) \\ &\quad + (1-2\xi) \left(\sum_{e \in p_1 \cap p_2} (\alpha_e n_e + \beta_e) + \sum_{e \in p_2 \setminus p_1} (\alpha_e (n_e + 1) + \beta_e) \right). \end{aligned}$$

Since player i has no incentive to change her strategy from p_1 to p_2, we obtain that $cost_i(A) \leq cost_i(A')$, i.e.,

$$\xi \sum_{e \in p_1 \ominus p_2} (\alpha_e n_e^2 + \beta_e n_e) + (1-2\xi) \sum_{e \in p_1 \setminus p_2} (\alpha_e n_e + \beta_e) \leq$$

$$\xi \left(\sum_{e \in p_1 \setminus p_2} \left(\alpha_e (n_e - 1)^2 + \beta_e (n_e - 1)\right) + \sum_{e \in p_2 \setminus p_1} \left(\alpha_e (n_e + 1)^2 + \beta_e (n_e + 1)\right)\right)$$

$$+ (1-2\xi) \sum_{e \in p_2 \setminus p_1} (\alpha_e (n_e + 1) + \beta_e),$$

which implies that

$$\sum_{e \in p_1 \setminus p_2} (\alpha_e (n_e - \xi) + \beta_e (1-\xi)) \leq \sum_{e \in p_2 \setminus p_1} (\alpha_e (n_e + 1 - \xi) + \beta_e (1-\xi))$$
$$= \sum_{e \in p_2 \setminus p_1} (\alpha_e (n'_e - \xi) + \beta_e (1-\xi)),$$

and, equivalently,

$$\sum_{e \in p_1} (\alpha_e (n_e - \xi) + \beta_e (1-\xi)) \leq \sum_{e \in p_2} (\alpha_e (n'_e - \xi) + \beta_e (1-\xi)).$$

Observe that when $\xi = 0$, the above inequality is merely the Nash condition. In general, this condition implies that, given an assignment A_{-i} of the remaining players, a ξ-altruistic player i aims to select a strategy s from S_i such that the expression

$$\sum_{e \in s} (\alpha_e (n_e(A_{-i}, s) - \xi) + \beta_e (1-\xi))$$

is minimized.

In the rest of this paper, we will assume, without loss of generality, that $\beta_e = 0$ for all resources. Our lower bound constructions exhibit this property, while the proofs of our upper bounds carry over even with non-zero values of β_e.

3 Upper Bounds for Atomic Congestion Games

In this section we describe our upper bounds concerning the price of anarchy for atomic congestion games and ξ-altruistic players. In our proofs we use the following two technical lemmas.

Lemma 1. *For all integers $x, y \geq 0$ and $\xi \in [0, 1/2]$ it holds that*

$$xy + (1-\xi)y + \xi x \leq \frac{1+\xi}{3} x^2 + \frac{5-\xi}{3} y^2.$$

Proof. Consider the function

$$f(x,y) = \frac{1+\xi}{3}x^2 + \frac{5-\xi}{3}y^2 - xy - (1-\xi)\,y - \xi x.$$

It suffices to prove that $f(x,y) \geq 0$ when x, y are non-negative integers and $\xi \in [0, 1/2]$.

We start with the case $x = y = k$. Then,

$$f(x,y) = f(k,k) = k^2 - k \geq 0.$$

We now consider the case $x = k$ and $y = k + z$, where $k \geq 0$ and $z \geq 1$. Then,

$$\begin{aligned} f(x,y) &= f(k,k+z) \\ &= f(k,k) + \frac{5-\xi}{3}\left(z^2 + 2zk\right) - kz - (1-\xi)\,z \\ &= f(k,k) + z\left(\frac{5-\xi}{3}z + \frac{7-2\xi}{3}k - 1 + \xi\right). \end{aligned}$$

Since $f(k,k) \geq 0$, $z \geq 1$ and $\xi \in [0, 1/2]$, we conclude that $f(x,y) \geq 0$, when $y > x$.

Finally, we consider the case where $x = k + z$ and $y = k$, where $k \geq 0$ and $z \geq 1$. Then,

$$\begin{aligned} f(x,y) &= f(k+z,k) \\ &= \frac{1+\xi}{3}(k+z)^2 + \frac{5-\xi}{3}k^2 - (k+z)\,k - (1-\xi)\,k - \xi\,(k+z) \\ &= k^2 - k + z\left(\frac{1+\xi}{3}(z+2k) - k - \xi\right). \end{aligned}$$

If $z > k$, then

$$f(x,y) \geq k^2 - k + z\left((1+\xi)\,k + \frac{1+\xi}{3} - k - \xi\right) \geq 0,$$

since $k \geq 0$ and $\xi \in [0, 1/2]$.

If $z = k$, then

$$f(x,y) = k^2 - k + k\left((1+\xi)\,k - k - \xi\right) \geq 0,$$

since $k = z \geq 1$ and $\xi \in [0, 1/2]$.

Finally, if $z < k$, then

$$f(x,y) = k^2 - k + z\left(\frac{1+\xi}{3}z - \xi\right) + z\left(\frac{1+\xi}{3}2k - k\right).$$

Since $z\left(\frac{1+\xi}{3}z - \xi\right) \geq 0$ for $z \geq 1$ and $\xi \in [0, 1/2]$, and $k^2 - k - zk \geq 0$ for $z \leq k - 1$, the lemma follows. □

Lemma 2. *For all integers $x, y \geq 0$ and $\xi \in [1/2, 1]$ it holds that*

$$xy + (1-\xi)\,y + \xi x \leq \xi x^2 + (2-\xi)\,y^2.$$

Proof. Consider the function

$$f(x,y) = \xi x^2 + (2-\xi)\,y^2 - xy - (1-\xi)\,y - \xi x.$$

To prove the lemma it suffices to show that $f(x,y) \geq 0$ when x, y are non-negative integers and $\xi \in [1/2, 1]$.

We first consider the case where $x = y = k$. Then,

$$f(x,y) = f(k,k) = k^2 - k \geq 0.$$

We now consider the case $x > y$ and let $x = k + z$ and $y = k$, where $k \geq 0$ and $z \geq 1$. Then,

$$\begin{aligned} f(x,y) &= f(k+z,k) \\ &= f(k,k) + \xi\left(z^2 + 2kz\right) - kz - \xi z \\ &= f(k,k) + z\,(z\xi + 2\xi k - k - \xi) \\ &= f(k,k) + z\,(\xi\,(z-1) + k\,(2\xi - 1)). \end{aligned}$$

Since $f(k,k) \geq 0$, $z \geq 1$ and $\xi \in [1/2, 1]$, it holds that $f(x,y) \geq 0$ when $x > y$.

Finally, we consider the case $y > x$ and let $x = k$ and $y = k + z$, where $k \geq 0$ and $z \geq 1$. Then,

$$\begin{aligned} f(x,y) &= f(k,k+z) \\ &= f(k,k) + (2-\xi)\left(z^2 + 2kz\right) - kz - (1-\xi)z \\ &= f(k,k) + z\,((2-\xi)\,(z+2k) - k - 1 + \xi) \\ &= f(k,k) + z\,((2-\xi)\,z + (3-2\xi)\,k - 1 + \xi). \end{aligned}$$

Since $f(k,k) \geq 0$, $z \geq 1$ and $\xi \in [1/2, 1]$, it holds that $f(x,y) \geq 0$ also when $y > x$. □

We note that the above lemmas also hold for the more general case of possibly negative x and y, but it suffices to consider non-negative values for our purposes. We are now ready to state the main result of this section.

Theorem 1. *The price of anarchy of atomic congestion games with ξ-altruistic players is at most $\frac{5-\xi}{2-\xi}$ if $\xi \in [0, 1/2]$ and at most $\frac{2-\xi}{1-\xi}$ if $\xi \in [1/2, 1]$.*

Proof. Consider a pure Nash equilibrium and an optimal assignment, and denote by n_e and o_e the number of players using resource e in the two assignments. Furthermore, let p_{i_1} and p_{i_2} be the strategies of player i in the two assignments. Since player i is a ξ-altruistic player, it holds that

$$\sum_{e \in p_{i_1}} \alpha_e\,(n_e - \xi) \leq \sum_{e \in p_{i_2}} \alpha_e\,(n_e + 1 - \xi).$$

For the total latency of the pure Nash equilibrium, it holds that

$$\begin{aligned}
cost &= \sum_e \alpha_e n_e^2 = \sum_i \sum_{e \in p_{i_1}} \alpha_e n_e \\
&= \sum_i \sum_{e \in p_{i_1}} \left(\alpha_e \left(n_e - \xi\right) + \alpha_e \xi\right) \\
&\leq \sum_i \sum_{e \in p_{i_2}} \alpha_e \left(n_e + 1 - \xi\right) + \sum_i \sum_{e \in p_{i_1}} \alpha_e \xi \\
&= \sum_e \alpha_e n_e o_e + (1 - \xi) \sum_e \alpha_e o_e + \xi \sum_e \alpha_e n_e \\
&= \sum_e \alpha_e \left(n_e o_e + (1 - \xi)\, o_e + \xi n_e\right).
\end{aligned}$$

So, for the case where $\xi \in [0, 1/2]$, from Lemma 1 we obtain that

$$\sum_e \alpha_e \left(n_e o_e + (1 - \xi)\, o_e + \xi n_e\right) \leq \frac{1 + \xi}{3} \sum_e \alpha_e n_e^2 + \frac{5 - \xi}{3} \sum_e \alpha_e o_e^2,$$

and, thus,

$$\sum_e \alpha_e n_e^2 \leq \frac{1 + \xi}{3} \sum_e \alpha_e n_e^2 + \frac{5 - \xi}{3} \sum_e \alpha_e o_e^2$$

which leads to

$$\frac{2 - \xi}{3} \sum_e \alpha_e n_e^2 \leq \frac{5 - \xi}{3} \sum_e \alpha_e o_e^2.$$

So, we obtain that the price of anarchy for this case is

$$\frac{\sum_e \alpha_e n_e^2}{\sum_e \alpha_e o_e^2} \leq \frac{5 - \xi}{2 - \xi}.$$

Similarly, for the case where $\xi \in [1/2, 1]$, from Lemma 2 we obtain that

$$\sum_e \alpha_e \left(n_e o_e + (1 - \xi)\, o_e + \xi n_e\right) \leq \xi \sum_e \alpha_e n_e^2 + (2 - \xi) \sum_e \alpha_e o_e^2,$$

and, thus,

$$\sum_e \alpha_e n_e^2 \leq \xi \sum_e \alpha_e n_e^2 + (2 - \xi) \sum_e \alpha_e o_e^2$$

which leads to

$$(1 - \xi) \sum_e \alpha_e n_e^2 \leq (2 - \xi) \sum_e \alpha_e o_e^2.$$

So, we obtain that the price of anarchy for this case is

$$\frac{\sum_e \alpha_e n_e^2}{\sum_e \alpha_e o_e^2} \leq \frac{2 - \xi}{1 - \xi}.$$

□

We observe that altruism is actually harmful, since the price of anarchy is minimized when $\xi = 0$, i.e., in the absence of altruism. Furthermore, when $\xi = 1$, i.e., players are completely altruistic, the price of anarchy is unbounded.

4 Lower Bounds for Atomic Congestion Games

In this section we state our lower bounds on the price of anarchy. The constructions in the proofs are load balancing games and are similar to a construction used in [4]. In these constructions, we represent the load balancing game as a graph. In this graph, each node represents a machine, and each edge represents a player having as possible strategies the machines corresponding to the nodes defining the edge.

Theorem 2. *For any $\epsilon > 0$ and $\xi \in [0, 1/2]$, there is a load balancing game with ξ-altruistic users whose price of anarchy is at least $\frac{5-\xi}{2-\xi} - \epsilon$.*

Proof. We construct a graph G, consisting of a complete binary tree with $k+1$ levels and $2^{k+1}-1$ nodes, with a line of $k+1$ edges and $k+1$ additional nodes hung at each leaf. So, graph G has $2k+2$ levels $0, \ldots, 2k+1$, with 2^i nodes at level i for $i = 0, \ldots, k$ and 2^k nodes at levels $k+1, \ldots, 2k+1$. The machines corresponding to nodes of level $i = 0, \ldots, k-1$, have latency functions $f_i(x) = (\frac{2-\xi}{3-\xi})^i x$, the machines corresponding to nodes of level $i = k, \ldots, 2k$, have latency functions $f_i(x) = (\frac{2-\xi}{3-\xi})^{k-1}(\frac{1-\xi}{2-\xi})^{i-k}x$, and the machines corresponding to nodes of level $2k+1$, have latency functions $f_{2k+1}(x) = (\frac{2-\xi}{3-\xi})^{k-1}(\frac{1-\xi}{2-\xi})^k x$. Consider the assignment where all players select machines corresponding to the endpoint of their corresponding edge which is closer to the root of graph G. It is not hard to see that this is a Nash equilibrium, since machines corresponding to nodes of level $i = 0, \ldots, k-1$, have two players and latency $2(\frac{2-\xi}{3-\xi})^i$, machines corresponding to nodes of level $i = k, \ldots, 2k$, have one player and latency $(\frac{2-\xi}{3-\xi})^{k-1}(\frac{1-\xi}{2-\xi})^{i-k}$, and machines corresponding to nodes of level $2k+1$, have no player. Therefore, due to the definition of the latency functions, a player assigned to a machine corresponding to a node of level $i = 0, \ldots, 2k$, would experience exactly the same latency if she changed her decision and chose the machine corresponding to the node of level $i+1$. The cost of the assignment is

$$\begin{aligned}
cost &= \sum_{i=0}^{k-1} 4 \cdot 2^i \left(\frac{2-\xi}{3-\xi}\right)^i + \sum_{i=k}^{2k} 2^k \left(\frac{2-\xi}{3-\xi}\right)^{k-1} \left(\frac{1-\xi}{2-\xi}\right)^{i-k} \\
&= 4\frac{\left(\frac{2(2-\xi)}{3-\xi}\right)^k - 1}{\frac{4-2\xi}{3-\xi} - 1} + 2^k \left(\frac{2-\xi}{3-\xi}\right)^{k-1} \left(\frac{1 - \left(\frac{1-\xi}{2-\xi}\right)^{k+1}}{1 - \frac{1-\xi}{2-\xi}}\right) \\
&= \frac{4(3-\xi)}{1-\xi}\left(\left(\frac{2(2-\xi)}{3-\xi}\right)^k - 1\right) + (2-\xi)\left(\frac{3-\xi}{2-\xi}\right)\left(\frac{2(2-\xi)}{3-\xi}\right)^k \\
&\quad -(2-\xi)2^k \left(\frac{2-\xi}{3-\xi}\right)^{k-1} \left(\frac{1-\xi}{2-\xi}\right)^{k+1} \\
&= (3-\xi)\left(\frac{5-\xi}{1-\xi}\right)\left(\frac{2(2-\xi)}{3-\xi}\right)^k - \frac{(3-\xi)(1-\xi)}{2-\xi}\left(\frac{2-2\xi}{3-\xi}\right)^k - \frac{4(3-\xi)}{1-\xi}.
\end{aligned}$$

To compute the upper bound on the cost of the optimal assignment it suffices to consider the assignment where all players select the machines corresponding to nodes which are further from the root. We obtain that the cost *opt* of the optimal assignment is

$$\begin{aligned}
opt &\leq \sum_{i=1}^{k-1} 2^i \left(\frac{2-\xi}{3-\xi}\right)^i + \sum_{i=k}^{2k} 2^k \left(\frac{2-\xi}{3-\xi}\right)^{k-1} \left(\frac{1-\xi}{2-\xi}\right)^{i-k} \\
&\quad +2^k \left(\frac{2-\xi}{3-\xi}\right)^{k-1} \left(\frac{1-\xi}{2-\xi}\right)^k \\
&= \frac{3-\xi}{1-\xi}\left(\left(\frac{2(2-\xi)}{3-\xi}\right)^k - 1\right) - (2-\xi)2^k \left(\frac{2-\xi}{3-\xi}\right)^{k-1} \left(\left(\frac{1-\xi}{2-\xi}\right)^{k+1} - 1\right) \\
&\quad +2^k \left(\frac{2-\xi}{3-\xi}\right)^{k-1} \left(\frac{1-\xi}{2-\xi}\right)^k - 1 \\
&= \frac{3-\xi}{1-\xi}\left(\left(\frac{2(2-\xi)}{3-\xi}\right)^k - 1\right) - 1 + (2-\xi)\left(\frac{3-\xi}{2-\xi}\right)\left(\frac{2(2-\xi)}{3-\xi}\right)^k \\
&\quad -2(2-\xi)\left(\frac{1-\xi}{2-\xi}\right)^{k+1}\left(\frac{2(2-\xi)}{3-\xi}\right)^{k-1} + 2^k \left(\frac{2-\xi}{3-\xi}\right)^{k-1}\left(\frac{1-\xi}{2-\xi}\right)^k \\
&= \left(\frac{3-\xi}{1-\xi} + 3 - \xi\right)\left(\frac{2(2-\xi)}{3-\xi}\right)^k - 2(2-\xi)\left(\frac{1-\xi}{2-\xi}\right)^{k+1}\left(\frac{2(2-\xi)}{3-\xi}\right)^{k-1} \\
&\quad +2^k \left(\frac{2-\xi}{3-\xi}\right)^{k-1}\left(\frac{1-\xi}{2-\xi}\right)^k - \frac{3-\xi}{1-\xi} - 1.
\end{aligned}$$

Hence, for any $\epsilon > 0$ and for sufficiently large k, the price of anarchy of the game is larger than

$$\frac{cost}{opt} \geq \frac{\frac{(3-\xi)(5-\xi)}{1-\xi}}{\frac{(3-\xi)(2-\xi)}{1-\xi}} - \epsilon = \frac{5-\xi}{2-\xi} - \epsilon.$$ □

We notice that this lower bound is tight for $\xi \in [0, 1/2]$. In order to prove a tight lower bound for the case $\xi \in [1/2, 1]$, it suffices to focus on one line of $k+2$ nodes and $k+1$ edges hanging from the binary tree of the aforementioned graph (including the corresponding leaf).

Theorem 3. *For any $\epsilon > 0$ and $\xi \in [1/2, 1]$, there is a load balancing game with ξ-altruistic users, whose price of anarchy is at least $\frac{2-\xi}{1-\xi} - \epsilon$.*

Proof. Consider the construction used in the proof of the previous theorem. We remind that the machine located at the node of the $2k+1$ level, has latency function $f_{2k+1}(x) = (\frac{2-\xi}{3-\xi})^{k-1}(\frac{1-\xi}{2-\xi})^k x$, and the machines corresponding to nodes of levels $i = k, \ldots, 2k$ have latency functions $f_i(x) = (\frac{2-\xi}{3-\xi})^{k-1}(\frac{1-\xi}{2-\xi})^{i-k} x$. Similarly, the assignment, where all players select the machine corresponding to the node closer to the root, is a Nash equilibrium, whereas the players are optimally assigned to the machine corresponding to the node further from the root (considering the endpoints of the corresponding edge). Using similar analysis, we obtain that

$$\begin{aligned}
cost &= \sum_{i=k}^{2k} \left(\frac{2-\xi}{3-\xi}\right)^{k-1} \left(\frac{1-\xi}{2-\xi}\right)^{i-k} \\
&= \sum_{i=0}^{k} \left(\frac{2-\xi}{3-\xi}\right)^{k-1} \left(\frac{1-\xi}{2-\xi}\right)^{i} \\
&= \left(\frac{2-\xi}{3-\xi}\right)^{k-1} \frac{(\frac{1-\xi}{2-\xi})^{k+1} - 1}{\frac{1-\xi}{2-\xi} - 1} = (2-\xi)\left(\frac{2-\xi}{3-\xi}\right)^{k-1} \left(1 - \left(\frac{1-\xi}{2-\xi}\right)^{k+1}\right),
\end{aligned}$$

and

$$\begin{aligned}
opt &\leq \sum_{i=k+1}^{2k} \left(\frac{2-\xi}{3-\xi}\right)^{k-1} \left(\frac{1-\xi}{2-\xi}\right)^{i-k} + \left(\frac{2-\xi}{3-\xi}\right)^{k-1} \left(\frac{1-\xi}{2-\xi}\right)^{k} \\
&= \sum_{i=1}^{k} \left(\frac{2-\xi}{3-\xi}\right)^{k-1} \left(\frac{1-\xi}{2-\xi}\right)^{i} + \left(\frac{2-\xi}{3-\xi}\right)^{k-1} \left(\frac{1-\xi}{2-\xi}\right)^{k} \\
&= \left(\frac{2-\xi}{3-\xi}\right)^{k-1} \frac{(\frac{1-\xi}{2-\xi})^{k+1} - \frac{1-\xi}{2-\xi}}{\frac{1-\xi}{2-\xi} - 1} + \left(\frac{2-\xi}{3-\xi}\right)^{k-1} \left(\frac{1-\xi}{2-\xi}\right)^{k} \\
&= (2-\xi)\left(\frac{2-\xi}{3-\xi}\right)^{k-1} \frac{1-\xi}{2-\xi} \left(1 - \left(\frac{1-\xi}{2-\xi}\right)^{k}\right) + \left(\frac{2-\xi}{3-\xi}\right)^{k-1} \left(\frac{1-\xi}{2-\xi}\right)^{k} \\
&= (1-\xi)\left(\frac{2-\xi}{3-\xi}\right)^{k-1} \left(1 - \left(\frac{1-\xi}{2-\xi}\right)^{k}\right) + \left(\frac{2-\xi}{3-\xi}\right)^{k-1} \left(\frac{1-\xi}{2-\xi}\right)^{k}.
\end{aligned}$$

We conclude, that for any $\epsilon > 0$, and sufficiently large k, the price of anarchy of the game is larger than $\frac{2-\xi}{1-\xi} - \epsilon$. □

5 Symmetric Load Balancing Games

In this section, we consider the important class of symmetric load balancing games with ξ-altruistic players. In our proof, we make use of the following two technical lemmas.

Lemma 3. *For any integers $x, y \geq 0$ and any $\xi \in [0, 1/2]$ it holds that, when $x < y$,*

$$xy + (1-\xi)\,y - (1-\xi)\,x \leq \frac{1+2\xi}{4}x^2 + (1-\xi)\,y^2,$$

and, when $x \geq y$,

$$xy + \xi x - \xi y \leq \frac{1+2\xi}{4}x^2 + (1-\xi)\,y^2.$$

Proof. We begin with the case $x < y$. Consider the function

$$f(x,y) = \frac{1+2\xi}{4}x^2 + (1-\xi)\,y^2 - xy - (1-\xi)\,y + (1-\xi)\,x.$$

It suffices to show that $f(x,y) \geq 0$. Let $y = x + z$, where z is a positive integer. Then

$$\begin{aligned} f(x,y) &= f(x, x+z) \\ &= \frac{1+2\xi}{4}x^2 + (1-\xi)\left(x^2 + z^2 + 2xz\right) - x^2 - xz + (1-\xi)\,x - (1-\xi)\,x \\ &\quad - (1-\xi)\,z \\ &= \left(\frac{1+2\xi}{4} + 1 - \xi - 1\right)x^2 + (1-\xi)\,z^2 + (2-2\xi-1)\,xz - (1-\xi)\,z \\ &= \frac{1-2\xi}{4}x^2 + (1-\xi)\,z^2 + (1-2\xi)\,xz - (1-\xi)\,z \\ &\geq 0, \end{aligned}$$

since $x \geq 0$, $z \geq 1$ and $\xi \in [0, 1/2]$.

We now consider the case $x \geq y$. Consider the function

$$g(x,y) = \frac{1+2\xi}{4}x^2 + (1-\xi)\,y^2 - xy - \xi x + \xi y.$$

In order to complete the proof, we have to show that $g(x,y) \geq 0$. Since $x \geq y$, let $x = y + z$, where z is a non-negative integer. Then,

$$\begin{aligned} g(x,y) &= g(y+z, y) \\ &= \frac{1+2\xi}{4}\,(y+z)^2 + (1-\xi)\,y^2 - (y+z)\,y - \xi\,(y+z) + \xi y \\ &= \frac{1+2\xi}{4}y^2 + \frac{1+2\xi}{4}z^2 + \frac{1+2\xi}{2}yz - \xi y^2 - yz - \xi z \\ &= \frac{1-2\xi}{4}y^2 + \frac{1+2\xi}{4}z^2 - \frac{1-2\xi}{2}yz - \xi z \\ &= \frac{1}{4}(y^2 + z^2 - 2yz) - \frac{\xi}{2}(y^2 - z^2 - 2yz) - \xi z \\ &= \frac{1}{4}(y-z)^2 - \frac{\xi}{2}(y^2 + z^2 - 2yz) + \xi z^2 - \xi z \\ &= \frac{1}{4}(y-z)^2 - \frac{\xi}{2}(y-z)^2 + \xi z(z-1) \\ &\geq 0 \end{aligned}$$

since $z \geq 0$ and $\xi \in [0, 1/2]$. □

Lemma 4. *For any integers $x, y \geq 0$ and any $\xi \in [1/2, 1]$ it holds that when $x < y$*

$$xy + (1-\xi)\,y - (1-\xi)\,x \leq \xi x^2 + \frac{3-2\xi}{4}y^2,$$

and when $x \geq y$

$$xy + \xi x - \xi y \leq \xi x^2 + \frac{3-2\xi}{4} y^2.$$

Proof. The proof follows from Lemma 3. Note that the two inequalities of Lemma 3 can be transformed to those of Lemma 4 by replacing ξ by $1-\xi$ and exchanging x and y. Furthermore, the two inequalities become identical when $x = y$. □

Again, these two lemmas also hold when x, y can be negative. We are now ready to prove the main result of this section.

Theorem 4. *The price of anarchy for symmetric load balancing games with* ξ*-altruistic players is* $\frac{4(1-\xi)}{3-2\xi}$ *when* $\xi \in [0, 1/2]$ *and* $\frac{3-2\xi}{4(1-\xi)}$ *when* $\xi \in [1/2, 1]$.

Proof. Consider a pure Nash equilibrium and an optimal assignment and let n_j and o_j be the number of players in machine j in the equilibrium and the optimal assignment, respectively. Consider the sets H and L of machines j such that $n_j > o_j$ and $n_j < o_j$, respectively. Denote by S the set of players consisting of $n_j - o_j$ players that are in machine $j \in H$ in equilibrium, for every machine $j \in H$. Observe that $\sum_{j \in H} (n_j - o_j) = \sum_{j \in L} (o_j - n_j)$. Hence, we can associate each player of S with a machine in L such that $o_j - n_j$ players of S are associated to each machine $j \in L$.

Consider a player in S that lies in machine $j \in H$ in equilibrium and let $j' \in L$ be the machine of L she is associated with. By the ξ-altruistic condition, we have that $\alpha_j(n_j - \xi) \leq \alpha_{j'}(n_{j'} - \xi + 1)$. By summing up the ξ-altruistic conditions for each player in S, we obtain that

$$\sum_{j:n_j>o_j} \alpha_j(n_j - \xi)(n_j - o_j) \leq \sum_{j:n_j<o_j} \alpha_j(n_j - \xi + 1)(o_j - n_j). \qquad (1)$$

Now using (1), the fact that n_j and o_j are integers, and the definition of the latency functions, we obtain that

$$\begin{aligned}
\sum_j \alpha_j n_j^2 &= \sum_{j:n_j>o_j} \alpha_j n_j^2 + \sum_{j:n_j \leq o_j} \alpha_j n_j^2 \\
&= \sum_{j:n_j>o_j} \alpha_j (n_j - \xi)(n_j - o_j) + \sum_{j:n_j>o_j} (\alpha_j n_j o_j + \alpha_j \xi n_j - \alpha_j \xi o_j) \\
&\quad + \sum_{j:n_j \leq o_j} \alpha_j n_j^2 \\
&\leq \sum_{j:n_j<o_j} \alpha_j (n_j - \xi + 1)(o_j - n_j) + \sum_{j:n_j>o_j} (\alpha_j n_j o_j + \alpha_j \xi n_j - \alpha_j \xi o_j) \\
&\quad + \sum_{j:n_j \leq o_j} \alpha_j n_j^2 \\
&= \sum_{j:n_j<o_j} (\alpha_j n_j o_j - \alpha_j n_j^2 - \alpha_j \xi o_j + \alpha_j \xi n_j + \alpha_j o_j - \alpha_j n_j)
\end{aligned}$$

$$+ \sum_{j:n_j>o_j} (\alpha_j n_j o_j + \alpha_j \xi n_j - \alpha_j \xi o_j) + \sum_{j:n_j \le o_j} \alpha_j n_j^2$$

$$= \sum_{j:n_j<o_j} \alpha_j (n_j o_j - \xi o_j + \xi n_j + o_j - n_j) + \sum_{j:n_j>o_j} \alpha_j (n_j o_j + \xi n_j - \xi o_j)$$

$$+ \sum_{j:n_j=o_j} \alpha_j n_j^2$$

$$= \sum_{j:n_j<o_j} \alpha_j (n_j o_j + (1-\xi)(o_j - n_j)) + \sum_{j:n_j \ge o_j} \alpha_j (n_j o_j + \xi (n_j - o_j)).$$

When $\xi \in [0, 1/2]$, by Lemma 3 we obtain that

$$\sum_j \alpha_j n_j^2 \le \sum_j \alpha_j \left(\frac{1+2\xi}{4} n_j^2 + (1-\xi) o_j^2 \right)$$

which yields that the price of anarchy is

$$\frac{\sum_j \alpha_j n_j^2}{\sum_j \alpha_j o_j^2} \le \frac{4(1-\xi)}{3-2\xi}.$$

When $\xi \in [1/2, 1]$, by Lemma 4 we obtain that

$$\sum_j \alpha_j n_j^2 \le \sum_j \alpha_j \left(\xi n_j^2 + \frac{3-2\xi}{4} o_j^2 \right)$$

which yields that the price of anarchy is

$$\frac{\sum_j \alpha_j n_j^2}{\sum_j \alpha_j o_j^2} \le \frac{3-2\xi}{4(1-\xi)}.$$

□

We note that when $\xi = 0$, i.e., for the case of totally selfish players this result implies the known 4/3 upper bound on the price of anarchy [11], while when $\xi = 1$, i.e., for completely altruistic players, the ratio is unbounded. Furthermore, as ξ increases from 0 to 1/2 the ratio improves from 4/3 to 1, and then deteriorates as ξ approaches 1; note that when $\xi = 0.7$ the ratio is again 4/3.

It is not hard to show that these bounds are tight. It suffices to consider a load balancing game with two machines with latency functions $f_1(x) = (2-\xi)x$ and $f_2(x) = (1-\xi)x$ and two players. Two assignments are equilibria in this setting: either assigning both players to the second machine (where the total latency is $4(1-\xi)$) or assigning one player at each machine (where the total latency is $3-2\xi$).

6 Extensions and Open Problems

In this paper, we have studied the impact of altruism on the system performance in atomic congestion games and have noticed that, surprisingly, altruism can be harmful in general. For the special case of symmetric load balancing games, we observe that altruism can be helpful in some cases; in particular, compared to selfishness, we have shown that altruism helps in decreasing the price of anarchy when $\xi \in [0, 0.7]$ but is harmful when $\xi \in (0.7, 1]$. We note that for $\xi = 1/2$, symmetric load balancing games with ξ-altruistic players admit only optimal solutions as equilibria.

Following [6], we have also briefly considered the case in which players are simultaneously selfish and spiteful (as opposed to altruistic). Similarly to the model in the current paper, we can define ξ-spiteful players for particular values of the parameter ξ. In this setting, player i aims to select a strategy $s \in S_i$ so that the quantity

$$\sum_{e \in s} (\alpha_e (n_e(A_{-i}, s) + \xi) + \beta_e (1 + \xi))$$

is minimized given the strategies A_{-i} of the other players. This is equivalent to assuming that all players are selfish and each of them is forced to pay a tax equal to $\xi \alpha_e$ for each resource e she uses (this particular tax definition is called a universal tax function in [5]). Then, the cost of a player is the sum of her latency and the taxes she pays and the equilibria of the corresponding game are those assignments in which no player has an incentive to deviate in order to decrease her cost. Caragiannis et al. [5] have proved that the universal tax function with $\xi = \frac{3}{2}\sqrt{3} - 2 \approx 0.598$ yields the best possible price of anarchy which is equal to $1 + 2/\sqrt{3} \approx 2.155$. This result implies the rather surprising conclusion that ξ-spiteful behavior for the particular value of ξ leads to the best possible price of anarchy.

In our study herein, we have assumed that all players are unweighted, i.e., each controls a unit demand, and *homogeneous*, i.e., each player is ξ-altruistic (or ξ-spiteful) for the same value of ξ. It would be interesting to study the case of *heterogeneous* players with different behavior, i.e., each player i is ξ_i-altruistic (or ξ_i-spiteful). Furthermore, an interesting question from the system designer's point of view is whether the behavior of the players can be coordinated in order to always force them to reach efficient equilibria. Even in this case, one cannot hope to achieve a price of anarchy smaller than 2.012 in general. This value matches the tight bound on the price of anarchy of load balancing games with identical latency functions of the form $f(x) = x$ on all resources [4,14]; in this case, any combination of selfish and altruistic or spiteful behavior of a player is actually equivalent to selfishness.

We plan to elaborate on the two claims above in the final version of the paper.

References

1. Aland, S., Dumrauf, D., Gairing, M., Monien, B., Schoppmann, F.: Exact price of anarchy for polynomial congestion games. In: Durand, B., Thomas, W. (eds.) STACS 2006. LNCS, vol. 3884, pp. 218–229. Springer, Heidelberg (2006)

2. Awerbuch, B., Azar, Y., Epstein, A.: The price of routing unsplittable flow. In: Proceedings of the 37th Annual ACM Symposium on Theory of Computing (STOC 2005), pp. 57–66 (2005)
3. Bilò, V., Caragiannis, I., Fanelli, A., Flammini, M., Kaklamanis, C., Monaco, G., Moscardelli, L.: Game-theoretic approaches to optimization problems in communication networks. In: Graphs and Algorithms in Communication Networks, pp. 241–263. Springer, Heidelberg (2009)
4. Caragiannis, I., Flammini, M., Kaklamanis, C., Kanellopoulos, P., Moscardelli, L.: Tight bounds for selfish and greedy load balancing. In: Bugliesi, M., Preneel, B., Sassone, V., Wegener, I. (eds.) ICALP 2006, Part I. LNCS, vol. 4051, pp. 311–322. Springer, Heidelberg (2006)
5. Caragiannis, I., Kaklamanis, C., Kanellopoulos, P.: Taxes for linear atomic congestion games. ACM Transactions on Algorithms (to appear)
6. Chen, P.-A., Kempe, D.: Altruism, selfishness and spite in traffic routing. In: Proceedings of the 9th ACM Conference on Electronic Commerce (EC 2008), pp. 140–149 (2008)
7. Christodoulou, G., Koutsoupias, E.: The price of anarchy of finite congestion games. In: Proceedings of the 37th Annual ACM Symposium on Theory of Computing (STOC 2005), pp. 67–73 (2005)
8. Fotakis, D., Spirakis, P.: Cost-balancing tolls for atomic network congestion games. In: Deng, X., Graham, F.C. (eds.) WINE 2007. LNCS, vol. 4858, pp. 179–190. Springer, Heidelberg (2007)
9. Hoefer, M., Skopalik, A.: Altruism in atomic congestion games. In: Fiat, A., Sanders, P. (eds.) ESA 2009. LNCS, vol. 5757, pp. 179–189. Springer, Heidelberg (2009)
10. Koutsoupias, E., Papadimitriou, C.: Worst-case equilibria. In: Meinel, C., Tison, S. (eds.) STACS 1999. LNCS, vol. 1563, pp. 404–413. Springer, Heidelberg (1999)
11. Lücking, T., Mavronicolas, M., Monien, B., Rode, M.: A new model for selfish routing. Theoretical Computer Science 406(2), 187–206 (2008)
12. Papadimitriou, C.: Algorithms, games and the internet. In: Proceedings of the 33rd Annual ACM Symposium on Theory of Computing (STOC 2001), pp. 749–753 (2001)
13. Rosenthal, R.: A class of games possessing pure-strategy Nash equilibria. International Journal of Game Theory 2, 65–67 (1973)
14. Suri, S., Tóth, C., Zhou, Y.: Selfish load balancing and atomic congestion games. Algorithmica 47(1), 79–96 (2007)

Stressed Web Environments as Strategic Games: Risk Profiles and Weltanschauung*

Joaquim Gabarro[1], Peter Kilpatrick[2], Maria Serna[1], and Alan Stewart[2]

[1] ALBCOM, LSI Dept., Universitat Politècnica de Catalunya, Barcelona
{gabarro,mjserna}@lsi.upc.edu
[2] School of Computer Science, The Queen's University of Belfast, Belfast
{a.stewart,p.kilpatrick}@qub.ac.uk

Abstract. We consider the behaviour of a set of services in a stressed web environment where performance patterns may be difficult to predict. In stressed environments the performances of some providers may degrade while the performances of others, with *elastic* resources, may improve. The allocation of web-based providers to users (brokering) is modelled by a strategic non-cooperative angel-daemon game with risk profiles. A risk profile specifies a bound on the *number* of unreliable service providers within an environment without identifying the names of these providers. Risk profiles offer a means of analysing the behaviour of broker agents which allocate service providers to users. A Nash equilibrium is a fixed point of such a game in which no user can locally improve their choice of provider – thus, a Nash equilibrium is a viable solution to the provider/user allocation problem. Angel daemon games provide a means of reasoning about stressed environments and offer the possibility of designing brokers using risk profiles and Nash equilibria.

1 Introduction

A web-based computation involves the discovery and utilisation of services. It is often the case that a service is made available by a number of providers. The performance of a provider can vary greatly over time (although service level agreements (SLAs) may provide information about "normal" expected performance). Brokers [2] are often used to monitor provider performance and to provide an interface to the "best" current provider.

It is usually the case that the performance of a provider deteriorates as demand increases (although "elastic" providers may call on extra servers in times of peak demand – thus, in such (stressed) situations performance can conceivably improve). The goal of this paper is to study the behaviour of a set of service providers in a stressed environment with the hope that a clearer understanding of stressed behaviour may aid the design of intelligent brokers.

* J. Gabarró and M. Serna are partially supported by FET pro-active Integrated Project 15964 (AEOLUS), TIN-2007-66523 (FORMALISM), TIN-2005-25859-E and SGR 2009-2015 (ALBCOM).

M. Wirsing, M. Hofmann, and A. Rauschmayer (Eds.): TGC 2010, LNCS 6084, pp. 189–204, 2010.

Here we adopt the point of view that providers should be treated *in toto* since web users alternate between providers in times of high usage. We also assume that users behave in a non-cooperative way (in that the behaviour of others is, usually, irrelevant). Given these assumptions it is reasonable to model the behaviour of a set of providers (resources) in a stressed environment as a strategic situation in algorithmic game theory [8,11,12]. The notion of a Nash equilibrium is used to derive an efficient broker allocation of providers to users (see Example 1).

Example 1. **Brokering in an idealised environment.** Consider a situation where a set of users $\{1, \ldots, n\}$ submit jobs for execution to a broker. Suppose that the broker uses multiple *predictable* service providers (resources) $R = \{r_1, \ldots r_k\}$ to meet demand. The broker allocates service providers to jobs in such a way as to minimise user delay. This situation can be modelled by a *non-cooperative* game with n players in which users *"move"* in sequence by allocating (or reallocating) their job to a provider. Providers may have modified work loads and delays as a consequence of a sequence of "moves". A Nash equilibrium is an allocation schedule in which no user can improve their situation by making a move[1]. □

The web is comprised of a very diverse range of resources. Such heterogeneity contributes to the complexity of a web environment. Performance variability and sporadic unavailability of underlying networks provide further complications. Conventionally, unreliability is treated from a probabilistic viewpoint [9,1,10]. In contrast, we investigate a variety of provider behaviours within a stressed web environment using non-cooperative game theory (see Example 2).

Example 2. **Brokering in a stressed environment.** Now consider a more realistic refinement of the brokering example 1 where provider and network behaviour is less predictable. The following assumptions are made about stressed web environments:

1. stress is non-uniformly distributed across the web;
2. patches of stress can move dynamically in response to users moving jobs from stressed regions to more responsive providers;
3. the performance of certain providers may be highly vulnerable to heavy work loads; other providers may incorporate autonomic behaviour which increases the number of servers on offer in response to increased demand (elasticity). Consequently, some providers may be associated with increased unreliability at times of stress while others may exhibit robust behaviour.

An extended form of non-cooperative game is used to reason about brokering in stressed environments; in addition to the n users the game additionally contains two extra players: a daemon player who selects a number of sites to be stressed so as to maximise the delay associated with the game (in a sense the daemon player

[1] A set of users may individually find service providers without utilising a broker; this process also corresponds to a game which may reach a Nash equilibrium. The broker model acts as an abstraction of this alternative allocation problem.

models the deterioration of a stressed network at a set of vulnerable points); and an angel who selects a number of sites so as to minimise delay (in some sense the angel models the capacity of a network to modify its behaviour so as to improve throughput). Unreliability is described by the notion of a risk profile which specifies (a priori) possible angel and daemon behaviours; given a risk profile the behaviour of a broker in a stressed environment can be described by an associated $n + 2$ player game. □

Risk profiles were introduced in [3,4,5] to analyse network behaviour when a bounded number of services failed. However, risk profiles are sufficiently rich to allow the analysis of stressed web environments where networks may be under the influence of competing tendencies (one destructive, the other self-correcting). In a risk profile bounds are placed on both the constructive and destructive capacities (for example, an unreliable network may have no self-correcting behaviour and no angel player). As far we know the use of risk profiles to model stressed web environments is new.

The paper is structured as follows. Basic models of resource allocation games are given in § 2, with particular attention placed on uniform unit allocation games. In § 3 risk profiles are defined and Weltanschauungs are used to model stress in allocation problems. In § 4 angel-daemon games are defined and used to analyse stressed resource allocation problems. Snapshots are used in § 5 to provide a condensed description of strategy profiles; these are used to study pure Nash equilibria. In § 6 we consider the structure of pure Nash equilibria in angel-daemon games. In § 7 the idea of a risk-aware broker is developed. Finally in § 8 some open questions are raised.

2 Resource Allocation Games

We consider a basic resource allocation game introduced by Koutsoupias and Papadimitriou in [11,8] as a means of modelling simple competitive situations.

A *resource allocation game* (also called load balancing game) is a tuple

$$C = \langle N, R, (w_i)_{i\in N}, (d_r)_{r\in R}, (A_i)_{i\in N}, \rangle$$

where the set of players is $N = \{1, \ldots, n\}$. Player $i \in N$ has to execute a job (or work) w_i. The set of resources is $R = \{1, \ldots, k\}$. Each resource $r \in R$ has a *delay* function d_r. For each player $1 \leq i \leq n$, A_i is the set of possible allocations for work w_i, with $A_i \subseteq R$. A strategy s_i (or action) for a player i is an element of A_i, (player i chooses a resource). A strategy profile is a tuple $s = (s_1, \ldots, s_n)$. Given a player i and a strategy profile $s = (s_1, \ldots, s_n)$ we denote by $s_{-i} = (s_1, \ldots, s_{i-1}, s_{i+1}, \ldots, s_n)$ the profile where the strategy s_i is missing. Given a strategy profile $s = (s_1, \ldots, s_n) \in A_1 \times \cdots \times A_n$, the set of players using resource $r \in R$ is $L_r(s) = \{i \in N \mid r = s_i\}$ and the *load* of resource r is the weight of the players using r, that is $\ell_r(s) = \sum_{i\in L_r(s)} w_i$. The *cost* for player i of strategy profile s, is defined as $c_i(s) = d_{s_i}(\ell_{s_i}(s))$. Following J. Bentham, 1748-1832, the *social cost* of a strategy profile s is defined additively as $c_{\mathfrak{s}}(s) = \sum_{i \in N} c_i(s)$. In some examples, in order to simplify matters, costs are defined as $c_i(s) = \lceil d_{s_i}(\ell_{s_i}(s)) \rceil$ and $c_{\mathfrak{s}}(s) = \sum_{i \in N} \lceil d_{s_i}(\ell_{s_i}(s)) \rceil$.

Given a strategy profile $s = (s_1, \ldots, s_n)$ we define the *load map* of strategy s as the vector $\ell(s) = (\ell_1(s), \ldots, \ell_k(s))$ which describes macroscopically the load of each resource under strategy profile s. Observe that in load maps part of the information contained in a strategy profile is lost: we do not know which player is using a given resource.

Resource allocation games are a particular case of *strategic games* [6]. Strategic games can be used to model non-cooperative behaviour: a solution to a game corresponds to identifying Nash equilibria [6]. A *pure Nash equilibrium* (PNE for short) is a strategy profile s^* such that for any player $i \in N$ and for any strategy $s_i \in A_i$, $c_i(s^*) \leq c_i(s^*_{-i}, s_i)$, where (s^*_{-i}, s_i) denotes the strategy profile in which s^*_i is replaced by s_i.

We are interested in analysing some specific natural types of delay functions, non-negative and monotone, and in particular *affine* functions, that is $d_r(x) = d_r\, x$ with $0 < d_r < \infty$.

Example 3. Consider an allocation game *Fortran&MPI_Servers* defined in Figure 1. The web environment comprises four servers $R = \{1, 2, 3, 4\}$ with delays $d_1 = 1/2$, $d_2 = 1/4$, $d_3 = 1/4$ and $d_4 = 1/8$. Cost functions and social cost are defined using ceiling functions. Resources 1, 2, 3 can execute Fortran programs. Resources 1, 3, 4 can execute MPI programs. There are 5 jobs to be executed (superindices are used to denote the type of a job).

$$w_1^{\mathtt{MPI}} = 10,\ w_2^{\mathtt{F}} = 5,\ w_3^{\mathtt{F}} = 6,\ w_4^{\mathtt{MPI}} = 15,\ w_5^{\mathtt{F}} = 3$$

Thus job 1 can be executed using resources (servers) 1, 2 and 3 etc. and so $A_1 = A_4 = \{1, 3, 4\}$ and $A_2 = A_3 = A_5 = \{1, 2, 3\}$. Consider a strategy profile $s = (1, 1, 1, 4, 3)$, where $s_5 = 3$ denotes that "job $w_5^{\mathtt{F}}$ is mapped to resource 3". The load map of this profile is $\ell(s) = (21, 0, 3, 15)$. In s the cost of player 1 is high because $c_1(s) = \lceil \frac{1}{2}(w_1^{\mathtt{MPI}} + w_2^{\mathtt{F}} + w_3^{\mathtt{F}}) \rceil = 11$, therefore player 1 has a strong incentive to move his job to another server with lower current cost. Suppose that player 1 moves to server 3 (denoted by $1 \xrightarrow{w_1^{\mathtt{MPI}}} 3$): the cost to player 1 improves from 11 to 4 and therefore s is not a PNE. By performing a sequence of similar kinds of move we finally get a PNE $(3, 2, 3, 4, 1)$ with social cost 13. This PNE is non-unique: for instance $(4, 2, 3, 4, 2)$ is a PNE having a social cost 14. □

In some cases (*uniform*) all the resources have the same capability. This forces $A_i = R$ for $1 \leq i \leq n$, and moreover all the resources have the same delay function. We are specially interested in *uniform affine delays* $d_r(x) = dx$, $0 < d < \infty$. We distinguish the case where all players have the same *unit* weight works (or jobs), i.e. $w_i = 1$ for all $i \in N$. Inspired by [11], let $Unit_{n,k,d}$ be the unit resource allocation game with n players, k resources and uniform affine delays with coefficient d. For unit weight games load maps provide enough information to describe a family of "equivalent" strategy profiles. The following lemma captures a widely-observed result.

Fortran&MPI_Servers	Resources			
	1	2	3	4
	Services			
	`F, MPI`	`F`	`F, MPI`	`MPI`
	Delay			
	1/2	1/4	1/4	1/8
Initial strategy				
s	$w_1^{\mathtt{MPI}} = 10$ $w_2^{\mathtt{F}} = 5$ $w_3^{\mathtt{F}} = 6$		$w_5^{\mathtt{F}} = 3$	$w_4^{\mathtt{MPI}} = 15$
Cost	11		1	2
Moves				
$1 \xrightarrow{w_1^{\mathtt{MPI}}} 3$	$w_2^{\mathtt{F}} = 5$ $w_3^{\mathtt{F}} = 6$		$w_1^{\mathtt{MPI}} = 10$ $w_5^{\mathtt{F}} = 3$	$w_4^{\mathtt{MPI}} = 15$
Cost	6		4	2
$1 \xrightarrow{w_3^{\mathtt{F}}} 3$	$w_2^{\mathtt{F}} = 5$		$w_1^{\mathtt{MPI}} = 10$ $w_3^{\mathtt{F}} = 6$ $w_5^{\mathtt{F}} = 3$	$w_4^{\mathtt{MPI}} = 15$
Cost	3		5	2
$3 \xrightarrow{w_5^{\mathtt{F}}} 1$	$w_2^{\mathtt{F}} = 5$ $w_5^{\mathtt{F}} = 3$		$w_1^{\mathtt{MPI}} = 10$ $w_3^{\mathtt{F}} = 6$	$w_4^{\mathtt{MPI}} = 15$
Cost	4		4	2
$1 \xrightarrow{w_2^{\mathtt{F}}} 2$	$w_5^{\mathtt{F}} = 3$	$w_2^{\mathtt{F}} = 5$	$w_1^{\mathtt{MPI}} = 10$ $w_3^{\mathtt{F}} = 6$	$w_4^{\mathtt{MPI}} = 15$
Cost	2	2	4	2
$3 \xrightarrow{w_3^{\mathtt{F}}} 2$	$w_5^{\mathtt{F}} = 3$	$w_2^{\mathtt{F}} = 5$ $w_3^{\mathtt{F}} = 6$	$w_1^{\mathtt{MPI}} = 10$	$w_4^{\mathtt{MPI}} = 15$
Cost	2	3	3	2

Fig. 1. Allocation game *Fortran&MPI_Servers*. Servers 1 and 3 offer `Fortran` and `MPI` services. Server 2 offers `Fortran` services and server 4 offers `MPI` services. An initial allocation $s = (1, 1, 1, 4, 3)$ is displayed. A sequence of moves which end with the PNE $(3, 2, 2, 4, 1)$ is also displayed.

Lemma 1. *In the $Unit_{n,k,d}$ game, a strategy profile $s = (s_1, \ldots, s_n)$ is a PNE, iff $\ell(s)$ has $n\%k$ resources with load $\lceil n/k \rceil$ and the remaining resources have load $\lfloor n/k \rfloor$ and the social cost is $(\lceil n/k \rceil\, n + \lfloor n/k \rfloor\, n\%k)\, d$.*

Proof. Consider a game $Unit_{n,k,d}$ with n unit jobs (or works) $w_i = 1$, $1 \leq i \leq n$ and r servers (or resources). The broker allocates $\lfloor n/k \rfloor$ jobs into each server. After that there remain $n\%k$ jobs to allocate. As $n\%k < n$, the broker spreads these into the different servers (one per server). After such allocation, there are $n\%k$ servers with load $\lceil n/k \rceil$ and $r - n\%k$ server with load $\lfloor n/k \rfloor$. We can easily prove that such allocation is a PNE. Moreover any other "type" of allocation is not a PNE. In such cases there exists an oveloaded server and any job in such a server has interest to migrate.

Let us consider the social cost. The $n\%k$ servers contribute a social cost of $(n\%d)\lceil n/k\rceil^2 d$. The remaining $k-n\%k$ servers contribute a cost $(n-n\%k)\lfloor n/k\rfloor^2 d$. The social cost is $dk\lfloor n/k\rfloor^2 + d(n\%k)(\lceil n/k\rceil^2 - \lfloor n/k\rfloor^2)$ A little thought allows us to see $(n\%k)(\lceil n/k\rceil^2 - \lfloor n/k\rfloor^2) = (n\%k)(2\lfloor n/k\rfloor + 1)$ and the social cost is rewritten as $dk\lfloor n/k\rfloor^2 + d(n\%k)(2\lfloor n/k\rfloor + 1)$. As $k\lfloor n/k\rfloor + n\%k = n$ we rewrite as $d\lfloor n/k\rfloor(n\%k) + dn\%k$. As $n\%k(\lfloor n/k\rfloor + 1) = n\%k\lceil n/k\rceil$ we get the final expression. □

3 Risk Profiles and Weltanschauung

Risk profiles [5] are used to describe stressed environments in which two competing forces act on resources. Assume that the set of resources R in an allocation game is partitioned into two subsets $\mathcal{A}$ and $\mathcal{D}$ such that $R = \mathcal{A} \cup \mathcal{D}$ and $\mathcal{A} \cap \mathcal{D} = \emptyset$.

Subset $\mathcal{A}$ is controlled by an agent $\mathfrak{a}$ called *the angel*; $\mathcal{A}$ is used to model resources which behave robustly under stress. When a resource r is selected by the angel it runs under the angelic delay function $d_r^{\mathcal{A}}$. The angel can force angelic behaviour only for a limited number of resources $f_{\mathcal{A}}$. The angel's objective is to improve system behaviour as much as possible.

Subset $\mathcal{D}$ is controlled by another agent $\mathfrak{d}$ called *the daemon* that exhibits malicious behaviour. When r is selected by the daemon it runs under the daemonic delay function $d_r^{\mathcal{D}}$. Again the daemon can affect only a limited number of resources, $f_{\mathcal{D}}$. The daemon's objective is to maximise system delay.

We summarize all these ideas into the following definition of risk profile:

Definition 1. *Given* $C = \langle N, R, (w_i)_{i \in N}, (d_r)_{r \in R}, (A_i)_{i \in N} \rangle$, *a* risk profile *for* C *is a tuple* $\mathcal{R} = \langle C, \mathcal{A}, \mathcal{D}, f_{\mathcal{A}}, f_{\mathcal{D}}, (d_r^{\mathcal{A}})_{r \in \mathcal{A}}, (d_r^{\mathcal{D}})_{r \in \mathcal{D}} \rangle$.

Risk profiles can model highly non-uniform network behaviour with extreme and diverse stress levels. For instance, consider two resources r and r', with delays d_r and $d_{r'}$, controlled by the angel. The way that the angel influences r and r' may be very different: it may be the case that $d_r^{\mathcal{A}} = \lfloor \sqrt{d_r} \rfloor$ while $d_{r'}^{\mathcal{A}} = \lfloor \ln d_{r'} \rfloor$.

Some concrete instances of abnormal (angel and daemon) uniform delay functions are considered and the resulting situations (world views) are analysed using the notion of Weltanschauung. A Weltanschauung defines one uniform type of stress for the angel and another uniform stress for the daemon. The set of Weltanschauungs $\mathfrak{W}$ that are used in the paper are formalised below:

In the first classification the angel and daemon have two possible *sensitivities* [2] with respect to the environment: an *extreme* sensitivity (denoted by $\mathbb{E}$) or a *moderate* one (denoted by $\mathbb{M}$). The set $\mathfrak{W}$ combines these sensitivity types. The set of joint sensitivities is $\mathbb{S} = \{\mathbb{E}\text{-}\mathbb{E}, \mathbb{E}\text{-}\mathbb{M}, \mathbb{M}\text{-}\mathbb{E}, \mathbb{M}\text{-}\mathbb{M}\}$. At a second level, both

[2] In this paper the words *sensitivity* and *moral* are used in a mathematical context which, nevertheless, mimics the usual meaning of these words. In [7] *sensitive* is defined as *quick to detect, respond to, or be affected by slight changes, signals, or influences.* An alternative meaning (especially well-adapted to the daemon) is *easily offended or upset.* It is assumed that angel and daemon act instantaneously on the environment.

the angel and the daemon have a joint psychological view of the environment called here *the moral*[3]. A moral is associated with both, the angel **and** the daemon conjointly; the set of morals formed by the basic types is:

$$\mathsf{M} = \{\mathsf{Crash}, \mathsf{Benevolent}, \mathsf{Polarized}, \mathsf{Schizophrenic}\}$$

Formally the set of Weltanschauungs is $\mathfrak{W} = \mathbb{S} \times \mathsf{M}$ and a Weltanschauung is written as $\mathfrak{w} \in \mathfrak{W}$. Depending on the sensitivity and moral, the angel and the daemon stress the delay functions of a resource in the following way:

	Crash	Benevolent	Polarized	Schizophrenic
$\mathbb{E}$-$\mathbb{E}$	$d_r^{\mathcal{A}} = \infty$ $d_r^{\mathcal{D}} = \infty$	$d_r^{\mathcal{A}} = 0$ $d_r^{\mathcal{D}} = 0$	$d_r^{\mathcal{A}} = 0$ $d_r^{\mathcal{D}} = \infty$	$d_r^{\mathcal{A}} = \infty$ $d_r^{\mathcal{D}} = 0$
$\mathbb{E}$-$\mathbb{M}$	$d_r^{\mathcal{A}} = \infty$ $d_r^{\mathcal{D}} = \beta d_r$	$d_r^{\mathcal{A}} = 0$ $d_r^{\mathcal{D}} = \beta d_r$	$d_r^{\mathcal{A}} = 0$ $d_r^{\mathcal{D}} = \beta d_r$	$d_r^{\mathcal{A}} = \infty$ $d_r^{\mathcal{D}} = \beta d_r$
$\mathbb{M}$-$\mathbb{E}$	$d_r^{\mathcal{A}} = \alpha d_r$ $d_r^{\mathcal{D}} = \infty$	$d_r^{\mathcal{A}} = \alpha d_r$ $d_r^{\mathcal{D}} = 0$	$d_r^{\mathcal{A}} = \alpha d_r$ $d_r^{\mathcal{D}} = \infty$	$d_r^{\mathcal{A}} = \alpha d_r$ $d_r^{\mathcal{D}} = 0$
$\mathbb{M}$-$\mathbb{M}$	$d_r^{\mathcal{A}} = \alpha d_r$ $d_r^{\mathcal{D}} = \beta d_r$	$d_r^{\mathcal{A}} = \alpha d_r$ $d_r^{\mathcal{D}} = \beta d_r$	$d_r^{\mathcal{A}} = \alpha d_r$ $d_r^{\mathcal{D}} = \beta d_r$	$d_r^{\mathcal{A}} = \alpha d_r$ $d_r^{\mathcal{D}} = \beta d_r$
	$1 < \alpha < \infty$ $1 < \beta < \infty$	$0 < \alpha < 1$ $0 < \beta < 1$	$0 < \alpha < 1$ $1 < \beta < \infty$	$1 < \alpha < \infty$ $0 < \beta < 1$

A Weltanschauung $\mathfrak{w}$ for the case $\mathbb{E}$-$\mathbb{E}$ is the list of pairs: (∞, ∞), $(0, 0)$, $(0, \infty)$ and $(\infty, 0)$. When the angel and daemon have a moderate behaviour (case $\mathbb{M}$-$\mathbb{M}$) we assume that $d_r^{\mathcal{A}} = \alpha d_r$ $d_r^{\mathcal{D}} = \beta d_r$. The values that α and β take depend on the morals. As we can associate a risk profile to a given $\mathfrak{w} \in \mathfrak{W}$ and as we know how to stress d_r into $d_r^{\mathcal{A}}$ or $d_r^{\mathcal{D}}$, then we can extend the definition of risk profile to incorporate Weltanschauung:

Definition 2. *Let* $C = \langle N, R, (w_i)_{i \in N}, (d_r)_{r \in R}, (A_i)_{i \in N} \rangle$ *be a resource allocation game and let* $\mathfrak{w} \in \mathfrak{W}$ *be a Weltanschauung. A* risk profile *is a tuple* $\mathcal{R} = \langle C, \mathcal{A}, \mathcal{D}, f_{\mathcal{A}}, f_{\mathcal{D}}, \mathfrak{w} \rangle$ *where* $\mathcal{A} \cap \mathcal{D} = \emptyset$ *and* $\mathcal{A} \cup \mathcal{D} = R$.

Example 4. Consider a risk profile for the game *Fortran&MPI_Servers* (see Example 3). Suppose that the angel $\mathfrak{a}$ controls servers 1 and 2 (i.e. $\mathcal{A} = \{1, 2\}$) and the daemon $\mathfrak{d}$ controls servers 3 and 4 (i.e. $\mathcal{D} = \{3, 4\}$). Assume that both the angel and the daemon have limited capacity to act over the game: for instance $f_{\mathcal{A}} = f_{\mathcal{D}} = 1$. Consider the following scenario (where cost functions are again rounded by the ceiling function):

- The angel $\mathfrak{a}$ controls a number of servers: assume that one of these servers fails when put under stress i.e. $d_r^{\mathcal{A}} = \infty$.
- The daemon $\mathfrak{d}$ controls a number of robust servers. However, one server's performance is degraded under stress and so $d_r^{\mathcal{D}} = \beta d_r$ where $\beta = 3/2$ (note that $\beta > 1$).

[3] In [7] *moral* is defined as *conforming to accepted standards of behaviour*. In this paper the moral determines the joint social behaviour of the angel and the daemon.

This situation is a Crash Weltanschauung $\mathfrak{w} = (\infty, 3/2)$ of type $\mathbb{E}$-$\mathbb{M}$ and can be used to describe the risk profile

$$Stop\&Slow = \langle Fortran\&MPI\_Servers, \{1,2\}, \{3,4\}, 1, 1, (\infty, 3/2)\rangle. \qquad \square$$

Example 5. A dual scenario arises when the roles of $\mathfrak{a}$ and $\mathfrak{d}$ are interchanged: $\mathcal{A} = \{3,4\}$, $\mathcal{D} = \{1,2\}$ and $f_{\mathcal{A}} = f_{\mathcal{D}} = 1$. Now the angel $\mathfrak{a}$ increases its delay by a factor 3/2. The daemon $\mathfrak{d}$ can close a service ($\mathfrak{d}$ is delighted with such a possibility). This situation is a Crash Weltanschauung $(3/2, \infty)$ with risk profile $Slow\&Stop = \langle Fortran\&MPI\_Servers, \{3,4\}, \{1,2\}, 1, 1, (3/2, \infty)\rangle$. $\square$

Both scenarios are analysed using game theory below.

4 Angel-Daemon Games

A risk profile $\mathcal{R}$ reflects a strategic situation that can be analysed by an angel-daemon game[4]. In such a game, the stress actions are taken by two active players the angel $\mathfrak{a}$ and the daemon $\mathfrak{d}$. The subset of resources $\mathcal{A}$ in $\mathcal{R}$ is controlled by an agent $\mathfrak{a}$ called *the angel*. The angel tries to improve the behaviour as much as possible. To do that, $\mathfrak{a}$ selects a subset a of $f_{\mathcal{A}}$ resources in $\mathcal{A}$. When a resource r is selected (formally $r \in a$) it runs under the angelic delay function $d_r^{\mathcal{A}}(x)$. The angelic cost $c_{\mathfrak{a}}$ is defined as the (entire) social network cost calculated using updated (stressed) delays. Thus, $c_{\mathfrak{a}}(\sigma) \geq 0$. Dually, $\mathcal{D}$ in $\mathcal{R}$ is controlled by another agent $\mathfrak{d}$ called *the daemon* $\mathcal{D}$. The daemon tries to make the situation deteriorate as much as possible by choosing $f_{\mathcal{D}}$ resources in $\mathcal{D}$. When r is selected by $\mathfrak{d}$, it has a delay $d_r^{\mathcal{D}}(x)$. The cost to the daemon is defined as $c_{\mathfrak{d}} = -c_{\mathfrak{a}}$. Note that the definition of the angel and daemon cost functions give rise to opposite behaviours of $\mathfrak{a}$ and $\mathfrak{d}$: the goal of $\mathfrak{a}$ is to minimise the overall social cost whereas $\mathfrak{d}$ has the opposite strategy. Below is the formal definition of an angel-daemon game with an associated risk profile:

Definition 3. *Given* $C = \langle N, R, (w_i)_{i\in N}, (d_r)_{r\in R}, (A_i)_{i\in N}\rangle$ *and a risk profile* $\mathcal{R} = \langle C, \mathcal{A}, \mathcal{D}, f_{\mathcal{A}}, f_{\mathcal{D}}, \mathfrak{w}\rangle$, *the* angel-daemon game *associated to* $\mathcal{R}$ *is* $\Gamma(\mathcal{R}) = \langle N \cup \{\mathfrak{a}, \mathfrak{d}\}, (A_i)_{i\in N}, A_{\mathfrak{a}}, A_{\mathfrak{d}}, (c_i)_{i\in N}, c_{\mathfrak{a}}, c_{\mathfrak{d}}\rangle$ *where* $A_{\mathfrak{a}} = \{a \subseteq \mathcal{A} \mid |a| = f_{\mathcal{A}}\}$ *and* $A_{\mathfrak{d}} = \{b \subseteq \mathcal{D} \mid |b| = f_{\mathcal{D}}\}$. *Given* $(a, d) \in A_{\mathfrak{a}} \times A_{\mathfrak{d}}$ *the cost function of a resource* r *is defined as follows.*

$$d_r[a,d] = \begin{cases} d_r^{\mathcal{A}} & \text{if } r \in a. \\ d_r^{\mathcal{D}} & \text{if } r \in d. \\ d_r & \text{if } r \notin (a \cup d). \end{cases}$$

Given a strategy profile $\sigma = (s, a, d)$, *player* $i \in N$ *incurs a cost* $c_i(\sigma) = d_{s_i}[a,d](\ell_{s_i}(s))$, *the angel cost is* $c_{\mathfrak{a}}(\sigma) = \sum_{i\in N} c_i(\sigma)$ *and the daemon cost is* $c_{\mathfrak{d}}(\sigma) = -c_{\mathfrak{a}}(\sigma)$.

[4] We define a game using the notation given in [6]. A game is a tuple $\Gamma = \langle N, (A_i)_{i\in N}, (c_i)_{i\in N}\rangle$ such that N is the set of players, A_i is the set of actions for player i and c_i is the cost of player i.

Example 6. Consider a one player game *SimpleCloud* in which a cloud *user* wishes to execute a job w with weight 16. Two cloud services can execute w (i.e. $R = \{1, 2\}$ and $A_1 = \{1, 2\}$). The services have delays $1/2$ and $1/8$, respectively (i.e. $d_1 = 1/2$ and $d_2 = 1/8$). The two possible strategies for job placement are $s_1 = 1$ or $s_1 = 2$. Suppose that *SimpleCloud* is stressed using a moderate sensitivity (type $\mathbb{M}$-$\mathbb{M}$) Crash Weltanschauung $\mathfrak{w} = (2, 2)$ with two associated risk profiles, *Angel* and *Daemon*.

In the *Angel* profile the angel controls both resources, $\mathcal{A} = R$, but can act over only one, $f_{\mathcal{A}} = 1$. Since $\mathcal{D} = \emptyset$ (and $f_{\mathcal{D}} = 0$) the only strategy for $\mathfrak{d}$ is $d = \emptyset$. As $\mathfrak{d}$ cannot "move" the game $\Gamma(Angel)$ has only two "active players", the *user* and the angel $\mathfrak{a}$. If the angel chooses the first service ($a = \{1\}$) then the delays are $d_1[\{1\}, \emptyset] = 2 * 1/2$ and $d_2[\{1\}, \emptyset] = 1/8$; otherwise $a = \{2\}$ and $d_1[\{2\}, \emptyset] = 1/2$ and $d_2[\{2\}, \emptyset] = 1/4$. Game $\Gamma(Angel)$ is

		$\mathfrak{a}$: $\{1\}$	$\mathfrak{a}$: $\{2\}$
user	1	$16, 16$	$8, 8$
	2	$2, 2$	$4, 4$

$\Gamma(Angel)$

		$\mathfrak{d}$: $\{1\}$	$\mathfrak{d}$: $\{2\}$
user	1	$16, -16$	$8, -8$
	2	$2, -2$	$4, -4$

$\Gamma(Daemon)$

The strategy $(2, \{1\}, \emptyset)$ is the only PNE in $\Gamma(Angel)$. In this equilibrium, $\mathfrak{a}$ increases the delay of the slower service while the job is placed on the faster one.

Given $Daemon = \langle Small, \emptyset, \{1, 2\}, 0, 1, \mathfrak{w} \rangle$, the associated game $\Gamma(Daemon)$, has again only two effective players (the *user* and $\mathfrak{d}$); $\Gamma(Daemon)$ has only one PNE: $(2, \emptyset, \{2\})$. In this case $\mathfrak{d}$ increases the delay of the faster service and job w is also allocated to service 2. □

Example 7. Consider *SimpleCloud* again (see Example 6). Suppose that a moderate beneficial stress is applied to the game, $\mathfrak{w} = (1/2, 1/2)$. With risk profile $Angel' = \langle SimpleCloud, \{1, 2\}, \emptyset, 1, 0, \mathfrak{w} \rangle$, game $\Gamma(Angel')$ has a PNE $(2, \{2\}, \emptyset)$. With $Daemon' = \langle SimpleCloud, \emptyset, \{1, 2\}, 0, 1, \mathfrak{w} \rangle$ game $\Gamma(Daemon')$ has a unique PNE, $(2, \emptyset, \{1\})$. □

Example 8. Consider game $\Gamma(Stop\&Slow)$ (from Example 4). Consider a risk profile for *Fortran&MPI_Servers* (Example 3) where the set of players is $N \cup \{\mathfrak{a}, \mathfrak{d}\}$, $f_{\mathcal{A}} = f_{\mathcal{D}} = 1$ $A_{\mathfrak{a}} = \{\{1\}, \{2\}\}$ and $A_{\mathfrak{d}} = \{\{3\}, \{4\}\}$. Suppose that jobs are allocated using the schedule $s = (3, 2, 3, 4, 1)$. The angel $\mathfrak{a}$ closes site 1 ($a = \{1\}$) while the daemon $\mathfrak{d}$ chooses to deteriorate the performance of site 3 ($d = \{3\}$). The stressed delay functions $d_r[a, d]$ are:

$$d_1[\{1\}, \{3\}] = \infty, \quad d_2[\{1\}, \{3\}] = d_2 = 1/4,$$
$$d_3[\{1\}, \{3\}] = \beta d_3 = 3/4 \times 1/4, \quad d_4[\{1\}, \{3\}] = d_4 = 1/8$$

The preceding profile is not a PNE because $w_5^{\mathfrak{F}}$ can improve its situation by moving from server 1. However, $\sigma = ((3, 2, 2, 4, 2), \{1\}, \{3\})$ is a PNE. We have $c_1(\sigma) = 4$, $c_2(\sigma) = c_3(\sigma) = c_5(\sigma) = 4$, $c_4(\sigma) = 2$ with an associated social cost $c_{\mathfrak{s}}(\sigma) = 18$: in this case $c_{\mathfrak{a}} = 18$ and $c_{\mathfrak{d}} = -18$. In order to prove that σ is a

PNE we need to show that no player in $N \cup \{\mathfrak{a}, \mathfrak{d}\}$ is interested in changing its strategy.

- It is easy to see that no job $i \in N$ can improve their (private) cost c_i by moving to another server.
- If $\mathfrak{a}$ changes from $\{1\}$ to $\{2\}$, the new profile is $\tau = ((3,2,2,4,2),\{2\},\{3\})$ and the new cost is $c_2(\tau) = c_3(\tau) = c_5(\tau) = \infty$. Clearly, the angel $\mathfrak{a}$ will not make such a move.
- If $\mathfrak{d}$ changes from $\{3\}$ to $\{4\}$, the profile is $\tau' = ((3,2,2,4,2),\{1\},\{4\})$ and the new daemon delay functions are $d_3[\{1\},\{4\}] = 1/4$ and $d_4[\{1\},\{4\}] = 3/2 \times 1/8$. The costs are $c_1(\tau') = 3$, $c_2(\tau') = c_3(\tau') = c_5(\tau') = 4$, $c_4(\tau') = 3$. and the social cost $c_{\mathfrak{s}}(\tau') = 18$. As social cost of τ' is the same as the social cost of σ, the agent $\mathfrak{d}$ does not conduct this move. □

Example 9. Consider the game $\Gamma(\mathit{Slow\&Stop})$ (Example 5) again. As before $\mathcal{A} = \{3,4\}$, $\mathcal{D} = \{1,2\}$ and $f_{\mathcal{A}} = f_{\mathcal{D}} = 1$. $\Gamma(\mathit{Slow\&Stop})$ has no PNE. Proof by case analysis.

- Consider profile $\sigma = (s, a, \{1\})$ where $d_1[a,\{1\}] = \infty$. Suppose that there is an $i \in N$ such that $s_i = 1$ (at least one work is placed on server 1). Profile σ cannot be a PNE because work i can be placed elsewhere to reduce the social cost.
- Consider profile $\sigma = (s, a, \{1\})$ where no jobs are allocated to server 1 but there is at least one job allocated to server 2. The daemon $\mathfrak{d}$ would select server $\{2\}$ (rather than 1) to increase the social cost (to infinity). Thus, we can assume that in a PNE no jobs are placed on servers 1 or 2.
- Consider a profile $\sigma = (s, a, \{1\})$ with no jobs allocated to servers 1 and 2. Now server 2 works and is free and so the existing `Fortran` job prefers to move to server 2 and so we get a contradiction.

Case $(s, a, \{2\})$ is similar. □

5 Snapshots and Anonymous Pure Nash Equilibria

Now we extend the notion of load of a resource $\ell_r(s)$ to obtain information about the situation of r in relation to $\mathfrak{a}$ and $\mathfrak{d}$. We also add the delay function being currently used in this resource to obtain an adequate snapshot of the system occupancy. When we need to make explicit the Weltanschauung we replace $d_r[a,d]$ with $d_r[a,d,\mathfrak{w}]$.

Definition 4. *Let $\Gamma(\mathcal{R})$ be an angel-daemon resource allocation game, $\mathcal{R} = \langle C, \mathcal{A}, \mathcal{D}, f_{\mathcal{A}}, f_{\mathcal{D}}, \mathfrak{w}\rangle$, with profile $\sigma = (s, a, d)$. For a resource $r \in R$ define two properties:*

$$\mathsf{affiliation} = \begin{cases} \mathfrak{a} & \text{if } r \in \mathcal{A} \\ \mathfrak{d} & \text{otherwise} \end{cases} \qquad \mathsf{selected} = \begin{cases} \mathsf{y} & \text{if } r \in a \cup d \\ \mathsf{n} & \text{otherwise} \end{cases}$$

Property affiliation *indicates whether r is controlled by the angel or the daemon. Property* selected *denotes whether r's behaviour is abnormal or not (i.e. whether r has been chosen by either angel or daemon). A* snapshot *is a tuple* $\delta(\sigma, \mathfrak{w}) = (\delta_1(\sigma, \mathfrak{w}) \mid \cdots \mid \delta_k(\sigma, \mathfrak{w}))$ *which provides information about the current state of each of the resources where* $\delta_r(\sigma, \mathfrak{w}) = (\mathsf{affiliation}_{\mathsf{selected}}, \ell_r(s), d_r[a, d, \mathfrak{w}])$

Snapshots provide a clear picture of (i) the occupancy of resources, (ii) the strategies of $\mathfrak{a}$ and $\mathfrak{d}$, and (iii) the delay functions applicable to each resource. When the context is known we abbreviate the notation of a snapshot to $\delta(\mathfrak{w})$.

Example 10. Consider $Unit_{2,4,d}$ under a risk profile $\mathcal{A} = \{1, 2\}$, $\mathcal{D} = \{3, 4\}$ and $f_{\mathcal{A}} = f_{\mathcal{D}} = 1$. Given $\sigma = (s, a, d) = ((2, 4), \{1\}, \{4\})$ and $\mathfrak{w} = (\infty, \infty)$, the snapshot is $\delta(\sigma, (\infty, \infty)) = (\mathfrak{a}_{\mathsf{y}}, 0, \infty \mid \mathfrak{a}_{\mathsf{n}}, 1, d\,x \mid \mathfrak{d}_{\mathsf{n}}, 0, d\,x \mid \mathfrak{d}_{\mathsf{y}}, 1, \infty)$ □

Lemma 2. *Let* $\mathcal{R} = \langle Unit_{n,k,d}, \mathcal{A}, \mathcal{D}, f_{\mathcal{A}}, f_{\mathcal{D}}, \mathfrak{w}\rangle$, *be a risk profile associated with a unit resource allocation game and Weltanschauung* $\mathfrak{w}$ *and let* $\sigma = (s, a, d)$, $\sigma' = (s', a', d')$ *be two strategy profiles of the angel-daemon game* $\Gamma(\mathcal{R})$. *Then* $\delta(\sigma, \mathfrak{w}) = \delta(\sigma', \mathfrak{w})$ *iff* $a = a'$ *and* $d = d'$ *and there is a permutation* π *of* $\{1, \ldots, n\}$ *such that* $\pi(L_r(s)) = L_r(s')$ *for any* $1 \leq r \leq k$.

Proof. Define $R = \{1, \ldots, k\}$ and $N = \{1, \ldots, n\}$. Observe that $\delta(\sigma, \mathfrak{w}) = \delta(\sigma', \mathfrak{w})$ implies that $a = a'$ and $d = d'$ and that for any $r \in R. \ell_r(\sigma) = \ell_r(\sigma')$. Therefore, for any $r \in R$ the number of players in N that select r is the same for s and s'. Thus there is a bijection between $L_r(s)$ and $L_r(s')$. The permutation π is obtained by composing the bijection defined for each resource. Given $\mathcal{R} = \langle C, \mathcal{A}, \mathcal{D}, f_{\mathcal{A}}, f_{\mathcal{D}}, \mathfrak{w}\rangle$, and strategies $\sigma = (s, a, d)$, $\sigma' = (s', a', d')$ with $a = a'$ and $d = d'$ such that there exists a permutation $\pi : N \to N$ satisfying $\pi(L_r(s)) = L_r(s')$ for $r \in R$, then $\delta(\sigma, \mathfrak{w}) = \delta(\sigma', \mathfrak{w})$.

Let π be a permutation fulfilling the conditions given in the lemma. As we have $\pi(L_r(s)) = \{\pi(i) \mid s_i = \{r\}\} = \{j \mid s'_j = \{r\}\}$, for every i there exists j such that $\pi(i) = j$ and $s_i = s'_j = \{r\}$. Take i and r such that $s_i = s_{\pi(i)} = \{r\}$, then

$$c_i(\sigma) = d_r[a, d, \mathfrak{w}](\ell_r(s)) = d_r[a', d', \mathfrak{w}](\ell_r(s')) = c_{\pi(i)}(\sigma')$$

As π is a permutation $c_{\mathfrak{a}}(\sigma) = \sum_{i \in N} c_i(\sigma) = \sum_{i \in N} c_{\pi(i)}(\sigma') = c_{\mathfrak{a}}(\sigma')$ and similarly for $\mathfrak{d}$. The conditions on cost follow. Finally, given $\mathcal{R}$, s and s' such that $a = a'$ and $d = d'$, for any r the parts $\mathsf{affiliation}_{\mathsf{selected}}$ and $d_r[a, d, \mathfrak{w}]$ coincide in $\delta_r(\sigma, \mathfrak{w})$ and in $\delta_r(\sigma', \mathfrak{w})$. Finally, as $\pi(L_r(s)) = L_r(s')$, we have $\ell(s) = \ell(s')$ and both strategies have the same snapshot. □

Lemma 3. *Given* $\Gamma(\mathcal{R})$ *for* $\mathcal{R} = \langle Unit_{n,k,d}, \mathcal{A}, \mathcal{D}, f_{\mathcal{A}}, f_{\mathcal{D}}, \mathfrak{w}\rangle$, *and* $\sigma = (s, a, d)$, $\sigma' = (s', a, d)$ *such that* $\delta(\sigma, \mathfrak{w}) = \delta(\sigma', \mathfrak{w})$ *then* σ *is a PNE iff* σ' *is a PNE.*

Proof. There exists π such that the role of player i in s is mapped into the role of player $\pi(i) = j$ in s'. We can imagine j as an alias of i. Imagine that i is interested in changing from r to $\hat{r}$, that is change $s_i = \{r\}$ into $\hat{s}_i = \{\hat{r}\}$, because $c_i(\sigma_{-i}, \hat{s}_i) < c_i(\sigma)$. Note that $\ell_{\hat{r}}(\sigma) = \ell_{\hat{r}}(\sigma')$ and $\ell_{\hat{r}}(\sigma_{-i}, \hat{s}_i) = \ell_{\hat{r}}(\sigma) + 1$.

As $s_i = s'_{\pi(i)} = \{r\}$, defining $\hat{s}_{\pi(i)} = \{\hat{r}\}$ we have the loads $\ell_{\hat{r}}(\sigma'_{-\pi(i)}, \hat{s}_{\pi(i)}) = \ell_{\hat{r}}(\sigma') + 1 = \ell_{\hat{r}}(\sigma_{-i}, \hat{s}_i)$ and

$$c_{\pi(i)}(\sigma'_{-\pi(i)}, \hat{s}_{\pi(i)}) = d_{\hat{r}}[a,b](\ell(\sigma'_{-\pi(i)}, \hat{s}_{\pi(i)})) = c_i(\sigma_{-i}, \hat{s}_i)$$

and player $\pi(i)$ has an interest in changing the strategy. Suppose that $\mathfrak{a}$ is interested in changing in $\sigma = (s, a, d)$ from a to $\hat{a}$ because $c_{\mathfrak{a}}(s_{-\mathfrak{a}}, \hat{a}) < c_{\mathfrak{a}}(s)$. Note that $\ell_r(s) = \ell_r(s_{-\mathfrak{a}}, \hat{a})$ for any $r \in R$, therefore

$$c_{\mathfrak{a}}(s_{-\mathfrak{a}}, \hat{a}) = \sum_{r \in R} \ell_r(s) d_r[\hat{a}, d](\ell_r(s)) = c_{\mathfrak{a}}(s'_{-\mathfrak{a}}, \hat{a})$$

and $\mathfrak{a}$ has an interest in changing also in s'. The daemon has similar behaviour. □

In snapshots resource loads are important but the player of the load is not. Thus, by lemmas 2 and 3, snapshots describe Nash equilibria in an "anonymous way". This idea is at the root of the following definition.

Definition 5. *A snapshot δ is called an* anonymous Nash equilibrium iff there exists a PNE σ such that $\delta(\sigma) = \delta$.

The following lemma demonstrates that, even in simple cases, the existence of a set of resources under the control of a daemon prohibits the existence of a pure Nash equilibrium.

Lemma 4. *For any $\mathfrak{w} \in \mathfrak{W}$, the game $\Gamma(\mathcal{R}_{\mathfrak{w}})$ corresponding to the profile $\mathcal{R}_{\mathfrak{w}} = \langle Unit_{1,2,d}, \emptyset, \{1,2\}, 0, 1, \mathfrak{w}\rangle$ has no pure Nash equilibria.*

Proof. The game $Unit_{1,2,d}$ without an angel or daemon has two Nash equilibria, namely, $s_1 = \{1\}$ or $s_1 = \{2\}$. The introduction of a daemon changes the situation completely. Now there are no anonymous Nash equilibria.

Define $R = \{1,2\}$. As in $\mathcal{R}_{\mathfrak{w}}$ we have $\mathcal{A} = \emptyset$, $\mathcal{D} = R$, $f_{\mathcal{A}} = 0$ and $f_{\mathcal{D}} = 1$, by symmetry we have to consider only the snapshots $(\mathfrak{d}_{\mathsf{y}}, 1, d^{\mathcal{D}}(x) \mid \mathfrak{d}_{\mathsf{n}}, 0, d(x))$, $(\mathfrak{d}_{\mathsf{y}}, 0, d^{\mathcal{D}}(x) \mid \mathfrak{d}_{\mathsf{n}}, 1, d(x))$. As usual $d(x) = dx$. The possible values for a demonic delay function are $d^{\mathcal{D}}(x) = \infty$, $d^{\mathcal{D}}(x) = 0$, $d^{\mathcal{D}}(x) = \alpha dx$ with $1 < \alpha < \infty$ and $d^{\mathcal{D}}(x) = \alpha dx$ with $0 < \alpha < 1$. Let us consider each case separately.

(1) When $d^{\mathcal{D}}(x) = \infty$ we have to consider two snapshots, $(\mathfrak{d}_{\mathsf{y}}, 1, \infty \mid \mathfrak{d}_{\mathsf{n}}, 0, dx)$ and $(\mathfrak{d}_{\mathsf{y}}, 0, \infty \mid \mathfrak{d}_{\mathsf{n}}, 1, dx)\}$. The first one is not an anonymous Nash because the player located at $r = 1$ has an interest in moving to $r = 2$ improving the cost from ∞ to $2d$. The second one is not an anonymous Nash because $\mathfrak{d}$ has interest to abandon $r = 1$ and select (destroy) $r = 2$ increasing the delay from d to ∞.
(2) When $d^{\mathcal{D}}(x) = 0$ neither $(\mathfrak{d}_{\mathsf{y}}, 1, 0 \mid \mathfrak{d}_{\mathsf{n}}, 0, dx)$ nor $(\mathfrak{d}_{\mathsf{y}}, 0, 0 \mid \mathfrak{d}_{\mathsf{n}}, 1, dx)$ are anonymous Nash. In the first one $\mathfrak{d}$ has interest to select the second resource because nobody is using it. In the second one, the user of the resource 2 has interest to use resource 1.
(3) When $d^{\mathcal{D}}(x) = \alpha dx$ with $1 < \alpha < \infty$, the analysis of the snapshots $(\mathfrak{d}_{\mathsf{y}}, 1, \alpha dx \mid \mathfrak{d}_{\mathsf{n}}, 0, dx)$ and $(\mathfrak{d}_{\mathsf{y}}, 0, \alpha dx \mid \mathfrak{d}_{\mathsf{n}}, 1, dx)$ is similar to the case $d^{\mathcal{D}}(x) = \infty$.
(4) When $d^{\mathcal{D}}(x) = \alpha dx$ with $0 < \alpha < 1$ the analysis is similar to $d^{\mathcal{D}}(x) = 0$. □

6 On Pure Nash Equilibria

As a consequence of the preceding lemma we have the following theorem

Theorem 1. *There are tuples* $\langle Unit_{n,k,d}, \mathcal{A}, \mathcal{D}, f_{\mathcal{A}}, f_{\mathcal{D}} \rangle$ *such that for any* $\mathfrak{w} \in \mathcal{W}$*, the profile* $\mathcal{R}_{\mathfrak{w}} = \langle Unit_{n,k,d}, \mathcal{A}, \mathcal{D}, f_{\mathcal{A}}, f_{\mathcal{D}}, \mathfrak{w} \rangle$ *describes a game* $\Gamma(\mathcal{R}_{\mathfrak{w}})$ *with no pure Nash equilibria.*

However, when the game has an angel but no daemon $\mathfrak{d}$, there are anonymous Nash equilibria (see below):

Example 11. Given $\mathcal{R}_{\mathfrak{w}} = \langle Unit_{1,2,d}, \{1,2\}, \emptyset, 1, 0, \mathfrak{w} \rangle$ for any $\mathfrak{w} \in \mathfrak{W}$. It is easy to see that, $(\mathfrak{a}_{\mathsf{y}}, 0, d^{\mathcal{A}}(x) \mid \mathfrak{a}_{\mathsf{n}}, 1, dx)$ is an anonymous pure Nash equilibrium when $d^{\mathcal{A}}(x) = \infty$ or $d^{\mathcal{A}}(x) = \alpha dx$ when $1 < \alpha < \infty$ (this corresponds to a crash moral). The following snapshot $(\mathfrak{a}_{\mathsf{y}}, 1, d^{\mathcal{A}}(x) \mid \mathfrak{a}_{\mathsf{n}}, 0, dx)$ is an anonymous Nash when $d^{\mathcal{A}}(x) = 0$ or $d^{\mathcal{A}}(x) = \alpha dx$ when $0 < \alpha < 1$ (under a benevolent moral) □

When $Unit_{n,k,d}$ is under control of both $\mathfrak{a}$ and $\mathfrak{d}$ a variety of situations can arise (as in the following example):

Example 12. Consider $\mathcal{R}_{\mathfrak{w}} = \langle Unit_{2,4,d}, \{1,2\}, \{3,4\}, 1, 1, \mathfrak{w} \rangle$ for any $\mathfrak{w}$ having extreme sensitivity. Under Crash there is no pure Nash. In this moral, no player wishes to allocate work to resources selected by $\mathfrak{a}$ or $\mathfrak{d}$ (infinite delay). The snapshot $(\mathfrak{a}_{\mathsf{y}}, 0, \infty \mid \mathfrak{a}_{\mathsf{n}}, 1, dx \mid \mathfrak{d}_{\mathsf{n}}, 1, dx \mid \mathfrak{d}_{\mathsf{y}}, 0, \infty)$ is not an anonymous Nash because $\mathfrak{d}$ would select resource 3. Similarly $(\mathfrak{a}_{\mathsf{y}}, 0, \infty \mid \mathfrak{a}_{\mathsf{n}}, 0, dx \mid \mathfrak{d}_{\mathsf{n}}, 0, dx \mid \mathfrak{d}_{\mathsf{y}}, 2, \infty)$ is not an anonymous pure Nash. The snapshot $(\mathfrak{a}_{\mathsf{y}}, 0, \infty \mid \mathfrak{a}_{\mathsf{n}}, 2, dx \mid \mathfrak{d}_{\mathsf{n}}, 0, dx \mid \mathfrak{d}_{\mathsf{y}}, 0, \infty)$ is not stable because one player has an interest in moving to resource 3. When the moral is benevolent $(\mathfrak{a}_{\mathsf{y}}, 2, 0 \mid \mathfrak{a}_{\mathsf{n}}, 0, dx \mid \mathfrak{d}_{\mathsf{n}}, 0, dx \mid \mathfrak{d}_{\mathsf{y}}, 0, 0)$ is the only anonymous pure Nash equilibrium. When the moral is polarised the anonymous Nash is $(\mathfrak{a}_{\mathsf{y}}, 2, 0 \mid \mathfrak{a}_{\mathsf{n}}, 0, dx \mid \mathfrak{d}_{\mathsf{n}}, 0, dx \mid \mathfrak{d}_{\mathsf{y}}, 0, \infty)$. Finally, when the moral is schizophrenic there is no Nash. In this case no player chooses a resource selected by $\mathfrak{a}$ (infinite delay). As the resource selected by $\mathfrak{d}$ has delay 0 players will move to this resource but $\mathfrak{d}$ will subsequently select the other resource. □

When there are enough resources to locate all the players on the angelic side, sometimes there are Nash equilibria.

Theorem 2. *If* $\mathcal{R}_{\mathfrak{w}} = \langle Unit_{n,k,d}, \mathcal{A}, \mathcal{D}, f_{\mathcal{A}}, f_{\mathcal{D}}, \mathfrak{w} \rangle$ *such that* $\mathfrak{w}$ *has moral* Crash *or* Polarized*,* $f_{\mathcal{A}} + n \leq \#\mathcal{A}$*, then* $\Gamma(\mathcal{R}_{\mathfrak{w}})$ *has always a pure Nash equilibrium.*

Proof. Given $N = \{1, \ldots, n\}$, When there is enough place on the angelic side and no player $i \in N$ is tempted to use a resource in the demonic side the angel and the players $i \in N$ are in agreement.

We consider separately the morals Crash and Polarized. In the case of a Crash moral, $d_r^{\mathcal{A}} = \alpha d$ with $1 < \alpha \leq \infty$ and $d_r^{\mathcal{D}} = \beta d$ with $1 < \beta \leq \infty$. Both, $\mathfrak{a}$ and $\mathfrak{d}$ strictly increases de delay (degradates the performance) of $f_{\mathcal{A}}$ and $f_{\mathcal{D}}$ servers respectivelly. Consider the possibilities offered to the broker in such a risk profile. Whenever possible, the broker allocates jobs in undegradated servers. As $n \leq \#\mathcal{A} - f_{\mathcal{A}}$ the angel has enough undegrated services to allocate the n jobs.

The broker spreads the n jobs in different servers and the social cost is dn. Let us see that such an allocation is a PNE.

- As a job i is located in non-degradeted server, job i is not interested to move into one of the $f_{\mathcal{A}} + f_{\mathcal{D}}$ servers because delay increases.
- The angel $\mathfrak{a}$ having selected $f_{\mathcal{A}}$ servers has no interest no change the initial choice. For instance if it degradates a site containing a job, the social cost becomes $(n-1)d + \alpha d$ and therefore it increases in $(\alpha - 1)d > 0$.
- Any change in $\mathfrak{d}$ makes no change in the social cost.

Consider the case of a Polarized moral. In this case $d_r^{\mathcal{A}} = \alpha d$ with $0 \leq \alpha < 1$ and $d_r^{\mathcal{D}} = \beta d$ with $1 < \beta \leq \infty$. The angel $\mathfrak{a}$ improves $f_{\mathcal{A}}$ servers and $\mathfrak{d}$ degradates $f_{\mathcal{D}}$ servers. Initially the broker could locate the jobs into the untouched serves from the angelic side, this give a social cost of dn. This allocation is far from to be a PNE. For instance, $\mathfrak{a}$ will select and improve $\min\{n, f_{\mathcal{A}}\}$ servers containing a job and the social cost improves to $\alpha d \min\{n, f_{\mathcal{A}}\} + (n - \min\{n, f_{\mathcal{A}}\})d$. In many cases this situation is not yet a PNE. For instance, in the case of α being "really small", the jobs remaining in normal servers have interes to move to a server improved by the angel. Suppopse that such one server contains x jobs with cost αdx. A job in an a normal server has cost d. This job has interest to move into an improved server if $\alpha d(x+1) < d$. This process will continue until a PNE is reached. □

7 Brokering

The use of risk profiles and Weltanschauungs may be extended from modelling stressful grid environments to deriving resource allocation strategies for brokers. Given an resource allocation problem C and an adequate risk profile $\mathcal{R}$ of a web environment it is possible to determine if there is a pure Nash equilibrium in $\Gamma(\mathcal{R})$; if so the PNE (s, a, d) with *optimal cost* can be sent from the broker to each player. Even in cases where there are no PNE the risk profiles for the environment still provide an abstract description of web interactions which may provide insights into which resources the broker should utilise.

Different brokers can have different criteria about the adequacy of risk profiles and which parameters are critical. Depending on the brokers, different criteria for optimality can be adopted. The following example illustrates how risk profiles might be utilised by brokers.

Example 13. Consider the allocation problem given by a $Unit_{3,4,d}$. With no information about network stress players should (eventually) choose any Nash equilibrium. A Nash equilibrium is obtained allocating different players in different resources. For instance $s_1 = 1, s_2 = 2, s_3 = 3$ is a Nash.

Suppose that the allocation problem for $Unit_{3,4,d}$ is submitted to a broker. The current stress situation about the resources is known by the broker and is summarised in the risk profile $\mathcal{R} = \langle Unit_{3,4,d}, \{1,2\}, \{3,4\}, 1, 1, \mathfrak{w}\rangle$ with a benevolent Weltanschauung $\mathfrak{w} = (1/2, 1/2)$. In $\Gamma(\mathcal{R})$ the snapshot

$$(\mathfrak{a}_{\mathsf{y}}, 1, dx/2 \mid \mathfrak{a}_{\mathsf{n}}, 0, dx \mid \mathfrak{d}_{\mathsf{y}}, 1, dx/2 \mid \mathfrak{d}_{\mathsf{n}}, 1, dx)$$

is an anonymous Nash. The broker forwards to the four players any allocation consistent with the anonymous Nash. For instance $s_1 = 1$, $s_2 = 3$ and $s_3 = 4$ is a possible allocation and $s_1 = 3$, $s_2 = 4$, $s_3 = 1$ is other possible suggestion. Note that:

1. In a given allocation some players will have better outcomes than others; for example, in the first allocation players 1 and 2 have delay $d/2$ but player 3 has delay d.
2. In different allocations players can have different delays. For example, player 3 has delays d and $d/2$ in the first and second allocations, respectively.

In this case the behaviour of the broker is clear: it should never propose the allocation $s_1 = 1, s_2 = 2, s_3 = 3$ since here is no snapshot consistent with this allocation which corresponds to an anonymous Nash. If resources 1 and 2 are selected, the angel $\mathfrak{a}$ can improve one of them, say the first, giving the initial snapshot $(\mathfrak{a}_{\mathsf{y}}, 1, dx/2 \mid \mathfrak{a}_{\mathsf{n}}, 1, dx \mid \cdots, 1, \cdots \mid \ldots, 0, \ldots)$. $\mathfrak{d}$ will elect to damage the allocation by choosing resource 4 giving snapshot $(\mathfrak{a}_{\mathsf{y}}, 1, dx/2 \mid \mathfrak{a}_{\mathsf{n}}, 1, dx \mid \mathfrak{d}_{\mathsf{n}}, 1, dx \mid \mathfrak{d}_{\mathsf{y}}, 0, dx/2)$ which does not correspond to an anonymous Nash (player 3 now has an incentive to allocate into resource 4). □

8 Discussion

Conventionally the behaviour of a web service is captured by treating the service in isolation. For example, a service level agreement (SLA) might provide information about the expected behaviour of a service. In this paper an alternative view of web services is presented; here the behaviour of a *set of services* within a stressed web environment is modelled by a strategic angel daemon game. Two different abstractions for modelling stressed web environments are presented, namely, risk profiles and Weltanschauungs. Risk profiles partition web services into angel and daemon sets. Weltanschauungs consider the various scenarios that can arise when angels and daemons have uniform abnormal delay functions at a number of sensitivities. The use of risk profiles and Weltanschauungs raises a number of questions about how the model should be interpreted in a concrete situation:

1. How can a set of services be partitioned into angel and daemon controlled sets?
2. How can a service's performance improve under stress?
3. How can abnormal bounds for the angel and the daemon be set?

Perhaps one way to interpret the angel/daemon partition is by means of a cost model: sets of low cost services are liable to be severely affected by stressed environments – such sets of services may be considered to be under the control of a daemon. On the other hand expensive services may be responsive even when the surrounding environment becomes stressed. Note that some services may be implemented on *elastic clouds* – as demand increases a service may call upon more servers to facilitate ongoing requests. In this way it may be the case that behaviour in abnormal stressed conditions may even be better than under normal conditions. However, it seems likely that the choice of the abnormal bound parameters would have to be made on the basis of experimental evidence.

The work reported in this paper provides insights into the dynamic behaviour of sets of services embedded within a (stressed) web environment. Treating network stress as a non-cooperative game clearly reflects the experience of web users and brokers.

References

1. Babaioff, M., Kleinberg, K., Papadimitriou, C.: Congestion games with malicious players. In: ACM Conference on Electronic Commerce, pp. 103–112 (2007)
2. Baraglia, R., Laforenza, D., Ferrini, R., Adami, D., Giordano, S., Yahyapour, R.: A study on network resources management in grids. In: CoreGRID-IW, pp. 213–224 (2006)
3. Gabarro, J., García, A., Clint, M., Stewart, A., Kilpatrick, P.: Bounded Site Failures: an Approach to Unreliable Grid Environments. In: Danelutto, M., Fragopoulou, P., Getov, V. (eds.) Making Grid Works, pp. 175–187. Springer, Heidelberg (2007)
4. Gabarro, J., García, A., Serna, M.: On the Complexity of Equilibria Problems in Angel-Daemon Games. In: Hu, X., Wang, J. (eds.) COCOON 2008. LNCS, vol. 5092, pp. 31–40. Springer, Heidelberg (2008)
5. Gabarro, J., García Serna, M., Stewart, A., Kilpatrick, P.: Analysing Orchestrations with Risk Profiles and Angel daemon Games. In: Gorlatch, S., Fragopoulou, P., Priol, T. (eds.) Grid Computing Achievements and Prospects, pp. 121–132. Springer, Heidelberg (2008)
6. Osborne, M., Rubinstein, A.: A Course on Game Theory. MIT Press, Cambridge (1994)
7. Oxford Dictionaries, `http://www.askoxford.com/?view=uk`
8. Nisan, N., Roughgarden, T., Tardos, E., Vazirani, V.: Algorithmic Game Theory, Cambridge (2007)
9. Penn, M., Maria Polukarov, M., Tennenholtz, M.: Congestion games with failures. In: ACM Conference on Electronic Commerce, pp. 259–268 (2005)
10. Penn, M., Maria Polukarov, M., Tennenholtz, M.: Congestion games with load-dependent failures: identical resources. In: ACM Conference on Electronic Commerce, pp. 210–217 (2007)
11. Koutsoupias, E., Papadimitriou, C.: Worst-case Equilibria. In: Meinel, C., Tison, S. (eds.) STACS 1999. LNCS, vol. 1563, pp. 404–413. Springer, Heidelberg (1999)
12. Rosenthal, R.: A class of games possessing pure-strategy Nash equilibria. Int. J. Game Theory 2, 65–67 (1973)

An Algebra of Hierarchical Graphs*

Roberto Bruni[1], Fabio Gadducci[1], and Alberto Lluch Lafuente[2]

[1] Department of Computer Science, University of Pisa, Italy
[2] IMT Institute for Advanced Studies Lucca, Italy

Abstract. We define an algebraic theory of hierarchical graphs, whose axioms characterise graph isomorphism: two terms are equated exactly when they represent the same graph. Our algebra can be understood as a high-level language for describing graphs with a node-sharing, embedding structure, and it is then well suited for defining graphical representations of software models where nesting and linking are key aspects.

1 Introduction

As witnessed by a vast literature, graphs offer a convenient ground for the specification and analysis of software systems. Roughly, graphical models expose the structure of a system in terms of its computational components, their ports and their connectivity. Using *plain hypergraphs* (i.e. graphs where nodes and edges form just sets, with no additional structure), components and connectors become hyperedges and their ports become nodes. Moreover, nodes, hyperedges and their tentacles can be *typed* so to discard erroneously linked systems.

In [1] we argue that *structured* graphs are most suited for service-oriented systems, where scalable techniques and open-ended specifications are important issues that are not immediately met by plain hypergraphs alone. Structured graphs offer better support for "understanding" graphs (like parsing and browsing large systems), for designing systems (like expressing requirements and specifications, facilitating abstraction and refinement, allowing modularity and seamless aggregation), supporting automated analysis and verification (like model construction, model conformance, behavioural analysis, assessing sound reconfiguration and refactoring transformations) and last but not least, for sound and complete visual encoding of computational systems.

Different kinds of structures can be super-imposed on graphs. First, a graph G can be enclosed in some sort of box whose label L implicitly defines some properties of the enclosed graph, i.e., its *style* (e.g. see the graph transformation framework in [2]). Figure 1 (left) shows one example of "topologically" labelled graph, that can be written, e.g., $Seq[G]$ (for the obvious plain graph G derivable from the figure) or, equivalently, as a membership annotation $G : Seq$, where Seq can be read as the set of all (well-linked) sequential graphs.

The "graphs within boxes" view can be enhanced into a "graphs within edges" view, where boxes have their own tentacles and boxing can be iterated. For example, Fig. 1 (right) shows that the sequential composition of sequential graphs

* Research supported by the EU, FET integrated project IST-2005-016004 SENSORIA.

M. Wirsing, M. Hofmann, and A. Rauschmayer (Eds.): TGC 2010, LNCS 6084, pp. 205–221, 2010.

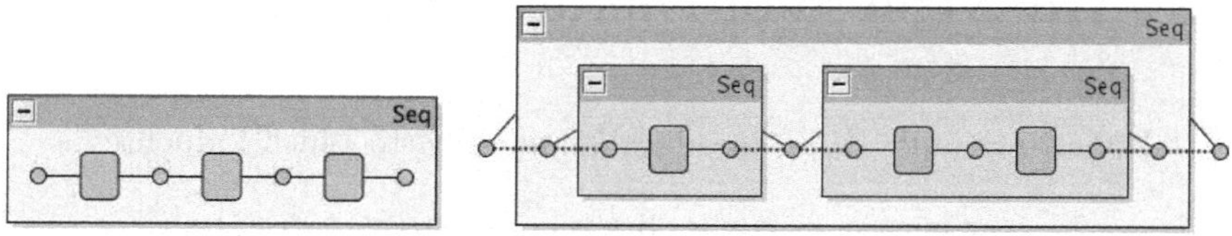

Fig. 1. Graphs within boxes (left) and graphs within edges (right) views

still yields a sequential graph. Note that the boxed interfaces are equipped with tentacles and dotted lines make explicit the link between inner nodes, exposed by interfaces, and actual nodes (analogous notation will be used in Fig. 6 (right) and Fig. 7). This way, boxes can be read as enhanced interfaces allowing for more sophisticated forms of containment, (well-typed) composition, modular specification, logical hierarchies or node sharing.

The encoding of configurations given with an algebraic specification language (e.g. as in process calculi) is best defined by structural induction. In absence of an algebraic presentation for the target model, an ad-hoc algebraic syntax must be developed in order to benefit from structural induction in proofs, transformations or definitions. An example of this is the algebraic presentation of MOF (Meta Object Facility) metamodels of [3]. Still, most graph models are not equipped with an algebraic syntax and those that exist require advanced skills to deal with sophisticated models involving set-theoretic definitions of graphs with interfaces (e.g. [4]) or complex type systems (e.g. [5]), hampering definitions and proofs. Moreover, one encounters a severe drawback: namely, the syntax of a graph formalism is often very different from the source language and not provided with suitable primitives to deal with features that commonly arise in algebraic specifications, like names (e.g. references, channels), name restrictions (e.g. hiding, nonce generation) or hierarchical aspects (e.g. ambients, scopes) in the case of process calculi. Additionally, any graphical encoding involves the challenge of preserving structural equivalence of system configurations, i.e. ensuring that structurally equivalent configurations are mapped to isomorphic graphs. For example, in graph transformation approaches [6] the soundness of the encoding is necessary to model dynamic aspects like operational semantics, reconfigurations, refactorings or model transformations, because the matching of redexes is based on (sub)graph isomorphism.

In order to overcome such challenges, we have developed a handy syntax for representing nested graphs and reducing the representation distance w.r.t. specification languages. The syntax has been first presented in [7] together with a methodology to encode process calculi like, among other case studies, a sophisticated calculus for the description of service-oriented applications, CaSPiS [8], whose features posed further challenges to visualisation, due to the interplay of name handling, nested sessions and a pipeline operator.

The contribution of this paper is to equip the syntax with a set of axioms and a suitable domain of interpretation, thus resulting in a novel algebra of hierarchical graphs. The domain of interpretation is a (sound and complete) initial

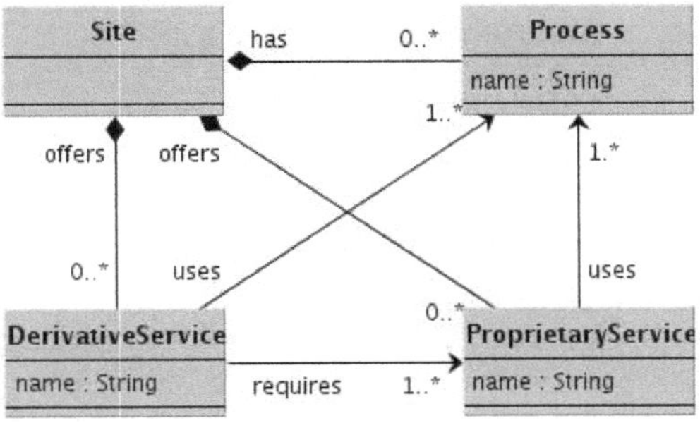

Fig. 2. SPS metamodel for our running scenario

model that serves as an original flavour of (layered) graphs: the axioms allow for term normalization and the interpretation of terms over set-theoretical models allow us to use the algebra as some sort of intermediate language, reducing the representation distance between specification languages and structured graph models. This paper, hence, is the foundational counterpart of our methodological approach to the visual specification of systems initiated in [7].

Synopsis. We take a scenario based on a simple metamodel of service oriented entities as a running example, introduced in § 2. The algebra of nested graphs is defined in § 3 and its set-theoretical interpretation is defined in § 4, together with the main result establishing the soundness and completeness of the interpretation. Finally, related and future works are discussed in § 5 together with some concluding remarks. A short appendix addresses a practical issue, raised in [7], concerning the possibility of flattening certain layers of a hierarchical graph.

2 Sites, Processes and Services

Nesting and linking are two key structural aspects that arise repeatedly in computer systems: consider e.g. the structure of file systems, composite diagrams, networks, membranes, sessions, transactions, locations, structured state machines or XML files. Identifying the right structure and level of abstraction is fundamental to enjoy scalability. In particular, nesting (called composition in MOF) plays a fundamental role for abstracting the complexity of a system by offering different levels of detail. We argue that nesting and linking must be treated as first-class concepts, conveniently represented with a suitable syntax that allows one to express and exploit them. Various graphical models of nesting and sharing structures already exist but (as we argue in § 5) it seems to us that none of them offers a syntax as simple and intuitive as the one proposed in this paper.

As a simple running example, we consider the metamodel SPS (for sites, processes and services) shown in Fig 2. It fixes an alphabet of (attributed) entities (sites, processes, derivative and proprietary services) and their possible relations: processes and services are associated to sites (containment is given by *composition relations*, which are denoted by lines decorated with diamonds on the

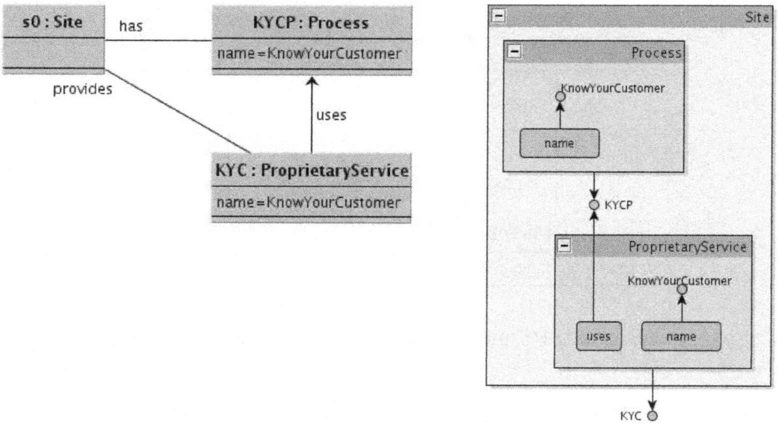

Fig. 3. An SPS instance as a flat diagram (left) and as a nested graph (right)

container end), proprietary services may *use* processes, and derivative services may also *require* services (*association relations* are denoted with ordinary arrows). The algebraic presentation of [3] basically consists of representing models as multisets of (typed) objects with some attributes used for their interrelations (i.e. references to object identifiers). Roughly, each configuration (object multiset) corresponds to a flat graph where nodes and edges are used to represent objects and their relations as depicted in the example instance of Fig. 3 (left), where a site provides a client certification service (Know Your Customer) built out from an internal process. Composition is represented just as any other relation (the *has* and *provides* relations) which makes it difficult to exploit the compositional structure to abstract or manipulate such models. For instance, it is not easy to write a term **site**(x) that matches a site with any possible configuration x of processes and services because the multiset representation requires us to see the configuration as **site**$(x), C$, where **site**(x) is a configuration containing the process and all its contents for which we need to check that C (the rest of the configuration) does not contain any object referring to the site as its container. Matching a term like **site**(x) in a graphical representation would mean to match an entire subgraph which is clearly facilitated when graphs are structured (e.g. hierarchical). For instance, the graph on Fig. 3 (right) offers an explicit, visual representation of composition by containment. Now, **site**(x) can be used to denote a *Site*-labelled box embedding x (the content of the site).

3 An Algebra of Hierarchical Graphs

We introduce here our algebra of (typed) hierarchical graphs with edge-like interfaces that we call *designs*. The algebraic presentation of designs has emerged during our studies on *Architectural Design Rewriting* [9] (hence the name) and it has been inspired by the graph algebra of [10].

Definition 1 (design). *A* design *is a term of sort* $\mathbb{D}$ *generated by the grammar*

$$\mathbb{D} \ ::= \ L_{\overline{x}}[\mathbb{G}] \qquad \mathbb{G} \ ::= \ \mathbf{0} \ \mid \ x \ \mid \ l\langle\overline{x}\rangle \ \mid \ \mathbb{G} \mid \mathbb{G} \ \mid \ (\nu x)\mathbb{G} \ \mid \ \mathbb{D}\langle\overline{x}\rangle$$

where l and L are drawn from alphabet $\mathcal{E}$ and $\mathcal{D}$ of edge *and* design *labels, respectively, x is taken from a set $\mathcal{N}$ of nodes and $\overline{x} \in \mathcal{N}^*$ is a list of nodes.*

As a matter of notation, we let $\lfloor\overline{x}\rfloor$ denote the set of elements of a list $\overline{x}$ and overload $|\cdot|$ to denote both the length of a list and the cardinality of a set.

Terms generated by $\mathbb{G}$ and $\mathbb{D}$ are meant to represent (possibly hierarchical) graphs and "edge-encapsulated" hierarchical graphs, respectively. The syntax has the following informal meaning: $\mathbf{0}$ represents the empty graph, x is a discrete graph containing node x only, $l\langle\overline{x}\rangle$ is a graph formed by an l-labeled (hyper)edge attached to nodes $\overline{x}$ (the i-th tentacle to the i-th node in $\overline{x}$, sometimes denoted by $\overline{x}[i]$), $\mathbb{G} \mid \mathbb{H}$ is the graph resulting from the parallel composition of graphs $\mathbb{G}$ and $\mathbb{H}$ (their disjoint union up to shared nodes), $(\nu x)\mathbb{G}$ is the graph $\mathbb{G}$ after making node x not visible from the outside (borrowing nominal calculus jargon we say that the node x is *restricted*), and $\mathbb{D}\langle\overline{x}\rangle$ is a graph formed by attaching design $\mathbb{D}$ to nodes $\overline{x}$ (the i-th node in the interface of $\mathbb{D}$ to the i-th node in $\overline{x}$).

A term $L_{\overline{x}}[\mathbb{G}]$ is a design labeled by L, with body graph $\mathbb{G}$ whose nodes $\overline{x}$ are exposed in the interface. To clarify the exact role of the interface of a design, we can use a programming metaphor: a design $L_{\overline{x}}[\mathbb{G}]$ is like a procedure declaration where $\overline{x}$ is the list of formal parameters. Then, term $L_{\overline{x}}[\mathbb{G}]\langle\overline{y}\rangle$ represents the application of the procedure to the list of actual parameters $\overline{y}$; of course, in this case the length of $\overline{x}$ and $\overline{y}$ must be equal (more precisely, the applicability of a design to a list of nodes must satisfy other requirements to be detailed later in the definition of well-formedness).

Restriction $(\nu x)\mathbb{G}$ acts as a binder for x in $\mathbb{G}$ and similarly $L_{\overline{x}}[\mathbb{G}]$ binds $\lfloor\overline{x}\rfloor$ in $\mathbb{G}$, leading to the usual (inductively defined) notion of *free* nodes $\mathit{fn}(\cdot)$

$$\mathit{fn}(L_{\overline{x}}[\mathbb{G}]) = \mathit{fn}(\mathbb{G}) \setminus \lfloor\overline{x}\rfloor \qquad \mathit{fn}(\mathbf{0}) = \emptyset \quad \mathit{fn}(x) = \{x\} \quad \mathit{fn}(l\langle\overline{x}\rangle) = \lfloor\overline{x}\rfloor$$
$$\mathit{fn}(\mathbb{G} \mid \mathbb{H}) = \mathit{fn}(\mathbb{G}) \cup \mathit{fn}(\mathbb{H}) \quad \mathit{fn}((\nu x)\mathbb{G}) = \mathit{fn}(\mathbb{G}) \setminus \{x\} \quad \mathit{fn}(\mathbb{D}\langle\overline{x}\rangle) = \mathit{fn}(\mathbb{D}) \cup \lfloor\overline{x}\rfloor$$

Example 1. Let $a, b \in \mathcal{E}$, $A \in \mathcal{D}$, $u, v, w, x, y \in \mathcal{N}$. We write and depict in Fig. 4 some terms of our algebra. Nodes are represented by circles, edges by small rounded boxes, and designs by large shaded boxes with a top bar. The first tentacle of an edge is represented by a plain arrow with no head, while the second one is denoted by a normal arrow. If a node is exposed in the interface we put it on the outermost layer and overlap the edges of the various layers denoting this with black squares on design borders. In the particular examples only free nodes are annotated with their identities. Note that this representation

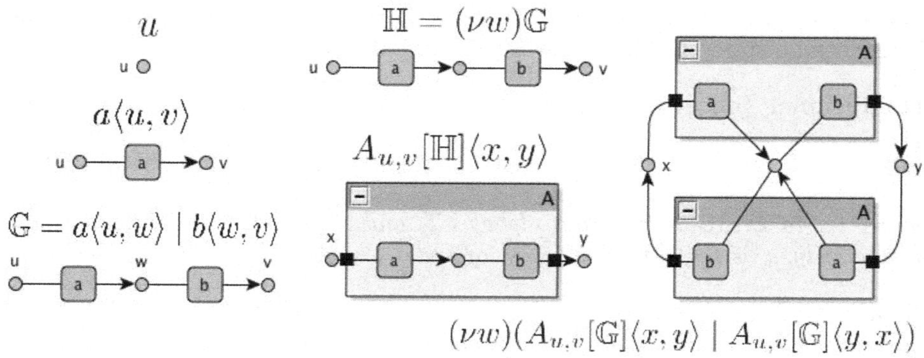

Fig. 4. Some terms of the graph algebra

is informal (alike Fig. 3 (right) and Fig. 5) to give a first intuition of our model of hierarchical graphs. Next section offers the formal representation of the rightmost term.

In practice, it is very frequent that one is interested in disciplining the use of edge and design labels so to be attached only to a specific number of nodes (possibly of specific sorts) or to contain graphs of a specific topology. To this aim it is typically the case that: 1) nodes are sorted, in which case their labels take the form $n : s$ for n the *name* and s the *sort* of the node; 2) each label of $\mathcal{E}$ and $\mathcal{D}$ has a fixed arity and for each rank a fixed node sort; 3) designs can be partitioned according to their top-level labels (i.e. the set of design labels $\mathcal{D}$ can be seen as the set of sorts, with a membership predicate $\mathbb{D} : L$ that holds whenever $\mathbb{D} = L_{\overline{x}}[\mathbb{G}]$ for some $\overline{x}$ and $\mathbb{G}$). When this is the case, we say that a design (or a graph) is *well-typed* if for each sub-term $L_{\overline{x}}[\mathbb{G}]$ we have that the (lists of) sorts of $\overline{x}$ and L coincide, and similarly for sub-terms $\mathbb{D}\langle\overline{x}\rangle$ and $l\langle\overline{x}\rangle$. From now on, we restrict our attention to well-formed designs.

Definition 2 (well-formedness). *A design or graph is* well-formed *if (1) it is well-typed; (2) for each occurrence of design $L_{\overline{x}}[\mathbb{G}]$ we have $\lfloor\overline{x}\rfloor \subseteq fn(\mathbb{G})$; and (3) for each occurrence of graph $L_{\overline{x}}[\mathbb{G}]\langle\overline{y}\rangle$, the substitution $^{\overline{y}}/_{\overline{x}}$ induces a bijection.*

Intuitively, the restriction on the mapping $^{\overline{y}}/_{\overline{x}}$ allows $\overline{x}$ to account for matching and mismatching of nodes in the interface: distinct nodes in $\overline{y}$ must correspond to distinct nodes in $\overline{x}$, and if the list $\overline{x}$ contain repetitions, then all the occurrences of the same node x in $\overline{x}$ must correspond to the same node y in $\overline{y}$, and vice versa.

In order to have a notion of syntactically equivalent designs (i.e. to consider designs up to isomorphism), the algebra includes the structural graph axioms of [10] such as associativity and commutativity for | (with identity **0**) and node restriction (respectively, axioms DA1–DA3 and DA4–DA6). In addition, it includes axioms to α-rename bound nodes (DA7–DA8), an axiom for making immaterial the addition of a node x to a graph where x is already free (DA9) and another one that makes sure global names are not local (DA10).

Definition 3 (design axioms). *The structural congruence* $\equiv_{\mathrm{D}}$ *over well-formed designs and graphs is the least congruence satisfying*

$$\begin{array}{rlrll}
\mathbb{G} \mid \mathbb{H} \equiv \mathbb{H} \mid \mathbb{G} & (\mathsf{DA1}) & \mathbb{G} \mid (\nu x)\mathbb{H} \equiv (\nu x)(\mathbb{G} \mid \mathbb{H}) & \textit{if } x \notin \mathit{fn}(\mathbb{G}) & (\mathsf{DA6})\\
\mathbb{G} \mid (\mathbb{H} \mid \mathbb{I}) \equiv (\mathbb{G} \mid \mathbb{H}) \mid \mathbb{I} & (\mathsf{DA2}) & L_{\overline{x}}[\mathbb{G}] \equiv L_{\overline{y}}[\mathbb{G}\{^{\overline{y}}/_{\overline{x}}\}] & \textit{if } \lfloor \overline{y} \rfloor \cap \mathit{fn}(\mathbb{G}) = \emptyset & (\mathsf{DA7})\\
\mathbb{G} \mid \mathbf{0} \equiv \mathbb{G} & (\mathsf{DA3}) & (\nu x)\mathbb{G} \equiv (\nu y)\mathbb{G}\{^{y}/_{x}\} & \textit{if } y \notin \mathit{fn}(\mathbb{G}) & (\mathsf{DA8})\\
(\nu x)(\nu y)\mathbb{G} \equiv (\nu y)(\nu x)\mathbb{G} & (\mathsf{DA4}) & x \mid \mathbb{G} \equiv \mathbb{G} & \textit{if } x \in \mathit{fn}(\mathbb{G}) & (\mathsf{DA9})\\
(\nu x)\mathbf{0} \equiv \mathbf{0} & (\mathsf{DA5}) & L_{\overline{x}}[z \mid \mathbb{G}]\langle \overline{y} \rangle \equiv z \mid L_{\overline{x}}[\mathbb{G}]\langle \overline{y} \rangle & \textit{if } z \notin \lfloor \overline{x} \rfloor & (\mathsf{DA10})
\end{array}$$

where in axiom (DA7) *the substitution is required to be a function (to avoid node coalescing) and to respect the typing (to preserve well-formedness).*

Note that $\equiv_{\mathrm{D}}$ respects free nodes, i.e. $\mathbb{G} \equiv_{\mathrm{D}} \mathbb{H}$ implies $\mathit{fn}(\mathbb{G}) = \mathit{fn}(\mathbb{H})$. Being $\equiv_{\mathrm{D}}$ a congruence, we remark e.g. that $L_{\overline{x}}[\mathbb{G}] \equiv_{\mathrm{D}} L_{\overline{x}}[\mathbb{H}]$ whenever $\mathbb{G} \equiv_{\mathrm{D}} \mathbb{H}$.

In the following, we shall often write $L[\mathbb{G}]\langle \overline{y} \rangle$ as a shorthand for $L_{\overline{y}}[\mathbb{G}]\langle \overline{y} \rangle$.

Example 2. Recall the example of Section 2 and consider the graph on the right of Fig. 3. Its syntactical representation **site0** is defined as

$$\begin{array}{l}
\mathrm{Site}[(\nu \mathrm{KYCP})(\ \mathrm{Process}[\mathrm{KYCP} \mid \mathbf{attr}(\mathrm{name}, \mathrm{KnowYourCustomer})]\langle \mathrm{KYCP} \rangle \\
\ \mid \mathrm{ProprietaryService}[\mathrm{KYC} \mid \mathbf{attr}(\mathrm{name}, \mathrm{KnowYourCustomer}) \mid \mathrm{uses}\langle \mathrm{KYCP} \rangle]\langle \mathrm{KYC} \rangle\ )\ ]
\end{array}$$

where $\mathbf{attr}(l, y) \stackrel{\mathrm{def}}{=} (\nu y)l\langle y \rangle$ is an abbreviation for the representation of an attribute as an edge with the name of the attribute as label attached to a new node representing the value. Note that other representations can be chosen for a pure graphical representation of attributes (for instance sharing values).

The syntactical presentation is very compact and clean. Note for instance how some structural constraints are captured: the impossibility for a service to use a process of another site (an OCL constraint not shown in Fig 2 for brevity) is ensured by the restriction of the identity of processes inside sites. Now, recall the convenience of being able to express a term like $\mathbf{site}(x)$. In our syntax we can define $\mathbf{site}(x) \stackrel{\mathrm{def}}{=} \mathrm{Site}[x]$, i.e., a Site-labelled design with some graph x in it. Clearly, our **site0** matches $\mathbf{site}(x)$ with x being the graph representing processes and services of the site. We can then perform some proof based on induction on the compositional structure of sites but also define rewrite rules like $\mathbf{site}(x) \mid \mathbf{site}(y) \rightarrow \mathbf{site}(x \mid y)$ for fusing two sites, which would require a cumbersome set of rules when working with plain graphs or multisets.

Let us now consider the more complex instance of Fig. 5, with some non-trivial linking modelling the fact that a derivative service (a certified mini credit service) is built using an external client certification service (KYC). The term underlying the graphical representation is **site0** | **site1** where **site1** is defined as

$$\begin{array}{l}
\mathrm{Site}[(\nu \mathrm{MCP})(\ \mathrm{Process}[\mathrm{MCP} \mid \mathbf{attr}(\mathrm{name}, \mathrm{MiniCredit})]\langle \mathrm{MCP} \rangle \\
\ \mid \mathrm{DerivativeService}[\mathrm{CMC} \mid \mathbf{attr}(\mathrm{name}, \mathrm{CertifiedMiniCredit}) \\
\qquad\qquad\qquad\qquad \mid \mathrm{uses}\langle \mathrm{MCP} \rangle \mid \mathrm{requires}\langle \mathrm{KYC} \rangle]\langle \mathrm{CMC} \rangle \\
\ \mid \mathrm{ProprietaryService}[\mathrm{MC} \mid \mathbf{attr}(\mathrm{name}, \mathrm{UncertifiedMiniCredit}) \mid \mathrm{uses}\langle \mathrm{MCP} \rangle]\langle \mathrm{MC} \rangle\ )\ ]
\end{array}$$

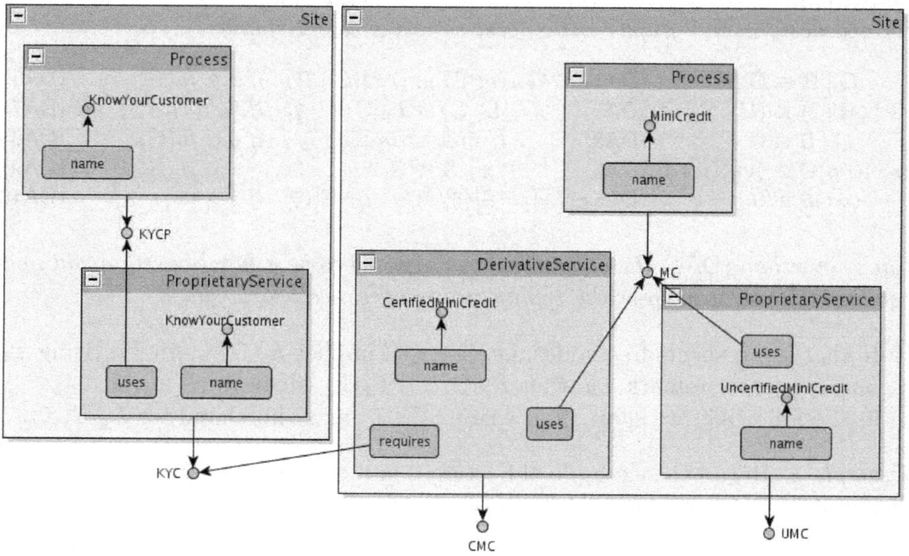

Fig. 5. An instance of the SPS metamodel as a hierarchical graph

It is worth to observe how the model is structured by the graph, hiding the processes inside sites and allowing for cross-references to services only, as in the case of the derivative service CMC of **site1** that requires the proprietary service KYC of **site0**.

One important aspect of our algebra is allowing the derivation of standard representatives for the equivalence classes induced by $\equiv_{\mathrm{D}}$.

Definition 4 (Normalized form). *A term* $\mathbb{G}$ *is in* normalized form *if it is* **0** *or it has the shape (for some* $n+m+p+q \geq 1$*, nodes* x_j *and* z_k*, and edges* $l_h\langle \overline{v}_h \rangle$ *and* $L^i_{\overline{y}_i}[\mathbb{G}_i]\langle \overline{w}_i \rangle$*)*

$$(\nu x_1)\ldots(\nu x_m)(\, z_1 \mid \ldots \mid z_n \mid l_1\langle \overline{v}_1 \rangle \mid \ldots \mid l_p\langle \overline{v}_p \rangle \mid L^1_{\overline{y}_1}[\mathbb{G}_1]\langle \overline{w}_1 \rangle \mid \ldots \mid L^q_{\overline{y}_q}[\mathbb{G}_q]\langle \overline{w}_q \rangle\,)$$

where all terms $\mathbb{G}_i$ *are in normalized form, all nodes* x_j *are pairwise distinct, all nodes* z_k *are pairwise distinct and letting* $X = \{x_1, \ldots, x_m\}$ *and* $Z = \{z_1, \ldots, z_n\}$ *we have* $X \subseteq Z$*,* $fn(\mathbb{G}) = Z \setminus X$ *and* $fn(L^i_{\overline{y}_i}[\mathbb{G}_i]\langle \overline{w}_i \rangle) = Z$ *for all* $i = 1...q$*.*

Proposition 1. *Any term* $\mathbb{G}$ *admits a* $\equiv_{\mathrm{D}}$*-equivalent term* $norm(\mathbb{G})$ *in normalized form.*

Roughly, in $norm(\mathbb{G})$ the top-level restrictions are grouped to the left, and all the global names z_k are made explicit and propagated inside each single component $L^i_{\overline{y}_i}[\mathbb{G}_i]\langle \overline{w}_i \rangle$. Up to α-renaming and to nodes and edges permutation, the normalized form is actually proved to be unique.

4 A Model of Hierarchical Graphs

The family of hierarchical graphs. We first present the set of *plain* graphs and graph *layers*, upon which we build our novel notion of *hierarchical* graphs. In the following, $\mathcal{N}$ and $\mathcal{A} = \mathcal{A}_\mathcal{E} \uplus \mathcal{A}_\mathcal{D}$ denote the universe of nodes and edges, respectively, for $\mathcal{A}$ indexed over the alphabets $\mathcal{E}$ and $\mathcal{D}$.

Definition 5 (graph layer). *The set $\mathcal{L}$ of* graph layers *is the set of tuples $G = \langle N_G, E_G, t_G, F_G\rangle$ where $E_G \subseteq \mathcal{A}$ is a (finite) set of edges, $N_G \subseteq \mathcal{N}$ a (finite) set of nodes, $t_G : E_G \to N_G^*$ a tentacle function, and $F_G \subseteq N_G$ a set of free nodes. The set $\mathcal{P}$ of* plain graphs *contains those graph layers G such that $E_G \subseteq \mathcal{A}_\mathcal{E}$.*

Thus, we just equipped the standard notion of hypergraph with a chosen set of *free* nodes, intuitively denoting those nodes that are available to the environment, mimicking free names of our algebra. Next, we build the set of hierarchical graphs.

Definition 6 (hierarchical graph). *The set $\mathcal{H}$ of* hierarchical graphs *is the smallest set*[1] *containing all the tuples $G = \langle N_G, E_G, t_G, i_G, x_G, r_G, F_G\rangle$ where*

1. *$\langle N_G, E_G, t_G, F_G\rangle$ is a graph layer;*
2. *$i_G : E_G \cap \mathcal{A}_\mathcal{D} \to \mathcal{H}$ is an embedding function (we say that $i_G(e)$ is the inner graph of $e \in E_G \cap \mathcal{A}_\mathcal{D}$);*
3. *$x_G : E_G \cap \mathcal{A}_\mathcal{D} \to \mathcal{N}^*$ is an exposure function ($x_G(e)$ tells which nodes of $i_G(e)$ are exposed and in which order), such that for all $e \in E_G \cap \mathcal{A}_\mathcal{D}$*
   (a) $\lfloor x_G(e) \rfloor \subseteq N_{i_G(e)} \setminus F_{i_G(e)}$, i.e. free nodes of inner graphs are not exposed
   (b) $|x_G(e)| = |t_G(e)|$, i.e. exposure and tentacle functions have the same arity[2]
   (c) $\forall n, m \in \mathbb{N}$ we have that $x_G(e)[n] = x_G(e)[m]$ iff $t_G(e)[n] = t_G(e)[m]$, i.e. it is not possible to expose a node twice without attaching it to the same external node (and vice versa);
4. *$r_G : E_G \cap \mathcal{A}_\mathcal{D} \to (N_G \hookrightarrow \mathcal{N})$ is a renaming function ($r_G(e)$ tells how nodes N_G are named in $i_G(e)$), such that for all $e \in E_G \cap \mathcal{A}_\mathcal{D}$ $r_G(e)(N_G) = F_{i_G(e)}$, i.e. the nodes of the graph are (after renaming) the free nodes of inner layers.*

Thus, a hierarchical graph G is either a plain graph, or it is equipped with a function associating to each edge in $E_G \cap \mathcal{A}_\mathcal{D}$ another graph. The tuple $\langle N_G, E_G, t_G, i_G\rangle$ recalls the layered model of hierarchical graphs of [2], with i_G being the function that embeds a graph (of a lower layer) inside an edge. Node sharing is introduced by the graph component F_G and the renaming function r_G, inspired by the graphs with (cospan-based) interfaces of [4]. In practice, we shall often assume that $r_G(e)$ (when defined) is the ordinary inclusion: the general case is useful to embed and reuse graphs without renaming their nodes.

[1] Taking the least set we exclude cyclic dependencies from containment, like a graph being embedded in one of its edges.

[2] We shall not put any emphasis on the typing of the graph, but clearly if the set of nodes is many-sorted an additional requirement should force the exposure and tentacle functions to agree on the node types.

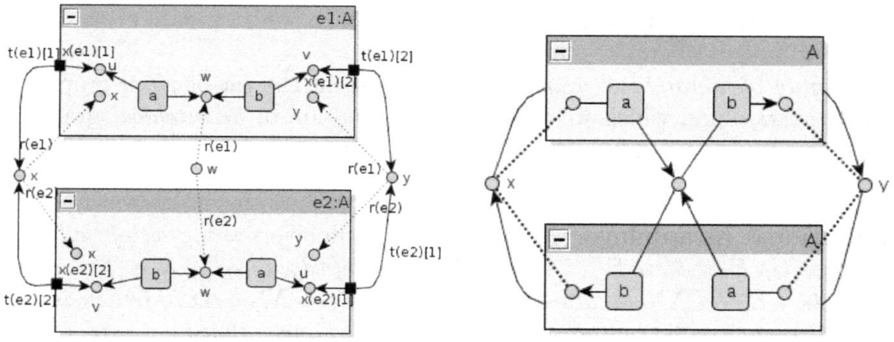

Fig. 6. A hierarchical graph (left) and its simplified representation (right)

An intuitive way to understand our model is a programming metaphor where each hierarchical edge e is seen as a procedure declaration: $t_G(e)$ are the actual arguments, $x_G(e)$ the formal parameters, $F_{i_G(e)}$ the global variables for which $r_G(e)$ acts as aliasing, and $N_{i_G(e)} \setminus (F_{i_G(e)} \cup \lfloor x_G(e) \rfloor)$ the local variables.

Example 3. Consider the last term of Example 1 and its informal graphical representation on Fig. 4 (right). Its actual interpretation as a hierarchical graph appears in Fig. 6 (left) decorated with the most relevant annotations (the tentacle, exposition and renaming functions for the two hierarchical edges). As witnessed by Fig. 6 (right), we can introduce convenient shorthands, such as dotted lines for mapping parameters, node-sharing represented by unique nodes and tentacles crossing the hierarchy levels, dropping the order of tentacles in favour of graphical decorations (missing or different heads and tails) to get a simplified notation (reminiscent of Fig. 1 (right)) that still retains all the relevant information. Note that such a simplified representation is very close to the informal notation of terms of our graph algebra shown in Fig. 4 and Fig. 5.

Example 4. Recall our example of services and the instance with two sites for which we gave its syntactical representation as **site0** | **site1** (see Example 2) and its informal graphical representation (see Fig. 5). Its actual hierarchical graph is depicted in Fig. 7 where we do not offer all the annotations as in the previous example and we hide some useless copies of global nodes (just to allow the reader to focus on the relevant part of the example). To a certain extent, it might be argued that our formal model is redundant, in the sense that global nodes require a copy at each subgraph. As we will see, this is necessary for the completeness result. In the informal presentation, as well as e.g. in a visualising tool, all copies are put together at the intuitively "right" level.

These examples should hopefully outline how our model of hierarchical graphs works and the comparison with the informal representation should suggest how they could be used to obtain an intuitive, clear visualisation. The examples should also highlight that the algebra is providing a simple syntax that hides the complexities of hierarchical models. The syntax can then be used in definitions,

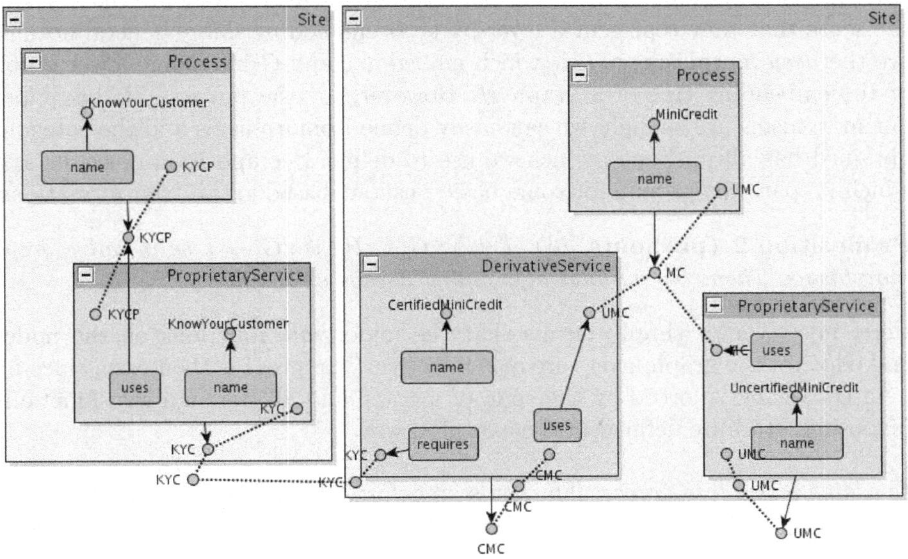

Fig. 7. An instance of our SPS metamodel as a formal hierarchical graph

proofs and transformations in a much more friendly way than would be the case when working directly with actual graphs.

In the rest of the section we explain how such graphs are obtained out of terms, but first we have to fix some notation and concepts. In the following, we shall just use *graph* in place of *hierarchical graph.* Note that the embedding structure forms a directed acyclic graph, whose unfolding we call *embedding tree.* The *height* (resp. *depth* or *layer*) of a graph is the height (resp. depth) of its embedding tree. The leaves of the embedding tree are actually plain graphs. In the following, $\mathcal{H}$ denotes both the set of all such graphs or the category having such graphs as objects and the following graph morphisms as arrows.

Definition 7 (graph morphism). *Let G, H be graphs such that $F_G \subseteq F_H$. A* graph morphism *$\phi : G \to H$ is a tuple $\langle \phi_N, \phi_E, \phi_I \rangle$ where $\phi_N : N_G \to N_H$ is a node morphism, $\phi_E : E_G \to E_H$ an edge morphism, and $\phi_I = \{\phi^e \mid e \in E_G \cap \mathcal{A}_\mathcal{D}\}$ a family of graph morphisms $\phi^e : i_G(e) \to i_H(\phi_E(e))$ such that*[3]

1. *$\forall e \in E_G$, $\phi_N(t_G(e)) = t_H(\phi_E(e))$, i.e. the tentacle function is respected;*
2. *$\forall e \in E_G \cap \mathcal{A}_\mathcal{D}$, $\phi^e_N(x_G(e)) = x_H(\phi_E(e))$, i.e. the exposure function is respected;*
3. *$\forall e \in E_G \cap \mathcal{A}_\mathcal{D}$, $\forall n \in N_G$, $\phi^e_N(r_G(e)(n)) = r_H(\phi_E(e))(\phi_N(n))$, i.e. the renaming function is respected;*
4. *$\forall n \in F_G$, $\phi_N(n) = n$, i.e. the free nodes are preserved.*

In the above definition we abuse the notation by lifting morphisms to sets and vectors. It is worth to observe that our morphisms are not the most general form

[3] Again, many-sorted alphabets would require the morphisms to be type consistent.

one can define. In particular, using the terminology of [11] they are *root-level* in the sense that they represent a layer-by-layer embedding. More general notions are the *deep* morphisms of [11] which embed a graph G into some lower graph of the embedding tree of a graph H. However, for the purpose of this paper our morphisms are enough: we can easily define isomorphisms and the category obtained has all pushouts, which we use to define a composition operator and which prepare the ground for some basic pushout-based graph transformations.

Proposition 2 (pushouts [6]). *Let $\phi : G \to H$, $\psi : G \to I$ be injective graph morphisms. Then, the pushout of ϕ and ψ always exists.*

Here, injectiveness simply means that the underlying functions on the nodes and edges of the graph layers are also injective. The proof is then easy, since no item coalescing is forced by the span of arrows, and all the auxiliary functions (exposure, etc.) are defined in the expected way.

Encoding terms into graphs. The last step before introducing the algebraic characterisation of graphs is the definition of a composition operator. We need however a few auxiliary definitions.

Definition 8. *Let $N \in \mathcal{N}$ be a subset of nodes of graph G. Then, $\widehat{N}$ is the hierachical graph given by the tuple $\langle N, \emptyset, \bot, \bot, \bot, \bot, N\rangle$, and $in_N : \widehat{N} \to G$ is the obviously defined, injective graph morphism.*

We denote the empty function with $\bot$, distinguishing it from the empty set $\emptyset$.

Definition 9 (graph composition). *Let G, H be graphs. Then, the* composition *of G and H, denoted $G \oplus H$, is the (codomain of the) pushout of the span $\widehat{F_G \cap F_H} \to G$ and $\widehat{F_G \cap F_H} \to H$.*

Graph composition is always defined, thanks to Proposition 2. We are now ready to see how terms of our algebra can be interpreted as graphs. We assume that subscripts refer to the corresponding encoded graph. For instance, $[\![\mathbb{G}]\!] = \langle N_\mathbb{G}, E_\mathbb{G}, t_\mathbb{G}, i_\mathbb{G}, x_\mathbb{G}, r_\mathbb{G}, F_\mathbb{G}\rangle$.

Definition 10 (graph interpretation). *The encoding $[\![\cdot]\!]$, mapping well-formed terms into graphs, is the function inductively defined as*

$$
\begin{aligned}
[\![x]\!] &= \langle \{x\}, \emptyset, \bot, \bot, \bot, \bot, \{x\}\rangle & [\![l\langle\overline{x}\rangle]\!] &= \langle \lfloor\overline{x}\rfloor, \{e'\}, e' \mapsto \overline{x}, \bot, \bot, \bot, \lfloor\overline{x}\rfloor\rangle \\
[\![\mathbb{G} \mid \mathbb{H}]\!] &= [\![\mathbb{G}]\!] \oplus [\![\mathbb{H}]\!] & [\![\mathbf{0}]\!] &= \langle \emptyset, \emptyset, \bot, \bot, \bot, \bot, \emptyset\rangle \\
[\![(\nu x)\mathbb{G}]\!] &= \langle N_\mathbb{G}, E_\mathbb{G}, t_\mathbb{G}, i_\mathbb{G}, x_\mathbb{G}, r_\mathbb{G}, F_\mathbb{G} \setminus x\rangle
\end{aligned}
$$

$$
[\![L_{\overline{x}}[\mathbb{G}]\langle\overline{y}\rangle]\!] = \langle N_\mathbb{G}, \{e\}, e \mapsto \overline{y}, e \mapsto [\![\mathbb{G}]\!] \oplus [\![\lfloor\overline{y}\rfloor]\!], e \mapsto \overline{x}, e \mapsto id_N, (F_\mathbb{G} \setminus \lfloor\overline{x}\rfloor) \cup \lfloor\overline{y}\rfloor\rangle
$$

where $e' \in \mathcal{A}_\mathcal{E}$ and $e \in \mathcal{A}_\mathcal{D}$.

The encoding into (plain) graphs of the empty design, isolated nodes and single edges is trivial. Node restriction consists of removing the restricted node from the set of free nodes. The encoding of the parallel composition is as expected: a disjoint union of the corresponding hierarchical graphs up to common free nodes, plus a possible saturation of the sub-graphs with the nodes now appearing in the top graph layer. A hierarchical edge (last row) is basically a graph with a single edge (which is mapped to the corresponding body graph) and a copy of the free nodes of the body graph (properly mapped to the corresponding copies in the body), while adding the names $\lfloor \overline{y} \rfloor$ among the free ones.

It is worth to remark that the encoding is surjective, i.e. every graph can be denoted by a term of the algebra.

Proposition 3. *Let G be a graph. Then, there exists a well-formed term $\mathbb{G}$ generated by the design algebra such that G is isomorphic to $[\![\mathbb{G}]\!]$.*

Moreover, our encoding is sound and complete, meaning that equivalent terms are mapped to isomorphic graphs and vice versa.

Theorem 1. *Let $\mathbb{G}_1$, $\mathbb{G}_2$ be well-formed terms generated by the design algebra. Then, $\mathbb{G}_1 \equiv_d \mathbb{G}_2$ if and only if $[\![\mathbb{G}_1]\!]$ is isomorphic to $[\![\mathbb{G}_2]\!]$.*

The proof proceeds by exploiting the normalized form of well-formed terms. In fact, by Prop. 3 each graph has associated a well-formed term in normalized form, and this can be further exploited to prove the uniqueness of such term.

5 Conclusions and Related and Future Works

We introduced a novel specification formalism based on a convenient algebra of hierarchical graphs: its features make it well-suited for the specification of systems with inherently hierarchical aspects ranging from process calculi with notion of scopes and containments (like ambients, membranes, sessions and transactions) to metamodels with composition relations. Some advantages of our approach are due to the graph algebra. Most importantly, its syntax resembles standard algebraic specifications and, in particular, it is close to the syntax found in nominal calculi. The key point is to exploit the algebraic structure of both designs and graphs when proving properties of an encoding, i.e. to facilitate proofs by structural induction. Indeed, the main result of the paper already guarantees that equivalent terms correspond to isomorphic graphs.

On the algebra of graphs. Our most direct source of inspiration is an approach for the reconfiguration of software architectures called *Architectural Design Rewriting* (ADR) [9], where architectures are encoded as terms of a particular graph algebra and reconfigurations are defined using standard term rewriting techniques. Our model of hierarchical graphs extends ADR graphs with node sharing and our algebra equips ADR with a suitable syntax. In particular, original ADR specifications can be seen as rewrite theories over a signature formed by derived operations defined by terms closed with respect to nodes. Our algebra, hence, inherits the characteristics of ADR, like the ability to nicely model style-preserving architectural reconfigurations [9].

Our syntax is inspired by the graph algebra proposed in [10]. The main idea there was to have constructors such as the empty graph, single edges, and parallel composition, and axioms like associativity and commutativity of such composition, in order to consider graphs up to isomorphism. Our richer design algebra includes hierarchical features and it is intended to enable a more suitable representation for nominal calculi and their behaviour. A key difference is that in our initial model, a node restriction cannot cross the boundaries of hierarchical edges in which it is contained. Adding the corresponding axiom is feasible, even if it would result in a quite different set-theoretic notion of hierarchical graph. A less demanding, yet quite useful alternative is linked with the possibility of "flattening" some of the designs, in order to consider them just as type annotations. Accomodating for these axioms, fruitfully used in [7], would not change our class of hierarchical class, as shown in the Appendix of the present paper.

Concerning set-theoretical formalisms, a direct reference is the framework for hierarchical graph transformation introduced in [2], of which our proposal can be considered an extension, dealing with free names, along the lines of so-called graph with interfaces discussed in e.g. [4]. Indeed, as far as the mapping of processes is concerned, our solution follows closely [4]: the operators verifying the AC1 axioms basically disappear, while name restriction is dealt with by handling the interfaces. Other models of hierarchical graphs exist in the line of [2] (e.g. [12,11]), but most of them lack an algebraic syntax and an associated set of axioms.

On structured graphical models. Our approach is closely related to other formalisms that adopt a graphical representation of concurrent systems. Among those, we mention Bigraphical Reactive Systems (BRSs) [13] and Synchronized Hyperedge Replacement (SHR) [14].

The syntax of SHR is basically the one of [10], and it is subsumed by our algebra. Instead, the SHR approach focuses on the description of the operational behaviour of a system by a set of suitably labelled inference rules, which may involve complex synchronisations. We discuss later some of the rewriting features we intend to add to our approach. However, we can safely say that so far the concerns of the two proposals have been largely orthogonal.

A bigraph is given by the superposition of two independent graphs, representing the locality and the connectivity structure of a system, respectively. In our terms, the first specifies the hierarchical structure of the system, while the second the naming topology. We believe that the two approaches have the same expressiveness, but argue for the better usability of our syntax and the small, intuitive set of axioms. Most importantly, BRSs have been mostly studied in connection with the relative pushout (RPO) technique [15], in order to distill a bisimilarity congruence from a set of rewrite rules. Our hierarchical graphs form a category with pushouts (indeed, possibly an adhesive one), and the DPO approach could be then lifted, as in [2]. Hence, they should be amenable to the borrowed context technique for distilling RPOs [16]. Our proposal thus fits in the standard graph-theoretic mold, while its slender syntax provide a simple intermediate language between process calculi and their graphical models. Obviously, a possible integration is to use our syntax in order to characterise certain classes of bigraphs (e.g. *pure* bigraphs). Such an integration is suggested in [17], where the authors propose an algebraic syntax for denoting bigraphs and present type systems to characterise those terms that correspond to particular sub-classes.

On rewriting mechanisms. Concerning the operational behaviour of our specifications, we would like to find a term rewriting-like technique for the reconfiguration of designs, and prove it compatible with a graph theoretical approach for rewriting hierarchical graphs. In other words, the correspondence holding between designs and hierarchical graphs should be lifted at the level of rewriting. The standard notions of term rewriting can be applied to our algebra of designs, simply considering sets of (name and design) variables. The corresponding technique for graph rewriting is more complex, since most of these techniques are eminently local, thus making it difficult to simulate the replication of an unspecified design. Nevertheless, since our category admits pushouts, a clear path is laid down by the use of rule schemata in the DPO approach, as in [2].

Applications. We are applying our technique to various languages, focusing on process calculi exhibiting nested features. A preliminary proof of the flexibility of our approach for this purpose is found in [7], offering an encoding of a session-centered calculus. Another focus is on metamodels, we plan to develop a technique to distill algebraic specifications out of MOF metamodels, along the lines of [3] but capturing composition as nesting.

An implementation of our approach and its integration in our prototypical implementation of ADR [18] in the rewrite engine Maude is under current work. A preliminary version is available (at `http://www.albertolluch.com/adr2graphs/`) as a visualiser that considers our design algebra and some encodings of process calculi like the π-calculus and CaSPiS.

Acknowledgements. We are grateful to Andrea Corradini for his many suggestions and to Artur Boronat for fruitful discussions.

References

1. Bruni, R., Lluch Lafuente, A.: Ten virtues of structured graphs. In: Boronat, A., Heckel, R. (eds.) Proceedings of the 8th International Workhshop on Graph Transformation and Visual Modeling Technique (GT-VMT 2009). Electronic Communications of the EASST, vol. 18. EASST, Berlin (2009)
2. Drewes, F., Hoffmann, B., Plump, D.: Hierarchical graph transformation. Journal on Computer and System Sciences 64, 249–283 (2002)
3. Boronat, A., Meseguer, J.: An algebraic semantics for MOF. In: Fiadeiro, J.L., Inverardi, P. (eds.) FASE 2008. LNCS, vol. 4961, pp. 377–391. Springer, Heidelberg (2008)
4. Gadducci, F.: Term graph rewriting for the pi-calculus. In: Ohori, A. (ed.) APLAS 2003. LNCS, vol. 2895, pp. 37–54. Springer, Heidelberg (2003)
5. Bundgaard, M., Sassone, V.: Typed polyadic pi-calculus in bigraphs. In: Bossi, A., Maher, M.J. (eds.) Proceedings of the 8th International Symposium on Principles and Practice of Declarative Programming (PPDP 2006), pp. 1–12. ACM, New York (2006)

6. Corradini, A., Montanari, U., Rossi, F., Ehrig, H., Heckel, R., Löwe, M.: Algebraic Approaches to Graph Transformation - Part I: Basic Concepts and Double Pushout Approach. In: Rozenberg, G. (ed.) Handbook of Graph Grammars and Computing by Graph Transformations. Foundations, vol. 1, pp. 163–246. World Scientific, Singapore (1997)
7. Bruni, R., Gadducci, F., Lluch Lafuente, A.: A graph syntax for processes and services. In: Jianwen, S., Laneve, C. (eds.) WS-FM 2009. LNCS, vol. 6194, pp. 46–60. Springer, Heidelberg (2010)
8. Boreale, M., Bruni, R., De Nicola, R., Loreti, M.: Sessions and pipelines for structured service programming. In: Barthe, G., de Boer, F.S. (eds.) FMOODS 2008. LNCS, vol. 5051, pp. 19–38. Springer, Heidelberg (2008)
9. Bruni, R., Lluch Lafuente, A., Montanari, U., Tuosto, E.: Style Based Architectural Reconfigurations. Bulletin of the European Association for Theoretical Computer Science (EATCS) 94, 161–180 (2008)
10. Corradini, A., Montanari, U., Rossi, F.: An abstract machine for concurrent modular systems: CHARM. Theoretical Computer Science 122, 165–200 (1994)
11. Palacz, W.: Algebraic hierarchical graph transformation. Journal of Computer and System Sciences 68, 497–520 (2004)
12. Busatto, G., Kreowski, H.J., Kuske, S.: Abstract hierarchical graph transformation. Mathematical Structures in Computer Science 15, 773–819 (2005)
13. Milner, R.: Pure bigraphs: Structure and dynamics. Information and Computation 204, 60–122 (2006)
14. Ferrari, G.L., Hirsch, D., Lanese, I., Montanari, U., Tuosto, E.: Synchronised hyperedge replacement as a model for service oriented computing. In: de Boer, F.S., Bonsangue, M.M., Graf, S., de Roever, W.-P. (eds.) FMCO 2005. LNCS, vol. 4111, pp. 22–43. Springer, Heidelberg (2006)
15. Leifer, J.J., Milner, R.: Deriving bisimulation congruences for reactive systems. In: Palamidessi, C. (ed.) CONCUR 2000. LNCS, vol. 1877, pp. 243–258. Springer, Heidelberg (2000)
16. Ehrig, H., König, B.: Deriving bisimulation congruences in the DPO approach to graph rewriting with borrowed contexts. Mathematical Structures in Computer Science 16, 1133–1163 (2006)
17. Grohmann, D., Miculan, M.: Graph algebras for bigraphs. In: Boronat, A., Heckel, R. (eds.) Proceedings of the 10th International Workshop on Graph Transformation and Visual Modeling Techniques (GT-VMT 2010). Electronic Communications of the EASST. EASST, Berlin (2010) (to appear)
18. Bruni, R., Lluch Lafuente, A., Montanari, U.: Hierarchical design rewriting with Maude. In: Rosu, G. (ed.) Proceedings of the 7th International Workshop on Rewriting Logic and its Applications (WRLA 2008). Electronic Notes in Theoretical Computer Science, vol. 238(3), pp. 45–62. Elsevier, Amsterdam (2009)
19. Drewes, F., Kreowski, H.J., Habel, A.: Hyperedge replacement graph grammars. In: Rozenberg, G. (ed.) Handbook of Graph Grammars and Computing by Graph Transformations. Foundations, vol. 1, pp. 95–162. World Scientific, Singapore (1997)

Appendix: Flattening

We call a graph *flat* whenever there is no design in its body. Flattening a design is done by a kind of hyper-edge replacement [19] in the form of axioms that are sometimes useful to be included in the structural congruence.

Example 5. Suppose that we want to characterise the set of a-labelled, acyclic, and connected sequences (see Example 1). We can define an algebra with an element α in the sequence, and a binary sequential composition $\_;\_$. Both are derived operators defined by $\alpha \stackrel{\text{def}}{=} A_{(u,v)}[a(u,v)]$ and $X;Y \stackrel{\text{def}}{=} A_{(u,v)}[(\nu w)(X\langle u,w\rangle \mid Y\langle w,v\rangle)]$, where X and Y have type A. Clearly, the algebra as such constructs hierarchical sequences, where e.g. $(\alpha;(\alpha;\alpha))\langle x,y\rangle$ and $((\alpha;\alpha);\alpha)\langle x,y\rangle$ are not equivalent graphs due to different nestings.

Definition 11 (flattening axiom). *Given a design label* $L \in \mathcal{D}$, *its* flattening *axiom* $\mathsf{flat_L}$ *is* $L_{\overline{x}}[\mathbb{G}]\langle\overline{y}\rangle \equiv \mathbb{G}\{^{\overline{y}}/_{\overline{x}}\}$.

Example 6. By introducing $\mathsf{flat_A}$ in the algebra of Example 5, the two former terms $(\alpha;(\alpha;\alpha))\langle x,y\rangle$ and $((\alpha;\alpha);\alpha)\langle x,y\rangle$ are identified, and correspond to the plain graph $(\nu w_1,w_2)(a(x,w_1) \mid a(w_1,w_2) \mid a(w_2,y))$.

The above example illustrates the two roles of the nesting operator: as a means to enclose a graph and as a sort of typed interface to enable disciplined graph compositions. The presence of flattening axioms makes the first role implicit. The example also illustrates how graphical encodings of existing (algebraic) languages are defined and exploited: the main trick is to see the constructors of the original language as derived operators of the graph algebra.

In the presence of flattening, our main result can be extended just by a minor change in the graph interpretation of Definition 10, by letting

$$\llbracket L_{\overline{x}}[\mathbb{G}]\langle\overline{y}\rangle\rrbracket = \langle N_{\mathbb{G}}, \{e\}, e \mapsto \overline{y}, e \mapsto \llbracket\mathbb{G}\rrbracket \oplus \llbracket\lfloor\overline{y}\rfloor\rrbracket, e \mapsto \overline{x}, e \mapsto id_N, N'\rangle \quad \text{if } \mathsf{flat_L} \not\in \equiv_D$$
$$\llbracket L_{\overline{x}}[\mathbb{G}]\langle\overline{y}\rangle\rrbracket = \langle N_{\mathbb{G}}\{^{\overline{y}}/_{\overline{x}}\}, E_{\mathbb{G}}\{^{\overline{y}}/_{\overline{x}}\}, t_{\mathbb{G}}\{^{\overline{y}}/_{\overline{x}}\}, i_{\mathbb{G}}\{^{\overline{y}}/_{\overline{x}}\}, x_{\mathbb{G}}, r_{\mathbb{G}}, N'\rangle \quad \text{if } \mathsf{flat_L} \in \equiv_D$$

where $e \in \mathcal{A}_{\mathcal{D}}$ and N' abbreviates $(F_{\mathbb{G}} \setminus \lfloor\overline{x}\rfloor) \cup \lfloor\overline{y}\rfloor$.

Property-Preserving Refinement of Concurrent Systems

Liliana D'Errico and Michele Loreti

Dipartimento di Sistemi e Informatica
Università di Firenze

Abstract. Verification of concurrent systems within the process algebraic approach can be performed by checking that processes enjoy properties described by formulae of a temporal logic. However, to use these approach a complete description of the considered system has to be provided. In a previous work we propose a formal framework based on an assumption-guarantee approach where each system component is not considered in isolation, but in conjunction with assumptions about the context of the component. In the present paper we propose a procedure to refine the set of context assumptions. In each of the refinement steps the environment is partially instantiated with a process algebraic term while formulae satisfaction is preserved.

1 Introduction

Process algebras [14,15,3,1] are a set of mathematically rigourous languages with well defined semantics that permit describing and verifying properties of concurrent communicating systems. They provide a number of constructors for system descriptions and are equipped with an operational semantics that describes systems evolution.

Process algebras and modal logics have been largely used as tools for specifying and verifying properties of concurrent systems. This also thanks to model checking algorithms that permit verifying whether a given specification satisfies the expected properties.

Verification of concurrent systems within the process algebraic approach can be performed by checking that processes enjoy properties described by some temporal logic's formulae [10,4]. In this case, concurrent systems are specified as terms of a process description language, Labelled Transition Systems are associated with terms via a set of structural operational semantics rules and model checking is used to determine whether the transition systems associated with those terms enjoy the property specified by the given formulae.

However, it is not always possible to specify (or know) all the details of a system. Typical examples are network and distributed systems. These are composed of heterogeneous computational units that interact with each other following a predefined protocol. Even if the protocol governing the interactions among the system components is completely specified, the precise implementation of each component is not known.

In a previous work [6] we propose a formal framework based on an assumption-guarantee approach where the verification of a system (a *mixed composition* $\Gamma \triangleright P$)

M. Wirsing, M. Hofmann, and A. Rauschmayer (Eds.): TGC 2010, LNCS 6084, pp. 222–236, 2010.

is decomposed into the verification of a subset of the system components (P). These components are not considered in isolation, but in conjunction with assumptions (Γ) on the behaviour of the context where the components will be executed.

In this paper we introduce a set of reduction rules that can be considered the heart of a Local Model Checking Algorithm. The rules are sound and complete in the sense that their application permits verifying whether for each process Q satisfying assumptions Γ, the composition of P and Q satisfies a property φ.

The proposed framework naturally induces a notion of *refinement*. We say that $\Gamma_2 \triangleright Q$ refines assumption Γ_1 if and only $\Gamma_2 \triangleright Q$ satisfies Γ_1. At the same time, if $\Gamma_1 \triangleright P$ satisfies φ the same is for $\Gamma_2 \triangleright Q|P$. By iterating the proposed approach we obtain a methodology that permits obtaining a complete description of a system starting from a high level logical based specification. Moreover, in each step of the refinement procedure the satisfaction of the expected properties is preserved.

To enable the refinement procedure we introduce a set of rules to compute the *Most General Assumption* $\mathcal{W}$, that is the assumptions we have to impose on the environment to see a given process satisfying the expected formulae. Function $\mathcal{W}$ enables the refinement procedure for the definition of a whole system starting from a more general specification.

Related Works. In [2,5] analysis on automated assume-guarantee reasoning are evaluated. Verification is implemented through LTSA and FLAVERS (both based on finite state automata) and results are not encouraging. In their analysis, assume-guarantee reasoning is advocated as a way to lessen the effects of the state-explosion problem. The decomposition of the system is not driven by the environment, but is just a "*divide et impera*". As a consequence, the verification based on automata does not take advantage of such decomposition.

In [11,12,13] we found an approach similar to the one we have introduced, addressed from a different point of view. We imagine a well known process *immersed* into a context not completely known. They describe a system, whose architecture is well known, composed by a context (well described) containing *holes*. They introduce a method (similar to the ours) to obtain a weakest precondition that is used to check if a composed system satisfies a property. Their methodology avoids the definition of an operational semantics of formulae, but forces to be aware of the system architecture.

Structure of the paper. The rest of the paper is organised as follows. In Section 2 we recall the basics of the *Calculus of Communicating Systems* and the *Hennessy-Milner logic* (HML). In Section 3 we recall the dialect of HML [6] that we use to specify the properties we assume satisfied by the environment. Section 4 presents the proposed Reduction Rules for the Local Model Checking. In section 5 we present the refinement procedure and the *Weakest Environment* function $\mathcal{W}$. Section 6 gives an example of what one can describe through the introduced framework. Section 7 concludes the paper with a few final considerations. In the present paper all the proof are only sketched, detailed proofs can be found in [7].

2 Calculus of Communicating Systems

The *Calculus of Communicating Systems* (CCS) [14,15], one of the most popular process calculi, provides a set of operators that permit describing the behaviour of a system starting from the specification of its subcomponents. Components interact with each other by means of *actions*, atomic and not interruptible steps, which represent input/output operations on communication ports or internal computations of the system.

Let Λ be an infinite numerable set of channels or ports, a CCS action α can be: an input over $a \in \Lambda$, denoted by a; an output on $a \in \Lambda$, denoted by $\bar{a}$; an internal computational step, denoted by τ. We assume $\bar{\bar{\alpha}} \triangleq \alpha$, where $\alpha \in \mathcal{A} = \{\Lambda \cup \{\bar{a} \mid a \in \Lambda\} \cup \{\tau\}\}$. Actions $\bar{\alpha}$ and α are said complementary, they represent input and output actions on the same channel.

The syntax of CCS processes is defined by the following grammar:

$$P, Q ::= nil \mid X \mid \alpha.P \mid P + Q \mid P \mid Q \mid P \backslash A \mid P[f]$$
$$\alpha ::= \bar{a} \mid a \mid \tau$$

CCS processes and operators have the following meaning:

- *nil* is the *inactive* process.
- X is a *constant* which is assumed defined by an appropriate equation $X \triangleq P$ for some process term P, where *constants* occur only guarded in P, i.e. under the scope of an action prefix.
- $\alpha.Q$ is the *action prefixing* and describes a process that after the execution of action α behaves like P.
- $P + Q$ is the *choice or sum* operator and identifies a process that can behave either like P or like Q.
- $P \mid Q$ is the *parallel composition* operator and represents the concurrent execution of processes P and Q. A synchronisation, generating a τ action, can occur when P and Q execute complementary actions.
- $P \backslash A$ is the *restriction* operator and models a process that behaves like P, but for the impossibility of interacting using actions in $A \subseteq \Lambda$.
- $P[f]$ is the *relabelling* operator where $f : \mathcal{A} \to \mathcal{A}$ is a function that "renames" actions performed by P.

The operational semantics of CCS is formally defined in Table 1. In the rest of the paper we will use $P \xrightarrow{\alpha}$ to denote that there exists P' such that $P \xrightarrow{\alpha} P'$. Similarly, $P \stackrel{\alpha}{\nrightarrow}$ if $\neg(P \xrightarrow{\alpha})$. We will also write $P \to P'$ if there exists α such that $P \xrightarrow{\alpha} P'$; $\to^*$ is the transitive and reflexive closure of $\to$. Finally, we adopt the following notation:

- *Proc* is the set of all CCS processes;
- $\mathsf{Ch}(P)$ denotes the set of channels occurring in P;
- $\mathsf{Act}(P)$ denotes the set of actions that P can perform during a computation;
- $\mathsf{Init}(P)$ denotes the set of actions that P can immediately perform;
- $\mathsf{Der}(P) = \{Q | P \to^* Q\}$.

Table 1. CCS Operational Semantics

$$\frac{}{\alpha.P \xrightarrow{\alpha} P} \qquad \frac{P \xrightarrow{\alpha} P'}{P + Q \xrightarrow{\alpha} P'} \qquad \frac{Q \xrightarrow{\alpha} Q'}{P + Q \xrightarrow{\alpha} Q'}$$

$$\frac{P \xrightarrow{\alpha} P'}{P|Q \xrightarrow{\alpha} P'|Q} \qquad \frac{Q \xrightarrow{\alpha} Q'}{P|Q \xrightarrow{\alpha} P|Q'} \qquad \frac{P \xrightarrow{\alpha} P' \quad Q \xrightarrow{\overline{\alpha}} Q'}{P|Q \xrightarrow{\tau} P'|Q'}$$

$$\frac{P \xrightarrow{\alpha} P'}{P[f] \xrightarrow{f(\alpha)} P'[f]} \qquad \frac{P \xrightarrow{\alpha} P'}{X \xrightarrow{\alpha} P'}(X \triangleq P) \qquad \frac{P \xrightarrow{\alpha} P'}{P\backslash A \xrightarrow{\alpha} P'\backslash A}(\alpha, \overline{\alpha} \notin A)$$

Example 1. A Jobber [15] can assemble three kinds of objects: *easy*, *normal* and *hard*. To do his work a Jobber can use a *hammer* or a *mallet*. *Easy* objects are done by hand, *hard* objects need a *mallet* whereas *normal* jobs are built either with a *mallet* or with a *hammer*. This agent can be modeled as follows:

$$\begin{aligned} \mathsf{Jobber} &\triangleq \mathsf{inE}.\overline{\mathsf{outE}}.\mathsf{Jobber} \\ &\quad +\mathsf{inN}.\mathsf{doNormal} \\ &\quad +\mathsf{inH}.\mathsf{doHard} \end{aligned}$$

$$\begin{aligned} \mathsf{doNormal} &\triangleq \overline{\mathsf{geth}}.\overline{\mathsf{puth}}.\overline{\mathsf{outN}}.\mathsf{Jobber} \\ &\quad +\overline{\mathsf{getm}}.\overline{\mathsf{putm}}.\overline{\mathsf{outN}}.\mathsf{Jobber} \end{aligned}$$

$$\mathsf{doHard} \triangleq \overline{\mathsf{geth}}.\overline{\mathsf{puth}}.\overline{\mathsf{outH}}.\mathsf{Jobber}$$

A signal is received on channels inE, inN or inH to select the kind of object to assemble. To get hammer and mallet, actions $\overline{\mathsf{geth}}$ and $\overline{\mathsf{getm}}$ are executed. Tools are released by sending a signal over channels puth and putm. When the job is completed a signal is sent on channels outE, outN or outH depending on the kind of requested object.

2.1 Hennessy-Milner Logic

Hennessy-Milner Logic (HML) is a modal logic introduced by Hennessy and Milner to provide a logical characterisation of bisimulation [9]. The syntax of the HML formulae is the following:

$$\varphi \ ::= \ tt \mid \langle \mathcal{A} \rangle \varphi \mid \neg\varphi \mid \varphi_1 \vee \varphi_2 \mid X \mid \nu X.\varphi$$

A process satisfies $\langle \alpha \rangle \varphi$ ($\alpha \in \mathcal{A}$) if and only if action α can be executed leading to a process satisfying φ. Greatest fix-point ($\nu X.\varphi$) can be used for specifying recursive properties. Greatest fixed-point operator $\nu X.\varphi$ acts as a binder for the recursive variable occurring in φ. We say that X occurs *free* in φ if it does not occur under the scope of $\nu X.\cdot$. A formula φ is *closed* if no free variable occurs in φ; φ is *well-formed* if it is closed and in each sub-formula of the form $\nu X.\varphi$, X is *positive*, i.e. X appears under an even number of symbols of negation. From now on we will consider only well-formed formulae.

Other operators can be defined as macro in the HML. In the sequel we let $\varphi_1 \wedge \varphi_2$ be $\neg(\neg\varphi_1 \vee \neg\varphi_2)$ and $[\alpha]\varphi$ be $\neg\langle\alpha\rangle\neg\varphi$. The former is the logical conjunction operator whereas the latter is a modal operator satisfied by all the processes that after α, satisfy φ. Formula ff is defined as $\neg tt$ and the minimum fixed-point $\mu X.\varphi$ is derived from $\neg\nu X.\neg\varphi[\neg X/X]$. Macros $\Box^{\mathcal{A}}$, $\varphi_1 \;{}_{\mathcal{A}}\mathcal{U}\; \varphi_2$ and $\Diamond^{\mathcal{A}}$ are introduced to simplify properties specification:

$$\varphi_1 \;{}_{\mathcal{A}}\mathcal{U}\; \varphi_2 \triangleq \mu X.\varphi_2 \vee (\varphi_1 \wedge [\mathcal{A}]X \wedge \langle\mathcal{A}\rangle\mathbf{true})$$

$$\Box^{\mathcal{A}}\varphi \triangleq \nu X.\varphi \wedge [\mathcal{A}]X \qquad \Diamond^{\mathcal{A}}\varphi \triangleq \mathbf{true} \;{}_{\mathcal{A}}\mathcal{U}\; \varphi$$

Semantics of HML formulae is formally defined through an interpretation function $[\![\cdot]\!]$ that takes a formula φ and a *recursion environment* δ, i.e. a function mapping recursion variable to set of processes, and yields the set of processes satisfying φ. Function $[\![\cdot]\!]$ is formally defined as follows:

- $[\![tt]\!]\delta = Proc$
- $[\![\neg\varphi]\!]\delta = Proc - [\![\varphi]\!]\delta$
- $[\![\varphi_1 \vee \varphi_2]\!]\delta = [\![\varphi_1]\!]\delta \cup [\![\varphi_2]\!]\delta$
- $[\![\langle\alpha\rangle\varphi]\!]\delta = \left\{P \middle| \exists P' : P \xrightarrow{\alpha} P' \;\&\; P' \in [\![\varphi]\!]\delta\right\}$
- $[\![X]\!]\delta = \delta(X)$
- $[\![\nu X.\varphi]\!]\delta = \bigcup\left\{S \middle| S \subseteq [\![\varphi]\!]\delta\left[{}^{S}/_{X}\right]\right\}$

where $\delta[S/X]$ denotes the function associating S to X and $\delta(Y)$ to each variable $Y \neq X$.

A process P satisfies a formula φ ($P \models \varphi$) if and only if $P \in [\![\varphi]\!](\lambda X.\emptyset)$. To properly handle recursive properties in proof systems, it is convenient to extend the syntax of HML so to annotate recursive variables with set of processes:

$$\nu X\{P_1, \ldots, P_n\}.\varphi$$

where $\nu X.\varphi$ can be viewed as a shorthand for $\nu X\{\,\}.\varphi$. Interpretation function is then modified as follows:

$$[\![\nu X\{\mathcal{P}\}.\varphi]\!]\delta = \mathcal{P} \cup \bigcup\left\{S \middle| S \subseteq [\![\varphi]\!]\delta\left[{}^{S}/_{X}\right]\right\}$$

The Lemma below guarantees preservation of formulae semantics.

Lemma 1 (Reduction lemma [16]). *For each set of processes $\mathcal{P}$,*

$$P \models \nu X.\varphi \Leftrightarrow P \models \varphi[\nu X\{\mathcal{P}\}.\varphi/X]$$

Example 2. HML can be used to specify properties of the Jobber of Example 1. If one considers the complete specification of a *jobshop*, where different jobbers and tools act and interact with each other in order to satisfies the incoming requests, it could be interesting to verify that every request is eventually satisfied. This property is formalised as follows:

$$\begin{array}{l} \nu X.[\mathsf{inE}]\Diamond^{\tau}[\overline{\mathsf{outE}}]X \\ \quad \wedge \\ \quad [\mathsf{inN}]\Diamond^{\tau}[\overline{\mathsf{outN}}]X \\ \quad \wedge \\ \quad [\mathsf{inH}]\Diamond^{\tau}[\overline{\mathsf{outH}}]X \end{array} \tag{1}$$

3 Formalising Assumptions for Process Environments

In this section we recall the dialect of HML introduced in [6], thought to specify the set of properties we assume satisfied by the environment where a process is executed. Indeed, we consider system specifications composed of two parts: a CCS process P that specifies the behaviour of a known component, and a set of formulae Γ that identifies the set of properties we assume satisfied by the environment where P is executed.

Assumptions on the environment are formalised through a dialect of HML. For this dialect of HML we are able to define a precise operational semantics, i.e. a relation of the form $\Gamma \xrightarrow{\alpha} \Gamma'$. The proposed semantics guarantees that a Γ exhibits a given behaviour if and only it is shared among all the processes satisfying Γ.

Let $\mathcal{L}_\chi$ be the set of formulae Φ, Ψ, ... defined by the following syntax:

$$\Phi, \Psi \ ::= tt \mid \dagger(\alpha) \mid (\!|\ \alpha\ |\!)\Phi \mid \neg\Phi \mid \Phi \vee \Psi \mid X \mid \nu X.\Phi$$

where for each $\nu X.\Phi$ we assume each free occurrence of X in Φ always occurring under the scope of a modal even operator.

In $\mathcal{L}_\chi$ modal operators of HML are replaced by $\dagger(\cdot)$ and $(\!|\ \cdot\ |\!)$ that have the following meaning: $\dagger(\alpha)$ states that action α cannot be performed, while $(\!|\ \alpha\ |\!)\Phi$ guarantees the execution of action α and ensures that after α, Φ is always satisfied. For instance, $(\!|\ \alpha\ |\!)\dagger(\beta)$ is satisfied by $\alpha.nil$ and it is not satisfied by $\alpha.\beta.nil|\alpha.nil$.

Interpretation function of HML is then extended in order to consider new modal operators:

- $[\![\ \dagger(\alpha)\ ]\!]\delta = \left\{P \middle| P \stackrel{\alpha}{\not\rightarrow}\right\}$
- $[\![\ (\!|\ \alpha\ |\!)\Phi\ ]\!]\delta = \left\{P \middle| P \xrightarrow{\alpha}\ \&\ \forall P' : P \xrightarrow{\alpha} P', P' \in [\![\ \Phi\ ]\!]\delta\right\}$

It is easy to prove that modal operators $\langle\cdot\rangle$ and $[\cdot]$ can be easily expressed, and then considered as macros, by using those in $\mathcal{L}_\chi$:

$$\langle\alpha\rangle\varphi \equiv \neg((\!|\ \alpha\ |\!)\neg\varphi \vee \dagger(\alpha)) \qquad [\alpha]\varphi \equiv (\!|\ \alpha\ |\!)\varphi \vee \dagger(\alpha)$$

at the same time, it is easy to prove that modal operators in $\mathcal{L}_\chi$ can be expressed through HML operators:

$$(\!|\ \alpha\ |\!)\Phi \equiv [\alpha]\Phi \wedge \langle\alpha\rangle tt \qquad \dagger(\alpha) \equiv [\alpha]ff$$

Assumptions on environments are then specified through a set Γ of sets of formulae in $\mathcal{L}_{\mathcal{X}}$. A process P satisfies an assumption Γ if and only if for each $\Phi \in \Gamma$, $P \models \Phi$. Formally:

$$[\![\Gamma]\!]\delta = \bigcap_{\Phi \in \Gamma} [\![\Phi]\!]\delta$$

Even if HML could be used to specify the properties we assume for an environment, this approach is not suitable for deriving the possible behaviours of the specified environment. On the contrary, the proposed dialect permits directly characterising the behaviour that is shared among all the processes satisfying given assumption Γ.

We let $\rightarrow \subseteq \mathcal{L}_{\mathcal{X}} \times \mathsf{Act} \times \mathcal{L}_{\mathcal{X}}$ be the transition relation defined in Table 2. Notice that, a transition can be derived for a Γ only when each $\Phi \in \Gamma$ has only modal operators at top level. We will refer to this kind of assumptions as *determined*.

Definition 1.

- *For each* $\Phi \in \mathcal{L}_{\mathcal{X}}$, $\mathsf{Init}(\Phi)$ *is inductively defined as follows:*

$$\mathsf{Init}(tt) = \mathsf{Init}(X) = \emptyset \qquad \mathsf{Init}(\neg\Phi) = \mathsf{Init}(\Phi)$$
$$\mathsf{Init}((\!|\, \alpha \,|\!)\Phi) = \mathsf{Init}(\dagger(\alpha)) = \{\alpha\} \qquad \mathsf{Init}(\nu X.\Phi) = \mathsf{Init}(\Phi)$$
$$\mathsf{Init}(\Phi_1 \vee \Phi_2) = \mathsf{Init}(\Phi_1) \cup \mathsf{Init}(\Phi_2)$$

- *For each* $\Gamma \subseteq \mathcal{L}_{\mathcal{X}}$*:*

$$\mathsf{Init}(\Gamma) = \bigcup_{\Phi \in \Gamma} \mathsf{Init}(\Phi)$$

Definition 2.

- *An environment* Γ *is* determined *if and only if* $\Gamma \neq \emptyset$ *and for each* $\Phi \in \Gamma$, $\Phi = (\!|\, \alpha \,|\!)\Psi, \dagger(\alpha)$.
- *An environment* Γ *is* inconsistent *if and only if either* $ff \in \Gamma$ *or both* $\dagger(\alpha)$ *and* $(\!|\, \alpha \,|\!)\Phi$ *belong to* Γ*, for some* α *and* Φ.

Indeed, we cannot directly derive a transition for every Γ. For instance, let Γ be:

$$((\!|\, \alpha \,|\!)\Phi_1 \wedge \dagger(\beta)) \;\vee\; ((\!|\, \beta \,|\!)\Phi_1 \wedge \dagger(\alpha))$$

This identifies all the environments where either α or β can be executed. In both the cases, after α (or β), satisfaction of Φ_1 is guaranteed. The point is that $\vee$ can combine "behaviours" that do not provide a "coherent" specification. In the example above, $(\!|\, \alpha \,|\!)\Phi_1 \wedge \dagger(\beta)$ states that α can be executed and β can not, while $(\!|\, \beta \,|\!)\Phi_1 \wedge \dagger(\alpha)$ does the contrary.

In the rest of the paper $\Gamma \rightarrow \Gamma'$ indicates that there exists α such that $\Gamma \xrightarrow{\alpha} \Gamma'$ and $\Gamma \rightarrow^* \Gamma'$ is the transitive and reflexive closure of $\rightarrow$. The interpretation function of Section 2.1 can be extended in order to consider the assumptions where a process is executed. The set of processes satisfying φ under the assumptions Γ ($[\![\varphi]\!]_\Gamma$) can be defined as:

$$[\![\varphi]\!]_\Gamma =_{def} \left\{ P \middle| \forall Q.\ Q \models \Gamma,\ P|Q \in [\![\varphi]\!] \right\} \tag{2}$$

Table 2. The operational semantics of $\mathcal{L}_\chi$

$$\{(\!|\, \alpha \,|\!)\Phi\} \xrightarrow{\alpha} \{\Phi\} \qquad \frac{\Gamma \xrightarrow{\beta} \Gamma'}{\Gamma \cup \{\dagger(\alpha)\} \xrightarrow{\beta} \Gamma'}(\alpha \neq \beta)$$

$$\frac{\Gamma \xrightarrow{\alpha} \Gamma'}{\Gamma \cup \{(\!|\, \alpha \,|\!)\Phi\} \xrightarrow{\alpha} \Gamma' \cup \{\Phi\}} \quad \frac{\Gamma \xrightarrow{\beta} \Gamma'}{\Gamma \cup \{(\!|\, \alpha \,|\!)\Phi\} \xrightarrow{\beta} \Gamma'}(\alpha \neq \beta)$$

We introduce another interpretation function, less restrictive than the one above. This function will turn out to be useful for the definition of a model checking algorithm.

$$[\![\, \varphi \,]\!]_\Gamma^\exists =_{def} \left\{P \,\middle|\, \exists Q.\ Q \models \Gamma,\ P|Q \in [\![\, \varphi \,]\!]\right\} \tag{3}$$

Example 3. Process Jobber, defined in Example 1, completely describes the behaviour of a part of the *Jobbershop*. To specify the rest of the system, formulae in $\mathcal{L}_\chi$ can be used. We can assume that a *hammer* and a *mallet* are always available:

$$\nu X.(\!|\, \mathsf{geth} \,|\!)(\!|\, \mathsf{puth} \,|\!)X \ \wedge \ (\!|\, \mathsf{getm} \,|\!)(\!|\, \mathsf{putm} \,|\!)X$$

4 Assume-Guarantee Based Local Model Checking

We present a Local Model Checking Algorithm that permits verifying whether a process P satisfies a formula φ under the assumption that the environment where P is executed satisfies a given set of formulae $\Gamma \subseteq \mathcal{L}_\chi$.

In [6] we proposed a tableau based proof system, in this section this proof system is defined through the *satisfaction* function (Sat). This is syntax-driven and can be considered the heart of a model checking algorithm.

The operational semantics of Table 1 is extended in order to consider *mixed specifications* $\Gamma \triangleright P$, with the following rules:

$$\frac{P \xrightarrow{\alpha} P'}{\Gamma \triangleright P \xrightarrow{\alpha} \Gamma \triangleright P'} \qquad \frac{\Gamma \xrightarrow{\alpha} \Gamma'}{\Gamma \triangleright P \xrightarrow{\alpha} \Gamma' \triangleright P} \qquad \frac{\Gamma \xrightarrow{\alpha} \Gamma' \quad P \xrightarrow{\overline{\alpha}} P'}{\Gamma \triangleright P \xrightarrow{\tau} \Gamma' \triangleright P'} \tag{4}$$

Definition 3. Sat : $\mathcal{L}_\chi \times Proc \times \Phi_{HML} \rightarrow$ {***true, false***} *is a function that starting from a set of assumptions Γ, a process P and a property φ, returns* ***true*** *if* for each *process Q satisfying Γ, $P|Q$ satisfies the property φ. Otherwise it returns* ***false****.* Sat *is inductively defined in Table 3.*

To prove completeness of Sat it is convenient to introduce $\mathsf{Sat}_\exists$ function, we will prove that $\mathsf{Sat}_\exists(\Gamma, P, \varphi)$ returns **true** if there *exists* a process satisfying Γ such that φ is verified. Sometimes $\mathsf{Sat}_\exists$ and Sat coincide, when this is not the case, we distinguish the two modalities introducing $\mathsf{Sat}_\forall$, with the obvious meaning.

The inductive definition of Sat in Table 3 shows some progress passing from the left- to the right-hand-side, in fact either the right-hand-side is a truth value, or concerns the satisfaction of reducible assertions or strictly smaller assertions than that on

Table 3. Reduction rules for the Local Model Checking Algorithm

$\mathsf{Sat}(\,\Gamma, P, tt\,) = \textbf{true}$	if Γ is consistent
$\mathsf{Sat}(\,\Gamma, P, \nu X\,\{\mathcal{H}\}\,\psi\,) = \textbf{true}$	if $\Gamma \triangleright P \in \mathcal{H}$ and Γ is consistent
$\mathsf{Sat}_{\forall}(\,\Gamma, P, \psi\,) = \textbf{true}$	if Γ is inconsistent.
$\mathsf{Sat}_{\exists}(\,\Gamma, P, \psi\,) = \textbf{false}$	if Γ is inconsistent.
$\mathsf{Sat}_{\forall}(\,\Gamma, P, \neg\psi\,) = \neg\,\mathsf{Sat}_{\exists}(\,\Gamma, P, \psi\,)$	
$\mathsf{Sat}_{\exists}(\,\Gamma, P, \neg\psi\,) = \neg\,\mathsf{Sat}_{\forall}(\,\Gamma, P, \psi\,)$	
$\mathsf{Sat}(\,\Gamma, P, \langle\alpha\rangle\psi\,) = \mathsf{Sat}(\,\mathcal{S}_1, \psi\,) \vee \ldots \vee \mathsf{Sat}(\,\mathcal{S}_n, \psi\,)$ where $\{\mathcal{S}_1, \ldots, \mathcal{S}_n\} = \left\{\mathcal{S}' \mid \Gamma \triangleright P \xrightarrow{\alpha} \mathcal{S}'\right\}$	if $^{(*)}$
$\mathsf{Sat}(\,\mathcal{S}, \psi_1 \vee \psi_2\,) = \mathsf{Sat}(\,\mathcal{S}, \psi_1\,) \vee \mathsf{Sat}(\,\mathcal{S}, \psi_2\,)$	
$\mathsf{Sat}(\,\mathcal{S}, \nu X\{\mathcal{H}\}.\psi\,) = \mathsf{Sat}(\,\mathcal{S}, \psi[\nu X\{\mathcal{H}, \mathcal{S}\}.\psi/X]\,)$	if $\mathcal{S} \notin \mathcal{H}$
$\mathsf{Sat}(\,\Gamma \cup \{tt\}, P, \psi\,) = \mathsf{Sat}(\,\Gamma, P, \psi\,)$	
$\mathsf{Sat}(\,\Gamma \cup \{\neg\neg\Phi\}, P, \psi\,) = \mathsf{Sat}(\,\Gamma \cup \{\Phi\}, P, \psi\,)$	
$\mathsf{Sat}(\,\Gamma \cup \{\neg\dagger(\alpha)\}, P, \psi\,) = \mathsf{Sat}(\,\Gamma \cup \{(\!\mid \alpha \mid\!) tt\}, P, \psi\,)$	
$\mathsf{Sat}_{\forall}(\,\Gamma \cup \{\Phi_1 \vee \Phi_2\}, P, \psi\,) = \mathsf{Sat}_{\forall}(\,\Gamma \cup \{\Phi_1\}, P, \psi\,) \wedge \mathsf{Sat}_{\forall}(\,\Gamma \cup \{\Phi_2\}, P, \psi\,)$	
$\mathsf{Sat}_{\exists}(\,\Gamma \cup \{\Phi_1 \vee \Phi_2\}, P, \psi\,) = \mathsf{Sat}_{\exists}(\,\Gamma \cup \{\Phi_1\}, P, \psi\,) \vee \mathsf{Sat}_{\exists}(\,\Gamma \cup \{\Phi_2\}, P, \psi\,)$	
$\mathsf{Sat}(\,\Gamma \cup \{\neg(\Phi_1 \vee \Phi_2)\}, P, \psi\,) = \mathsf{Sat}(\,\Gamma \cup \{\neg\Phi_1, \neg\Phi_2\}, P, \psi\,)$	
$\mathsf{Sat}_{\forall}(\,\Gamma \cup \{\neg(\!\mid \alpha \mid\!)\Phi\}, P, \psi\,) = \mathsf{Sat}_{\forall}(\,\Gamma \cup \{\dagger(\alpha)\}, P, \psi\,) \wedge \mathsf{Sat}_{\forall}(\,\Gamma \cup \{(\!\mid \alpha \mid\!) tt\}, P, \psi\,)$	
$\mathsf{Sat}_{\exists}(\,\Gamma \cup \{\neg(\!\mid \alpha \mid\!)\Phi\}, P, \psi\,) = \mathsf{Sat}_{\exists}(\,\Gamma \cup \{\dagger(\alpha)\}, P, \psi\,) \vee \mathsf{Sat}_{\exists}(\,\Gamma \cup \{(\!\mid \alpha \mid\!) tt\}, P, \psi\,)$	
$\mathsf{Sat}_{\forall}(\,\Gamma, P, \psi\,) = \mathsf{Sat}_{\forall}(\,\Gamma \cup \{\dagger(\alpha)\}, P, \psi\,) \wedge \mathsf{Sat}_{\forall}(\,\Gamma \cup \{(\!\mid \alpha \mid\!) tt\}, P, \psi\,)$	if $^{(**)}$
$\mathsf{Sat}_{\exists}(\,\Gamma, P, \psi\,) = \mathsf{Sat}_{\exists}(\,\Gamma \cup \{\dagger(\alpha)\}, P, \psi\,) \vee \mathsf{Sat}_{\exists}(\,\Gamma \cup \{(\!\mid \alpha \mid\!) tt\}, P, \psi\,)$	if $^{(**)}$
$\mathsf{Sat}(\,\Gamma \cup \{\nu X.\Phi\}, P, \psi\,) = \mathsf{Sat}(\,\Gamma \cup \{\Phi[\nu X.\Phi/X]\}, P, \psi\,)$	
$\mathsf{Sat}(\,\Gamma \cup \{\neg\nu X.\Phi\}, P, \psi\,) = \mathsf{Sat}(\,\Gamma \cup \{\neg\Phi[\neg\nu X.\Phi/X]\}, P, \psi) \vee \mathsf{Sat}(\,\Gamma \cup \{\neg\phi[tt/X]\}, P, \psi\,)$	

(*) Γ determined, $\alpha \in \mathsf{Init}(\Gamma)$ and if $(\alpha = \tau)\ \forall\beta \in \mathsf{Init}(P).\overline{\beta} \in \mathsf{Init}(\Gamma)$
(**) $\alpha \notin \mathsf{Init}(\Gamma)$ and $\overline{\alpha} \in \mathsf{Init}(P) \vee \alpha \in \mathsf{Init}(\psi)$.

the left. We find an exception in the case of reduction rules concerning recursive formulae (FIX, E-FIX, E-NOTFIX). We can say that these reductions terminate, with the correct answer, because we check the satisfaction of assertions by finite-state processes which means that we cannot go on extending the sets tagging the recursions forever. The following lemma enables the completeness for the algorithm generated from Sat:

Lemma 2. *For any ψ, if* Der(P) *is finite then*

$$\mathsf{Sat}_{\forall}(\ \Gamma, P, \psi\ ) \ = \ \textit{true} \qquad \textit{or} \qquad \mathsf{Sat}_{\exists}(\ \Gamma, P, \neg\psi\ ) \ = \ \textit{true}$$

Proof. First we prove that the computation of Sat terminate. Hence we prove the lemma by induction on the syntax of ψ and on the length of the computation of Sat (see [7]).

Sat rules are sound and complete in the sense of the theorem below.

Theorem 1. *For each process P, Γ, φ, where* Der(P) *is finite,*

$$P \in [\![\ \varphi\ ]\!]_{\Gamma} \iff \mathsf{Sat}(\ \Gamma, P, \varphi\ ) \ = \ \textit{true}$$

Proof. First, by induction on the length of the computation of Sat(Γ, P, φ), it is proved that if Sat(Γ, P, φ) $=$ **true** then $P \in [\![\ \varphi\ ]\!]_{\Gamma}$. Then, Lemma 2 is used to prove completeness (See [7]).

Example 4. Using the Local Model Checking algorithm with the Sat function in Table 3, we are able to verify that the process Jobber under the assumptions of Example 3 satisfies the property in Equation 1.

5 Specification Refinement

The approach defined in the previous section naturally induces a notion of *refinement*. We say that $\Gamma_2 \triangleright Q$ refines assumption Γ_1 if and only $\Gamma_2 \triangleright Q$ satisfies Γ_1. At the same time, if $\Gamma_1 \triangleright P$ satisfies φ the same is for $\Gamma_2 \triangleright Q|P$. By iterating the proposed approach we obtain a methodology that permits obtaining a complete description of a system starting from a high level logical based specification. In each step of the refinement procedure, the satisfaction of the expected properties is preserved.

In a refinement step, part of the environment (described through a set of assumptions) is replaced with a process algebra term modelling a specific behaviour.

To automate this procedure we need a mechanism that starting from a formula φ and a process P identifies the most general assumption we have to impose on the environment, to see φ be satisfied by P. The idea is reminiscent of the *weakest precondition* [8] ensuring the satisfaction of a wished *postcondition*.

In this section we define the *Weakest Environment* function $\mathcal{W}$ that takes a process P, a formula φ and a set of logical variables Δ and yields a logical formula $\mathcal{W}^{\Delta}(\ P, \varphi\ )$ identifying the assumptions on the environment in order to let P satisfy φ that is, $\mathcal{W}^{\Delta}(\ P, \varphi\ ) \triangleright P \vdash \varphi$. The set of logical variables Δ is crucial to properly handle recursive formulae. For each variable X and process P we univocally identify the variable X_P, we let $Var_{Proc} = \{X_P | X \in Var, P \in Proc\}$. Function $\mathcal{W} : Proc \times \Phi_{HML} \times 2^{Var_{Proc}} \rightarrow \mathcal{L}_X$ is inductively defined in Table 4.

Table 4. Weakest Environment Function

$$\mathcal{W}^{\Delta}(P, tt) = tt$$

$$\mathcal{W}^{\Delta}(P, ff) = ff$$

$$\mathcal{W}^{\Delta}(P, \neg\neg\phi) = \mathcal{W}^{\Delta}(P, \phi)$$

$$\mathcal{W}^{\Delta}(P, \langle\alpha\rangle\phi) = \langle\alpha\rangle\mathcal{W}^{\Delta}(P, \phi) \vee \left(\bigvee_{Q:P\xrightarrow{\alpha}Q} \mathcal{W}^{\Delta}(Q, \phi)\right) \qquad (\alpha \neq \tau)$$

$$\mathcal{W}^{\Delta}(P, [\alpha]\phi) = [\alpha]\mathcal{W}^{\Delta}(P, \phi) \wedge \left(\bigwedge_{Q:P\xrightarrow{\alpha}Q} \mathcal{W}^{\Delta}(Q, \phi)\right) \qquad (\alpha \neq \tau)$$

$$\mathcal{W}^{\Delta}(P, \langle\tau\rangle\phi) = \langle\tau\rangle\mathcal{W}^{\Delta}(P, \phi) \vee \left(\bigvee_{Q:P\xrightarrow{\tau}Q} \mathcal{W}^{\Delta}(Q, \phi)\right) \vee \left(\bigvee_{\alpha\in A\setminus\tau} \bigvee_{P':P\xrightarrow{\alpha}P'} \langle\overline{\alpha}\rangle\mathcal{W}^{\Delta}(P', \phi)\right)$$

$$\mathcal{W}^{\Delta}(P, [\tau]\phi) = [\tau]\mathcal{W}^{\Delta}(P, \phi) \wedge \left(\bigwedge_{Q:P\xrightarrow{\tau}Q} \mathcal{W}^{\Delta}(Q, \phi)\right) \wedge \left(\bigwedge_{\alpha\in A\setminus\tau} \bigwedge_{P':P\xrightarrow{\alpha}P'} [\overline{\alpha}]\mathcal{W}^{\Delta}(P', \phi)\right)$$

$$\mathcal{W}^{\Delta}(P, \phi_1 \vee \phi_2) = \mathcal{W}^{\Delta}(P, \phi_1) \vee \mathcal{W}^{\Delta}(P, \phi_2)$$

$$\mathcal{W}^{\Delta}(P, \neg\langle\alpha\rangle\phi) = \mathcal{W}^{\Delta}(P, [\alpha]\neg\phi)$$

$$\mathcal{W}^{\Delta}(P, \phi_1 \wedge \phi_2) = \mathcal{W}^{\Delta}(P, \phi_1) \wedge \mathcal{W}^{\Delta}(P, \phi_2)$$

$$\mathcal{W}^{\Delta}(P, \neg[\alpha]\phi) = \mathcal{W}^{\Delta}(P, \langle\alpha\rangle\neg\phi)$$

$$\mathcal{W}^{\Delta}(P, \nu X\{\mathcal{P}\}.\phi) = \begin{cases} X_P & \text{if } X_P \in \Delta \\ \nu X_P\{\mathcal{P}\}.\mathcal{W}^{\Delta\cup\{X_P\}}(P, \phi[\nu X\{\mathcal{P}\}.\phi/X]) & \text{otherwise} \end{cases}$$

The derivation of a most general assumption implies that for all processes Q satisfying the computed assumption, $P|Q$ will satisfy the property represented by φ.

To make the most general assumption useful to the refinement purpouse, we need to show that when $\mathcal{W}^{\Delta}(P, \varphi) = \phi$, for each Q satisfying ϕ, $P|Q$ satisfies φ (i.e. $\mathsf{Sat}(\phi, P, \varphi) = \mathbf{true}$); and viceversa that for each Q such that $P|Q$ satisfies φ, Q satisfies $\mathcal{W}^{\Delta}(P, \varphi)$. This will directly hold for the existential version.

Theorem 2 (Most General Guarantee Environment). *Let $P \in Proc$ ($\mathsf{Der}(P)$ finite), $\varphi \in \Phi_{HML}$ and $\phi \in \mathcal{L}_X$.*

$$\mathcal{W}^{\Delta}(P, \varphi) = \phi \iff \forall Q.\ P|Q \models \varphi,\ Q \models \phi$$

Proof. We prove, by induction on the syntax of φ and on the length of the computation of $\mathcal{W}^{\Delta}(P, \varphi)$, that $\mathsf{Sat}(\mathcal{W}^{\Delta}(P, \varphi), P, \varphi) = \mathbf{true}$. Moreover, we also show that a proof for $Q \models \mathcal{W}^{\Delta}(P, \varphi)$ can be obtained from a proof for $Q|P \models \varphi$,

Example 5. To obtain a refinement of the *Jobbershop* we can take out a *Hammer* from the environment satisfying the property in example 3. We describe the *Hammer* through a CCS process and hence we compute the *weakest assumption* guaranteeing the preservation of property (1) in Example 4:

$$\mathsf{Hammer} \triangleq \mathsf{geth.puth.Hammer}$$

$$\mathcal{W}^{\Delta}(\,\mathsf{Hammer}, \nu X.(\!|\,\mathsf{geth}\,|\!)(\!|\,\mathsf{puth}\,|\!)X \wedge (\!|\,\mathsf{getm}\,|\!)(\!|\,\mathsf{putm}\,|\!)X\,) \quad =$$

$$\mathcal{W}^{\Delta\cup\{X_H\}}(\,\mathsf{Hammer}, (\!|\,\mathsf{geth}\,|\!)(\!|\,\mathsf{puth}\,|\!)X_H \wedge (\!|\,\mathsf{getm}\,|\!)(\!|\,\mathsf{putm}\,|\!)X_H\,) \quad =$$

$$\nu X_H.(\!|\,\mathsf{getm}\,|\!)(\!|\,\mathsf{putm}\,|\!)X_H \;\wedge\; [\mathsf{geth}](\!|\,\mathsf{puth}\,|\!)X_H \;\wedge\; [\mathsf{puth}]X_H \;\wedge\; X_H$$

Through the Sat function introduced in Table 3 we can easily prove that the obtained formula is an environment where the execution of the process Jobber|Hammer satisfies property (1).

6 Refinement at Work

In this section we provide an example of application of the refinement framework. The example chosen for this purpouse is *Mutual Exclusion*, a well known tecnique to avoid the simultaneous use of common resources in concurrent programming.

Mutual exclusion algorithms are based on the definition of a critical section (a piece of code enclosing the common resource) and on the implementation of structures able to protect from simultaneous accesses that could cause inconsistency errors. Access to critical sections can be regulated by a *binary semaphore*: any process that wants enter the critical section must obtain the semaphore, and releases it when leaving the critical section.

Implementing mutual exclusion can give rise to side-effects, e.g. deadlock or starvation, due to the wait for the *semaphore*. We can describe them and many other interesting properties in HML. In other words, we are able to characterize and verify the behaviour of a system that implements mutual exclusion. The following are examples of representable properties:

- A process eventually enters the critical section

$$\psi_1 = \Diamond^{\tau}\langle\overline{\mathsf{enter}}\rangle\mathbf{true}$$

- The critical section is protected until a process releases it

$$\psi_2 = \Box^{\tau}[\overline{\mathsf{enter}}]([\overline{enter}]\mathbf{false}\ {}_{\tau}\mathcal{U}\ \langle\overline{exit}\rangle\mathbf{true})$$

We can describe a system where processes share a critical section through a *Mixed Specification*. The part of the system known in detail is defined through a CCS process, whereas the part of the system not completely known is defined through a set of HML formulae (the assumption). The process that waits for the lock to enter the critical section can be described by Ag:

$$\mathsf{Ag} \triangleq \overline{\mathsf{p}}.\overline{\mathsf{enter}}.\overline{\mathsf{exit}}.\overline{\mathsf{v}}.\mathsf{Ag}$$

Assumptions on the environment can be described as the set Γ_{ME} of properties ϕ_1 and ϕ_2:

- A semaphore is available in the environment. No process enters in critical section until semaphore is released:

$$\phi_1 = \nu X.\dagger(\mathsf{v}) \wedge \langle\!|\ \mathsf{p}\ |\!\rangle \left(\dagger(\overline{\mathsf{enter}}) \wedge \dagger(\mathsf{p}) \wedge \langle\!|\ \mathsf{v}\ |\!\rangle (X \wedge \phi_2)\right)$$

- Another process should enter the critical section. In that case, the semaphore will be available only after the exit from critical section:

$$\phi_2 = \nu Y.[\tau]\dagger(\mathsf{p}) \wedge \langle\!|\ \overline{\mathsf{enter}}\ |\!\rangle \left(\dagger(\overline{\mathsf{enter}}) \wedge \dagger(\mathsf{p}) \wedge \langle\!|\ \overline{\mathsf{exit}}\ |\!\rangle \langle\!|\ \tau\ |\!\rangle (Y \wedge \phi_1)\right)$$

We can verify that Ag satisfies properties ψ_1 and ψ_2, when we assume $\Gamma_{ME} = \{\phi_1, \phi_2\}$ for the environment, running the following:

$$\mathsf{Sat}(\Gamma_{ME}, \mathsf{Ag}, \psi_1)$$

and

$$\mathsf{Sat}(\Gamma_{ME}, \mathsf{Ag}, \psi_2)$$

Notice that these proofs can be performed without taking care of the exact number of processes in the system.

Once we have given a representation of the system implementing mutual exclusion, we can be interested in refining it, taking out the semaphore from the environment. The first step of refinement lies in concretely describing the process that represents the semaphore S:

$$\mathsf{S} \triangleq \mathsf{p.v.S}$$

The second step lies in determining new assumptions by function $\mathcal{W}$:

$$\mathcal{W}(S, \phi_1) = \phi_1' = \dagger(\mathsf{v}) \wedge \dagger(\mathsf{p}) \wedge \dagger(\mathsf{enter})$$

$$\mathcal{W}(S, \phi_2) = \phi_2' = \nu Y_S.\dagger(\tau) \wedge [\overline{\mathsf{p}}] \left(\dagger(\mathsf{p}) \wedge \langle\!|\ \overline{\mathsf{enter}}\ |\!\rangle (\dagger(\mathsf{p}) \wedge \phi_3)\right)$$

where:

$$\phi_3 = \langle\!|\ \overline{\mathsf{exit}}\ |\!\rangle \dagger(\tau) \wedge \langle\!|\ \overline{\mathsf{v}}\ |\!\rangle (Y_S \wedge \phi_1')$$

By iterating the refinement procedure, we can obtain a complete description of the system starting from a high level logical based specification. Moreover, in each step of the refinement procedure, the satisfaction of the expected properties is preserved. After a refinement step, we obtain:

$$\{\phi_1', \phi_2'\} \triangleright \mathsf{Ag}|\mathsf{S}$$

while satisfaction of considered formulae $(\psi_1 \wedge \psi_2)$ is preserved.

Since both Ag and *nil* satisfy $\phi_1' \wedge \phi_2'$ we are guaranteed that, for each $i > 0$:

$$\mathsf{Ag}^i|S \models \psi_1 \wedge \psi_2$$

where $\mathsf{Ag}^i = \underbrace{\mathsf{Ag}|\cdots|\mathsf{Ag}}_{i \text{ times}}$

7 Conclusions and Future Works

In this paper we have presented a formal framework that permits verifying properties of concurrent and communicating systems by using a refinement procedure based on the assumption-guarantee approach presented in a previous work [6].

Each system component under the analysis is not considered in isolation, but in conjunction with assumptions about the context of the component. The iteration of the refinement procedure gives a methodology that permits obtaining a complete description of a system, starting from a high level logical based specification. The proposed refinement procedure preserves the satisfaction of the expected properties in each step of the iteration.

In the paper we have also introduced a sound and complete set of reduction rules (Sat) for a local model checking algorithm that permits verifying whether a process, executed in an environment for which we provide some assumptions, satisfies a given formula. It is also ensured that property satisfaction is preserved whenever the context is partially instantiated (implemented) as a concrete process that verifies the assumptions we have for the environment.

To enable the refinement procedure we have introduced the *Weakest Environment* function $\mathcal{W}$. Such function, starting from a process and a formula, returns the right assumption for the environment where the starter process satisfies the requested property. The introduced function $\mathcal{W}$ is sound and complete in relation to the Sat function for the model checking.

In the future we plan of introducing the value-passing modality as well as probabilistic and stocastic additions for the proposed framework.

We will look for ways to exploit the Most General Assumption to simplify the specification of the environment, after each step of refinement, by eliminating what is redundant thanks to the new process. Moreover we will implement the local model checking algorithm whose rules have been introduced in this paper.

References

1. Bergstra, J.A., Klop, J.W.: Process algebra for synchronous communication. Information and Control 60(1-3), 109–137 (1984)
2. Bobaru, M.G., Pasareanu, C., Giannakopoulou, D.: Automated assume-guarantee reasoning by abstraction refinement. In: Gupta, A., Malik, S. (eds.) CAV 2008. LNCS, vol. 5123, pp. 135–148. Springer, Heidelberg (2008)
3. Brookes, S.D., Hoare, C.A.R., Roscoe, A.W.: A theory of communicating sequential processes. J. ACM 31(3), 560–599 (1984)
4. Clarke, E.M., Emerson, E.A.: Design and synthesis of synchronization skeletons using branching-time temporal logic. In: Proceedings of Logic of Programs, pp. 52–71. Springer, Heidelberg (1982)
5. Cobleigh, J.M., Avrunin, G.S., Clarke, L.A.: Breaking up is hard to do: An evaluation of automated assume-guarantee reasoning. ACM Trans. Softw. Eng. Methodol. 17(2), 1–52 (2008)
6. D'Errico, L., Loreti, M.: Assume-Guarantee Verification of Concurrent Systems. In: Field, J., Vasconcelos, V.T. (eds.) COORDINATION 2009. LNCS, vol. 5521, pp. 288–305. Springer, Heidelberg (2009)

7. D'Errico, L., Loreti, M.: Property-preserving refinement of concurrent systems. Technical report, Università di Firenze (2009), at
http://www.dsi.unifi.it/~loreti/
8. Dijkstra, E.W.: A Discipline of Programming. Prentice Hall PTR, Upper Saddle River (1997)
9. Hennessy, M., Milner, R.: Algebraic laws for nondeterminism and concurrency. J. ACM 32(1), 137–161 (1985)
10. Kozen, D.: Results on the propositional μ-calculus. Theor. Comput. Sci. 27, 333–354 (1983)
11. Larsen, K.G.: Compositional Theories Based on an Operational Semantics of Contexts. In: de Bakker, J.W., de Roever, W.-P., Rozenberg, G. (eds.) REX 1989. LNCS, vol. 430, pp. 487–518. Springer, Heidelberg (1989)
12. Larsen, K.G., Milner, R.: A compositional protocol verification using relativized bisimulation. Information and computation 99(1), 80–108 (1992)
13. Larsen, K.G., Xinxin, L.: Compositionality through an operational semantics of contexts. Journal of Logic and Computation 1(6), 761–795 (1991)
14. Milner, R.: A Calculus of Communication Systems. LNCS, vol. 92. Springer, Heidelberg (1980)
15. Milner, R.: Communication and Concurrency. Prentice-Hall, Englewood Cliffs (1989)
16. Winskel, G.: Topics in concurrency. Lecture notes. University of Cambridge, Cambridge (2008), http://www.cl.cam.ac.uk/~gw104/TIC08.ps

Certificate Translation for the Verification of Concurrent Programs*

César Kunz

IMDEA Software, Spain
FirstName.LastName@imdea.org

Abstract. The increasing presence of multicore execution environments is stimulating the development of concurrent software, an inherently error-prone task that affects the trust on the reliability of third-party code. There is thus a pressing need of providing verifiable evidence on a concurrent software correctness. Certificate Translation provides a means to generate verification certificates for complex functional properties. This technique, consists on progressively transferring verification results for source programs along a sequence of compilation steps. In previous work, we have shown how to transform certificates of a sequential program in the presence of compiler optimizations. In this article, we have shown that it is possible to extend certificate translation to the verification of concurrent programs, based on an Owicki/Gries-like proof system for a shared memory model.

1 Introduction

In the last years, there has been an increasing deployment of computational environments with several processing units. Following this trend, there has been a strong motivation to take advantage of the computational facilities offered by these modern architectures. There is an already widespread awareness of the risks coupled to concurrent program development: program bugs are more likely to occur due to the complexity of such systems, and the unpredictability of the scheduler hinders the reproduction of errors and thus program fixing. There is thus a pressing need to exploit verification methods during code development in order to provide trust on the reliability of the executable code.

Program certification provides a means to efficiently guarantee that a piece of executable code satisfies a required policy. Whereas certificate checking is well understood, certificate generation remains an open problem. In traditional Proof Carrying Code [8], certificates are generated during the code generation by a new module incorporated to the compiler. A negative consequence in this approach is that enforceable properties must be restricted to basic safety policies. In order to extend the set of enforceable properties to more complex specifications, we have proposed to rely on source code verification, with the potential cost of human

* This work is partially funded by the EU projects Mobius and HATS, and by the Spanish project Desafios 10, and by the Community of Madrid project Prometidos.

M. Wirsing, M. Hofmann, and A. Rauschmayer (Eds.): TGC 2010, LNCS 6084, pp. 237–252, 2010.

interaction, and then transfer these verification results to certify the correctness of the compiled code.

A program compiler is commonly defined as a chain of independent stages that transforms a source program into executable code. First, the source program is transformed into a lower-level representation, preserving its overall structure. Subsequent compiler steps transform the code, inserting, moving and removing instructions, and possibly affecting the program structure. Finally, in the last steps, the executable code is generated from the intermediate representations.

In previous work [2,3,1], we have shown that verification conditions are not preserved in the presence of compiler optimizations, and that they can even turn the original program specifications invalid. We have proposed then a technique, *certificate translation*, that transforms simultaneously the specification and certificate, for each optimization step.

This article extends previous results on certificate transformation for sequential programs to a concurrent setting. In particular, we consider a concurrent program execution as the interleaved semantics of its sequential components, in a shared-memory model. We adopt a verification infrastructure similar to an Owicki-Gries logic [11]: verification is split in two independent tasks: for each component, one first verifies that it satisfies its specification in isolation and then one must verify that the other concurrent components do not invalidate this specification. Since the number of verification conditions is exponential in the size of parallel components, practical applications of Owicki-Gries logics aim to reduce the number of verification conditions. This is done in general by grouping code fragments that are known to be atomically executed or by omitting proof obligations that are trivially provable. However, in this article, we do not refer to any criteria to reduce the number of proof obligations. Instead, we deal exclusively with the problem of transferring verification evidence in the presence of optimizations applied to the parallel program components.

Paper overview. In Section 2, we formalize the program representation and provide a simplified verification framework for concurrent programs. In Section 3, we show the existence of certificate translators for the verification framework of the previous section. In Section 3.1, we extend our results on proof-producing analyzers, a main component in a certificate translation process, to a concurrent setting. In Section 3.2, we deal with the transformation of verification results in the presence of compiler optimizations. We conclude and suggest future work in Section 5.

2 Preliminaries

In this section, we formalize the representation of sequential programs and the interleaving semantics of the parallel composition. We define a weakest precondition based verification framework for sequential components and extend it later to deal with concurrent programs.

integer expressions	$e ::= n \mid x \mid e + e \mid e * e \mid \ldots \mid a[e]$
boolean expressions	$b ::= \mathsf{true} \mid \mathsf{false} \mid e = e \mid e \leq e \mid b \wedge b \mid \ldots$
statements	$c ::= \mathbf{skip} \mid x := e \mid a[e] := e \mid \mathtt{return}\ e \mid b?$

Fig. 1. Sequential Program Statements

Definition 1. *A sequential program is defined as a directed graph $\langle \mathcal{N}, \mathcal{E}, G \rangle$, with the set of nodes $\mathcal{N}$ representing the program points. The graph edges are defined by the finitely branching relation $\mathcal{E} \subseteq \mathcal{N} \times \mathcal{N}$. The function G maps every edge $\mathfrak{e}$ in $\mathcal{E}$ to a statement from the grammar in Fig. 1.*

The set of execution environments Env is defined as mappings from scalar and array variables to integer and vector values, respectively. The non-deterministic program semantics is formalized by the relation $\rightsquigarrow \subseteq \mathsf{State} \times \mathsf{State}$, where State stands for the set $\mathcal{N} \times \mathsf{Env}$. Given a program $\langle \mathcal{N}, \mathcal{E}, G \rangle$, we define the relation $\langle l, \eta \rangle \rightsquigarrow \langle l', \eta' \rangle$ in terms of the statement $G[\langle l, l' \rangle]$. For the conditional statement $b?$, $\langle l, \eta \rangle \rightsquigarrow \langle l', \eta' \rangle$ iff $\eta = \eta'$ and b evaluates to true in η. For the assignment $x := e$, $\langle l, \eta \rangle \rightsquigarrow \langle l', \eta' \rangle$ iff $\eta' = [\eta : x \mapsto n]$ where n is the result of evaluating e in η. We assume that there is a distinguished node l_{init} from which execution starts. Also, for simplicity, we assume there is a single output node $l_{\mathsf{out}} \in \mathcal{N}$, such that for every $l \in \mathcal{N}$, $\langle l_{\mathsf{out}}, l \rangle \notin \mathcal{E}$. A program reaches a final environment η' if $\langle l_{\mathsf{init}}, \eta \rangle \rightsquigarrow^{\star} \langle l_{\mathsf{out}}, \eta' \rangle$, where $\rightsquigarrow^{\star}$ denotes the reflexive and transitive closure of the relation $\rightsquigarrow$.

Concurrent programs. A concurrent program is defined as the parallel composition of a set of sequential programs. In the sequel, for readability, we consider the parallel composition of two sequential programs P_{a} and P_{b}. The definitions and results of this section can be easily generalized to an arbitrary number of sequential components.

We model the interleaved semantics of sequential programs by a new sequential program with an equivalent non-deterministic semantics. That is, from the sequential components P_{a} and P_{b}, we define a new sequential program P whose non-deterministic semantics formalizes the interleaving semantics of $P_{\mathsf{a}} \parallel P_{\mathsf{b}}$.

Definition 2 (Concurrent Program). *Consider the two sequential programs $P_{\mathsf{a}} = \langle \mathcal{N}_{\mathsf{a}}, \mathcal{E}_{\mathsf{a}}, G_{\mathsf{a}} \rangle$ and $P_{\mathsf{b}} = \langle \mathcal{N}_{\mathsf{b}}, \mathcal{E}_{\mathsf{b}}, G_{\mathsf{b}} \rangle$. We define the parallel composition $P_{\mathsf{a}} \parallel P_{\mathsf{b}}$ as the tuple $\langle \mathcal{N}_{\mathsf{a}} \times \mathcal{N}_{\mathsf{b}}, \mathcal{E}, G \rangle$, where:*

- $\mathcal{E} = \{\langle (l_{\mathsf{a}}, l_{\mathsf{b}}), (l_{\mathsf{a}}, l'_{\mathsf{b}}) \rangle \mid (l_{\mathsf{a}} \in \mathcal{N}_{\mathsf{a}}) \wedge \langle l_{\mathsf{b}}, l'_{\mathsf{b}} \rangle \in \mathcal{E}_{\mathsf{b}}\} \ \cup$
  $\{\langle (l_{\mathsf{a}}, l_{\mathsf{b}}), (l'_{\mathsf{a}}, l_{\mathsf{b}}) \rangle \mid (l_{\mathsf{b}} \in \mathcal{N}_{\mathsf{b}}) \wedge \langle l_{\mathsf{a}}, l'_{\mathsf{a}} \rangle \in \mathcal{E}_{\mathsf{a}}\}$
- $G[\langle (l_{\mathsf{a}}, l_{\mathsf{b}}), (l'_{\mathsf{a}}, l_{\mathsf{b}}) \rangle] = G_{\mathsf{a}}[\langle l_{\mathsf{a}}, l'_{\mathsf{a}} \rangle]$
- $G[\langle (l_{\mathsf{a}}, l_{\mathsf{b}}), (l_{\mathsf{a}}, l'_{\mathsf{b}}) \rangle] = G_{\mathsf{b}}[\langle l_{\mathsf{b}}, l'_{\mathsf{b}} \rangle]$

From the definition, an execution point in the concurrent program $P_{\mathsf{a}} \parallel P_{\mathsf{b}}$ will be determined by the current execution point in each of its components (i.e., $\mathcal{N} = \mathcal{N}_{\mathsf{a}} \times \mathcal{N}_{\mathsf{b}}$). An execution step in any of the program components is considered an execution step of the whole program. Finally, the entry (output)

$$
\begin{aligned}
G[\langle l,l'\rangle] &= \texttt{skip} \Rightarrow \mathsf{wp}_{\langle l,l'\rangle}(\varphi) = \varphi \\
G[\langle l,l'\rangle] &= x := e \Rightarrow \mathsf{wp}_{\langle l,l'\rangle}(\varphi) = \varphi[^{e}/_{x}] \\
G[\langle l,l'\rangle] &= a[e] := e' \Rightarrow \mathsf{wp}_{\langle l,l'\rangle}(\varphi) = \varphi[^{[a:e\mapsto e']}/_{a}] \\
G[\langle l,l'\rangle] &= \texttt{return}\ e \Rightarrow \mathsf{wp}_{\langle l,l'\rangle}(\varphi) = \varphi[^{e}/_{\mathsf{res}}] \\
G[\langle l,l'\rangle] &= b? \Rightarrow \mathsf{wp}_{\langle l,l'\rangle}(\varphi) = b \Rightarrow \varphi
\end{aligned}
$$

Fig. 2. Definition of function wp

point of the composed program is set as the execution point in which every component is at its initial (final) node. Here we assume that the semantics of P_{a} and P_{b} are modeled with the finest possible granularity level in order to safely capture every possible semantics interleaving.

Program verification. Given a program $\langle \mathcal{N}, \mathcal{E}, G\rangle$, we formalize a program specification as a partial function from the set of program nodes $\mathcal{N}$ to first-order logical formulae. For a program node $l \in \mathcal{N}$, the annotation associated to l characterizes the set of states that can reach the program point l.

Definition 3. *We say that a specification* annot *is a sufficient annotation for a program* $\langle \mathcal{N}, \mathcal{E}, G\rangle$ *if the nodes* l_{init} *and* l_{out} *are in the domain of* annot, *and every cycle in the graph* $\langle \mathcal{N}, \mathcal{E}, G\rangle$ *contains at least one node in the domain of* annot.

The definition above requires a specification annot to provide not only a pre and postcondition $\mathsf{annot}(l_{\mathsf{init}})$ and $\mathsf{annot}(l_{\mathsf{out}})$ but also at least one invariant for every program loop. A sufficient annotation provides an induction principle (with $\mathsf{dom}(\mathsf{annot})$ the set of base cases) that is useful to prove the results presented in this article. In the following, we implicitly require specifications to be sufficient annotations.

From a program $\langle \mathcal{N}, \mathcal{E}, G\rangle$ and a sufficient annotation annot, one can define a total annotation $\overline{\mathsf{annot}}$ by setting:

- $\overline{\mathsf{annot}}(l) = \mathsf{annot}(l)$ if $l \in \mathsf{dom}(\mathsf{annot})$
- $\overline{\mathsf{annot}}(l) = \bigwedge_{\langle l,l'\rangle \in \mathcal{E}} \mathsf{wp}_{\langle l,l'\rangle}(\overline{\mathsf{annot}}(l'))$

where the standard function $\mathsf{wp}_{\langle l,l'\rangle}$ is defined in Fig. 2.

In order to provide efficiently verifiable evidence of a program correctness, we incorporate a notion of certificates to the wp-based verification framework:

Definition 4. *A sequential program is certified to satisfy the specification* annot, *if for every* $l \in \mathsf{dom}(\mathsf{annot})$ *there is a certificate* c_l *of the following proof goal:*

$$\mathsf{annot}(l) \Rightarrow \bigwedge_{\langle l,l'\rangle \in \mathcal{E}} \mathsf{wp}_{\langle l,l'\rangle}(\overline{\mathsf{annot}(l')})$$

The concrete certificate representation may vary. In this article, we do not base our exposition on a particular implementation of certificates. Instead, we rely on an abstract domain of certificates, closed under basic operations.

$$\begin{array}{lll}
\mathsf{axiom} & : & \mathcal{C}(a \Rightarrow a) \\
\mathsf{weak}_\wedge & : & \mathcal{C}(a \Rightarrow b) \rightarrow \mathcal{C}(a \wedge c \Rightarrow b) \\
\mathsf{weak}_\vee & : & \mathcal{C}(a \Rightarrow b) \rightarrow \mathcal{C}(a \Rightarrow b \vee c) \\
\mathsf{elim}_\wedge & : & \mathcal{C}(c \wedge a \Rightarrow b) \rightarrow \mathcal{C}(c \Rightarrow a) \rightarrow \mathcal{C}(c \Rightarrow b) \\
\mathsf{intro}_\vee & : & \mathcal{C}(a \Rightarrow c) \rightarrow \mathcal{C}(b \Rightarrow c) \rightarrow \mathcal{C}(a \vee b \Rightarrow c) \\
\mathsf{intro}_\wedge & : & \mathcal{C}(a \Rightarrow b) \rightarrow \mathcal{C}(a \Rightarrow c) \rightarrow \mathcal{C}(a \Rightarrow b \wedge c)
\end{array}$$

Fig. 3. Proof Algebra

Definition 5 (Certificate infrastructure). *A certificate infrastructure consists of an algebra $\mathcal{C}$ that assigns to all formulae a, a' a set of certificates $\mathcal{C}(a \Rightarrow a')$ such that:*

- *$\mathcal{C}$ is closed under the operations of Fig. 3, where a, b, c are formulae;*
- *$\mathcal{C}$ is sound, that is, for every a, a', if $a \not\Rightarrow a'$, then $\mathcal{C}(a \Rightarrow a') = \emptyset$.*

In the following, we write $c : a \Rightarrow a'$ to denote $c \in \mathcal{C}(a \Rightarrow a')$.

The soundness of the wp-based verification environment requires proving, for all $\langle l, l' \rangle \in \mathcal{E}$ and assertion ϕ, that if $\mathsf{wp}_{\langle l,l' \rangle}(\phi)$ holds in η and $\langle l, \eta \rangle \rightsquigarrow \langle l', \eta' \rangle$ then ϕ holds in η'. Assume that the certificate infrastructure is sound. Then, from the soundness of the verification framework, if the program $\langle \mathcal{N}, \mathcal{E}, G \rangle$ is certified to satisfy a specification annot, then every execution $\langle l_{\mathsf{init}}, \eta \rangle \rightsquigarrow^\star \langle l_{\mathsf{out}}, \eta' \rangle$ with η satisfying $\mathsf{annot}(l_{\mathsf{init}})$ is such that η' satisfies $\mathsf{annot}(l_{\mathsf{out}})$.

Example 1. Consider as example the verification of the producer-consumer program shown in Fig. 4, represented in a simple imperative language. We assume the variables `in` and `out` are initially equal to 0. A representation of the producer component as a directed graph is given in Fig. 5.

The specification annot for the program graph of Fig. 5 is defined as:

$$\begin{array}{ll}
\mathsf{annot}(l_1) = \mathsf{Inv} \wedge \mathtt{in} \leq M & \mathsf{annot}(l_2) = \mathsf{Inv} \wedge \mathtt{in} < M \\
\mathsf{annot}(l_5) = \mathsf{annot}(l_4) & \mathsf{annot}(l_f) = \mathsf{Inv} \wedge \mathtt{in} = M \\
\multicolumn{2}{l}{\mathsf{annot}(l_3) = \mathsf{Inv} \wedge \mathtt{in} < M \wedge \mathtt{in} - \mathtt{out} < N} \\
\multicolumn{2}{l}{\mathsf{annot}(l_4) = \mathsf{Inv} \wedge \mathtt{in} < M \wedge \mathtt{in} - \mathtt{out} < N \wedge \mathtt{buffer}[\mathtt{in}\ \mathsf{mod}\ N] = \mathsf{a}[\mathtt{in}]}
\end{array}$$

In order to attest that the **producer** component satisfies the specification above, one must provide, among others, a formal certificate for the following proof obligations:

- $\mathsf{annot}(l_2) \Rightarrow \mathsf{wp}_{\langle l_2,l_3 \rangle}(\mathsf{annot}(l_3))$, and
- $\mathsf{annot}(l_5) \Rightarrow \mathsf{wp}_{\langle l_5,l_1 \rangle}(\mathsf{annot}(l_1))$;

that is,

- $\mathsf{Inv} \wedge \mathtt{in} < M \Rightarrow \mathtt{in} - \mathtt{out} < M \Rightarrow \mathsf{Inv} \wedge \mathtt{in} < M \wedge \mathtt{in} - \mathtt{out} < N$, and
- $\mathsf{Inv} \wedge \mathtt{in} < M \wedge \mathtt{in} - \mathtt{out} < N \wedge \mathtt{buffer}[\mathtt{in}\ \mathsf{mod}\ N] = \mathsf{a}[\mathtt{in}]$
  $\Rightarrow \forall k.\ \mathtt{out} \geq k < \mathtt{in} + 1 \Rightarrow \mathsf{a}[k] = \mathtt{buffer}[k\ \mathsf{mod}\ N] \wedge \mathtt{in} + 1 = M$

Producer :

l_1 : while in $< M$ $\{\mathsf{Inv} \wedge \mathtt{in} \leq M\}$ do
l_2 : $\{\mathsf{Inv} \wedge \mathtt{in} < M\}$
(in $-$ out $< N$)?
l_3 : $\{\mathsf{Inv} \wedge \mathtt{in} < M \wedge \mathtt{in} - \mathtt{out} < N\}$
buffer[in mod N] := a[in]
l_4 : $\{\mathsf{Inv} \wedge \mathtt{in} < M \wedge \mathtt{in} - \mathtt{out} < N \wedge \mathtt{buffer}[\mathtt{in} \bmod N] = \mathtt{a}[\mathtt{in}]\}$
in := in + 1
l_f : $\{\mathsf{Inv} \wedge \mathtt{in} = M\}$

Consumer :

while out $< M$ $\{\mathsf{Inv}_2 \wedge \mathtt{out} \leq M\}$ do
$\{\mathsf{Inv}_2 \wedge \mathtt{out} < M\}$
(out $<$ in)?
$\{\mathsf{Inv}_2 \wedge \mathtt{out} < M \wedge \mathtt{out} < \mathtt{in}\}$
b[out] := buffer[out mod N]
$\{\mathsf{Inv}_2 \wedge \mathtt{out} < M \wedge \mathtt{out} < \mathtt{in} \wedge \mathtt{b}[\mathtt{out}] = \mathtt{a}[\mathtt{out}]\}$
out := out + 1
$\{\mathsf{Inv}_2 \wedge \mathtt{out} = M\}$

where

$$\mathsf{Inv} \stackrel{\mathrm{def}}{=} \forall k.\ \mathtt{out} \leq k < \mathtt{in} \Rightarrow \mathtt{a}[k] = \mathtt{buffer}[k \bmod N]$$
$$\mathsf{Inv}_2 \stackrel{\mathrm{def}}{=} \mathsf{Inv} \wedge \forall j.\ 0 \leq j < \mathtt{out} \Rightarrow \mathtt{a}[j] = \mathtt{b}[j]$$

Fig. 4. Producer-Consumer Program

Verification of concurrent programs. We illustrate with a short example the set of proof obligations required for the verification of a concurrent program. Consider the short code fragment at the left, containing a statement y := 2 ∗ x at node l with successor node l'.

l : $\{x \geq 0\}$	l_{b} : $\{\mathsf{even}(y)\}$
y := 2 ∗ x	x := $\mathtt{z}^{\mathtt{y}}$
l' : $\{y \geq 0\}$	...

A specification $\mathsf{annot_a}$ such that $\mathsf{annot_a}(l) = x \geq 0$ and $\mathsf{annot_a}(l') = y \geq 0$, can be certified to hold for the component at the left from the validity of the verification condition $\mathsf{annot_a}(l) \Rightarrow \mathsf{wp}_{\langle l,l' \rangle}(\mathsf{annot_a}(l'))$, that is $x \geq 0 \Rightarrow 2 * x \geq 0$. In a concurrent environment, however, the execution of the code at the right may invalidate the local specification $\mathsf{annot_a}$. In this example, this is the case of the assertion $\mathsf{annot_a}(l) = x \geq 0$ and the execution of the statement x := $\mathtt{z}^{\mathtt{y}}$.

In order to verify that the local specification $\mathsf{annot_a}$ is not invalidated by the code at the right, one must rely on the local specification $\mathsf{annot_b}$. In this example, one can show that $x \geq 0$ is preserved by the execution of x = $\mathtt{z}^{\mathtt{y}}$, assuming the precondition $\mathsf{annot_b}(l_{\mathsf{b}}) = \mathsf{even}(y)$. Formally, this requires discharging the verification condition $\mathsf{annot_b}(l_{\mathsf{b}}) \wedge \mathsf{annot_a}(l') \Rightarrow \mathsf{wp}_{\langle l_{\mathsf{b}},l'_{\mathsf{b}} \rangle}(\mathsf{annot_a}(l'))$. Proving the preservation of $y \geq 0$ is straightforward. Reciprocally, $\mathsf{annot_b}(l_{\mathsf{b}})$ must also be proved stable with respect to the assignment at the edge $\langle l, l' \rangle$ of program P_{a}.

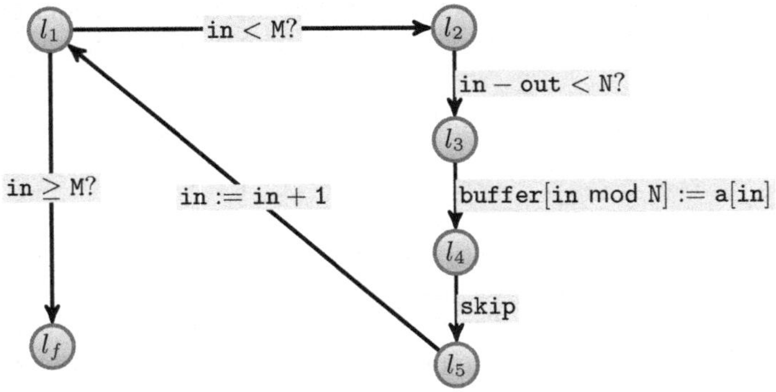

Fig. 5. Graph representing the *Producer* component

Notice that in contrast to previous definitions we must require the specifications $\mathsf{annot_a}$ and $\mathsf{annot_b}$ to be total.

Definition 6. *Let P the parallel composition of the sequential components P_1,.., P_k. P is certified to satisfy the specification $\langle \mathsf{annot}_1, \ldots, \mathsf{annot}_k \rangle$ if for all $i \in [1, \ldots, k]$:*

- *there is a certificate c_i for program P_i and specification annot_i, and*
- *for all $j \neq i$, annot_i is certified to be stable under the execution of P_j modulo annot_j. That is, for every $l \in \mathcal{N}_i$ and $\langle l_j, l'_j \rangle \in \mathcal{E}_j$ we have a certificate*

$$c'_i(l, l_j, l'_j) : \mathsf{annot}_i(l) \wedge \mathsf{annot}_j(l_j) \Rightarrow \mathsf{wp}_{\langle l_j, l'_j \rangle}(\mathsf{annot}_i(l))$$

Example 2. In this example, we proceed with the verification of the parallel composition of the sequential components **producer** and **consumer**.

Among the verification condition to prove the stability of the annotations for the consumer with respect to the producer, we have to prove for instance

$$\begin{aligned} \mathsf{Inv}_2 \wedge \mathtt{in} - \mathsf{out} < N \wedge \mathtt{buffer}[\mathtt{in} \bmod N] = \mathsf{a}[\mathtt{in}] \wedge \mathsf{annot}(l_1) \\ \Rightarrow \mathsf{wp}(\mathsf{out} := \mathsf{out} + 1, \mathsf{annot}(l_1)) \end{aligned}$$

that is, we must provide a certificate for the following goal:

$$\begin{aligned} \mathsf{Inv}_2 \wedge \mathtt{in} - \mathsf{out} < N \wedge \mathtt{buffer}[\mathtt{in} \bmod N] = \mathsf{a}[\mathtt{in}] \wedge \mathsf{Inv} \wedge \mathtt{in} \leq M \\ \Rightarrow \forall k.\ \mathsf{out} + 1 \leq k < \mathtt{in} \Rightarrow \mathsf{a}[k] = \mathtt{buffer}[k \bmod N] \end{aligned}$$

3 Certificate Translation for Compiler Optimizations

A compiler optimization is commonly performed in two phases. First, an analyzer computes static information from the program representation. Based on this analysis result, a second phase performs a semantic preserving transformation.

We have shown that verification conditions are not preserved in the presence of program optimizations [2], and thus the original certificates cannot be reused.

Furthermore, even semantics-preserving optimizations may render the original specification invalid. Consider the following sequential program transformation:

```
x = 0;                      x = 0;
while (x < N)               while (x < N)
  x = x + 1;      ⟶           x = x + 1;
y := x                      y := N
```

Assuming $0 \leq N$, the transformation is semantics preserving. Suppose that the program in the left has been verified against a postcondition x = y and loop invariant true. That involves discharging, among others, the proof obligation $\mathsf{true} \wedge \neg(\mathtt{x} < \mathtt{N}) \Rightarrow \mathtt{x} = \mathtt{x}$. After the program transformation, however, this proof obligation becomes invalid: $\mathsf{true} \wedge \neg(\mathtt{x} < \mathtt{N}) \Rightarrow \mathtt{x} = \mathtt{x}$.

For many program optimizations, certificate translation solves this problem by strengthening the original specification with the information provided by the analysis that justifies the optimization. In the example above, this consists of replacing the original invariant by $x \leq N$. However, whereas invariant strengthening enables one to preserve verification results in the presence of optimizations, it requires the automatic generation of certificates for analysis results. First, one must require the information provided by the analyzer to be representable as a program specification. Then, an automatic process must be defined in order to discharge the verification conditions computed from the result of the analysis as specification.

In the rest of this section, we postulate a set of sufficient conditions for the existence of certifying analyzers. We then proceed to explain a certificate transformation procedure that merges the original specification with the result of the analysis justifying the program transformation.

3.1 Certifying Analyzers

In this section, we first provide an abstract formalization of program analyzers and briefly review previous results on certifying analyzers. We then consider the existence of certifying analyzers for a concurrent programming setting. The existence of such analyzers is conditioned by a set of verification conditions formulated in our abstract setting.

Definition 7. *An analysis framework for a program* $\langle \mathcal{N}, \mathcal{E}, G \rangle$ *is defined as a tuple* $I = \langle \mathbf{A}, \{T_e\}_{e \in \mathcal{E}}, f \rangle$ *where:*

- $\mathbf{A} = \langle A, \sqsubseteq, \sqcap, \sqcup, \bot, \top \rangle$ *is the lattice domain of the analysis. Every element in* A *is interpreted as a property on execution states.*
- *for every* $e \in \mathcal{E}$, $T_e : A \to A$ *is a transfer function that approximates the program semantics in the abstract domain* A.
- f *is the flow of the interpretation, either backwards* ($f = \uparrow$) *or forwards* ($f = \downarrow$).

Although standard, we illustrate this definition with the formalization of a static analysis that determines whether variables hold even or odd values.

Let Par stand for the set $\{\mathsf{even}, \mathsf{odd}, \top\}$ with an order relation $\preceq$ defined as $\{(\mathsf{odd}, \top), (\mathsf{even}, \top)\}$ (the $\top$ symbol indicates that nothing is known about a value). We define the abstract analysis domain as $\mathbf{A} = \langle A, \sqsubseteq, \sqcup, ..\rangle$, where A is the set of stores that map variables to elements in Par plus a special symbol $\bot$, and $\rho \sqsubseteq \rho'$ if and only if $\rho = \bot$ or, otherwise, for all variable x we have $\rho x \preceq \rho' x$. Suppose we have an interpretation function $[\![.]\!]$ that takes an integer expression and an abstract store and returns an element in Par. For instance, for an abstract store mapping y and z to even and $\top$, respectively, the expressions $y + 1$ and $z + y$ are interpreted as odd and $\top$, respectively. Then, for an edge holding an assignment $x := e$, one can define a corresponding forward transfer function mapping every abstract store ρ to $[\rho \mid x \mapsto [\![e]\!]_\rho]$.

For every abstract domain $\mathbf{A}$, we assume a satisfaction relation $\models_A \subseteq \mathsf{Env} \times A$ (we omit the underscore A in the rest of the article), and denote $\models \eta : a$ when $\eta \in \mathsf{Env}$ "satisfies" the property $a \in A$. In addition, we assume the existence of a representation function γ, mapping elements in A to its representation as a logical formula.

Given an analysis with domain A for a program $\langle \mathcal{N}, \mathcal{E}, G\rangle$, an analysis result is provided by a labeling $S : \mathcal{N} \to A$ (for simplicity we assume every analysis result to be a total function on $\mathcal{N}$). Commonly, an analysis result is computed by iterative approximations until a fixpoint is reached. However, in this article we do not consider any particular method for the computation of analysis results. Instead, we characterize valid analysis results as labellings that satisfy a set of conditions defined in terms of the transfer functions.

Definition 8 (Solution). *A labeling $S : \mathcal{N} \to A$ is a solution of the analysis framework $\langle A, \{T_e\}_{e \in \mathcal{E}}, f\rangle$ if for all $\langle l, l'\rangle$ in $\mathcal{E}$:*

- *$f = \downarrow$ and $T_{\langle l,l'\rangle}(S(l)) \sqsubseteq S(l')$, or*
- *$f = \uparrow$ and $S(l) \sqsubseteq T_{\langle l,l'\rangle}(S(l'))$.*

In order to ensure that a solution of the analysis is valid over-approximation of the program semantics, one must require a consistency relation between each abstract transfer function T_e and the corresponding semantics relation for the edge e. Instead of stating the consistency relation with respect to the concrete semantics, we formalize it in this article in terms of the verification framework. In the following, we show that one can define a certifying analyzer provided there is a certificate of the consistency of the analyzer with respect to the verification framework.

Consider a program analysis $\langle \mathbf{A}, \{T_e\}_{e \in \mathcal{E}}, f\rangle$, and a representation function γ mapping elements in A to first-order formulae. This consistency property is formulated as a relation between the wp and the analysis transfer functions.

Definition 9 (Consistency). *Let $I = \langle \mathbf{A}, \{T_e\}_{e \in \mathcal{E}}, f\rangle$ be a program analysis and γ a representation function. The analysis I is consistent with the verification framework if for all $a, a' \in A$ and $\langle l, l'\rangle \in \mathcal{E}$, we have a certificate* cons *s.t.:*

- *$f = \uparrow$ and $\mathsf{cons} : \mathsf{wp}_e(\gamma(a)) \Rightarrow \gamma(T_e(a))$, or*
- *$f = \downarrow$ and $\mathsf{cons} : \mathsf{wp}_e(\gamma(T_e(a))) \Rightarrow \gamma(a)$.*

$$
\begin{aligned}
&\mathsf{monot}_\gamma : \mathcal{C}(\gamma(a_1) \Rightarrow \gamma(a_2)) \qquad \text{if } a_1 \sqsubseteq a_2 \\
&\mathsf{monot}_{\mathsf{wp}} : \mathcal{C}(a_1 \Rightarrow a_2) \to \mathcal{C}(\mathsf{wp}(a_1) \Rightarrow \mathsf{wp}(a_2)) \\
&\mathsf{distr}_{(\gamma,\sqcap)} : \gamma(a_1) \wedge \gamma(a_2) \Rightarrow \gamma(a_1 \sqcap a_2) \\
&\mathsf{distr}^{\leftarrow}_{(\mathsf{wp},\wedge)} : \mathsf{wp}(a_1) \wedge \mathsf{wp}(a_2) \Rightarrow \mathsf{wp}(a_1 \wedge a_2) \\
&\mathsf{distr}^{\rightarrow}_{(\mathsf{wp},\wedge)} : T(a_1 \wedge a_2) \Rightarrow T(a_1) \wedge T(a_2)
\end{aligned}
$$

Fig. 6. Certificates required for certificate translation (excerpt)

Provided there are certificates for the monotonicity of the representation function γ and for the distributivity of the transfer functions with respect to the operator $\sqcap$, we know from previous results that a *consistent* analyzer is certifying:

Lemma 1. *Let* $I = \langle A, \{T_e\}_{e \in \mathcal{E}}, f \rangle$ *be a program analysis and* γ *a representation function, such that* I *is consistent with the verification framework. Suppose that there are certificates* $\mathsf{monot}_\gamma(a, a')$ *(for every* $a, a' \in A$ *such that* $a \sqsubseteq a'$*) and* $\mathsf{distr}_{(\gamma,\sqcap)}$*, as defined in Fig. 6. If the labeling* $S : \mathcal{N} \to A$ *is a solution of* I*, then one can generate a certificate for the specification* $\gamma \circ S$*.*

In the rest of this section, we present an extension of the result above to consider the existence of certifying analyzers for concurrent programs.

Analysis of concurrent programs. As with program verification, one must refine the definition of analysis result to require not only the validity of a labeling with respect to a sequential program execution, but also its stability with respect to the execution of the other components.

Suppose an execution of P_{a} in a concurrent environment from the initial label $l_{\mathsf{init_a}}$ to a final label $l_o \in \mathcal{N}_{\mathsf{a}}$, that is, $\langle (l_{\mathsf{init_a}}, l), \eta \rangle \rightsquigarrow^\star \langle (l_o, l'), \eta' \rangle$ for some $\eta, \eta' \in \mathsf{Env}$. From the definition of $\rightsquigarrow$, the execution may traverse an arbitrary number of edges in $\mathcal{E}_{\mathsf{b}}$, affecting the execution of P_{a}. In that situation, we cannot ensure that $\models \eta : S_{\mathsf{a}}(l_{\mathsf{init_a}})$ implies $\models \eta' : S_{\mathsf{a}}(l_o)$.

We say that a condition a at node $l \in \mathcal{N}_{\mathsf{a}}$ is stable with respect to P_{b} and labeling S_{b} if the concurrent execution of P_{b} does not invalidate a as long as P_{b} satisfies S_{b}. The following definition formalizes this requirement.

Definition 10 (globally-stable solution). *A labeling* S_{a} *for program* P_{a}*, is a stable solution of* I_{a}*, with respect to program* P_{b} *with labeling* S_{b}*, if it is a solution of* I_{a} *and for every edge* $\langle l_{\mathsf{b}}, l'_{\mathsf{b}} \rangle \in \mathcal{E}_{\mathsf{b}}$ *and node* $l \in \mathcal{N}_{\mathsf{a}}$ *the following condition holds:*

- $f = \uparrow$ *and* $S_{\mathsf{b}}(l_{\mathsf{b}}) \sqcap S_{\mathsf{a}}(l) \sqsubseteq T_{\langle l_{\mathsf{b}}, l'_{\mathsf{b}} \rangle}(S_{\mathsf{a}}(l))$ *or,*
- $f = \downarrow$ *and* $T_{\langle l'_{\mathsf{b}}, l_{\mathsf{b}} \rangle}(S_{\mathsf{b}}(l'_{\mathsf{b}}) \sqcap S_{\mathsf{a}}(l)) \sqsubseteq S_{\mathsf{a}}(l)$*.*

We define a labeling for a concurrent program as a tuple of labellings, one for each of the parallel components. Consider the sequential programs P_{a} and P_{b} and the corresponding analyzers $I_{\mathsf{a}} = \langle \mathbf{A}, \{T^{\mathsf{a}}_e\}_{e \in \mathcal{E}_{\mathsf{a}}}, f \rangle$ and $I_{\mathsf{b}} = \langle \mathbf{A}, \{T^{\mathsf{b}}_e\}_{e \in \mathcal{E}_{\mathsf{b}}}, f \rangle$. Let the labellings S_a and S_b be specifications for the programs P_a and P_b, respectively. We define then a labeling for the parallel composition.

Definition 11 (Solution for a Concurrent Program). *A labeling $\langle S_a, S_b \rangle$ is a solution of the analysis (I_a, I_b) for the concurrent program $P_a \parallel P_b$, if S_a and S_b are solutions of I_a and I_b, respectively, and S_a is stable w.r.t. P_b and S_b, and S_b is stable w.r.t. P_a and S_a.*

Suppose that I_a and I_b are consistent with the semantics of P_a and P_b respectively. It follows from Definition 11 that, if (S_a, S_b) is a solution for (I_a, I_b), and that $\langle (l_{inita}, l_{initb}), \eta \rangle \leadsto^\star \langle (l_{o_a}, l_{o_b}), \eta' \rangle$ and that $\models \eta : S_a(l_{inita})$ and $\models \eta : S_b(l_{initb})$ then $\models \eta' : S_a(l_{o_a})$ and $\models \eta' : S_b(l_{o_b})$.

The following result states that the abstract conditions required over sequential program analyzers to be certifying are enough to guarantee certificate generation for concurrent program analyzers.

Lemma 2 (Certifying Analyzers for Globally-stable Solutions). *Consider a solution S_a for the analysis $I_a = \langle \mathbf{A}, \{T_e\}_{e \in \mathcal{E}_a}, f \rangle$. Assume that I_a is consistent with the verification framework. Suppose also that there are certificates $\mathsf{monot}_\gamma(a, a')$ (for every $a, a' \in A$ such that $a \sqsubseteq a'$) and $\mathsf{distr}_{(\gamma,\sqcap)}$, as defined in Fig. 6. Then, one can compute a certificate $\vec{c'}$ witnessing the stability of $\gamma \circ S_a$ with respect to program P_b and specification $\gamma \circ S_b$, provided S_a is stable with respect to P_b and S_b.*

Proof. *In Fig. 7 we define $\vec{c'}(l, l', l_1)$ in terms of* $\mathsf{monot}_{\mathsf{wp}}$ *and* $\mathsf{distr}_{(\gamma,\sqcap)}$.

case $f = \uparrow$

$$
\begin{aligned}
\mathsf{hyp} &:= S_b(l) \sqcap S_a(l_1) \sqsubseteq T_{\langle l,l' \rangle}(S_a(l_1))\\
p_1 &:= \mathsf{monot}_\gamma : \gamma(S_b(l) \sqcap S_a(l_1)) \Rightarrow \gamma(T_{\langle l,l' \rangle}(S_a(l_1)))\\
p_2 &:= \mathsf{distr}_{(\gamma,\sqcap)} : \gamma(S_b(l)) \wedge \gamma(S_a(l_1)) \Rightarrow \gamma(S_b(l) \sqcap S_a(l_1))\\
p_3 &:= \mathsf{trans}(p_2, p_1) : \gamma(S_b(l)) \wedge \gamma(S_a(l_1)) \Rightarrow \gamma(T_{\langle l,l' \rangle}(S_a(l_1)))\\
p_4 &:= \mathsf{cons} : \gamma(T_{\langle l,l' \rangle}(S_a(l_1))) \Rightarrow \mathsf{wp}_{\langle l,l' \rangle}(\gamma \circ S_a(l_1))\\
\vec{c'}(l, l', l_1) &:= \mathsf{trans}(p_3, p_4) : \gamma \circ S_b(l) \wedge \gamma \circ S_a(l_1) \Rightarrow \mathsf{wp}_{\langle l,l' \rangle}(\gamma \circ S_a(l_1))
\end{aligned}
$$

case $f = \downarrow$

$$
\begin{aligned}
\mathsf{hyp} &:= T_{\langle l,l' \rangle}(S_b(l) \sqcap S_a(l_1)) \sqsubseteq S_a(l_1)\\
p_1 &:= \mathsf{monot}_\gamma : \gamma(T_{\langle l,l' \rangle}(S_b(l) \sqcap S_a(l_1))) \Rightarrow \gamma(S_a(l_1))\\
p_2 &:= \mathsf{monot}_{\mathsf{wp}}(p_1) : \mathsf{wp}_{\langle l,l' \rangle}(\gamma(T_{\langle l,l' \rangle}(S_b(l) \sqcap S_a(l_1)))) \Rightarrow \mathsf{wp}_{\langle l,l' \rangle}(\gamma(S_a(l_1)))\\
p_3 &:= \mathsf{cons} : \gamma(S_b(l) \sqcap S_a(l_1)) \Rightarrow \mathsf{wp}_{\langle l,l' \rangle}(\gamma(T_{\langle l,l' \rangle}(S_b(l) \sqcap S_a(l_1))))\\
p_4 &:= \mathsf{distr}_{(\gamma,\sqcap)} : \gamma \circ S_b(l) \wedge \gamma \circ S_a(l_1) \Rightarrow \gamma(S_b(l) \sqcap S_a(l_1))\\
\vec{c'}(l, l', l_1) &:= \mathsf{trans}(p_4, \mathsf{trans}(p_3, p_2)) : \gamma \circ S_b(l) \wedge \gamma \circ S_a(l_1) \Rightarrow \mathsf{wp}_{\langle l,l' \rangle}(\gamma(S_a(l_1)))
\end{aligned}
$$

Fig. 7. Certifying Analyzers for parallel program composition

The existence of certifying analyzers for concurrent programs follows directly from Lemma 1 and 2.

3.2 Certificate Translation

In the rest of this section, we consider a fundamental program transformation from which many compiler optimizations are built: a program $P'_j = \langle \mathcal{N}'_j, \mathcal{E}'_j, G' \rangle$ is a transformation of a program $P_j = \langle \mathcal{N}_j, \mathcal{E}_j, G \rangle$ if $\mathcal{N}'_j \subseteq \mathcal{N}_j$ and $\mathcal{E}'_j \subseteq \mathcal{E}_j$. For readability, we consider the case in which only one of the parallel components is transformed, that is, $P_1 \parallel \ldots \parallel P_j \parallel \ldots \parallel P_k$ is transformed into $P_1 \parallel \ldots \parallel P'_j \parallel \ldots \parallel P_k$. We let the tuple $\langle S, \vec{c}_S, \vec{c'}_S \rangle$ represent the analysis result that motivated the transformation to the component P'_j. The generalization of the following results to transformations that operate simultaneously in several program components is straightforward.

In the rest of this section, we extend the results on certificate transformation to the concurrent programming setting presented in this paper.

Proposition 1 (Existence of certificate transformers). *Let I'_j be the certificate infrastructure $I'_j = \langle A, \{T'_e\}_{e \in \mathcal{E}_j}, f \rangle$ associated to P'_j. Assume the existence of the certificate $\mathsf{distr}_{(\mathsf{wp},\wedge)}$ defined in Fig. 6. Let $\langle S, \vec{c}_S, \vec{c'}_S \rangle$ be a certified globally stable specification of I_j such that for every $\langle l, l' \rangle \in \mathcal{E}_j$ and formula ϕ we have a certificate*

$$\mathsf{justif}(l, l') : S(l) \wedge \mathsf{wp}_{\langle l,l' \rangle}(\phi) \Rightarrow \mathsf{wp}'_{\langle l,l' \rangle}(\phi)$$

Then one can transform every certified specification $(\langle \mathsf{annot}_i, \vec{c_i}, \vec{c'_i} \rangle)_{1 \leq i \leq k}$ of the concurrent program $P_1 \parallel \ldots \parallel P_j \parallel \ldots \parallel P_k$ into a certified solution $(\langle \mathsf{annot}_1, \vec{d_1}, \vec{d'_1} \rangle, \ldots, \langle \mathsf{annot}'_j, \vec{d_j}, \vec{d'_j} \rangle, \ldots, \langle \mathsf{annot}_k, \vec{d_k}, \vec{d'_k} \rangle)$, where for all $l \in \mathcal{N}'_j$, $\mathsf{annot}'_j(l)$ is defined as $\mathsf{annot}_j(l) \wedge S(l)$.

Proof. *We show that for any $i \neq j$ one can transform every certified globally stable labellings $\langle \mathsf{annot}_i, \vec{c_i}, \vec{c'_i} \rangle$ for P_i and $\langle \mathsf{annot}_j, \vec{c_j}, \vec{c'_j} \rangle$ for P_j into the certified labellings $\langle \mathsf{annot}_i, \vec{d_i}, \vec{d'_i} \rangle$ for P_i and $\langle \mathsf{annot}'_j, \vec{d_j}, \vec{d'_j} \rangle$ for P'_j.*

First of all, notice that for $i \neq j$ we can let $\vec{d_i} = \vec{c_i}$ and that it is not hard to define $\vec{d'_j}$ from $\vec{c'}_j$ and $\vec{c'}_S$, since $\{\mathsf{wp}_e\}_{e \in \mathcal{E}_i}$ have not changed for $i \neq j$.

Building the certificates $\vec{d_j}$ that ensures that annot'_j is a local solution is exactly the same procedure as in Section 3.2. The case for the certificates $\vec{d'_i}$ for $i \neq j$ can be found in Fig. 8 and 9, for the cases $f = \uparrow$ and $f = \downarrow$, respectively. Notice that the certification of the solution $\langle S, \vec{c}_S, \vec{c'}_S \rangle$ is only required to define the certificates $\vec{d_j}$ and $\vec{d'_j}$.

Intuitively, for all $\langle l, l' \rangle \in \mathcal{E}$, the $\mathsf{justif}(l, l')$ certificate states that, assuming the result of the analysis $S(l)$ valid, the transformation is a semantics refinement, expressed in terms of the predicate transformer wp. For the particular case of textbook optimizations one can see that the justif certificate is easily discharged.

The following example shows a particular case of the justif certificate for an optimization applied to the running example.

Example 3. We illustrate a certificate translation for induction variable strength reduction. A first simple transformation consists of inserting extra statements

Let $\mathsf{wp} = \mathsf{wp}_{\langle l_j, l'_j \rangle}$ and $\mathsf{wp}' = \mathsf{wp}'_{\langle l_j, l'_j \rangle}$ in:

$$
\begin{array}{l}
p_1 := \vec{c'}_i : \mathsf{annot}_j(l_j) \wedge \mathsf{annot}_i(l) \Rightarrow \mathsf{wp}(\mathsf{annot}_i(l)) \\
p_2 := \mathsf{justif}(l_j, l'_j) : S(l_j) \wedge \mathsf{wp}(\mathsf{annot}_i(l)) \Rightarrow \mathsf{wp}'(\mathsf{annot}_i(l)) \\
p_3 := \mathsf{weak}_\wedge(p_1) : \mathsf{annot}_j(l_j) \wedge \mathsf{annot}_i(l) \wedge S(l_j) \Rightarrow \mathsf{wp}(\mathsf{annot}_i(l)) \\
p_4 := \mathsf{weak}_\wedge(\mathsf{axiom}) : \mathsf{annot}_j(l_j) \wedge \mathsf{annot}_i(l) \wedge S(l_j) \Rightarrow S(l_j) \\
p_5 := \mathsf{intro}_\wedge(p_3, p_4) : \mathsf{annot}_j(l_j) \wedge \mathsf{annot}_i(l) \wedge S(l_j) \Rightarrow \mathsf{wp}(\mathsf{annot}_i(l)) \wedge S(l_j) \\
\vec{d}_i(l_j, l'_j, l) := \mathsf{trans}(p_5, p_2) : \mathsf{annot}'_j(l_j) \wedge \mathsf{annot}_i(l) \Rightarrow \mathsf{wp}'(\mathsf{annot}_i(l))
\end{array}
$$

Fig. 8. Definition of $\vec{d}_i(l_1, l'_1, l_2)$. Case $f = \uparrow$

Let $\mathsf{wp} = \mathsf{wp}_{\langle l_j, l'_j \rangle}$ and $\mathsf{wp}' = \mathsf{wp}'_{\langle l_j, l'_j \rangle}$ in:

$$
\begin{array}{l}
p_1 := \mathsf{axiom} : \mathsf{annot}_j(l_j) \wedge \mathsf{annot}_i(l) \Rightarrow \mathsf{annot}_j(l_j) \wedge \mathsf{annot}_i(l) \\
p_2 := \mathsf{weak}_\wedge(p_1) : \mathsf{annot}'_j(l_j) \wedge \mathsf{annot}_i(l) \Rightarrow \mathsf{annot}_j(l_j) \wedge \mathsf{annot}_i(l) \\
p_3 := \mathsf{monot}_{\mathsf{wp}}(p_2) : \mathsf{wp}(\mathsf{annot}'_j(l_j) \wedge \mathsf{annot}_i(l)) \Rightarrow \mathsf{wp}(\mathsf{annot}_j(l_j) \wedge \mathsf{annot}_i(l)) \\
p_4 := \vec{c'}_i : \mathsf{wp}(\mathsf{annot}_j(l_j) \wedge \mathsf{annot}_i(l)) \Rightarrow \mathsf{annot}_i(l) \\
p_5 := \mathsf{trans}(p_3, p_4) : \mathsf{wp}(\mathsf{annot}'_j(l_j) \wedge \mathsf{annot}_i(l)) \Rightarrow \mathsf{annot}_i(l) \\
p_6 := \mathsf{weak}_\wedge(p_5) : R(l'_j) \wedge \mathsf{wp}(\mathsf{annot}'_j(l_j) \wedge \mathsf{annot}_i(l)) \Rightarrow \mathsf{annot}_i(l) \\
p_7 := \mathsf{justif} : \mathsf{wp}'(\mathsf{annot}'_j(l_j) \wedge \mathsf{annot}_i(l)) \Rightarrow R(l'_j) \wedge \mathsf{wp}(\mathsf{annot}'_j(l_j) \wedge \mathsf{annot}_i(l)) \\
\vec{d'}_i(l_j, l'_j l) := \mathsf{trans}(p_7, p_6) : \mathsf{wp}'(\mathsf{annot}'_j(l_j) \wedge \mathsf{annot}_i(l)) \Rightarrow \mathsf{annot}_i(l)
\end{array}
$$

Fig. 9. Definition of $\vec{d'}_i(l_j, l'_j l)$. Case $f = \downarrow$

that affect a fresh variable `r`. The motivation of this transformation is to ensure the validity of the condition $\mathtt{r} = \mathtt{in} \bmod N$ enabling, thus, a further transformation. In the graph, the transformation consists in introducing the nodes l, l_6 and l_7, together with the edges $\{\langle l, l_1 \rangle, \langle l_5, l_6 \rangle, \langle l_5, l_7 \rangle\}$. Translating the certificate in this step is straightforward since `r` is a fresh variable and hence does not appear in the program annotations. The freshness of `r` is formalized by the fact that transfer functions T_e for $e \in \{\langle l, l_1 \rangle, \langle l_4, l_5 \rangle, \langle l_5, l_6 \rangle, \langle l_5, l_7 \rangle\}$ are defined as the identity function on the original specification. As a result, the labeling S is extended to l as $S(l) = S(l_1)$ and to l_6, l_7 as $S(l_6) = S(l_7) = S(l_5)$.

At this point, we assume that an analysis is able to compute a solution S with $S(l)$ defined as $(\mathtt{r} = \mathtt{in} \bmod N)$ for l in $\{l_1, l_2, l_3, l_4\}$. It is not hard to verify that this labeling can be certified: $\gamma \circ S$ is locally valid for the producer component and stable with respect to transfer functions on the consumer side (since `r` is a fresh variable and `in` is local to the producer side).

As shown in Fig. 11, the transformation consists in replacing the assignment $\mathtt{buffer}[\mathtt{in} \bmod N] := \mathtt{a}[\mathtt{in}]$ by $\mathtt{buffer}[\mathtt{r}] := \mathtt{a}[\mathtt{in}]$. By Lemma 1, it is sufficient to provide for every edge e a certificate justif. In the example, since $\langle l_3, l_4 \rangle$ is the only edge that is modified, it is sufficient to provide a certificate for the goal

$$\gamma(R(l_3)) \wedge \phi[{}^{[a|\mathtt{in} \bmod N \mapsto \mathtt{a}[\mathtt{in}]]}/_{a}] \Rightarrow \phi[{}^{[a|\mathtt{r} \mapsto \mathtt{a}[\mathtt{in}]]}/_{a}]$$

which is valid since $\gamma(R(l_3))$ is defined as $\mathtt{r} = \mathtt{in} \bmod N$.

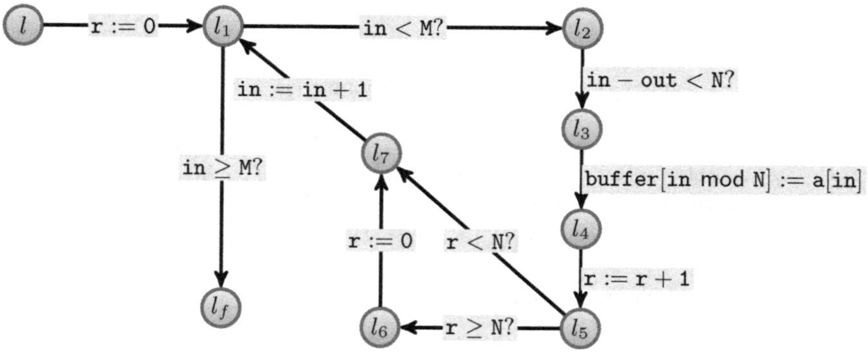

Fig. 10. *Producer* component after node insertion

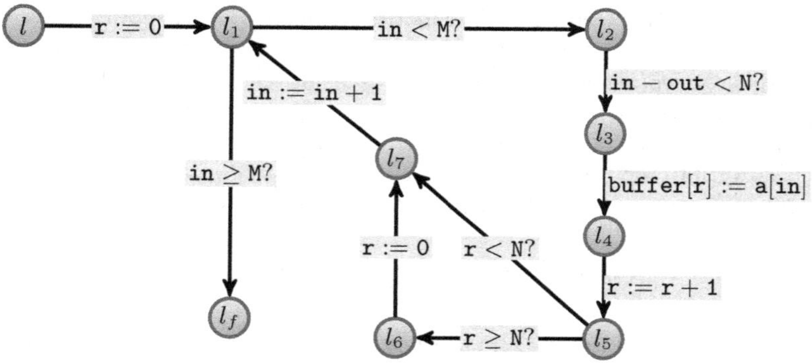

Fig. 11. *Producer* component after induction variable strength reduction

4 Related Work

Certificate translation. Recently, there has been some progress on transferring correctness evidence from source programs to compiled code, but none of them considered the verification of concurrent programs.

In particular, Müller and Nordio [7] describe a proof transforming compiler from Java to Java Bytecode. In this work, they pay special attention to the occurrence of abrupt termination in the presence of `try-catch-finally` statements, but they do not consider compiler optimizations. In a more recent work [9], Nordio, Müeller, and Meyer have formalized a proof transforming procedure from a contract-equipped Eiffel program to the Microsoft CIL language.

In another line of work, Saabas and Uustalu [12] study the existence of proof transformers in a type-based setting. In particular, they consider optimizations such as common subexpression elimination, code elimination, and partial redundancy optimization. For each optimization, they show how to derive Hoare proof of the transformed program from a Hoare derivation tree of the source program.

Certifying analyzers. Seo et al. [13] presented an approach to derive verification certificates from static analysis results. In this work, analysis results are formalized as abstract interpretations of a simple sequential and structured language. They propose an algorithm that, from an abstract interpretation result, can automatically construct a Hoare derivation tree. One noticeable difference is that no notion of certificate is used to support the validity of a Hoare derivation tree. In a more recent work [14], Seo et al. propose a mechanism for slicing analysis results to remove redundant information. Removing irrelevant information from the analysis result avoids unnecessary growth of the final certificate size.

In a different line of work, Chaieb [4] implemented a proof generating analyzer in the Isabelle system. The verification framework is based on a weakest precondition calculus and the certificate infrastructure is interpreted as Isabelle/HOL theorems. Chaieb's work considers program analyzers as backwards abstract interpretations, enabling automatic proof generation of safety properties.

5 Conclusion

In this article, we presented an extension of previous results on certificate translation to a concurrent programming setting. Under an abstract formalization of analysis frameworks and an Owicki-Gries like logic, we have identified a set of verification conditions that ensure the existence of proof-producing analyzers, a crucial component for the transformation of certificates. For a class of optimizations that preserve the overall program structure, we have shown that it is feasible to transfer verification results in the presence of program optimizations.

The number of proof obligations to be discharged when using the Owicki-Gries technique can be exponential on the number of program components. The applicability of Owicki/Gries like proof systems relies on proposing criteria to overlook a significant number of trivial proof obligations. For instance, one should only consider global stability under statements that may modify part of the shared memory. An issue that must be checked is whether the verification conditions that originally satisfy these criteria fail to do it after a semantics-preserving program transformation, affecting the applicability of the framework.

One disadvantage of the Owicki-Gries logic is that it forces the verification of a concurrent component with respect to the concrete context in which it will be executed. One alternative approach consists of verifying each concurrent component relying on a specification of the effect that may have the execution context on this component. One such proof systems that have been proposed as a more practical alternative to Owicki-Gries, are rely-guarantee methods [6,5]. A further extension would be restricting interference points with concurrent separation logics [10], and combining both [15].

References

1. Barthe, G., Grégoire, B., Heraud, S., Kunz, C., Pacalet, A.: Implementing a direct method for certificate translation. In: Breitman, K., Cavalcanti, A. (eds.) ICFEM 2009. LNCS, vol. 5885, pp. 541–560. Springer, Heidelberg (2009)

2. Barthe, G., Grégoire, B., Kunz, C., Rezk, T.: Certificate translation for optimizing compilers. ACM Transactions on :Programming Languages and Systems 31(5), 18:1–18:45 (2009)
3. Barthe, G., Kunz, C.: Certificate translation in abstract interpretation. In: Drossopoulou, S. (ed.) ESOP 2008. LNCS, vol. 4960, pp. 368–382. Springer, Heidelberg (2008)
4. Chaieb, A.: Proof-producing program analysis. In: Barkaoui, K., Cavalcanti, A., Cerone, A. (eds.) ICTAC 2006. LNCS, vol. 4281, pp. 287–301. Springer, Heidelberg (2006)
5. Flanagan, C., Freund, S.N., Qadeer, S.: Thread-modular verification for shared-memory programs. In: Le Métayer, D. (ed.) ESOP 2002. LNCS, vol. 2305, pp. 262–277. Springer, Heidelberg (2002)
6. Jones, C.B.: Tentative steps toward a development method for interfering programs. ACM Transactions on Programming Languages and Systems 5(4), 596–619 (1983)
7. Müller, P., Nordio, M.: Proof-transforming compilation of programs with abrupt termination. Technical Report 565, ETH Zurich (2007)
8. Necula, G.C.: Proof-carrying code. In: Principles of Programming Languages, pp. 106–119. ACM Press, New York (1997)
9. Nordio, M., Müller, P., Meyer, B.: Proof-transforming compilation of eiffel programs. In: Paige, R. (ed.) TOOLS-EUROPE. LNBIP. Springer, Heidelberg (2008)
10. O'Hearn, P.W.: Resources, concurrency and local reasoning. Theoretical Computer Science 375(1-3), 271–307 (2007)
11. Owicki, S., Gries, D.: An axiomatic proof technique for parallel programs. Acta Informatica Journal 6, 319–340 (1975)
12. Saabas, A., Uustalu, T.: Type systems for optimizing stack-based code. In: Huisman, M., Spoto, F. (eds.) Bytecode Semantics, Verification, Analysis and Transformation. Electronic Notes in Theoretical Computer Science, vol. 190(1), pp. 103–119. Elsevier, Amsterdam (2007)
13. Seo, S., Yang, H., Yi, K.: Automatic Construction of Hoare Proofs from Abstract Interpretation Results. In: Ohori, A. (ed.) APLAS 2003. LNCS, vol. 2895, pp. 230–245. Springer, Heidelberg (2003)
14. Seo, S., Yang, H., Yi, K., Han, T.: Goal-directed weakening of abstract interpretation results. ACM Transactions on Programming Languages and Systems 29(6), 39:1–39:39 (2007)
15. Vafeiadis, V., Parkinson, M.J.: A marriage of rely/guarantee and separation logic. In: Caires, L., Vasconcelos, V.T. (eds.) CONCUR 2007. LNCS, vol. 4703, pp. 256–271. Springer, Heidelberg (2007)

Certified Result Checking for Polyhedral Analysis of Bytecode Programs*

Frédéric Besson, Thomas Jensen, David Pichardie, and Tiphaine Turpin

INRIA Rennes - Bretagne Atlantique
Campus de Beaulieu, F-35042 Rennes, France

Abstract. Static analysers are becoming so complex that it is crucial to ascertain the soundness of their results in a provable way. In this paper we develop a certified checker in Coq that is able to certify the results of a polyhedral array-bound analysis for an imperative, stack-oriented bytecode language with procedures, arrays and global variables. The checker uses, in addition to the analysis result, certificates which at the same time improve efficiency and make correctness proofs much easier. In particular, our result certifier avoids complex polyhedral computations such as convex hulls and is using easily checkable inclusion certificates based on Farkas lemma. Benchmarks demonstrate that our approach is effective and produces certificates that can be efficiently checked not only by an extracted Caml checker but also directly in Coq.

1 Introduction

Bytecode verification is an important component for making Java a trustworthy platform for mobile computing. Several researchers have investigated how to develop machine-checked bytecode verifiers in order to increase the confidence in this component itself [13,2]. The standard bytecode verifier ensures one kind of security policy that is proved by a simple data flow analysis. The static verification of other security and safety policies (*e.g.*, to check that all array accesses are within bounds) requires more sophisticated static program analysers, which themselves are sophisticated pieces of software. A significant example of this is the state-of-the-art Astrée static analyser for C [9] which proves the absence of run-time errors for the primary flight control software of the Airbus A340 fly-by-wire system.

In this paper we show that it is possible to use advanced analysers to enhance the security of a mobile code platform by developing a machine-verified extended bytecode verifier that can check the result of such analysers. One approach would be to certify the analyser entirely within a proof checker, as done for the key components of the Java bytecode verifier [13,2]. In previous work, Pichardie *et. al* [18,6] formalised the theory of abstract interpretation inside the Coq proof assistant and proved the correctness of a variety of program analysers. This

* This work was partially funded by the FET Global Computing project MOBIUS, by the Brittany region project CERTLOGS and the FRAE project ASCERT.

M. Wirsing, M. Hofmann, and A. Rauschmayer (Eds.): TGC 2010, LNCS 6084, pp. 253–267, 2010.

approach is ambitious since it would require to program and certify in Coq the whole analyser with all its abstract operators (least upper bound, closure, widening...) and to prove termination of the fixpoint iteration process. Formally certifying a polyhedral analyser with this technique would require a tremendous certification effort. Moreover, efficiency is a major concern when considering the expensive symbolic manipulations of a polyhedral library [12] and the problem becomes even more perceptible in a pure lambda-calculus language such as Coq.

As noticed by Leroy in the context of certified compilation [15], static analyses and optimisation heuristics are algorithms for which it is generally easier to prove the correctness of a result verifier than the algorithm itself. In this paper we apply this *result certification* methodology [20] to a polyhedral analysis [10] for an imperative, stack-oriented bytecode language with procedures, arrays and global variables. We design in parallel a polyhedral analyser and a certified result checker using the abstract interpretation theory. The analyser and the checker share the same constraint-based specification whose soundness is formally proved in Coq. The analyser uses an optimised polyhedral C library [12] to compute a post-fixpoint solution while the checker uses a certified simplified abstract domain to check the post-fixpoint. One particularity of our approach is that, in addition to the program and the post-fixpoint, the checker receives hints that enable it to use a simplified abstract domain when verifying the fixpoint. In particular, the expensive operations of computing the convex hull of polyhedra is replaced by polyhedral inclusion checks which can be performed efficiently by an application of Farkas's lemma. More precisely, we propose the following three contributions:

- A certified constraint based specification of a polyhedral analysis for bytecode programs.
- A notion of certificate for result checking of polyhedral analysers.
- A certificate result checker, obtained by Coq extraction, able to perform static array bound checking on resource constrained devices.

2 Polyhedral Analysis of Bytecode

We consider a cut-down language of Java bytecode which includes integers, dynamically created (unidimensional) arrays of integers, static methods (procedures) and static fields (global variables). The formal syntax and small-step operational semantics are rather straightforward and can be found in the companion report [4].

The analysis is inter-procedural, relational and parametrised with respect to a numeric abstract domain used to abstract the values of the local and global variables of the program. The analyser automatically infers an invariant for each control point in the program, a pre-condition that must hold at the point of calling a procedure and a post-condition that is guaranteed to hold when the procedure returns.

2.1 Motivating Example

The Binary Search example (in source format here for readability considerations) given in Fig. 1 shows how our analysis will prove that the instruction that accesses the array `vec` with index `mid` will not index out of bounds. We have annotated the code of Binary Search with the invariants that have been inferred automatically. Invariants refer to values of local and global variables and can also refer to the length of an array. For example, the invariant (I_3) asserts among other properties that when entering the while loop, the relation $0 \leq \texttt{low} < \texttt{high} < |\texttt{vec}|$ is satisfied. Similarly, the post-condition ensures that the result is a valid index into the array being searched, or -1, indicating that the element was not found. In addition, the analysis introduces a 0-indexed variable (such as *e.g.* $\texttt{key}_0$ in the example) for each parameter in order to refer to its value when entering the procedure. As a result, the invariant on exit of the method defines a *summary relation* between its input and its output.

```
  //     PRE:  0 ≤ |vec0|
static int bsearch(int key, int[] vec) {
  // (I1) key0 = key ∧ |vec0| = |vec| ∧ 0 ≤ |vec0|
   int low = 0, high = vec.length - 1;
  // (I2) key0 = key ∧ |vec0| = |vec| ∧ 0 ≤ low ≤ high + 1 ≤ |vec0|
   while (0 < high-low) {
  // (I3) key0 = key ∧ |vec0| = |vec| ∧ 0 ≤ low < high < |vec0|
      int mid = low + (high - low) / 2;
  // (I4) key0 = key ∧ |vec0| = |vec|∧
  //        0 ≤ low < high < |vec0| ∧  low + high − 1 ≤ 2 · mid ≤ low + high
      if (key == vec[mid]) return mid;
      else if (key < vec[mid]) high = mid - 1;
      else low = mid + 1;
  // (I5) key0 = key ∧ |vec0| = |vec| ∧ −2 + 3 · low ≤ 2 · high + mid∧
  //        − 1 + 2 · low ≤ high + 2 · mid ∧ −1 + low ≤ mid ≤ 1 + high∧
  //        high ≤ low+mid∧1+high ≤ 2·low+mid∧1+low+mid ≤ |vec0|+high∧
  //        2 ≤ |vec0| ∧ 2 + high + mid ≤ |vec0| + low
   }
  // (I6) key0 = key∧|vec0| = |vec|∧low−1 ≤ high ≤ low∧0 ≤ low∧high < |vec0|
   return -1;
} //    POST:  −1 ≤ res < |vec0|
```

Fig. 1. Binary search

2.2 Numeric Relational Domain Specification

The bytecode analysis is specified with respect to an abstract numeric relational interface (defined below) that can be instantiated with standard relational abstract domains [10,16,17]. The numeric abstract domain $\mathbb{D}$ is a family of sets $\mathbb{D}_V$ indexed with a finite set V of variables. The abstract operators and associated properties listed below furnish the interface needed to specify and prove correct our generic numeric relational bytecode analysis.

To establish the connection between abstract elements and sets of numeric environments $\mathcal{P}(V \to \mathbb{Z})$, $\mathbb{D}$ is equipped with a concretisation function $\gamma : \mathbb{D}_V \to \mathcal{P}(V \to \mathbb{Z})$ compatible with a decidable partial order relation $\sqsubseteq$ *i.e.*, $d \sqsubseteq d' \Rightarrow \gamma(d) \subseteq \gamma(d')$. The domain $\mathbb{D}$ provides an upper-bound ($\sqcup$) and a lower bound ($\sqcap$) operators. To handle variable scopes, the domain is also equipped with a renaming and a projection operator. The renaming operator $[\cdot]_{W \to W'} : \mathbb{D}_{V+W} \to \mathbb{D}_{V+W'}$ is purely syntactic and maps a variable w_i in the ordered set W to the corresponding variable w'_i in W' (+ denotes disjoint union here). The projection operator $\exists_{V'} : \mathbb{D}_{V+V'} \to \mathbb{D}_V$ allows to project an abstract element onto a subset of the variables. For instance, $\exists_{\{y\}}.x \leq y \leq z$ would (by transitivity) compute $x \leq z$.

All the previous operators are language independent. The interface of the numeric domain with the programming language is made through expressions (*Expr*) and guards (*Guard*).

$$\begin{array}{ll} \mathit{Expr}_V \ni e ::= n \mid x \mid ? \mid e \diamond e & x \in V,\ \diamond \in \{+, -, \times, /\} \\ \mathit{Guard}_V \ni t ::= e \bowtie e & \bowtie \in \{=, \neq, <, \leq, >, \geq\} \end{array}$$

In the rest of the paper $\overline{\bowtie}$ will denotes the negation of a binary test $\bowtie$. Expressions denote sets of numerical values (due to the question mark symbol ? that is used to model an arbitrary value) while guards denote predicates on environments. The meaning $[\![\cdot]\!]_\rho$ of such expressions is defined relative to an environment $\rho \in V \to \mathbb{Z}$.

$$\begin{array}{c} [\![n]\!]_\rho = \{n\} \qquad [\![x]\!]_\rho = \{\rho(x)\} \qquad [\![?]\!]_\rho = \mathbb{Z} \\ [\![e_1 \diamond e_2]\!]_\rho \quad = \quad \{n_1 \diamond n_2 \mid n_1 \in [\![e_1]\!], n_2 \in [\![e_2]\!]\} \\ [\![e_1 \bowtie e_2]\!]_\rho \iff \exists\, n_1 \in [\![e_1]\!]_\rho, n_2 \in [\![e_2]\!]_\rho.\ n_1 \bowtie n_2 \end{array}$$

The abstract assignment of an expression $e \in \mathit{Expr}_V$ to a variable $x \in V$ is modelled by the operator $[\![x := e]\!]^\sharp : \mathbb{D}_V \to \mathbb{D}_V$.

$$\{\rho[x \mapsto v] \mid \rho \in \gamma(d) \wedge v \in [\![e]\!]_\rho\} \subseteq \gamma([\![x := e]\!]^\sharp(d))$$

The set of environments for which a guard $t \in \mathit{Guard}_V$ is true may be over-approximated by $\mathit{assume}^\sharp(t)$. Formally, the following holds:

$$\{\rho \mid [\![t]\!]_\rho\} \subseteq \gamma(\mathit{assume}^\sharp(t)).$$

The analyser used in the benchmarks is obtained by instantiating the operators described above with the domain of convex polyhedra [10]. In addition, the analyser uses a widening operator whose purpose is to ensure the termination of fixpoint iterations—this operator is therefore not needed at checking time.

2.3 Constraint-Based Specification

The bytecode analysis is defined by specifying for each bytecode an abstract transfer function which maps abstract states to abstract states (for non-jumping intraprocedural instructions at least). The abstract states are pairs of the form $(s^\sharp, l^\sharp)$ where $l^\sharp$ is a relation between local, global and auxiliary variables and $s^\sharp$ is an abstract stack whose elements are symbolic expressions built from these variables. More precisely, the analysis manipulates the following sets of variables:

R: set of local variables $r_0, \dots, r_{|R|-1}$ of methods,
R_0: set of old local variables $r_0^{old}, \dots, r_{|R|-1}^{old}$ of methods, representing their initial values at the beginning of method execution,
S: set of static fields $f_0, \dots, f_{|S|-1}$ of the program,
S_0: set of old static fields $f_0^{old}, \dots, f_{|S|-1}^{old}$ of the program used to model values of static fields at the beginning of method execution,
A: set of auxiliary variable $aux_0, \dots, aux_{|A|-1}$ used to keep track of results of methods in the symbolic operand stack.

Moreover, we use a "primed" version X' of the variable set X for renaming purposes. For each method the analysis computes a signature *Pre* $\rightarrow$ *Post* whose informal meaning is

> if the method is called with in a context where its arguments and the static fields satisfy the property *Pre* then if the method returns, then its result, its arguments, and the initial and final values of static fields satisfy the property *Post*.

Preconditions are chosen by over-approximating the context in which each method may actually be invoked. Additionally the analysis computes at each control point of each method a local invariant between the current (R) and initial (R_0) values of local variables, the current (S) and initial (S_0) values of static fields, and some auxiliary variables (A) which are used temporarily to remember results of method calls which are still on the stack.

The stack of symbolic expressions is used to "decompile" the operations on the operand stack. For example, for the instruction *Load* r that fetches the value of local variable r, the analysis just pushes the symbolic expression r onto the abstract stack $s^\sharp$. More generally, the effect of most instructions can be represented symbolically and only the comparisons and assignment to variables require updating the relation $l^\sharp$ between variables. In a polyhedron-based analysis this kind of symbolic manipulation [24,21] is a substantial saving.

Definition 1 (Abstract domain). *The abstract value for a program P is described by an element $(Pre, Post, Loc)$ of the lattice*

$$\begin{aligned} State^\sharp &= (Meth \rightarrow \mathbb{D}_{R_0+S_0}) \times \big(Meth \rightarrow \mathbb{D}_{R_0+S_0+S+\{res\}}\big) \\ &\times \big(Meth \times \mathbb{N} \rightarrow \big(Expr^\star_{R+S+A} \times \mathbb{D}_{R_0+S_0+R+S+A}\big) + \{\bot\}\big) \end{aligned}$$

The analysis result is specified as a solution of a constraint (inequation) system associated to each program. The constraint system is given in Fig. 2. Array references are abstracted by the length of the array they point to. As a consequence, the instruction *Newarray* which takes an integer n on top of the stack and replaces it with a reference to a newly allocated array of length n, is simply

instr	F_{instr}
Nop	$(s^\sharp, l^\sharp) \to (s^\sharp, l^\sharp)$
Ipush n	$(s^\sharp, l^\sharp) \to (n :: s^\sharp, l^\sharp)$
Pop	$(e :: s^\sharp, l^\sharp) \to (s^\sharp, l^\sharp)$
Dup	$(e :: s^\sharp, l^\sharp) \to (e :: e :: s^\sharp, l^\sharp)$
Iadd	$(e_2 :: e_1 :: s^\sharp, l^\sharp) \to (e_2 + e_1 :: s^\sharp, l^\sharp)$
Isub	$(e_2 :: e_1 :: s^\sharp, l^\sharp) \to (e_2 - e_1 :: s^\sharp, l^\sharp)$
Imult	$(e_2 :: e_1 :: s^\sharp, l^\sharp) \to (e_2 \times e_1 :: s^\sharp, l^\sharp)$
Idiv	$(e_2 :: e_1 :: s^\sharp, l^\sharp) \to (e_2 / e_1 :: s^\sharp, l^\sharp)$
Ineg	$(e :: s^\sharp, l^\sharp) \to (0 - e :: s^\sharp, l^\sharp)$
Iinput	$(s^\sharp, l^\sharp) \to (? :: s^\sharp, l^\sharp)$
Load r	$(s^\sharp, l^\sharp) \to (r :: s^\sharp, l^\sharp)$
Store r	$(e :: s^\sharp, l^\sharp) \to (s^\sharp[?/r], [\![r := e]\!]^\sharp(l^\sharp))$
Getstatic f	$(s^\sharp, l^\sharp) \to (f :: s^\sharp, l^\sharp)$
Putstatic f	$(e :: s^\sharp, l^\sharp) \to (s^\sharp[?/f], [\![f := e]\!]^\sharp(l^\sharp))$
Iinc r n	$(s^\sharp, l^\sharp) \to (s^\sharp[r - n/r], [\![r := r + n]\!]^\sharp(l^\sharp))$
Newarray	$(e :: s^\sharp, l^\sharp) \to (e :: s^\sharp, l^\sharp)$
Arraylength	$(e :: s^\sharp, l^\sharp) \to (e :: s^\sharp, l^\sharp)$
Iaload	$(e_2 :: e_1 :: s^\sharp, l^\sharp) \to (? :: s^\sharp, l^\sharp)$
Iastore	$(e_3 :: e_2 :: e_1 :: s^\sharp, l^\sharp) \to (s^\sharp, l^\sharp)$

$$\frac{m[p] = instr \notin \{Goto\ p', If\_icmp\ cond\ p', Invoke\ m', Return\}}{F_{instr}(Loc(m,p)) \sqsubseteq Loc(m, p+1)}\,[\mathsf{Intra}]$$

$$\frac{m[p] = Goto\ p'}{Loc(m,p) \sqsubseteq Loc(m,p')}\,[\mathsf{Goto}]$$

$$\frac{m[p] = If\_icmp \bowtie p' \quad Loc(m,p) = (e_2 :: e_1 :: s^\sharp, l^\sharp)}{(s^\sharp, assume^\sharp(e_1 \bowtie e_2) \sqcap^\sharp l^\sharp) \sqsubseteq Loc(m,p')}\,[\mathsf{If1}]$$

$$\frac{m[p] = If\_icmp \bowtie p' \quad Loc(m,p) = (e_2 :: e_1 :: s^\sharp, l^\sharp)}{(s^\sharp, assume^\sharp(e_1 \overline{\bowtie} e_2) \sqcap^\sharp l^\sharp)) \sqsubseteq Loc(m,p+1)}\,[\mathsf{If2}]$$

$$\frac{m[p] = Invoke\ m' \quad n = nbArgs(m') \quad Loc(m,p) = (e_{n-1} :: \cdots :: e_0 :: s^\sharp, l^\sharp)}{\left(\exists_{R+S_0+A}\left(\bigsqcap_{i=0}^{n-1} assume^\sharp(e_i = r_i^{old}) \sqcap \exists_{R_0}(l^\sharp)\right)\right)_{S \to S_0} \sqsubseteq Pre(m')}\,[\mathsf{Call1}]$$

$$\frac{\begin{array}{c} m[p] = Invoke\ m' \quad Loc(m,p) = (e_{n-1} :: \cdots :: e_0 :: s^\sharp, l^\sharp) \\ l^\sharp_{m'} = \exists_{R_0}\left(\bigsqcap_{i=0}^{n-1} assume^\sharp(e_i = r_i^{old})_{S \to S'} \sqcap Post(m')_{S_0 \to S'}\right) \end{array}}{\left(aux_j :: s^\sharp[?/aux_j], \exists_{S'+\{res\}}[\![aux_j := res]\!]\left(l^\sharp_{S \to S'} \sqcap\ l^\sharp_{m'}\right)\right) \sqsubseteq Loc(m,p+1)}\,[\mathsf{Call2}]$$

where p is the index of the j–th *Invoke* in m

$$\frac{m[p] = Return \quad Loc(m,p) = (e :: s^\sharp, l^\sharp)}{\exists_{R+A}([\![res := e]\!]^\sharp(l^\sharp)) \sqsubseteq Post(m)}\,[\mathsf{Return}]$$

$$\frac{m \in P \quad n = nbArgs(m)}{\bigsqcap_{i=0}^{|S|-1} assume^\sharp(f_i = f_i^{old}) \bigsqcap_{i=0}^{n-1} assume^\sharp(r_i^{old} = r_i) \sqcap Pre(m) \sqsubseteq Loc(m,0)}\,[\mathsf{Init}]$$

$$\frac{}{\top \sqsubseteq Pre(\mathrm{main})}\,[\mathsf{PreMain}]$$

Fig. 2. Analysis specification

abstracted by the identity function. The constraints [Call1] and [Call2] associated with a method call are the most complicated parts of the analysis. The complications partly arise because we have several kinds of variables (static fields, local and auxiliary variables) whose different scopes must be catered for. The analysis gives rise to two constraints: one that relates the state before the call to the pre-condition of the method ([Call1]) and one that registers the impact of the call on the state immediately following the call site ([Call2]).

When invoking a method m' from method m, we compute an abstract state that holds before starting executing m' and which constrains the $Pre(m')$ component of the abstract element describing P. This state registers that the n topmost expressions $e_1, \ldots, e_n$ on the abstract stack corresponds to the actual arguments that will be bound to the local variables of the callee m', by injecting the constraints $e_i = r_i^{old}$ into the relational domain and adding them to the current state as given by $l^\sharp$. Care must be exercised not to confound the parameters R_0 of the caller with the parameters of the callee, hence the projecting out of R_0 before joining the constraints. Furthermore, the local variables R, the initial values of static fields S_0 and the auxiliary variables A of method m have a different meaning in the context of method m' and are removed from the abstract state at the start of m' too. Finally, the current value of static fields S in m at the point of the method call becomes the initial value of the static fields when analysing m', hence the renaming of S into S_0.

The second rule [Call2] for *Invoke* describes the impact of the method call on its successor state. We use an auxiliary variable aux_j (chosen to be free in $s^\sharp$) to name the result of the method call which is pushed onto the stack. This variable is constrained to be equal to the variable *res* which receives the value returned by m'. The rest of the left-hand side expression of the constraint $l^\sharp_{S \to S'} \sqcap \exists_{R_0} (\ldots)$ serves to link the post-condition $Post(m')$ of the method with the state $l^\sharp$ of the call site. These are linked via the local variables r_i constrained to be equal to the argument expressions e_i and via the global static fields S. Again, some renaming and hiding of variables is required: *e.g.*, the initial values of the static fields in m', referred to by S_0, correspond to the values of the static fields before the call in the state $l^\sharp$ and in the expressions e_i, referred to by S. The renamings $S_0 \to S'$ and $S \to S'$, respectively, ensure that these values are identified.

The purpose of the invariants specified by the analysis is to enforce a suitable safety policy. In a context of array bound checking we must check that each array access is within the bounds of the array. As a consequence, for each occurence of an instruction *Iaload* or *Iastore* at a program point (m, pc), we test if the local invariant $Loc(m, pc)$ computed by the analysis ensures a safe array access. If these tests succeed we say that *Loc satisfies all safety checks.*

2.4 Inference

The constraint system presented in the previous section can be turned into a post-fixpoint problem by standard techniques. Consequently, the solutions of the system can be characterised as the set of post-fixpoints $\{x \mid F^\sharp(x) \sqsubseteq x\}$ of a suitable monotone function $F^\sharp$ operating on the global abstract domain

$State^\sharp$ of the analysis. Computing such a post-fixpoint is then the role of chaotic iterations [8]. Iteration is sped up by using widening on well-chosen control points. Neither the iteration strategy nor the widening operators belong to the Trusted Computing Base (TCB) since the validity of the result can be checked with a post-fixpoint test.

2.5 Soundness of the Analysis

To prove the soundness of the analysis we prove that for each method of the program, the signature *Pre* → *Post* and the local invariants in *Loc* that are specified by the constraint system, are correct with respect to the semantics of the execution of the method. The full proof has been machine checked in Coq (see [23]) in order to prove the soundness of the result checker. Details (see [4]) are omitted here for lack of space but we comment the main theorems now.

First we define the safety policy using semantic ingredients. A program is safe if all reachable states w.r.t. to the small-step semantics are distinct from the error state. The semantics enters the error state when an array is accessed via the instructions *Iaload* and *Iastore* with a value outside the array bounds.

```
Definition safe (p:program) : Prop :=
  ∀ st, reachable p st → st <> error.
```

The constraint based specification of Fig. 2 is turned into a suitable Coq predicate `AnalysisSolution` (including safety checks) and we prove that the existence of a suitable (*Pre*, *Post*, *Loc*) solution implies the safety of the program.

```
Theorem sound_analysis : ∀ p loc pre post,
   AnalysisSolution p loc pre post → safe p.
```

The purpose of Section 3 is to define an executable checker able to check if a candidate (*Pre*, *Post*, *Loc*) is a solution to the constraint based specification. The candidate is included in a certificate `cert` with extra information that we will describe in the next section.

```
Theorem bin_checker_correct_wrt_analysis_spec : ∀ p cert,
  checker p cert = true →
  ∃ loc, ∃ pre, ∃ post, AnalysisSolution p loc pre post.
```

Combined together these two theorems prove the semantic soundness of the executable checker that can be run in Coq or extracted into a Caml version.

```
Theorem bin_checker_correct_wrt_semantic :
  ∀ p cert, checker p cert = true → safe p.
```

3 Result Checking of Polyhedral Operations

In this section, we show how to efficiently implement convex polyhedra operators using a result checking approach.

3.1 The Polyhedral Domain Revisited

Polyhedra can be represented as sets of linear constraints. For efficiency, it is desirable to keep these sets in normal form *i.e.,* without redundant constraints. For this purpose, polyhedra libraries maintain a dual description of polyhedra based on *generators* in which a convex polyhedron is the convex hull of a (finite) set of *vertices*, *rays* and *lines*. Vertices, rays and lines are respectively extremal points, infinite directions and bi-directional infinite directions of the polyhedron.

At the origin of the efficiency (and complexity) of convex polyhedra algorithms is Chernikova's algorithm which is used to maintain the coherence of the double description of polyhedra [7]. The main insight of our approach is that we develop a checker which only uses the constraint description of polyhedra and which never needs to detect redundant constraints. Moreover, projections are not computed but delayed using a set of extra *existential* variables. More precisely, our polyhedra are represented by a list of linear expression over two disjoint sets of variables V and E. Variables in $v \in V$ are genuine variables. The set E is fixed. Variables $e \in E$ are (existential) variables that represent dimensions which have been projected out.

Definition 2. *Let V and E be disjoint sets of variables.*

$$\mathbb{P}_V = Lin^{\star}_{V+E}$$

where $Lin_X = \{c_0 + c_1 \times x_1 + \cdots + c_n \times x_n \mid c_i \in \mathbb{Z}, x_i \in X\}$.

Given $es \in \mathbb{P}_V$, the concretisation function is defined by

$$\gamma(es) = \{\rho_{|V} \mid \rho \in (V+E) \to \mathbb{Z} \wedge \forall lc \in es, [\![lc \geq 0]\!]_\rho\}$$

Efficient Coq implementation of $\mathbb{P}_V$. We have implemented (and proved correct) a result checker for convex polyhedra based on an efficient implementation of $\mathbb{P}_V$. To ensure the efficiency of the checker, we have carefully fine-tuned algorithms and data-structures. Variables are coded by binary integers *i.e.,* the Coq `positive` type.

```
Inductive positive : Set
  := xH | x0 (p:positive) | xI (p:positive).
```

Variables in $v \in V$ start with a `x0` constructor while existential variables $v \in E$ start with a `xI` constructor. A linear expression $e \in Lin$ is coded by a radix tree whose node labels record integer coefficients of the linear expression.

```
Inductive tree : Set :=
  | Leaf
  | Node (left:tree) (label:Z) (right:tree).
```

Therefore, looking-up a variable coefficient can be done by following a path in the tree. This operation executes in time linear in the length of the variable *i.e.,* logarithmic in the number of variables. For efficiency again, Coq polyhedra $p \in \mathbb{P}_V$ are not simply lists of linear expressions but are dependent records which store: i) a list `lin_cstr` of linear constraints coded as trees, ii) a variable `fresh_v` $\in V$ for which all successors are fresh, iii) a variable `fresh_e` $\in E$ for which all successors are fresh, iv) a set `used_v` that stores the variables $v \in V$ that are used in `lin_cstr`, v) and all the proofs *i.e.*, the data-structure invariants, that ensure that `fresh_v` and `fresh_e` are really fresh and that the set `used_v` indeed over-approximates the variables used in `lin_cstr`.

Checking convex polyhedra operations. In the following, we show how to implement the polyhedral operations using (only) polyhedra in constraint form.

Renaming simply consists in applying the renaming to the expressions within the polyhedron. Because the existential variables belong to a disjoint set, no capture can occur.

Using Fourier-Motzkin elimination (see *e.g.*, [19]), **projections** can be computed directly over the constraint representation of polyhedra. However, in the worst case, the number of constraints grows exponentially in the number of variables to project. To solve this problem, we delay the projection and simply register them as existentially quantified. This is done by renaming these variables to fresh existential variables.

To compute **intersections**, care must be taken not to mix up the existential variables. To avoid captures, existentially variables are renamed to variables that are fresh for both polyhedra. Interestingly, with our tree encoding, renaming all the existential variables is a constant time operation. Thereafter, the intersection is obtained by concatenating the lists of linear expressions.

To implement the **assume** operator, the involved expressions are first linearised and the obtained linear inequalities are put into the form $e \geq 0$ where e now belongs to the set *Lin* defined above. A special care is taken to precisely handle euclidean division (which is the semantics we give to the division operator in this work). For instance, the expression $x = y/c$ where c is a strictly positive constant, gives rise to a polyhedron made of the linear constraints $c \cdot x \leq y$ and $y \leq c \cdot x + c - 1$. Dealing with the round-to-zero integer division can be done via a program transformation that does case analysis on the signs of the arguments. We do not detail this here.

Assignment can be expressed in terms of the previous operators. Given x' a fresh existential variable, we have:

$$[\![x := e]\!]^\sharp(P) = \left(\exists_{\{x\}} \left(P \sqcap \mathit{assume}^\sharp(x' = e)\right)\right)_{\{x'\} \to \{x\}}$$

The **least upper bound** operator *i.e.*, convex hull is the typical operation that is straightforward to implement using the generator representation of polyhedra. Instead of computing a convex hull, we follow the result certification methodology and provide a certificate polyhedron that is the result of the convex hull computation. Furthermore, our result checker need not check that the result is exactly the convex hull but only that it is an upper bound by doing a two inclusion tests.

To implement **inclusion tests**, we push the methodology further and use inclusion certificates. The form of certificates and their generation are described below.

3.2 Result Certification for Polyhedral Inclusion

Our inclusion checker $\sqsubseteq_{check}$ takes as input a pair of polyhedra (P, Q) and an inclusion certificate. It will only return true if the certificate contains enough information to conclude that P is indeed included in Q ($P \sqsubseteq Q$).

In practice, we only use our checker where Q does not contain existential variables (because Q is computed by the untrusted analyser). This allows us to reduce the problem of inclusion into n problems of polyhedron emptiness where n is the number of constraints in Q. Such a problem admits a nice result certification technique thanks to Farkas's lemma (see for instance [19]) that gives a notion of *emptiness* certificate for polyhedra.

Lemma 1 (Farkas Lemma). *Let $A \in \mathbb{Q}^{m \times n}$ and $b \in \mathbb{Q}^m$. The following statements are equivalent:*

- *For all $x \in \mathbb{Q}^n$, $\neg(A \cdot x \geq b)$*
- *There exists $ic \in \mathbb{Q}^{+m}$ satisfying $A^t \cdot ic = \bar{0}$ and $b^t \cdot ic > 0$.*

The soundness ($\Leftarrow$) proof is the easy part and is all that is needed in the machine-checked proof. The existence of a certificate ensures the infeasibility of the linear constraints and therefore that the corresponding polyhedron is empty.

Thus, an *inclusion certificate* $ic_1 :: \cdots :: ic_n$ for an entry (P, Q) is a collection of n vectors of $\mathbb{Q}^m$ (with $n = |Q|$) and checking each emptiness certificate ic_k consists of 1) computing a matrix-vector product ($A^t \cdot ic$); 2) verifying that the result is a null vector; 3) computing a scalar product ($b^t \cdot ic_k$); and 4) verifying that the result is strictly positive. All in all, the certificate checker runs in quadratic-time in terms of arithmetic operations for each emptiness certificate.

Moreover, certificate generation can be recast as a linear programming problem that can be efficiently solved by either the Simplex or interior point methods.

4 Implementation and Experiments

The relational bytecode analysis has been implemented in Caml and instantiated with the efficient NewPolka polyhedral library [12] as its relational abstract domain. The programs we analyse are genuine Java programs where unsupported instructions have been automatically replaced by conservative numerical instructions (*e.g.*, a *Getfield* is replaced by a sequence *Pop*; *Iinput*). *Iinput* is a dummy instruction placing an arbitrary value on top of the operand stack. The analyser then computes a solution to the constraint system generated from a program. From these invariants, loop headers and join points are extracted and the inclusion certificates required by the checker are produced using the Simplex algorithm. A binary form of loop headers, join point invariants and their inclusion certificates constitute the final program certificate.

As invariants computed by static analysers often contain more information than necessary for proving a particular safety policy *i.e.*, the absence of array out-of-bounds accesses, it is interesting to *prune* the analysis result and eliminate invariants that are useless for proving a given safety property. The advantages are twofold: invariants to check are smaller and their verification cheaper. We have applied the technique described in [5] for pruning constraint-based invariants, with some adaptations to deal with the interprocedural aspects of our polyhedral analysis. The algorithm is not described here for space reasons but can be found in the companion report [4].

The result checker for polyhedral analysis described in Section 2 and Section 3 has been implemented in Coq. For our benchmarks we consider a refined version of the safety property where all but a designated subset of array accesses are required to be correct.

For each program we compare the checking time with (before) and without (after) fixpoint pruning, using either an extracted checker (Caml) or the checker running in Coq. In the first approach the Coq result checker is automatically transformed into a Caml program by the Coq extraction mechanism. In the second approach, the result checker is directly run inside the reduction engine of Coq to compute a foundational proof of safety of the program (using the technique of proof by *reflection* [1]). Fig. 3 presents our experimental results. The benchmarks are relatively modest in size and it is well known that full-blown polyhedral analyses have scalability problems. Our analyser will not avoid this but can be instantiated with simpler relational domains such as *e.g.*, octagons, without having to change the checker. The programs and the analysis results can be found online [23] and replayed in Coq or with an extracted Caml checker. We consider two families of programs. The first one consists of benchmarks used by Xi to demonstrate the dependent type system for Xanadu [24]. For this family we automatically prove the absence of out-of-bound accesses. The second is taken from the Java benchmark suite SciMark for scientific and numerical computing where our polyhedral analysis prove safety for array accesses except for the more intricate multi-dimensional arrays representing matrices.

Two things are worth noticing. First, the checking time is very small (less than one second), which is especially noteworthy given that the checker is run in Coq. We clearly benefit here from our efficient implementation and the optimised reduction engine of Coq [11]. Compared to the extracted version, the Coq verifier has at most a factor 10 of efficiency penalty. Second, pruning can halve the

	size	score	certificate size		checking time (Caml)		checking time (Coq)	
Program			before	after	before	after	before	after
BSearch	80	100%	20	11	2.0	1.4	14.1	11.6
HeapSort	143	100%	65	25	6.1	3.7	45.0	35.5
QuickSort	276	100%	90	42	144.5	128.7	1036.7	974.0
Random	883	83%	50	31	7.3	8.0	46.9	44.3
Jacobi	135	50%	31	10	1.6	1.7	12.8	9.2
LU	559	45%	206	96	20.1	17.4	100.5	91.5
SparseCompRow	90	33%	34	6	1.5	1.1	10.3	6.1
FFT	591	78%	194	50	38.8	22.7	263.2	193.8

Fig. 3. Size in number of instructions, score in ratio succeeded checks / total checks, certificates in number of constraints, time in milliseconds

number of constraints to verify. This reduction can sometimes but not always produce a similar reduction in checking time. The reduction is especially visible when the analyser tends to generate huge invariants which cannot be exploited. This is *e.g.*, the case for FFT where the analyser approximates an exponential with a complex polyhedron.

As part of the Mobius project and collaboration with Pierre Crégut from France Télécom, we have experimented with using the polyhedral result checker to check array bounds on a mobile phone. This is part of the Mobius demo that is available online[1]. The experiment shows that it is feasible to perform extended bytecode verification with the polyhedral certificates that we have developed.

5 Related Work

A number of relational abstract domains (octagons [16], convex polyhedra [10], polynomial equalities [17]) have been proposed with various trade-offs between precision and efficiency, and intra-procedural relational abstract interpretation for high-level imperative languages is by now a mature analysis technique. However, to the best of our knowledge the present work is the first extension of this to an inter-procedural analysis for bytecode. Dependent type systems for Java-style bytecode for removing array bounds checks have been proposed by Xi and Xia [25]. The analysis of the stack uses singleton types to track the values of stack elements, in the same spirit as our symbolic stack expressions. The analysis is intra-procedural and does not consider methods (they are added in a later work [24] which also adds a richer set of types). The type checking relies on loop invariants. We have run our analysis on the example Xanadu programs given by Xi and have been able to infer the invariants necessary for verifying safe array access automatically.

The area of certified program verifiers is an active field. Wildmoser, Nipkow *et al.* [22] were the first to develop a fully certified VCGen within Isabelle/HOL for verifying arithmetic overflow in Java bytecode. The certification of abstract interpreters has been developed by Pichardie *et al.* [18,6]. Lee *et al.* [14] have certified the type analysis of a language close to Standard ML in LF and Leroy [15] has certified some of the data flow analyses of a compiler back-end. Wildmoser *et al.* [21] certify a VCGen that uses untrusted interval analysis for producing invariants and that relies on Isabelle/HOL decision procedures to check the verification conditions generated with the help of these invariants. Their technique for analysing bytecode is close to ours in that they also use symbolic expressions to analyse the operand stack and the main contribution of the work reported here with respect to theirs is to develop this result checking approach for a fully relational analysis.

6 Conclusions and Future Work

This paper demonstrates the feasibility of an interprocedural relational analysis which automatically infers polyhedral loop invariants and pre-/post-condition for

[1] `http://mobius.inria.fr/`

programs in an imperative bytecode language. To simplify the checking of these invariants, we have devised a result checker for polyhedra which uses inclusion certificates (issued from a result due to Farkas) instead of computing convex hulls of polyhedra at join points. This checker is much simpler to prove correct mechanically than the polyhedral analyser and provides a means of building a foundational proof carrying code that can make use of industrial strength relational program analysis.

Future work concerns extensions to incorporate richer domains of properties such as disjunctive completions of linear domains or non-linear (polynomial) invariants. Using propositional reasoning, checking disjunctive invariants can be reduced to emptiness tests. As a result, parts of the polyhedral checker could be reused. Emptiness certificates from Section 3.2 can be generalised to deal with non-linear inequalities [3]. However, the analyses for *inferring* such properties are in their infancy. On a language level, the challenge is to extend the analysis to cover the object oriented aspects of Java bytecode. The inclusion of static fields and arrays in our framework provides a first step in that direction but a full extension would notably require an additional alias analysis.

References

1. Allen, S.F., Constable, R.L., Howe, D.J., Aitken, W.E.: The semantics of reflected proof. In: Proceedings of the Fifth Annual IEEE Symposium on Logic in Computer Science, pp. 95–105. IEEE Computer Society, Los Alamitos (1990)
2. Barthe, G., Dufay, G.: A tool-assisted framework for certified bytecode verification. In: Wermelinger, M., Margaria-Steffen, T. (eds.) FASE 2004. LNCS, vol. 2984, pp. 99–113. Springer, Heidelberg (2004)
3. Besson, F.: Fast reflexive arithmetic tactics: the linear case and beyond. In: Altenkirch, T., McBride, C. (eds.) TYPES 2006. LNCS, vol. 4502, pp. 48–62. Springer, Heidelberg (2006)
4. Besson, F., Jensen, T., Pichardie, D., Turpin, T.: Result certification for relational program analysis. Research Report 6333, Inria (2007), `http://hal.inria.fr/inria-00166930/`
5. Besson, F., Jensen, T., Turpin, T.: Small witnesses for abstract interpretation based proofs. In: De Nicola, R. (ed.) ESOP 2007. LNCS, vol. 4421, pp. 268–283. Springer, Heidelberg (2007)
6. Cachera, D., Jensen, T., Pichardie, D., Rusu, V.: Extracting a Data Flow Analyser in Constructive Logic. Theoretical Computer Science 342(1), 56–78 (2005)
7. Chernikova, N.V.: Algorithm for finding a general formula for the non-negative solutions of a system of linear inequalities. U.S.S.R Comp. Mathematics and Mathematical Physics 5(2), 228–233 (1965)
8. Cousot, P., Cousot, R.: Abstract interpretation: A unified lattice model for static analysis of programs by construction of approximations of fixpoints. In: Proc. of 4th ACM Symp. on Principles of Programming Languages, pp. 238–252. ACM Press, New York (1977)
9. Cousot, P., Cousot, R., Feret, J., Mauborgne, L., Miné, A., Monniaux, D., Rival, X.: The Astrée analyser. In: Sagiv, M. (ed.) ESOP 2005. LNCS, vol. 3444, pp. 21–30. Springer, Heidelberg (2005)

10. Cousot, P., Halbwachs, N.: Automatic discovery of linear restraints among variables of a program. In: Proc. of 5th ACM Symp. on Principles of Programming Languages (POPL 1978), pp. 84–97. ACM Press, New York (1978)
11. Grégoire, B., Leroy, X.: A compiled implementation of strong reduction. In: Proc. of the 7th ACM international conference on Functional programming (ICFP 2002), pp. 235–246. ACM Press, New York (2002)
12. Jeannet, B., the Apron team: The Apron library (2007)
13. Klein, G., Nipkow, T.: Verified Bytecode Verifiers. Theoretical Computer Science 298(3), 583–626 (2002)
14. Lee, D.K., Crary, K., Harper, R.: Towards a mechanized metatheory of Standard ML. In: Proc. of 34th ACM Symp. on Principles of Programming Languages (POPL 2007), pp. 173–184. ACM Press, New York (2007)
15. Leroy, X.: Formal certification of a compiler back-end or: programming a compiler with a proof assistant. In: Proc. of the 33rd ACM Symp. on Principles of Programming Languages, pp. 42–54. ACM Press, New York (2006)
16. Miné, A.: The octagon abstract domain. Higher-Order and Symbolic Computation 19, 31–100 (2006)
17. Müller-Olm, M., Seidl, H.: Precise interprocedural analysis through linear algebra. In: Proc. of 31st ACM Symp. on Principles of Programming Languages (POPL 2004), pp. 330–341. ACM Press, New York (2004)
18. Pichardie, D.: Interprétation abstraite en logique intuitioniste: extraction d'analyseurs Java certifiés. PhD thesis, Université de Rennes 1 (2005)
19. Schrijver, A.: Theory of Linear and Integer Programming. Wiley, Chichester (1998)
20. Wasserman, H., Blum, M.: Software reliability via run-time result-checking. Journal of the ACM 44(6), 826–849 (1997)
21. Wildmoser, M., Chaieb, A., Nipkow, T.: Bytecode analysis for proof carrying code. In: Proc. of 1st Workshop on Bytecode Semantics, Verification and Transformation, ENTCS (2005)
22. Wildmoser, M., Nipkow, T.: Asserting bytecode safety. In: Sagiv, M. (ed.) ESOP 2005. LNCS, vol. 3444, pp. 326–341. Springer, Heidelberg (2005)
23. The Coq development of the work, `http://www.irisa.fr/celtique/ext/polycert/`
24. Xi, H.: Imperative Programming with Dependent Types. In: Proc. of 15th IEEE Symposium on Logic in Computer Science (LICS 2000), pp. 375–387. IEEE, Los Alamitos (2000)
25. Xi, H., Xia, S.: Towards Array Bound Check Elimination in Java Virtual Machine Language. In: Proc. of CASCOON 1999, pp. 110–125 (1999)

A Novel Resource-Driven Job Allocation Scheme for Desktop Grid Environments*

Paolo Bertasi, Alberto Pettarin, Michele Scquizzato, and Francesco Silvestri

Department of Information Engineering,
University of Padova, Padova, Italy
{bertasi,pettarin,scquizza,silvest1}@dei.unipd.it

Abstract. In this paper we propose a novel framework for the dynamic allocation of jobs in grid-like environments, in which such jobs are dispatched to the machines of the grid by a centralized scheduler. We apply a new, full resource-driven approach to the scheduling task: jobs are allocated and (possibly) relocated on the basis of the matching between their resource requirements and the characteristics of the machines in the grid. We provide experimental evidence that our approach effectively exploits the computational resources at hand, successfully keeping the completion time of the jobs low, even without having knowledge of the actual running times of the jobs.

1 Introduction

Groups of distributed, heterogeneous computational resources, called *Grids* [9], have recently emerged as popular platforms to tackle large-scale computationally-intensive problems in science, engineering, and commerce. The desktop grid computing technology permits to exploit the idle computational resources of a large amount of non-dedicated heterogeneous machines within a single organization or scattered across several administrative domains.

In order to properly exploit the potential of these grid systems, key services such as resource management and scheduling are needed. Indeed, effectively matching tasks with the available resources is a major challenge for a grid computing system because of the heterogeneous, dynamic and autonomous nature of the grid, and a great deal of research concerning scheduling strategies capable of fully exploiting computational grids has been conducted.

In this paper, we propose a novel allocation scheme in which job and resource characteristics are captured together in the scheduling strategy, without resorting to the knowledge of the running times of the jobs, which usually are not known in advance. To this end, each machine that joins the grid is represented

* This work was supported, in part, by the European Union under the FP6-IST/IP Project AEOLUS, by MIUR of Italy under project AlgoDEEP, and by University of Padova under Projects CPDA099949 and STPD08JA32. Part of this work was done while the second author was visiting the Department of Computer Science of Brown University, USA, supported by "Fondazione Ing. Aldo Gini", Padova, Italy.

M. Wirsing, M. Hofmann, and A. Rauschmayer (Eds.): TGC 2010, LNCS 6084, pp. 268–283, 2010.

by a d-dimensional *speed vector*, whose components are numerical values which quantify features of the system such as CPU clock, and disk/network bandwidth. Similarly, each user submitting a job characterizes the computational properties of his task by giving the estimated percentages of how the operations of the job will "distribute" among the features of the machines. For example, and with respect to the three aforementioned features, a pure CPU intensive task might be described with a triplet similar to $\langle 1, 0, 0 \rangle$, while a job dealing with a local large data set might be represented by $\langle 0.4, 0.6, 0 \rangle$. Then, a quantity similar, in spirit, to the inner product between the vector of the job and the speed vector of a machine m provides a quantitative measure of the suitability of the machine for the job, with the job being dispatched to the machine which guarantees the highest score. Allocation is *centralized*, that is, one node in the system acts as a scheduler and makes all the load balancing decisions, and *on-line*, as jobs must be assigned upon their arrival. Moreover, scheduling is *dynamic*, since we allow the grid scheduler to migrate a job (we assume we are dealing with *preemptable* jobs) as soon as the completion of a job in a host or a variation of the load due to the machine owner might make some re-assignments fruitful. (Hence, load re-balancing is event-driven, while in most systems it is simply performed through periodic rescheduling.) We consider a finite-size temporal window of job arrivals with the implicit goal of keeping as low as possible the *makespan* of the schedule, that is, the completion time of the job that finishes last.

Previous work already showed how taking into account all features of the jobs in the scheduling activity leads to good performances. However, we argue that no one of the existing resource-aware allocators relies upon a score mechanism for machine-job pairs which is effective (in that it fully leverages knowledge about job and machine characteristics to assign the former to the host that best meets the user requirements), fair, dynamic, and easy to use at the same time.

Related work. Since most variants of the task scheduling problem are NP-complete [10], a great deal of effort has been devoted to the development of approximation and heuristic algorithms (see, e.g., [12,17,20,5,15]). However, these works make the strong assumption that perfect knowledge of how long each job will run is known at the time of scheduling, while our strategy does not require this knowledge; indeed users' runtime estimates are notoriously inaccurate [7], and it seems that users are generally incapable of providing more accurate estimates [14], with the problem being worsened by the heterogeneity of the machines of a grid. Moreover, the estimates required by our allocator to the user are completely machine-independent.

For these reasons, most real grid brokering strategies rely on a suitable mapping of user jobs to hosts according to the requirements of the former and to the properties of the latter. A number of grid middleware and management mechanisms have been designed to this end. Condor [18] provides a general resource selection mechanism based on the ClassAd [21], a language that allows resource owners to describe their resource and users to describe resource requests for their jobs. Specifically, all machines in the Condor pool use a resource offer ad to advertise their resource properties, both static and dynamic, such as CPU type, CPU speed, available RAM memory, physical location, and current average load, and users specify a resource request ad when submitting a job. The request consists of the set of minimal resources needed to run the job, along with a field in which the user specifies the function to be maximized by the broker. (ClassAd has also been extended to allow users to specify aggregate resource properties, e.g., in [19].) Condor acts as a broker by matching user requests with appropriate resources. However, we notice that our approach is simpler to use for the user, as the information required for the matching is simply an estimated repartition of the machine capabilities to be exploited. In Globus [8], users describe required resources through a resource specification language (RSL) that is based on a predefined schema of the resources database. The task of mapping specifications to actual resources is performed by a resource allocator, which is responsible for coordinating the allocation and management of resources at multiple sites. The RSL allows users to provide very sophisticated resource requirements (while no analogous mechanism for resources exists), but this comes at the price of ease-of-use. The Application Level Scheduling project (AppLeS [3]) uses the performance model provided by users to schedule applications. Key to the AppLeS approach is that resources in the system are evaluated in terms of predicted capacities at execution time, as well as their potential for satisfying application resource requirements. In the Nimrod/G system [1] the scheduling policy is driven by an economic model which supports user-defined deadline and "budget" constraints for schedule optimizations, and maps a job to the lowest-cost resource able to meet its deadline. Again, an effective utilization by the user is not immediate. In the work of Khoo *et al.* [13], jobs and resources are mapped in a multi-dimensional space, and nearest neighbor searches are conducted by the scheduling algorithm, with a job being dispatched to its nearest machine in such a space. While being quite similar to ours, their strategy does not consider job relocation.

Our contribution. In this paper we introduce a new resource-driven allocation scheme for grid environments, in which the scheduling mechanism assigns jobs to machines that are best suited for their resource requirements without knowing their actual running times. We describe two different schemes: the first, called GREEDY allocation scheme, greedily maps and relocates job to the machine which represents the best match, while the second, termed SOCIAL allocation scheme, performs the choice that best affect the "social welfare". We set up a grid simulation environment to demonstrate the efficacy of the proposed scheduling solution. Indeed, experimental results give evidence that our algorithms perform effectively the allocation task, that is, the allocation is fair, balanced, and the resulting makespan is kept low. Moreover, we show that the second outperforms the first in many cases of interest for real-life scenarios.

Paper organization. The rest of the paper is organized as follows. Section 2 describes the model and our algorithms for allocation and relocation. In Section 3, experimental results are presented which provide evidence of the effectiveness of our approach. Finally, in Section 4 we draw some conclusions and discuss directions for future work.

2 The Framework

In this section we first provide a simple but effective model of a desktop grid environment, and then describe two procedures for job allocation and relocation which assign a job to the machine that best suits the job requirements according to two different criteria: a selfish one (from the point of view of the job), which we simply call GREEDY allocator, and a "more altruistic" one, the SOCIAL allocator.

2.1 The Model

We represent a computational grid as a collection of heterogeneous machines: each machine $m \in \mathcal{M}$ can perform $d > 0$ types of "real-world" operations (e.g., CPU instructions, read/write data from/to disk, receive/send data through the network) at rates defined by its *speed vector* $\boldsymbol{S}_m$. Specifically, $\boldsymbol{S}_m$ is a d-dimensional vector where component $\boldsymbol{S}_m[i]$, for $0 \leq i < d$, represents the number of *type-i* operations that can be performed by m in a time unit (e.g., CPU frequency, disk, network bandwidth). Each machine performs at most one operation at a given time instant, that is, we ignore any form of concurrency among operations: this is a worst-case scenario since in general some operation types can be (partially) performed in parallel on modern machines. To model the fact that some of the computational power of machine m is used by its *owner*, we introduce the *owner load* λ_m, with $0 \leq \lambda_m \leq 1$, which represents the fraction of resources of m devoted to the owner's needs: in other words, we suppose that all the rates in $\boldsymbol{S}_m$ are multiplied by a factor $(1 - \lambda_m)$. We allow the owner load to change dynamically over time. Note that we are implicitly assuming that the owner load impacts on *each* component of the machine. Of course, this might not be true in specific scenarios, for example when the machine owner always requires only a given type of resources (e.g. she just needs the CPU but not the disk resources). However, since the grid does not know the owner's computational requests, we choose to simply scale down *all* the components of a machine by the same factor. It deserves to be remarked that in most of previous work, a machine is either completely available (i.e., $\lambda_m = 0$) or completely not available (i.e., $\lambda_m = 1$), and any intermediate status is not taken into account.

A job j, which consists of $\ell_j \geq 1$ operations of the various types, is described by its *composition vector*, a d-dimensional unit vector whose component $\boldsymbol{C}_j[i]$, for $0 \leq i < d$, represents the percentage of type-j operations, measured as multiples of $\boldsymbol{W}[i]$, where $\boldsymbol{W}$ is the d-dimensional *weight vector*. The weight vector, which we assume to fix a priori, can be seen as a sort of "operation-exchange" unit system between the various components. Indeed, it implicitly defines a common "logical concurrency" between the various components, where one "logical operation" corresponds to $\boldsymbol{W}[i]$ "real-world" operations of the i-th component. Then, job j contains at most $\ell_j \cdot \boldsymbol{W}[i] \cdot \boldsymbol{C}_j[i]$ type-i operations. We observe that the model can be defined without the vector $\boldsymbol{W}$, however weights are needed for tuning the composition vector to reflect the actual effect on performance of each component. For example, suppose type-0 operations are numerous but fast and type-1 operations are few but slow: if $\boldsymbol{W}$ is not used (i.e., $\boldsymbol{W}[i] = 1$ for each i), we have $\boldsymbol{C}_j[0] >> \boldsymbol{C}_j[1]$ even if their influences on performance are comparable. Intuitively, $\boldsymbol{C}_j$ characterizes the computational properties of job j by giving the estimated percentages of utilization of each machine subsystem.

A machine can execute an arbitrary number of jobs[1], which are performed according to a round robin scheduler which assigns fixed-size time slices to each job, handling all processes without priority. For simplicity, we assume the time slice to be small in comparison to the overall task length. Under these assumptions, the *execution time* $t(j, m)$ of a new job j which starts on machine m can be reasonably estimated by

$$t(j,m) = \frac{\ell_j(n_m+1)}{1-\lambda_m} \sum_{i=0}^{d-1} \frac{\boldsymbol{W}[i]\boldsymbol{C}_j[i]}{\boldsymbol{S}_m[i]}, \tag{1}$$

where n_m is the number of jobs other than j running on m. (Note that both n_m and λ_m change dynamically, but we omit their dependence on time for ease of notation.) Clearly, the execution time of a job j has to be proportional to its length ℓ_j and it has to grow at the same rate of (n_m+1), due to the fair resource sharing mechanism. Conversely, it must be inversely proportional to the fraction $(1-\lambda_m)$ of the machine power not utilized by the owner and thus at the grid user's disposal. Finally, the summation is justified by the assumption that the execution time is split among the various components without overlapping.

Whenever n_m or λ_m change during the execution of j, we first calculate the number of remaining operations ℓ'_j, and then update the estimated execution time by replacing ℓ_j with ℓ'_j in Equation (1). (We assume that the composition of the non-executed operations reflects the composition vector $\boldsymbol{C}_j$.) Throughout the paper we denote by $\mathcal{J}_m$ the set of jobs running on machine m at the time instant under consideration.

When a new job is submitted to the grid, it is handled by the *allocator*, which reads its composition vector and assigns the job to a suitable machine according to the allocation scheme of choice[2]. The allocation is *dynamic* because we allow relocation of jobs upon the occurrence of events that modify the load of a machine, in particular when a machine completes the execution of a job, or when a owner load varies. In both cases, we suppose that the involved machine notifies the allocator of the change taking place.

It is important to recall that the parameters that characterize machines and jobs can be quickly estimated in a real scenario. The speed vector $\boldsymbol{S}_m$ of a new machine m can be determined automatically, reducing the burden of its owner willing to share the machine, through a *microbenchmarking* suite such as that of [4]: specifically, once a machine m joins the grid, the system performs a round

[1] Clearly, a job j cannot be executed on a machine m whose owner load λ_m is 1 (i.e., the machine is not available). Furthermore, if $\boldsymbol{S}_m[i] = 0$ for some $0 \le i < d$, then machine m cannot execute a job j with $\boldsymbol{C}[i] \ne 0$; for this reason, we suppose that $0/0 = 0$ (e.g., in the subsequent equation).

[2] For simplicity, in our model the allocation task is performed in a centralized fashion, however nothing impedes to implement it in a distributed way, for example, to improve the robustness of the whole system.

of microbenchmarking to derive the peak performance of m, which will be used to derive its $\boldsymbol{S}_m$. The same microbenchmarking suite, or faster heuristics on the CPU usage, can be used periodically for computing the owner load λ_m of the machine. To further reduce the specification burden to the user, the composition vector $\boldsymbol{C}_j$ of a new job j may be chosen by the user submitting the job by associating it to a label, corresponding to a certain composition vector. The label might be selected from a small, predefined set of labels, each related to the most common job types (e.g., CPU intensive jobs, jobs dealing with local large data sets, etc.), thus relieving the user of explicitly specifying the composition vector for his job (which additionally requires the knowledge of the weight vector). The aforementioned set of labels and the weight vector $\boldsymbol{W}$ can be determined in the initial set-up of the grid environment. We argue that we do not require the user submitting a job j to provide an estimation of ℓ_j, as the allocators we are going to describe do not rely upon its knowledge.

2.2 Allocation Procedures

In this section we describe two allocation procedures for our model which differ on the score function used to assign jobs to machines. When a new job j arrives, both allocators assign j to the machine m maximizing a given score function $f(j,m)$, which is differently defined in the two procedures. A key element in our allocators is the notion of affinity which is a measure of the suitability of a machine to execute a certain job. The *affinity* $\tau(j,m)$ of job j on machine m is defined as

$$\tau(j,m) = \frac{1-\lambda_m}{(n_m+1)\sum_{i=0}^{d-1} \boldsymbol{W}[i]\boldsymbol{C}_j[i]/\boldsymbol{S}_m[i]},$$

where n_m is the number of other jobs that are executing on m. The affinity depends on the time instant in which it is computed, since n_m and λ_m change dynamically; however, for notational simplicity, we omit the dependence on time from $\tau(j,m)$. As one can easily recognize, the affinity and the estimated completion time are related by the following formula:

$$t(j,m) = \frac{\ell_j}{\tau(j,m)}. \tag{2}$$

The GREEDY allocator relies on Equation (2), and simply sets its score function to $f(j,m) = \tau(j,m)$. Therefore, job j is assigned to the machine maximizing its affinity, and thus minimizing its execution time (despite of the allocator being unaware of the actual job length ℓ_j). However, this selfish approach ignores the fact that the execution times of the jobs running on m grow (or, by our definition, their affinities decrease).

In order to reduce the latter negative effect, we can correct the score function as follows, obtaining what we dubbed SOCIAL allocator:

$$f(j,m) = \tau(j,m) - \sum_{k\in\mathcal{J}_m} \frac{\tau(k,m)}{n_m+1}.$$

The term $\tau(k,m)/(n_m+1)$ denotes the decrease in affinity of job $k \in \mathcal{J}_m$ (i.e., already executing on m) if the new job j is assigned to m. The above equation provides a trade-off between the selfish approach where the job minimizes its execution time, and a social approach where the job is assigned to the machine where the execution times of preexisting jobs do not increase excessively.

In Section 3 we analyze experimentally the two approaches without relocation, and provide evidence that the makespan obtained with the SOCIAL allocator is in general better than the one with the GREEDY one.

2.3 Relocation Procedures

In this section we describe two relocator procedures, namely the GREEDY and SOCIAL relocators, which are similar to their allocation counterparts. They act similarly when a machine status changes, but differ on the implementation of function $f(j,m,m')$, which is used as a score for evaluating the migration of job j from machine m to machine m'. We describe how $f(j,m,m')$ is implemented by the two procedures after explaining the relocation mechanism.

The events that cause the invocation of the relocator are the following:

- The owner load of machine m increases. In this case, the relocator migrates a job in $\mathcal{J}_m$ into another machine m' in order to reduce the effect of the variation; job $j \in \mathcal{J}_m$ and machine m' are chosen so that $f(j,m,m')$ is maximized.
- The owner load of machine m decreases or a job in m terminates its execution. In this case, the relocator moves a job j from machine m' into m in order to use the available computational resources of machine m and at the same time to reduce the load of machine m'. Machine m' and job $j \in \mathcal{J}_{m'}$ are chosen so that function $f(j,m',m)$ is maximized.

To ensure that a prospective action leads to an actual improvement of the system state, function $f(j,m,m')$ is expressed as a relative gain with respect to the previous system state. This gain has to be greater than a given constant threshold $\theta > 0$. The meaning of θ is easy to understand: the lower θ, the more likely relocations occur, and vice versa. This stipulated relative threshold aims at modeling the cost of job migration, which also includes the intrinsic overhead of each preemption-and-resume step. Moreover, after a single event, the above procedure can be iterated until no improvement can be obtained or the maximum number of iterations N is reached (being N an a priori fixed constant).

In the GREEDY relocator, $f(j,m,m')$ is given by

$$f(j,m,m') = \frac{\tau(j,m') - \tau(j,m)}{\tau(j,m)},$$

where the affinities are computed at the instant where the load of m changes. In other words, the GREEDY relocator moves the job j which maximizes its relative affinity increment, that is, the job reaches the biggest relative decrease in execution time. As for the GREEDY allocator, this procedure does not take into account jobs already present on the machine where the job is migrated, whose execution times increase (and affinities decrease).

On the contrary, the SOCIAL relocator takes into account also the difference between the increase in affinity of jobs on m (since the number of jobs decreases) and the decrease in affinity of jobs on m' (since the number of jobs increases). The proposed score function takes the form

$$f(j, m, m') = \frac{\alpha_0(\Sigma_m - \Sigma'_m) + \alpha_1(\Sigma_{m'} - \Sigma'_{m'})}{\Sigma_m + \Sigma'_m},$$

where Σ'_m (respectively, $\Sigma'_{m'}$) and Σ_m (respectively, $\Sigma_{m'}$) denote the sum of affinities of jobs in m (respectively, m') before and after the migration of job j from m to m'. The coefficients

$$\alpha_0 = \frac{|\mathcal{J}_m|}{|\mathcal{J}_m| + |\mathcal{J}_{m'}|} \quad \text{and} \quad \alpha_1 = \frac{|\mathcal{J}_{m'}|}{|\mathcal{J}_m| + |\mathcal{J}_{m'}|}$$

are used for balancing the number of jobs among machines when m and m' contain similar workloads.

In the next section we show that the GREEDY and the SOCIAL relocators attain the same performances, independently of the adopted allocation procedure.

3 Experimental Results

In this section we experimentally compare the allocators and relocators described in previous section with a simple allocation scheme, referred to as MIN-NUM. The MIN-NUM allocator assigns a new job to the machine with the minimum number of running jobs at the arrival time, independently of job and machine characteristics. Similarly, the MIN-NUM relocator invoked on machine m moves a job from the machine m' with maximum $\mathcal{J}_{m'}$ to m if the load on m decreases (i.e., a job terminates its execution, or the owner load decreases), or moves a job from machine m into the machine m' with minimum $\mathcal{J}_{m'}$ if the load on m increases (i.e., the owner load increases); this invocation is executed at most N times for each invocation, where N is a suitable constant. This allocator scheme can be efficiently implemented, however it performs poorly as shown in the following examples. All the experiments are carried out through a Java simulator, whose source code might be obtained upon request to the authors.

We consider three types of operations: the components of a speed vector represent, in order, CPU frequency (in GHz), disk bandwidth (in MB/s), and network bandwidth (in KB/s). We consider two machine sets. The first one, named *synthetic grid*, consists of four machines characterized by the speed vectors $\boldsymbol{S}_0 = \langle 4, 100, 250 \rangle$, $\boldsymbol{S}_1 = \boldsymbol{S}_2 = \langle 2, 100, 250 \rangle$, and $\boldsymbol{S}_3 = \langle 1, 800, 250 \rangle$. The second one, named *AEOLUS grid*, models the AEOLUS testbed [2] and consists of 70 machines, whose speed vectors are given in Table 3 in the Appendix. The synthetic grid is used to enlighten some properties of allocators and relocators, while the simulations of the AEOLUS grid provide evidence of their performance in a real-world scenario.

To the best of our knowledge, publicly available workloads like those in Feitelson's Parallel Workloads Archive [6] do not consider job features such as those required by our framework, and hence the composition vectors used in our experiments are artificial, and described in Table 1. We note that $\boldsymbol{C}_0$ denotes a CPU intensive job, $\boldsymbol{C}_1$ a generic job which uses all operations, $\boldsymbol{C}_2$ a network intensive job, $\boldsymbol{C}_3$ and $\boldsymbol{C}_4$ disk intensive jobs. For simplicity, we say that a job is of type i, for $0 \leq i \leq 4$, if its composition vector is $\boldsymbol{C}_i$. The weight vector used in the experiments is $\boldsymbol{W} = \langle 2 \cdot 10^{-5}, 10^{-1}, 10^{-1} \rangle$. Since some studies (e.g., [16,11]) show that durations of real jobs are distributed according to a power law, we generate job lengths using a discrete representation of a power law.

Table 1. Job composition vectors adopted in this section.

Type	CPU	Disk	Network	Description
$\boldsymbol{C}_0$	1.0	0.0	0.0	CPU intensive
$\boldsymbol{C}_1$	0.7	0.1	0.2	Generic (all operations)
$\boldsymbol{C}_2$	0.6	0.0	0.4	Network intensive
$\boldsymbol{C}_3$	0.5	0.5	0.0	Disk intensive I
$\boldsymbol{C}_4$	0.2	0.8	0.0	Disk intensive II

We remind that, when the load of a machine changes, the Greedy and Social relocators perform job migration until the relative gain of the score function $f(j, m, m')$ is bigger than θ (e.g., 5%), and no more than N job relocations might occur. In Figure 1, we analyze the behavior of Greedy and Social relocators for different values of N and θ, and of Min-Num for different N's. Each relocator is associated with its respective allocator. We use the synthetic grid described above, with the owner loads set to 0, and jobs described by composition vectors $\boldsymbol{C}_0$ and $\boldsymbol{C}_1$, which arrive uniformly in the time interval $[0, 100]$ s and whose lengths are generated according to a three-step discretization of a power law distribution (the exact description[3] is available in section "Job set 0" of Table 2). We notice that all the relocators exhibit small fluctuations (about 1%) when N or θ changes, and the Greedy and Social relocators are almost equivalent. For these reasons in the following experiments we set $N = 3$ for decreasing the computational cost of relocation, and $\theta = 10\%$ for justifying the migration cost (moving jobs with small score increments is not convenient since the migration costs may be bigger than the execution time saved after relocation). The difference between our relocators and the Min-Num one is small in the analyzed data set, however we later show that in a more general scenario the gap considerably increases. We performed other experiments, which are not reported for lack of space, where we analyze any allocator/relocator combination: in all cases the makespan remains almost constant changing N and θ and the Greedy and Social relocators provide the best makespans independently of the used allocator.

[3] In the paper we denote by $\mathcal{N}(\mu, \sigma)$ a Gaussian random variable with mean μ and standard deviation σ, and by $\mathcal{U}(i, j)$ an uniform random variable in the interval $[i, j]$.

Table 2. Lengths and arrival times of the job sets used in the three experiments.

Job type	Number of jobs	Length	Arrival time (in s)
		Job set 0 (Figure 1)	
C_0	200	24% with length $\mathcal{N}(400\text{k}, 8\text{k})$, 38% with length $\mathcal{N}(200\text{k}, 4\text{k})$, 38% with length $\mathcal{N}(100\text{k}, 2\text{k})$	$\mathcal{U}(0, 100)$
C_1	800	24% with length $\mathcal{N}(100\text{k}, 4\text{k})$, 38% with length $\mathcal{N}(50\text{k}, 2\text{k})$, 38% with length $\mathcal{N}(25\text{k}, 1\text{k})$	$\mathcal{U}(0, 100)$
		Job set 1 (Figure 2)	
C_0, C_4	500 per type	24% with length $\mathcal{N}(500\text{k}, 40\text{k})$, 38% with length $\mathcal{N}(250\text{k}, 20\text{k})$, 38% with length $\mathcal{N}(125\text{k}, 10\text{k})$	$\mathcal{U}(0, 1000)$
		Job set 2 (Figures 3 and 4)	
C_0, C_1 C_2, C_3	500 per type	20% with length $\mathcal{N}(250\text{k}, 75\text{k})$, 30% with length $\mathcal{N}(100\text{k}, 30\text{k})$, 30% with length $\mathcal{N}(40\text{k}, 12\text{k})$, 20% with length $\mathcal{N}(10\text{k}, 3\text{k})$	0, 25, 50, 75

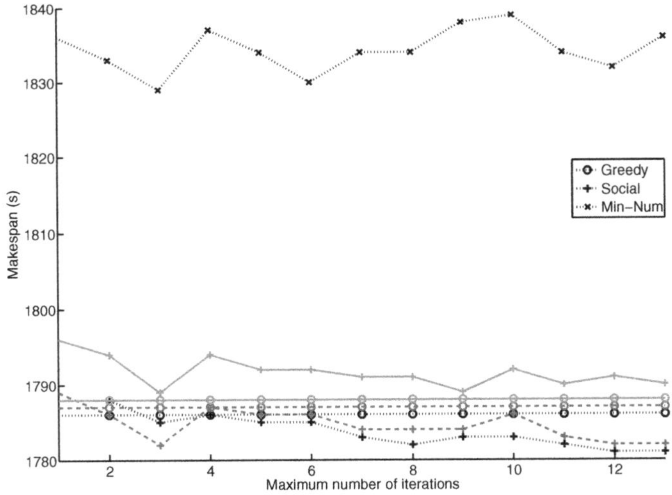

Fig. 1. Behavior of the GREEDY, SOCIAL and MIN-NUM with varying N (on x-axis) and θ (cyan solid curves $\theta = 10\%$, magenta dashed curves $\theta = 5\%$, black dotted curves $\theta = 1\%$). θ is not defined for MIN-NUM.

In Figure 2 we compare how the SOCIAL and MIN-NUM relocators respond to a variation of the owner load of a machine. We use the synthetic grid, and the job set composed of two job types, namely C_0 and C_4: jobs arrive uniformly in the interval $[0, 1000]$ s and their lengths are represented by a three-step discretization of a power law (more details described in section "Job set 1" of Table 2). The

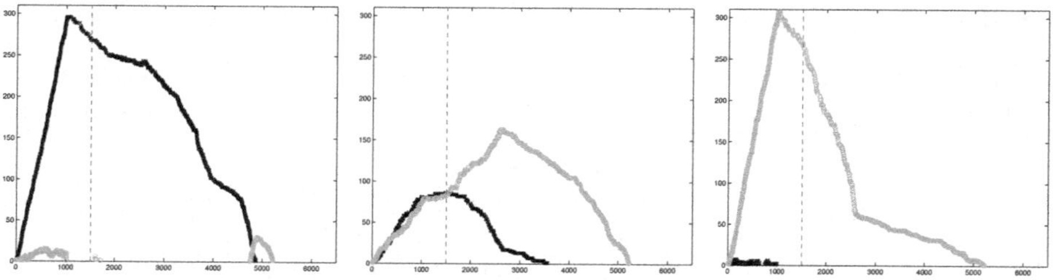

(a) The machine with S_0. **(b)** The machine with S_1. **(c)** The machine with S_3.

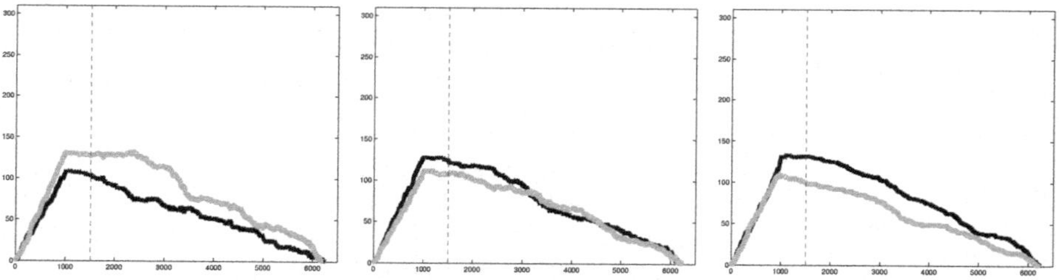

(d) The machine with S_0. **(e)** The machine with S_1. **(f)** The machine with S_3.

Fig. 2. Job distribution on the synthetic grid on machines described by speed vectors $\boldsymbol{S}_0$, $\boldsymbol{S}_1$, and $\boldsymbol{S}_3$ (we remind that $\boldsymbol{S}_1 = \boldsymbol{S}_2$): in (a), (b), and (c) under the SOCIAL relocator; in (d), (e), and (f) under the MIN-NUM relocator. In cyan jobs with composition vector $\boldsymbol{C}_4$; in black jobs with composition vector $\boldsymbol{C}_0$. The x-axis reports the elapsed time (range $[0, 6500]$ s), the y-axis the number of jobs on the machine (range $[0, 310]$).

owner load of all the four machines is initially set to 0, but the owner load of machine m with speed vector $\boldsymbol{S}_3$ increases to 0.95 at the time instant 1500 s, that is, it becomes *essentially* unavailable to the grid users. Plots in Figures 2(a), 2(b), and 2(c) show how jobs are distributed among machines with speed vectors $\boldsymbol{S}_0$, $\boldsymbol{S}_1$, and $\boldsymbol{S}_3$, respectively, under the SOCIAL relocator (the plot for machine $\boldsymbol{S}_2$ is omitted because it is identical to that of $\boldsymbol{S}_1$). A similar job distribution holds for the GREEDY relocator as well. Figures 2(d), 2(e), and 2(f) show job distribution under the MIN-NUM relocators in machines with speed vectors $\boldsymbol{S}_0$, $\boldsymbol{S}_1$, and $\boldsymbol{S}_3$, respectively. We notice that after the time instant 1500 s, the SOCIAL relocator begins to migrate jobs from m to other machines (with the GREEDY relocator exhibiting a similar behavior): indeed, the increasing number of jobs on the other machines is not due to new jobs, since no new job arrives after the time instant 1000 s. It is also interesting to note that jobs are distributed on machines according to their compositions: in particular, we observe that jobs of type $\boldsymbol{C}_4$ (in cyan), dealing with large local data sets (i.e., $\boldsymbol{C}_4[1] = 0.8$), are assigned by the allocator/relocator to m (i.e., $\boldsymbol{S}_3$), which has the fastest disk, until the change in its owner load makes it essentially unavailable.

We now analyze a more general scenario using the AEOLUS grid. Jobs are described by composition vectors $\boldsymbol{C}_0$, $\boldsymbol{C}_1$, $\boldsymbol{C}_2$, and $\boldsymbol{C}_3$; job lengths follow a four-step discrete discretization of a power law distribution, equal for all job types (see section "Job set 2" of Table 2). Since similar jobs in this environment are typically submitted in bursts, we consider four arrival times (0 s, 25 s, 50 s, and 75 s), and in each one only jobs described by the same composition vector arrive. Figure 3 provides the makespan (averaged on 5 simulation runs) of six allocation schemes (GREEDY, SOCIAL, MIN-NUM, each with and without the respective relocator), for any of the 4! orderings of job arrival times by job type. The mapping between permutation ID and the actual order of job types is provided in the Appendix (Table 4).

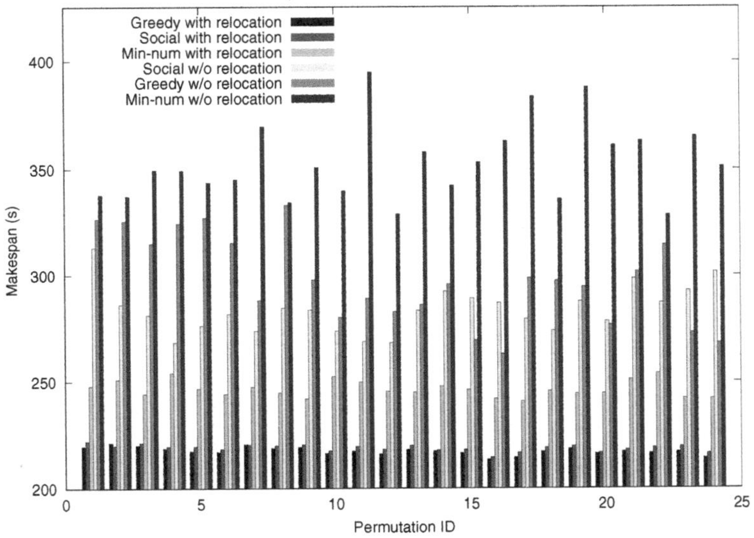

Fig. 3. Makespan on the AEOLUS grid of six allocation schemes (GREEDY, SOCIAL, MIN-NUM, each with and without the respective rebalancing), for each of the 4! permutations of job arrival times by job type (permutation IDs are listed in Table 4).

In the analyzed scenario, the GREEDY and SOCIAL relocators exhibit similar performances as noted before; in contrast, the MIN-NUM relocator experiences an average 10% performance loss. The experiment also provides evidence that, when relocation is not used for its high computational cost, the MIN-NUM should be avoided and the SOCIAL allocator is preferable to the GREEDY one: indeed, GREEDY wins over SOCIAL in 21% of the permutations with at most a 11% gap, while SOCIAL outperforms GREEDY on 79% of these instances, and the gap is more than 11% in 37% of the instances. It deserves to be noticed that SOCIAL beats GREEDY in particular in the first permutations, that is, when jobs with composition vector $\boldsymbol{C}_3$ are the last jobs submitted into the grid. The new jobs are allocated by the GREEDY allocator to machines with speed vector $\boldsymbol{S}_0$, since these machines have a smaller number of assigned jobs. However, the affinities of these jobs decrease considerably (then, their execution times increase) and they cannot be migrated to other machines since the relocator is disabled. This problem is minimized in the Social allocator since the decrease in affinity of other jobs is taken into account in the score function.

We conclude this section with Figure 4, where we added to the previous scenario some owner load variations. Specifically, the owner load of the four machines characterized by speed vectors $\boldsymbol{S}_0$, $\boldsymbol{S}_6$, $\boldsymbol{S}_{26}$, $\boldsymbol{S}_{19}$ increases to 0.95 at time instants 0 s, 60 s, 100 s, 125 s, respectively. With relocation, performances are similar to those described above regarding Figure 3 since the relocations spread jobs from the four "nearly unavailable" machines to the remaining 66 machines. In contrast, disabling relocations yields huge makespans, in particular under the Min-Num allocator since it does not take into account the owner load of a machine.

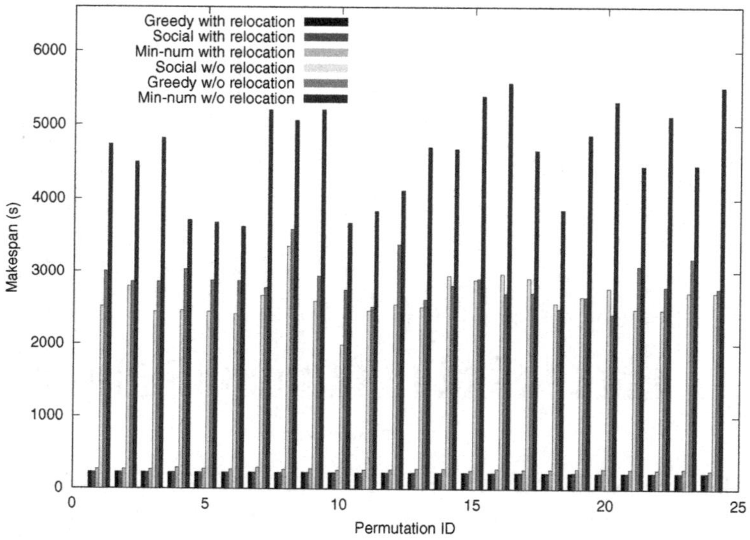

Fig. 4. Makespan on the AEOLUS grid of six allocation schemes (Greedy, Social, Min-Num, each with and without the respective rebalancing), for each of the 4! permutations of job arrival times by job type. The owner load of the four machines characterized by speed vectors $\boldsymbol{S}_0$, $\boldsymbol{S}_6$, $\boldsymbol{S}_{26}$, $\boldsymbol{S}_{19}$ increases to 0.95 at time instants 0 s, 60 s, 100 s, 125 s, respectively (permutation IDs are listed in Table 4).

4 Conclusions and Future Work

In this paper, we have proposed a new framework for resource allocation in desktop grid environments based on the idea of performing job assignments to the machines which best meet the computational requirements of the jobs. Within this framework, we have developed and compared two different allocation schemes, which attempt to minimize the overall system makespan, even without knowing the actual durations of the jobs submitted to the system. We have argued that our strategy results in a proper, fair, and balanced allocation of the jobs processed by the grid, and this translates into good results in terms of completion time of the jobs. The proposed framework can be extended in several ways: first, by introducing the concept of *domain* of a job, that is, allowing a job to choose, on the basis of their hardware or software capabilities (e.g., CPU architecture, amount of RAM and disk space, operating system installed, available software libraries), the subset of machines on which its computation can be carried out (notice that this simple extension would add a new combinatorial dimension to the problem, since both the allocation and the relocation choices would have to deal with intersecting domains); then, it would be useful, for robustness and scalability purposes, to implement our scheduler in a distributed fashion; finally, this approach deserves to be implemented in a real grid environment (such as the AEOLUS testbed), and possibly to compare its performances with other state-of-the-art resource brokering systems and time-driven scheduling strategies.

Acknowledgments. The authors would like to thank Andrea Pietracaprina and Geppino Pucci for helpful discussions and comments, and Joachim Gehweiler for his help on the AEOLUS testbed.

References

1. Abramson, D., Giddy, J., Kotler, L.: High performance parametric modeling with Nimrod/G: Killer application for the global grid? In: Proceedings of the 14th International Parallel & Distributed Processing Symposium, pp. 520–528. IEEE Computer Society, Los Alamitos (2000)
2. AEOLUS testbed website, `http://aeolus.cs.upb.de`
3. Berman, F., Wolski, R., Casanova, H., Cirne, W., Dail, H., Faerman, M., Figueira, S.M., Hayes, J., Obertelli, G., Schopf, J.M., Shao, G., Smallen, S., Spring, N.T., Su, A., Zagorodnov, D.: Adaptive computing on the grid using AppLeS. IEEE Transactions on Parallel & Distributed Systems 14(4), 369–382 (2003)
4. Bertasi, P., Bianco, M., Pietracaprina, A., Pucci, G.: Obtaining performance measures through microbenchmarking in a peer-to-peer overlay computer. International Journal of Computational Intelligence Research 4(1), 1–8 (2008)
5. Casanova, H., Legrand, A., Zagorodnov, D., Berman, F.: Heuristics for scheduling parameter sweep applications in grid environments. In: Proceedings of the 9th Heterogeneous Computing Workshop, pp. 349–363. IEEE Computer Society, Los Alamitos (2000)
6. Parallel Workloads Archive, `http://www.cs.huji.ac.il/labs/parallel/workload`
7. Feitelson, D.G., Weil, A.M.: Utilization and predictability in scheduling the IBM SP2 with backfilling. In: Proceedings of the 12th International Parallel Processing Symposium / 9th Symposium on Parallel and Distributed Processing, pp. 542–546. IEEE Computer Society, Los Alamitos (1998)
8. Foster, I., Kesselman, C.: Globus: A meta-computing infrastructure toolkit. International Journal of Supercomputer Applications 11(2), 115–128 (1997)
9. Foster, I., Kesselman, C. (eds.): The Grid 2: Blueprint for a New Computing Infrastructure, 2nd edn. Morgan Kaufmann, San Francisco (2003)
10. Garey, M.R., Johnson, D.S.: Computers and Intractability: A Guide to the Theory of NP-Completeness. W. H. Freeman, New York (1979)

11. Harchol-Balter, M., Downey, A.B.: Exploiting process lifetime distributions for dynamic load balancing. ACM Transactions on Computer Systems 15(3), 253–285 (1997)
12. Ibarra, O.H., Kim, C.E.: Heuristic algorithms for scheduling independent tasks on nonidentical processors. Journal of the ACM 24(2), 280–289 (1977)
13. Khoo, B.B., Veeravalli, B., Hung, T., Simon See, C.W.: A multi-dimensional scheduling scheme in a grid computing environment. Journal of Parallel and Distributed Computing 67(6), 659–673 (2007)
14. Lee, C.B., Schwartzman, Y., Hardy, J., Snavely, A.: Are user runtime estimates inherently inaccurate? In: Feitelson, D.G., Rudolph, L., Schwiegelshohn, U. (eds.) JSSPP 2004. LNCS, vol. 3277, pp. 253–263. Springer, Heidelberg (2005)
15. Lee, Y.C., Zomaya, A.Y.: Practical scheduling of bag-of-tasks applications on grids with dynamic resilience. IEEE Transactions on Computers 56(6), 815–825 (2007)
16. Leland, W., Ott, T.J.: Load-balancing heuristics and process behavior. ACM SIGMETRICS Performance Evaluation Review 14(1), 54–69 (1986)
17. Lenstra, J.K., Shmoys, D.B., Tardos, É.: Approximation algorithms for scheduling unrelated parallel machines. Mathematical Programming 46, 259–271 (1990)
18. Litzkow, M.J., Livny, M., Mutka, M.W.: Condor – a hunter of idle workstations. In: Proceedings of the 8th International Conference on Distributed Computing Systems, pp. 104–111. IEEE Computer Society, Los Alamitos (1988)
19. Liu, C., Yang, L., Foster, I., Angulo, D.: Design and evaluation of a resource selection framework for grid applications. In: Proceedings of the 11th IEEE International Symposium on High Performance Distributed Computing, pp. 63–72. IEEE Computer Society, Los Alamitos (2002)
20. Maheswaran, M., Ali, S., Siegel, H.J., Hensgen, D., Freund, R.F.: Dynamic mapping of a class of independent tasks onto heterogeneous computing systems. Journal Parallel and Distributed Computing 59(2), 107–131 (1999)
21. Raman, R., Livny, M., Solomon, M.: Matchmaking: Distributed resource management for high throughput computing. In: Proceedings of the 7th IEEE International Symposium on High Performance Distributed Computing, pp. 140–146. IEEE Computer Society, Los Alamitos (1998)

Appendix

In this appendix we provide the speed vectors of the machines in the AEOLUS grid, listed in Table 3, while Table 4 shows the mapping between permutation IDs and arrival times, used in Figures 3 and 4.

Table 3. Speed vectors of the 70 machines in the AEOLUS grid.

Speed vector	CPU (GHz)	Disk (MB/s)	Network (KB/s)
S_0	0.70	50	500
S_1	0.80	50	500
S_2	0.87	50	500
S_3	0.90	50	500
$S_4 - S_5$	0.93	50	500
S_6	1.00	60	500
S_7	1.30	60	500
S_8	1.40	60	500
S_9	1.67	75	500
$S_{10} - S_{15}$	1.70	70	500
S_{16}	1.80	70	500
$S_{17} - S_{19}$	2.00	100	500

Speed vector	CPU (GHz)	Disk (MB/s)	Network (KB/s)
S_{20}	2.20	100	500
S_{21}	2.40	100	500
S_{22}	2.40	100	1000
$S_{23} - S_{24}$	2.53	90	1000
S_{25}	2.60	90	1000
$S_{26} - S_{55}$	2.66	105	1000
$S_{56} - S_{61}$	2.80	85	500
$S_{62} - S_{63}$	2.83	100	500
$S_{64} - S_{65}$	3.00	80	500
$S_{66} - S_{67}$	3.10	80	500
$S_{68} - S_{69}$	3.20	80	500

Table 4. Arrival time of each job type for each permutation ID (see Figures 3 and 4).

ID	0 s	25 s	50 s	75 s
1	C_0	C_1	C_2	C_3
2	C_1	C_0	C_2	C_3
3	C_0	C_2	C_1	C_3
4	C_2	C_0	C_1	C_3
5	C_2	C_1	C_0	C_3
6	C_1	C_2	C_0	C_3
7	C_0	C_1	C_3	C_2
8	C_1	C_0	C_3	C_2

ID	0 s	25 s	50 s	75 s
9	C_0	C_3	C_1	C_2
10	C_3	C_0	C_1	C_2
11	C_3	C_1	C_0	C_2
12	C_1	C_3	C_0	C_2
13	C_0	C_3	C_2	C_1
14	C_3	C_0	C_2	C_1
15	C_0	C_2	C_3	C_1
16	C_2	C_0	C_3	C_1

ID	0 s	25 s	50 s	75 s
17	C_2	C_3	C_0	C_1
18	C_3	C_2	C_0	C_1
19	C_3	C_1	C_2	C_0
20	C_1	C_3	C_2	C_0
21	C_3	C_2	C_1	C_0
22	C_2	C_3	C_1	C_0
23	C_2	C_1	C_3	C_0
24	C_1	C_2	C_3	C_0

A Framework for Rule-Based Dynamic Adaptation*

Ivan Lanese[1], Antonio Bucchiarone[2], and Fabrizio Montesi[1]

[1] Lab. Focus, Università di Bologna/INRIA, Bologna, Italy
{lanese,fmontesi}@cs.unibo.it
[2] Fondazione Bruno Kessler - IRST, Trento, Italy
bucchiarone@fbk.eu

Abstract. We propose a new approach to dynamic adaptation, based on the combination of *adaptation hooks* provided by the adaptable application specifying where adaptation can happen, and *adaptation rules* external to the application, specifying when and how adaptation can be performed. We discuss different design choices that have to be considered when using such an approach, and then we propose a possible solution. We describe the solution in details, we apply it to a sample scenario and we implement it on top of the language Jolie.

1 Introduction

Adaptation, evolvability and reconfiguration are hot topics today. Adaptable systems change their behavior, reconfigure their structure and evolve over time reacting to changes in the operating conditions, so to always meet users' expectations [3]. This is fundamental since those systems live in distributed and mobile devices, such as mobile phones, PDAs, laptops, etc., thus their environment may change frequently. Also, user goals and needs may change dynamically, and systems should adapt accordingly, without intervention from technicians.

To achieve the required degree of flexibility, different research groups have proposed frameworks for programming more adaptable applications [1,13,20,17,23]. For instance, the application code may include constraints on the environment conditions or on the user behavior, and may specify how to change the application logic if those constraints are violated [5]. This approach is called *built-in adaptation*, and allows to adapt the application if the conditions change in some expected way. However, since the adaptation logic is hard-wired into the application, it is not possible to adapt to unforeseen changes in the operating conditions. *Dynamic adaptation* instead aims at adapting the system to unexpected changes [4]. Dynamic adaptation is challenging since information on the update to be performed is not known at application development time.

We propose a new approach to dynamic adaptation, based on the separation between the application and the adaptation specification. An adaptable

* Research supported by Projects FP7 EU FET ALLOW IST-324449, FET-GC II IST-2005-16004 Sensoria and FP7-231620 HATS.

M. Wirsing, M. Hofmann, and A. Rauschmayer (Eds.): TGC 2010, LNCS 6084, pp. 284–300, 2010.

Table 1. List of possible (Travelling) domain activities

Activity	**Functional Parameters**			**Non-functional Parameters**	
`Activity Name`	`Number`	`Source`	`Destination`	`Time`	`Cost`
Take Train	IC2356	Bologna Train Station	Trento Train Station	2 h 41 m	20 euros
Take Bus	13	Trento Train Station	Univ. of Trento	30 m	1 euro
Take Taxi	25	Trento Train Station	Univ. of Trento	10 m	15 euros
Go To Meeting	-	Bob's House	Univ. of Trento	4 h	50 euros

application should provide some *adaptation hooks*, i.e. information on part of its structure and its behavior. The adaptation logic should be developed separately, for instance as a set of adaptation rules, by some adaptation engineer, and can be created/changed after the application has been deployed without affecting the running application. Adaptation should be enacted by an *adaptation manager*, possibly composed by different *adaptation servers*. At runtime, the adaptation manager should check the environment conditions and the user needs, control whether some adaptation rule has to be applied to the application, and exploit the adaptation hooks provided by the application to reconfigure it.

We describe now a scenario that will be used to validate our proposal.

1.1 Travelling Scenario

Consider Bob travelling from Bologna to University of Trento for a meeting. He may have on his mobile phone an application instructing him about what to do, taking care of the related tasks. A set of possible tasks are in Table 1. For instance, the activity *Take Train* connects to the information system of Bologna train station to buy the train ticket. It also instructs Bob to take the train.

Assume that such an application has been developed for adaptation. This means that its *adaptation interface* specifies that some of the activities are adaptable. Each adaptable activity has a few parameters, e.g. *Number* specifying the code of the train, bus or taxi to be taken, *Source* specifying the desired leaving place and *Destination* specifying the desired arrival place, all visible from the adaptation interface. Also, a few non-functional parameters for the activities may be specified as *Time* and *Cost*. We show now a few examples of adaptation.

Example 1. When Bob arrives to Bologna train station, its Travelling application connects to the adaptation server of the train station. Assume that a new "*FrecciaRossa*"(Italian high speed train) connection has been activated from Bologna to Trento providing a connection with *Time=1 h 23 m* and *Cost=32 euros*. This is reflected by the existence of an adaptation rule specifying that all the applications providing an activity *Take Train* for a train for which the new connection is possible may be adapted. Adaptation may depend on Bob's preferences for comparing the old implementation and the new one, or may be forced if, for instance, the old connection is no more available. In case adaptation has to be performed, the new code for the activity is sent by the adaptation server to the application, and replaced as new definition of activity *Take Train*. Thus Bob can immediately exploit the new high speed connection, which was not expected when the application has been created.

Example 2. Suppose that the train from Bologna to Trento is one hour late. Bob mobile phone may have an adaptation server taking care of adapting all Bob's applications to changing environment conditions. The adaptation server will be notified about the train being late, and it may include an adaptation rule specifying that if Bob is late on his travel, he can take a taxi instead of arriving to the University by bus. The adaptation rule thus replaces the activity *Take Bus* of the travelling application with a new activity *Take Taxi*.

Example 3. Suppose that the train from Bologna to Trento is cancelled and there is no other train to reach Trento. Bob receives this event from the train station information system. The unique way to reach Trento is thus to rent a car (i.e., a *Rent a Car* activity) from his house. Bob's adaptation server provides adaptation rules specifying that if a resource needed by the activity *Go To Meeting* is not available, the whole activity has to be replaced by a different one. Again, adaptation depends on Bob's preferences for choosing the best offer from various car rental proposals. The code of the chosen one is sent by the adaptation manager to the application, and replaced for the *Go To Meeting* activity.

1.2 Overview

Both the described Travelling scenario and the technical solution that we propose can be applied to applications written in any language, e.g. Java, C++ or even BPEL. Thus we will discuss the general aspects in a language-independent setting, then move to more and more concrete settings to deal with aspects more related to the implementation. We will validate our approach using the Travelling scenario in Section 1.1 and the Jolie [16] language.

The main contributions of this paper are:

- the description of an approach able to realize the scenario;
- a discussion of different design choices for the realization of the approach;
- JoRBA (Jolie Rule-Based Adaptation framework), a proof-of-concept implementation based on the language Jolie.

The rest of the paper is structured as follows: Section 2 presents the rule-based approach that we propose to realize dynamic adaptation. In Section 3 we introduce the algorithm for enacting dynamic adaptations and we put it at work on the Travelling scenario. Section 4 describes JoRBA, a proof-of-concept implementation of our adaptation mechanisms based upon the Jolie language. The paper concludes with related works and conclusions.

2 A Rule-Based Approach to Dynamic Adaptation

In this section we discuss a possible solution for implementing the scenario described in Section 1.1. Our approach can be applied to applications developed using any language, provided that (i) the application exposes the desired adaptation interface and (ii) the application is able to support the code mobility mechanism necessary for performing adaptation. In Section 4 we will show how this can be done for instance in the case of Jolie, a language for programming service-oriented applications.

Thus we want to build an *adaptable application* using some language L and following our approach to dynamic adaptation. The application must expose a set of *adaptable domain activities* (or, simply, activities) $\{A_i\}_{i \in I}$, together with some additional information. Activities A_i are the ones that may require to be updated to adapt the application to changes in the operating conditions. While it is necessary to guess where adaptation may be possible, it is not necessary to know at the application development time which actual conditions will trigger the adaptation, and which kind of adaptation should be performed.

The adaptable application will interact with an *adaptation manager*, possibly implemented as a set of *adaptation servers*, providing the adaptation rules. More precisely, it provides a set of rules $\{R_j\}_{j \in J}$, each of them specifying a possible adaptation. The environment has full control over the set of rules $\{R_j\}_{j \in J}$, and may change them at any time, regardless of the state of the running applications. Each such rule R includes a description D_R of the activity to be adapted, an applicability condition c_R specifying when the rule is applicable, the new code P_R of the activity, the set V_R of variables required by the activity, and some information NF_R on the non-functional properties of the activity.

At runtime, rule R is matched against application activity A to find out whether adaptation is possible/required. In particular:

- the description of the activity to be adapted in the rule (i.e., D_R) should be compatible with the description of the activity D_A in the application;
- the applicability condition c_R should evaluate to true; the applicability condition may refer to both variables of the adaptation manager and variables published by the adaptation interface of the application;
- the non-functional properties NF_R guaranteed by the new code provided by the adaptation rule should be better than the ones guaranteed by the old implementation, according to some user specified policy;
- the variables V_R required by the new code P_R should be a subset of the variables provided by the application for the activity.

If all these conditions are satisfied then adaptation can be performed, i.e. the new code of the activity should be sent by the adaptation manager to the application, and installed by the application replacing the old one. Since the update may also influence the state, we also allow the adaptation rule to specify a state update for the adaptable application.

Even if the approach presented so far is quite simple, a few technical decisions have to be taken to implement it in practice. We consider them below.

When is the applicability of rules checked?

We have two kinds of approaches to this problem: either adaptation is *application-triggered*, or it is *manager-triggered*.

If the adaptation is application-triggered then the application asks the adaptation manager to check whether activities have to be adapted. Application-triggered approaches ensure that updates are performed when they are more needed, and are best suited when the required updates strongly depend on the application state. There are three main possibilities:

On Initialization: when the application starts, it checks its environment for updates. This approach allows to build configurable applications, which adapt themselves to the environment where they are deployed. However, they do not react to changes in the environment occurring after start-up.

On Wait: when the application is idle, it checks for possible adaptations. This can be useful if the updates are particularly time-consuming.

On Activity Enter: when the application is about to enter a new activity, it checks whether some update for the activity to be executed is available. This is the most useful pattern, since activity enter is the last point in time when adaptation is possible. In this way one is guaranteed that the most updated implementation of the activity is executed. We do not deal with adaptation of ongoing activities, since this will require to consider how to adapt the state and the point of execution according to the current state of the activity. We leave the issue for future work.

Dually, adaptation can also be manager-triggered, i.e. the adaptation manager decides when to check whether applications need to be adapted. Manager-triggered approaches are best suited for adaptations that do not depend on the state of the application. Three approaches dual to the ones above are possible:

On Registration: when an application enters the range of an adaptation server, it registers onto the adaptation server itself, and rules are checked for applicability. This allows location adaptation, i.e. it allows to adapt mobile applications to the different environments they move in.

At Time Intervals: at fixed points in time, applicability of rules is checked for all the applications in the range. This allows to ensure that applications are updated within a predefined time bound.

On Rule Update: each time a new rule is added to the adaptation server, it is checked for applicability. This ensures that new rules are applied as soon as possible. This is useful for instance to update mobile applications before they leave the range of an adaptation server. The On Registration and On Rule Update approaches combined allow one to perform all the adaptations that are state-independent with the smallest possible number of checks.

The two kinds of approaches can be combined for maximal flexibility.

How to choose the order of application of rules?

Different rules may be applicable to the same activity at the same time. In this case the choice of which rule to apply first may change the time required for performing adaptation, or even the final result. For instance, if two updates enhance the same non-functional property, the best one will make the other superfluous. In case of updates that do not influence the applicability of each other, only the last one will affect the final behavior.

Non-deterministic Update: updates are applied in non-deterministic order. This is the simplest possibility, in particular for distributed implementations. In fact, an application can be in the range of different adaptation servers, and this policy does not require them to synchronize (but for mutual exclusion during the updates). However this policy is applicable only in some cases, and may lead to troubles in others. Essentially, this approach is applicable when the order of application of the rules does not change the final result. A general analysis of when this approach is applicable is left for future work.

Priority Update: adaptation rules can be given a priority (static or dynamic): if many rules apply, the one with highest priority is applied first, and this forbids later applications of rules with lower priority. This approach guarantees that the smallest number of updates is performed, but it requires to check all the rules for applicability, and its distributed implementation is quite difficult. Some simplifications of the priority mechanism may be implemented in a more easy way. For instance, if one allows to apply rules in a random order, but does not want the effect of high priority rules to be reverted by low priority rules, it is enough to include priority of the adaptation rule as most significant factor in the non-functional properties, and to use the non-deterministic approach. Priority can also be applied only for rules managed by the same adaptation server, using the non-deterministic approach for rules of different servers. **Sequential Update**, where rules are ordered, is a particular case of priority update, where priority coincides with the position of the rule in the order.

Why is the application of an adaptation rule needed?

There are two classes of rules, and they have to be treated in different ways:

Corrective Rules: these rules take care of adapting the application when the current implementation is not viable in the current conditions; this is, e.g., the case of Example 3 in the Introduction, where the train has been cancelled. These rules will be identified thanks to a compulsory flag set to true, and they will be applied regardless of the non-functional properties of the previous available implementation.

Enhancing Rules: these rules enhance an existing activity which may however work; this may for instance change the non-functional properties of the activity, or provide new functionalities. These rules are identified since their compulsory flag is set to false, and they are applied only if the non-functional properties of the activity described by the rule are better than the ones of the previous activity according to the user-specified preferences. Even if the update does not involve (only) the non-functional behavior, the same approach can be used, since a version number can be added to the non-functional properties and used to distinguish the different levels of functionalities.

3 Algorithm and Example

In this section we formalize the algorithm for applying the adaptation rules, and discuss the example in more detail.

As we have seen, our adaptation framework is composed by two main interacting parts: a set of adaptable applications, each one exposing an adaptation interface, and an adaptation manager providing a set of adaptation rules.

Definition 1 (Adaptable application). *An* adaptable application *is an application exposing an adaptation interface (defined in more detail below) defining its set of domain activities and the public part of its state, and providing functionalities for accessing the public part of its state and for replacing its domain activities with external activities.*

Thus, the main feature of an adaptable application is its adaptation interface.

Definition 2 (Adaptation interface). *The* adaptation interface *of an application $\mathcal{A}$ is a set of quadruples $\langle D_A, V_A, NF_A, COMP_A \rangle$, one for each domain activity A, where D_A is a description of the activity, V_A its set of public variables, NF_A the values of non-functional properties provided by the current implementation, and $COMP_A$ a boolean function that given two sets of non-functional values decides which one is more desirable.*

The description D_A of the activity may have different forms. The only requirement is that it must be possible to check two descriptions for compatibility. We assume to this end a function $MATCH$, returning *true* if the two descriptions match, $false$ otherwise. For instance, one can consider as part of the description of each activity its *goal* in the sense of [22], and assume that two descriptions are compatible if the goal is the same. We will consider more complex definitions of activity compatibility in future work.

The set V_A in the adaptation interface contains the names of the public variables of the activity. They are used both to evaluate the applicability condition of the adaptation, which may depend on the current state of the application, and for the activity code to access the state of the whole application.

The set NF_A describes the non-functional properties of the activity A. It is a set of labelled values, one for each non-functional dimension. Examples of these dimensions can be ExecutionTime, Cost, SecurityLevel, and others. The set NF_A can be used also for more general purposes, including dimensions such as Priority and CodeVersion.

Function $COMP_A$ describes the user preferences concerning the non-functional properties of the activity. In particular, given two sets of non-functional properties, it checks which is the most desirable one. This function depends on the user preferences, thus it must be part of the starting application.

In the following we show examples of the adaptation interfaces of some activities introduced in Table 1.

Example 4 (Take Train Activity). The adaptation interface of the activity *Take Train* is a quadruple, defined as:

$$\langle D_{TakeTrain}, \{Number, Source, Destination\}, \\ \{Time = 161m, Cost = 20euros\}, COMP_{TakeTrain}\rangle$$

Here $D_{TakeTrain}$ is a description of an activity for going from *Source* to *Destination* using train number *Number*. These last are also the variables in the public interface of the activity. The actual values of those variables, which in this case are *Source=Bologna*, *Destination=Trento* and *Number=IC2356*, are retrieved at runtime from the state of the application. The third component describes the non-functional properties. In this case we have two dimensions, *Time*, describing the time required for the travel (in minutes) and *Cost*, describing the cost of the ticket (in euros). Finally, $COMP_{TakeTrain}$ is a function expressing the user preferences. For instance, given two pairs $\langle Time_1, Cost_1\rangle$ and $\langle Time_2, Cost_2\rangle$ it may return *true* (i.e., adaptation will improve) if $Time_2 < Time_1$ (i.e., the new solution is faster) and $(Cost_2 - Cost_1)/(Time_1 - Time_2) < 0,3$, i.e. each saved minute costs less than 30 cents.

Example 5 (Go To Meeting Activity). The adaptation interface of the activity *Go To Meeting* is a quadruple, defined as:

$$\langle D_{GoToMeeting}, \{Resources, Source, Destination\}, \\ \{Time = 240m, Cost = 50euros\}, COMP_{GoToMeeting}\rangle$$

Here $D_{GoToMeeting}$ is a description of an activity for going from *Source* (Bob's House) to *Destination* (University of Trento) using resources described by variable *Resources* (train IC2356, bus 13). These last are also the variables in the public interface of the activity. The time required is 4 hours while the cost is 50 euros. Finally, $COMP_{GoToMeeting}$ is a function expressing the user preferences.

The other component of our framework is the adaptation manager. It includes a state, which may be used to check the environment conditions (e.g., time, temperature, etc.), and the set of adaptation rules, one for each possible adaptation. It may be implemented in a distributed way as a set of adaptation servers.

Definition 3 (Adaptation Manager). *An* adaptation manager ρ *is a pair* $\langle V_\rho, \mathcal{R}_\rho\rangle$ *where* V_ρ *is a set of variables and* R_ρ *a set of rules.*
Each rule R *in* $\mathcal{R}_\rho$ *has the form* $D_R, c_R \vdash P_R(S_R, V_R, NF_R, CF_R)$ *where:*

- D_R *is a description of an activity,*
- c_R *is a boolean expression,*
- P_R *is a program,*
- S_R *is a state update,*
- V_R *is the set of variables required by* P_R *to work,*
- NF_R *is the set of non-functional properties guaranteed by* P_R, *and*
- CF_R *is the compulsory flag specifying whether the adaptation is compulsory.*

D_R describes the set of activities the rule can be applied to. This will be compared to the description D_A of the activity to be adapted. Condition c_R is the applicability condition for the rule: a boolean condition evaluated over the set of variables of the adaptation manager and the set of public variables of the activity. If this evaluates to *true* then the rule can be applied. P_R is the new code for the activity. P_R may use the public variables of the activity. S_R is a state update. Upon adaptation some values in the application state may require to be updated to reflect the change (see Example 6). V_R is the set of public variables expected by the new activity P_R. Finally, NF_R is the set of non-functional properties that will be provided by the new implementation P_R and CF_R the compulsory flag, specifying whether the update is compulsory or not.

Example 6. The Example 1 in the Introduction can be implemented by:

$$D_R, Number = IC2356 \vdash P_R(\{Number = FR82\},$$
$$\{Number, Source, Destination\}, \{Time = 83m, Cost = 32euros\}, false)$$

where the description D_R matches with D_A. Here the applicability condition c_R is just $Number = IC2356$, i.e. we assume to have such a rule for each train that could be replaced by a different connection, and that the train number is enough to identify it. If adaptation has to be performed, then the new code P_R will be installed, for booking and taking the FrecciaRossa train. In this case, the state will be updated by setting $Number$ to $FR82$, the number of the FrecciaRossa train (it is not enough to add an assignment to P_R, since in this last case the state update will be executed only when the new activity will be scheduled). The new activity will require to exploit the public variables $\{Number, Source, Destination\}$ and will guarantee as new non-functional properties $\{Time = 83m, Cost = 32euros\}$. Since the old train connection is still available, this update is not compulsory (i.e., the compulsory flag is set to false).

When Bob enters the train station and its Travelling application registers to the adaptation server of the train station (if the On Registration approach is used), or before the activity Take Train is started (if the On Activity Enter approach is used), or at some other point in time (depending on the used approach), the check for adaptation is performed according to the algorithm in Table 1. We show now how Algorithm 1 is applied to Example 1.

1. the description D_R in the rule is matched with the description $D_{TakeTrain}$ of the activity using function $MATCH$; the two description matches;
2. it is checked whether the public variables of the application are enough for running the new code, i.e. whether $V_R \subseteq V_A$;
3. the applicability condition $Number = IC2356$ is evaluated; this holds;
4. the compulsory flag CF_R is checked; we assume here that it is false, i.e. the old train connection is still available;
6. the non-functional properties of the new implementation are compared with the old ones, i.e. $COMP_{TakeTrain}(\langle 161, 11\rangle, \langle 83, 32\rangle)$ is computed; this evaluates to true.

Algorithm 1. Rule matching algorithm

Require: Activity definition $\langle D_A, V_A, NF_A, COMP_A \rangle$, rule definition $D_R, c_R \vdash (S_R, V_R, NF_R, CF_R)$, adaptation manager state V_ρ

if $MATCH(D_R, D_A) ==$ **true then**
  if $V_R \subseteq V_A$ **then**
    if $c_R(V_A, V_\rho)$ **then**
      if $CF_R ==$ **true then**
        return true
      else if $COMP_A(NF_A, NF_R) ==$ **true then**
        return true
      else
        return false
      end if
    end if
  end if
end if

After these checks have been performed and succeeded, adaptation has to be performed. This requires the following steps:

1. the adaptation server sends the new code P_R to the application, which replaces the old code of the activity P_A;
2. the adaptation interface of the application is updated, with the new non-functional properties NF_R replacing the old non-functional properties NF_A;
3. the state of the application is updated by setting variable $Number$ to $FR82$, the number of the FrecciaRossa train.

The first step is the more tricky, since the new code P_R needs to be sent from the adaptation server to the application and integrated with the rest of the application. For instance, it should be able to exploit the public variables of the application. To show how this issue can be solved, and how the whole approach can be applied in practice in a service-oriented setting we move in the next section to a practical example.

4 Dynamic Adaptation in Service-Oriented Applications

In this section we describe JoRBA (Jolie Rule-Based Adaptation framework), a proof-of-concept implementation of our adaptation mechanisms based upon the Jolie (Java Orchestration Language Interpreter Engine) language. Jolie [16,11] is a full-fledged programming language based upon the service-oriented programming paradigm, suited for rapid prototyping of service-oriented applications.

The service-oriented paradigm offers an easy way to model loosely coupled interactions such as the ones between our adaptation manager and the adaptable applications interacting with it. As such, each adaptation server offers a set of public interfaces that the adaptable applications can exploit in order to check when and whether adaptation is needed and to apply it. We have chosen

Jolie since it offers native primitives that are based upon the service-oriented paradigm, which simplify the implementation of the complex interactions required by our approach. For instance, the use of *dynamic embedding* has been fundamental to perform the replacement of activities during adaptation. Embedding is a Jolie mechanism that allows for the creation of private instances of services. Jolie allows to embed new services at runtime.

Jolie is an open source project released under the LGPL license, whose reference implementation is an interpreter written in the Java language.

The Jolie language takes inspiration from both sequential languages and concurrent calculi. It includes in fact assignments, if-then-else, while and other statements with a syntax similar to those, e.g., of C and Java, but it also provides parallel composition as a native operator and allows message passing communications by means of its One-Way and Request-Response communication patterns, inspired by WSDL [24] and WS-BPEL [18]. Jolie allows to easily manipulate structured data such as trees and XML-like structures. In fact, Jolie variables are labelled trees, where nodes can be added and removed dynamically.

4.1 JoRBA Architecture

We describe now the overall architecture of JoRBA, the Jolie prototype implementing the approach for dynamic adaptation described in the paper. For simplicity, JoRBA is based on the **On Activity Enter** approach for triggering adaptations, and on the **Sequential** approach for rule order. JoRBA includes both an adaptation manager composed by different distributed adaptation servers and a general skeleton for adaptable applications (together with a sample instance). JoRBA and the implementation of the Travelling scenario are available at [12]. The overall architecture of JoRBA is represented in Fig. 1 using a Collaboration Diagram (see [6]) and described below.

The adaptation server is composed by two roles: *AdaptationManager* and *AdaptationServer*. An AdaptationServer handles a set of adaptation rules and their related functionalities. We allow for many AdaptationServer instances to run simultaneously coordinated by the AdaptationManager service. The AdaptationManager service is also responsible for managing a global state, including information on the environment conditions, and handling requests coming from the adaptable applications.

The adaptable applications are implemented as *Client* services, which implement the behavior of the application relying on two other services for managing the adaptation mechanisms:

- ActivityManager: handles the execution of adaptable activities; in particular it provides an operation `run` to execute an adaptable activity when requested by Client; since JoRBA is based on the **On Activity Enter** approach, before starting the execution of the activity the ActivityManager invokes the AdaptationManager service to look for updates;
- State: manages the state of the application and allows the adaptation manager (as well as the application code itself) for accessing it when needed.

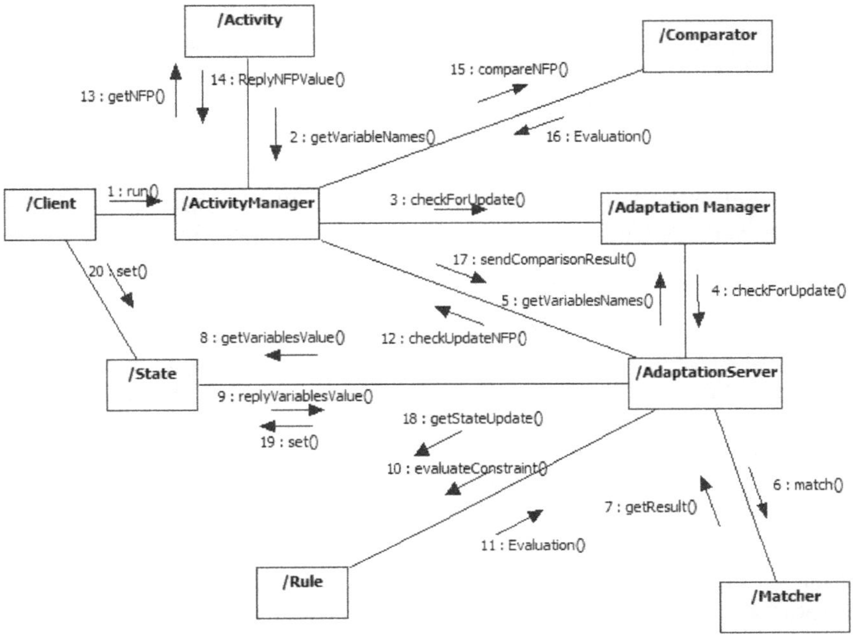

Fig. 1. Collaboration Diagram of JoRBA

Client services can easily be implemented by extending the *AbstractClient* definition, and complementing it with the user-defined behavior of the application. More specifically, the client application must include the `AbstractClient.iol` file, which in turn embeds the ActivityManager and State services. The code of the application should initialize the public variables by interacting with the private State service. Also, activities should be defined in separate files and executed by calling the `run` operation of the private ActivityManager service.

Whenever a Client service invokes the AdaptationManager service via the ActivityManager, the AdaptationManager queries all the registered AdaptationServer services in sequential order. When an AdaptationServer starts, it registers itself to the AdaptationManager service, and initialize itself. In particular, it scans its `rules` subdirectory for rule definitions. Each rule is defined as a service extending the `AbstractRule.iol` file. Each rule should define three procedures:

- `dataInit`: initializes the data structure with the information concerning the rule, including a reference to the new code for the activity;
- `onEvaluateConstraint`: implements the applicability condition c;
- `onGetStateUpdate`: specifies the state update for the client.

Upon invocation, each AdaptationServer service scans its rules in sequential order, checking if each of them is applicable using Algorithm 1. The implementation of this algorithm relies on Matcher, an internal auxiliary service that implements the *MATCH* function for comparing the activity description with the corresponding description in the rule. In the current implementation the Matcher service just performs an equality check between the two descriptions, however one can easily refine it by implementing his preferred matching policy. The AdaptationServer interacts with the states of the AdaptationManager and of the Client to get the values necessary for checking the applicability conditions. It also interacts with the ActivityManager of the Client for checking if the non-functional properties provided by the new activity are better than the ones provided by the current activity, according to the user-specified policies (which are encoded in the Comparator service embedded by the ActivityManager). If all the checks succeed then the AdaptationServer updates the State of the Client with the new values specified by the adapted activity and, finally, sends back to the invoking ActivityManager the updated code for the activity. The latter is dynamically embedded by the ActivityManager, replacing thus the old code. A sample execution of the Travelling scenario implemented using JoRBA can be found in Appendix A.

5 Related Works and Conclusions

Most of the approaches to adaptation found in the literature concern built-in adaptation, i.e. the adaptation logic is completely specified at design time. They concentrate on how to specify adaptation mechanisms and adaptable applications, exploiting different tools. For instance, the specification may be performed by extending standard notations (such as BPEL [18]) with adaptation-specific tools [13], using event-condition-action like rules [2,7], variability modeling [10] or aspect-oriented approaches [14]. Other works extend Software Architectures [19] to deal with adaptation, giving rise to *Dynamic Software Architectures* (DSAs) [15,8]. Other approaches to built-in adaptation instead define novel languages to specify structural reconfiguration aspects [9,15,21], that have been proposed with the objective of architecture-based dynamic adaptations.

There is a main difference between the proposals listed above and ours, since their adaptation logics are hard-wired into the application and defined at design-time, while we separate the running application from the adaptation logic, allowing to create and update the latter after application deployment (i.e., at runtime).

In the literature there are however proposals of frameworks for dynamic adaptation, all featuring an adaptation manager separated from the application. We will compare with them below, considering the following aspects: *(i)* whether the set of adaptation rules can be created and modified during the execution of the application; *(ii)* whether the choice of which rule to apply is static or dynamic; *(iii)* whether adaptation is aimed at changing the functionalities of the application or *(iv)* optimizing the non-functional properties. The results of the comparison are depicted in Table 2. Notably, all the listed approaches are in the service-oriented field.

In [20] the authors consider the problem of adapting the application by replacing malfunctioning services at runtime. The adaptation rule is fixed at design time, but it is dynamically applied by a *manager* component that monitors

Table 2. Features of frameworks for dynamic adaptation

Framework	Dynamic adaptation rules	Dynamic rule selection	Functional improvement	Non-functional optimization
Spanoudakis et al.[20]	–	+	+	+
Narendra et al.[17]	–	+	–	+
METEOR-S[23]	–	–	–	+
PAWS[1]	–	+	+	+
Our framework	+	+	+	+

functional and non-functional properties, creates queries for discovering malfunctioning services and replaces them with dynamically discovered replacements.

[17] proposes an aspect-oriented approach for runtime optimization of non-functional QoS measures. Here aspects replace our adaptation rules. They are statically defined, but dynamically selected.

The METEOR-S framework [23] supports dynamic reconfiguration of processes, based on constraints referring to several QoS dimensions. Reconfiguration is performed essentially at deployment-time.

PAWS [1] is a framework for flexible and adaptive execution of web service-based applications. At design-time, flexibility is achieved through a number of mechanisms, i.e., identifying a set of candidate services for each process task, negotiating QoS, specifying quality constraints, and identifying mapping rules for invoking services with different interfaces. The runtime engine exploits the design-time mechanisms to support adaptation during process execution, in terms of selecting the best set of services to execute the process, reacting to a service failure, or preserving the execution when a context change occurs.

As can be seen, there is a lot of work on dynamic adaptation, but still lot of space for improvements. Some of our directions for future work have been already cited throughout the paper. For instance, we want to update running activities, preserving their state. This requires to put more information in the adaptation interface of applications. We also want to apply our approach outside the service-oriented area, where most of the approaches are, moving to the object-oriented paradigm. Finally, we want to define type systems on rules and on adaptable activities to guarantee that during all the evolution some basic properties (e.g., security, deadlock freeness,...) are preserved.

Acknowledgments. Authors thank the anonymous reviewers for valuable comments and suggestions.

References

1. Ardagna, D., Comuzzi, M., Mussi, E., Pernici, B., Plebani, P.: PAWS: A framework for executing adaptive web-service processes. IEEE Software 24(6), 39–46 (2007)
2. Baresi, L., Guinea, S., Pasquale, L.: Self-healing BPEL processes with Dynamo and the JBoss rule engine. In: Proc. of ESSPE 2007, pp. 11–20. ACM Press, New York (2007)

3. Brun, Y., et al.: Engineering self-adaptive systems through feedback loops. In: Cheng, B.H.C., de Lemos, R., Giese, H., Inverardi, P., Magee, J. (eds.) SESAS 2009. LNCS, vol. 5525, pp. 48–70. Springer, Heidelberg (2009)
4. Bucchiarone, A., et al.: Design for adaptation of service-based applications: Main issues and requirements. In: Proc. of WESOA 2009 (2009) (to appear)
5. Bucchiarone, A., Lluch Lafuente, A., Marconi, A., Pistore, M.: A formalisation of Adaptable Pervasive Flows. In: Proc. of WS-FM 2009 (2009) (to appear)
6. Bultan, T., Fu, X.: Specification of realizable service conversations using collaboration diagrams. Service Oriented Computing and Applications 2(1), 27–39 (2008)
7. Colombo, M., Di Nitto, E., Mauri, M.: SCENE: A service composition execution environment supporting dynamic changes disciplined through rules. In: Dan, A., Lamersdorf, W. (eds.) ICSOC 2006. LNCS, vol. 4294, pp. 191–202. Springer, Heidelberg (2006)
8. Floch, J., Hallsteinsen, S., Stav, E., Eliassen, F., Lund, K., Gjorven, E.: Using architecture models for runtime adaptability. IEEE Software 23(2), 62–70 (2006)
9. Garlan, D., Schmerl, B.: Model-based adaptation for self-healing systems. In: Proc. of WOSS 2002, pp. 27–32. ACM Press, New York (2002)
10. Hallerbach, A., Bauer, T., Reichert, M.: Managing process variants in the process life cycle. In: Proc. of ICEIS, vol. (3-2), pp. 154–161 (2008)
11. Jolie team. Jolie website, `http://www.jolie-lang.org/`
12. Jorba v0.1., `http://www.jolie-lang.org/examples/tgc10/JoRBAv0.1.zip`
13. Karastoyanova, D., Houspanossian, A., Cilia, M., Leymann, F., Buchmann, A.P.: Extending BPEL for run time adaptability. In: Proc. of EDOC 2005, pp. 15–26. IEEE Press, Los Alamitos (2005)
14. Kongdenfha, W., Saint-Paul, R., Benatallah, B., Casati, F.: An aspect-oriented framework for service adaptation. In: Dan, A., Lamersdorf, W. (eds.) ICSOC 2006. LNCS, vol. 4294, pp. 15–26. Springer, Heidelberg (2006)
15. Kramer, J., Magee, J.: Self-managed systems: an architectural challenge. In: Proc. of FOSE 2007, pp. 259–268 (2007)
16. Montesi, F., Guidi, C., Zavattaro, G.: Composing services with JOLIE. In: Proc. of ECOWS 2007, pp. 13–22. IEEE Press, Los Alamitos (2007)
17. Narendra, N.C., Ponnalagu, K., Krishnamurthy, J., Ramkumar, R.: Run-time adaptation of non-functional properties of composite web services using aspect-oriented programming. In: Krämer, B.J., Lin, K.-J., Narasimhan, P. (eds.) ICSOC 2007. LNCS, vol. 4749, pp. 546–557. Springer, Heidelberg (2007)
18. OASIS. Web Services Business Process Execution Language Version 2.0., `http://docs.oasis-open.org/wsbpel/2.0/wsbpel-v2.0.html`
19. Perry, D.E., Wolf, A.L.: Foundations for the study of software architecture. SIGSOFT Softw. Eng. Notes 17(4), 40–52 (1992)
20. Spanoudakis, G., Zisman, A., Kozlenkov, A.: A service discovery framework for service centric systems. In: Proc. of SCC 2005, pp. 251–259. IEEE Press, Los Alamitos (2005)
21. Taylor, R.N., van der Hoek, A.: Software design and architecture: The once and future focus of software engineering. In: Proc. of FOSE 2007, pp. 226–243 (2007)
22. van Lamsweerde, A.: Requirements Engineering: From System Goals to UML Models to Software Specifications. Wiley, Chichester (2009)
23. Verma, K., Gomadam, K., Sheth, A.P., Miller, J.A., Wu, Z.: The meteor-s approach for configuring and executing dynamic web processes. Technical report, University of Georgia, Athens (2005)
24. World Wide Web Consortium. Web Services Description Language (WSDL) 1.1., `http://www.w3.org/TR/wsdl`

A The Travelling Scenario in Jolie

The JoRBA prototype [12] includes not only the basic services implementing the adaptation manager and the skeleton for adaptable applications described

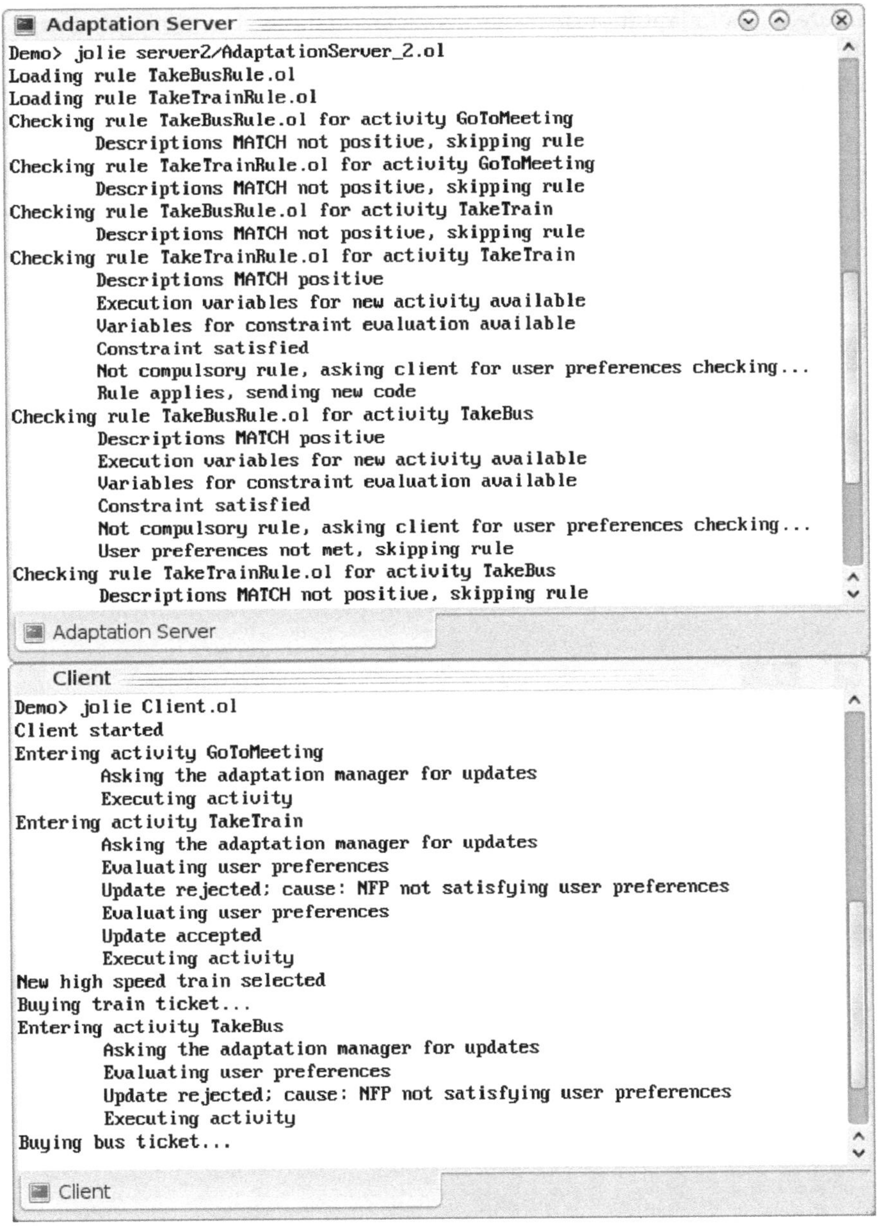

Fig. 2. Screenshot of prototype execution

in Section 4, but it also contains the sample Travelling application described in the examples presented throughout the paper and a few adaptation servers.

The main application has an adaptation interface including three different activities: the main activity Go To Meeting and the two subactivities Take Train and Take Bus. A sample execution is in Figure 2.

The client is executing in the bottom console. First the activity Go To Meeting is entered. The adaptation manager looks for updates, but there is no update matching this activity (as can be seen from the adaptation server console, in the top part of the figure). When the activity Take Train is started instead, two matching rules are found. All the checks are performed. The first one is discarded because of non-functional properties that do not satisfy user preferences. The second one instead is applied. Later on updates are checked also for activity TakeBus. The only update available is not applied because of the non-functional properties.

CarPal: Interconnecting Overlay Networks for a Community-Driven Shared Mobility*

Vincenzo Ciancaglini, Luigi Liquori, and Laurent Vanni

INRIA Sophia Antipolis Méditerranée, France
firstName.lastName@sophia.inria.fr

Abstract. Car sharing and car pooling have proven to be an effective solution to reduce the amount of running vehicles by increasing the number of passengers per car amongst medium/big communities, like schools or enterprises. However, the success of such practice relies on the ability of the community to effectively share and retrieve information about travelers and itineraries. Structured overlay networks, such as Chord, have emerged recently as a flexible solution to handle large amounts of data without the use of high-end servers, in a decentralized manner. In this paper we present CarPal, a proof-of-concept for a mobility sharing application that leverages a Distributed Hash Table to allow a community of people to spontaneously share trip information, without the costs of a centralized structure. Moreover the peer-to-peer architecture allows for deployment on portable devices, and opens new scenarios in which trips and sharing requests can be updated in real time. By using an already developed original protocol that allows to interconnect different overlays/communities, the success rate (number of shared rides) can be boosted up, thus increasing the effectiveness of our solution. Simulations results are shown to give a possible estimate of this effectiveness.

Keywords: Peer to peer, overlay networks, case study, information retrieval, car sharing.

1 Introduction

1.1 Context

Car pooling is the shared use of a driver's personal car with one or more passengers, usually, but not exclusively, colleagues or friends, for commuting (usually small-medium recurring trips, e.g. home-to-work or home-to-school). Amongst its many advantages, it decreases traffic congestion and pollution, reduces trip expenses by alternating the use of the personal vehicle amongst different drivers, and enables the use of dedicated lanes or reserved parking places where made available by countries aiming to reduce global dependency on petrol.

Car sharing is a model of car rental for short periods of time (rather than the classical car rental companies), where a number of cars, often small and energy-efficient, are spread across a small territory, for instance a city. Customers subscribe with a company which exploits and maintains the car park, and use those cars for their personal

* Supported by AEOLUS FP6-IST-15964-FET Proactive.

M. Wirsing, M. Hofmann, and A. Rauschmayer (Eds.): TGC 2010, LNCS 6084, pp. 301–317, 2010.

purposes. Service fees are normally per kilometer, and insurance and fuel costs are included in the rates. Car sharing is an interesting option for families in need of a second car who do not wish to buy one. Modern geolocation technologies, using GPS and mobile phones, assist locating the closest car to pick. The same economic/ecological advantages of car pooling apply here as well, and, mathematically speaking, they are parameters of the same function we would like to minimize.

1.2 Problem Overview

In Car sharing/pooling services, an Information System (IS) has been shown to be essential to match the offers, the requests, and the resources. The Information System is, in most cases, a front-end web site connected to a back-end database. A classical client-server architecture is usually sufficient to manage those services. Users register their profile to one Information System, and then post their offers/requests. In presence of multiple services, for technical and/or commercial reasons, it is not possible to share content across different providers, despite the evident advantage. As a simple example, the reader can have a quick look on Equipage06 [Éq] and OttoEtCo [Ott], two websites concerning car pooling in the French Riviera. At the moment the two do not communicate, share any user profile nor requests, even if they operate on the same territory and with the same objectives. Since both services are non-profit, the reason for this lack of cooperation would probably be found in the client-server nature of both Information Systems that, by definition, are not designed to collaborate with each other. Although, in principle this does not affect the correct behavior of both services, it is clear that interoperability between the two would increase the overall quality of the service. Moreover, the classical shortcomings of client-server architectures would make both services unavailable if both servers were to be down.

1.3 Contributions

As main contributions of this paper:

- we design and implement a peer-to-peer based Carpool information system, which we call *CarPal*: this service is suitable for deployment in a very low infrastructure and can run on various devices, spanning from PCs to small intelligent devices, like smartphones;
- we customize the Arigatoni protocol [CCL08] and its evolution, the Synapse protocol [LTV$^+$10], both specialized for resource discovery in overlay networks in order to allow two completely independent CarPal-based Information Systems to communicate without the need of merging one CarPal system into the other or, even worse, build a third CarPal system including both.

1.4 Outline

The rest of the paper is organized as follows: in Section 2, we introduce our CarPal service and we show how it is mapped onto a Distributed Hash Table. In Section 3 we describe the interconnection of different CarPal systems by means of the Synapse protocol developed in our team and tested over the Grid'5000 platform[1] In Section 4

[1] See `http://www-sop.inria.fr/teams/lognet/synapse`

we show, as proof-of-concept, a running example, that we have implemented in our team on the basis of a real case study in our French Riviera area of Sophia Antipolis, a technological pole of companies and research centers. A GUI is also available[2]. In Section 5 we present our conclusions and ides for further work.

2 Application Architecture

2.1 Application Principles

One of the most important features for a car share application is to be able to maximize the chances of finding a match between one driver and one or more travelers. From this comes the choice of arranging the database by communities, in order to put in touch people who most likely share the same traveling patterns in space and time (e.g. work for the same company, attend the same university and so on). Another important aspect is to be able to update the planned itinerary information as quickly as possible, so that a last minute change in plans can be easily managed and updated, and may eventually lead in finding a new match.

For the above reasons, CarPal has been intended as a desktop and mobile application running on a peer-to-peer overlay network. This allows a community of people to spontaneously create their own travel DB (which, as it will be shown later, can be interconnected with sibling communities) and manage it in a distributed manner. Furthermore, it constitutes a flexible infrastructure within which, by deployment on connected mobile devices, it will be possible to develop more advanced info-mobility solutions which might take into account the position of the user/vehicle (via an internal GPS), geographically-aware network discovery or easy network join, or vehicle tracking through checkpoints with the use of Near Field Communications technologies [NFC].

2.2 CarPal in a Nutshell

A user running CarPal on his mobile device or desktop computer can connect to one or more communities of which he is member (i.e. he has been invited or a request of his has been accepted). Two operations would then be available, namely (i) publishing a new itinerary and (ii) finding a matching itinerary.

Publishing a new itinerary. When a CarPal user has a one-time or recurring trip that he wants to optimize cost-wise, he can publish his route in the community in hope of finding someone looking for a place in the same route and time-window, to share the ride with. A planned itinerary is usually composed by the following data:

- *Trip date and number of repetitions*, in case of a recurring trip;
- *Place of departure and place of arrival*, whose representation is critical, since high granularity might lead to the omission of similar results;
- *Time of departure*;
- *Time of arrival* or, at least, an estimate given by the user;

[2] See `http://www-sop.inria.fr/teams/lognet/carpal`

- *Number of available seats* to be updated when another passenger asks for a place;
- *Contact*, usually an e-mail or a telephone number;
- Further useful information, i.e. pet allergies, other specific needs etc.;

Moreover, from a functional point of view, a trip, e.g. from place A to place D may include several checkpoints, meaning that the user offering a ride can specify one or more intermediate stops in the itinerary where he is willing to pick up or leave passengers.

Once the user has inserted all the required data (date, place and time of departure and arrival, number of seats and optional checkpoints), the trip is decomposed to all possible combinations: for example, a trip containing the stops A-B-C-D (where B and C are checkpoints specified by the user) will generate the combinations A-B, A-C, A-D, B-C, B-D and C-D. This operation is commonly known as *Slice and Dice*. Since the number of possible combinations can increase exponentially with the number of checkpoints, there is a software limitation to 3 maximum stops in the trip.

Each combination is then stored in the DHT as an individual segment; furthermore all of the segments which do not start from A are marked as estimated in departure time since, given a trip made of different checkpoints, only the effective departure time can be considered reliable, while the others are subject to traffic conditions and contingencies. Geographic and time information must be encoded in such a way that it is precise enough to still be relevant for our purposes (someone leaving from the same city but 10 km far is not a useful match) yet broad in the sense that a precise query will not omit any relevant results.

Every checkpoint (including departure and arrival point) could either be inserted directly through geographical coordinates (using the GPS capabilities of modern mobile devices) or as an address that would then be converted in geographical coordinates using Reverse Geolocation APIs made available by services such as Google Maps [Goo]. Such coordinates would then be rounded before the hash key encoding in order to group together locations within a given radius (around 5 kilometers). Concerning time approximation, a 20-minute-window is used to approximate departure times. Both during an insertion or a query, anything within the 0-19 minute interval would be automatically set at 10 minutes, 20-39 will be set at 30 minutes and 40-59 at 50.

Finding a matching itinerary and one seat. A user wishing to find a ride can perform a search by inserting the following information:

- *Date* of the trip;
- *Departure* place and time (picked on a map between the proposed points;
- *Arrival* place and wished time, picked in the same manner as the departure.

To increase the chances of finding a match, only part of the search criteria can be specified, allowing e.g. to browse for all the trips leading to the airport in a certain day disregarding the departure time (giving the user the chance of finding someone leaving the hour before) or the departure point (giving the user, in case of nobody leaving from the same place as him, to find someone leaving nearby to join with other means of transportation). Furthermore, it is possible to specify checkpoints in the search criteria too, in order to have the system look for multiple segments and create aggregated responses out of publications from multiple users.

Table 1. Different data structures stored in the DHT for each entry

Criteria	Key	Value	Grouping criteria
1	"I" ⌣TRIP_ID	♣	Individual trip
2	"T" ⌣DATE ⌣DEP ⌣TOD ⌣ARR ⌣TOA	list[TRIP_ID]	Departure, Arrival & Time
3	"B" ⌣DATE ⌣DEP ⌣ARR	list[TRIP_ID]	Departure & Arrival
4	"D" ⌣DATE ⌣DEP	list[TRIP_ID]	Departure
5	"A" ⌣DATE ⌣ARR	list[TRIP_ID]	Arrival
6	"U" ⌣USER_ID	list[TRIP_ID]	User

where ♣ = [DATE,DEPARTURE,TOD,ARRIVAL,TOA,SEATS,CONTACT,PUBLIC]

Negotiation. Once the itinerary has been found, it would be possible to contact the driver in order to negotiate and reserve a seat. If the trip is an aggregation of different drivers' segments, all of them would be notified through the application. The individual trip records will then be updated by decreasing the number of available seats.

2.3 Encoding CarPal in a DHT

The segments are stored in the DHT according to Table 1. The "⌣" symbol represents, with a little abuse of notation, the concatenation of multiple values for one key.

Multiple keys, representing different sets of trips grouped according to different criteria, are updated for each entry (or created if they do no already exist):

1. Is the actual trip record, associated to a unique TRIP_ID, that will be updated, e.g., when someone books a seat. The information stored concerns trip date - DATE, place and time of departure - DEPARTURE and TOD, place and time of arrival - ARRIVAL and TOA, number of available seats (or cargo space, in case of shared goods transportation) - SEATS, a reference to contact the driver - CONTACT, and if the trip has to be public or not - PUBLIC. Depending on the needs more information can be appended to this record; the key is created by appending the token "I" to the TRIP_ID.
2. Represents a set of trips having the same date, place and time of departure and arrival. The key is created by concatenating the token "T", trip date - DATE, place and time of departure - DEPARTURE and TOD, place and time of arrival - ARRIVAL and TOA. Its value is a list of TRIP_ID pointing to the corresponding trip records.
3. Is a set of trips grouped by date and place of departure and arrival. It will be used to query in one request all the trips of the day on a certain itinerary. The key to store them in the DHT is consequently made by appending to the token "B" the trip date, place of departure and place of arrival;

4-5. Are two sets of trips arranged by day and by point of departure or arrival. The key is therefore made by concatenating either the token "D" (for departure) or "A" (for arrival) to the date - DATE and point of departure or arrival - DEP or ARR. This set can be used, e.g., to query in one request all the trips of the day leaving from a company or all the trips of the day heading to the airport;

6. Is a set of trips for a given user. The key is the token "U" prepending the USER_ID itself.

2.4 Network Architecture

The overlay chosen for the proof of concept is Chord [SMK+01] although other protocols could be used to exploit the locality of the application or a more direct geographical mapping (see Section 5.2). Even on a simple Chord, several mechanisms to ensure fault tolerance can be put in place, like data replication using multiple hash keys or request caching. To allow a new community to be start up, a *public tracker* has been put in place on the Internet. The public tracker is a server whose tasks can be summed up as follow:

- It allows for the setup of a new community, by registering the IP of certain reliable peers, in a YOID-like fashion [Fra00];
- It acts as a central database of all the communities, keeping track of them and their geographical position;
- consequently, it can propose nearby overlays to improve the matches by placing co-located peers;
- It acts as a third party for the invitation of new peers into an overlay;
- It can provide statistical data about the activity of an overlay, letting a user know if a certain community has been active lately (and thus if it is worth joining);
- It acts as an entry point for downloading the application and getting updates.

3 Interconnecting Different Communities

3.1 Context and Motivations

As previously stated, CarPal has been conceived as a service where new communities of Car poolers can be put in place without the need for an existing IT infrastructure (e.g. a dedicated online service to join like [Éq] and [Ott]).

- As a first effect, we would expect to see is the birth and growing of different overlays around communities sharing the same interests, activities, jobs and, in general, anything which could lead to a common travel pattern (e.g. company employees, universities personnel, sports club members).
- Another expected consequence however will be to have multiple CarPal communities *geographically overlapping* i.e. residing in the same area and *not being aware of each other*, and thus, not taking advantage of each other's offerings. Often, companies are very close geographically and they have the same working timetable. If nearby communities put in place different CarPal overlays, those possible matches will not be taken into account.

Under certain conditions, in order to overcome such a limitation, a search operation for a given itinerary within a community can be extended to other overlays being geographically close.

3.2 Query Extension to Nearby Communities

A request for an itinerary can be routed through co-located nodes that are members of different CarPal overlays. The interconnection of a node to overlays other than his original is established via a social mechanism, where a user can ask for or receive an invitation to join other communities. Since every community shares the same structure for the hash key, the node will then be able to query all of his communities and act as a proxy as well for any requests going through it. Furthermore, as mentioned in Section 5, it will be possible to have a node interacting even with existing online services such as Equipage06 [Éq] and OttoEtCo [Ott]. The query extension mechanism is implemented using the Synapse protocol developed in our team and described in details in [LTV+10]. We hereby present a summary of its capabilities.

3.3 Synapse in a Nutshell

The protocol is based on co-located nodes, also called *Synapses*, serving as low-cost natural candidates for inter-overlay bridges. In the simplest case (where overlays to be interconnected are ready to adapt their protocols to the requirements of interconnection), every message received by a co-located node can be forwarded to other overlays the node belongs to. In other words, upon receipt of a search query, in addition to its forwarding to the next hop in the current overlay (according to their routing policy), the node can possibly start a new search, according to some given strategy, in some or all of the other overlay networks it belongs to. This obviously implies the presence of a Time-To-Live value and the detection of already processed queries, to avoid infinite looping within the networks, as in unstructured peer-to-peer systems. Applications of top of Synapse can see those inter-overlay as a unique overlay.

In case of concurrent overlay networks, inter-overlay routing becomes harder, as intra-overlays are provided as black boxes: a *control* overlay-network made of co-located nodes maps one hashed key from one overlay into the original key that, in turn, will be hashed and routed in other overlays to which the co-located node belongs to. This extra structure is unavoidable for routing queries along closed overlays and for preventing routing loops.

3.4 Synapse Performance and Exhaustiveness

Our experiments and simulations show that a small number of well-connected synapses is sufficient in order to achieve almost exhaustive searches in a set of structured overlay networks interconnected together.

In order to test our inter-overlay protocol on real platforms, we have initially developed JSynapse, a Java prototype which fully implements a Chord-based inter-overlay network. We have experimented with JSynapse on the Grid'5000 platform connecting more than 20 clusters on 9 different sites. Again, Chord was used as the intra-overlay protocol. The created Synapse network was first made of up to 50 processors uniformly distributed among 3 Chord intra-overlays. Then, still on the same cluster, as nodes are quad-core, we deployed up to 3 logical nodes by processor, thus creating a 150 nodes overlay network, with nodes dispatched uniformly over 6 overlays. During the deployment, overlays were progressively bridged by synapses (the degree of which was always 2).

Figure 1 (left) shows the satisfaction ratio when increasing the number of synapses (for both white and black box versions). A quasi-exhaustiveness is achieved, with only

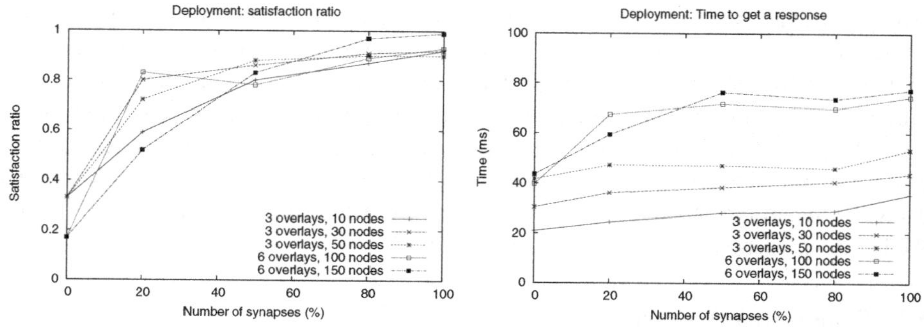

Fig. 1. Deploying Synapse : Exhaustiveness (left) and Latency (right)

a connectivity of 2 overlays per synapse. Figure 1 (right) illustrates the very low latency (a few milliseconds) experienced by the user when launching a request, even when a lot of synapses may generate a lot of messages. Obviously, this result has to be considered while keeping the performances of the underlying hardware and network used in mind. However, this suggests the viability of our protocols, the confirmation of simulation results, and the efficiency of the software developed.

3.5 Implementation in CarPal

For our scope, we decided to adopt the so called *black box* version of the Synapse protocol. The difference with the original Synapse approach is that, being aimed at routing through non collaborative networks, instead of embedding the additional data needed for the inter-overlay routing in the request packets themselves, it actually uses a parallel Control Network. The reasons for this design choice, disregarding the fact that every CarPal overlay would be collaborative by definition, with only CarPal peers within it, are the follwing:

- it offers the possibility to query an existing online service as if it were a non-collaborative network, by having one or more synapses acting as clients
- it allows for more control over the inter-overlay routing, by offering the possibility to perform selective flooding of specific networks only.

To achieve this the Control Network handles two different data structures: a Key Table and a Cache Table. Both are implemented as Distributed Hash Tables on a global overlay to which every CarPal node is connected.

- **The Key Table** is responsible for storing the unhashed keys circulating in the underlying overlays. When a synapse-enabled peer performs a GET which has to be replicated in other networks, it makes the unhashed key available to the other synapses through the Key Table. The key K is stored using an index formed by a networks identifier as a prefix, and the hashed key itself as a suffix. In this way, when a synapse on the overlay with e.g. ID = A will have to replicate e.g. H(K) = 123, it will be able to retrieve, if available, the unhashed key K from the Key Table by performing a get of the key A⌣123.

- **The Cache Table** is used to implement the replication of get requests, cache multiple responses and control the flooding of foreign networks. It stores entries in the form of [H(KEY),TTL,[NETID],[CACHE]]. In a nutshell: NETID are optional and used to perform selective flooding on specific networks. When another synapse receives a GET requests, it checks if there is an entry in the Key Table (to retrieve the unencrypted key), and an entry in the Cache Table; if so, it replicates the GET in the [NETID] networks it is connected to, or in all its networks if no [NETID] are specified. All of the responses are stored in the [CACHE], and only one is forwarded back, in order not to flood the other nodes having performed the same request. A TTL is specified to manage cache expiration and block the flooding of networks. When the synapse originating the request receives the first response, it can retrieve the rest of the results from the Cache Table. The cached responses should be sent back with the associated NETID. This might allow for a node to define a strategy of selective flooding to the networks which are better responding to a synapse request.

The **inter-overlay routing** takes place when a synapse peer wish to perform an extended query: before routing the request in its own community it adds an entry in the Key Table, containing the unhashed key to be searched, and an empty entry in the Cache Table. When another synapse in the first overlay receives the request, it looks for the unhashed key in the Key Table and the corresponding entry in the Cache Table. If those are found, the co-located synapse will query for the same key in all its communities and store the results in the Cache Table, in order not to pollute the originating network with too many results. The requesting peer in the first network will then collect the results from the Cache Table, upon receipt of the first response.

Controlling the data. Since different CarPal overlays use different hash functions to map their keys a first level of privacy and control is guaranteed in case a community wish to have some control over the visibility of their information. At present, there are two possible scenarios for accessing the data:

- A user can search for trips marked as both public and private in every overlay he is directly connected to. As previously stated, the connection to an overlay happens via invitation through a mechanism similar to certain social networks;
- If certain nodes of his own networks are members of other overlays, they can act as synapses and route queries from one network to another. However, only the trips marked as "public" will be made available to a foreign request.

4 A Running Example

We hereby present a first proof-of-concept for a CarPal application implementing the concepts discussed above. The software is still at an initial development stage but it has already been proven to be working in posting new routes and querying them across multiple networks. A basic user interface is proposed, showing a first attempt to integrate a mapping service (namely, Google Maps [Goo]) in the application to render the user experience more pleasant and efficient, although no GPS capabilities and no reverse geolocation are in place yet.

4.1 Building the Scenario

Let us turn to a practical example in order to better explain the logic behind the application. As a real world scenario for our proof-of-concept we chose the area of Sophia Antipolis in the department of Provence-Alpes-Cote d'Azur, France. The area (Figure 2 left) constitutes an ideal study case, being a technological pole with a high concentration of IT industries and research centers, thus providing several potential communities of people working in the same area and living in nearby towns (such as Antibes, Nice and Cagnes sur Mer).

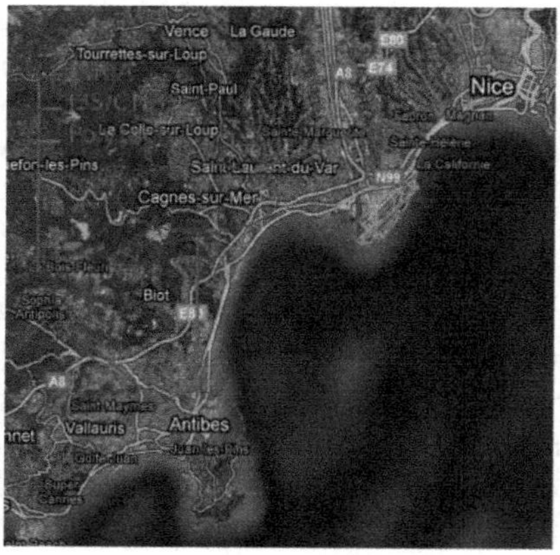

Trip date	15/01/2010
Departure	Nice
Departure Time	8.00
Checkpoint	Cagnes sur Mer
Checkpoint Time	8.30
Arrival	Sophia Antipolis
Arrival Time	9.00
Seats available	4
Contact	jsmith@email.com

Nice-Sophia	8.00-9.00
Nice-Cagnes sur Mer	8.00-8.30
Cagnes sur Mer-Sophia	8.30-9.00

Fig. 2. The geographical set-up (left), journey data (right) and sliced & diced segments (bottom right)

An engineer working in the area and willing to do some car pooling in order to reduce his daily transfer costs can publish his usual route to the CarPal overlay specific to his company. We assume the network has been already put in place spontaneously by him or some colleague of his. He can then use the CarPal application to publish his route with an intermediate checkpoint (as shown in Figure 3). As previously described, there is a checkpoint where our user is willing to stop and pick up some passengers.

4.2 Slice and Dice and Encoding in the DHT

Starting from the above data all of the possible combinations are generated leading to the segments shown in Figure 2 (right). Only the differences are reported, with each of those segments sharing the same date, number of available seats and contact information. The 3 segments are then stored in the DHT by updating (or adding) the appropriate keys as shown in Table 2. For clarity purposes, in Table 2, date and time values are represented as strings and instead of the actual geographic coordinates a placeholder is shown (i.e. NICE, SOPH...).

A PUT operation represents the insertion of a not yet existing key whereas the APPEND operation assumes that the key might already be in the DHT, in which case the value is simply updated by adding the new entry to the list. After the insertion, the

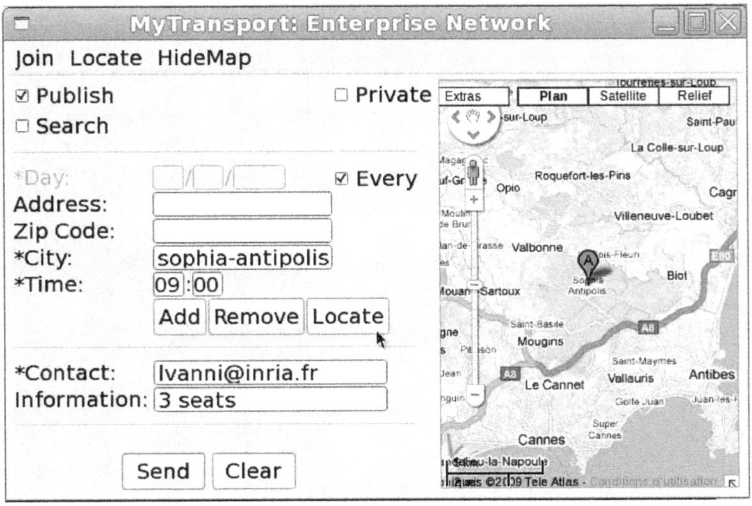

Fig. 3. CarPal application publishing a new trip

Table 2. DHT operations

Criteria (see Table 1)	Operation	Key	Value
1	PUT	"I"⌣123	♣
1	PUT	"I"⌣124	♠
1	PUT	"I"⌣125	■
2	APPEND	"T"⌣20100115⌣NICE⌣0800⌣SOPH⌣0900	123
2	APPEND	"T"⌣20100115⌣NICE⌣0800⌣CAGN⌣0830	124
2	APPEND	"T"⌣20100115⌣CAGN⌣0830⌣SOPH⌣0900	125
3	APPEND	"B"⌣20100115⌣NICE⌣SOPH	123
3	APPEND	"B"⌣20100115⌣NICE⌣CAGN	124
3	APPEND	"B"⌣20100115⌣CAGN⌣SOPH	125
4	APPEND	"D"⌣20100115⌣NICE	123
4	APPEND	"D"⌣20100115⌣NICE	124
4	APPEND	"D"⌣20100115⌣CAGN	125
5	APPEND	"A"⌣20100115⌣SOPH	123
5	APPEND	"A"⌣20100115⌣CAGN	124
5	APPEND	"A"⌣20100115⌣SOPH	125
6	APPEND	"U"⌣"jsmith@email.com"	[123,124,125]

where ♣ = [20100115, NICE, 0800, SOPH,0900, 3, jsmith@email.com, public=true]
where ♠ = [20100115, NICE, 0800, CAGN,0830,3, jsmith@email.com, public=true]
where ■ = [20100115, CAGN, 0830, SOPH, 0900, 3, jsmith@email.com, public=true]

trip is published and stands available to be searched. From Figure 3 we can see that it is possible to set the option of the the trip staying private. In that case, the segments will be discoverable only by members of the same network.

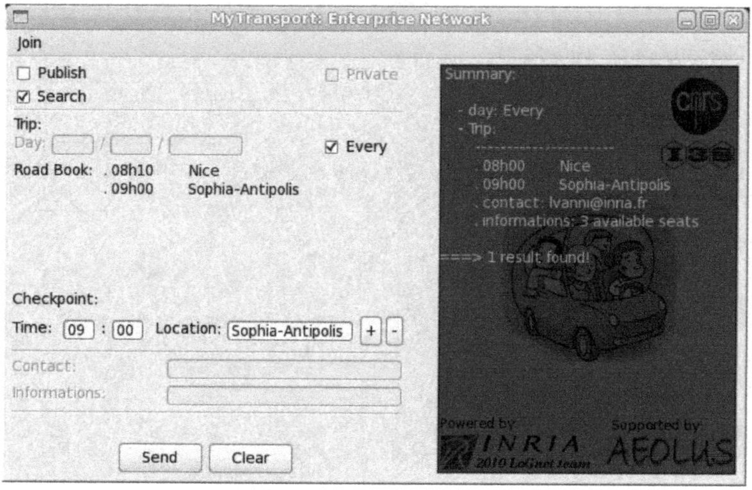

Fig. 4. Simple search

4.3 Searching for a Trip

A search for a trip follows a similar path as the trip submission. As we can see in Figure 4 the user can specify an itinerary, a specific time and even some intermediate segments, in order to find all the possible combinations. Depending on the search criteria specified, the application will perform a query for either a key made of Time of Departure and Time of Arrival, for a more exact match, a key with only Point of Departure and Arrival to browse through the day's trips or a key with only Departure

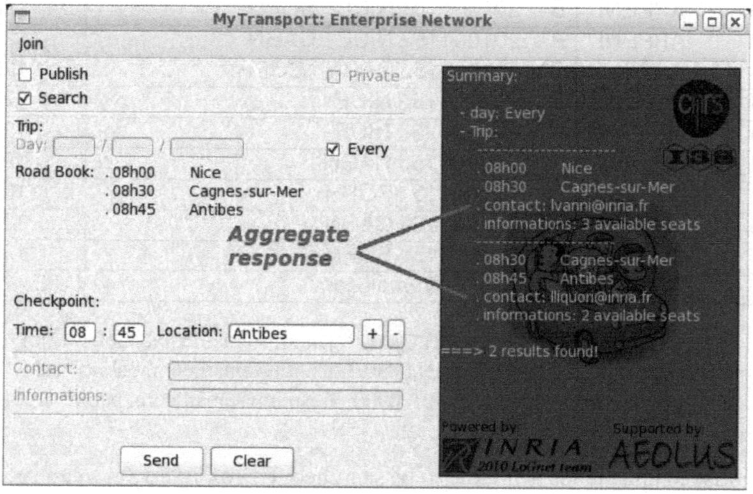

Fig. 5. Aggregate results

Fig. 6. Synapse creation

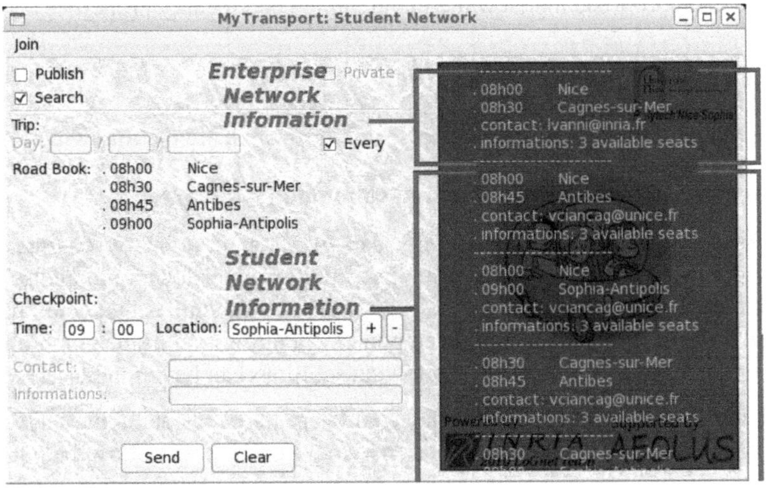

Fig. 7. CarPal Students accessing result from Enterprise Network

or Arrival for a broader search. Thanks to the Slice and Dice operation, it is possible to aggregate segments coming from different users as Figure 5 shows.

In this way the driver has more possibilities to find guests in his car. Despite that, there can still be some places available for his daily route. To optimize even further, he might share his information with, for example, students of nearby universities with their own carpool network (which has the same functions and technology).

By marking his published itinerary as public, a member of the Enterprise Network allows the students to get matching results via a synapse (Figure 8), i.e. somebody

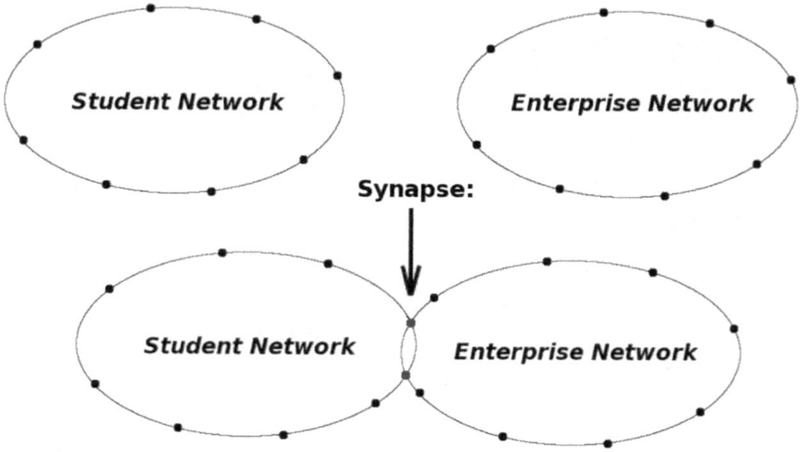

Fig. 8. Students, Enterprise and Synapsed Overlay Networks

registered to both networks (Figure 6). This allows the system to increase the chances of finding an appropriate match while maintaining good locality properties (Figure 7).

5 Conclusion and Further Work

There are several potential improvements, amongst which are the following:

5.1 Improved Network Bootstrap and Community Discovery

At the present state, a new community can be setup or joint by passing through the tracker. This keeps track of community activities, their location, handles the join negotiation and restrictions, and can suggest nearby communities that could be joined; however, it also constitutes a centralized point of failure for all of the communities. To further improve the mechanism, the following solutions can be put in place:

- Assuming that a community/overlay could very likely reside on the same network infrastructure (i.e. the enterprise intranet) a discovery protocol can be put in place leveraging existing technologies like Avahi [Ava] to discover new peers or new networks to join;
- Peer caching could be used to reconnect to previously connected peers whose activity is known to be reliable;
- An invitation to a new community could be handled physically via an Near Field Communications transaction [NFC]. A user with an NFC enabled phone could be invited by another user by simply swiping the phones together or touching a radio tag. Furthermore this could be an additional guarantee of user "reliability", as the a participant would need to be known and met by an existing member;
- The community database could as well be stored in the DHT itself, meaning that the new communities could simply be discovered through specific requests routed through existing synapses to other networks in a ping-like way.

5.2 Semantic Queries and Specialized Protocols

It appears clear that the current approach suffers from the limitation of a simple key-value approach. Such an approach does not fit well into an application that finds its strength in the possibility of performing searches according to many different criteria. The adoption of a semantic hash function (such as [SH09]) would allow for clustering of semantically close information (i.e. trips heading to sibling destinations or taking place in the same time window) in nearby peers. Needless to say, with such hashing in place the adoption of an overlay protocol more suited to range queries (like P-Ring [CLM$^+$07], P-Grid [ACMD$^+$03] or Skipnet [HJS$^+$03]) might lead to semantically significant range queries, where, for example, departure and arrivals can be geographically mapped and queried with a certain range in Km.

Another possible improvement (currently under study) would be to use a DHT protocol more suited for geo-located information. CAN [RFH$^+$01]) in a 2D configuration is a first example of how this could be achieved. Mapping CAN's Cartesian space over a limited geographic area (like in Placelab [CRR$^+$05]) could ease the query routing and eventually provide some strategic points to place synapsing nodes.

5.3 Overlay-Underlay Mapping Optimizations

The overlay-underlay network mapping to avoid critical latency issues due to the fact that one logical hop can correspond to many physical hops. This issue is under investigation and could involve e.g. the use of several always-on peers to triangulate the "position" of a peer over the Internet (according to latency metrics) and cluster together nearby peers (where by "nearby" we mean sharing similar latencies to the same given references). Another issue would be to make the service firewall-resilient, by implementing TCP Punch-hole techniques in the peer engine and in the tracker.

5.4 Backward Compatibility with Other Carpool Services

To take into account issues like access to non collaborative networks or backward compatibility the Synapse protocol also allows for a so called *black box* variant, whose first implementation is described in 3.5, that is suitable to interconnect overlays that, for different reasons, are not collaborative at all. This means that they only route packets according to their proprietary and immutable protocol. With the black box being more of a meta-protocol running on top of existing, and not necessarily peer-to-peer, structures, we can imagine strategically placed Synapse nodes being responsible of querying existing web services and returning the corresponding information as if they were coming from a foreign network. This would open new scenarios, where multimodality is easily integrated and made available to nearby communities. The system needs to be correctly designed, in order to avoid a situation in which too many peers act as a Distributed Denial Of Service, but the current infrastructure makes it rather feasible.

5.5 User Rating, Social Feedback

With CarPal being an application based on user-generated content and designed to put in touch people not necessarily acquainted to each other, it is important to implement some social feedback and security mechanism to promote proactive and good behavior by the users. Inspired by the most successful web applications of today, two solutions can be imagined:

- A user rating chould be put in place in order, for example, to allow passengers to evaluate a driver's punctuality, behavior and driving skills, and vice-versa. This feedback, similar to what systems like Ebay [Eba] have already from several years, can help maintaining a high level of quality of the service by giving an immediate picture of a driver's or passenger's reliability;
- Some points can be assigned to users based on their activity in the community. The more a user will be proactive by publishing or subscribing to new trips in an overlay, the more "karma points" he will receive. A similar approach can be verified in Social News website like Digg [Dig] or Reddit [Red] and has become pretty common in today's social media. With the deployment and integration of new distributed services, these points could act as a "virtual cash" and grant access to features normally reserved to paying customers, thus motivating drivers and passengers to keep a community alive.

5.6 Other Potential Applications

The Car sharing/pooling is not the exclusive applicative field for the overlay network technology we have designed; with the same final objective of minimizing traffic, pollution and energy a service interconnecting transportation companies Information Systems could be envisaged. A "BoxPal" system could be easily build using the same overlay network technology: the only difference being the (more difficult) 3D bin-packing combinatorial algorithms employed instead of a simple matching of drivers/cars/itinerary/car places.

References

[ACMD+03] Aberer, K., Cudré-Mauroux, P., Datta, A., Despotovic, Z., Hauswirth, M., Punceva, M., Schmidt, R.: P-grid: a self-organizing structured p2p system. SIGMOD Rec. 32(3), 29–33 (2003)

[Ava] Avahi project website, http://avahi.org/

[CCL08] Chand, R., Cosnard, M., Liquori, L.: Powerful resource discovery for Arigatoni overlay network. Future Generation Computer Systems 1(21), 31–38 (2008)

[CLM+07] Crainiceanu, A., Linga, P., Machanavajjhala, A., Gehrke, J., Shanmugasundaram, J.: P-ring: an efficient and robust p2p range index structure. In: SIGMOD 2007: Proceedings of the 2007 ACM SIGMOD international conference on Management of data, pp. 223–234. ACM, New York (2007)

[CRR+05] Chawathe, Y., Ramabhadran, S., Ratnasamy, S., LaMarca, A., Shenker, S., Hellerstein, J.: A case study in building layered dht applications. In: SIGCOMM 2005: Proceedings of the 2005 conference on Applications, technologies, architectures, and protocols for computer communications, pp. 97–108. ACM, New York (2005)

[Dig] Digg website, http://www.digg.com/

[Eba] Ebay website, http://www.ebay.com/

[Fra00] Francis, P.: Yoid: Extending the internet multicast architecture. Technical report, AT&T Center for Internet Research at ICSI, ACIRI (2000)

[Goo] Google maps website, http://maps.google.com

[HJS+03] Harvey, N.J.A., Jones, M.B., Saroiu, S., Theimer, M., Wolman, A.: Skipnet: a scalable overlay network with practical locality properties. In: USITS 2003: Proceedings of the 4th conference on USENIX Symposium on Internet Technologies and Systems, p. 9. USENIX Association (2003)

[LTV+10] Liquori, L., Tedeschi, C., Vanni, L., Bongiovanni, F., Ciancaglini, V., Marinković, B.: Synapse: A Scalable Protocol for Interconnecting Heterogeneous Overlay Networks. In: Crovella, M., Feeney, L.M., Rubenstein, D., Raghavan, S.V. (eds.) NETWORKING 2010. LNCS, vol. 6091, pp. 67–82. Springer, Heidelberg (2010)

[NFC] NFC forum website, http://www.nfc-forum.org/

[Ott] Otto et co. website, http://www.ottoetco.org/

[Red] Reddit website, http://www.reddit.com/

[RFH+01] Ratnasamy, S., Francis, P., Handley, M., Karp, R., Schenker, S.: A scalable content-addressable network. In: SIGCOMM 2001: Proceedings of the 2001 conference on Applications, technologies, architectures, and protocols for computer communications, pp. 161–172. ACM, New York (2001)

[SH09] Salakhutdinov, R., Hinton, G.: Semantic hashing. International Journal of Approximate Reasoning 50(7), 969–978 (2009)

[SMK+01] Stoica, I., Morris, R., Karger, D., Kaashoek, M.F., Balakrishnan, H.: Chord: A scalable peer-to-peer lookup service for internet applications. In: SIGCOMM 2001: Proceedings of the 2001 conference on Applications, technologies, architectures, and protocols for computer communications, pp. 149–160. ACM, New York (2001)

[Éq] Équipage 06 website, http://www.equipage06.fr/

Refactoring Long Running Transactions: A Case Study

Gianluigi Ferrari[1], Roberto Guanciale[1], Daniele Strollo[1], and Emilio Tuosto[2]

[1] Dipartimento di Informatica,
Università degli Studi di Pisa, Italy
{giangi,guancio,strollo}@di.unipi.it
[2] University of Leicester, Computer Science Department
University Road, LE17RH, Leicester, UK
et52@mcs.le.ac.uk

Abstract. Managing transactions is a key issue in Service Oriented Computing where particular relevance is given to the so called Long Running Transactions (LRT). Here, we show how to apply a formal approach to the specification and refactoring of LRT. Specifically, we consider a methodology arising on process calculi and show how it can be applied to a case study.

1 Introduction

Service Oriented Computing (SOC) envisages systems as combination of basic computational entities, called services, whose interfaces can be dynamically published and bound. Abstract composition/coordination mechanisms are necessary as SOC systems are typically executed on *overlay networks*, namely inter-networked communication infrastructures (e.g., wired and wireless networks, telecommunication networks or their combination). Such abstract mechanisms are divided in to *orchestration* and *choreography*. Services are orchestrated when their execution work-flow is described through an "external" process, called *orchestrator*. A *choreography* specifies how services should be connected and interact so to accomplish the overall choreography goals. Roughly, choreographies yield an abstract global view of SOC systems that must eventually be "projected" on the distributed components.

In this paper, we apply the theory defined in [4] to a case study taken from the SENSORIA project [9]. More precisely, in [4] it is shown how Long Running Transactions (LRT) can be refactored in a semantially sound way, namely a few refactoring rules for LRT are given and proved to preserve (weak) bisimilarity. An original contribution of this paper is the description of our methodology via an implemented programming framework, called ESC, based on the process calculi used in [4]. Our methodology consists of the following steps:

1. the software architect designs the LRT model in a semiformal notation (in this paper we adopt BPMN [8,10]);
2. programmers produce an initial implementation of the model in SCL, the programming language featured by ESC;
3. the initial implementation is refactored by repeatedly applying refactoring rules that automatically transform the implementation in an equivalent one.

M. Wirsing, M. Hofmann, and A. Rauschmayer (Eds.): TGC 2010, LNCS 6084, pp. 318–334, 2010.

The refactoring in the last step is applied according to the model-driven approach and allows the initial implementation to be adapted to choices/changes that may arise in a later stage of the development. For instance, the initial implementation can be given ignoring the execution platform; refactoring rules will then be applied to adapt the code to the underlying platform. Notice that this allows changes to the code to be done automatically for instance when the execution platform is decided or when it changes after the deployment.

Remarkably, the adoption of the ESC framework relieves software architects and programmers from the intricacies of the theoretical background. The ESC framework and its theoretical foundation guarantee the correctness, namely that refactored SCL code is equivalent to the initial implementation.

Synopsis. The ESC development framework on its underlying model are described in § 2; the SCL language is introduced in § 3; the SENSORIA case study and the LRT refactoring rules are discussed in § 4; the action of the refactoring rules on SCL code is given in § 5; final remarks are in § 6.

2 Background

We summarise the main ingredients of our framework illustrated in Figure 1 where ESC (left block), *SC* (middle block), and *NCP* (right block) are respectively a programming platform, its underlying formal model, and the choreography model all relying on event notification as the basic coordination paradigm.

The Event-based Service Coordination (ESC) platform provides a set of Eclipse plugins that offer a graphical and a textual representation of networks and is detailed below.

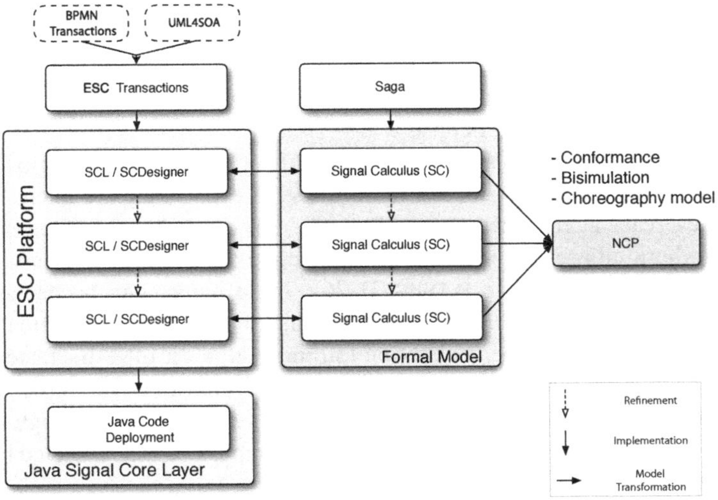

Fig. 1. ESC architecture

The Signal Calculus [5,3] (*SC*) yields a set of core primitives suitable and plays the key role of intermediate meta-model with respect to the other two layers. The calculus of Network Coordination Policies [1] (*NCP*) extends and equips our framework with a choreography model. In Figure 1, the arcs from *SC* to *NCP* represent the possibility to map *SC* models on *NCP* so that the conformance to *SC* designs can be verified.

The ESC framework relies on JSCL (a set of Java API realising *SC*) and offers two different perspectives of the network. The graphical representation presents a global view of the choreography by considering the components and their interconnections, without detailing their internal logics. The textual notation offers a closer view of components allowing designers to focus on the behavioral aspects. In a model driven metaphor, the aspects treated at these different levels of abstraction share a common meta-model. In this way a level can be easily transformed into another so that the resulting target model can be used for automatically generating (executable) JSCL code. In fact, the ESC platform supplies a set of model transformation tools that, starting from the high level specifications (cf. blocks BPMN transactions and UML4SOA [11] in Figure 1), automatically build their corresponding representation in the SCL model.

The event-notification model featured by SCL is based on components that asynchronously emit typed events; events are called *signals* and their types are called *topics*. A component may react to signals through *reactions* installed in their interface; each reaction has an associated behaviour executed when a signal triggering the reaction is received. Additionally, events are associated with *sessions* allowing to distinguish the different workflows. Intuitively, a session yields a "virtual communication link" among distributed components. Sessions are transparent to programmers and have a *scope* (i.e., the components participating in some interactions) that are dealt with by the SCL semantics. In other words, the semantics of SCL guarantees that components outside the scope of a session do not react to the events related to such session.

3 Signal Core Language

The textual representation supported by ESC is the *Signal Core Language* (SCL) implemented as a textual plug-in for Eclipse[1].

An SCL model defines a *network* by aggregation of *components*, described in terms of "reactive" software modules declaring the class of events they are interested to and the way they react at the occurrence of events. An example of SCL network is in Code 1.1 (where ellipses stand for immaterial code); the network consists of components `a` (LINES 3-20) and `b` (LINES 21-26). Topic names can be declared either **`restricted`** or (LINE 1 and LINE 2). A component has to declare its intention to refer a restricted name using the declaration **`knows`** (e.g., `a` on LINE 6). Instead, global names can be referred by all components in the network. Moreover, topic names can be declared **`local`** (LINE 4) or during in the body of a component through the primitive **`with`** (LINE 17). Similarly, component names can be declared restricted by tagging components with the **`protected`** clause (LINE 21).

[1] The textual editor has been implemented by using OpenArchitectureWare (oAW) [7], a modular MDA/MDD generator framework and supports code completion, error checking and code generation.

```
1  restricted: s1,s2;
2  global: t1, t2, t3;
3  component a {
4   local: lt1, lt2;
5   flows: [t1->a], [lt1->b];
6   knows: s1,b;
7   reaction lambda (t1@ws){
8    addFlow ([ws->b]);
9    addReaction (
10    reaction check (lt1@lt2){
11     emit (t1@lt1);
12    }
13   );
14   nop;
15   do ... or ...
16   split ... || ...
17   with (nlt1) ...
18   skip;
19  }
20 }
21 protected component b {
22  knows: s1;
23  main {
24    ...
25  }
26 }
```

Code 1.1: An SCL network of two components

Besides local names, components declare topics of their flows (LINE 5) and reactions. The flows of a component specify where the signals have to be routed (e.g., signals of topic `lt1` emitted by `a` are rooted towards `b`). Reactions specify what signals a component can react to and the corresponding code to be executed upon reaction. There are two kind of reaction; a **`reaction lambda`**, activated for a topic regardless its related session, and **`reaction check`**, triggered only within a specific session. For instance, `a` reacts to any signal on topic `t1` (LINE 7) while can react to signals on topic `lt1` only if they are related to session `lt2` (see LINE 10).

The computational steps described inside reactions, declare their *behaviors*. The basic primitives are

- **`emit`** (LINE 11), used to send out notification for an occurred event,
- **`addFlow`** (LINE 8) and **`addReaction`** (LINE 9) that allow flows and reactions of a component to be dynamically updated,
- **`nop`** (LINE 14) to indicate a block of code externally defined through host language instructions that do not interfere the coordination patterns (e.g. the access to the database),
- **`skip`** (LINE 18) represents the empty action (the *SC* silent action).

Furthermore, behaviors can be composed in sequence (using, as usual the semicolon) or with **do-or** (LINE 15) and **split** (LINE 16) constructs. The former constructs is used to implement the non deterministic execution of two branches, the latter allows the parallel composition of two behavioral activities.

Notice that component b declares a **main** block (LINES 23-25) that specifies its initial behavior.

4 A Case Study: The Car Repair Scenario

We apply our methodology to the SENSORIA automotive case study [11] and show how it can be developed in the ESC framework. We briefly describe the case study.

A car manufacturer offers a service that, once a user's car breaks down, the system attempts to locate a garage, a tow truck and a rental car service so that the car is towed to the garage and repaired meanwhile the car owner may continue his travel. The following requirements are specified:

- before any service lookup is made, an amount of money is reserved on the user's credit card;
- before looking for a tow truck, a garage must be found as it poses additional constraints to the candidate tow trucks;
- if no tow truck is found, the garage booking must be revoked;
- if a car rental (with an available car) is found succeeds while the search of either a tow truck or a garage fails, the car rental must be redirected to the broken down car's actual location;
- the failure of the search for a car rental should not affect the tow truck and garage booking.

Such requirements impose the adoption of LRT as coordination with compensations is needed; also it is worth pointing out some peculiarities of the scenario. The application consists of different services that dynamically federate in order to provide new functionalities. Specifically, services (e.g., financial institutions, garages and car rental or taxi companies) team up to help the customer. This service composition is dynamic and cannot be anticipated in the code. Moreover, the scenario requires distributed transactional behavior to be dealt with. In fact, interactions among services can fail for many reasons and, of course, the customer should not be charged when the service cannot be provided. Finally, SOC systems usually have to be deployed on heterogeneous platforms and have to be executed on *overlay computers*, namely networks of many different kinds (e.g., wired networks, wireless ones or, telecommunication networks). For instance, the car-repair scenario requires software interfacing GPRS system, mobile phone, the Internet, and dedicated networks for financial transactions. The complexity of such applications requires in fact a rather sophisticated development methodology that can help programmers in facing the complexity of underlying and platform specific aspects.

The LRT graphical model of this scenario is presented in Figure 2 (see Appendix A for an overview of LRT). The model exploits the transactional and compensation facilities of LRT; for instance, the car rental service is a sub-transaction, since (as required) it does not affect other activities.

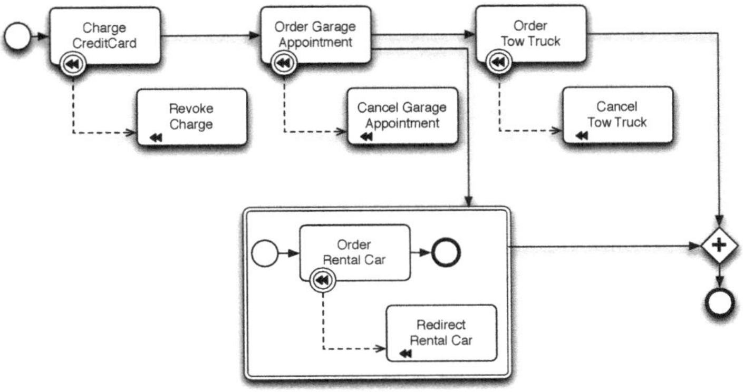

Fig. 2. Car repair scenario: the LRT model

Notice that initial design in Figure 2 simply describes the transactional aspects of the main activities. In this phase, it is not relevant to describe service distribution or (refined decomposition of the main activities).

4.1 LRT to SCL Model Transformation

The ESC platform comes up with a set of tools that permit to transform the platform independent LRT models to the platform specific SCL models.

The SCL implementation of transactional behaviors exploits two public names, `f` and `r`, respectively for *forward* and *rollback* events. Forward events propagate the successful completion from an activity to the next ones in the work-flow. Backward events are emitted on failures to trigger compensations. In the first step the model transformation generates an SCL component for every atomic process (aka an activity and the corresponding compensation).

Subsequently, the model transformation can generate *glue* components and update the existing flows, however the behavior of components generated in the previous steps cannot be altered. This permits to transform a transactional process to an SCL network independently by the context, and reuse it as building block just changing its connections (SCL flows).

The SCL snippets presented in the following contain unspecified behavior which is specific to the application (represented with comments in the code); this missing behaviours are supposed to be added by the programmers once the SCL code is compiled into JSCL API (e.g. Java).

Atomic process. Figure 3(a) gives a pictorial intuition of the internal structure of atomic processes; Figure 3(b) illustrates a black-box view of atomic processes where solid (resp. dashed) arrows represent the forward (resp. backward) flow of LRT; finally, the sequential composition of `a` and `b` their forward and backward flows as in Figure 3(c).

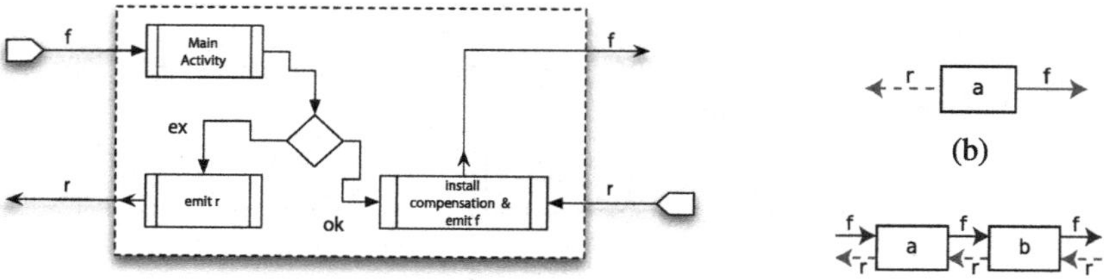

(a) Internal view of atomic process

(b)

(c)

Fig. 3. Atomic and sequential compensatable processes

In Code 1.2 we report the SCL coding of transactional activity GARAGE where (according to Figure 3(a)) two private topics, `ok` and `ex`, (LINE 2) are declared so to be able to determine the termination of the main activity of the component. Notice that all events on topics `ok` and `ex` are delivered to GARAGE itself (LINE 3). Initially the component can react only to `f` events (BLOCK 5-24). When reacting to forward events (signals on topic `f`), GARAGE receives the session identifier `s` and execute the behavior corresponding to the LRT main activity (LINE 7). Such behavior is not explicitly

```
1  component garage {
2   local: ok, ex;
3   flows: [(ok->garage), (ex->garage),
4           (r->creditCard), (f->dispatcherPar)];
5   reaction lambda (f@s) {
6    split {
7      /* coding of the main activity */
8      do {emit <ok@s>;} or {emit <ex@s>;}
9    } || {
10     addReaction (reaction check (ok@s) {
11       split {
12         emit <f@s>;
13       }||{
14         addReaction (reaction check (r@s) {
15           /*  Compensation */
16           emit <r@s>;
17         });
18       }
19     });
20   } || {
21     addReaction (reaction check (ex@s) {
22       emit <r@s>;
23     });
24   }
25 }
```

Code 1.2: SCL compensatable activity

given, it is just assumed to issue an `ok` event on successful termination and send an `ex` event otherwise. Concurrently with the main activity GARAGE installs a reactions to check when the main activity terminates (BLOCKS 10- 19 and 21-23). On successful termination (LINE 10), a signal on topic `f` is propagated (LINE 12) and a check reaction waiting for a possible rollback is installed (LINE 14-17); when a `r` event for the session `s` arrives, the activity is compensated (abstracted by `nop` on LINE 15) and the rollback signal propagated to previous stages (LINE 16).

If the execution of the activity fails (LINE 21), the handler simply starts the backward flow, raising a rollback event (LINE 22). Since the transformation of an atomic task generates only one SCL component, this component is both the entry point and the exit point of the generated network. Notice that the generated component has only flow to itself, since it is generated independently by the context.

Parallel composition. The parallel composition of two LRT processes `a` and `b` is represented in Figure 4(a) where two additional components `d` and `c` represent the *dispatcher* and *collector*.

A dispatcher propagates the forward flows to all the components executed in parallel and propagates the backward flows to the previous stage of the workflow. Similarly, the collector waits for the outcome of each parallel component before propating the forward flow and send rollback signals when subsequent stages of the workflow fail.

The SCL code for dispatcher is Code 1.3 and 1.4, respectively. Such code is generated for the parallel composition of the TOWTRUCK and RENTALCAR services.

The dispatcher (c.f. Code 1.3) represents the entry point of the parallel branch. Basically, it activates the forward flow of next components, and synchronizes their backward flows. Upon reactions to forward events (LINE 4), the collector emits two events: one having topic `f` (LINE 6) and the other one having topic `n` (LINE 8). The former event is delivered to the components representing the parallel activities. The latter event is delivered to the collector, informing it of the received session that will be later used by it to implement its synchronization. Concurrently, the collector activates its the synchronization mechanism by installing two nested reactions for the topic `r` in the work-flow session `s` (LINES 10 and 11). When the synchronization of the backward flow takes place, the emitter backwardly forwards the rollback event (LINE 12).

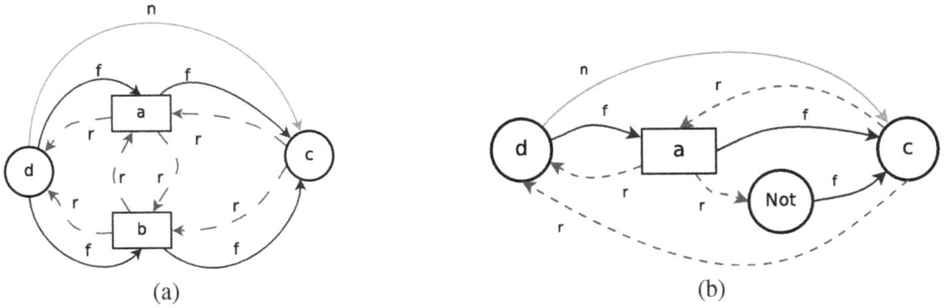

Fig. 4. Parallel composition and transactional enclosure

```
component dispatcherPar {
  flows: [f->towTruck],[f->dispatcherTrans],
         [r->garage],[n->collectorPar];
  reaction lambda (f@s) {
    split {
      emit (f@s);
    } || {
      emit (n@s);
    } || {
      addReaction (reaction check (r@s) {
        addReaction (reaction check (r@s) {
          emit (r@s);
        });
      });
    }
  }
}
```

Code 1.3: SCL parallel dispatcher

```
1  component collectorPar {
2   flows: [r->towTruck],[r->collectorTrans],[f->...];
3   reaction lambda (n@s) {
4     addReaction check (f@s) {
5       addReaction check (f@s) {
6         split {
7           emit <f@s>;
8         } || {
9           addReaction check (r@s) {
10            emit <r@s>;
11          }
12        }
13      }
14    }
15  }
16 }
```

Code 1.4: SCL parallel collector

Similarly, the collector component (in Code 1.4) is responsible to implement the synchronization mechanism for the forward flows (LINES 4 and 5) and to activate the backward flows of the parallel components when a `r` event is received (BLOCK 9-11). Once both the internal components have sent their forward messages, the collector sends out a `f` event (LINE 7). Notice that the collector exploits a `n` event to get information about the session `s` of the work-flow (LINE 3). After the generation of the new components, the flows of the two networks are updated (the flow for `f` in LINE 2). Moreover the backward flow is suitable connected to the internal parallel components as given in LINE 2). The dispatcher and the collector components represent the entry and exit point of the parallel component, respectively.

Isolated transaction. The intended meaning of transactional enclosure construct is that its internal failure does not affect other activities. For this reason, regardless the outgoings of a transactional activity a (see Figure 4(b)) the collector will receive a notification of forward event (f). The *Not* agent ensures that rollback requests from a are converted into forward requests so that the flow is passed to the next stages of the transaction. Conversely, if from the outside c receives a rollback, the component a must be informed and activate its compensation. Two cases are possible: *i)* a has previously successful terminated, so it has a compensation installed *ii)* a internally failed and no compensations are needed.

On its turn, d has to consume two instances of r events before activating the backward flow while c, for the same session, consumes only a f event and ignores the further instances of f.

Similarly to the parallel encoding previously exposed, the topic n is used from d to inform c that a new work-flow instance has been initiated so that the latter component can install the proper check reactions to consume two distinct instances of f events coming from a.

The generated SCL code for the sub-transaction containing the RENTALCAR component is provided by three internal components according to the schema given in Figure 4(b).

The DISPATCHERTRANS (c.f. Code 1.5) receives from the external activities the forward events (LINE 3), informs the COLLECTORTRANS that a new transactional session has been initiated (LINE 4), redirects the forward event to the RENTALCAR (LINE 5) and installs the rollback handler for the current session (BLOCK 6-10). Notice that, the rollback will be sent out (LINE 8) after the reception of two `r` notifications.

```
1  component dispatcherTrans {
2   flows [n->collectorTrans],[f->RentalCar];
3   reaction lambda (f@s) {
4     emit (n@s);
5     emit (f@s);
6     addReaction (reaction check (r@s){
7       addReaction (reaction check (r@s){
8         emit (r@s);
9       });
10    });
11  }
12 }
```

Code 1.5: SCL transactional enclosure dispatcher

```
component Not {
  flows [f->collectorTrans];
  reaction lambda (r@s) {
    emit <f@s>;
  }
}
```

Code 1.6: SCL transactional enclosure not

The NOT port has the obvious meaning, it inverts the topic from `r` to `f`, without altering the session, as given in Code 1.6.

```
1  component collectorTrans {
2    flows: [f->collectorPar],[r->RentalCar],
3           [r->dispatcherTrans];
4    reaction lambda (n@s) {
5      addReaction( reaction check  (f@s) {
6        emit(f@s);
7        addReaction (reaction check (r@s) {
8          emit (r@s);
9        });
10     });
11   }
12 }
```

Code 1.7: SCL transactional enclosure collector

The COLLECTORTRANS (c.f. Code 1.7) waits until the dispatcher communicates the new working session (LINE 4). Consequently, it installs the handler for the `f` notifications coming from the RENTALCAR (BLOCK 5-10). Once received the `f` event it is delivered outside (LINE 6) and an handler for the rollback coming from the outside is installed (BLOCK 7-9).

5 Scl Model Refactoring

In § 4.1 we have shown how to "compile" BPMN diagrams into SCL networks. Arguably, a similar mapping can be given also for other formalisms for LRT as [11]. Nevertheless, the automatically generated models may require some modifications either (*i*) to refine the code to consider those aspects not addressable in LRT (e.g., platform dependent issues) or (*ii*) to optimise the generated code.

Figure 5 pictorially represents the structure of the coding automatically generated by SCL to be subsequently refined to better adhere to additional requirements that are

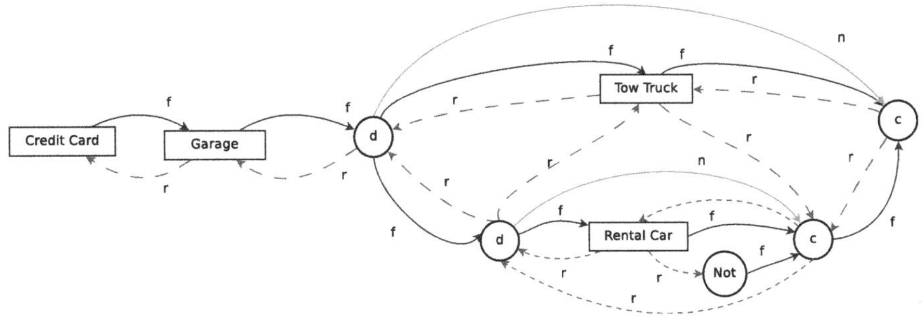

Fig. 5. A representation of the network generated in SCL

not taken into account at abstract level. For instance, the component distribution on the network, are not explicitly modeled at higher levels of abstraction, both at formal and specification levels. In fact, either LRT meta-models are not concerned with such aspects or, more pragmatically, they can more suitably considered at later stages of the development. For example, BPMN designs sketches how the overall transaction among transactional components should proceed without making any further assumption on which services implement such components (or where they are located).

A possible solution to the problem described abovev is to refineme the code. The refinement process has to provide sound refactoring rules as those introduces in [4] and adopted here. Our translation of LRT into SCL models provides the suitable level of abstraction to which these refactoring steps can be applied. For example, deployment of distributed components or rearrangement of points of control can be automatically transformed at the SCL level respecting the original semantics of automatically translated designs.

5.1 Refactoring Transactional Components

The first refactoring rule consists in delegating the compensation of SCL transactional components; the rule is applied to the GARAGE (cf. Code 1.2, § 4.1).

As already pointed out, both the main activity and the compensation of a transactional component are embedded into a single SCL component that manages `ok` and `ex` events in order to propagate forward or backward flows. However, it might be useful to delegate the compensation task to a different component. For example, the compensation should run on a different host than the main activity, because it involves a remote service. Usually, this aspect is not specified in the model of the business process. In the ESC framework, this issue can be tackled at deployment time, indeed implementation of JSCL [5] permits to orthogonally distribute components on the network topology.

The refactoring rule generates a component, called CMP (Code 1.8, lines 20-29), that handles the compensation managing the backward flow and is reachable only by GARAGE (line 5). For this reason, GARAGE directs `r` and `ex` events as specified in the refactored set of flows (line 4). The refactored GARAGE component needs only to check the termination of its main activity. In fact, its check reaction (line 9) propagates the

```
1  restricted ex;
2  component garage {
3   local: ok;
4   flows: [(ok->garage),(ex->cmp),(r->cmp),(f->dispatcherPar)];
5   knows: cmp;
6   reaction lambda (f@s) {
7    split { do {emit <ok@s>;} or {emit <ex@s>;} }
8       || {
9      addReaction (reaction check (ok@s) {
10       split {
11         emit <f@s>;
12       }||{
13         addReaction (reaction check (r@s) {
14           emit <r@s>;
15         });
16       }
17     });
18   }
19 }
20 protected component cmp {
21  flows: [(r->creditCard)];
22  reaction lambda (ex@s) {
23    emit <r@s>;
24  }
25  reaction check (r@s) {
26    /* Coding of Compensation.
27    Defined by host language API. */
28    nop;
29    emit <r@s>;
30  }
31 }
```

Code 1.8: Delegating compensation in SCL

forward flow and activates a listener for the rollback notifications possibly sent by subsequent transactional components. Notice that the reaction implicitly delegates the execution of the compensation to CMP. Once a rollback is captured by GARAGE it is automatically forwarded to CMP according to the flows defined in line 4. Hence, CMP is informed if something goes wrong either during the execution of the main activity (ex events) or, after its successful execution, when r events is be delivered by other components.

The component CMP waits the notification of an exception (line 7) or a rollback request coming from subsequent components. In the former case, CMP simply activates the backward flow while, in the latter case, CMP executes the compensation that, upon termination, starts the backward flow (lines 26-29).

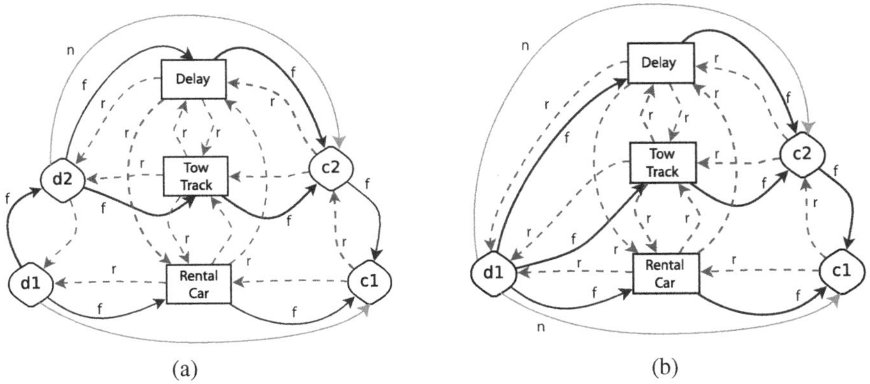

Fig. 6. Parallel composition and its refactoring

5.2 Refactoring Parallel Composition

The mapping of the parallel composition of transactions introduces two additional components, a dispatcher and a collector, respectively acting as the entry and exit point of the parallel composition.

To illustrate the refactoring of parallel SCL transactions the scenario of § 4 is extended by adding a new activity (DELAY) that informs the Information System of the driver company about a possible delay. This activity can be performed after GARAGE has been contacted. Namely, the resulting business process contains three concurrent activities: the DELAY, the TRACK and the sub-transaction that encloses RENTALCAR. Figure 6(a) depicts the flows and components required to implement this parallel composition. Two distinct dispatchers (D1 and D2) are involved in the coordination. Dispatcher D2 is responsible to forward the received requests to components DELAY and TRACK and results externally the entry point of their parallel composition. As result, the dispatcher D1 is connected to the entry point of the sub-transaction RENTALCAR and to D2, acting as entry point for the whole parallel block. Similar considerations can be made for the exit points C1 and C2.

The notification of events to dispatchers D1 and D2 are not relevant to the semantic of the implementing network (more precisely these are hidden notification, since the dispatchers are not visible outside the network). The generation of two different dispatchers can provide a mechanism to optimize the communications among components. For example, if D2, DELAY, and TOWTRACK reside on the same host, the generated dispatcher permits to reduce the inter-host communications for the forward and backward flow, since it receives only one inter-host signal and generates two intra-host signals for DELAY and TOWTRACK.

If DELAY, TOWTRACK, and RENTALCAR are remotely executed, the two dispatchers can be fused applying our next refactoring rule. Such rule can be applied in two directions, namely (i) it can merge two parallel dispatchers into one (simplifying the SCL code) or (ii) it can split a dispatcher into two parallel ones (refining inter-hosts communication). In the following we summarize the refactoring of parallel dispatchers.

Noteworthy, the same strategy can provide a similar refactoring mechanism for the collectors. The refactoring merges the dispatcher D2 with D1 as follows:

- Migrates any flow targeted to the dispatcher D2 to the dispatcher D1. For example, the flows of TowTrack becomes

```
flows: [(ok->TowTrack), (ex->TowTrack),
        (r->RentalCar,Delay,d1), (f->c2)]
```

- Add all flows of the dispatcher D2 to the dispatcher D1 (Code 1.9, line 2)
- Removes the component D2
- Extends the synchronization of D1 in order to wait the reception of three rollback events (Code 1.9, line 10).

```
1  component D1 {
2    flows: [f->Delay,TowTruck,dispatcherTrans],
3           [r->garage],[n->C1,C2];
4    reaction lambda (f@s) {
5      split {
6        emit (f@s);
7      } || {
8        emit (n@s);
9      } || {
10       addReaction (reaction check (r@s) {
11         addReaction (reaction check (r@s) {
12           addReaction (reaction check (r@s) {
13             emit (r@s);
14           });
15         });
16       });
17     }
18   }
19 }
```

Code 1.9: Resulting dispatcher of the refactoring

6 Concluding Remarks

Service manageability is a key issue that must be solved to widely adopt SOC. This paradigm can simplify software adaptation when changes in the business relations occur. However, the size of systems obtained by aggregating services can impose high costs possibly not affordable by small-medium enterprises. Of course, this may prevent SOA (service oriented architecture) to be largely adopted and limit its success.

To reduce costs and the efforts of adopting SOA solutions, developers and designers should separately manage different aspects a system. This goal can be achieved by the adoption of the Model Driven Development. Framework and tools should provide specific formalisms and languages suitable to manage a subset of the whole aspects of an application.

We focused on the issues related to the management of transactional aspects of SOA systems. In the last years several toolkits have been developed to handle these specific issues (e.g. Eclipse/BPEL [2,12]). However, these proposals lack solid foundational grounds, making it difficult to provide reasoning techniques and to prove correctness of applications.

In this paper we presented some of the main benefits provided by the strict interplay between theoretical results and programming practice. A key feature of our proposal is that any language involved by the development process has a formal description, allowing us to clearly define the semantics of systems and to provide sound tools. For example, our tool is equipped with refactoring rules that (i) support the designer in the refinement process (ii) do not affect the semantics of the system.

We plan to adopt the same methodology to provide further extension to our framework. We want to investigate formal methods to manage different aspects of the system (e.g. quality of service). These models can drive the definition of domain specific languages that allow the developer to separately manage the corresponding domains.

References

1. Ciancia, V., Ferrari, G., Guanciale, R., Strollo, D.: Global coordination policies for services. ENTCS 260, 73–89 (2010)
2. Eclipse Modeling Framework, `http://www.eclipse.org/modeling/emf/`
3. Ferrari, G.L., Guanciale, R., Strollo, D., Tuosto, E.: Coordination via types in an event-based framework. In: Derrick, J., Vain, J. (eds.) FORTE 2007. LNCS, vol. 4574, pp. 66–80. Springer, Heidelberg (2007)
4. Ferrari, G.L., Guanciale, R., Strollo, D., Tuosto, E.: Refactoring long runing transactions. In: WSFM (2008)
5. Ferrari, G.L., Guanciale, R., Strollo, D.: Jscl: A middleware for service coordination. In: Najm, et al. [6], pp. 46–60
6. Najm, E., Pradat-Peyre, J.-F., Donzeau-Gouge, V. (eds.): FORTE 2006. LNCS, vol. 4229. Springer, Heidelberg (2006)
7. OpenArchitectureWare MDA/MDD generator framework, `http://www.openarchitectureware.org/`
8. Business Process Modeling Notation (2002), `http://www.bpmn.org`
9. SENSORIA project, `http://sensoria.fast.de/`
10. White, S.: Introduction to BPMN (May 2004), `http://www.bpmn.org/Documents/Introduction%20to%20BPMN.pdf`
11. Wirsing, M., Clark, A., Gilmore, S., Hölzl, M.M., Knapp, A., Koch, N., Schroeder, A.: Semantic-based development of service-oriented systems. In: Najm, et al. [6], pp. 24–45
12. Wohed, P., van der Aalst, W.M., Dumas, M., ter Hofstede, A.H.: Pattern Based Analysis of BPEL4WS. Technical report, Department of Computer and Systems Sciences Stockholm University/The Royal Institute of Technology, Sweden (November 2003)

A Overview of BPMN

The graphical notation of BPMN permits to describe the work-flow of a distributed system by a global point of view. The software architect can abstract from the distribution of the processes, the communication mechanisms and the technologies that will implement each process. We focus on the transactional part of BPMN that in the following we indicate as LRT. Specifically, LRT encloses only the subset of BPMN necessary to model LRT.

The basic elements of LRT are *compensable activities*, namely pairs of activities and compensations that can be composed sequentially or in parallel.

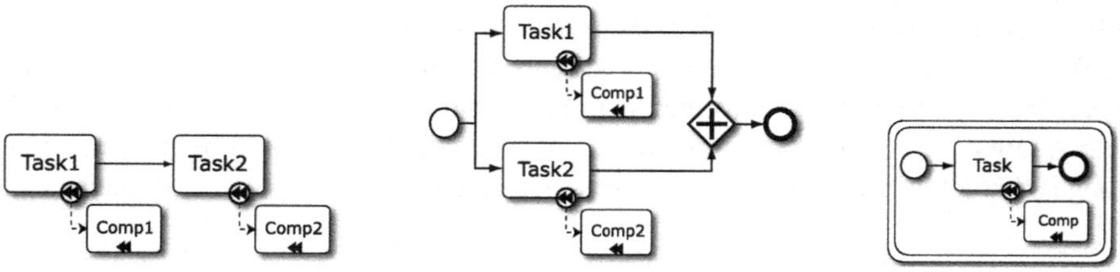

(a) Sequence (b) Parallel (c) Transactional scope

Fig. 7. Composition of compensable activities

Figure 7 depicts the designs respectively for sequential (a) and parallel (b) composition of compensable activities.Main activities and their compensations are represented as boxes linked by dashed arrows (for instance, `Task1` has a "compensation" entry point to which its compensation `Comp1` is attached). The sequential composition is performed by linking together the main activities (cf. Figure 7(a)), while the parallel composition makes use of "fork" and "join" operators.

In Figure 7(b) it is reported a parallel composition of two transactional activities. The two circles represent the start event and the end event of the whole process, while the diamond with the plus operation represents the join of the two parallel activities. The fork operation is implicit in the multiple connections on the start event.

Finally, compensable activities, and their compositions, can be enclosed inside transactional boundaries as shown in Figure 7(c).

All the elements presented at this layer are inherited from the core meta-models of BPMN and UML4SOA [11] and have the usual meaning of flowchart designs. Processes are built by composing activities as in Figure 7. BPMN does not specify the internal behaviour of activities and the interactions among components.

Approximate Model Checking of Stochastic COWS

Paola Quaglia and Stefano Schivo

Dipartimento di Ingegneria e Scienza dell'Informazione, Università di Trento

Abstract. Given the description of a model and a probabilistic formula, approximate model checking is a verification technique based on statistical reasoning that allows answering whether or not the model satisfies the formula. Only a subset of the properties that can be analyzed by exact model checking can be attacked by approximate methods. These latest methods, though, being based on simulation and sampling have the advantage of not requiring the generation of the complete state-space of the model.

Here we describe an efficient tool for the approximate model checking of services written in a stochastic variant of COWS, a process calculus for the orchestration of services.

1 Introduction

Stochastic process calculi have been mainly defined to ground the formal quantitative analysis of both performance and reliability aspects of concurrent distributed systems. When specializing the distributed paradigm to the case of service-oriented computation, performance issues suddenly become even more demanding by clearly expressing features like, e.g., quality of service, resource usage, and dependability. That is why recent research work in the concurrency community focussed on the definition of probabilistic/stochastic extensions of calculi explicitly meant to specify services and hence natively equipped with primitives for rendering basic service operations as sessioning or protection [3,15].

On the quantitative analysis side, the primary techniques to be applied are Monte Carlo simulation and probabilistic model checking. The first one, which is mostly used to reason about really huge systems (e.g., biological ones), consists in running a number of execution traces of the system, and then inferring the relevant information by applying statistical methods. Model checking, which can be either *exact* or *approximate*, grounds on a quite distinctive point of view. Both in the exact and in the approximate case, indeed, model checking consists in contrasting the behaviour of the system against a specific property expressed as a formula of a given probabilistic or stochastic logic (e.g., CSL [1]).

In more detail, exact model checking numerically checks the complete state-space of the system against a formula and returns a totally accurate result. Approximate model checking, instead, is based on simulation and sampling. The estimation if the given property holds is rather based on statistical reasoning on the generated samples. Different approaches offer a choice between *a priori* setting a fixed number of samples or not. In the first case, the generation of samples is stopped when the predetermined maximum is reached and an answer is given based on the available data. When the number

M. Wirsing, M. Hofmann, and A. Rauschmayer (Eds.): TGC 2010, LNCS 6084, pp. 335–347, 2010.

of samples is not fixed, the user can set a desired error probability (confidence level). The lower the confidence level, the bigger the number of samples to be generated.

Approximate model checking cannot have the same high level of accuracy as the result of the numerical methods of exact model checking. Also, given that samples are deemed to have finite length, approximate model checking cannot be used to check as many kinds of formulae as those checked by exact techniques. Building the complete state-space of the system, though, is not necessary. This is the good point of approximate model checking: memory requirements are negligible if compared to those imposed by numerical methods. Indeed, especially for loosely coupled interacting systems as those used for representing service computations, the size of the corresponding model typically suffers an exponential blow-up leading to state-space explosion.

This paper describes a tool for the approximate model checking of services described in Scows [17], the stochastic extension of COWS [14] (Calculus for Orchestration of Web Services), a calculus for service-oriented computation strongly inspired by WS-BPEL. We first overview the source language (Section 2) which extends the work presented in [15] to polyadic communication. Then we describe the tool, called Scows_amc, together with the foundational theory it is based upon (Section 3). Further, in Section 4, based on a simple service describing the classical scenario of the dining philosophers, the efficiency of Scows_amc is compared to the results obtained by applying Scows_lts [2], a tool that builds the complete Continuos Time Markov Chain (CTMC) corresponding to Scows services and allows their exact model checking through PRISM [13].

2 Scows Overview

Scows is a stochastic extension of COWS, to which the capability to represent quantitative aspects of services (in particular, execution time) has been added. The semantics of Scows reflects the one of the basic calculus, where an original communication paradigm is used. This paradigm is based on a mechanism of *best-matching* of the parameters of complementary invoke (send) and request (receive) activities.

The COWS communication paradigm is best illustrated by a simple example. To this purpose, let us consider the following term composed of three parallel services:

$$[\,n_1, n_2, y_1, y_2\,]\,(p.o\,!\,\langle n_1, n_2\rangle \mid p.o\,?\langle n_1, y_2\rangle.\, s_1 \mid p.o\,?\langle y_1, y_2\rangle.\, s_2) \qquad (1)$$

where $[\,n_1, n_2, y_1, y_2\,]$ is a scope delimiter for n_1, n_2, y_1, and y_2. The leftmost subcomponent $p.o\,!\,\langle n_1, n_2\rangle$ can send the tuple of names $\langle n_1, n_2\rangle$ over the endpoint $p.o$ (an endpoint is given by a *partner name* and an *operation name*, respectively p and o in this case). In (1) the middle service $p.o\,?\langle n_1, y_2\rangle.\, s_1$ is a request-guarded term. It is waiting to receive over the endpoint $p.o$ a pair of actual parameters matching the formal tuple $\langle n_1, y_2\rangle$, where y_2 is a variable. Names and variables play quite distinctive roles in the matching policy. Names can be thought of as constants or ground objects: each name can only match itself. Variables instead can match any name. Briefly put, matching two tuples means finding a substitution of names for variables that, applied to the tuple of the receiving service, makes it equal to the tuple of actual parameters offered by the sending service. So, for instance, the tuples $\langle n_1, n_2 \rangle$ and $\langle n_1, y_2 \rangle$ match because the substitution of n_2 for y_2, written $\{^{n_2}/_{y_2}\}$, when applied to $\langle n_1, y_2 \rangle$ results in $\langle n_1, n_2 \rangle$. Going back to the behaviour of the service $p.o\,?\langle n_1, y_2 \rangle.\, s_1$, the execution of the request activity would unblock the continuation service s_1 and would make it dependent on the substitution induced by the matching. For instance, a communication between the leftmost parallel services in (1) would result in running $s_1\{^{n_2}/_{y_2}\}$. The rightmost parallel component $p.o\,?\langle y_1, y_2 \rangle.\, s_2$ is much similar in its structure to the middle one. It is a request-guarded term with potentials for interaction with whichever service can offer over $p.o$ a tuple matching $\langle y_1, y_2 \rangle$, where y_1 is yet another variable. The tuple $\langle n_1, n_2 \rangle$ offered by the leftmost service matches $\langle y_1, y_2 \rangle$ by inducing the substitution $\{^{n_1}/_{y_1}, ^{n_2}/_{y_2}\}$. Out of a set of potential communications, the *best-matching* mechanism adopted by COWS amounts to allow only those communications that induce substitutions as small as possible. So in our example $p.o\,!\langle n_1, n_2 \rangle$ can only communicate with $p.o\,?\langle n_1, y_2 \rangle.\, s_1$. Here notice that if the global service were augmented by adding a fourth parallel component $p.o\,?\langle y_1, n_2 \rangle.\, s_3$, then $p.o\,!\langle n_1, n_2 \rangle$ could communicate with either $p.o\,?\langle n_1, y_2 \rangle.\, s_1$ or $p.o\,?\langle y_1, n_2 \rangle.\, s_3$. So the best-matching policy is not a cure against non-determinism. It rather serves the purpose of implementing sessioning: opening a session is rendered by passing a unique name as session identifier, and all the communications relative to that session will carry on that identifier as parameter. Moreover, in the same way as the interaction of $p.o\,!\langle n_1, n_2 \rangle$ with $p.o\,?\langle n_1, y_2 \rangle.\, s_1$ pre-empties the communication with $p.o\,?\langle y_1, y_2 \rangle.\, s_2$, concluding the operations relative to an open session will have priority over opening a new session (just think of n_1 as of a session identifier).

In the stochastic extension of COWS, each basic action (the two communicating primitives request and invoke, plus a special killing activity used for process termination) is enriched by a real number representing the rate of an exponential distribution, which models the time taken by the service to execute the corresponding action. For example, letting $\delta_1, \delta_2, \delta_3$ to stay for rates, the term in (1) would be written as follows in Scows:

$$[\, n_1, n_2, y_1, y_2 \,]\, (\, (p.o!\langle n_1, n_2 \rangle, \delta_1) \mid (p.o?\langle n_1, y_2 \rangle, \delta_2).\, s_1 \mid (p.o?\langle y_1, y_2 \rangle, \delta_3).\, s_2 \,).$$

The interaction paradigm adopted in the basic calculus, and retained in Scows, is responsible of a rather complex rate computation method for communications. Indeed, the competition induced by the best-matching policy for pairing invoke and request activities has to be correctly reflected in the rate of the resulting action. In particular, polyadicity makes rate computation quite more intricate in Scows than what can be seen in [15] where a monadic version of the basic calculus was considered. On the other hand, polyadic communication allows the user to explicitly render the use of session identifiers.

We will briefly illustrate the main issues about rate computation by means of a simple example. Consider the following service definition:

$$\begin{aligned} S = [\, m, n, n', x, y \,]\, (&\underbrace{(p.o!\langle m, n \rangle, \delta_1)}_{S_1} \mid \underbrace{(p.o!\langle m, n' \rangle, \delta_2)}_{S_2} \mid \underbrace{(p.o!\langle n, n' \rangle, \delta_3)}_{S_3} \mid \underbrace{(p.o!\langle n, n \rangle, \delta_4)}_{S_4} \\ &\mid \underbrace{(p.o?\langle m, x \rangle, \gamma_1).\, \mathbf{0}}_{S_5} \mid \underbrace{(p.o?\langle y, n' \rangle, \gamma_2).\, \mathbf{0}}_{S_6}) \end{aligned}$$

Using the notation $S_j \rhd S_k$ to mean that services S_j and S_k communicate (with S_j sending and S_k receiving), we list below all the communications allowed in S by the matching paradigm:

- $S_1 \rhd S_5$, matching m with m and substituting x by n;
- $S_2 \rhd S_5$, matching m with m and substituting x by n';
- $S_2 \rhd S_6$, substituting y by m and matching n' with n';
- $S_3 \rhd S_6$, substituting y by n and matching n' with n';
- no service can successfully match S_4's tuple, so S_4 does not communicate.

Observing the interaction capabilities of the processes in the example, we suggest an asymmetric way to intend the communication paradigm in Scows in the sense that the choice of an invoke action also determines the set of possible communications. For instance, one single communication is possible when choosing the invoking service S_1, and the same holds when selecting S_3. On the other hand, if the sending service S_2 is chosen, then there are two possible communications: $S_2 \rhd S_5$ and $S_2 \rhd S_6$. Note that, as both $S_2 \rhd S_5$ and $S_2 \rhd S_6$ induce one substitution, they are equally viable from the non-stochastic point of view, while the stochastic rates of the two transitions can determine different probabilities for the execution of the two distinct actions.

In case of communications, the rate computation also depends on the so-called *apparent rate* of the participants. The apparent rate represents the rate at which actions of the same type are perceived by an observer located outside the service. We consider two actions to be indistinguishable from the point of view of an external observer if these actions are competing to participate with the same role in the same communication. In the case of an invoke action the actions competing with it are all the send-actions available on the same endpoint. The case of a request action is more complicated, as it requires to take into account also all the actions which would have been in competition with the chosen one if another invoke action would have been selected. The formal definition of the Scows operational semantics is outside the scope of the present paper. For more details on the actual computation of apparent rates the interested reader is referred to [17].

The rate of a communication event is obtained by multiplying the apparent rate of the communication by the probability to choose exactly the two participants involved in that communication. Adopting a classical way of approximating exponential rates [9], we take the apparent rate of a communication to be the minimum between the apparent rates of the participating services (i.e., the communication proceeds at the speed of the "slowest" of the participants). So, the formula for the rate of a communication between the invoking service S_j and the requesting service S_k has the following form:

$$\mathcal{P}(S_j \rhd S_k) \cdot \mathtt{min}\Big(\mathtt{appRate}(S_j), \mathtt{appRate}(S_k)\Big),$$

where $\mathcal{P}(S_j \rhd S_k)$ is the probability that services S_j and S_k are involved in the communication, and $\mathtt{appRate}(S_j)$ (resp. $\mathtt{appRate}(S_k)$) represents the apparent rate of the invoke (request) action computed considering the whole service containing S_j and S_k. As we consider request actions to be dependent on invoke actions, the probability to choose a particular invoke-request pair is computed as a conditional probability:

$$\mathcal{P}(S_j \rhd S_k) = \mathcal{P}(S_j) \cdot \mathcal{P}(S_k \mid S_j).$$

This means that the probability of a communication between the invoke S_j and the request S_k is given by the product of the probability to have chosen S_j among all possible invoke actions on endpoint $p.o$ and the probability to choose S_k among the request actions made available by the choice of S_j (i.e., the request actions best-matching S_j).

In the above example, the probability that a communication occurs between S_2 and S_5 is calculated as follows:

$$\begin{aligned}\mathcal{P}(S_2 \rhd S_5) &= \mathcal{P}(S_2) \cdot \mathcal{P}(S_5 \mid S_2)\\ &= \frac{\delta_2}{\delta_1 + \delta_2 + \delta_3} \cdot \frac{\gamma_1}{\gamma_1 + \gamma_2}\,.\end{aligned}$$

Given that S_4 cannot take part into any communication, the rate δ_4 of service S_4 is not taken into account. On the other hand, as S_5 is the single request action matching with S_1, the probability of a communication between S_1 and S_5 is basically the probability of choosing S_1:

$$\begin{aligned}\mathcal{P}(S_1 \rhd S_5) &= \mathcal{P}(S_1) \cdot \mathcal{P}(S_5 \mid S_1)\\ &= \frac{\delta_1}{\delta_1 + \delta_2} \cdot 1\,.\end{aligned}$$

Here notice that we do not take into account the rate δ_3 of service S_3, as S_3 cannot communicate with S_5 ($n \neq m$) and thus cannot influence the above communication.

3 Scows_amc

Generating a CTMC from a Scows term, as required by exact model checking, can be a computationally costly task, and could even lead to state-explosion when building the underlying transition system. This issue is most evident when a model comprises a number of loosely coupled components, as it is often the case when dealing with distributed systems. A compositional generation of the transition system might help minimizing the state space, thanks to the fact that parallel components could be considered in isolation and then merged with less-than-exponential execution time. Unfortunately, this type of approach cannot be applied in the case of Scows. This is due to the adopted communication paradigm which requires the complete knowledge of the model to calculate each single communication action, de facto preventing a compositional generation of the transition system. In languages with multi-way synchronization and not featuring name-passing, like e.g. in PEPA [9], the compositional approach can be applied and is in fact feasible: for instance, such an approach is used for the generation of CTMCs from PEPA models in PRISM, which is based on MTBDD (Multi-Terminal Binary Decision Diagrams [4,8]) representations. Another example of application of the same principle can be seen in CASPA [12], a tool which generates a MTBDD representation from YAMPA, a stochastic process algebra based on TIPP [7].

Below we present a tool, called Scows_amc, that allows statistical model checking of Scows terms while maintaining acceptable computation time and approximation values. In order not to generate complete transition systems, we base our approach on direct simulations of Scows models. In particular, we generate a number of simulation traces by applying the operational semantics rules directly to Scows services, and then perform the computations necessary to check the desired formula against these traces. As a single execution trace of a stochastic model is by definition a random walk on the transition system of the model, we resort to statistical reasoning in order to estimate the size of the error we make in evaluating the requested property through a finite number of random walks. The theories behind the reasoning on which the approach used by Scows_amc is based are the one adopted in Ymer [11], and the one adopted in APMC [5,6]. In particular, letting $\bowtie \in \{<, \leqslant, >, \geqslant\}$, $t_0, t_1 \in \mathbb{R}^+$, and $\theta \in [0, 1]$, Scows_amc can model check Scows terms against the usual CSL time-bounded until properties of the form:

$$\mathcal{P}_{\bowtie\theta}\,[\Psi_1 \ \mathcal{U}^{[t_0,t_1]} \ \Psi_2] \tag{2}$$

and their numerical corresponding in the following shape:

$$\mathcal{P}_{=?}\,[\Psi_1 \ \mathcal{U}^{[t_0,t_1]} \ \Psi_2] \tag{3}$$

which can be read as:

> "Is there a probability $p \bowtie \theta$ that state formula Ψ_1 will hold until, inside the time interval $[t_0, t_1]$, state formula Ψ_2 holds?"

and, respectively,

> "What is the probability that state formula Ψ_1 will hold until, inside the time interval $[t_0, t_1]$, state formula Ψ_2 holds?"

where the state formulae Ψ_1 and Ψ_2 are to be intended as state labels.

The truth value of CSL probabilistic formulae of the type (2) is calculated through the *sequential probability ratio test* [18]. This method requires to perform a sequence of observations of the hypothesis to be tested. After each observation an error estimation is made, taking into account the results of all the previous observations. When a given error threshold is crossed, the hypothesis is either accepted or rejected. In our case, performing an observation corresponds to testing the formula over an execution trace, which is generated on demand. This kind of approach does not require to have an exact estimation of the real probability to have the property verified: it only checks whether the probability lies below or beyond the specified threshold. The algorithm implemented to apply the sequential probability ratio test and to evaluate formulae of type (2) is reported as pseudocode in Algorithm 1. The applied method computes estimations based on three approximation parameters: α (the probability to get a false negative), β (the probability to get a false positive), and δ (the semi-distance from θ used to define the indifference region). These parameters must be chosen making a trade-off between the execution time and the answer confidence.

In order to obtain the approximate model checking of formulae of type (3), we rely on a method presented in [5] and based on [10]. As in the case of formulae of type (2), the value of properties is estimated by means of a series of observations on random walks over the transition system. This time, however, the number of observations necessary to obtain the desired approximation level is determined *before* observations are made. This allows the user to make trade-offs between speed and approximation with

Algorithm 1. The algorithm used to perform the sequential probability ratio test

```
input α, β, δ, Φ = P_{⋈θ}[φ]
p0 ← θ + δ
p1 ← θ − δ
logA ← ln (1−β)/α
logB ← ln β/(1−α)
nSamples ← 0
d ← 0
while logB < d ∧ d < logA do
   generate a random walk σ
   if σ ⊨ φ then
      d ← d + ln p1/p0
   else
      d ← d + ln (1−p1)/(1−p0)
   end if
   nSamples ← nSamples + 1
end while
if ⋈ ∈ {>, ⩾} then
   return d ⩽ logB
else
   return d > logB
end if
```

a deeper insight on the effects of his choices. Two main parameters are used for error estimation: the *approximation parameter* ε, and the *confidence parameter* δ. It can be shown that the evaluation of the given formula on $O\left(\frac{1}{\varepsilon^2} \cdot \log \frac{1}{\delta}\right)$ random walks brings to a probability estimation differing from the real value by less than ε with probability $1 - \delta$. The number of random walks necessary to obtain the desired result is given by the following formula:

$$nObservations = 4 \cdot \frac{\log \frac{2}{\delta}}{\varepsilon^2}. \tag{4}$$

Algorithm 2 is used in Scows_amc for the estimation of type (3) formulae and it is in fact the one presented in [5]. The idea on which the algorithm is based in order to compute the probability estimation for $\mathcal{P}_{=?}[\varphi]$ is to execute a fixed number of observations of the truth value of the formula φ, and then count the number of positive results. The probability that φ is true is given by the ratio between the number of positive observations and the total number of observations.

A final observation is about what is involved in checking until path formulae. Algorithm 3 is used to obtain the truth value for one of such formulae on a single simulation trace of the model. Notice that the algorithm performs the checking of the formula as the generation of the trace goes along. This is a solution which has a better average execution time w.r.t. an approach in which a complete simulation trace is generated and then checked against the path formula. This is possible thanks to the fact that the until formula has time bounds, which allows us to stop the generation of a trace when "time is up" or when a truth value for the formula has been found, even if the simulation could proceed further.

Algorithm 2. The algorithm used in Scows_amc for the estimation of a CSL formula in the form $\mathcal{P}_{=?}[\varphi]$.

---

input δ, ε
$nObservations \leftarrow 4\log\left(\frac{2}{\delta}\right)/\varepsilon^2$
$count \leftarrow 0$
for $i = 1$ to $nObservations$ **do**
  generate a random walk σ
  if $\sigma \models \varphi$ **then**
    $count \leftarrow count + 1$
  end if
end for
return $count/nObservations$

Algorithm 3. Verification of a bounded until formula

1: **input** α, β, δ, Scows*model*, $\varphi = \Phi_1\,\mathcal{U}^{[tmin,tmax]}\,\Phi_2$
2: $totalTime \leftarrow 0$
3: $nextTime \leftarrow 0$
4: $currState \leftarrow$ initialState(Scows*model*)
5: $transitions \leftarrow$ computeTransitions($currState$)
6: **while** $\neg$isEmpty($transitions$) **do**
7:   $(nextState, \tau) \leftarrow$ computeNextState($transitions$)
8:   $nextTime \leftarrow totalTime + \tau$
9:   **if** $tmin \leq totalTime$ **then**
10:     **if** verify(Φ_2, $currState$, α, β, δ) **then**
11:       **return** true
12:     **else if** $\neg$verify(Φ_1, $currState$, α, β, δ) **then**
13:       **return** false
14:     **end if**
15:   **else**
16:     **if** $\neg$verify(Φ_1, $currState$, α, β, δ) **then**
17:       **return** false
18:     **else if** $tmin < nextTime \wedge$ verify(Φ_2, $currState$, α, β, δ) **then**
19:       **return** true
20:     **end if**
21:   **end if**
22:   $currState \leftarrow nextState$
23:   $totalTime \leftarrow nextTime$
24:   **if** $tmax < totalTime$ **then**
25:     **return** false
26:   **end if**
27:   $transitions \leftarrow$ computeTransitions($currState$)
28:   **if** isEmpty($transitions$) **then**
29:     **return** verify(Φ_2, $currState$, α, β, δ)
30:   **end if**
31: **end while**
32: **return** false

---

4 Comparison with CTMC Generation

To the best of our knowledge, the single other tool available for the quantitative model checking of Scows is Scows_lts [2], which takes an approach orthogonal to that of Scows_amc. Indeed Scows_lts performs probabilistic model checking by generating a CTMC from a Scows model and then by using PRISM to obtain an assessment of the model.

In what follows, we show a test for the performance of Scows_amc by comparing it against Scows_lts. As a test-bed for the comparison we use a simple model of the system of the dining philosophers, an instance of which is presented in Table 1 using the Scows syntax accepted by Scows_amc. We model the problem using knives and forks as cutlery, and coupling right-handed philosophers with left-handed ones, in order to have an alternating pattern allowing each philosopher to eat with the preferred hand. The rates `r1`, `r2`, `r3`, ... are defined as parameters of the model. This feature is meant to foster sensitivity analysisis, and indeed Scows_lts can itself handle parametric rates.

The model in Table 1 is used in the experiment varying the number of dining philosophers between 2 and 12, properly adapting the available cutlery. As we differentiate between right-handed and left-handed philosophers, the resulting models will include an even number of philosophers. The CSL formula against which all the models are checked is the following one:

$$\mathcal{P}_{=?}\,[\texttt{true}\;\mathcal{U}^{[0,\mathtt{T}]}\;\texttt{fed} = \mathtt{N}]$$

meaning

"What is the probability that `N` philosophers are fed at time `T`?".

The formula has been checked with parameters `N` and `T` varying between 0 and the number of philosophers in the model, and, respectively, between 0 and 40 time units. The settings for Scows_amc have been chosen so to obtain results with approximation of 10^{-2} with confidence of 0.9, and hence are $\varepsilon = 0.01$ and $\delta = 0.1$. This implies that 52042 simulation traces need to be computed for each configuration of the CSL formula. Actually, the number of computed traces is 52042 in total, as our tool uses an optimization which allows us to reduce the number of simulation traces needed to obtain the requested evaluations. Basically, we reuse the same trace for testing all the formulae which we need to test before proceeding with the computation of a new simulation trace.

As said, Scows_amc is compared against Scows_lts, which actually exploits PRISM for the analysis of CTMCs. The version of PRISM employed in our tests is the 3.3.1, available for download from the PRISM web site [16]. The CSL property has been checked against the relevant CTMCs by means of both the numerical (exact) and the simulation-based (approximate) approaches available in PRISM. As the approximate model checking used in PRISM is the same as the one used in Scows_amc, we have used the same parameters also for PRISM. All the tests have been executed on a workstation equipped with an Intel (R) Pentium (R) D 3.40 GHz CPU and 2 Gigabyte of RAM, running Ubuntu Linux 9.10.

The results of the comparison are shown in Table 2, where we report the execution time of Scows_amc against that of Scows_lts together with PRISM, when checking

Table 1. An instance of the dining philosophers system modelled in Scows

```
//Agents

//RHphil: right-handed philosopher
RHphil(right#, left#) =
[fork][knife]( (right#.take#?<fork>,r1) . (left#.take#?<knife>,r2) .
    [eat#][food#]( (eat#.eat#!<food#>,r3) | (eat#.eat#?<food#>,r4) .
         ( (left#.release#!<knife>,r5) | (right#.release#!<fork>,r6) )
    )
);

//LHphil: left-handed philosopher
LHphil(right#, left#) =
[knife][fork]( (right#.take#?<knife>,r7) . (left#.take#?<fork>,r8) .
    [eat#][food#]( (eat#.eat#!<food#>,r9) | (eat#.eat#?<food#>,r10) .
         ( (left#.release#!<fork>,r11) | (right#.release#!<knife>,r12) )
    )
);

Cutlery(f#) = [p#] ( (f#.take#!<p#>,r13)
                   | (f#.release#?<p#>,r14).Cutlery(f#) );

$
//initial process

[fork1#][knife1#][fork2#][knife2#][take#][release#] (
      RHphil(fork1#, knife1#) | LHphil(knife1#, fork2#)
    | RHphil(fork2#, knife2#) | LHphil(knife2#, fork1#)
    | Cutlery(fork1#) | Cutlery(knife1#)
    | Cutlery(fork2#) | Cutlery(knife2#)
)

$

//counter definitions

fed : [ 0 .. 4 ];

$
//cows actions <-> counter modifications

eat#.eat#<*>: fed < 4 : (fed' = fed + 1);
```

Table 2. Computational time results for the example model checking (time is expressed in seconds). The two columns for PRISM correspond to the numerical (exact) and simulation-based (approximate) model checking approaches.

Philosophers	State space size	Scows_lts	PRISM		Scows_amc
			Exact	Approx.	
2	20	0.9	1.9	95.5	395.6
4	249	345.4	153.5	1871.2	5537.8
6	3247	523173.0	138749.0	73729.4	31109.4
8	-	-	-	-	113603.0
10	-	-	-	-	309769.1
12	-	-	-	-	719487.9

the models against the CSL formula. The time taken to model check the CTMC with PRISM is shown separately in order to highlight the actual time taken to produce the relevant CTMC. The execution time results are plotted in Figure 1. Data for 8, 10, and 12 philosophers are not available for the case of CTMC-based model checking, as the estimated computational times for the generation of the CTMCs was too high. Relative to this issue, we notice here that Scows_lts undergoes a number of computationally heavy optimizations mainly related to congruence checking of the states of the labelled transition system the CTMC is based upon. These optimizations, which involve, e.g., verifying α-equivalence of Scows terms, are fundamental to keep the state-space as small as possible and hence to limit the effects of memory usage.

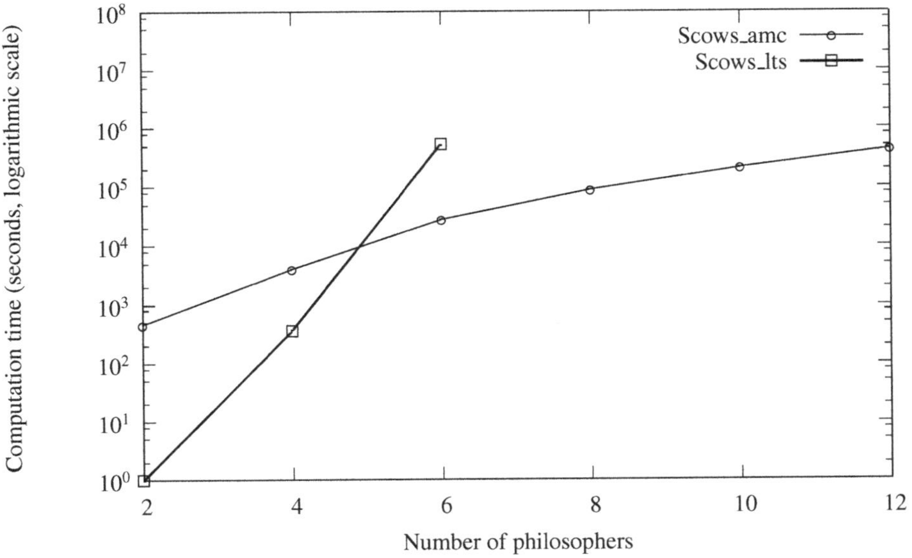

Fig. 1. Graph plotting execution time performances of the two approaches for model checking Scows models

Our comparison in Table 2 shows that when the number of states in the model is anticipated to be at most in the order of hundreds, the most convenient approach to model checking is to build a CTMC from the Scows model and use CTMC-based tools to perform the desired performance measures (either exact or approximate). Conversely, when the size of the state-space is estimated to be larger than few hundreds, the execution time of Scows_amc is expected to be lower. This execution speed comes at the price of precision, which however can be adjusted as necessity dictates.

5 Concluding Remarks

A tool for the approximate model checking of Scows was described. An application of the tool was also presented, measuring its performances in terms of execution time. The example clearly shows, whenever applicable, the advantage of approximated model checking over its exact counter-part which involves the generation of the full state-space of the term.

Acknowledgements. This work has been partially sponsored by the project SENSORIA, IST-2005-016004.

References

1. Aziz, A., Sanwal, K., Singhal, V., Brayton, R.: Model-checking continous-time Markov chains. ACM Trans. on Computational Logic 1(1), 162–170 (2000)
2. Cappello, I., Quaglia, P.: A Tool for Checking Probabilistic Properties of COWS Services. In: Proceedings of TGC 2010 (2010), http://disi.unitn.it/~cappello/
3. De Nicola, R., Latella, D., Loreti, M., Massink, M.: MarCaSPiS: a Markovian Extension of a Calculus for Services. Electronic Notes in Theoretical Computer Science 229(4), 11–26 (2009)
4. Fujita, M., McGeer, P.C., Yang, J.C.-Y.: Multi-Terminal Binary Decision Diagrams: An efficient data structure for matrix representation. Formal Methods in System Design 10, 149–169 (1997)
5. Hérault, T., Lassaigne, R., Magniette, F., Peyronnet, S.: Approximate probabilistic model checking. In: Steffen, B., Levi, G. (eds.) VMCAI 2004. LNCS, vol. 2937, pp. 307–329. Springer, Heidelberg (2004)
6. Hérault, T., Lassaigne, R., Peyronnet, S.: APMC 3.0: Approximate Verification of Discrete and Continuous Time Markov Chains. In: Proc. 3rd Int. Conf. on Quantitative Evaluation of Systems, QEST 2006, pp. 129–130. IEEE, Los Alamitos (2006)
7. Hermanns, H., Herzog, U., Katoen, J.-P.: Process algebra for performance evaluation. Theoretical Computer Science 274(1-2), 43–87 (2002)
8. Hermanns, H., Meyer-Kayser, J., Siegle, M.: Multi terminal binary decision diagrams to represent and analyse continuous time Markov chains. In: Plateau, B., Stewart, W., Silva, M. (eds.) Proc. 3rd International Workshop on Numerical Solution of Markov Chains (NSMC 1999), pp. 188–207. Prensas Universitarias de Zaragoza (1999)
9. Hillston, J.: A compositional approach to performance modelling. Cambridge University Press, New York, NY, USA (1996)
10. Hoeffding, W.: Probability inequalities for sums of bounded random variables. Journal of the American Statistical Association 58(301), 13–30 (1963)

11. Younes, H.L.: Verification and Planning for Stochastic Processes with Asynchronous Events. PhD thesis, Computer Science Department, Carnegie Mellon University, Pittsburgh, Pennsylvania (2005)
12. Kuntz, G.W.M.: Symbolic Semantics and Verification of Stochastic Process Algebras. PhD thesis, Friedrich-Alexander-Universitaet Erlangen-Nuernberg, Erlangen (March 2006)
13. Kwiatkowska, M., Norman, G., Parker, D.: PRISM: Probabilistic Model Checking for Performance and Reliability Analysis. ACM SIGMETRICS Performance Evaluation Review 36(4), 40–45 (2009)
14. Lapadula, A., Pugliese, R., Tiezzi, F.: Calculus for Orchestration of Web Services. In: De Nicola, R. (ed.) ESOP 2007. LNCS, vol. 4421, pp. 33–47. Springer, Heidelberg (2007), `http://rap.dsi.unifi.it/cows/`
15. Prandi, D., Quaglia, P.: Stochastic COWS. In: Krämer, B.J., Lin, K.-J., Narasimhan, P. (eds.) ICSOC 2007. LNCS, vol. 4749, pp. 245–256. Springer, Heidelberg (2007)
16. PRISM homepage, `http://www.prismmodelchecker.org/`
17. Schivo, S.: Statistical model checking of Web Services. PhD thesis, Int. Doctorate School in Information and Communication Technologies, University of Trento (2010)
18. Wald, A.: Sequential tests of statistical hypotheses. The Annals of Mathematical Statistics 16(2), 117–186 (1945)

Probabilistic Aspects: Checking Security in an Imperfect World

Chris Hankin[1], Flemming Nielson[2], and Hanne Riis Nielson[2]

[1] Department of Computing, Imperial College London
clh@imperial.ac.uk
[2] DTU Informatics, Technical University of Denmark
{nielson,riis}@imm.dtu.dk

Abstract. We address the challenges arising from enforcing security policies in an imperfect world – in a system involving humans, a determined attacker always has a chance of circumventing any security. We motivate our approach by two examples: an on-line auction house; and a airport security system. In our work, security policies are enforced using a probabilistic aspect-oriented approach; policies are combined using a rich set of policy composition operators. We present the examples using a process-based language in which processes and local data are distributed across a number of locations (network addresses). The formal definition of the language gives rise to Markov Decision Processes.

1 Introduction

The usual view on security in IT systems is that the security policies should be enforced at all times. This presents a mostly static and deterministic view of security policies, except that it is widely recognised that at certain times the security policies need to be modified, which may present security problems of its own. It is less common to consider the possibility that the enforcement of security policies may depend on factors outside of our control and hence be imperfect. This may be due to human involvement, e.g. in providing basic input to the system based on an interview with an applicant, or may be due to distributed databases not yet fully synchronised, e.g. in propagating the revocation of a credit card throughout the banking sector.

In this paper we address the challenges arising from enforcing security policies in an imperfect world. For example, airport security is not perfect and, even at heightened security levels, there is a probability that terrorists will evade the checks. We perform our development in a distributed setting where processes and local data are distributed on a number of locations (e.g. network addresses) and where the security policies govern whether or not to allow certain actions to proceed. Our proposal makes use of probabilities to describe the potential imperfections in enforcing the security policy of interest. To obtain a flexible specification of security policies, that can be changed as the need arises, we follow the aspect oriented approach of specifying the security policies using aspects that can then be "woven into" the program [11,7]. In contrast to conventional aspects,

M. Wirsing, M. Hofmann, and A. Rauschmayer (Eds.): TGC 2010, LNCS 6084, pp. 348–363, 2010.

our aspects do not perform any actions but act as predicates which either allow or disallow the interrupted action. Whilst a policy decision is boolean, policy composition is often better expressed using a four-valued logic (allowing underspecification and inconsistency as additional outcomes) [4].

Our proposal therefore is to develop a notion of aspects that can express security policies using a four-valued probabilistic logic. We perform this development in a setting inspired by the primitives found in the distributed coordination language Klaim [2]. This should be contrasted to the approaches of StoKlaim [5], where the actions have rates, and pKlaim [10], where operators in the process language have probabilities associated with them. Our intention is to stimulate and contribute to a study of how to model security policies in a distributed, imperfect world.

Overview. Our presentation is primarily based on two examples: a simple on-line auction house, and a model of airport security; these are presented in Section 2. Our technical development is based on our previous work where a distributed coordination language with features from Klaim is extended with aspects using a four-valued logic for security policies [8]. It is extended with a probabilistic four-valued logic (developed in Section 3) to express probabilistic policies and their composition in a distributed manner. The syntax and semantics of the language is overviewed in Section 4 while the formal details are left for Appendix A; as we shall see, the probabilistic four-valued logic gives rise to Markov Decision Processes. Section 5 presents our conclusions and pointers to future work.

2 Examples

The language that we use to model our examples is a distributed process calculus. Processes are located (i.e. have an address), and each location also has a local memory. The simplest form of process is a sequence of actions but we also use the standard process algebra operations to combine processes. Communication between processes is achieved by the source process placing a tuple in the target process' local memory.

In addition to basic process calculus features, every address has a "policy" associated with it. This policy is a combination of primitive aspects and each aspect is of the form $[rec \ \underline{\text{if}} \ \ cut : cond]$. Here *cut* is the action to be trapped by the aspect: the location of the subject and the action (including the operation and the location of the target). Actions can output tuples to an address (**out**) and read tuples from an address, either destructively (**in**), or not (**read**). The *rec* component is a probabilistic four-valued policy recommendation and *cond* is a boolean applicability condition. When a process attempts to perform an action at an address, the policies for the process and for the address are both checked. If an aspect applies to the action (i.e. the action matches and *cond* is true), the recommendation is evaluated to give the probability with which the action is allowed to proceed. This may be viewed as a way of recording the effectiveness of enforcing the intended security policies. We dispense with a more formal account of the syntax until presenting Tables 1 and 2 in Section 4.

2.1 The On-Line Auction

We shall be modelling a small electronic auction system pBuy; the system consists of a single location for pBuy and a location for each buyer and seller registered with the auction house. The local memory of pBuy contains six kinds of data:

- $\langle \mathsf{buyer}, \mathit{name}, \mathit{profile} \rangle$ records that *name* is a registered buyer and has feedback profile $\mathit{profile} \in \{\mathsf{good}, \mathsf{moderate}, \mathsf{new}\}$;
- $\langle \mathsf{seller}, \mathit{name} \rangle$ records that *name* is a registered seller;
- $\langle \mathsf{safepay}, \mathit{seller} \rangle$ records that *seller* is registered to receive secure payments;
- $\langle \mathsf{monthly}, \mathit{seller} \rangle$ records that *seller* is registered to receive payments by monthly installments;
- $\langle \mathsf{object}, \mathit{number}, \mathit{seller}, \mathit{range} \rangle$ indicates that *seller* is offering an object with identification *number* for sale in the price range $\mathit{range} \in \{\mathsf{cheap}, \mathsf{affordable}, \mathsf{expensive}\}$; and
- $\langle \mathsf{bid}, \mathit{number}, \mathit{buyer}, \mathit{value} \rangle$ indicates a bid from *buyer* for object *number* at value *value*.

We concentrate on the policies to be associated with the different kinds of locations in the system while paying less attention to the processes for the locations; for example a simple, but rather compulsive, process for a buyer, b, might be:

$$*(\mathsf{read}(\mathsf{object}, n, s, r)@\mathsf{pBuy}.\mathsf{out}(\mathsf{bid}, n, b, 100)@\mathsf{pBuy})$$

which repeatedly selects some item from the auction and bids 100 currency units for the item.

We proceed by defining policies for the auction house, potential buyers and potential sellers.

The auction house. The following policy, which is actually deterministic, expresses that only registered buyers may place bids for objects that are up for auction and that they can only place bids on behalf of themselves. The rule applies to any matching output action (indicated by the use of true in the applicability condition). The predicate test(_)@_ tests whether there is a tuple at the location (second argument) which matches the tuple pattern (first argument) – _ is used to represent a don't care pattern:

$$\mathsf{Pol}_{\mathsf{buy}} \triangleq \left[\begin{array}{l} \mathsf{test}(\mathsf{object}, n, \_, \_)@\mathsf{pBuy} \wedge \\ \quad \mathsf{test}(\mathsf{buyer}, u, \_)@\mathsf{pBuy} \wedge u = b \\ \underline{\mathsf{if}}\ u :: \mathsf{out}(\mathsf{bid}, n, b, \_)@\mathsf{pBuy} : \\ \quad \mathsf{true} \end{array}\right]$$

This policy deals with all attempts to place bids in the data base of pBuy and imposes the conditions mentioned; in all other cases no conditions are imposed. The policy recommendation actually evaluates to (the probabilistic four-valued representation of) true or false depending on whether the conditions are met or not. The idea is that the action is only allowed to proceed if the recommendation cannot give false (except perhaps with low probability).

Similarly, only registered sellers can put objects up for auction:

$$\mathsf{Pol}_{\mathsf{sell}} \triangleq \begin{bmatrix} \mathsf{test}(\mathsf{seller}, l)@\mathsf{pBuy} \ \wedge u = l \\ \underline{\mathsf{if}}\ u :: \mathsf{out}(\mathsf{object}, \_, l, \_)@\mathsf{pBuy} : \\ \quad \mathsf{true} \end{bmatrix}$$

On top of this the auction house will want to impose a number of policies that express that buyers and sellers are in general "well behaved" in not attempting to place entries in the data base that conflict with the prescribed form above; while it is straightforward to model this using aspects this is not central to our concerns in this paper.

The overall policy for the auction house, that is, the location pBuy, therefore is:

$$\mathsf{Pol}_{\mathsf{house}} \triangleq \mathsf{Pol}_{\mathsf{buy}} \oplus \mathsf{Pol}_{\mathsf{sell}}$$

We will give a precise definition of $\oplus$ in Section 3.

Buyers. The overall policy for the buyers is composed from two components.

There may be some circumstances when the buyer is concerned that the seller has a mechanism for secure payment – this might be relevant when the object is not cheap. In order to model this, we need a new unary operator on four-valued values, $?_s$, that with probability s returns its argument and with probability $1 - s$ gives true. The policy can then be modelled as follows:

$$\mathsf{Pol}^{sp}_{\mathsf{secure}} \triangleq \begin{bmatrix} ?_{sp}\, \mathsf{false} \\ \underline{\mathsf{if}}\ u :: \mathsf{out}(\mathsf{bid}, n, b, \_)@\mathsf{pBuy} : \\ \quad u = b \ \wedge \exists r, s : (\mathsf{test}(\mathsf{object}, n, s, r)@\mathsf{pBuy} \ \wedge \\ \qquad \neg(r = \mathsf{cheap}) \ \wedge \neg(\mathsf{test}(\mathsf{safepay}, s)@\mathsf{pBuy})) \end{bmatrix}$$

The applicability condition identifies the situation where a bid refers to a non-cheap object and the seller is not registered for secure payments. Whenever this condition fails, the action is allowed to proceed (the policy does not apply). Otherwise, in a certain proportion, sp, of the cases the policy will prevent the buyer from making the bid; in the remaining proportion, $1 - sp$, of cases the buyer takes his chances and makes the bid while disregarding the policy.

Furthermore, for expensive items, some buyers may not consider bidding unless the seller is able to take payment by installments:

$$\mathsf{Pol}^{pi}_{\mathsf{monthly}} \triangleq \begin{bmatrix} ?_{pi}\, \mathsf{false} \\ \underline{\mathsf{if}}\ u :: \mathsf{out}(\mathsf{bid}, n, b, \_)@\mathsf{pBuy} : \\ \quad u = b \ \wedge \exists r, s : (\mathsf{test}(\mathsf{object}, n, s, r)@\mathsf{pBuy} \ \wedge \\ \qquad (r = \mathsf{expensive}) \ \wedge \neg(\mathsf{test}(\mathsf{monthly}, s)@\mathsf{pBuy})) \end{bmatrix}$$

Here the buyer is insistent on the ability to perform monthly installments in a certain proportion, pi, of cases but is willing to make use of whatever payment scheme is offered in the remaining proportion, $1 - pi$, of cases.

We combine these policies to capture the extent to which the buyer is willing to disregard a policy when making a bid:

$$\mathsf{Pol}^{sp,pi}_{\mathsf{buyer}} \triangleq \mathsf{Pol}^{sp}_{\mathsf{secure}} \oplus \mathsf{Pol}^{pi}_{\mathsf{monthly}}$$

Sellers. Sellers may want to do spot checks in a certain proportion, *sc*, of the cases to ensure that new buyers do not bid for expensive items:

$$\mathsf{Pol}^{sc}_{\mathsf{seller}} \triangleq \left[\begin{array}{l} ?_{sc}\,\mathsf{false} \\ \underline{\mathsf{if}}\ u :: \mathbf{in}(\mathsf{bid}, n, b, \_)@\mathsf{pBuy} : \\ \quad \mathsf{test}(\mathsf{buyer}, b, \mathsf{new})@\mathsf{pBuy} \wedge \\ \quad\quad \mathsf{test}(\mathsf{object}, n, u, \mathsf{expensive})@\mathsf{pBuy} \end{array}\right]$$

Here the seller is insistent on the ability to perform spot checks in a certain proportion, *sc*, of cases but is willing to waive this check in the remaining proportion, $1 - sc$, of cases.

2.2 Airport Security

As a second example, we consider a very simplified model of an airport, Port containing six kinds of data:

- $\langle\mathsf{traveller}, \mathit{name}, \mathit{profile}\rangle$ records that *name* is a potential traveller and *profile* $\in \{\mathsf{unchecked}, \mathsf{low}, \mathsf{high}\}$ where:
  - unchecked indicates that the traveller's documents have not been inspected
  - low indicates that the documents are in order and the traveller is from a low risk group
  - high indicates that the documents are in order and the traveller is from a high risk group;
- $\langle\mathsf{passenger}, \mathit{name}\rangle$ records that *name* is a traveller who has been allowed to proceed to the departure lounge;
- $\langle\mathsf{scan}, \mathit{name}, \mathit{gate}\rangle$ records that *name* has passed through a walkthrough scanner at gate *gate*;
- $\langle\mathsf{fullscan}, \mathit{name}, \mathit{gate}\rangle$ records that *name* has been subjected to a full body scan at gate *gate*;
- $\langle\mathsf{frisk}, \mathit{name}, \mathit{gate}\rangle$ records that *name* has been manually frisked at gate *gate*; and
- $\langle\mathsf{threat}, \mathit{level}\rangle$ with $\mathit{level} \in \{\mathsf{normal}, \mathsf{severe}\}$ records the current security threat level; we assume that only one such tuple is present.

We now proceed to define a policy for the security gates. In general, one is only permitted to pass through to the Departures lounge if the travelling documents have been checked and one passes through a standard scanner. This policy is expressed in the following way:

$$\mathsf{Pol}_{\mathsf{default}} \triangleq \left[\begin{array}{l} (\mathsf{test}(\mathsf{traveller}, t, \mathsf{low})@\mathsf{Port} \vee \mathsf{test}(\mathsf{traveller}, t, \mathsf{high})@\mathsf{Port}) \wedge \\ \quad \mathsf{test}(\mathsf{scan}, t, g)@\mathsf{Port} \\ \underline{\mathsf{if}}\ g :: \mathsf{out}(\mathsf{passenger}, t)@\mathsf{Port} : \\ \quad \mathsf{true} \end{array}\right]$$

In times of heightened security, the airport might want to subject certain high risk travellers to full body scans before allowing them into the Departures lounge.

Since this delays the flow of passengers, the airport only subjects a certain proportion, *fs*, of this category of travellers to the full check:

$$\mathsf{Pol}^{fs}_{\mathsf{security}} \triangleq \left[\begin{array}{l} ?_{fs}\ \mathsf{false} \\ \underline{\text{if}}\ g :: \mathsf{out}(\mathsf{passenger}, t)@\mathsf{Port} : \\ \quad \exists p : (\mathsf{test}(\mathsf{traveller}, t, p)@\mathsf{Port}\ \wedge p = \mathsf{high}\ \wedge \\ \quad\quad \mathsf{test}(\mathsf{threat}, \mathsf{severe})@\mathsf{Port} \wedge \neg(\mathsf{test}(\mathsf{fullscan}, t, g)@\mathsf{Port})) \end{array}\right]$$

It might also be the case that, in such circumstances, some proportion (say *fr*) of passengers might be subjected to a manual frisking, regardless of their profile:

$$\mathsf{Pol}^{fr}_{\mathsf{manual}} \triangleq \left[\begin{array}{l} ?_{fr}\ \mathsf{false} \\ \underline{\text{if}}\ g :: \mathsf{out}(\mathsf{passenger}, t)@\mathsf{Port} : \\ \quad \exists p : (\mathsf{test}(\mathsf{traveller}, t, p)@\mathsf{Port}\ \wedge \\ \quad\quad \mathsf{test}(\mathsf{threat}, \mathsf{severe})@\mathsf{Port} \wedge \neg(\mathsf{test}(\mathsf{frisk}, t, g)@\mathsf{Port})) \end{array}\right]$$

We combine these policies to give an overall policy for the Port:

$$\mathsf{Pol}^{fs,fr}_{\mathsf{airport}} \triangleq \mathsf{Pol}_{\mathsf{default}} \oplus \mathsf{Pol}^{fs}_{\mathsf{security}} \oplus \mathsf{Pol}^{fr}_{\mathsf{manual}}$$

3 Probabilistic Belnap Logic

3.1 Two-valued Logic and Probabilistic Two-valued Logic

In a *deterministic* system, policy decisions eventually result in either *granting* an action or *denying* it. Two-valued logic, be it propositional logic or some fragment of predicate logic, is suitable for expressing the result of the policy. We write **Bool** for the set $\{\mathbf{t}, \mathbf{f}\}$ of two-valued truth values.

As we have seen, in a *probabilistic* system, policy decisions result in a certain probability for granting the action. One approach is to use a simple probability p and interpret it to mean that the action is granted with probability p whereas the action is denied with probability $(1-p)$. In this approach $\mathbf{t}$ corresponds to 1 and $\mathbf{f}$ corresponds to 0. We shall prefer to write (p, q) where p gives the probability for granting the action and q gives the probability for denying the action; in this approach $\mathbf{t}$ corresponds to $(1, 0)$ and $\mathbf{f}$ corresponds to $(0, 1)$. Clearly we impose the condition on the probabilistic two-valued boolean (p, q) that $p + q = 1$ (as well as p and q being real numbers in the interval $[0, 1]$) in which case it becomes a discrete *probability distribution* over the outcomes $(\mathbf{t}, \mathbf{f})$.

The standard logical operators can be reinterpreted over probabilistic two-valued booleans. For this we shall write v_1 for $\mathbf{t}$ and v_2 for $\mathbf{f}$; for each operator ϕ its extension, also denoted ϕ, to probabilistic truth values is given by:

$$(p_1, p_2)\phi(q_1, q_2) = (r_1, r_2) \text{ where } r_k = \Sigma_{(i,j)|v_k = v_i \phi v_j}\ p_i q_j$$

This expresses that r_k is the sum of those products of probabilities $p_i q_j$ for which the corresponding value $v_i \phi v_j$ gives v_k (where both i and j range over $\{1, 2\}$). So, for example, the conjunction of $(p, 1-p)$ and $(q, 1-q)$ is $(pq, 1-pq)$, whereas the disjunction of $(p, 1-p)$ and $(q, 1-q)$ is $(p+q-pq, 1-p-q+pq)$, and the negation of $(p, 1-p)$ is $(1-p, p)$.

3.2 Four-Valued Logic

As has been discussed in many places (e.g. [4,8]), two-valued logic is not equally satisfactory for expressing the *policies* according to which the granting of an action should be made. The reason is that in general policies may be both incomplete, in providing no answer for a given request, as well as being contradictory, in providing conflicting answers for a given request. In this paper we follow the approach of a number of papers [3,4,8] of using a four-valued logic over which to express policies. In addition to the truth values **t** and **f** from **Bool** we also have the value $\bot$ for indicating absence of information and the value $\top$ for indicating conflicting information. It is useful to write **Four** for the set $\{\bot, \mathbf{t}, \mathbf{f}, \top\}$ of four-valued truth values.

The four-valued truth values can be turned into a so-called bilattice – first suggested by Belnap. In this approach we equip **Four** with two partial orders: $\leq_k$ and $\leq_t$ as illustrated in Figure 1 and explained below.

The partial order $\leq_k$ denotes the *knowledge* ordering that has $\bot$ as the least element, $\top$ as the greatest element, and **t** and **f** as two incomparable elements. This turns **Four** into a lattice as displayed in the left hand Hasse diagram in Figure 1. We shall write $\oplus$ for the least upper bound with respect to $\leq_k$ and $\otimes$ for the greatest lower bound with respect to $\leq_k$. Clearly $\oplus$ and $\otimes$ are commutative and associative.

The partial order $\leq_t$ denotes the *truth* ordering that has **f** as the least element, **t** as the greatest element, and $\bot$ and $\top$ as two incomparable elements. This also turns **Four** into a lattice as displayed in the right hand Hasse diagram in Figure 1. We shall write $\vee$ for the least upper bound with respect to $\leq_t$ and $\wedge$ for the greatest lower bound with respect to $\leq_t$. Clearly $\vee$ and $\wedge$ are commutative and associative. There is no risk of confusion from this notation as $\vee$ coincides with disjunction when interpreted over **Bool** and $\wedge$ coincides with conjunction when interpreted over **Bool**.

Negation $\neg$ is familiar from two-valued logic and is extended to four-valued logic by leaving the elements $\bot$ and $\top$ unchanged. This turns **Four** into a *bilattice* [1]: it is a lattice with respect to each of the two partial orderings and negation preserves the knowledge ordering (i.e. if $f_1 \leq_k f_2$ then $\neg f_1 \leq_k \neg f_2$) while it dualises the truth ordering (i.e. if $f_1 \leq_t f_2$ then $\neg f_1 \geq_t \neg f_2$).

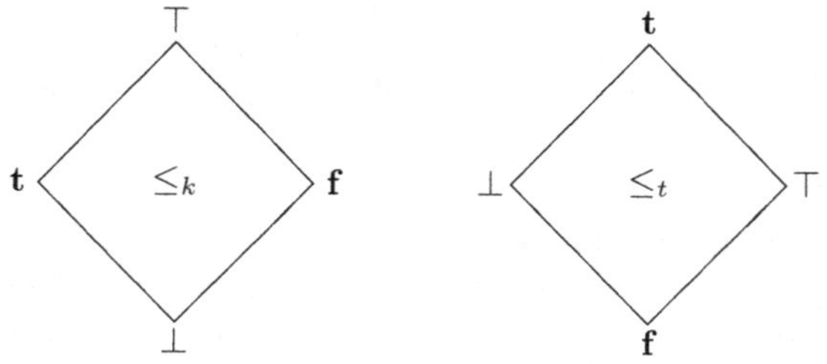

Fig. 1. The Belnap bilattice **Four**: $\leq_k$ and $\leq_t$.

We also need the following notion of implication denoted $\Rightarrow$:

$$(f_1 \Rightarrow f_2) = \begin{cases} f_2 & \text{if } f_1 \leq_k \mathbf{t} \\ \mathbf{t} & \text{otherwise} \end{cases}$$

It coincides with ordinary implication when interpreted over **Bool**.

Example 1. Returning to the On-line Auction example, consider the policy:

$$\mathsf{Pol}_{\mathsf{house}} \triangleq \mathsf{Pol}_{\mathsf{buy}} \oplus \mathsf{Pol}_{\mathsf{sell}}$$

Both $\mathsf{Pol}_{\mathsf{buy}}$ and $\mathsf{Pol}_{\mathsf{sell}}$ will evaluate to four-valued truth values: if the action of the policy matches and the recommendation evaluates to true then the result is $\mathbf{t}$, if the action matches but the recommendation evaluates to false then the result is $\mathbf{f}$ and if the action does not match then the result is $\perp$ since the policy does not apply.

The use of $\oplus$ takes care of the correct combination of the four-valued truth values. For actions that matches neither $u :: \mathsf{out}(\mathsf{bid}, n, b, \_)@\mathsf{pBuy}$ nor $u :: \mathsf{out}(\mathsf{object}, n, l, \_)@\mathsf{pBuy}$ the overall policy will give the four-valued truth value $\perp$ indicating inapplicability as far as the action is concerned. For actions matching $u :: \mathsf{out}(\mathsf{bid}, n, b, \_)@\mathsf{pBuy}$ it will give one of the four-valued truth values $\mathbf{t}$ or $\mathbf{f}$ indicating acceptance or rejection of the action. Finally, for actions matching $u :: \mathsf{out}(\mathsf{object}, n, l, \_)@\mathsf{pBuy}$ it will give one of the four-valued truth values $\mathbf{t}$ or $\mathbf{f}$ indicating acceptance or rejection of the action.

Indeed, had we used $\wedge$ in place of $\oplus$ in the definition of $\mathsf{Pol}_{\mathsf{house}}$ we could never get the value $\mathbf{t}$ since an action cannot match both $u :: \mathsf{out}(\mathsf{bid}, n, b, \_)@\mathsf{pBuy}$ and $u :: \mathsf{out}(\mathsf{object}, n, l, \_)@\mathsf{pBuy}$ at the same time. □

As discussed in [8] there are many ways in which to map four-valued truth values into two-valued booleans. The choice used in [8] has $\mathsf{grant}(f) = \neg(f \Rightarrow \mathbf{f})$ and maps $\perp$ and $\mathbf{t}$ to $\mathbf{t}$ whereas $\mathbf{f}$ and $\top$ are mapped to $\mathbf{f}$; this can also be written $\mathsf{grant}(f) = (f \leq_k \mathbf{t})$. This is based on the idea that an operation should be denied only if there is some evidence to suggest so.

3.3 Probabilistic Four-Valued Logic

By analogy with our consideration of probabilistic two-valued logic we shall now introduce probabilistic four-valued truth values as probability distributions over the outcomes $(\perp, \mathbf{t}, \mathbf{f}, \top)$. These will be quadruples (p_1, p_2, p_3, p_4) of real numbers in the interval $[0, 1]$ subject to the condition that $p_1 + p_2 + p_3 + p_4 = 1$. In this setting $\perp$ corresponds to $(1, 0, 0, 0)$, $\mathbf{t}$ corresponds to $(0, 1, 0, 0)$, $\mathbf{f}$ corresponds to $(0, 0, 1, 0)$, and $\top$ corresponds to $(0, 0, 0, 1)$.

The four-valued operators can be reinterpreted over probabilistic four-valued truth values. For example, the negation of (p_1, p_2, p_3, p_4) is (p_1, p_3, p_2, p_4).

Before giving further examples of operators we shall describe the methodology used for reinterpreting the operators. For this it is helpful to write $v_1 = \perp$, $v_2 = \mathbf{t}$, $v_3 = \mathbf{f}$, and $v_4 = \top$. For a binary four-valued operator ϕ its extension, also denoted ϕ, to probabilistic four-valued truth values is given by:

$$(p_1, p_2, p_3, p_4)\phi(q_1, q_2, q_3, q_4) = (r_1, r_2, r_3, r_4) \text{ where } r_k = \Sigma_{(i,j)|v_k = v_i \phi v_j}\ p_i q_j$$

Much as before this expresses that r_k is the sum of all those products of probabilities $p_i q_j$ for which the corresponding value $v_i \phi v_j$ gives v_k (where both i and j range over $\{1, 2, 3, 4\}$). It is straightforward to check that (r_1, r_2, r_3, r_4) is indeed a probabilistic four-valued truth value (as each (i, j) is used for exactly one k).

We need one more operator in order to actually introduce probabilistic four-valued truth values. This is the operator $?_s$, which we saw in Section 2, that with probability s returns its argument and with probability $1 - s$ gives $\mathbf{t}$; it is defined as follows:

$$?_s(q_1, q_2, q_3, q_4) = (sq_1, (1 - s) + sq_2, sq_3, sq_4)$$

Example 2. Let us return to the On-line Auction example of Section 2 and consider the policy

$$\mathsf{Pol}^{0.9,0.2}_{\mathsf{buyer}} \triangleq \mathsf{Pol}^{0.9}_{\mathsf{secure}} \oplus \mathsf{Pol}^{0.2}_{\mathsf{monthly}}$$

where the buyer, in the case of non-cheap objects, in 90% of the cases will check that the seller offers secure payment and, in the case of expensive objects, in 20% of the cases will check that the seller accepts monthly payments.

In the case of an action that does not match it will give the probabilistic four-valued truth value $(1, 0, 0, 0)$ indicating inapplicability as far as the action is concerned. For actions that do match and where the conditions of the two actions are satisfied, the $\mathsf{Pol}^{0.9}_{\mathsf{secure}}$ policy will give the value $(0, 0.1, 0.9, 0)$ whereas the $\mathsf{Pol}^{0.2}_{\mathsf{monthly}}$ policy will give $(0, 0.8, 0.2, 0)$. The combined policy therefore gives the value $(0, 0.08, 0.18, 0.74)$ meaning that in 8% of the cases the action is granted, in 18% of the cases it will be denied and in 74% of the cases the two policies give conflicting information. □

There are many ways in which to map probabilistic four-valued truth values into probabilistic two-valued booleans. The choice corresponding to that used in [8] is given by

$$\mathsf{grant}(p_1, p_2, p_3, p_4) = (p_1 + p_2, p_3 + p_4)$$

and adds the probabilties on $\perp$ and $\mathbf{t}$ to give the one on $\mathbf{t}$, and similarly adds the probabilities on $\mathbf{f}$ and $\top$ to give the one on $\mathbf{f}$.

Example 3. Continuing the above example we see that with this definition of grant the combined policy will allow the buyer to proceed with the bidding action in 8% of the cases (assuming that the relevant conditions are fulfilled) and deny it in 92% of the cases. □

Example 4. Consider now the policy of the Airport example of Section 2:

$$\mathsf{Pol}^{fs,fr}_{\mathsf{airport}} \triangleq \mathsf{Pol}_{\mathsf{default}} \oplus \mathsf{Pol}^{fs}_{\mathsf{security}} \oplus \mathsf{Pol}^{fr}_{\mathsf{manual}}$$

In the case of severe security threat and a passenger with high security profile the three policies will evaluate to the probabilistic four-valued truth values $(0, 1, 0, 0)$.

$(0, 1 - fs, fs, 0)$ and $(0, 1 - fr, fr, 0)$ respectively. The combined policy therefore evaluates to the value $(0, 1 - fs - fr + fs \cdot fr, 0, fs + fr - fs \cdot fr)$ meaning that the action will be granted in $100(1 - fs - fr + fs \cdot fr)\%$ of the cases and denied in the remaining $100(fs + fr - fs \cdot fr)\%$ of the cases. We may note that if, for example, $fs = 1$ (so a full body scan is always performed) then there is no need to combine it with frisk (so fr can be taken to 0). □

4 Design of The Language

Table 1 displays the computational part of the workflow language AspectKP. A net is a parallel composition of located processes and/or located tuples. Locations are annotated with a policy, the form of which is described below. We impose a *well-formedness* condition on nets: each location is assigned a unique policy, i.e. if a location has multiple occurrences in a net expression, each occurrence must be annotated with the same policy – this property is preserved by the semantics. A process can be a parallel composition of processes, a guarded sum of action prefixed processes, or a replicated process (indicated by the * operator); we shall write **0** for the empty sum. An action operates on tuples: a tuple can be output to, input from (read and delete the source) and read from (read and keep the source) a location. The actual operation performed by an action is called a *capability*. We do not distinguish real locations and data, and all of them are called locations in our setting, which can be location constants l, defining occurrences of location variable $!u$ (where the scope is the entire process to the right of the occurrence), and applied occurrences of a location variable u. The $\uplus$ operator adds elements to the tuple space at a location, whilst keeping track of the number of occurrences; in other words, a tuple space is a multi-set of tuples.

Table 2 extends the syntax of Table 1. It introduces the syntax for policies which are constructed from aspects, corresponding to the basic policies of [3,4], using the Belnap operators. An aspect declaration takes the form $[rec\ \underline{\text{if}}\ \ cut : cond]$. Here cut is the action to be trapped by the aspect: the location of the subject and the action (including the operation and the location of the target). Furthermore rec is a probabilistic four-valued policy recommendation and $cond$ is a boolean applicability condition. We allow a don't care pattern in the parameters to the cut and the test operation.

Table 1. AspectKP Syntax – Nets, Processes and Actions.

$N \in$ **Net**	$N ::= N_1 \mid\mid N_2 \mid l ::^{pol} P \mid l ::^{pol} T$
$P \in$ **Proc**	$P ::= P_1 \mid P_2 \mid \sum_i a_i.P_i \mid *P$
$a \in$ **Act**	$a ::= \mathbf{out}(\overrightarrow{\ell})@\ell \mid \mathbf{in}(\overrightarrow{\ell^\lambda})@\ell \mid \mathbf{read}(\overrightarrow{\ell^\lambda})@\ell$
$T \in$ **Tuplespace**	$T ::= \varepsilon \mid T \uplus \langle \overrightarrow{l} \rangle$
$\ell, \ell^\lambda \in$ **Loc**	$\ell ::= u \mid l \qquad \ell^\lambda ::= \ell \mid !u$

Table 2. AspectKP Syntax - Aspects and Policies (where $\phi \in \{\oplus, \otimes, \Rightarrow, \wedge, \vee\}$)

$$\begin{array}{ll}
pol \in \mathbf{Pol} & pol ::= asp \mid \neg pol \mid pol\,\phi\,pol \mid \ \mathsf{true} \mid \mathsf{false} \\
asp \in \mathbf{Asp} & asp ::= [rec\ \underline{\mathsf{if}}\ \ cut : cond] \\
cut \in \mathbf{Cut} & cut ::= \ell :: a^t \\
a^t \in \mathbf{Act}^t & a^t ::= \mathbf{out}(\overrightarrow{\ell^t})\,@\,\ell \ \mid\ \mathbf{in}(\overrightarrow{\ell^{t\lambda}})\,@\,\ell \ \mid\ \mathbf{read}(\overrightarrow{\ell^{t\lambda}})\,@\,\ell \\
rec \in \mathbf{Rec} & rec ::= \ell_1 = \ell_2 \mid \mathsf{test}(\overrightarrow{\ell^t})@\ell \mid \neg rec \mid rec\,\phi\,rec \mid ?_x\, rec \mid \mathsf{true} \mid \mathsf{false} \\
cond \in \mathbf{Cond} & cond ::= \ell_1 = \ell_2 \mid \mathsf{test}(\overrightarrow{\ell^t})@\ell \mid \neg cond \mid cond_1 \wedge cond_2 \mid cond_1 \vee cond_2 \mid \\
 & \qquad\qquad \exists x : cond \mid \mathsf{true} \mid \mathsf{false} \\
\ell^t, \ell^{t\lambda} \in \mathbf{Loc}^t & \ell^t ::= \ell \mid _ \qquad\qquad \ell^{t\lambda} ::= \ell^\lambda \mid _
\end{array}$$

The semantics is given by a Markov Decision Process (MDP) on nets. Non-determinism arises because of the non-deterministic selection of tuples, the choice operator (Σ) and parallelism; probabilities arise from the probabilistic aspects. The detailed semantics is defined in Appendix A.

5 Conclusion

We have built on our previous work in [8] to show how probabilistic aspects can be used to model the enforcement of security policies in an imperfect world.

- Probabilities are introduced in the sub-language for policy recommendations rather than in the actual primitives of the programming language.
- Four-valued logic has been used for obtaining a compositional specification of the policies.
- Policy recommendations are expressed using aspects in order to obtain a flexible specification that can be changed as the need arises to revise the security policy.

Our objective in this paper has been to demonstrate the feasibility of such an approach. Hence we have focussed on examples although the appendix does give the details of the language design, including a formal semantics in the form of a Markov Decision Process.

In subsequent work we would like to develop a logic for reasoning about global behaviour of the system; one approach, which extends our work in [8], would be to develop a probabilistic variant of ACTL [6] to be interpreted over Markov Decision Processes.

In the case of the On-line Auction this would allow us to check properties like

$$\begin{array}{l}
\forall b, n, v.\ P_{\leq 0.1}(\mathsf{true}\ {}_{\mathcal{C}}\mathbf{U}_{\{b::\mathsf{out}(\mathsf{bid}, n, b, v)@\mathsf{pBuy}\}} \exists r, s. \\
\qquad (\mathsf{test}(\mathsf{object}, n, s, r)@\mathsf{pBuy} \wedge \\
\qquad \neg(r \neq \mathsf{cheap} \Rightarrow \mathsf{test}(\mathsf{safepay}, s)@\mathsf{pBuy}) \wedge \\
\qquad \neg(r = \mathsf{expensive} \Rightarrow \mathsf{test}(\mathsf{monthly}, s)@\mathsf{pBuy})))
\end{array}$$

which says that there is at most 10% chance that a buyer actually places a bid without checking that the seller supports safe payment for non-cheap objects, and without checking that the seller offers monthly installments for expensive objects. It follows from the calculations in Example 3 that this is indeed the case (as $0.08 \leq 0.10$).

In the case of the Airport Security a suitable property might be:

$$\begin{aligned}\forall g, t.\ P_{\leq tr}(&\mathsf{true}\ {}_{C}\mathbf{U}_{\{g::\mathsf{out}(\mathsf{passenger},t)@\mathsf{Port}\}}\exists p.\\ &(\mathsf{test}(\mathsf{traveller}, t, p)@\mathsf{Port} \wedge \mathsf{test}(\mathsf{threat}, \mathsf{severe})@\mathsf{Port}\wedge\\ &\neg(p = \mathsf{high} \Rightarrow \mathsf{test}(\mathsf{fullscan}, t, g)@\mathsf{Port})\wedge\\ &\neg(\mathsf{test}(\mathsf{frisk}, t, g)@\mathsf{Port})))\end{aligned}$$

which says that there is some threshold probability (tr) above which, at times of heightened security, it is not possible for a passenger to get into the Departures lounge without having been through a full body scanner (if a high risk traveller) or being manually frisked. Then, based on the calculation in Example 4, we might aim to minimise fs and fr such that $1 - fs - fr + fs \cdot fr \leq tr$.

To carry out this development we would need to extend the formal semantics of our programming notation (given in the Appendix) with a formal syntax and interpretation of a probabilistic variant of ACTL. This is mostly standard and requires clarifying the role of schedulers in order to turn "scheduled Markov Decision Processes" into Markov Chains; the schedulers are intended to resolve the non-determinism in the nets and processes of AspectKP and has no bearing on the semantics of aspects and policies. This would allow to automate the model checking of formula illustrated above.

Another line of development would be to include BEFORE and AFTER actions into aspects in order that security policies can express remedial actions for an intended action to succeed (e.g. [9]). This would allow an even more pertinent treatment of enforcing security in an imperfect world than our current proposal.

Acknowledgment. This work was supported in part by the Danish Strategic Research Council (project 2106-06-0028) "Aspects of Security for Citizens". We should like to thank Alejandro Hernandez for useful comments.

References

1. Arieli, O., Avron, A.: The value of the four values. Artif. Intell. 102(1), 97–141 (1998)
2. Bettini, L., Bono, V., De Nicola, R., Ferrari, G., Gorla, D., Loreti, M., Moggi, E., Pugliese, R., Tuosto, E., Venneri, B.: The Klaim Project: Theory and Practice. In: Priami, C. (ed.) GC 2003. LNCS, vol. 2874, pp. 88–150. Springer, Heidelberg (2003)
3. Bruns, G., Dantas, D.S., Huth, M.: A simple and expressive semantic framework for policy composition in access control. In: Proceedings of the ACM workshop on Formal methods in security engineering, pp. 12–21. ACM Press, New York (2007)
4. Bruns, G., Huth, M.: Access-control policies via Belnap logic: Effective and efficient composition and analysis. In: Proceedings of the 21st IEEE Computer Security Foundations Symposium, pp. 163–176. IEEE, Los Alamitos (2008)

5. De Nicola, R., Katoen, J.-P., Latella, D., Massink, M.: StoKlaim: A Stochastic Extension of Klaim. Technical Report 2006-TR-01, Università degli Studi di Firenze (2006)
6. De Nicola, R., Vaandrager, F.W.: Action versus state based logics for transition systems. In: Guessarian, I. (ed.) LITP 1990. LNCS, vol. 469, pp. 407–419. Springer, Heidelberg (1990)
7. Georg, G., Ray, I., France, R.: Using aspects to design a secure system. In: 8th International Conference on Engineering of Complex Computer Systems, pp. 117–126. IEEE Computer Society, Los Alamitos (2002)
8. Hankin, C., Nielson, F., Riis Nielson, H.: Advice from Belnap policies. In: Proceedings of the 22nd IEEE Computer Security Foundations Symposium, pp. 234–247. IEEE, Los Alamitos (2009)
9. Hankin, C., Nielson, F., Riis Nielson, H., Yang, F.: Advice for coordination. In: Lea, D., Zavattaro, G. (eds.) COORDINATION 2008. LNCS, vol. 5052, pp. 153–168. Springer, Heidelberg (2008)
10. Di Pierro, A., Hankin, C., Wiklicky, H.: Probabilistic Klaim. In: De Nicola, R., Ferrari, G.-L., Meredith, G. (eds.) COORDINATION 2004. LNCS, vol. 2949, pp. 119–134. Springer, Heidelberg (2004)
11. De Win, B., Joosen, W., Piessens, F.: Developing secure applications through aspect-oriented programming. In: Aspect-Oriented Software Development, pp. 633–650. Addison-Wesley, Reading (2005)

A Appendix

The semantics is given by a Markov Decision Process (MDP) on nets. We formulate the semantics as a one-step reduction function $\Rightarrow$: $\mathbf{Net} \to \mathcal{P}_{\neq\emptyset}(\mathcal{D}(\mathbf{Net}))$ where $\mathcal{D}(\mathbf{Net})$ denotes the set of probability distributions on nets that satisfy the well-formedness condition detailed below. The $\Rightarrow$ function is derived from $\to$ (Table 7) with cycling on the stuck state which results from all locations containing the $\mathbf{0}$ process; alternatively, this state could be declared as being absorbing.

A probability distribution on nets is a function $\mu : \mathbf{Net} \to [0,1]$ such that $\Sigma_{N\in\mathbf{Net}}\mu(N) = 1$. To take proper account of the congruence we shall say that a probability distribution μ is *well-formed* whenever it satisfies the property

$$\mu(N) > 0 \wedge \mu(N') > 0 \wedge N \equiv N' \Rightarrow N = N'$$

which means that all probability belonging to one equivalence class of the structural congruence is assigned to just one representative. Since $\mathbf{Net}$ is countable we can write probability distributions in the form $\bigodot_i^{p_i} N_i$, subject to $\Sigma_i\, p_i = 1$ and $N_i \equiv N_j \Rightarrow i = j$. This denotes the probability distribution μ given by $\mu(N) = \Sigma_{i|N_i=N}\, p_i$. When the index set for i is finite we write $\odot^{p_1} N_1 \cdots \odot^{p_n} N_n$; we can safely dispense with entries having $p_i = 0$, as in $\odot^1 N \odot^0 M = \odot^1 N$.

We shall write $N \to \bigodot_{p_i}^{i} N_i$ whenever one non-deterministic step in the evaluation of N might produce the probability distribution $\bigodot_{p_i}^{i} N_i$ where N_i is chosen with probability p_i.

The semantics uses a structural congruence on nets, which is an associative and commutative (with respect to $||$) equivalence relation that is a congruence

Table 3. Structural Congruence

$$l ::^{pol} P_1 \mid P_2 \equiv l ::^{pol} P_1 \mid\mid l ::^{pol} P_2$$
$$l ::^{pol} *P \equiv l ::^{pol} P \mid *P$$
$$l ::^{pol} P \equiv l ::^{pol} P \mid\mid l ::^{pol} \mathbf{0}$$
$$\frac{N_1 \equiv N_2}{N \mid\mid N_1 \equiv N \mid\mid N_2}$$

Table 4. Matching Input Patterns to Data

$$\begin{aligned} match(\,!u, \overrightarrow{\ell^\lambda}\,;\, l, \overrightarrow{l}\,) &= match(\,\overrightarrow{\ell^\lambda}\,;\, \overrightarrow{l}\,) \circ [l/u] \\ match(l, \overrightarrow{\ell^\lambda}\,;\, l, \overrightarrow{l}\,) &= match(\,\overrightarrow{\ell^\lambda}\,;\, \overrightarrow{l}\,) \\ match(\,\epsilon\,;\,\epsilon\,) &= id \\ match(\,\cdot\,;\,\cdot\,) &= \mathsf{fail} \qquad \text{otherwise} \end{aligned}$$

(with respect to $||$) and with some additional rules defined in Table 3. It also makes use of an operation *match*, for matching input patterns to actual data, defined in Table 4.

The reaction rules are defined in Table 7 and are straightforward for nets. We shall discuss the rules for actions. When executed, **out** puts the tuple $\overrightarrow{l}$ into location l_0 and continues with the following process P if the action is granted; otherwise, it enters a busy waiting state (taking the view that since aspects are probabilistic the action might get granted at a later point in time). For the actions **in** and **read** there are two possibilities. One is that the formal parameters $\overrightarrow{\ell^\lambda}$ match some tuple $\overrightarrow{l}$ that is currently present – here we use the operation *match* defined in Table 4. In this case the action inputs the tuple if the action is granted; otherwise, it enters a busy waiting state. The other possibility is that no matching tuple is present, in which case a busy waiting state is entered.

The probabilistic four-valued meaning $[\![pol]\!]$ of a policy *pol* is defined in Table 6 relative to the action $l :: a$ being performed and the local environment. The function *check*, defined in Table 5, checks the applicability of a basic policy, and produces the corresponding bindings of actual parameters of actions to the formal parameters of the policy. The function *extract* facilitates this checking by producing a list of names: the location where the trapped action is; the capability (**out**, **in** or **read**); the parameters of the action; and the target location of the action. As an example,

$$extract(\ell :: \mathbf{out}(\ell_1^t, \cdots, \ell_n^t)@\ell') = (\ell, \mathbf{out}, \ell_1^t, \cdots, \ell_n^t, \ell')$$

Table 5. Checking Formals to Actuals

$$\begin{aligned} check(\,\alpha, \overrightarrow{\alpha}\,;\, \alpha', \overrightarrow{\alpha'}\,) &= check(\,\overrightarrow{\alpha}\,;\, \overrightarrow{\alpha'}\,) \circ do(\alpha; \alpha') \\ check(\,\epsilon\,;\,\epsilon\,) &= id \\ check(\,\cdot\,;\,\cdot\,) &= \mathsf{fail}\ \text{otherwise} \end{aligned}$$

$$\begin{aligned} do(u\,;\,l) &= [l/u] & do(!u\,;\,!u') &= [u'/u] \\ do(\_;\,l) &= id & do(\_;\,!u) &= id \\ do(X\,;\,P) &= [P/X] & do(l\,;\,l) &= id \\ do(c\,;\,c) &= id & do(\cdot\,;\,\cdot) &= \mathsf{fail}\ \text{otherwise} \end{aligned}$$

Table 6. Meaning of Policies in **Pol** (where $\phi \in \{\oplus, \otimes, \Rightarrow, \wedge, \vee\}$)

$$[\![rec \ \underline{\text{if}} \ \ cut : cond]\!](l :: a) = \left(\begin{array}{l} \text{case } check(\, extract(cut)\, ;\, extract(l :: a)) \text{ of} \\ \qquad \left(\begin{array}{ll} \mathsf{fail}: & \bot \\ \theta : & \left\{ \begin{array}{ll} (\!| rec\ \theta |\!) & \text{if } (\!| cond\ \theta |\!) \\ \bot & \text{if } \neg (\!| cond\ \theta |\!) \end{array} \right. \end{array} \right) \end{array} \right)$$

$$[\![pol_1 \ \phi \ pol_2]\!](l :: a) = ([\![pol_1]\!](l :: a)) \ \phi \ ([\![pol_2]\!](l :: a))$$

$$[\![\neg pol]\!](l :: a) = \neg([\![pol]\!](l :: a))$$

$$[\![\mathsf{true}]\!](l :: a) = \mathbf{t} \qquad [\![\mathsf{false}]\!](l :: a) = \mathbf{f}$$

Table 7. Markov Decision Processes from AspectKP

$$\frac{N \rightarrow \bigodot_i^{p_i} N_i}{N \,||\, M \rightarrow \bigodot_i^{p_i} N_i \,||\, M} \qquad \frac{N \equiv M \quad M \rightarrow \bigodot_i^{p_i} M_i \quad \bigwedge_i M_i \equiv N_i}{N \rightarrow \bigodot_i^{p_i} N_i}$$

$$\begin{array}{l} l_s ::^{pol_s} (\mathbf{out}(\overrightarrow{l})@l_t.P \,+\, Q) \,||\, l_t ::^{pol_t} T \\ \rightarrow \odot^p \, l_s ::^{pol_s} P \,||\, l_t ::^{pol_t} T \uplus \langle \overrightarrow{l} \rangle \\ \quad \odot^q \, l_s ::^{pol_s} (\mathbf{out}(\overrightarrow{l})@l_t.P \,+\, Q) \,||\, l_t ::^{pol_t} T \\ \qquad \text{if } (p, q) = \mathsf{grant}([\![pol_s]\!](l_s :: \mathbf{out}(\overrightarrow{l})@l_t) \oplus [\![pol_t]\!](l_s :: \mathbf{out}(\overrightarrow{l})@l_t)) \end{array}$$

$$\begin{array}{l} l_s ::^{pol_s} (\mathbf{in}(\overrightarrow{\ell^\lambda})@l_t.P \,+\, Q) \,||\, l_t ::^{pol_t} T \uplus \langle \overrightarrow{l} \rangle \\ \rightarrow \odot^p \, l_s ::^{pol_s} P\theta \,||\, l_t ::^{pol_t} T \\ \quad \odot^q \, l_s ::^{pol_s} (\mathbf{in}(\overrightarrow{\ell^\lambda})@l_t.P \,+\, Q) \,||\, l_t ::^{pol_t} T \uplus \langle \overrightarrow{l} \rangle \\ \qquad \text{if } (p, q) = \mathsf{grant}([\![pol_s]\!](l_s :: \mathbf{in}(\overrightarrow{\ell^\lambda})@l_t) \oplus [\![pol_t]\!](l_s :: \mathbf{in}(\overrightarrow{\ell^\lambda})@l_t)) \\ \qquad \text{and } match(\overrightarrow{\ell^\lambda}; \overrightarrow{l}) = \theta \\ l_s ::^{pol_s} (\mathbf{in}(\overrightarrow{\ell^\lambda})@l_t.P \,+\, Q) \,||\, l_t ::^{pol_t} T \\ \rightarrow \odot^1 \, l_s ::^{pol_s} (\mathbf{in}(\overrightarrow{\ell^\lambda})@l_t.P \,+\, Q) \,||\, l_t ::^{pol_t} T \\ \qquad \text{if } \forall \langle \overrightarrow{l} \rangle \in T : match(\overrightarrow{\ell^\lambda}; \overrightarrow{l}) = \mathsf{fail} \end{array}$$

$$\begin{array}{l} l_s ::^{pol_s} (\mathbf{read}(\overrightarrow{\ell^\lambda})@l_t.P \,+\, Q) \,||\, l_t ::^{pol_t} T \uplus \langle \overrightarrow{l} \rangle \\ \rightarrow \odot^p \, l_s ::^{pol_s} P\theta \,||\, l_t ::^{pol_t} T \uplus \langle \overrightarrow{l} \rangle \\ \quad \odot^q \, l_s ::^{pol_s} (\mathbf{read}(\overrightarrow{\ell^\lambda})@l_t.P \,+\, Q) \,||\, l_t ::^{pol_t} T \uplus \langle \overrightarrow{l} \rangle \\ \qquad \text{if } (p, q) = \mathsf{grant}([\![pol_s]\!](l_s :: \mathbf{in}(\overrightarrow{\ell^\lambda})@l_t) \oplus [\![pol_t]\!](l_s :: \mathbf{in}(\overrightarrow{\ell^\lambda})@l_t)) \\ \qquad \text{and } match(\overrightarrow{\ell^\lambda}; \overrightarrow{l}) = \theta \\ l_s ::^{pol_s} (\mathbf{read}(\overrightarrow{\ell^\lambda})@l_t.P \,+\, Q) \,||\, l_t ::^{pol_t} T \\ \rightarrow \odot^1 \, l_s ::^{pol_s} (\mathbf{read}(\overrightarrow{\ell^\lambda})@l_t.P \,+\, Q) \,||\, l_t ::^{pol_t} T \\ \qquad \text{if } \forall \langle \overrightarrow{l} \rangle \in T : match(\overrightarrow{\ell^\lambda}; \overrightarrow{l}) = \mathsf{fail} \end{array}$$

If *check* returns fail, it means that this policy does not apply to the action; otherwise, it returns a substitution, θ, which is applied to the policy recommendation (*rec* in Table 6) if the applicability condition (*cond* in Table 6) holds, otherwise the policy does not apply.

The two-valued meaning $[\!(cond)\!]$ for an applicability condition *cond* is defined in the usual way; it is straightforward to adapt it to define the four-valued meaning $[\!(rec)\!]$ of a policy recommendation *rec*.

A Tool for Checking Probabilistic Properties of COWS Services

Igor Cappello and Paola Quaglia

Dipartimento di Ingegneria e Scienza dell'Informazione, Università di Trento

Abstract. We present a tool developed for fostering probabilistic model checking of services formally specified in Scows, a stochastic enrichment of the Calculus for Orchestration of Web Services. The tool, called Scows_lts, derives the Labelled Transition System associated to the term, and further generates the corresponding Continuous Time Markov Chain in the same notation adopted by the PRISM model checker. Scows_lts is first described and then seen at work against a small, yet representative, application scenario.

1 Introduction

Recently defined process calculi for the specification of service behaviours (see, e.g., [7,10,2]), provide a solid formal underpinning to the service oriented computing paradigm. Although the adopted languages are a bit far from those of the most well-known WS-BPEL, WSFL, WSCI, or WSDL, these calculi bring in the advantage of introducing clear mathematical structures for reasoning about service coordination and orchestration. For instance, given that processes are associated with a structural operational semantics, the dynamic behaviour of a term of the language can be represented by a connected oriented graph whose nodes are the reachable states of the system, and whose paths stay for its possible runs. Also, the generation of such graphs can be automatized, and this fosters the verification of qualitative properties of the specified services: Enquiries about the behaviour of any given service (e.g. "Can a given state ever be reached?") can be solved by running algorithms over the corresponding graph.

Quantitative analysis of services (like, e.g., quality of service, resource usage, service level agreement, dependability, quantification of trust, or more generally uncertainty and performance) can be as interesting as its qualitative counterpart. To ease this sort of analysis, some of the above mentioned calculi have been extended to accommodate quantitative measures and probabilistic/stochastic semantics so to also allow modelling and verification of non-functional aspects of computation [4,12]. In particular, in the case of stochastic service calculi, each basic action is often enriched by the rate of an exponential distribution which models the time taken to complete its execution. The directed graph representing the semantics of the given service can then be converted into a Continuous-Time Markov Chain (CTMC), and probabilistic reasoning about the service behaviour can be carried on by applying standard numerical techniques to this mathematical structure.

In this paper we present a Java tool developed for fostering the quantitative analysis of COWS [10] (Calculus for Orchestration of Web Services), a calculus strongly

M. Wirsing, M. Hofmann, and A. Rauschmayer (Eds.): TGC 2010, LNCS 6084, pp. 364–378, 2010.

inspired by WS-BPEL which combines primitives of well-known process calculi (like, e.g., the π-calculus [11,15]) with constructs meant to model web services orchestration. More specifically, the described software takes as input terms of Scows [16], a stochastic version of COWS which extends the work presented in [12] to the case of polyadic communication. The tool, called Scows_lts, derives the *Labelled Transition System* (LTS) associated to the term, and further generates the corresponding CTMC which is provided in the same notation adopted by the PRISM probabilistic model checker [9,13]. Also, when building the CTMC, the user can specify which transitions of the LTS affect the state variables of the model checker.

By providing a suitable interface to PRISM, Scows_lts allows the verification of the behaviour of Scows terms against properties expressed in Continuous Stochastic Logic (CSL) [1], a temporal logic based on CTL [3]. In particular, those properties refer to both the *transient* and the *steady-state* behaviour of the given chain, i.e., they relate to the probability of being in a certain state either at a given time instant or in the long-run. In fact, besides formulas built from atomic propositions and the obvious boolean operators, letting $\sim \in \{<, \leqslant, \geqslant, >\}$ and $p \in [0, 1]$, CSL can express the following properties:

- $P_{\sim p}[\phi]$ which asserts that the probability of the path formula ϕ being satisfied from a given state meets the bound $\sim p$. Here notice that time is naturally embedded in until path formulae which take shape $\Phi \; U_I \; \Psi$, where I is an interval of $\mathbb{R}^+$, so that $\Phi \; U_I \; \Psi$ holds if Ψ is satisfied at some time instant in I and Φ holds at all preceding time instants. Precisely, these path formulae are referred to as *time-bounded until* formulae when I is bounded, and *unbounded until* when $I = [t, \infty)$ for some $t \geqslant 0$.
- $S_{\sim p}[\Phi]$ which indicates that the steady-state probability of being in a state satisfying the CSL formula Φ meets the bound $\sim p$.

Besides CSL properties and those written using derived operators (like, e.g., implication and timed temporal operators), PRISM can also check properties evaluating to a numerical value and written $P_{=?}[\phi]$ and $S_{=?}[\Phi]$, respectively.

A small sample of properties that can be checked by PRISM and their corresponding intuitive meaning is listed below.

- $P_{>0.8}[\mathit{true} \; U_{[0,5.7]} \; a_1]$: the probability that a_1 holds within the first 5.7 time units is greater than 0.8.
- $P_{=?}[\mathit{true} \; U_{[0,5.7]} \; a_1]$: which is the probability that a_1 holds within the first 5.7 time units.
- $a_2 \longrightarrow P_{>0.6}[a_3 \; U_{[1,7]} \; a_4]$: when a_2 becomes true, the probability that a_4 holds in the time interval $[1, 7]$, with a_3 holding at all the preceding time instants is greater than 0.6.
- $S_{\leqslant 0.1}[a_5]$: in the long-run, the probability that a_5 holds is less than 0.1.

By producing input to PRISM, Scows_lts allows interesting probabilistic properties of closed Scows services to be analyzed, and, to the best of our knowledge, Scows_lts is at the moment the single tool offering the ability to carry over exact probabilistic checking for such language. Although the reader might object that what the tool produces is just the interface to an existing model checker, it should be noticed that developing an efficient implementation for such interface is far from trivial. First, w.r.t. naming, COWS is a calculus in the π-calculus style, and this immediately brings in all the operative issues related to either α-conversion or generation of new names. Second, given that the actual communication paradigm adopted by Scows is based on a *best-matching* policy, finding the communicating pairs imposes a quite time-consuming processing when the moment of understanding whether the matching of the involved input/output actions is really among the "best" ones comes. Third, to overcome the state explosion problem which could be raised even by systems not particularly big, a number of optimization techniques have to be implemented to keep the LTS size as small as possible. Concluding, the approach taken by Scows_lts is intrinsically less efficient than, e.g., carrying over approximate statistical model checking of Scows [14]. It must be observed, however, that approximate checking is based on hypothesis testing performed over simulation runs obviously of finite length. Then, by its own nature, statistical model checking cannot be used to verify either unbounded until formulae or steady-state properties.

Another tool that can be partially compared to Scows_lts is CMC [6], an on-the-fly model checker supporting the verification of qualitative (vs. quantitative) properties of COWS services. CMC generates only those fragments of the state space which are relevant to the verification of the considered property. Hence the approach adopted in CMC is quite different from the one taken in Scows_lts, where the whole state space is generated. Here we observe that this feature of Scows_lts, although computationally demanding, is crucial, e.g., to reuse the resulting structures for the verification of properties with different instantiations of the involved quantitative parameters.

Outline of the paper. The source language of the Scows_lts is briefly presented in Section 2. The description of Scows focuses on the main semantic points impacting on the complexity of the LTS generation. Section 3 provides a description of the tool, and contains details about the implementation of structural congruence checking, one of the main optimization techniques applied to keep the number of states as small as possible. In Section 4, we present an application scenario and a few examples of the results obtained by model checking its probabilistic properties in PRISM. Conclusions and plans for future work are reported in Section 5.

2 Scows

Below we provide a short presentation of Scows, the source language of the tool whose description is the main subject of the paper.

Scows services (ranged over by $S, S', \ldots, S_1, S_2, \ldots$) are based on two countable and disjoint sets of entities: the set of names $\mathcal{N}$ (ranged over by $m, n, o, p, m', \ldots$) and the set of variables $\mathcal{V}$ (ranged over by $x, y, z, x', \ldots$). We will indicate elements of $\mathcal{N} \cup \mathcal{V}$ by the metavariables $u, v, w, u', \ldots$, which will be collectively called *identifiers*. The set of identifiers occurring in service S will be denoted by $ids(S)$. Also, tuples of the shape $\langle u_1, \ldots, u_n \rangle$ will be denoted by $\tilde{u}$.

The terms of the Scows language are generated by the grammar in Table 1. For simplicity, we do not present here the support for service termination through the killing and protection primitives as presented in [12,16]. Following a common approach in stochastic extensions of process calculi, we associate a stochastic delay to each basic action of the language. These delays are determined via exponentially distributed

Table 1. Grammar of Scows

$$s ::= (u.u!\tilde{u}, \delta) \mid g \mid s \mid s \mid [\,u\,]\,s \mid \mathsf{S}(m_1, \ldots, m_j)$$
$$g ::= \mathbf{0} \mid (p.o?\tilde{u}, \gamma).\,s \mid g + g$$

random variables, the rates of which are included in the syntax of basic actions. The two basic actions are invoke $(u.u'!\tilde{u}, \delta)$ and request $(p.o?\tilde{u}, \gamma)$, and represent respectively the capacity to send an output tuple $\tilde{u}$ through the *endpoint* $u.u'$ with rate δ, and to receive an input on the tuple $\tilde{u}$ through the endpoint $p.o$ with rate γ. The basic activities are assembled through the classical combinators of parallel composition $s \mid s$, *guarded* choice $g + g$ (the classical nondeterministic choice, in which each service has to start with a request action) and service identifier $\mathsf{S}(m_1, \ldots, m_j)$. The last constructor allows the representation of recursive behaviour and is associated with a service definition of the form $\mathsf{S}(n_1, \ldots, n_j) = s$. The *delimiter* of u, written $[\,u\,]\,s$, defines the scope of u to be s. An identifier under the scope of a delimiter is said to be *bound* by that delimiter. For example, in the service $S = [\,x\,]((p.o?x, \gamma).\,(p.o!x, \delta))$ the variable x is bound by the delimiter $[\,x\,]$, while names p and o are free. A Scows service S is termed *closed* if every entity appearing in S is bound by a delimiter.

The main goal of the operational semantics of Scows terms is the generation of Continuous Time Markov Chains (CTMCs) grounding the analysis of the behaviour of the specified systems. Although the detailed presentation of the Scows semantics lies outside the scope of this paper, we briefly recall here the main assumptions that have been taken in order to both allow the definition of finitely branching transition systems and ease the computation of transition rates. First, it is assumed that service identifiers do not occur unguarded. Second, we assume that there is no homonymy both among bound identifiers and among free and bound identifiers of the service under consideration. This condition can be initially met by appropriately refreshing the term, and is dynamically kept true by a suitable management of the unfolding of recursion (new versions of bound identifiers are generated and used when a recursively defined service is instantiated). Third, as for the stochastic extension of monadic COWS [12], and differently from the original work on COWS [10], the semantics of Scows [16] is not given in reduction style, but rather as a labelled transition system making use of rules for opening and closing the scope of delimiters.

In order to give an intuitive flavour of the Scows semantics, we comment on a simple service specified in Table 2 which is a fragment of the application scenario analyzed later on in Section 4. In the example reported in Table 2, like in other examples below, we use intuitive identifiers instead of metavariables and metanames. Variables can still be distinguished from names for the fact that identifiers for variables have a leading `v`. The service in Table 2 models the behaviour of a customer performing a login attempt on a loan granting service, and then waiting for the outcome of the operation. The delimiters `[id]`, `[name]`, and `[pwd]` define the scope where the identifiers are defined and valid. An invoke action on channel `creditReq.initialize` allows the service to communicate with other services able to perform a request action on the same endpoint.

Table 2. Example of a Scows service

```
[id][name][pwd]
 (creditReq.initialize!<id,name,pwd>,1)
    | [vuserOK]
        (portal.initialize?<id,vuserOK>,1).
        [if][then](
            (if.then!<vuserOK>,1)
            | (if.then?<false>,1).
                   ...
            + (if.then?<true>,1).
                   ...      )
```

In case of communication, the names are exchanged, extending the scope of the private names if needed. The invoke activity is in parallel with a second subservice. The second subservice is composed of a request activity, which receives the result of the login attempt and stores it in the variable `vuserOk`. After this information is received, the service can perform one of the two internal synchronizations over the endpoint `if.then`. This behaviour is obtained by using the nondeterministic choice operator, and by exploiting the communication paradigm, which is based on correlation sets and adopts a *best-matching* policy. The basic ingredient of best-matching is that each name matches both with itself and with any variable. That said, a communication between an invoke and a request can take place only if all of the following conditions hold:

1. the invoke and the request activities occur at the same endpoint;
2. the parameters of the invoke (actual parameters) can really match with the parameters of the request (formal parameters);
3. among all the requests occurring at the same endpoint as the invoke, the chosen request is one of those that induce the least number of substitutions of actual parameters for formal parameters.

Going back to the example in Table 2, the nondeterministic choice

```
(if.then?<false>,1).... + (if.then?<true>,1)....
```

defines a mutually exclusive choice between two possible prosecutions. The two branches of the choice model different behaviours of the customer, based on the result of the login procedure. The two possible outcomes are handled by defining two request actions on the same channel but with different parameters. If `vuserOk` gets substituted by `false`, the service continues with the actions needed to manage a failed login. Conversely, if `vuserOk` is set to `true`, the logged customer and the loan granting service continue with the protocol defined to initialize, assess and then define the loan request.

The Scows operational semantics [16] defines the possible transitions of closed services. Transitions take the form $S \xrightarrow[\rho]{\alpha} S'$ where α is the action label, and ρ is the rate associated to the action. Accounting for the best-matching communication paradigm in a polyadic setting makes rate computation quite a heavy task, and this has an obvious impact over Scows_lts. To highlight this point, we informally illustrate the foundational ideas and main issues related to rate computation. As in [12], invoke and request activities are dealt with in an asymmetric way. In fact, differently from what happens in CCS or in π-calculus, the actual pairing of two sending and receiving actions depends not only on the equality of their endpoints (item 1 above), but also on two further conditions relative to parameters: a local one (item 2 above) and a global one (item 3 above). Then, fixed an endpoint, the selection of a specific invoke activity, and hence a particular tuple of actual parameters, filters the request activities which are eligible for communication with the chosen invoke. This policy is reflected in the quantitative semantics. From the probabilistic point of view, the act of sending is considered an independent event, while receiving depends on the chosen invoke activity. Consider for instance the service below.

$$S = [\,m,n,x,y\,]\;((\underbrace{p.o!\langle m,n\rangle,1)}_{S_1} \mid \underbrace{(p.o?\langle x,y\rangle,2).\mathbf{0}}_{S_2} \mid \underbrace{(p.o!\langle n,n\rangle,3)}_{S_3} \\ \mid \underbrace{(p.o?\langle m,y\rangle,4).\mathbf{0}}_{S_4} \mid \underbrace{(p.o?\langle x,y\rangle,5).\mathbf{0}}_{S_5})$$

Matching the invoke action labelled S_1 with the request guarding S_2 involves the two substitutions $\{{}^{m}/_{x}\}$ and $\{{}^{n}/_{y}\}$, and the same happens for matching S_1 with the request guarding S_5. The single substitution $\{{}^{n}/_{y}\}$ instead is induced by pairing S_1 with the request $(p.o?\langle m,y\rangle,4)$ in S_4. Using conditional probabilities, the rate of the communication between S_1 and S_4, named $\rho_{1,4}$, is computed as follows:

$$\rho_{1,4} = \mathcal{P}(S_1)\,\mathcal{P}(S_4 \mid S_1)\,\min\,(app(S_1), app(S_4)) = \frac{1}{1+3}\,\frac{4}{4}\,\min\,(1+3,4)$$

where $app(S_i)$ stays for the *apparent rate* of S_i and is computed taking into account the rates of those actions in S which might compete to communicate over the same endpoint. As usual, we take the minimum of the apparent rates of the involved invoke and request actions. This amounts to assuming that synchronization occurs at the (apparent) pace of the slowest participant.

We observe here that the computation of apparent rates faithfully reflects the best-matching communication paradigm of Scows. In the above example for instance, the apparent rate of S_1 is given by the sum of the rates of both S_1 and S_3, while the computation of the apparent rate of S_4 takes into account the fact that $(p.o?\langle m,y\rangle,4)$ is indeed the single best-matching request for the invoke $(p.o!\langle m,n\rangle,1)$.

3 Overview of Scows_lts

Scows_lts is a Java tool freely available at [17] for the derivation of CTMCs from Scows services. Given the input service, its Labelled Transition System is first derived. The LTS is then used to build a CTMC expressed in the syntax accepted by the PRISM model checker [9]. As detailed below, when building the CTMC, a manual input can specify which transitions of the LTS affect the variables defining the state of the system in the model checker tool.

Table 3. Structural congruence rules for Scows_lts

$$s_1 \equiv s_2 \text{ if } s_1 \text{ is an } \alpha\text{-converse of } s_2$$

$$s_1 \mid [u]\, s_2 \equiv [u](s_1 \mid s_2) \text{ if } u \notin ids(s_1), \qquad [u_1][u_2]\, s \equiv [u_2][u_1]\, s, \qquad [u]\mathbf{0} \equiv \mathbf{0}$$

$$s_1 \mid (s_2 \mid s_3) \equiv (s_1 \mid s_2) \mid s_3, \qquad s_1 \mid s_2 \equiv s_2 \mid s_1, \qquad s \mid \mathbf{0} \equiv s$$

$$(g_1 + g_2) + g_3 \equiv g_1 + (g_2 + g_3), \qquad g_1 + g_2 \equiv g_2 + g_1, \qquad (p?\tilde{u}, \gamma).\, s + \mathbf{0} \equiv (p?\tilde{u}, \gamma).\, s$$

The automatic derivation of the LTS builds the graph structure in breadth-first order. A challenging and stimulating issue related to this process is the well-known state space explosion problem. In order to reduce its effects in terms of memory usage and execution time, we have chosen to implement a notion of structural congruence between Scows services, defined as the minimal relation following the laws presented in Table 3. These laws state the equality of terms that are α-converse of each other, i.e. that could be made syntactically identical by appropriately refreshing bound identifiers, and comprise the usual axioms for scope delimitation together with the monoidal laws for parallel composition and nondeterministic choice. A congruence check is performed when inserting the residual S' of service S in the transition system, so that this check is carried on *after* the transition $S \xrightarrow[\rho]{\beta} S'$ has been computed. At the time this transition is considered, S is already represented by a node in the LTS; a node S_1 such that $S_1 \equiv S'$ is searched for in the whole LTS. If the search is successful, the computed transition links S to S_1. A new node is created otherwise.

Consider the service S defined as in Table 4. This service can perform two distinct communications over the endpoint `s.o`, and evolve, respectively, to either S1 or S2 as defined below:

```
S1 = [id][b] (s.b ! <id>, 1) | [vid2] [vch2] ( ... )

S2 = [id][b] ( [vid1] [vch1] ( ... ) | (s.b ! <id>, 1) )
```

Table 4. A service S that can perform two distinct communications with congruent residuals

```
S = [id][b] (s.o ! <id, b>, 1)
    | [vid1] [vch1] (
        (s.o ? <vid1, vch1>, 1)
              .(s.vch1 ! <vid1>, 1)    )
    | [vid2] [vch2] (
        (s.o ? <vid2, vch2>, 1)
              .(s.vch2 ! <vid2>, 1)    )
```

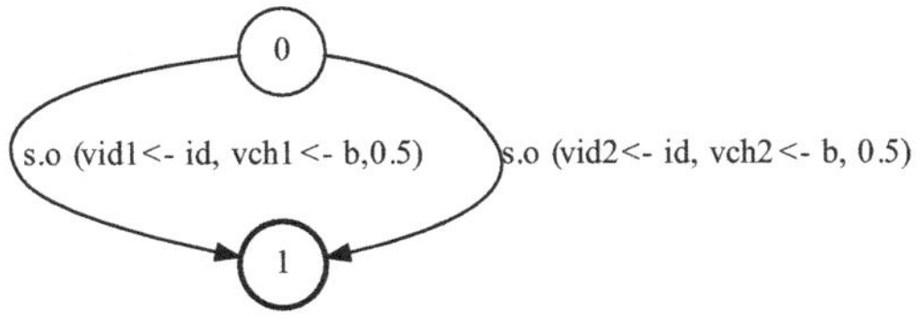

Fig. 1. Transition graph for service S: congruent residuals

Although the obtained residuals S1 and S2 are not syntactically identical, the tool recognizes that they can be equated by using two substitutions on bound entities and a rearrangement of the parallel components.

A graphical representation of the transition graph is obtained using the *dot* tool [5]. In this representation, the labels associated with states are integer numbers, defined at runtime, that uniquely identify services in the transition graph. The LTS obtained for service S in Table 4 is drawn in Figure 1. The labels associated with the two transitions leading to the same node show information about the endpoint over which the communication takes place, along with the substitutions induced by the communication mechanism and the rate associated with the transition.

Checking for structural congruence of services requires special care. In order to achieve the desired goal, it is necessary to abstract from the concrete representations (syntax trees) used in the operational semantics. The abstraction phase, called *flattening*, consists in the definition of a hashmap, relating each subservice to the list of bound identifiers used in that subprocess. A definition, given as pseudocode, of the $flatten$ function is presented in Table 5. Function $flatten$ is defined recursively on the structure of services: it considers the parallel composition and the name/variable binding as inductive cases, while all other constructs are treated as atomically resolved services. In the case of a parallel composition $S_1 \mid S_2$, the map obtained flattening S_1 is used as intermediate result when flattening S_2. In the case of a name/variable binding $[u]S'$, the bound identifier u is added to the list l of the encountered bound identifiers. In the general case of the definition of function $flatten$, a list $fid(S) \cap l$ is built. This list contains the bound identifiers used in the considered service S. Function *flatten* takes into account the case in which copies of the same service are composed in parallel: the flattening procedure adds a list of bound entities for each copy, so the mapped entities $\mathcal{L}, \mathcal{L}'$ are *lists of lists* of bound identifiers. The list $\mathcal{L}'$, which will be the object mapped by S, is composed taking into consideration if S was previously mapped to a list $\mathcal{L}$. When building and using the resulting hashmap, we are again assuming that bound and free names are all distinct.

Once both maps m_S and $m_{S'}$, for services S and S' respectively, are built, the actual congruence checking takes place. The idea underlying this procedure is that, if S and S' are congruent, then the subservices of S', that we will identify with $keys(m_{S'})$, can be arranged in an ordering $\left[S'_1, \ldots, S'_n\right]$ that matches the ordering $[S_1, \ldots, S_n]$ of $keys(m_S)$. This match, built considering the structure of subservices, takes into account the possibility of renaming of bound names: this is achieved by building a bijection, named sub, between the bound identifiers used in S and those used in S'.

Table 5. Pseudocode for the flattening function

```
flatten(S,l,m) =
if S = S1 | S2
    intermediate_map = flatten(S1,l,m)
    return flatten(S2,l,intermediate_map)
else if S = [u]S'
    l_new = l ∪ u
    return flatten(S',l_new,m)
else
    L = m.get(S)
    mapped = fid(S) ∩ l
    if L == null
        L = [mapped]
        m.put(S,L)
    else
        L' = L :: mapped
        m.put(S,L')
    return m
```

For example, consider S1 and S2, the two possible residuals of the service in Table 4. The flattening procedure, applied to the two services, creates two maps m_A and m_B such that the mappings of the invoke and residuals actions are as follows (where double-list notation has been omitted for clarity).

1. m_A([id][b](s.b!<id>,1)) = m_B([id][b](s.b!<id>,1)) = [id,b]
2. m_A([vid2][vch2] ((s.o?<vid2,vch2>,1). ...)) = [vid2,vch2]
3. m_B([vid1][vch1] ((s.o?<vid1,vch1>,1). ...)) = [vid1,vch1]

The congruence checking procedure builds a bijection *sub* between the bound identifiers mapped in m_A and those mapped in m_B, taking into account the use of these identifiers in the atomic services. For instance, m_A maps an invoke service into a list of two names, as does m_B. Since the types of the services are compatible, the bijection is initialized as *sub* = { b → b , id → id }. Again, m_A maps a request service into a list of two variables, as does m_B. Also in this case the types of the services are compatible, so the procedure updates *sub* accordingly: *sub* = { b → b , id → id , vid2 → vid1 , vch2 → vch1 }. The mapping given by *sub* is still valid (i.e. it is still a bijection) when considering the residuals of the two request services. Since there are no more mapped services to consider, S1 and S2 are recognized as congruent. If, for instance, the residual of S were S2' = (s.o?<vid1,vch1>,1).(s.vid1!<vch1>,1) instead of S2, then the construction of the bijection *sub* would fail. In fact, when considering the residuals of the request operations, *sub* would already contain { vid1 → vid2 } and { vid1 → vch2 } should be inserted for matching the trailing invoke directives. This mismatch is a sign that the ordering of mapped services cannot be used to conclude that S1 and S2' are congruent. Since this is the case for each permutation of mapped services for S1 and S2', we conclude that S1 and S2' are not congruent.

When the automatic procedure to build the transition system for a service S has considered all possible residuals, the obtained LTS is used to define a CTMC expressed in PRISM notation. The states in the chain, at this point, are represented only by the values of an integer variable. Different values of this variable uniquely identify each service. In order to express and check even simple quantitative properties, one would have to know the correspondence between the values of this variable and the residuals in the LTS. Even for small systems, this is too demanding. In order to easily express and check interesting and elaborated quantitative properties, the state description has to be enriched. The additional information, in terms of CTMC variable updates, can be obtained by user-provided descriptions (annotations) of Scows transitions.

4 Applying Scows_lts

We complete the presentation of Scows_lts by a detailed description of its application to an example derived from a Case-Study of the SENSORIA European Project. The setting for the scenario consists in a Bank Credit Request service, which can be invoked by customers to obtain a loan. Once the customer provides the information needed to compute the security assessment on the loan request, the bank service can either automatically grant the loan (e.g., if the required sum is below a threshold or if the security assessment is very favorable) or forward the request to a clerk for a manual review. If the security assessment is very unfavorable the manual review must be performed by a supervisor. A favorable response of this review process triggers the generation of a loan proposal, which is then sent to the customer, who can accept or decline the offer. In particular, the scenario is composed of the following phases: login, collection of information, rating computation, generation of the loan proposal/decline, customer decision, session closure.

The model, whose complete definition is reported in the full version of this paper, available at [17], is composed of various persistent services modeled as agents, and by a non-persistent service, named `Portal`, which mimics the behaviour of the customer: the adopted point of view is the one of the bank internal services, which receive requests and give response to the `Portal` service. The fact that the model has to contain persistent services dealing with sensitive information rises two issues that must be taken into account. First, at any time each persistent service has to be able to interact with whichever service is requiring its functionalities. Second, different instances of the same service have to execute transparently with respect to each other. The first aspect is addressed using guarded recursion, while the second is easily solved with private names modelling session identifiers used as communication parameters. Since the Scows communication paradigm is based on correlation sets, this choice ensures that sensitive data is not disclosed to unauthorized services.

Table 6 presents the service `CustomerManagement`, defined taking into account the two aspects above. The first request activity of the service guards a parallel composition of processes which comprises the recursive call needed to obtain service persistence. The first request activity is involved also in the second aspect underlined before: one of its parameters is `vid`, which will contain the value representing the session id that will be used in the following requests and invocations, whenever sensitive data have to

Table 6. Definition of the CustomerManagement service

```
CustomerManagement(vcustMgt) =
 [vid][vname][vpassword]
  (vcustMgt.checkUser?<vid,vname,vpassword>,1).
   [nonDet][choice]
    ( (nonDet.choice!<dummy>,1)
      | (nonDet.choice?<dummy>,loginFailRate).
           (creditReq.checkUser!<vid,false>,1)
        + (nonDet.choice?<dummy>,loginOkRate).
            ((creditReq.checkUser!<vid,true>,1)
              | (vcustMgt.getCustData?<vid,vname,vpassword>,1).
                  [login][first][last]
                   (creditReq.getCustData!<vid,login,first,last>,1)    )
      | CustomerManagement(vcustMgt)   )
```

be transmitted. The role of the presented service is involved in the first and partly in the second phase of the scenario (login and data collection); in particular, this service is responsible for the decision on the outcome of the login phase: a choice between two possible communications over the private channel `nonDet.choice` determines whether the login attempt is successful or not.

Scows_lts allows the use of *parameters* to denote action rates. In Table 6 this is the case for both *loginOkRate* and *loginFailRate*. Using parametric values, the actual computation of action rates is not performed when deriving the CTMC (as it happens when actual values are used), but rather an arithmetic expression is derived. The actual instantiation of parametric rates can be specified when using the model checking software; in this way the CTMC derivation phase can be performed once, and the result can be used to check for properties using different sets of rate values. In the application scenario at hand, we used this feature for both the login phase (*loginOkRate* and *loginFailRate*), and the manual review performed by clerks (*clerkDecisionRate*) and supervisors (*supDecisionRate*). All the other rates in the system are set equal to 1.

Another useful feature of Scows_lts is the possibility of specifying annotations of Scows transitions. These annotations can be used to enrich the state space description of the CTMC in the model checking software. For instance a communication on a particular endpoint can trigger the increment of a variable in the description of the PRISM CTMC.

Another possibility, shown in Table 7, is referring also to the parameters involved in the communication operation. In this example, a communication over the endpoint `portal.goodbye` with the placeholder parameter `@1`, triggers the assignment of a PRISM variable with the value 1. The actual name of the variable involved in this

Table 7. Definition of parametric annotations for Scows communications

```
portal.goodbye <@1> :: @1_finished' = 1 ;
creditReq.createNewCreditRequest <@1,*> :: @1_started' = 1;
```

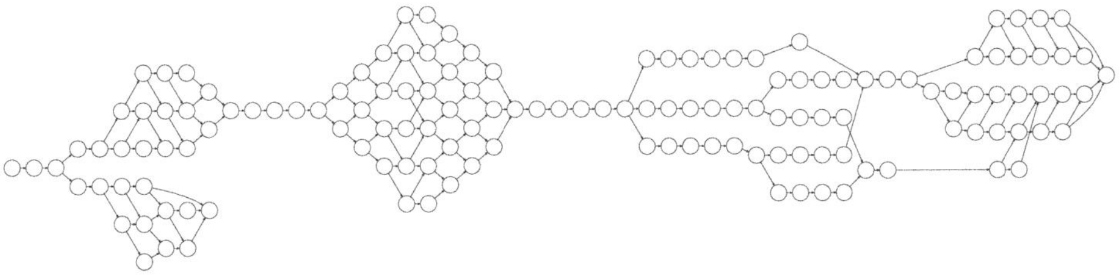

Fig. 2. Transition System for the Bank Credit Request scenario

assignment depends on the parameter of the communication `@1`, so that, e.g., if `@1` = `id0` then the PRISM variable that will be assigned the value 1 is the one named *id0_finished*. Similarly, the second annotation reported in Table 7 refers to communications over `creditReq.createNewCreditRequest`, which trigger the assignment `@1`*_started* = 1. Note that in this second case the list of parameters for the communication contains the wildcard *, which basically means that the possibly remaining parameters and their values are all irrelevant. The joint use of these two annotations allows the model checker to track the execution of one particular loan request from the moment it is initialized by communicating over `creditReq.createNewCreditRequest`, to the latest step involving an interaction over `portal.goodbye`. In both cases the first parameter of the communication (`@1`) is the session identifier of the logged in customer.

The complete LTS automatically generated by Scows_lts for the model of the Bank Credit Request scenario is reported in Figure 2, where state and transition labels have been omitted for readability. The LTS is used to build a model which is expressed in a format compatible with PRISM. The CTMC corresponding to the graph in Figure 2 is composed of 139 states and 195 transitions. Also, it has the four parameters used in the definition of the model: *loginFailRate*, *loginOkRate*, *supDecisionRate*, and *clerkDecisionRate*. The adoption of annotated transitions is responsible for the creation of two PRISM variables: *id0_started* and *id0_finished* which can both assume values in $\{0, 1\}$. These latest variables can be used when expressing probabilistic properties to be checked against the model. This happens, for instance, for property P1 below which tracks the probability that the loan request procedure is completed either with an accepted or with a refused loan request (i.e., either by the customer or by the bank) within time T.

$$P_{=?}\,[(true)\ U_{[0,T]}\ (id0\_finished = 1)] \qquad \text{(P1)}$$

Note that the probability of *eventually* reaching a state in which $id0\_finished = 1$ depends only on the ratio between *loginFailRate* and *loginOkRate*. Indeed, in the considered model, a successful login eventually leads to the generation of a message by the bank services, either containing a loan proposal or a decline. On the other hand, the transient behaviour of the system depends on all the four parametric rates. Property P1 was checked with the following settings: $loginFailRate = 0.5$, $loginOkRate = 1.5$, and $supDecisionRate, clerkDecisionRate \in \{0.05, 0.30, 0.55\}$. With these values, the probability of Property P1 being *eventually* true is

$$\frac{loginOkRate}{loginOkRate + loginFailRate} \times 100 = 75\%.$$

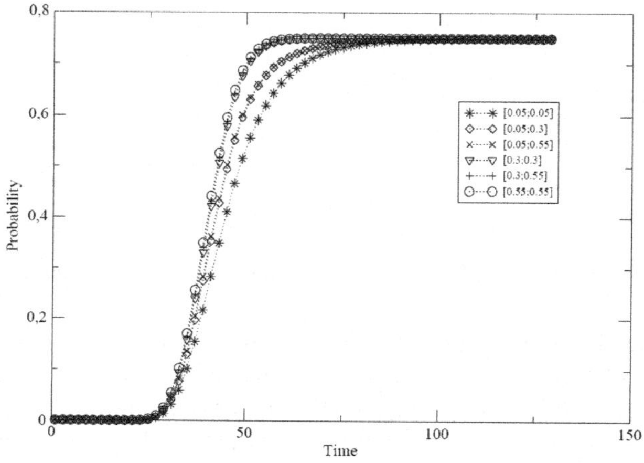

Fig. 3. Results of model checking for Property P1 using different values for the parametric rates *clerkDecisionRate* and *supDecisionRate*

Figure 3 presents the results of the model checking procedure for Property P1 for the time scale $T \in [1, 130]$, while Figure 4 shows a close-up on the time frame $T \in [44, 50]$, where the different probability outcomes in the transient part of the model are easier to see. For clarity, not all the generated series are reported in Figures 3 and 4. Indeed, the results given by series where the parameters *supDecisionRate* and *clerkDecisionRate* have interchanged values are equal. This is due to the fact that clerks and supervisors are modelled by identical terms, and the probabilities of requiring the service of either of them are exactly the same. For this same reason, in the legends of both Figures 3 and 4 we do not specify which element of the pairs refers to *supDecisionRate* and which refers to *clerkDecisionRate*. The interpretation of the obtained results allows the identification of potential performance issues. For instance, we notice that on average the system evolves faster (i.e. the customer gets a faster response) when both the clerk and the supervisor have a medium review rate (0.3) rather than when one of the two has a low review rate (0.05), whichever the review rate of the other bank employee.

If we wish to verify whether a customer receives a response (either a loan proposal or a decline message) within a time boundary with a certain probability, we can formulate a property such as Property P2:

$$init \longrightarrow \mathrm{P}_{>0.6} \left[true \ \mathrm{U}_{[0,T]} \quad id0\_finished = 1 \right] \qquad \text{(P2)}$$

which allows checking whether a logged customer will receive a response within time T with a probability greater than 60%.

We checked Property P2 with these settings: $loginFailRate = 0.5$; $loginOkRate = 1.5$; $supDecisionRate = clerkDecisionRate = 0.30$ and $T = 50$. With these settings, the model checking procedure verifies that the property holds, giving as result `true`. This can be visually verified looking at Figure 4 considering the series labelled [0.3; 0.3]

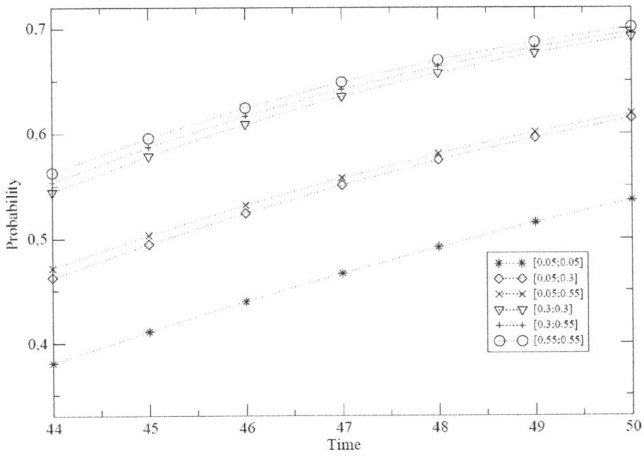

Fig. 4. Results of model checking for Property P1: close-up on the time frame $T \in [44, 50]$

at time $T = 50$. The actual probability value for which Property P2 holds, obtained performing model checking on Property P3 below, is approximately 0.69.

$$\mathrm{P}_{=?}\,[\mathit{true}\ \mathrm{U}_{[0,T]}\quad \mathit{id0\_finished} = 1] \qquad \text{(P3)}$$

5 Concluding Remarks

We presented Scows_lts, a software written in Java for the automatic derivation of LTSs for closed Scows terms. We outlined the main features of the software, such as the implementation of the congruence check for Scows services, the annotation of transitions and the possibility to use parametric rates. A loan-request application scenario was then used to show how to take advantage of the features of Scows_lts, and analyze probabilistic properties of the global model by using PRISM.

One aspect that will be taken into account in future work is the performance of the automatic LTS derivation process, in particular regarding the complexity of the structural congruence checking phase. Also, it should be observed that Scows_lts is engineered in a stratified way, so that the heaviest computational phase, i.e, the generation of the LTS, is separated from the module for the generation of the input to PRISM. We aim at extending the software by implementing different back-ends to plug to the LTS generation module to allow users to analyze Scows specification by means of other model checkers (e.g., MRMC [8]) and against other logics.

Acknowledgements. This work has been partially sponsored by the project SENSORIA, IST-2005-016004.

References

1. Aziz, A., Sanwal, K., Singhal, V., Brayton, R.: Model-checking continous-time Markov chains. ACM Trans. on Computational Logic 1(1), 162–170 (2000)
2. Boreale, M., Bruni, R., Caires, L., De Nicola, R., Lanese, I., Loreti, M., Martins, F., Montanari, U., Ravara, A., Sangiorgi, D., Vasconcelos, V.T., Zavattaro, G.: SCC: A Service Centered Calculus. In: Bravetti, M., Núñez, M., Zavattaro, G. (eds.) WS-FM 2006. LNCS, vol. 4184, pp. 38–57. Springer, Heidelberg (2006)
3. Clarke, E.M., Allen Emerson, E., Prasad Sistla, A.: Automatic verification of finite-state concurrent systems using temporal logics. ACM Trans. on Programming Languages and Systems 8(2), 244–263 (1986)
4. De Nicola, R., Latella, D., Loreti, M., Massink, M.: MarCaSPiS: a Markovian Extension of a Calculus for Services. Electronic Notes in Theoretical Computer Science 229(4), 11–26 (2009)
5. http://www.graphviz.com
6. Fantechi, A., Gnesi, S., Lapadula, A., Mazzanti, F., Pugliese, R., Tiezzi, F.: A model checking approach for verifying COWS specifications. In: Fiadeiro, J.L., Inverardi, P. (eds.) FASE 2008. LNCS, vol. 4961, pp. 230–245. Springer, Heidelberg (2008)
7. Guidi, C., Lucchi, R., Gorrieri, R., Busi, N., Zavattaro, G.: A Calculus for Service Oriented Computing. In: Dan, A., Lamersdorf, W. (eds.) ICSOC 2006. LNCS, vol. 4294, pp. 327–338. Springer, Heidelberg (2006)
8. Katoen, J.-P., Zapreev, I.S., Hahn, E.M., Hermanns, H., Jansen, D.N.: The Ins and Outs of The Probabilistic Model Checker MRMC. In: Quantitative Evaluation of Systems (QEST), pp. 167–176. IEEE Computer Society, Los Alamitos (2009), www.mrmc-tool.org
9. Kwiatkowska, M., Norman, G., Parker, D.: PRISM: Probabilistic Model Checking for Performance and Reliability Analysis. ACM SIGMETRICS Performance Evaluation Review 36(4), 40–45 (2009)
10. Lapadula, A., Pugliese, R., Tiezzi, F.: Calculus for Orchestration of Web Services. In: De Nicola, R. (ed.) ESOP 2007. LNCS, vol. 4421, pp. 33–47. Springer, Heidelberg (2007), http://rap.dsi.unifi.it/cows/
11. Milner, R.: Communicating and mobile systems: the π-calculus. Cambridge Universtity Press, Cambridge (1999)
12. Prandi, D., Quaglia, P.: Stochastic COWS. In: Krämer, B.J., Lin, K.-J., Narasimhan, P. (eds.) ICSOC 2007. LNCS, vol. 4749, pp. 245–256. Springer, Heidelberg (2007)
13. PRISM homepage, http://www.prismmodelchecker.org/
14. Quaglia, P., Schivo, S.: Approximate Model Checking of Stochastic COWS. In: Proceedings of TGC 2010 (2010)
15. Sangiorgi, D., Walker, D.: The π-calculus: a Theory of Mobile Processes. Cambridge Universtity Press, Cambridge (2001)
16. Schivo, S.: Statistical model checking of Web Services. PhD thesis, Int. Doctorate School in Information and Communication Technologies, University of Trento (2010)
17. http://disi.unitn.it/~cappello/

Author Index

GPSR Compliance

The European Union's (EU) General Product Safety Regulation (GPSR) is a set of rules that requires consumer products to be safe and our obligations to ensure this.

If you have any concerns about our products, you can contact us on ProductSafety@springernature.com

In case Publisher is established outside the EU, the EU authorized representative is:

Springer Nature Customer Service Center GmbH
Europaplatz 3
69115 Heidelberg, Germany

Batch number: 09504227

Printed by Printforce, the Netherlands